Legal aspects of care in the community

Legal aspects of care in the community

Bridgit Dimond

MACMILLAN

First published 1997 by
MACMILLAN PRESS LTD
Houndmills, Basingstoke, Hampshire RG21 6XS
and London
Companies and representatives
throughout the world

ISBN 0–333–53819–6 hardcover
ISBN 0–333–53820–X paperback

A catalogue record for this book is available
from the British Library.

This book is printed on paper suitable for recycling and
made from fully managed and sustained forest sources.

10   9   8   7   6   5   4   3   2   1
06   05   04   03   02   01   00   99   98   97

Printed in Great Britain by
Antony Rowe Ltd
Chippenham, Wiltshire

In memory of Stuart

Contents

Preface

Community care has always existed. Once it was provided on a formal basis as outdoor relief by the monasteries, later in history state support was provided through the Poor Law. Recently the term has been used to contrast with the care provided in institutions especially for the old, mentally ill and mentally impaired. The Community Care Plans published in 1963, which followed the Hospital Plans of 1962 overseen by the then Minister of Health Enoch Powell, envisaged that the large institutions provided by the National Health Service for long-stay patients would be reduced in size – even razed to the ground – and community care would take their place. The plans have been a long time in the implementing, each successive Government emphasising the priority which should be given to care in the community, and gradually the number of institutional places has been reduced with varying degrees of community provision being made. Important legal changes were made in 1983 enabling joint financing and funding to take place between health and local authorities to facilitate the discharge of patients.

The second Griffiths Report and the white paper, *Caring for People*, followed by the National Health Service and Community Care Act 1990 have made major changes in the responsibility for financing community care and shifted more responsibility from the health service to the local authorities. For the first time a statutory definition was given to community care which is set out in Chapter 2.

This book is specifically concerned with the health aspects of community care and seeks to identify some of the legal problems faced by the various professionals who work in the community caring for people. It is focused on five areas:

A. The rights of the client in relation to care, powers of entry and removal from premises, consent and confidentiality.

B. The duties and responsibilities of the many professionals providing care, initially in relation to their accountability and professional liability and then in relation to health and safety concerns (specific chapters deal with individual professional groups, volunteers and carers).

C. The statutory bodies and other organisations involved in the provision of care, also considering enforcement provisions.

D. The legal issues relating to the provision of accommodation.

E. The financing of individuals.

The aim is to provide a readable guide to the many issues which arise in the care of the client in the community with special emphasis on the practical problems and situations which are likely to occur. The law is explained in relation to specific situations which are frequently encountered by professionals. Inevitably any division of the subject area will lead to an artificial treatment of the topic in that there will be overlaps and omissions. The goodwill of the reader is sought in tolerating the cross references which are necessary to avoid repetition of such material.

The decision was taken not to divide the legal issues into client groups, for example mentally ill, learning disabilities, elderly, physically disabled and so on, since services are not necessarily categorised in that way and many professionals work across any such boundaries.

Two major areas of the law, those relating to children and education (except in the context of health care), are omitted. The reason for the omission is simply space. There are sufficient specialist books dealing with these areas to justify excluding them from this text. This has allowed more focused concentration on the issues of community care in the context of health and social services. Midwives have also been omitted from the health professionals considered in Section B, not because they do not have a community role, but because a specific book on midwifery law has just been published which deals more appropriately with issues particularly their concern.

Where possible the emphasis is on practical problems rather than academic niceties. It is a book for the practitioner rather than the lawyer. Where relevant cases have been cited and the facts given since this reveals clearly to the practitioner the extent to which their work is subject to oversight by the courts. To illustrate other problems, not yet the subject of court hearings, situations have been envisaged which are fictional but useful in illustrating potential hurdles. They do not represent any living persons.

The actual wording of statutes has been quoted where relevant, and this has been placed in the figures so that the continuity of the text is not destroyed. Those practitioners who are interested in the actual words of the sections concerned can study these. Reference material which should be of assistance to the practitioner is included in the appendices.

The aim is to make the law meaningful to the practitioner who cannot leave all legal knowledge to the lawyer. Practitioners must be aware of the legal framework within which they practice and know at which point they require to bring in the legal experts.

It is apparent that each chapter could be a book in its own right and omissions are inevitable. The book therefore includes a list for further reading confined to books on law. There is also in Appendix 3 limited specialist bibliographies on Health and Safety and HIV/Aids and on Community Care assessments. Such bibliographies, including current Health Circulars and so on, are maintained by major reference libraries and the libraries of educational establishments. The interested reader is referred to these.

In addition in this book a selective list of useful addresses is provided and a glossary to chart a way through the many technical terms. Terminology in relation to the recipient of services, variously called the client, consumer, customer, patient or resident, can cause difficulties and in the main the term 'client' has been used, except in relation to accommodation where the term resident was considered more appropriate.

Finally, the perennial problem of he or she, his or her has been resolved by generally referring to all in the plural or in the feminine gender unless the context is clearly to the contrary. So for 'she' read also 'he' and for 'her' read also 'him'.

Acknowledgements

It is impossible to mention all the numerous individuals who have assisted me in the completion of this book. Perhaps it is even invidious to mention some by name. However, I would like to give special thanks to Yvonne Apsitis, Mel Evans, Margaret Griffiths, Marilyn Tickner, Sally Kettle, Penny Llewellyn, Marion Way, Carol Tucker, Peter Williams, Ian Ferris, J. Donnally, M. Goodwin, Joan Harlow, A. Thomas, S. Dando, Margaret Williams, Kathy Hier, Margery Nawaz, Paul Morgan, Barbara Wilson, Richard Rowson and Chris Chaplin. Others to be added are Catherine Cotterill, librarian, Bevan Ashford who assisted in a library search, Tessa Shellens and Peter Edwards who read through the whole manuscript and made extremely helpful suggestions in the initial stages. I accept responsibility, however, for any errors and omissions that remain.

I am grateful to Richenda Milton-Thompson, my editor, for having the persistence to see this project through and acknowledge the considerable debt I owe to Tamsin Bacchus, my copy editor.

Finally, as always, I thank my family and friends for their support and patience and for whom 'community care' has quite a different meaning.

Abbreviations

CA	Court of Appeal
CHC	Community Health Council
CHP	Council for Health Professions
COSHH	Control of Substances Hazardous to Health
CPN	Community Psychiatric Nurse
CPSM	Council to the Professions Supplementary to Medicine
CSSD	Central Sterile Supply Department
DHA	District health authority
DSS	Department of Social Security
FHSA	Family Health Services Authority
GP	General practitioner
GPFH	GP fund-holder
HAG	Housing Association Grant
HCHS	Hospital and community health services
HIV	Human Immunodeficiency Virus
HL	House of Lords
HSC	Health Services Commissioner (Ombudsman)
HSE	Health and Safety Executive
JCC	Joint Consultative Committee
JP	Justice of the Peace
MDU	Medical Defence Union
NAA	National Assistance Act
NHSME	National Health Service Management Executive
PRN	As required (of medicines)
QBD	Queens Bench Division (of the High Court)
RHA	Regional Health Authority
RMO	Responsible Medical Officer
RPSGB	Royal Pharmaceutical Society of Great Britain.
RSC	Rules of the Supreme Court
SNMA	Special Needs Management Allowance
SPPA	Special Projects Promotional Allowance
SSD	Social Services Department
SSI	Social Services Inspectorate
UKCC	United Kingdom Central Council for Nursing, Midwifery and Health Visiting
WHC	Welsh Health Circular

CHAPTER 1

Introduction

It is not the purpose of this book to explore the long history of government attempts to shift patients from the institutional care of the National Health Service into the community. Instead attention will be concentrated upon the immediate steps leading to the National Health Service and Community Care Act 1990. These were the second report by Griffiths and the white paper, *Caring for People*. This chapter will consider these developments together with the main provisions of the 1990 Act.

THE GRIFFITHS REPORT

The development of care in the community had been the declared aim of successive Governments since the 1960s. Initiatives which speeded and informed government thinking included:

- the House of Commons Social Services Committee which reported on community care with special reference to adult mentally ill and mentally handicapped people in 1984–85 (HC 13 1984–85); and
- the Audit Commission Report in December 1986, *Making a reality of Community Care*.

In December 1986 the Secretary of State, Norman Fowler, asked Sir Roy Griffiths, who had undertaken the report into hospital management, to undertake a review of community care policy. His terms of reference were to 'review the way in which public funds are used to support community care policy and to advise . . . on the options for action that would improve the use of these funds as a contribution to more effective community care'. In addition he was instructed that 'the review should be brief and geared towards advice on action as was the review of management in the health service in 1983.'

In his letter of response[1] to the Government, presented in February 1988, Sir Roy Griffiths made some radical suggestions which were initially not enthusiastically received. His main recommendations are summarised in Figure 1.1.

Figure 1.1 Summary of Griffiths recommendations

- Strengthening and clarifying the role of central government.
- Clarifying the role of local social services authorities in assessing needs, developing local priorities and determining priorities.
- Transferring to local authorities the responsibility for funding residential and nursing home accommodation for those unable to pay.
- Enhancing the role of health authorities in the provision of medically required community health services and their role in the assessment of needs.

Basically the recommendations were for a radical change in the funding of accommodation in the community and greater emphasis on clear lines of managerial accountability. Provision in future had to be on the basis of assessment of need and the development of local plans, drawn up by the local authorities in conjunction with health authorities and the voluntary sector.

THE WHITE PAPER

Subsequently a white paper was published, *Caring for People: Community Care in the next decade and beyond*[2]. Figure 1.2 sets out the key objectives of the white paper's proposals.

Figure 1.2 Objectives of white paper *Caring for People*

- To promote the development of domiciliary, day and respite services to enable people to live in their own homes wherever feasible and sensible.
- To ensure that service providers make practical support for carers a high priority.
- To make proper assessment of need and good care management the cornerstones of high quality care.
- To promote the development of a flourishing independent sector alongside good quality public services.
- To clarify the responsibilities of agencies and so make it easier to hold them to account for their performance.
- To secure better value for taxpayers' money by introducing a new funding structure for social care.

This envisaged that certain key changes would be required. These were in brief:

- Local authorities were to become responsible, in collaboration with medical, nursing, and other interests, for assessing individual need, designing care arrangements and securing their delivery within available resources.

- Local authorities would be expected to produce and publish clear plans for the development of community care services, consistent with the plans of health authorities and other interested agencies. The Government would take new powers to ensure that plans are open to inspection, and to call for reports from social services authorities.

- Local authorities would be expected to make maximum use of the independent sector. The Government would ensure that they have acceptable plans for achieving this.

- There would be a new funding structure for those seeking public support for residential and nursing home care from April 1991 (subsequently changed to 1993). After that date local authorities would take responsibility for financial support of people in private and voluntary homes, over and above any general social security entitlements. The new arrangements would not, however apply to people already resident in homes before April 1991 – subsequently postponed to April 1993.

- Applicants with few or no resources of their own would be eligible for the same levels of Income Support and Housing Benefit, irrespective of whether they are living in their own homes or in independent residential or nursing homes.

- Local authorities would be required to establish inspection and registration units at arm's length from the management of their own services which would be responsible for checking on standards in both their own homes and in independent sector residential care homes.

- There would be a new specific grant to promote the development of social care for seriously mentally ill people.

The white paper explains how this would work in practice and outlines the roles and responsibilities of the social services authorities and also those of the health services. Emphasis is placed upon quality control and achieving high standards of care, collaborative working and service for people with a mental illness. It also considers the issue of resources and the links with social security. Separate chapters of the paper cover Wales and Scotland.

Subsequent to the publication of the white paper there has been a spate of guidance material published by government departments and agencies.

The status of these publications is not always clear. Certainly the sections of the Act itself must take precedence in any dispute, since any directions or guidance issued must be within the scope of the Act. However, should a local authority ignore these guidelines a government department could, through financial controls, implement its own views but this could be challenged by judicial review (see Chapter 27). It is not always clear whether a government circular is of persuasive or mandatory status. In *Beckwith*[3] the House of Lords declared that DoH guidance in LAC(93)10 stated the law incorrectly, but in a recent case the QBD has emphasised that a local authority could not depart without good reason from policy guidance issued by the Secretary of State (see page 399).

THE NHS AND COMMUNITY CARE ACT 1990

Many of the recommendations of the white paper were incorporated in the NHS and Community Care Act 1990. The main provisions of this Act are given in Figure 1.3 and for convenience the section number and chapter of the book in which the particular provision is discussed are also given.

Figure 1.3 NHS and Community Care Act 1990

The community care provisions

- **Section 46(3)** Statutory definition of community care. One of the most significant steps in the Act is that for the very first time there is a statutory definition of community care. (Discussed on page 11, Chapter 2)
- **Sections 42 to 45** The provision of accommodation and welfare services, charges for accommodation and the recovery of charges provided by local authorities. (Chapters 28 and 33)
- **Section 46** The provision of a community care plan by each local authority. (Chapter 25)
- **Section 47** Assessment of needs for community care services. (Chapter 25)
- **Section 48** Inspection of premises used for provision of community care services. (Chapter 25)
- **Section 49** Transfer of staff from health service to local authorities. (Chapter 13)
- **Section 50** Power of Secretary of State to give directions and instruct local authorities to set up complaints procedures. (Chapter 27)
- **Sections 51 to 58** Provisions for Scotland. (not discussed)

The NHS provisions

- Part I and Part II of the NHS and Community Care Act 1990 set up new statutory bodies in the form of NHS Trusts and Group Fundholding Practices and placed new duties upon health authorities in the context of the internal market. Family Health Services Authorities (now themselves replaced) replaced the Family Practitioner Committees. The following sections are discussed in the chapters shown below:
- **Sections 1, 3 and 4 and Schedule 1** Local management of Regional and District Health Authorities and NHS contracts. (Chapter 23)

- **Sections 2, 12 and 13 and Schedule 1** Family Health Services Authorities – now amended by the Health Authorities Act 1995. (Chapter 24)
- **Sections 5 to 11 and Schedule 2** NHS Trusts. (Chapter 23)
- **Sections 14 to 21** Fund-holding practices. (Chapter 24)
- **Part II Sections 27 to 41** Scotland. (not discussed)

Those sections relating to the establishment of the new health authorities and family health services authorities were implemented in 1991 when the first wave of NHS Trusts were approved. The structure has now been amended by the Health Authorities Act 1995 merging the FHSAs with new health authorities (see Figure 23.11). The implementation of the community care provisions of the 1990 Act was delayed and the main provisions did not come into force until 1 April 1993.

The NHS and Community Care Act 1990 introduced a new management and administrative structure into both secondary health care and primary health as well as implementing the basic principles of the Griffiths letter[4] in community care. However this book ranges beyond these statutory provisions and seeks to look at the wider legal issues confronting the client and the professional in the community. Topics such as accountability, patients' rights, health and safety and other legal issues not covered in the 1990 Act are therefore included.

REFERENCES

1. Sir Roy Griffiths *Community Care: Agenda for Action* HMSO, 1988
2. Command Paper 849, *Caring for People: Community Care in the next decade and beyond.* HMSO, November 1989
3. *R v. Wandsworth London Borough Council, ex parte Beckwith* [1996] 1 All ER 129 (HL)
4. Sir Roy Griffiths *Community Care: Agenda for Action* HMSO, 1988

SECTION A

Clients

This first section considers the provision of community care from the perspective of the client. The first chapter (Chapter 2 of the book) discusses what is meant by community care and looks at the basis in Acts of Parliament for services to be provided. Subsequent chapters consider the law relating to consent, powers of entry into client's property and removal from premises, confidentiality and access to health and social services records.

CHAPTER 2

Clients and community care

This chapter seeks an answer to the following questions:

- What is meant by community care?
- What right does a client have to community care?
- What specific statutory responsibilities exist from before 1990?
- What is the significance of the NHS and Community Care Act 1990 to clients' entitlement to community care?
- What is the significance of the Patient's and Citizen's Charters to the legal rights of the client?
- What effect would a Bill of Rights have?

DEFINITION OF COMMUNITY CARE

The term received its first statutory definition in section 46(3) of the NHS and Community Care Act 1990. This is set out in Figure 2.1.

Figure 2.1 Definition of community care services – section 46(3)

'Community care services' means services which a local authority may provide or arrange to be provided under any of the following provisions —

(a) Part III of the National Assistance Act 1948 [provision of accommodation for those over 18 who need it because of age, illness, disability or any other circumstances];

(b) section 45 of the Health Services and Public Health Act 1968 [arrangements for promoting the welfare of 'old people'];

(c) section 21 of and Schedule 8 to the National Health Service Act 1977 [the provision of services for the care of mothers and young children, prevention, care and after-care, and home help and laundry facilities]; and

(d) section 117 of the Mental Health Act 1983 [the duty of the health authority and local social services authority to provide, in co-operation with relevant voluntary agencies, after-care services for any person who has been detained under specified sections of the Mental Health Act 1983].

The statutory provisions referred to in section 46(3) are discussed in more detail in Chapter 25. The purpose of this chapter is to take a broad view of services which can be provided.

The definition of community care services under section 46 of the 1990 Act does not include those services provided to disabled persons under sections 1 and 2 of the Chronically Sick and Disabled Persons Act 1970 and section 3 of the Disabled Persons (Employment) Act 1958. Section 47(2) of the NHS and Community Care Act 1990 requires an assessment to be carried out under the 1970 Act if it is ascertained that a person is disabled (see below). There is also a duty to assess the needs of disabled persons under the Disabled Persons (Services, Consultation and Representation) Act 1986 and this and the other disabled persons legislation is discussed in Chapter 25. The services to be provided under these statutes will be considered in this book even though they do not come within the statutory definition given above, as will the community health services provided within the National Health Service. Thus all those services provided by health visitors, community psychiatric nurses, and other specialists will be considered.

RIGHT TO COMMUNITY CARE SERVICES

■ What right does a client have to community care services?

The simple answer to this question is that it depends upon what service is sought. There is no enforceable charter which sets out the basic services and rights to which clients are entitled. Thus, if a community service is demanded from a statutory body, the claimant must show that there is express legislation which gives a duty or power to that authority to provide that service and/or that directions have been issued by the Secretary of State requiring the authority to provide the service. The NHS and Community Care Act 1990 made no attempt to consolidate the earlier legislation, and therefore any client seeking to understand his rights to community care must

- identify the specific section of the 1990 Act and of earlier legislation which it amended, which appears to give a right to that service, then
- seek out any directions which have been issued in relation to the statutory provisions, and then
- analyse how that section is enforced and at the request of whom.

Even then, if the statute itself provides a remedy such as default powers given by the Secretary of State, a court action to enforce the right may not succeed.

The case of *Wyatt* (1978) (details on page 431) shows that in the court's view, where default powers (that is powers to take action in the event of a failure to implement the duties set out in the legislation) are given to the Secretary of State to investigate a breach of duty by the local authority, then it is not open to an individual claimant to bring an action for breach of the statutory duty to provide services under the Act. This case is discussed in detail in Chapter 27 where the problems of any single individual enforcing statutory duties are considered. The conclusion is that in general the courts have not supported individual patients or clients claiming specific services and bringing an action for breach of statutory duty against the Secretary of State and the health authorities – though there are some exceptions to this principle.

SPECIFIC STATUTORY RESPONSIBILITIES

The specific statutory responsibilities to provide services in the community will be considered. There is fuller discussion of these in relation to the functions of health authorities and local authorities in Chapters 23 and 25.

Community health services

The Secretary of State has a responsibility under the National Health Service Act 1977 (NHS Act 1977) to continue to promote in England and Wales

a comprehensive health service designed to secure improvement—
(a) in the physical and mental health of the people of those countries, and
(b) in the prevention, diagnosis, and treatment of illness
and for the purpose to provide or secure the effective provision of services in accordance with this Act (section 1(1)).

Under section 3 he has a duty to provide, to such extent as he considers necessary to meet all reasonable requirements, specific services listed in the section. These are shown in Chapter 23.

Though the provision of community services is not listed, such health services in the community would be included in the duty:

- to provide medical, dental, nursing and ambulance services (section 3(1)(c)); and
- to provide services for the care of expectant and nursing mothers and young children (section 3(1)(d)); and
- such facilities for the prevention of illness, the care of persons suffering from illness and the after-care of persons who have suffered from illness as the Secretary of State considers are appropriate as part of the health service (section 3(1)(e)).

The final provision (f) of subsection 3(1) of the NHS Act 1977 requires him to provide 'such other services as are required for the diagnosis and treatment of illness'. This can be used to cover any other community health service which does not directly fall under the previous provisions.

The Secretary of State also has a duty to provide specific primary health services such as general practitioners, dentists, and pharmaceutical services, which he does through the operation of the contracting authorities which are discussed in Chapter 24. From 1996 responsibility for holding the contracts for these primary health care services fell upon the new health authorities set up on 1 April 1996 which combined statutory responsibility for the services previously undertaken by health authorities and family health services authorities.

From the client's situation the duties placed upon the Secretary of State are extremely comprehensive and cover wide ranging services. However the duty under section 3 of the NHS Act 1977 is qualified by the words 'to such extent as he considers necessary' and 'to meet all reasonable requirements'. This places considerable discretion on the Secretary of State and ultimately the purchasers of health services to whom he delegates the task of negotiating with the providers of health care.

An example of the difficulties in assessing the extent to which patients can insist upon services being provided is the confusion relating to the provision of nursing services. This has been the subject of reports by the Health Service Commissioner (HSC), also known as the Ombudsman, which are considered in Chapter 23 where criticism has been levelled by the HSC on the failure of a health authority to provide accommodation for patients requiring nursing care. Confusion over the boundaries between the responsibilities of the NHS and those of non-NHS organisations is discussed in greater detail in Chapter 23. The respective responsibilities of health and local social services authorities were the subject of a consultation document on the care of long-stay patients being discharged into the community. The consultation document has been followed by guidance in which local authorities and health authorities are asked to develop local policies. This guidance is also discussed in Chapter 23.

Community social services

Several statutes place specific duties and/or powers on local authorities to provide specified services to different client groups. In some statutes the terminology is that the local authority must provide the service, that is the word 'shall' is used. However, this mandatory duty may be subject to the necessity for further direction by the Secretary of State. Other sections simply enable the local authority to provide a service, that is the word 'may' is used. This power may also be subject to directions and guidance by the Secretary of State.

Some of the relevant statutes covering the elderly, the disabled and the mentally ill are shown below.

Services for the elderly
Section 45(1) of the Health Services and Public Health Act 1968 enables the local authority to promote the welfare of old people. The section is discussed in Chapter 25. This section creates a power, not a duty.

In addition the elderly can obtain services under the provisions of section 29 of the National Assistance Act 1948 (NAA 1948) and (if disabled) under section 2 of the Chronically Sick and Disabled Persons Act 1970 which are set out below and discussed further in Chapter 25. These sections impose a duty on the social services departments.

Services for the disabled.
Section 29 of the NAA 1948 enables local authorities to provide services other than residential accommodation. The duty under this section is shown in Figure 2.2.

Figure 2.2 The NAA 1948 – section 29 (1)

A local authority may, with the approval of the Secretary of State, and to such extent as he may direct in relation to persons ordinarily resident in the area of the local authority *shall* [author's emphasis] make arrangements for promoting the welfare of persons to whom this section applies, that is to say persons aged eighteen or over who are blind, deaf or dumb, or who suffer from mental disorder of any description and other persons aged eighteen or over who are substantially and permanently handicapped by illness, injury or congenital deformity or such other disabilities as may be prescribed by the Minister.

The local authority has an express duty under this section.

Section 2 of the Chronically Sick and Disabled Persons Act 1970 also imposes duties and this section is summarised in Figure 2.3.

Figure 2.3 The 1970 Act – Summary of section 2

Where the local authority . . . are satisfied in the case of any person to whom [section 29 of the NAA 1948 applies] who is ordinarily resident in their area that it is necessary in order to meet the needs of that person for that authority to make arrangements for all or any of the following matters, namely [the provision of] —

(a) practical assistance for that person in his home;
(b) wireless, television, library or similar recreational facilities;
(c) lectures, games, outings or other recreational facilities outside his home or assistance to that person in taking advantage of educational facilities available to him;
(d) facilities for, or assistance in, travelling to and from his home [to participate] in any services provided under arrangements made by the authority under the said section 29 or, with the approval of the authority, [to participate] in any [similar] services provided otherwise than as aforesaid;
(e) any works of adaption in his home or the provision of any additional facilities designed to secure his greater safety, comfort or convenience;
(f) [facilitation for the] taking of holidays by that person, whether at holiday homes or otherwise and whether provided under arrangements made by the authority or otherwise;
(g) meals for that person whether in his home or elsewhere;
(h) a telephone and any special equipment necessary to enable him to use a telephone;

then . . . *it shall be the duty of that authority to make those arrangements in exercise of their functions under the said section 29.* [author's emphasis]

The emphasised words in Figure 2.3 show that a duty exists. However, this duty is qualified, being subject to the provisions of the Local Authority Social Services Act 1970. This requires local authorities, in exercising certain functions – including functions under section 29 of the NAA 1948 – to act under the general guidance of the Secretary of State. The duty is also subject to the provisions of section 7A of that Act (which refers to directions given by the Secretary of State). Directions on this have been issued and are consolidated in circular LAC(93)10 (see Chapter 25 and Appendix 1).

Section 2 of the Chronically Sick and Disabled Persons Act came under the scrutiny in a case heard before the High Court in 1995[1], when disabled persons complained of cuts in the social services provided to them. The court held that the local authority should have reassessed once it was established that cuts had to be made in the services but that this assessment could take into account the resources available. Once it was decided what arrangements were necessary, however, there was an absolute duty to provide the services. The case is discussed in full in Chapters 25 and 27.

Schedule 8 of the NHS Act 1977 lists local social services authorities' powers and (if directed by the Secretary of State) duties to make arrangements for the services summarised in Figure 2.4.

Figure 2.4 Duties and powers of local authorities under the NHS Act 1977 Schedule 8

To make arrangements generally:

- for the care of expectant and nursing mothers and of children under 5 years (Paragraph 1(1))
- for the prevention of illness, the care of persons suffering from illness and for the after-care of persons who have been so suffering (Paragraph 2(1))

To make arrangements particularly for

- centres or other facilities for training persons whose care is undertaken with a view to preventing them from becoming ill, persons suffering from illness or persons who have been so suffering, or keeping them suitably occupied and the equipment and maintenance of such centres (Paragraph 2(1)(b))
- ancillary or supplemental services for the benefit of such persons mentioned in Paragraph 2(1)(b) (Paragraph 2(1)(c)
- functions of the authority in respect of persons under guardianship under the Mental Health Act 1983 (Paragraph 2(1)(d))

In addition paragraph 3 of Schedule 8 places a duty upon local authorities to provide the services shown in Figure 2.5.

Figure 2.5 Duty of local authorities under Schedule 8 paragraph 3 of NHS 1977 Act

to provide on such a scale as is adequate for the needs of their area, or to arrange for the provision on such a scale as is so adequate, of home help for households where such help is required owing to the presence of —

(a) a person who is suffering from illness, lying-in, an expectant mother, aged, handicapped as a result of having suffered from illness or by congenital deformity, or
(b) a child [within compulsory school age],

and every such authority has power to provide or arrange for the provision of laundry facilities for households for which home help is being, or can be, provided.

Under section 21 the services described in Schedule 8 in relation to:

- care of mothers and young children
- prevention, care and after-care
- home help and laundry facilities

are stated to be functions exercisable by local social services authorities.

Section 2 of the Chronically Sick and Disabled Persons Act 1970 imposes a duty to gather information and publicise services to those to whom the local social services authority owes a duty under section 29 NAA 1948.

The Disabled Persons (Services, Consultation and Representation) Act 1986, section 4 requires an assessment to be made by the local authority when requested by such a person or by one of the other specified persons. This provision is discussed in Chapter 25.

Duties to provide accommodation are discussed in Chapter 28.

It should be noted that there are overlaps between the different statutory provisions for the disabled, for example there is a duty for local authorities to provide home helps under Schedule 8 of the NHS Act 1977 and also under section 2 of the 1970 Act which requires '(a) the provision of practical assistance for that person in his home'.

Services for the mentally ill

There are overlapping statutory provisions for the supply of services to the mentally ill. Such persons may come under the Chronically Sick and Disabled Persons legislation as well as the community health provisions of the NHS Act 1977. In addition both local authority and health authority have an overlapping duty. Section 22 of the NHS Act 1977 requires them to co-operate in the provision of services. Section 117 of the Mental Health Act 1983 also requires local authorities and health authorities to co-operate with the voluntary sector in the provision of after-care for certain categories of detained patients. A Court of Appeal case[2] shows that this duty is enforceable at the insistence of the patient (see page 244 for fuller discussion).

One major difference between the services provided within the NHS and those provided by the local social services authorities is that charges can be made for the latter, whilst the principle of the former is that they are free at the point of use (except for specific charges for which there is express statutory authority, for example prescriptions). The reason for the difference is that many of the duties placed on the local authorities derive from the NAA 1948 which enabled local authorities to charge for the services they provided. In contrast section 1(2) of the NHS Act 1977 (re-enacting 1946 Act) prohibits charging for NHS services without specific authority.

There are no nationally laid down charges for local social services and there are wide discrepancies. However, charges for residential and nursing home accommodation must be based upon the Charging for Residential Accommodation Guide (CRAG), which is the statutory guidance issued by the Secretary of State (see Chapter 33). Local authorities should not use high charges to reduce demand for the services. The Health and Social Services and Social Security Adjudication Act 1983 section 17 states that charges in relation to the service should take into account an individual's ability to pay. Complaints can be made to the Local Government Ombudsman if the charges are considered too high and if the review system which the local authority is required to set up is considered to be inadequate (see Chapter 28).

EFFECT OF THE 1990 ACT ON COMMUNITY CARE ENTITLEMENT

Sections 42 to 45 accommodation

The duty which local authorities have under the NAA 1948 to provide accommodation is extended by the substitution of the words 'illness' and 'disability' for 'infirmity' in section 21(1) of the NAA 1948, and by adding the provision of accommodation for 'expectant and nursing mothers who are in need of care and attention which is not otherwise available to them'.

The local authority also has a duty to provide accommodation under section 26 of the NAA 1948, using voluntary organisations and others for the provision and claiming refunds from the clients following means-testing (that is the assessment of contributions from the client in relation to his income and capital).

Before a local authority provides nursing home accommodation for a client there must be the consent of the health authority unless it is a matter of urgency in which case the consent must be obtained as soon as practicable.

Other changes are discussed in Chapter 28.

Section 46 – Community Care Plans

Each local authority has a duty to prepare and publish a plan for the provision of community care services in their area. Consultation is statutorily required and this should give the opportunity for groups representing those with specific needs in the community to ensure that these are taken into account in the determination of the priorities which form the basis of the community care plan. This is further discussed in Chapter 25.

Section 47 – Assessment

The local authority is required to provide an assessment of the needs of a person under section 47 of the NHS and Community Care Act where the local authority believes a person for whom it has a duty to provide services may be in need of any such service. This is discussed on pages 393–402. This section creates a duty but there are numerous difficulties relating to the interpretation of this duty. It should also be noted that whilst there is a duty to assess, there is not necessarily a duty to provide the service identified as needed in the assessment. The fact that there might not be the resources to meet identified needs is discussed in Chapter 25.

EFFECT OF THE PATIENT'S AND CITIZEN'S CHARTERS ON LEGAL RIGHTS

The existing legal system

One difficulty of the English legal system is that there is not in existence a Bill of Rights which is binding upon the courts of law. It is true that this country is a signatory of the European Convention of Human Rights but its declaration is not automatically enforceable in the English courts. The applicant who has failed to convince the English court of the existence of a right of action must take the case to Strasbourg. This can be a time wasting and costly procedure.

Instead of being able to turn to one source of law for the protection of an individual's rights, recourse must be made to two main sources of law:

- Statutes or Acts of Parliament and similar legislation including European Community legislation. These will take precedence over other sources which means that, where there is a conflict between a statutory and another source of law, the statute will prevail.
- The common law (that is decisions by judges in decided cases subject to precedent and hierarchy of the courts (see glossary)).

The result is a maze of statutes and cases, to which must now be added the European Community Legislation and decisions which cover the field of human rights and professional responsibilities and powers. Unfortunately the coverage is uneven with many gaps and overlaps. Yet every health and social work professional in the community should have an understanding of the main features, which is the purpose of this book.

The Charters

In the summer of 1991 the Citizen's Charter and the Patient's Charter were launched by the Government and have since been followed by many local charters. The Patient's Charter has been revised and expanded and implementation guidance was issued on 3 March 1995[3].This sets out new standards in relation to community care as shown in Figure 2.6.

Figure 2.6 Community care standards in the Patient's Charter

1. From 1 April 1995 if you need a home visit from a community nurse, health visitor or midwife, you can expect to be consulted about a convenient time. You can then expect a visit within a two-hour band. Exceptionally, your community nurse, health visitor or midwife may be unable to make this appointment or be delayed. In these cases, he/she should let you know and make another appointment.

2. You can expect to receive someone in the district nursing team or the mental health nurse:
   - within 4 hours (daytime), if you have been referred to them as an urgent patient;
   - within 2 working days, if you have been referred to them as a non-urgent patient and have not asked them to see you on any particular day; and
   - by appointment on the day you ask for, if you give the district nursing services more than 48 hours notice.

3. You can expect to receive a visit from your midwife if you and your midwife agree this is necessary. Together you and your midwife will discuss and agree the care you need both before and after your baby is born.

4. You can expect to receive a visit from your health visitor:
   - between 10 and 14 days after the birth of the baby;
   - within 5 working days if you are newly registered with a GP and have children under 5 years old.

In relation to community pharmacy services, standards provide the public with information about what pharmacists normally do in dispensing NHS prescriptions.

■ What is the significance of these documents in relation to the rights of the patient and the work of the professional in the community?

The charter movement can be related to the growth of the consumerist movement which perhaps began with the first Griffiths Report in 1988. The emphasis was upon the patient as the customer and the consumer. The emphasis on quality assurance which has been a feature in health care provision over the last decade, and the concern with the 'shop window' elements of hospital care can be seen as resulting from this preoccupation with the consumer.

Charter for primary health care

Guidance issued by the Welsh Office in December 1992 (WHC(92)88) advised the FHSAs and practitioners of ways in which the Patient's Charter should be developed in primary care. The guidelines include national standards and targets to be achieved for FHSAs and areas in which individual GP practices should consider setting standards, in consultation with and with the assistance of their FHSA. This initiative is designed to build on the existing work of local charters and practice-based standards. Although the FHSAs have now been replaced by the 1995 legislation this guidance in equally applicable to the new health authorities.

The standards have been drawn up in discussion with representatives of NHS management. Primary health care teams are encouraged to develop their own charters.

The circular (WHC(92)88) contained a timetable within which it was expected that each FHSA would:

- publish information on the conduct of its business including the standards to which it commits itself;
- be expected to produce several publications including:
  (a) revised local charters,
  (b) expanded local directories,
  (c) annual reports and other promotional material;
- discuss the arrangements for the publication of standards with the local Community Health Councils working jointly with DHAs and other health organisations.

A National Citizen's Charter Unit exists to monitor the success of the charters and to encourage new initiatives.

Since these charters do not appear to give additional enforceable legal rights, they could be written off as nothing but hype, and certainly the proliferation of charters from a wide range of service industries and manufacturers which are not necessarily accompanied by an improvement in standards can lead to some justified cynicism.

Charters and the internal market

The charters do however have a value in the context of the internal market created by the NHS and Community Care Act 1990.

In the agreements drawn up between purchaser and provider it is possible for the purchaser to define the standards of care to be provided and not just the quantity. The charters can be included in the terms of the agreement and specific targets set. For example, in the handling of complaints the purchaser can set a target time within which complaints should be investigated and resolved. The purchaser can define policies and practices which are designed to implement the principles of the charter. Even though NHS contracts (agreements between health service bodies) are not enforceable through the courts of law (see section 4, NHS and Community Care Act 1990 considered in Chapter 23), the terms of the contract are still relevant to the future provision of the services. If other providers are able to step in then failure by one provider to meet the terms of an agreement could mean that particular body ceasing to provide services in that area. Should there be a disagreement between purchaser and provider then the matter can be referred to the Secretary of State who can appoint an adjudicator.

There are now an increasing number of community NHS Trusts. These have agreements to provide health services for the community with local health service bodies who act as purchasers. In some districts one Trust provides both hospital and community health services.

Once standards are set, it is easier to gain information to check to see if they have been met and to monitor in a systematic and regular way the activities of the provider. Monitoring can also lead to more precise setting of standards and targets for the next round of negotiations on the NHS contract.

Another effect of the charter in combination with the internal market, is that the charter can raise the expectations of clients. It is easy for them to see if there has been compliance with the charter principles and complain to the provider if standards are not met. A complaints system is statutorily required for hospital complaints and, although complaints about community health services were not included in the Hospitals Complaints Procedure Act 1985, guidelines indicate that a procedure should be established for community services as well. The NHS and Community Care Act 1990 gives the Secretary of State the power to require local authorities to establish a procedure for considering any representations (including complaints) made to it in relation to the discharge of its social services functions and this is considered below.

The mechanism for handling complaints is discussed in Chapter 27.

The internal market within the Social Services Department

There is no statutorily prescribed internal market for social service provision, but under guidance given to local authorities they have been encouraged to establish within their services a purchaser/provider divide. The speed with which local authorities have moved towards the implementation of an internal market has varied considerably. In small units it is not always possible to ensure that the care manager is a purchaser rather than a provider. Also some professionals such as approved social workers do not have a clear purchasing or provider role and cross the boundary. However, the statutory duty to prepare a community care plan and to provide assessment of individual needs should ensure far greater consumer representation and consultation in the provision of social services.

Standard setting and the law

In the chapter on professional accountability it is explained that the courts use the standard of the Bolam test (see glossary) in determining whether there is a breach of the duty of care in a case of alleged negligence. This relates to the reasonable standards which would be expected of a specific professional working in a particular context – what would be the accepted approved practice reasonably expected of him, and whether there are any professionally acceptable reasons justifying a departure from this standard. Evidence would be given before the courts by experts to explain the acceptable expected practice. Where the experts were in conflict, the person bringing the action would have to show why the defendant acted unreasonably in following a different practice.

■ How does the Bolam test relate to the standards set in the local charter of health and to the standards set in the NHS agreements between purchasers and providers and to the standards set by individual NHS Trusts and directly managed units?

Clearly the Bolam test cannot be based on local standards: it would be no justification for one hospital to claim that, because of resources or lack of staff training, it could not be expected to diagnose fractures – the patient is entitled to receive the reasonable standard of care wherever he is treated. It would, however, be possible to use national standards of, for example, what particular services would be provided to a person suffering from a specific condition.

Limitations of the charters

There are some weaknesses and disadvantages of the charter movement. The first is that there are no legal powers of enforcing the provisions within a charter, whether national or local. If the provider fails to conform to the charter terms or NHS terms and if there are no other providers who can replace the provider at fault there is little the purchaser can do (other than ask the Secretary of State to terminate the Trust). Patients are similarly powerless; only if there is an existing legal right of action which covers some of the principles of the charter can they enforce its provisions. For example, the charter might state that the patient must be informed of the treatments available and be given appropriate advice before giving consent. This is a legally recognised right and is discussed in Chapter 3. On the other hand there is no legal right to insist that care is given and if the charter promises that a health professional will visit within a specified time this is not enforceable.

Clients or patients are not part of the internal market. Others negotiate on their behalf – the GP fund-holding practice, the purchaser and providers – but patients have no direct say in these negotiations. This is unlike the situation in private practice where a contract would exist between the patient and the professional who is providing private services and the terms of the contract can be enforced by and against the patient.

Nor does it follow that resources will necessarily be available to meet the decisions on health needs made by local purchasers or social services.

A BILL OF RIGHTS AND RELATED ISSUES

There has been an increasing number of calls for a Bill of Rights to be recognised and for charters for specific client groups to be drawn up. In its 1993 report the Select Committee of the House of Commons[4] expressed the view that there should be a Community Care Charter which would specify the minimum level of service under the community care reforms. The Charter would include the right to choose between public and private provision. It also advised that patients whose needs are assessed under the provisions of section 47 of the 1990 Act (see Chapter 25) should be given the results of their assessment even when there are no resources to meet the identified need. This is contrary to the earlier advice of the Department of Health. In this way the Select Committee considered that it would be possible to check whether the policy is working and adequately funded.

An example given of the varying standards between local authorities is that in one area the services of a home help are free while in another area a client could be paying up to £27 for less than three hours. The Select Committee suggested that there should be national guidelines for charges.

Another example of a call for a charter in care is contained in the report of a working party chaired by Lady Howe[5]. It recommended that those residents who live in residential homes should have a code of rights. The report suggested that a code of rights is fundamental to the delivery of a quality service. Each authority should draw up its own code. In the meantime the Inquiry has asked the Department of Health to gather together the appropriate bodies to discuss a national minimum code. (The report is further discussed in Chapter 31)

This call for the recognition of rights for persons in residential accommodation was foreshadowed in the report of the DHSS sponsored working party on *Home Life: a code of practice for residential care*[6]. See also the other calls for the development of codes and charters of rights discussed in Chapter 31.

The situation generally in relation to residential care homes and the rights of residents is considered further in Chapter 31.

Rights for disabled persons

An attempt by Alfred Morris to bring his Civil Rights (Disabled Persons) Bill into law in 1993 failed as a result of Government lack of support. It was given a third reading in the House of Lords but the Government obstructed its second reading in the House of Commons. This Bill would have given to disabled persons the right not to be discriminated against. A subsequent attempt to introduce similar legislation in 1994 failed for the same reasons. The situation contrasts strongly with such countries as Australia. In New South Wales a Disabilities Services Act 1993 No 3 aims at ensuring the provision of services necessary to enable persons with disabilities to achieve their maximum potential as members of the community. Amongst the specified objectives are to ensure that the provision of services furthers the integration of persons with disabilities into the community and enables them to achieve positive outcomes, such as increased independence, employment opportunities and integration, and to provide services in ways that promote in the community a positive image of persons with disabilities and enhance their self-esteem.

However, in 1995 the Disability Discrimination Act 1995 was finally passed.

This Act makes it unlawful to discriminate against disabled persons in connection with employment, the provision of goods, facilities and services or the disposal or management of premises. It also makes provision about the employment of disabled persons and establishes a National Disability Council. As with much of the health legislation, the bulk of the provisions are to come into force piecemeal on dates to be appointed by the Secretary of State.

A person has a disability if 'he has a physical or mental impairment which has a substantial and long-term adverse effect on his ability to carry out normal day-to day duties.' Guidance may be issued by the Secretary of State about the matters which must be taken into account in the application of this definition.

Part II covers discrimination in employment. It is unlawful for an employer to discriminate against a disabled person (that is unjustifiably treat the disabled person less favourably) in arrangements for recruitment, and also in the terms of employment which are offered – including opportunities for promotion, training and other benefits. The disabled employee is also protected against dismissal or other detriment. Regulations will be made to cover these provisions and also to define further the duties of the employer in relation to physical arrangements. Small businesses are exempt from these provisions if the employer has fewer than 20 employees.

The disabled person has the right to apply to an Industrial Tribunal over any discrimination. There are also provisions covering discrimination of contract workers and discrimination by trade union organisations. Discrimination by occupational pension schemes and insurance services is also made illegal.

Part III covers discrimination in the provision of goods, facilities and services. It is unlawful for a provider of services to discriminate against a disabled person by refusing to provide him with services, or in relation to the standard or terms of the service. There is a duty on service providers to take such steps as are reasonable to make alterations to buildings or the approach or access, and to provide auxiliary aids, such as audio tapes or sign language. Regulations will be passed to determine what is reasonable and on the implementation of this duty.

Part IV covers discrimination in education.

Part V deals with public transport.

Part VI establishes the National Disability Council. This Council will, following consultation, advise the Secretary of State on relevant matters as requested, and prepare Codes of Practice.

In theory the framework is in place for a major revolution to take place in the lives of disabled persons. However in practice the value of the Act will depend on the more detailed guidance and regulations still to be passed and the extent to which the Government of the day places its weight behind the legislation. Much, too, will depend upon the new National Disability Council acting as a pressure force to ensure that unjustified discrimination is attacked and the individual disabled person is protected.

There has been concern about the financial consequences of the implementation of the provisions. The Government has estimated that the cost to employers of taking on disabled persons will be £8 million and adapting buildings and improving access could cost between £380 million to £1.13 billion.

Consumerism in community care

Interesting experiments have developed to give individual consumers a greater voice in purchasing activity. For example in Newcastle consumer groups have been set up to inform purchasers of consumer requirements in the context of mental health services. In 1991 Newcastle's mental health group were invited by the Newcastle Health Authority to an all day strategy meeting entitled 'Purchasing for People'. The aim was to give users the opportunity to communicate directly with purchasers and explore how services might be changed to address problems which were identified. Also involved in the meeting were representatives from the Community Health Councils (CHCs) and GPs. Some of the problems identified were:

- patients being offered tranquillisers and being told that nothing else could be done;
- a lack of follow up after discharge;
- no counselling available as an alternative to referral to a psychiatrist.

In January 1992 a research officer was employed by the Newcastle CHC to follow up the problems identified by users in the field of support for people with mental health problems[7].

Incompetence and the protection of the rights of individuals

The community care management approach relies upon the involvement of the client in the assessment of needs and in the decision making over priorities. However, there is growing awareness of the numbers of adults receiving care who are incapable of making decisions relating to their medical care or treatment and their day to day lives. Nevertheless, for those with impaired cognitive skills it might be possible through various strategies to ensure that there is full participation in the decisions which are made[8].

The Law Commission in its consultation paper No. 119[9] has shown that we cannot be complacent about the protection of the rights of those adults who are mentally incapable of making decisions but that some mechanism is required, or at the very least a strengthening of existing machinery, in order to provide safeguards for this vulnerable group. Three consultation papers have been published following the initial overview in 1991. These cover the areas of private law, medical treatment and research and public law[10]. In 1995 the Law Commission published its conclusions from the consultation exercise[11] and drafted legislation to ensure the protection of the mentally incompetent adult over the whole area of decision making on their behalf and this will be discussed in the next chapter.

Even where clients would be capable of being involved in the assessment process, there is evidence from research undertaken by MENCAP[12] that there is a wide variation between local authorities on the extent to which clients are given the necessary information and involved in the assessment process. This is further discussed in Chapter 13. The MENCAP research is supported by research undertaken by the British Medical Association[13]. The BMA assistant secretary stated that 'whether you get a good package of care depends on the part of the country that you live in'. Two thirds of the 500 GPs who responded to the survey said the availability of home helps – the cornerstone of care in the community – had worsened. Increased efforts by social workers to keep dependent elderly people in their homes were using up available resources and denying help to others who previously received it.

Concern for carers

Many were concerned that the assessment provisions did not give a clear statutory responsibility to the local authority to assess the ability of the carers to provide help for the client, taking into account their own limitations and disabilities. This omission is now partly filled by the Carers (Recognition and Services) Act 1995. This Act provides for the assessment of the ability of the carers to provide care. This topic is considered in detail in Chapter 22.

CONCLUSIONS

It is not surprising that under the new legislation there is still no absolute right to receive community services, whether health or social services. The allocation is ultimately dependent upon the resources available and, in the light of earlier cases, it is probable that the courts will continue to be reluctant to interfere where the allocation is reasonable. However, there are likely to be new applications to the courts under the 1990 Act in relation to the duties of assessment and the community care plans. As assessments reveal needs for which resources are inadequate, complaints resulting from these increased expectations are likely to occur and the complaints mechanism which all social service departments and hospitals have a duty to carry out might not resolve all concerns.

A further complication which creates an imbalance in any discussion of a right to receive care is the fact that health care, when provided, must be on the basis that contributions from the client are not chargeable unless legislation expressly enables charges to be levied. In contrast social services provided under the NAA 1948 and subsequent legislation enable the recipient to be means-tested and required to contribute to the costs of the service. This major distinction will, as long as it remains, always cause a major impediment to the achievement of a 'seamless service' as clients and carers protest at the transfer of functions from health providers to social services or others.

In addition, the unevenness of social services provision across the country and the wide variations in the charges to the clients and carers emphasise the inequalities and the lack of any legal rights to enforce individual provision. This lack of uniformity is accentuated by the differences in the provision of voluntary services.

Such inequalities are bound to lead to further calls for charters, bills of rights and government intervention, and for further central funding of hard pressed local authority budgets. The Citizen's Charter, the Patient's Charter and the Primary Health Care Charter have not contained powers of enforcement of the locally agreed standards, but they do provide bench marks for evaluating and monitoring the services.

Ultimately the client or carer who requires an essential service cannot invoke charters but must look to the courts and the legal profession for assistance. Unfortunately, the changes to the contribution levels for the receipt of legal aid have meant that the numbers who can benefit from the legal aid scheme are considerably reduced. The introduction of payment of legal fees only on the basis of winning (the conditional fee system (see glossary) introduced 10 July 1995) may increase the numbers of law suits, but clarity of legislation and better identification of legal rights would still be of considerable advantage. (The difficulties over the enforcement of legal rights are considered further in Chapter 27.)

CHAPTER 3

Consent to treatment

This chapter considers the law which relates to the consent of the client to treatment and care. The chapter begins with general consideration of the law relating to trespass to the person and then looks at the defences to such an action which include the consent of the patient. The areas to be covered are shown in Figure 3.1.

Figure 3.1   Contents of chapter

- Trespass to the person
- Wilful act calculated to cause physical harm
- False imprisonment
- Defences:
    - Consent:
        - General principles
        - Special groups: Minors of 16 and 17
        - Minors under 16
        - The mentally disordered
    - Medical necessity
    - Statutory authorisation and common law rights
- The difference between trespass and negligence
    - The right to be informed
    - Withholding information

INTRODUCTION

Professionals are often perplexed at the extent and limit of their powers to assist their clients into accepting care and treatment. These issues are often heightened in the community where the professional may be dealing with basic issues relating to human rights without the support and advice or help of colleagues and also outside the institutionalising effect that hospital has upon residents. At the heart of this debate is the dilemma of the individual's autonomy and his legal and ethical right to make his own choice, and the professional desire and duty to act in the long term interests of the client even though this may mean using short term coercion to achieve such an outcome.

This chapter seeks to deal with these conflicts in the community setting, examining the law in relation to the practical problems which the various professionals face. Topics to be covered will include the basic principles of law relating to consent to treatment. The individual's right of action for trespass to the person, false imprisonment and negligence will also be considered.

Special areas will be considered in relation to minors and the mentally disordered. The following chapter will cover the statutory power of entry onto another person's land which will be considered together with the rights to remove a person from his home. Subsequent chapters look at the rights relating to confidentiality and access to health records.

TRESPASS TO THE PERSON

The basic remedy for any unauthorised touching of the person is an action for trespass to the person. Figure 3.2 sets out the main features.

Figure 3.2 Elements in an action for trespass to the person

Battery: An act of the defendant which
- directly intentionally or negligently
- causes physical contact with the person of the plaintiff
- without the plaintiff's consent.

Assault: An act of the defendant which
- directly intentionally or negligently
- causes fear of physical contact
- with the person of the plaintiff
- without the plaintiff's consent.

A writ of trespass is one of the oldest legal remedies dating from at least the thirteenth century. It is a right of action where there has been 'intentional interference with the interests in the person or the property of the plaintiff'. Social touching is excluded from this definition and the courts have held that there must be evidence of hostility if harm results from the touching in a social context[14]. Hostility would not be required to be shown, however, where a professional, wanting to act in the client's best interests, carried out treatment upon the client without his consent and possibly contrary to his expressed wishes.

A community physiotherapist considers that it is in the best interests of the client to receive a particular form of therapy, even though the client is not prepared to consent to it. Against the wishes of the client, the physiotherapist carries out the treatment skilfully and causes no harm.

The client could still bring an action for trespass to the person: there has been an unwanted physical contact with the patient. In addition, as can be seen from Figure 3.2, it is not essential that harm be established. The mere touching of the plaintiff's person is sufficient as the basis of an action in trespass. Clearly, however, if in addition harm is established compensation would be greater. Different considerations apply if the patient is incapable of making a decision and this is discussed below.

Battery

The main form of trespass to the person is known as 'battery'. This is any act of the defendant which directly and either intentionally or negligently causes some physical contact with the person of the plaintiff. Battery is both a civil and criminal wrong. This means that there can be a prosecution in the criminal courts as well as an action for compensation in the civil courts. There could be both, but usually if there has been a successful criminal prosecution (where compensation could be ordered to be paid to the victim) the defendant in the civil action would admit liability. This is because there is a higher standard of proof in the criminal courts where the prosecution must prove beyond all reasonable doubt that the accused is guilty. In contrast in the civil courts the standard of proof is on a balance of probabilities. For the most part we are concerned with the civil law in this chapter.

Turning back to the situation above, the physiotherapist who touched the client without the client's consent in order to carry out therapy is liable in battery to the client.

Situation

A care assistant wishes to cut the hair of an elderly person in a residential home. The elderly resident refuses. If the care assistant persists and the elderly person does not lack mental capacity then this would constitute a trespass to her person, that is a battery. However there may be a lawful exception to this trespass (see below under the heading 'Necessity').

Assault

Another form of trespass is an 'assault'. Here there is no actual touching but the plaintiff apprehends such contact as a result of an intentional or negligent act of the defendant. The care assistant in the situation described above who advances with the hair brush and scissors but does not actually touch the elderly person would be liable for assault if she knew the elderly person was refusing to give consent to having her hair cut and the elderly person feared that it would happen.

WILFUL ACT CALCULATED TO CAUSE PHYSICAL HARM

In addition to an action for trespass to the person it is possible to bring an action for a wilful act or statement by a defendant which is calculated to cause physical harm to the plaintiff. In this cause of action there must be evidence that the physical harm actually occurred.

Situation

A community nurse for the mentally impaired, exasperated with the lack of co-operation and awkwardness of her client, loses her temper shouts at the client (who is known to have a fear of lions ever since visiting the zoo) that unless he behaves himself he will be thrown to the lions for their supper. As a result of this the client suffers from serious nervous shock, nightmares, insomnia and feeding disorders.

In these circumstances the client would have a potential cause of action against the community nurse for her wilful statement which was calculated to cause physical harm. The client's representative would, however, have to prove that the defendants's act was so plainly calculated to produce some effect of that kind, that the intention to produce it ought to be imputed to the defendant.

The nurse would of course also face the possibility of proceedings before the professional conduct committee of the UKCC and also disciplinary proceedings from her employer.

FALSE IMPRISONMENT

Finally the client may have a claim against the professionals on the basis of a false imprisonment. More publicity is given to the false imprisonment of persons in institutions (see the *Code of Practice: Mental Health Act 1983* produced by the Department of Health, second edition 1993). However even in the community there could be situations where a client is locked in a room or in a house and an action for false imprisonment would be available.

Situation

A community psychiatric nurse attends a small family unit of four mentally ill long term chronic schizophrenic patients who have been discharged from the psychiatric ward to the family unit. She leaves the house and locks it. None of the residents have keys and they are thus effectively locked in. In theory, if they attempted to leave and found they were locked in, they would have an action for false imprisonment: the nurse has directly and either intentionally or negligently caused the residents to be confined to an area.

In order to succeed in an action for false imprisonment the residents would have to show the elements which are set out in Figure 3.3. On the nurse's behalf it could be argued that there was no intention to imprison them, it was merely an oversight – an accident. However, provided the residents could show negligence on her part even though they could not establish intention, that should be sufficient. The nurse, of course, could argue that it was done deliberately so that the clients would be safe overnight and that she was acting in their best interests. This defence is unlikely to succeed since it could be said that if that was necessary then there should have been 24 hour staffing cover. The residents would also have to establish that they were completely imprisoned. If, for example, there is a back door which is openable from the inside then there is no false imprisonment. What if there is no back door, but there is a ground floor window which could have been opened? This fact may prevent the imprisonment being complete and therefore actionable. However, account would be taken of the potential danger in using alternative methods of escape and the physical and mental competence of the residents. If the residents were too elderly and mentally disturbed to arrange for departure through the window, which was therefore impracticable as an exit, they are effectively falsely imprisoned.

Figure 3.3 Elements in an action for false imprisonment

An act of the defendant which
- intentionally or negligently directly causes
- the confinement of the plaintiff
- within a limited area.

Some residents in small community homes could be confined in a room as a punishment. Many fear that such abuses will be less easy to detect in the community and much depends upon the system for inspection. In hospitals the legal basis for using seclusion should be clarified: its use should be carefully scrutinised and records kept for inspection, and there should be regular examination by trained nursing and medical staff. In the community there is unlikely to be this level of supervision by trained staff and abuses may go undetected. In addition in ordinary family homes an elderly mentally infirm person or a mentally impaired person might lose her freedom in this way (see Chapter 17 on the health visitor and signs of elder abuse).

DEFENCES TO AN ACTION FOR TRESPASS TO THE PERSON

The following are the main defences against an action for trespass to the person which will be considered in this chapter:

- Consent
- Necessity
- Statutory authorisation.

Consent – general principles

The above causes of action can be successfully defended if there is evidence that the plaintiff gave consent.

■ What is meant by consent in relation to an action for trespass to the person?

Consent must be freely given, a non-coerced permission for the professional to carry out an action which would otherwise be a trespass to the person. It must be given by a mentally competent person who has the capacity to give a valid consent.

Difficulties arise since the law does not, except in very specific situations (such as the Mental Health Act 1983) insist that consent is given in a particular form. It could be given in writing, in spoken words or even by implication. Clearly, it is in the interests of the professional, in the light of the possibility of facing an action for trespass to the person, to be aware that the greater the risk to the patient and the more likely an action for trespass to the person, the more important it is to ensure that there is the best possible evidence that the patient consented.

Situation

A chiropodist attends an elderly person at home: the risk of harm to the patient is minimal but it seems to the chiropodist that the patient is hesitant.

The chiropodist might be well advised to ask the patient if he is happy for the treatment to proceed. If another person is present, then there would be a confirmatory witness. In exceptional circumstances, the chiropodist might consider asking for the patient's consent in writing. This would certainly be so if the treatment involved a local anaesthetic or minor surgery on a part of the patient's feet.

■ What if the chiropodist believes that the patient is incapable as a result of mental incapacity of giving a valid consent?

This is dealt with later in this chapter but here it must be emphasised that there is no power at the moment in law for one person to give consent on behalf of another adult. A relative or carer could not therefore be asked by the chiropodist to give consent on behalf of the client.

Once it is established that the client has given real consent to the treatment then the action for trespass to the person will fail.

Case: *Chatterton v. Gerson*[15]

Judge Bristow held that the plaintiff had to show that there had been a lack of real consent.

If the patient had been informed in broad terms of the nature of the intended treatment and has given consent the patient could not then say that there had been a lack of real consent.

In such circumstances, if the patient can show that the significant risks of substantial harm were not notified to him he might have an action in negligence on the basis of the professional's failure to inform him (see below) but an action founded in trespass will fail.

Implied consent

In practice community professionals rarely obtain the consent of the patient in writing. Indeed they may seldom seek an express statement by word of mouth that the patient is prepared for the treatment to proceed. Some therapies are, of course, by their very nature impossible to perform without the consent of the patient – if the patient is not prepared to undertake speech therapy then the speech therapist could not force this to be done (except possibly with threats of violence). Similarly occupational therapy usually relies upon the compliance, co-operation and willingness of the client, otherwise it cannot be performed. However other professionals might find it possible to carry out their care with a refusing client:

● a district nurse may attempt to bath an unwilling client with the help of an assistant, relative or friend;

● the community psychiatric nurse might attempt to administer medication by injection without the consent of the patient;

● a physiotherapist might try to encourage ambulation in a patient confined to bed.

Should they attempt to perform these tasks in the absence of consent or other authorisation (considered below) then they would be liable for trespass to the person.

Often, however, the situation is not so clear. There may be no consent in writing or by word of mouth, and there may be no evidence of refusal by the patient. In this situation there may be implied consent. Implied consent is non-verbal communication by the client that he agrees with the professional proceeding with the treatment. It may be the rolling up of a sleeve for an injection, taking off a shirt for a chest examination, holding out an arm for blood pressure to be taken. In such circumstances, the professional can rely on the implied consent to treatment. There can, however, be dangers since both the client and the professional can misread the situation: there may be no meeting of minds as to what is to occur. Implied consent is thus a more risky defence to an action for trespass to the person than express consent and very much more difficult to establish in evidence before the court.

Written consent
If a patient has signed a consent form for the treatment which took place, it is very difficult for him to argue that he did not read the form or had little idea of what he was signing for, and in the absence of fraud, coercion or some form of deceit, the patient's signature on the form will usually indicate that real consent has been given.

There are considerable advantages to the professional and also to clients in suggesting that consent should be in writing. One advantage is to make it expressly clear to clients that the proposed treatment is not without risks and that they are exercising their autonomy and choice in making the decision to go ahead. Many of the treatments, for example, which are administered by a practice nurse (such as ear syringing and vaccinations) do have risks and consent in writing by the client would seem a wise safeguard for both client and professional. The NHS Management Executive has designed a form for consent to treatments given by professionals other than doctors and dentists and this is reproduced in Appendix 2.

The competence of the client to give consent
Clearly a young child, or a severely mentally impaired client, may be incapable of giving a valid consent. It is a question of fact in each case as to whether the capacity exists. What happens with specific cases of incapacity is considered in more detail below. The general presumption is that an adult is capable of giving a valid consent. This presumption could, however, be rebutted in cases where there was evidence of incapacity. Unfortunately, it is often only when the treatment proposed by the professional is actually questioned by the adult client that the issue of capacity and competence to consent is raised. If the client agrees with the proposed treatment or shows no opposition to receiving it then his competence to consent is accepted: if he disagrees this competence is queried.

In the normal situation the professional determines both the competency of the client to give consent and also recommends the treatment which should be given. The Law Commission has recommended that statutory measures should be taken to enable decisions on behalf of the mentally incompetent adult to be made. These are discussed below.

Consent – special groups

So far we have considered the general principles of consent in relation to the mentally competent adult (that is a person of 18 and over). Now we shall consider variations on these in relation to special groups.

Minors of 16 and 17 years

Specific statutory provisions set out in Figure 3.5 enable minors of 16 and 17 to give consent to treatment in their own right. Treatment is widely defined as can be seen from subsection (2) in Figure 3.4.

Figure 3.4 Family Law Reform Act 1969 – section 8

(1) The consent of minor who has attained the age of sixteen years to any surgical, medical or dental treatment which, in the absence of consent, would constitute a trespass to his person, shall be as effective as it would be if he were of full age; and where a minor has by virtue of this section given an effective consent to any treatment it shall not be necessary to obtain any consent for it from his parent or guardian.

(2) In this section, 'surgical, medical or dental treatment' includes any procedure undertaken for the purposes of diagnosis, and this section applies to any procedure (including, in particular, the administration of an anaesthetic) which is ancillary to any treatment as it applies to that treatment.

(3) Nothing in this section shall be construed as making ineffective any consent which would have been effective if this section had not been enacted.

The statutory provision is in addition to pre-existing rights of consent (see section 8(3)) and therefore the parents still retain the right they had at common law to give consent on behalf of the 16 and 17 year old minor. In addition the mature, comprehending minor of under 16 years could in certain circumstances give a valid consent to treatment (see below).

■ Can parents overrule minors of 16 and 17 and insist that treatment be given against their wishes?

The point arose in the case of *Re W*.

Case: *Re W*[16]

In this case a 16 year old who suffered from anorexia refused to be treated. The question was could her refusal to accept treatment be overruled by the court or the parents or those acting *in loco parentis* (see glossary). The answer was held to be 'yes'. She could be compelled to accept the treatment. The 1969 Act which gave 16 and 17 year olds the right to give consent did not necessarily mean that their refusal could not be overruled. The

Court of Appeal held that this was correctly decided and did not conflict with the principles set out in the Children Act 1989.

One of the themes of the Children Act is the importance attached to the wishes of the child, but section 1(1) of the Act emphasises that in any decisions concerning a child the child's welfare shall be the Court's paramount consideration. Figure 3.5 sets out some of the provisions of the Children Act in relation to the involvement of the child in decision making.

Figure 3.5   The Children Act and the child's involvement in decision making

Section 1 *Welfare of the child*
(1) When a court determines any question with respect to—
(a) the upbringing of a child; or
(b) the administration of a child's property or the application of any income arising from it, *the child's welfare shall be the court's paramount consideration.* [author's emphasis]

(2) In any proceedings in which any question with respect to the upbringing of a child arises, the court shall have regard to the general principle that any delay in determining the question is likely to prejudice the welfare of the child.

(3) In the circumstances mentioned in subsection (4), [in deciding whether to make, vary, or discharge an order under section 8 (residence, contact, and other orders with respect to children) and under Part IV (Care and Supervision)] a court shall have regard in particular to—

(a) *the ascertainable wishes and feelings of the child concerned (considered in the light of his age and understanding)*; [author's emphasis]
(b) his physical, emotional and educational needs;
(c) the likely effect on him of any change in his circumstances; . . .

In general, the community professional is in the position of being able to rely on the consent of a minor of 16 or 17 years or the consent of the parent for treatment to be given. The statutory provisions enable the professional to discuss treatments, diagnosis, prognosis and so on with the 16 and 17 year old on their own without the parent's presence and to respect the patient's wish for information to be kept confidential (see Chapter 5).

This is of particular importance to the nurse working with the mentally disturbed adolescent, or in a family planning clinic or in a practice where the youngster might seek confidential advice and treatment and not be prepared, at least initially, for this to be disclosed to his parents.

Minors under 16 years

■ Can a minor so young give consent?

Parents have the right to give consent to treatment on behalf of their children where the proposed treatment is in the best interests of the child. However, minors who are capable of understanding the significance of the proposed treatment can, in exceptional circumstances, be regarded as competent in law to give consent. This was the issue considered by the House of Lords in the case of *Gillick* v. *West Norfolk and Wisbech Area Health Authority*[17]. The issues which were debated in that case are shown in Figure 3.6.

Figure 3.6 Issues in the *Gillick* case

- Did a minor under 16 years have the right to receive advice and treatment without the consent or knowledge of the parents?
- What were the parents' rights?
- Would a doctor be commission, aiding or abetting the commission of a criminal offence in giving contraceptive advice or treatment to a girl under 16 years?

The view of the majority was that in exceptional circumstances a doctor could give advice and contraceptive treatment to a girl under 16 years without the involvement and consent of her parents and in these exceptional circumstances the doctor would be justified in respecting the confidentiality of the girl. Lord Fraser emphasised that the doctor should be satisfied that:

- the girl would understand his advice
- he could not persuade her to inform her parents herself or to allow him to inform the parents that she was seeking contraceptive advice
- she was very likely to have sexual intercourse with or without contraceptive treatment
- unless she received contraceptive advice or treatment her physical or mental health or both were likely to suffer, and
- her best interests required him to give her contraceptive advice, treatment or both without parental consent.

It could be said that the actual decision of the case related only to contraceptive advice or treatment and cannot be authority for other forms of consent being given by the minor under 16 years. However, this would be to take too narrow a view of the House of Lords judgment. In their discussion of the legal basis for a minor giving a valid consent, they considered a wide range of precedents and situations. The exceptional circumstances would, of course, vary from situation to situation.

The Children Act 1989, which was passed since the *Gillick* case was decided, has of course, as can be seen in Figure 3.6, placed far greater emphasis on the involvement of the child in the decision making process.

Situation

A school nurse escorts a 14 year old child with a severely bleeding forehead to the accident and emergency department. Contact with the parents cannot initially be made. The child is conscious, mature and capable of understanding the options and is prepared to give his consent to having a general anaesthetic. The alternative is a series of local anaesthetics which the accident and emergency doctor does not favour. Could the doctor accept the consent given by the child as sufficient authorisation to perform the operation?

A simple answer cannot be given to this question without a lot more information. Clearly the more substantial the risks of harm arising from any proposed treatment the more unsafe it is to rely upon the child's consent alone. Time also is crucial: the possibility of waiting for contact to be made with the parents must be balanced against the risk of delay in carrying out the treatment. If the professional feared for the life of the child if treatment were delayed, treatment could proceed on the basis of the ruling of the House of Lords in *Re F* (see glossary) on the common law duty of the professional to act in the best interests of a patient who is incapable of giving a valid consent, or alternatively on the basis of the minor's consent should he be regarded as having the capacity to give a valid consent.

In the end it is a question of professional judgment as to the capacity of the child, the particular circumstances of the treatment required and the dangers in acting without the knowledge of the parents. (In the above situation, for example, it might be necessary to see the parents in case there has been any history of allergies or difficulties with anaesthetics.) As in all such cases of professional discretion, it is vital that comprehensive records are kept of the circumstances of the child giving consent and the basis of any course of action, so that if eventually the parents were to complain, or even sue for trespass to the child's person, detailed accounts of the events and the reasons for any decision are available.

■ Could the school nurse give consent on behalf of the child?

This situation may now be covered by section 3(5) of the Children Act 1989 which is set out in Figure 3.7.

Figure 3.7 Children Act 1989 – section 3(5)

A person who —

(a) does not have parental responsibility for a particular child; but
(b) has care of the child,

may (subject to the provisions of this Act) do what is reasonable in all the circumstances of the case for the purpose of safeguarding or promoting the child's welfare.

This provision would enable the school nurse to give consent to essential emergency treatment or routine stitches, subject to the necessity of finding out any background information about the child's allergies and so on (see above). It would probably not cover the situation of major elective surgery.

■ Can the parents' views be overruled?

The presumption behind the parents' right to give or withhold consent is that the parents will be making a decision which is in the child's best interests. Where this is not so, appropriate action can be taken. Two situations arise:

● where the parents have consented or are consenting to treatment and that treatment is not deemed to be in the best interests of the child; and

● where the parents are withholding their consent to treatment which the professionals consider is necessary for the child.

Case: Re D[18]

This is an example of the first situation. The parents and certain medical staff agreed that a sterilisation operation would be performed upon an eleven year old girl who was suffering from Sotos Syndrome, a degenerating condition which could lead to serious mental retardation. An educational psychologist and other teaching staff approached the area administrator of the health authority to stop the operation going ahead but without success. They eventually applied to the court for the child to be made a ward of court. Mrs Justice Heilbron decided that, in the interests of the child, the operation should not proceed. It was not therapeutically necessary (that is the girl was not suffering from a physical illness or disease which required immediate surgery involving sterilisation) and to perform the operation at this stage was unjustified.

One fact which emerged from the case was that the gynaecologist who was prepared to undertake the operation had in the past performed sterilisations on girls under 16 years on the basis of their parents' consent. It was fortuitous that in the case the girl was made a ward of court.

Case: Re B (1987)[19]

The House of Lords recommended in this case that a procedure should be set down to ensure that such decisions were not left in the hands of parents and doctors. They had to decide whether a sterilisation operation on a mentally handicapped girl of 17 years should proceed. In a unanimous judgment they agreed that it was in her best interests to have the operation.

Case: Re B (1981)[20]

The other situation – that where the parents are withholding consent to treatment which is deemed necessary – is illustrated by this case. Here the parents decided not to consent to an operation to relieve an intestinal blockage on a Down's Syndrome baby aged 10 days. The doctors contacted the local authority who made the child a ward of court. The court ordered the operation to proceed. The surgeons, on discussing the issue with the parents declined to perform it, and the judge revoked the order. The Court of Appeal, however, ordered the operation to proceed.

This problem arises when blood transfusions are required by children of Jehovah's Witnesses. DHSS guidance suggests that if doctors consider the blood to be essential in the interests of the child they should transfuse the blood. However, such a decision is not to be taken lightly since a child given a blood transfusion may be rejected by his Jehovah's Witness parents.

■ What steps can be taken?

Applying these legal principles to the community situation, there may be some occasions when a community professional such as a health visitor or educational/clinical psychologist comes across a decision which has been made relating to treatment of a child under 16 years and which does not appear to be in the best interests of the child. Any interested person is able to apply for wardship proceedings and the treatment decision can then be reviewed by the court to determine whether it is in the interests of the child. Obviously an application for wardship should not be undertaken lightly and full discussions should be held with those involved in the questionable decision. The important point is that, like section 47 of the National Assistance Act 1948 (see Chapter 4), it is another significant weapon in the armoury of the community professional, to be kept in reserve but available for use in extreme circumstances to protect the interests of the child.

The Children Act 1989 has made changes in the use of wardship to challenge local authority action in respect of children in care. The Act does not however directly affect the individual's right to invoke the jurisdiction of the High Court and as soon as the originating summons is issued the child becomes a ward of court and no important step can be taken with regard to the child's life without prior court sanction[21].

■ What if the minor is mentally disordered?

Mentally disordered minors would come under exactly the same principles discussed above. Account would, however, have to be taken of the limitations to their capacity in applying the *Gillick* ruling (see above).

The mentally disordered adult

■ How are the Courts involved?

Problems arise in relation to the mentally disordered adult who is incapable of giving a valid consent. This issue was considered in the following case.

Case: *Re F* [22]

The facts of this case are given on page 50 below. The conclusion was that where the adult was mentally incompetent, and therefore unable to give a valid consent, the doctor would not be acting unlawfully if he acted in her best interests and followed the accepted approved standard of care according to the Bolam test (see glossary). The House of Lords recommended that, where it was proposed to carry out treatment such as sterilisation, then the view of the court should be sought.

Case: *T* v. *T*[23]

The defendant in this case was a woman aged 19 who was epileptic and severely mentally handicapped. Her medical advisers recommended in her interests that her pregnancy be terminated and asked the court for a declaration that it was in order for them to proceed. The court held that there was no power in the Mental Health Act 1983 which enabled consent to be given. The court also said that there was no jurisdiction for the court as *parens patriae* to give consent to the operation. However, it was prepared to make a 'declaration' (see glossary) because the circumstances were special and proper medical practice demanded that the operation take place.

The decision in *Re F* was a landmark in providing the highest judicial authority to doctors acting in the best interests of the patient but what is also significant in these cases (and in the case *Re B* (1987) considered above) is not so much the decisions on the individual matters but the thread of commentary by the court on its role in filling the vacuum arising from the patients' incapacity to give valid consent.

■ What is the present situation?

As identified by the courts in the foregoing cases there is at present a vacuum in relation to the giving of consent on behalf of mentally disordered persons who are not under a section of the Mental Health Act 1983. No other individual has the right to give consent on their behalf. All the professional can do is act in the best interests of the client and follow the recognised professional practice according to the Bolam test, seeking the view of the court if the treatment is particularly risky or grave. However, as stated above the Law Commission has issued a Consultation Paper No. 129 on how this vacuum should be filled and this has been followed by draft proposals for a Bill (see below).

Situation

A resident in a community home for those with learning disabilities attends a dental surgery and the dentist advises the care assistant who accompanied him that an extraction is required. A further appointment is arranged and the care assistant is asked to sign the consent form on behalf of the 35 year old resident who is incapable of giving consent in his own right. She refuses. What is the legal position?

The care assistant is correct in refusing since at present there is no statute which gives to parents or other carers of mentally incapacitated adults the right to consent on their behalf. If the treatment is required then the dentist should act in the best interests of the patient and follow the recognised standard of professional practice on the basis of the ruling in *Re F*. Use of a specific form is recommended by the NHS Management Executive in such situations where the adult patient is incapable of giving consent and is not detained under the Mental Health Act 1983 and is shown in Appendix 2.

One of the major areas of difficulty in dealing with the incompetent adult is in the assessment and provision of services following that assessment. Where the client is incapable of giving valid consent to the choices available, the carers and professionals have to act in the best interests of the client, following acceptable standards of care. These choices might include decisions relating to the location and nature of residential or nursing home accommodation. The sections of the Disabled Persons (Services, Consultation and Representation) Act 1986 which relate to the appointment of representatives have not been implemented and are unlikely to be so (see further Chapter 25). Therefore, until the recommendations of the Law Commission are enacted, the carers and professionals will have to act on the common law authority given in *Re F*.

■ Can the gap be filled by current statutory provisions?

One of the hopes expressed in the white paper on mental health law which preceded the 1983 legislation was that guardianship orders under section 7 or section 37 of the Mental Health Act 1983 would become more widely used and enable more people who would otherwise have to be detained in hospital to be cared for in the community with guardianship supervision. That this has not occurred is partly due to the limited powers of a guardianship order. It may also be due to the fact that there is no compulsory power under the Mental Health Act 1983 to require a patient in the community to take medication. The guardian has three powers (see Figure 3.8) but these are difficult to enforce if the patient resists.

Figure 3.8   Mental Health Act 1983 – section 8 (guardian's powers)

- The power to require the patient to reside at a place specified by the authority or person named as guardian.
- The power to require the patient to attend at places and times so specified for the purpose of medical treatment, occupation, education or training.
- The power to require access to the patient to be given, at any place where the patient is residing, to any registered medical practitioner, approved social worker or other person so specified.

If the patient under guardianship absents himself without the permission of the guardian from any place where he is required to reside, he may be taken into custody and returned to that place by any officer on the staff of the local social services authority, any constable or any person authorised in writing by the guardian or local social services authority (section 18(3) Mental Health Act 1983). The previous provision for no recall after 28 days absence has been changed under the Mental Health (Patients in the Community) Act 1995.

Apart from this limited power to return the patient to the place where he is required to reside, there are few means of enforcing the other powers. The person required to visit the patient can attend but has no power under the Act to do more: even if she is a doctor or nurse she has no power to examine the patient physically or administer medication. Nor is it realistic or lawful to consider dragging the patient by force to the specified place for medical treatment, occupation, education or training.

Given the resource problems of many social services authorities together with these inherent weaknesses in the powers of guardianship, it is not surprising that the Mental Health Act 1983 did not lead to a resurgence in the popularity of guardianship orders. However, some use is made of it and professionals need therefore to be aware of its extent and implications, and their own responsibilities in relation to a client who is under guardianship. The Mental Health (Patients in the Community) Act 1995 makes provision for the introduction of an after-care supervision order which is discussed in the next chapter.

■ Why can't a spouse/cohabitee or relative give consent?

A few words are required to emphasise that the law does not recognise the right of one spouse to give or withhold consent on behalf of the other. Whilst there may have been authority in the past for the husband to give consent to treatment on behalf of his wife this is no longer so. Obviously the involvement, where appropriate, of a spouse or cohabitee in discussions relating to care and treatment is of value, but in the last resort, if the client refuses to consent or is incapable of consenting, the professional cannot rely on the substituted consent of the spouse or cohabitee. If there is a refusal to consent to necessary life saving treatment then this must be subjected to scrutiny by the professional as laid down in the case of Re T[24] discussed below and obviously discussions with spouse or cohabitee will be an important stage in analysing the refusal.

The same principles apply to other relatives. The views of the relatives on care, treatment and outcomes for the client may be of use to the professional but relatives do not have the legal powers either to insist on treatment or to refuse it.

Many professionals may have come across situations where they have been asked to 'let mother die' or not to carry out some form of care and treatment. However the relatives' views are not the determining factor. In the absence of a view expressed by the client, the professional must act according to the approved accepted practice in the light of the patient's prognosis: if the patient's medical condition justifies an operation or other treatment, the relatives' view that it should not take place should not prevail.

■ Can the client give or withhold consent in advance of becoming mentally incapable?

The Court of Appeal in the case of Re T[24] emphasised the right of a mentally competent adult to refuse treatment. In deciding whether a person who is at present incapable of giving consent would wish treatment to proceed the professional can consider the previously expressed wishes of the client. There is at present, however, no statutory system for people to define the extent or limits of treatment which they would wish to have in the future. Such declarations, which are legally recognised in certain states of America, are known as 'living wills', 'advance refusal of treatment' or 'advance statements/directives'. The Law Commission in its Consultation Paper[25] suggested that they should be formally recognised in English law and made proposals relating to the degree of formality and the legislation necessary. Their recommendations were considered by the House of Lords Select Committee on medical ethics[26] which supported the development of advance directives, but concluded that legislation was unnecessary. It recommended that a code of practice should be developed. However, the Law Commission has now drafted legislation[27] for statutory provision for an advance refusal of treatment. The Government has set up a working party to consider its proposals and legislation is expected. The BMA has in the meantime prepared a Code of Practice[28] in accordance with the suggestions of the House of Lords Select Committee.

Medical necessity

The best interests of the patient

One important defence to the professional in an action for trespass to the person is that the professional was acting out of necessity in the best interests of the person. This would be appropriate, for example, in an accident and emergency department when an unconscious patient is treated. In the community examples of acting out of necessity are likely to be less dramatic. Yet everyday care of the elderly mentally infirm who are unable to give consent to care will involve acting out of necessity.

Unfortunately, the legal basis for this defence at common law is not clearly spelt out. A case in 1909[29] which held that prison warders who force fed a suffragette acted out of necessity to save her life, so her action for battery failed, might well not be followed now. More significantly the refusal of a Broadmoor patient to have a gangrenous leg amputated was upheld by the court[29a] which found that his illness did not affect his competence to refuse consent. Medical opinion that the operation was necessary did not justify ignoring his express refusal and an injunction (see page 435) was granted against the doctors.

The House of Lords has provided some assistance in the case of *Re F*[30].

Case: *F* v. *West Berkshire Health Authority* (also known as *Re F*)

This case was concerned with the sterilisation of a mentally handicapped woman of 35 years. She was considered to have only a mental age of 4–5 years and to be incapable of giving a valid consent. Since she was over 18 years her parents could not give a consent on her behalf and an application was therefore made to the court to determine whether the sterilisation could proceed.

The court held unanimously that if the doctor acted in the best interests of the patient and followed the Bolam test he would not be acting unlawfully in performing the operation. This dictum has been applied to a wide range of situations of day to day care since the court emphasised that it was not only in life saving situations that these powers and duties existed. Acting in the best interests of the patient who was unable to give consent covered also those essential day to day tasks which were necessary for their health and to prevent deterioration of their condition. The duty also covered the emergency situation when the patient was unconscious.

What is not clear from the judgment is whether the duty covered those situations where the patient lacked the capacity to give consent and actually resisted care. The powers might for example justify short term detention of a mentally handicapped person to protect herself or others from harm but not long term detention since this would deny the patient the protection of the mental health legislation. For example the defence of necessity may justify the actions of a nurse who removes an elderly patient against her will from a blazing house. It would not justify the administration of medicines to a mentally disordered person in the community contrary to his wishes. It would probably be valid as a defence to a professional who prevents a patient from jumping from a third floor window in a suicide attempt, or who rushes an overdose patient to hospital for a washout. It would not however justify long term detention to protect the would-be suicide.

The lack of clarity and substantial guidelines is frustrating for the professional. Day to day care of patients who refuse to have their hair brushed, their nails cut, their bodies washed could, under the principles laid down in the case of *Re F*, be justified as acting in their best interests out of necessity. Yet there is little protection for the rights of patients and no check on the professionals' decisions. The situation is unsatisfactory both for client and professional.

The Law Commission papers
This vacuum has been addressed by the Law Commission in its papers dealing with decision making and the mentally incapacitated adult. In its Consultation Paper No. 129[31], which covers the area of medical treatment and research, it puts forward proposals for a new jurisdiction to be available for specified people who are incapacitated from making decisions. There should be a judicial forum with statutory jurisdiction:

● to make orders approving or disapproving the medical treatment of incapacitated patients; and

● to make declarations as to the patient's capacity or the scope or validity of the patient's own decisions.

This judicial forum could either make a single issue order or it could appoint a suitable person to discharge the duties of a medical treatment proxy for that person. Decisions relating to such major issues as sterilisation, donation of tissue, abortion, withdrawal of nutrition and hydration, and medical research could be subject to a special category of steps, which require advance approval by the judicial forum unless there is an emergency situation.

The Consultation Paper was followed by draft legislation drawn up by the Law Commission[32] which may be put before Parliament in 1996. The proposals contained in the draft legislation are summarised in Figure 3.9.

Figure 3.9 The Law Commission's proposals on incapacity

Part 1 – Mental incapacity

1. Incapacity should be given a statutory definition.
2. Actions should be taken in the best interests of persons without capacity, with regard to such circumstances as the person's past and present wishes and feelings, the need to encourage his participation.
3. It should be lawful to do anything for the welfare or health care of a person who is without capacity, including the use of their money.
4. The duty above does not authorise the use of force unless it is necessary to avert a substantial risk of serious harm to the person concerned.
5. Treatment can be given if authorised by a doctor as being in the best interests of the person, or authorised by the court.
6. An advance refusal of treatment should be given statutory recognition but cannot include the refusal of basic care.
7. Termination of life support procedures can be authorised by the court.
8. Any non-therapeutic research should be subject to the decision of a Mental Incapacity Research Committee.
9. The requirements for a continuing power of attorney are set down and it can extend to all personal welfare, health care, property or affairs, including the conduct of legal proceedings.
10. The powers of the court to make declarations and to appoint managers to make decisions on behalf of the incapacitated person are defined.
11. The manager's powers should be as limited in scope and duration as possible, but may include decisions on personal welfare matters and health care matters.
12. Certain decisions such as marriage, sexual relations and voting are excluded.
13. Codes of Practice are to be provided.
14. Offences are defined, including ill-treatment of mentally disabled person and concealing or destroying an advance refusal of treatment.

Part II – Persons in need of care or protection

1. Local authorities are given powers and duties to protect vulnerable persons.
2. The local authority should investigate if they have reason to believe that a vulnerable person is in need and make provision for community care services.
3. Powers of entry are given and warrants obtainable.
4. An assessment order can be made.
5. Temporary protection orders can be issued by the court.

Part III – Jurisdiction

1. A newly defined Court of Protection should be established to deal with Part I issues.
2. The newly defined Court of Protection, a magistrates court or justice of the peace should deal with matters arising under Part II.

Schedules cover:

- Payments due to persons without capacity.
- The mental incapacity research committee.
- Enduring powers of attorney.
- Property and affairs – supplementary provisions.

Refusal

Some assistance in the situation where the client refuses to give consent to a life saving treatment has been given by the Court of Appeal.

Case: *Re T.*[33]

Here a 20 year old pregnant woman told the nurse and midwife that she did not want a blood transfusion. She had been brought up by her mother who was a Jehovah's Witness. Her condition deteriorated to the point when a blood transfusion was necessary to save her life. Her father and her cohabitee sought the approval of the court for a blood transfusion to be given. The judge held that in the circumstances it was not clear that her refusal was based on clear capacity. There was evidence that her views had been overborne by her mother and he permitted the transfusion to go ahead. In reviewing the decision the Court of Appeal emphasised the right of the adult mentally competent person to refuse even life saving treatment. However, if there is evidence that the refusal is not properly that of a competent adult in that the adult is under the influence of drugs or drink or has had his or her mind overborne by the views of another, then the professional can proceed with the treatment in the best interests of the patient.

Statutory authorisation and common law rights

Treatment under the Mental Health Act 1983

Part IV of the Mental Health Act 1983 enables treatment for mental disorder to be given to certain detained patients if specific procedures are followed. However these provisions do not apply to the treatment of physical disorders and do not apply to those on short term sections (for example section 4, section 35, section 135 and section 136). Nor do they apply to informal patients except where it is proposed to undertake brain surgery as a treatment for mental disorder or to prescribe the implantation of hormones to reduce sexual drive. In these cases, informal patients have the same procedural protection as detained patients and the treatments can only be carried out with the consent of the patient and the consent of persons appointed by the Mental Health Act Commission (unless it is out of necessity and in the best interests of the patient).

To provide protection for the detained patient, where medication has been given for three months, it can only continue beyond that time with the consent of the patient or the referral to a second opinion doctor appointed by the Mental Health Act Commission. Electroconvulsive therapy can only be given with the consent of the patient or the supporting agreement of a second opinion appointed doctor unless a situation of urgency exists.

Where treatment is given to a detained patient under the provisions of the Mental Health Act 1983 the authorisation under the Act should be a valid defence against an action for trespass to the person.

Parental power to discipline

A concern with care assistants, social workers and community nurses for the mentally impaired is the extent to which they are authorised by law, *in loco parentis* (see glossary), to discipline those in their charge. If they were to exercise corporal punishment or lock up their charges temporarily could they be successfully sued for trespass to the person or false imprisonment? Would a defence of 'disciplining' succeed? The answer is probably not. Whilst parental power to discipline by corporal punishment or locking up was accepted as legal at common law, provided it is within reasonable limits, there is now statutory provision prohibiting the exercise of corporal punishment in maintained schools and against state funded pupils in independent schools. However, the common law cases justifying the defence of discipline in connection with schools and pupils not specified in the Education Act are still valid authorities. Until recently the cases did not cover situations outside the field of education: and there is still no direct authority for a nurse to exercise corporal punishment over a mentally impaired person or a care assistant to punish physically a resident, even though both these professionals may be deemed to be acting *in loco parentis*. A recent non-educational case[34] is where the local authority lost its appeal against a decision by the magistrates that a child minder should be reinstated on the authority's list of approved minders. She had been removed from the list on the ground that she had been prepared to exercise corporal punishment on her charges.

In spite of this case (where the element of choice available to the actual parents of the children concerned was relevant) the safest view is to assume that the defence of disciplining the client would be invalid in the nursing/care context and such measures should never be taken. This would probably be the view of the Professional Conduct Committee of the UKCC if it were asked to determine whether a registered nurse who used physical force against a client/resident was guilty of misconduct. This principle would apply to adults as well as to children.

Citizen's right to arrest
The private citizen has long enjoyed the right to make an arrest without a warrant and thus community professionals in their capacity as private citizens have this power. This power has now been placed on a statutory basis under the provisions of the Police and Criminal Evidence Act 1984. The details are set out in Figure 3.10.

Figure 3.10 Police and Criminal Evidence Act 1984 – section 24 (citizen's power to arrest)

(4) Any person may arrest without warrant —

(a) anyone who is in the act of committing an arrestable offence [see glossary];
(b) any one whom he has reasonable grounds for suspecting to be committing such an offence.

(5) Where an arrestable offence has been committed, any person may arrest without a warrant —

(a) anyone who is guilty of the offence;
(b) anyone whom he has reasonable grounds for suspecting to be guilty of it.

Where the power is exercised in accordance with the legal provisions and only reasonable force (see below) is used in effecting the arrest, the community professional should have a successful defence to an action for trespass to the person or false imprisonment.

However caution should be used. Every single word in the statutory power is essential. Thus if the citizen believes that an arrestable offence has been committed and arrests the person he believes to have committed it (under section 24(5)), and it so happens that there has not been an offence that is technically arrestable, then the citizen may be liable for false imprisonment and liable to pay compensation.

Situation

A social worker is called out in a crisis situation where a family are concerned at the behaviour of a mentally disordered member of the family. When the social worker arrives he finds the client threatening a person with a knife. There is no time to wait for the arrival of the police or doctor.

He has to act immediately to prevent a crime occurring. However, the force he uses must be reasonable in relation to the threat with which he or another person is faced. Clearly as soon as he has effected the arrest the social worker should arrange for the arrested person to be handed over to those who have the authority to detain. This could be the police or, in these circumstances, detention under the Mental Health Act might be considered. The statutory provisions do not give any powers of extended imprisonment by the private citizen.

Self-defence and reasonable force
All community professionals should be aware of their rights to defend themselves and others. With the increasing number of examples of violence suffered by the professionals (see Chapter 10 on health and safety), they need to take appropriate reasonable action to defend themselves against threatened violence from clients, relatives or others. They should also receive the appropriate training.
  In the case of *Beckford* v. *R*[35] Lord Griffiths said:

> The test to be applied for self-defence is that a person may use such force as is reasonable in the circumstances as he honestly believes them to be in the defence of himself or another.

How is 'reasonable' determined? It depends upon the nature of the threat with which the person is faced and also upon other circumstances such as the difference in their sizes, the need for speedy action, the possibility of help arriving promptly. It would be reasonable for the nurse to defend herself against a knife attack by, for example, knocking the hand carrying the knife.

The nurse might be prosecuted if she harms the aggressor and in such a prosecution she could raise the plea of self-defence as the justification for her actions. Once this defence is raised the burden is on the prosecution to show that the force used was excessive. The importance of the defendant's belief of what he thought was necessary is described by Lord Borth-y-Guest as follows:

> It will be recognised that a person defending himself cannot weigh to a nicety the exact measure of his necessary defensive action. If a jury thought that in a moment of unexpected anguish a person attacked had only done what he honestly and instinctively thought was necessary that would be most potent evidence that only reasonable defensive action had been taken. A jury will be told that the defence of self-defence, where the evidence makes its raising possible, will only fail if the prosecution show beyond reasonable doubt that what the accused did was not by way of self-defence.[36]

The judge has a duty to direct the jury in such cases that the test of the reasonableness of the actions must be based on what the defendant believed the circumstances to be. An objective test of what the reasonable person would think the circumstances to be is not used. Thus where the accused nurse was mistaken in her belief that she was being attacked, she may still be able to rely upon a defence of self-defence if her belief was nevertheless genuine.

All her actions however can only be defended on these grounds if they really are in defence. If, for example, the attacker was running off, she could not then hit him in self-defence. If he was injured in such circumstances she might face prosecution and the defence of acting in self-defence would not succeed. In the case of *Priestnall* v. *Cornish*[37] the initial aggressor had started to retreat and it was held not reasonable in the circumstances to use force.

Reasonable force in preventing a crime or effecting an arrest
A statutory reference to reasonable force in such circumstances is set out in Figure 3.11.

Figure 3.11 Criminal Law Act 1967 – section 3(1)

A person may use such force as is reasonable in the circumstances in the prevention of crime, or in effecting or assisting in the lawful arrest of offenders or suspected offenders or persons unlawfully at large.

Reasonableness in this context would be defined in the same way as it is in self-defence[38].

The Criminal Law Act 1967 must be read in conjunction with the Police and Criminal Evidence Act 1984 which places upon a statutory footing the citizen's right to arrest (see above).

TRESPASS OR NEGLIGENCE

The right to receive appropriate information

It has been explained that an adult has the right to consent to or refuse treatment and, if his refusal is ignored, he may, in the absence of any qualifying circumstances (see defences above), bring an action for trespass to his person. On the other hand once he has given real consent he cannot base a trespass to the person action on the fact that there were certain details of which he was not informed. If this situation occurs then the remedy for the client is not an action for trespass to the person, but rather an action in negligence on the basis that the professional was in breach of his duty of care to give information to the client of significant risks of substantial harm. The details of this action are shown in Figure 3.12.

Figure 3.12 Duty to give information

The plaintiff must establish that;

- there is a duty to inform,
- there is a breach of this duty, and
- as a reasonably foreseeable consequence of this breach
- the plaintiff has been harmed.

The professional's duty to provide information is part of the duty of care in the tort of negligence which is discussed in Chapter 7.

Situation

A practice nurse is asked by a doctor to syringe a patient's ears. The patient clearly conveys to her his agreement to have his ears syringed, but neither the nurse nor the doctor warn the patient of significant risks of harm.

If these risks arise and the patient is harmed, he could argue that had he known of these risks he would not have agreed to have the ear syringing and in failing to warn him neither doctor nor nurse followed the accepted approved professional practice. Figure 3.13 illustrates the difference between this form of action and that of trespass to the person.

Figure 3.13 Trespass to the person or negligence for breach of the duty to inform

1. In trespass the plaintiff does not need to show he has suffered harm or loss.
2. In trespass there must be a direct interference with the plaintiff's person.
3. In negligence harm or loss to the plaintiff must be established.
4. In negligence there must be 'fault' in the sense of a failure to meet the standard of the reasonable professional.
5. In negligence there must also be a causal link between the fault and the harm which has occurred.

(see Chapter 7 for further discussion on the law of negligence)

Case: *Sidaway*[39]

The leading case on the topic of the duty to inform the patient is that of *Sidaway* v. *Governors of Bethlem Royal Hospital and the Maudsley Hospital*[39]. The facts were that Mrs Amy Sidaway sued for damages for the personal injuries when she was paralysed after an operation to relieve back pain. She argued that the operation involved the risk of damage to the nerve root on to the spinal cord of between one and two per cent. and, had she been advised of this risk, she would not have consented to the operation. The House of Lords held that on the facts her claim must fail, but the majority confirmed that a doctor was under a duty to the patient to disclose any substantial risk involving grave adverse consequences inherent in the treatment he was proposing. The majority agreed that the test as to whether the doctor was in breach of this duty was the same as in any other case where professional negligence is alleged, that is the Bolam test.

To decide what risks the existence of which a patient should be voluntarily warned and the terms in which such a warning, if any, should be given, having regard to the effect that warning may have, is as much an exercise of professional skill and judgment as any other part of the doctor's comprehensive duty of care to the individual patient, and expert medical evidence on this matter should be treated in just the same way. The Bolam test should be applied. (Lord Diplock)

It cannot be said, therefore, that as the law stands the patient has an absolute right to be given information of potential risks although there are statutory provisions giving a qualified right of access to information and these are considered in Chapter 6. Rather the client/patient has a remedy if substantial harm arises from significant risks inherent in the treatment and the professional failed to inform the patient of these in accordance with the current approved accepted professional practice. If the failure to provide the relevant information is not so fundamental that it amounts to an invalidation of the patient's consent or if no harm occurs to the patient then there is no remedy.

Withholding information

As Lord Diplock pointed out, there is a further limitation on the patient's right to be informed. In the exercise of this duty the professional must take into account the particular character and personality of the patient and the effects of this information upon the patient and, in exceptional circumstances, the professional can withhold information which would normally be given. This withholding of information has been called 'therapeutic privilege'.

From the client's point of view the situation is unsatisfactory in that the law recognises no absolute right to be given information which the client may consider to be of extreme relevance to the decisions she is asked to make. From the professional's view point there is a weighting towards paternalism and the exercise of professional judgment on whether any information should be withheld from the patient.

Many community professionals are likely to be involved in carrying out treatments which have inherent risks of varying degrees of seriousness. They should ascertain what is the accepted approved practice in relation to the information which is given to the patient and ensure that they keep up to date with changes in the approved practice. They should ensure that they keep records of their decisions to meet any subsequent criticisms.

CHAPTER 4

Entry and removal from premises and compulsory detention

One of the most important areas of concern and confusion in the care of the individual relates to the powers and rights of entry when it is feared that a person may be in need of care and attention and is failing or refusing to respond to a request for entry. The first part of this chapter therefore looks at the various statutory provisions which enable entry to be made onto a person's premises. As in the area of consent considered in the last chapter, there must be a balance between the right of people to prevent unwanted persons coming onto their land or into their home and the public interest in ensuring that action is taken to prevent harm to an individual or to prevent harm to others if fire or other public health dangers are threatened. The second part of the chapter looks at means by which the law enables a person to be compulsorily admitted to hospital and the alternative to compulsory admission provided for in the Mental Health (Patients in the Community) Act 1995.

The areas to be covered in this chapter are shown in Figure 4.1.

Figure 4.1 Contents of chapter

- Right to prevent interference with land
- Defence – consent of the occupier
- Defence – statutory justification
- Compulsory admission to hospital
- Community supervision and the 1995 Act
- Conclusion

THE RIGHT TO PREVENT INTERFERENCE WITH LAND

Just as a someone can protect his person from unwanted touching by an action for trespass to the person, or his freedom of movement by an action for false imprisonment, so an individual can protect his property by an action for trespass to property. In addition the law allows an individual to use reasonable force to evict a trespasser from his land. Reasonable force means that the force used must be compatible with the nature and type of trespasser and the particular circumstances of the case. Figure 4.2 sets out the basic provisions in relation to an action for trespass to land.

Figure 4.2 Elements in an action for trespass to land
- Intentional or negligent
- entering onto or remaining on, or
- causing any physical object to come into contact with
- land
- in the possession of another
- without consent (implied or express).

Harm need not be established (that is an action for trespass is actionable *per se* (see glossary)).

Many people enter another's property with implied consent: for example the postman or milkman. Some have express agreement and may be there as a result of a contractual arrangement or licence. Others have a statutory right of entry in specified circumstances, for example police, or electricity, gas and other utility officers. Usually an express or implied right can be revoked (that is, withdrawn) by the occupier. If this occurs (and there is no statutory right to remain or other defence – see below) the person coming onto the land becomes a trespasser and the occupier/owner can use reasonable force to evict her if she refuses to go.

Community nurses frequently confront this problem: a nurse is visiting a patient and either the patient or the relative becomes aggressive and makes it clear that the professional is no longer welcome. In law the professional entered with implied consent, but when consent is withdrawn she becomes a trespasser. The professional is then in a dilemma: should she leave the premises as requested abandoning the patient or should she remain as a trespasser and attempt to provide treatment?

Obviously the different circumstances in each situation will determine the legal position. In the simplest situation where the patient asks the professional to leave, the latter should accept the instructions. Her continuing presence would be as a trespasser and any attempt to administer unwanted treatment would constitute a trespass to the person.

Special provisions, however, exist for the mentally disordered and other vulnerable groups (see below).

DEFENCE – CONSENT BY THE OCCUPIER

This will be one of the most important defences and is the one most usually relied upon. However as pointed out earlier it can be withdrawn at any time, in which case the visitor should leave unless one of the situations described below exists.

Where the premises are in multi-occupation, it would be a question of fact as to which occupier had the right to consent to or refuse a visitor's entry onto that particular part of the premises. This may be difficult where for example the client wishes the professional to stay but the relative/carer orders her off the property. In practice, since the professional would not wish to be involved in force, the safest step is for the professional to leave when requested but then seek the relevant statutory order discussed below to ensure the client is protected.

DEFENCE – STATUTORY JUSTIFICATION

The various statutory authorities for entering private premises and removing persons by force from such premises are shown in Figure 4.3.

Figure 4.3 Statutory justification

- Section 115 Mental Health Act 1983
- Danger from fire and other hazards
- Statutory powers of the police
- Children in danger
- National Assistance Act 1948
- Section 135 Mental Health Act 1983
- Section 136 Mental Health Act 1983

Section 115   Mental Health Act 1983

Section 115 of the Mental Health Act 1983 enables an approved social worker to enter and inspect premises and is set out in Figure 4.4. The exact wording of the Act is given, but it is broken down into bullet points as each element is vital to the legality of action taken under the authority of the section.

Figure 4.4 Mental Health Act 1983 – Section 115

Powers of entry and inspection
- An approved social worker of a local social services authority may
- at all reasonable times
- after producing,
- if asked to do so,
- some duly authenticated document showing that he is such a social worker,
- enter and inspect any premises (not being a hospital)
- in the area of that authority
- in which a mentally disordered patient is living,
- if he has reasonable cause to believe that
- the patient is not under proper care.

Section 115 does not give the social worker the power to force entry and therefore, if entry is refused, a warrant would be required under section 135(1) (see page 69 below).

The power is only available if a mentally disordered person is living on the premises. It does not give the right to search to see if there is a mentally disordered person there. Once it is established (by means other than section 115) that a mentally disordered person is there, then, if the approved social worker has reasonable cause to believe that the patient is not under proper care, he can enter and inspect. Although the section does not provide a means of forcing entry if the occupier refuses, any unreasonable refusal to allow inspection would be an offence under section 129.

Danger from fire and other hazards

The fire brigade has statutory authority to enter premises where there is a fire or danger from fire. Community professionals who fear for the life of a client in similar circumstances who are not covered by this statutory authority could use the defence of necessity in an action for trespass brought in respect of their entry onto the premises. The defence will only succeed if the professional could show that there was actual danger to persons or property and that she took reasonable steps in acting as she did. A defence of necessity could probably also be used by the professional when she enters a house outside of which milk bottles and papers have accumulated. In these circumstances section 115 of the Mental Health Act 1983 would not be appropriate. If this situation were to arise the professional would be well advised to seek the help of the police who have a more extensive power of entry and often as well the means to enforce it.

Statutory powers of the police

There are considerable advantages in the community professional seeking the assistance of the police who can act under the authority of their statutory powers, rather than relying on the undefined defence of necessity. Section 17 of the Police and Criminal Evidence Act 1984 (see Figure 4.5) allows a police constable to enter premises without a warrant for the purposes of protecting life and limb.

Figure 4.5 Police and Criminal Evidence Act 1984 – section 17

(1) ... a constable may enter and search any premises for the purpose –
(a) of executing a warrant ...;
(b) of arresting a person for an arrestable offence;
(c) of arresting a person for an offence [under specified provisions];
(d) of recapturing a person who is unlawfully at large and whom he is pursuing [see further discussion on this below in connection with section 135(2) of the Mental Health Act 1983]; or
(e) of saving life or limb or preventing serious damage to property.

Section 17(1)(e) gives extremely wide powers which should cover most of the situations where professionals are concerned about the safety of their clients and cannot obtain entry by consent. There should, however, be reasonable grounds for fearing that there is danger to life or limb otherwise the occupier could claim compensation for trespass, including the costs of any property damaged when the entry was effected.

Danger to children

The Children Act 1989 has replaced the earlier provisions under section 40 of the Children Act 1933. Part V of the 1989 Act provides statutory powers for the protection of children, section 46 of which gives powers to the police for the removal and accommodation of children in cases of emergency. Section 48 gives powers to assist in the discovery of children who may be in need of emergency protection. For further details on the operation of these sections reference should be made to the many publications on the Children Act 1989[40].

National Assistance Act 1948, section 47

The main provision of this section are summarised in Figure 4.6.

Figure 4.6 National Assistance Act 1948 – section 47

(1) The following provisions of this section shall have effect for the purposes of securing the necessary care and attention for persons who —
(a) are suffering from grave chronic disease or, being aged, infirm or physically incapacitated, are living in insanitary conditions, and
(b) are unable to devote to themselves, and are not receiving from other persons, proper care and attention.

● The powers are exercised by the Community Medical Specialist (replacing the Medical Officer of Health) who certifies in writing to the appropriate authority which applies to a Magistrates' Court on seven days notice to the person in respect of whom the application is made or to some person in charge of him (section 47(7)).

● The Community Specialist must provide certification that, after thorough inquiry and consideration, he is satisfied that, in the interests of any such person as defined in section 47(1), or for preventing injury to the health of, or serious nuisance to, others, it is necessary to remove that person from the premises.

● The court can order the removal to a suitable hospital or other place.

● The detention period cannot exceed three months but can be extended.

● There is a right to apply for the revocation of the order.

The problems resulting from the seven day notice provisions of section 47 of the NAA 1948 came to light when a woman lay on her kitchen floor during the seven day period of notice required under the 1948 Act and during that time developed a pressure sore which became infected with tetanus bacteria, with the result that she died of tetanus. Amendments were made in 1951 as summarised in Figure 4.7.

Figure 4.7 The National Assistance (Amendment) Act 1951

1. An order can be made under section 47 of the 1948 Act without notice if it is certified by the medical officer of health and another registered medical practitioner that in their opinion it is necessary in the interests of that person to remove him without delay.
2. The period of detention under this provision is three weeks and this would enable an application under section 47(3) to be made during this time.
3. The application can be made to the magistrates court and can be made *ex parte* (that is without the other party appearing).

Dr. Muir Gray[41] points out that only about 200 orders a year are made under this legislation but that this represents the tip of the iceberg and many more people, especially the elderly, are referred to community physicians and are not removed under section 47. His paper illustrates starkly the ethical dilemmas which arise in relation to the use of these compulsory powers. Even when the conditions required by the Act are present, a community physician may still be reluctant to obtain a place of safety order since the prognosis for the patient in the place of safety may be poor. Dr. Muir Gray quoted a number of detailed studies demonstrating the adverse effects of relocation and describing what is known as the 'relocation effect'.

The order must specify the officer who is to effect the removal and authorises the removal of the person to a suitable hospital or other place in, or within convenient distance of, the area of the appropriate authority. The manager of the premises must either have given evidence at the hearing or seven clear days notice must have been given to him of the intended application and of the time and place at which it is proposed to be made. Section 47(5) permits a court order substituting another suitable place for the one cited in the original order.

Safeguards for the individual
There are certain safeguards for the individual in section 47 of the 1948 Act. In the first place he must be given seven clear days notice of the intended application and of the time and place at which it is proposed to be made (section 47 (7)(a)). Secondly, at any time after the expiration of six clear weeks from the day the order was made, the person who is the object of the order or someone on his behalf can apply to the court for the revocation of the order. (Seven days notice of this application for revocation must go to the Community Medical Specialist.)

Expenses
Any expense which is incurred by the local authority in maintaining the individual in a place other than NHS hospital accommodation or by another local authority in residential accommodation (under section 47 (8)) is recoverable from the individual himself or any other person liable to maintain him, as is expenditure on maintenance in Part III accommodation by the removing authority.

Alternatives
Almost all community professionals are at some time liable to encounter a situation to which section 47 would apply. Whilst the decision to apply for an order is undoubtedly that of the community physician, the report of the professional who makes the initial referral may have a considerable bearing on the ultimate decision. Central to the issue are alternative options to compulsory removal. Community health and social services may be sufficient to support the individual in need and prevent compulsory removal. Doris Lessing in The Diaries of Jane Somers[42] paints a graphic picture of the degradation and shame to which a recluse can sink and how an unlikely friendship may provide a means of rescue. The fierce independence of the elderly recluse putting

up a barrier against charitable, neighbourly or social services assistance would be well known to many professionals in the community.

The importance of section 47 lies perhaps more in the fact that it exists than in its use. At least professionals know that in the extreme the necessary powers are available to ensure the transfer of the patient to a place of safety: it is a safeguard or a fall back for the professional. However, there are many alternatives available before that section is put into use. Dr Muir Gray also points out that the existence of section 47 should prevent the adoption of non-legal deceitful means of transferring the person to a place of safety: drugging tea, deception and so on should not be used to facilitate the removal of the client.

The future

The Law Commission in its Consultation Paper 130[43] suggested that section 47 of the NAA 1948 and the National Assistance (Amendment) Act 1951 should be repealed and replaced by a new scheme giving clearer and more appropriate powers to local social services authorities to intervene to protect incapacitated, mentally disordered or vulnerable people. It suggests that the local social services authority should be the agency responsible for investigating allegations of neglect or abuse of an incapacitated, mentally disordered or vulnerable person and for initiating proceedings. It should have a duty to make such enquiries as it reasonably can, including taking steps to gain access to that person, and to decide whether they should take any action to provide community care services for that person or otherwise protect him from harm (or exploitation). An officer of the local social services authority should have powers to enter premises where any person believed to be incapacitated, mentally disordered or vulnerable is living, if there is reasonable cause to suspect that the person is suffering, or is likely to suffer, significant harm (or serious exploitation). It would be an offence to refuse access. Warrants could be applied for to authorise a constable to enter any premises for this purpose. In addition the local social services authority should be able to apply for an order of limited duration authorising them to carry out an assessment of the individual's capacity and needs, either for protection or for community care services or both.

An emergency protection order should be available to remove to a place of safety a person believed to be incapacitated or mentally disordered or vulnerable, and likely to suffer significant harm or serious exploitation. The suggested duration of this order is seven days.

Following consultation these proposals were contained in draft legislation prepared by the Law Commission[44] (see Figure 3.9 above). The Government has as yet not indicated that these proposals will be incorporated in the present programme of legislation.

Mental Health Act 1983

Section 135(1) – Searching for and removing patients
The powers under this subsection are more likely to be used than an order under the National Assistance Act 1948. The provisions and other subsections applicable to it are set out in Figure 4.8.

Figure 4.8 The Mental Health Act 1983 – section 135

(1) If it appears to a justice of the peace,
- on information on oath
- laid by an approved social worker,
- that there is reasonable cause to suspect
- that a person believed to be suffering from mental disorder —
- (a) has been, or is being, ill-treated, neglected or kept otherwise than under proper control,
-     in any place within the jurisdiction of the justice, *or*
- (b) being unable to care for himself,
-     is living alone in any such place,
- the justice may issue a warrant
- authorising any constable . . . to enter, if need be by force,
- any premises specified in the warrant in which the person is believed to be, and,
- if thought fit,
- remove him to a place of safety
- with a view to the making of an application in respect of him under Part II of [the Mental Health Act],
- or of other arrangements for his treatment or care.

(2) [see below]
(3) A patient who is removed to a place of safety in the execution of a warrant issued under this section may be detained there for a period not exceeding 72 hours.
(4) [The constable *shall* be accompanied by an approved social worker and by a registered medical practitioner.]
(5) [The patient need not be named in the warrant.]
The above wording except where indicated by square brackets is precisely that of the Act but because each element of section 135(1) is crucial to the legality of the action taken these have been split out with bullet points. Emphasis indicated by italics is the author's.

Only an approved social worker can seek a warrant from a justice of the peace and that must be on the basis of a reasonable cause to suspect that a person is believed to be suffering from mental disorder and that one of the two conditions are satisfied. In section 135(1) either of the conditions can be met. In section 47 of the 1948 Act both specified conditions must be present. Section 135(1) can be used as a follow up to section 115 whether or not the premises were entered and inspected (see above).

Mental disorder is defined in section 1 of the Mental Health Act and is set out in Figure 4.9.

Figure 4.9 Definition of mental disorder, section 1 Mental Health Act 1983

'mental disorder' means mental illness, arrested or incomplete development of mind, psychopathic disorder and any other disorder or disability of mind and 'mentally disordered' shall be construed accordingly [see glossary for commentary on the different terms]

Section 135(2) – Taking of a patient into custody
The taking or retaking into custody of patients unlawfully at large is a different issue and covered by section 135(2) of the Act which makes similar provisions for the issue of a warrant to enter premises and remove a patient to those contained in section 135(1) with the following differences:

● the oath may be laid by any constable or any authorised person as well as an ASW;

● admission to the premises must have been refused or it must be apprehended that it will be refused;

● the patient must be named in the warrant;

● the constable need not be accompanied by medical or social services personnel (but he usually is so accompanied).

In the case of *D'Souza*[45] the House of Lords held that section 17(1)(d) of the Police and Criminal Evidence Act 1984 (see Figure 4.5) can also be used to enter and search any premises for a patient who has absconded.

A place of safety
The patient who is removed to a place of safety under section 135(1) can be detained for a period not exceeding 72 hours. After that the patient could remain in hospital (if that is the place of safety) as an informal patient (that is, free to leave) unless he is compulsorily admitted under section 2 or 3 or otherwise legally detained.

The definition of 'place of safety' is set out in Figure 4.10.

Figure 4.10 Mental Health Act 1983 – section 135(6)

- 'place of safety' means residential accommodation provided by a local social services authority under Part III of the National Assistance Act 1948 or under paragraph 2 of the Schedule 8 to the National Health Service Act 1977,
- a hospital as defined by [the Mental Health Act 1983],
- a police station,
- a mental nursing home or residential home for mentally disordered persons or
- any other suitable place the occupier of which is willing temporarily to receive the patient.

Section 136 Mental Health Act 1983

This section also provides for compulsory removal – in this case from a place to which the public have access. Figure 4.11 sets out the main elements of the section.

Figure 4.11 Section 136 – mentally disordered persons found in public places

(1) If a constable finds

- in a place to which the public have access
- a person who appears to him
- to be suffering from mental disorder *and*
- to be in immediate need of care or control,
- the constable may,
- if he thinks it necessary to do so in the interests of that person or for the protection of other persons
- remove that person to a place of safety [as defined by the Act].

(2) A person removed to a place of safety . . . may be detained there for a period not exceeding 72 hours

- for the purpose of enabling him to be examined by a registered medical practitioner *and*
- to be interviewed by an approved social worker *and*
-         of making any necessary arrangements for his treatment or care.

[It should be noted that many of these provisions are linked by 'and' rather than 'or'. This means that they must all be satisfied. The words of the section are quoted precisely but split out by bullet points for clarity.]

Most districts now have in existence a policy which has been jointly agreed with the health authority, social services and the police. There is considerable local variation in what is agreed to be the usual place of safety: sometimes the policy envisages that the patient will normally be brought to the hospital sometimes the place of safety is the police station. See the Department of Health revised *Code of Practice*[46] on the Mental Health Act 1983 for further information on this.

It should be noted that under section 136 the person can be kept up to 72 hours in a place of safety for the purpose of enabling him to be examined by a registered medical practitioner and to be interviewed by an approved social worker, and also for the purpose of making any necessary arrangements for his treatment or care.

The operation of this section has been the object of some concern. Uncertainties often cloud the exact legal authority being exercised by a police constable in removing someone from a place to which the public have access. It may be initially under the Public Order legislation or for a breach of the peace and it is not until the person arrives at the police station under arrest that it is decided to make use of section 136 and call in an approved social worker or convey the patient directly to a psychiatric hospital. Only recently has the recording of the time of admission to hospital, the number and name of the constable and the circumstances of the use of section 136 been urged upon all health service providers.

Reference should be made to the *Code of Practice* which gives useful guidance on how section 136 and all other sections of the Mental Health Act should be implemented.

It is essential that when compulsory removal is being discussed all the relevant professionals should consider other options which are available to ensure that the compulsory powers are only used when there is no adequate alternative.

COMPULSORY ADMISSION TO HOSPITAL FOR ASSESSMENT AND TREATMENT

Neither the National Assistance Acts of 1948 and 1951 nor the removal provisions under sections 135 or 136 of the Mental Health Act permit compulsory treatment. If, during or immediately following the 72 hours detention under section 135 or section 136, a patient is detained under section 2 or 3 then treatment can be given compulsorily under Part IV provisions of the Mental Health Act 1983. However, if treatment is proposed and compulsion necessary, then admission under section 2 or 3 as appropriate should be considered, unless of course entry on to the client's premises needs to be effected by force. It may, however, often be the case that, once the person has been removed to the place of safety, she then becomes prepared to accept treatment and can be admitted as an informal patient.

Compulsory admission under the Mental Health Act 1983

Requirements
Figure 4.12 sets out the provisions for compulsory admissions under the Mental Health Act 1983 and Figure 4.13 the medical requirements. The full details cannot adequately be described in a book of this kind and it is essential that any professional who has regular contact with the mentally disordered should be familiar with the details of the legislation and with the *Code of Practice* prepared by the Department of Health[47].

Figure 4.12 Provision for compulsory admission for the mentally disordered

	Maximum Duration	Application made by	No. of Medical Recommendations
Section 2 Admission for Assessment	28 days		two
Section 4 Emergency Admission for Assessment	72 hours	Approved Social Worker or nearest relative	one
Section 3 Admission for Treatment	6 months		two
		Power exercised by	
Section 5(2) Detention of Informal In-patient	72 hours	Registered medical practitioner	none
Section 5(4) Nurse's Holding Power	6 hours or earlier arrival of RMO	Prescribed nurse	none

Figure 4.13 Medical requirements

[For admission under section 2 or 4 it must be established that]

(a) the patient is suffering from mental disorder of a nature or degree which warrants the detention of the patient in a hospital for assessment ... for at least a limited period; and
(b) he ought to be so detained in the interests of his own health or safety or with a view to the protection of other persons.

[For admission under section 3 it must be established that]

(a) the patient is suffering from [a specified form of mental disorder] and his mental disorder is of a nature or degree which makes it appropriate for him to receive medical treatment in hospital; and

(b) in the case of psychopathic disorder or mental impairment, such treatment is likely to alleviate or prevent a deterioration of his condition; and

(c) it is necessary for the health or safety of the patient or for the protection of other persons that he should receive such treatment and it cannot be provided unless he is detained under this section.

It should be noted, as seen in Figure 4.13, that on admission for assessment under section 2 or section 4 simply evidence of mental disorder must be shown, whereas for admission under section 3 there must be evidence of one of the specific mental disorders requiring treatment in hospital. This is because admission under section 2 or 4 is for assessment of the patient, and so for a limited duration, whereas section 3 applies once that assessment has taken place, establishing what disorder the patient is suffering from and that he requires treatment in hospital, and the admission can last for up to six months and can then be renewed for a further six months and then for one year at a time.

A guardianship order requires the same medical evidence as that required for section 3, though of course here the patient does not need to be detained in hospital.

'Nearest relatives'

The applicant can be the nearest relative or an approved social worker. Figure 4.14 shows the hierarchy of nearest relatives, Figure 4.15 explains why some persons are disregarded and the powers and duties of the nearest relative are shown in Figure 4.16.

Figure 4.14 Definition of the nearest relative, section 26.

In order or priority:

1. Any relative the patient ordinarily resides with or is cared by (section 26(4))
2. husband or wife (including a person living as the husband or wife for at least six months (section 26(6))
3. son or daughter
4. father or mother
5. brother or sister
6. grandparent
7. grandchild
8. uncle or aunt
9. nephew or niece
10. a person other than a relative with whom the patient ordinarily resides and has been for a period of not less that five years (section 26(7)).

NB – any relationship of the half-blood shall be treated as a relationship of the whole blood and an illegitimate person shall be treated as the legitimate child of his mother (section 26(2)).
In determining priority:

- Relatives of the whole blood are preferred to relatives of the half-blood.
- The elder or eldest of two or more relatives in the same category are preferred to the other(s) of those relatives regardless of sex (section 26(3)).

Where the patient is a child or young person in the care of the local authority by virtue of a care order under the Children Act 1989, then the Children Act provides that the authority shall be deemed the nearest relative of the patient in preference to any person except the patient's husband or wife (Children Act 1989 Schedule 13 paragraph 48).

Where a guardian has been appointed for a person who has not attained the age of eighteen years, or a residence order is in force with respect to such a person, then the guardian (or guardians if there is more than one), shall, to the exclusion of any other person, be deemed to be his nearest relative.

Certain person's listed in Figure 4.15 are disregarded for the purposes of the definition of nearest relative.

Figure 4.15 Persons disregarded, section 26(5)

- A non-resident of the UK, Channel Islands or Isle of Man (where the patient is so resident).
- The husband or wife who is permanently separated or has deserted or been deserted by the patient.
- A person not being the husband, wife, father or mother who is under 18 years of age.
- A person subject to an order under section 38 of the Sexual Offences Act 1956 (incest with a minor) which divests him of authority over the patient.

Figure 4.16 Powers and duties of the nearest relatives

- Application for admission of the patient: under section 2 for assessment, or section 3 for treatment, or section 4, emergency admission for assessment.
- Application for the patient to be placed under guardianship (section 7).
- Must be consulted by the approved social worker if reasonably practicable and can object to an application by an approved social worker for admission for treatment or for a guardianship order.
- Must be notified of application for admission for assessment and in an emergency (sections 2 and 4).
- Can discharge the patient under section 23(2)(a) after giving to the hospital managers (or if appropriate social services authority) 72 hours notice of such an intention.
- Can appeal to the Mental Health Review Tribunal if discharge overruled by patient's responsible medical officer.

- Can authorise a registered medical practitioner at any reasonable time to visit and examine the patient in private, the Doctor then being able to require and inspect any relevant records.
- Can apply to a Mental Health Review Tribunal on specified occasions.
- Has to be informed of certain information unless the patient has requested that the information is not passed on.
- Can require the local social services authority to direct an approved social worker as soon as practicable to consider whether an application under the Mental Health Act 1983 should be made in respect of the patient (section 13(4)).

Whilst the general practitioner and approved social worker have the major role to play in decisions relating to the compulsory admission of a patient under the Mental Health Act, other professionals, especially community psychiatric nurses and community nurses for the mentally handicapped, community occupational therapists and others who have responsibility for the mentally disordered in the community, should have a clear understanding of the procedure and law relating to compulsory admission.

Readmission

Readmission of a detained patient may take place in several situations. The two most common will be considered here.

- Where there has been a grant of leave of absence under section 17.
- Where the patient has absconded without leave and is recaught.

Recall from section 17 leave
The responsible medical officer (RMO) may grant to any patient who is for the time being liable to be detained in a hospital under Part II of the Mental Health Act 1983 leave to be absent from the hospital subject to such conditions (if any) as that officer considers necessary in the interests of the patient or for the protection of other persons.

The details of section 17 leave are further discussed in Chapter 15 on the community psychiatric nurse together with the provisions for recall from leave by the RMO. (For the detained patient on section 17 leave in a nursing home registered to take detained patients see Chapter 30.)

Return of absconding patient
Where the patient is absent without leave there is provision for him to be returned to hospital under section 18.

This provision also covers the patient who fails to return to the hospital after section 17 leave expires or is revoked; or if he absents himself without permission from any place where he is required to reside.

The persons who can retake the patient are:

- any approved social worker;
- any officer on the staff of the hospital;
- any constable; or
- any person authorised in writing by the manager of the hospital.

The Mental Health (Patients in the Community) Act 1995 repealed the provision that 28 days or more absence without leave from the specified place or hospital brought to an end the patient's liability to be detained or subject to guardianship, extending the period to six months. In addition, section 21 of the 1983 Act provides special provisions for the patient who is absent without leave.

COMMUNITY SUPERVISION AND THE 1995 ACT

Pressures for reform

The absence of a power to treat patients compulsorily had led to suggestions that the Mental Health Act should be amended to permit some form of community order or community supervision. These arose from the concern about the numbers of chronic patients who, on discharge into the community, failed to keep up with the treatment regimes and eventually had to be returned to hospital for compulsory treatment.

In January 1993 a report of the Royal College of Psychiatrists[48] proposed a new community supervision order. This would enable patients to be cared for in their homes. The Secretary of State set up an internal review committee in response to consider the need for and nature of any supervision order which might be required in the community. The team was set up on 13 January 1993 and its report[49] was published in August 1993. It recommended the creation of a new power known as a supervised discharge order for non-restricted patients who had been detained in hospital under the Act and who would present a serious risk to their own health or safety, or to the safety of other people, unless their care was supervised.

Before the internal review reported, a report of the House of Commons Health Committee on Community Supervision Orders[50] was published. This was set up as a direct result of the incident on New Year's Eve 1992 when Mr Ben Silcock climbed into the lions' enclosure at London Zoo and was severely injured by a lioness. It subsequently emerged that he suffered from schizophrenia.

THE MENTAL HEALTH (PATIENTS IN THE COMMUNITY) ACT 1995

This Act was introduced to meet the concerns summarised above which arose from situations where long term mentally disordered patients who had been discharged from detention in hospital deteriorated in the community to the extent that they became a serious danger to themselves or other people. The Act introduced from 1 April 1996 an arrangement whereby after-care under supervision could be provided. This was done by the insertion of new sections 25A to 25J in the Mental Health Act 1983.

By section 25A an application can be made for a patient to ensure that he receives the after-care services provided for him under section 117 of the 1983 Act. The terms of the new section are set out in Figure 4.17.

Figure 4.17 After-care under supervision – section 25A

(1) Where a patient —

(a) is liable to be detained in a hospital in pursuance of an application for admission for treatment [that is, under section 3 or under sections 37, 47 and 48]; and

(b) has attained the age of 16 years,

an application may be made for him to be supervised after he leaves hospital, for the period allowed by the following provisions of this Act, with a view to securing that he receives the after-care services provided for him under section 117 below.

(2) [Explanation of the terms 'supervision application' and 'subject to after-care supervision']

(3) [Reference to sections 25B and 25C for the making of the supervision application]

(4) A supervision application may be made in respect of a patient only on the grounds that —

(a) he is suffering from mental disorder, being mental illness, severe mental impairment, psychopathic disorder or mental impairment [see glossary];

(b) there would be a substantial risk of serious harm to the health or safety of the patient or the safety of other persons, or of the patient being seriously exploited, if he were not to receive the after-care services to be provided for him under section 117 below after he leaves hospital; and

(c) his being subject to after-care under supervision is likely to help to secure that he receives the after-care services to be so provided.

The application can only be made by the responsible medical officer (section 25A(5)) and is addressed to the health authority which has the duty of providing the section 117 services (section 25A(6)). The health authority must consult with the local social services authority before accepting a supervision application (section 25A(7)).

The detailed provisions for making the supervision application are given in section 25B and set out in Figure 4.18.

Figure 4.18 Making of supervision application – section 25B

(1) The responsible medical officer shall not make a supervision application unless—

(a) subsection (2) below is complied with; and

(b) the responsible medical officer has considered [the after-care services to be provided and any requirements imposed by section 25D].

(2) This subsection is complied with if—

(a) the following persons have been consulted about the making of the supervision application—
   (i) the patient;
   (ii) one or more persons who have been professionally concerned with the patient's medical treatment in hospital;
   (iii) one or more persons who will be professionally concerned with the after-care services to be provided for the patient under section 117 below; and
   (iv) any person who the responsible medical officer believes will play a substantial part in the care of the patient after he leaves hospital but will not be professionally concerned with any of the after-care services to be so provided;

(b) such steps as are practicable have been taken to consult the person (if any) appearing to be the nearest relative of the patient about the making of the supervision application [although the patient can request that this provision does not apply (subsection (3))]; and

(c) the responsible medical officer has taken into account any views expressed by the persons consulted.

(6) A supervision application shall be accompanied by—

(a) the written recommendation in the prescribed form of registered medical practitioner who will be professionally concerned with the patient's medical treatment after he leaves hospital or, if no such practitioner other than the responsible medical officer will be so concerned, of any registered medical practitioner; and

(b) the written recommendation in the prescribed form of an approved social worker.

(9) A supervision application shall also be accompanied by—

(a) a statement in writing by the person who is to be the community responsible medical officer in relation to the patient after he leaves hospital that he is to be in charge of the medical treatment provided for the patient as part of the after-care services provided for him under section 117 below;

(b) a statement in writing by the person who is to be the supervisor in relation to the patient after he leaves hospital that he is to supervise the patient with a view to securing that he receives the after-care services so provided;

(d) details of any requirements to be imposed on him under section 25D below.

Section 25D(1) enables the responsible after-care bodies to impose requirements on the patient to ensure that he receives the after-care services provided. These are set out in Figure 4.19.

Figure 4.19 Requirements to secure receipt of after-care – section 25D(3)

(3) the requirements referred to in subsection (1) above are—

(a) that the patient reside at a specified place;

(b) that the patient attend at specified places and times for the purpose of medical treatment, occupation, education or training; and

(c) that access to the patient be given, at any place where the patient is residing, to the supervisor, any registered medical practitioner or any approved social worker or to any other person authorised by the supervisor.

These requirements can be enforced by an authorised person having the power to take or convey the patient to the place of residence or occupation.

The after-care services must be kept under review and can be modified by the responsible after-care bodies. The after-care supervision lasts for six months beginning with the day on which the application supervision application was accepted. It can be renewed for a further six months and then for further periods of one year at a time.

The community responsible medical officer may at any time direct that a patient subject to after-care supervision shall cease to be so subject. A patient subject to after-care under supervision shall cease to be so subject if he is admitted to a hospital following an application for admission for treatment or is received into guardianship. On the other hand the patient can apply to a Mental Health Review Tribunal if an application for after-care supervision is accepted, if his diagnosis is changed or if the after-care supervision is renewed.

Future change

In the meantime the Mental Health Act Commission has recommended a comprehensive review of the Mental Health Act 1983 to incorporate the changes necessary as a result of the implementation of community care and the changes which have taken place since 1983. Also, in response to public concern, the Secretary of State has issued guidance applicable in England requiring Supervision Registers to be kept in relation to patients who are likely to be a serious threat to the health or safety of themselves or other persons. There is, however, no provision to enforce this.

CONCLUSION

There are considerable complexities in the law relating to the removal of patients from their own homes. The principle underlying the white paper *Caring for People* was that people should be assisted in remaining in their own homes as far as is reasonably possible.

The nature of independence and the significance of the principle that older people should be able to live in their own homes as far as possible has been analysed by Andrew Sixsmith[52]. Like so many other rights, the right to be independent is negative. There is no right to live in one's own home. The right only comes into play when specific persons in society wish to remove one from that place. These powers are now the subject of draft legislation by the Law Commission[15] and it is hoped that there will eventually be in place a framework which on the one hand secures to individuals maximum independence to remain in their own homes and at the same time enables intervention to take place when essential to prevent harm. The line between the two is extremely difficult to draw.

CHAPTER 5

Confidentiality

The duty to maintain the confidentiality of information obtained from and about the patient/client/resident still exists whether the patient is in hospital or in the community. In the community different pressures exist: professionals may glean much information from visiting a person's home and the dilemmas as to whether to break the duty of confidentiality are great. This chapter is concerned with the nature of the duty of confidentiality and the occasions on which that duty can give way to other greater duties.

The duty of confidentiality arises from several sources. It is part of the duty of care owed in the tort (see glossary) of negligence and also part of those duties arising from a contract of employment between the health professional and the employer, whether NHS Trust, health authority, social services or private employer. It is also recognised by most professional registration bodies as part of the code of professional conduct which their registered members should follow and as such it is enforceable through professional conduct hearings, though some registration bodies are more zealous than others in this respect.

The basic duty is clear. Problems arise in determining whether it is lawful not to keep the duty of confidentiality because other duties justify disclosure. These may include the duty to obey the law, the duty to act in the public interest, or that the facts show that the patient's interests would suffer if there were no disclosure.

The main exceptions to the duty of confidentiality are shown in Figure 5.1.

Figure 5.1 Exceptions to the duty of confidentiality

- Consent of the patient/client
- Disclosure in the interests of the patient/client
- Court order for disclosure
- Statutory duty
- The public interest.

CONSENT OF THE PATIENT

The duty is owed to the patient and the patient has the right to agree that information could be passed on to other people and this consent would be a complete defence against any action for breach of confidentiality.

Situation

A well known actor was in the terminal stages of AIDS and was being nursed by Macmillan nurses. He had all along refused any information relating to his condition being made public since he was married with children and did not wish his family to be hurt. Shortly before his death he changed his mind and the press visited the cottage where he was living. His personal secretary made a public statement to the press in spite of the pressures of the family to keep silent. The family threatened to sue her for breach of confidentiality.

They are unlikely to win such an action since the patient gave consent to the disclosure of the information, which was confidential to the patient rather than to the family. Obviously evidence of the patient's consent should be available if this was required for a court hearing.

The patient can give consent to any disclosure. It is important, however, to be clear of the patient's capacity to give consent.

Situation

A psychiatric patient who had suffered from schizophrenia over many years had agreed to take part in a video comparing her care in the community to that in the hospital. She was asked to sign a form which gave the video makers the right to show the video without restriction wherever they wished. She took a major part in the video and described in graphic details the lack of support from her family and the difficulties which she had had in surviving in the community. The family discovered the existence of this video which they said was libellous of them and claimed that it was made when the patient was severely ill and was not giving a balanced view. The video makers relied upon the consent form signed by the patient arguing that this gave them the right to show the film for fund raising purposes for schizophrenics wherever and whenever they wished. The patient now says that she was ill when she signed the form consenting to the video being made and shown and it does not represent a true account of the circumstances of her life in the community. She has asked for the film never to be shown again.

There are two separate issues here: an action for defamation and an action for breach of confidentiality. In the first action the consent of the patient is irrelevant in a claim for defamation brought by her family if it is established that the facts are wrong and the patient was not telling the truth. In the second, evidence of the patient's mental condition would be vital in determining the validity of her consent. A contract with a person who is mentally disordered would be binding if at the time the contract was agreed she had the capacity to make that agreement. It would be for the video makers to prove that capacity since they were aware of the prevailing mental disability. If it is established that the patient was incapable of knowing what she was doing when she signed the form and when the filming was done, then she would not be bound by it and the video makers would have to withdraw the video.

DISCLOSURE OF INFORMATION IN THE INTERESTS OF THE PATIENT

To other professionals

Professionals do not work in isolation. They need to relate on a multi-disciplinary basis and ensure that relevant information is given to each so that they can act in the best interests of the patient. Traditionally it has been the 'medical notes' which have been the most significant in the care of the patient and doctors have been rightly zealous over who should have access to them. In some hospitals it is not until recently that other professional staff, even nurses, have had such access.

In the community there is a similar need to ensure that relevant information is passed on to other professionals whilst at the same time protecting the confidential nature of that information. The task is more difficult in the community. There are no ward rounds where the professionals meet together to discuss the patient's care and even when there are several different professionals all visiting the patient's home it is far more difficult to ensure that the appropriate meetings and discussions take place. The individual professionals have to be aware of the role and therefore the needs of their colleagues in different professions.

Situation

A community nurse, who has been trained to prescribe specific medications as a result of recent changes in the law, was asked by a general practitioner to visit a patient who had telephoned in for a home visit with suspected influenza. The nurse asked for the patient's notes but these were not made available to her. The receptionists said that the practice did not like the notes being taken out of the surgery.

She visited the patient and decided that the patient was probably suffering from a mild form of tonsillitis together with a headache. She decided to prescribe an analgesic. She asked the patient if she were aware of any allergies and the patient said no. When the patient began the course of treatment she suffered a violent reaction to the analgesic and it was then discovered that this allergy was known from treatment given a few years before and was clearly identified in the notes had the nurse obtained access to them.

From these events it is clear that the community nurse must take most of the responsibility for the harm which occurred to the patient. In addition there would be some blame for the general practitioners in failing to set up a safe system of practice to prevent such incidents occurring and not ensuring good communication in their practice. The prescribing powers of the nurse had obviously led to the need for a review of relationships within the practice and the communication systems between doctors/ nurses and other health and social services professionals. Also the patient must bear some responsibility for the events. However, the extent of her contributory negligence will depend upon her mental and physical condition and the extent to which the nurse was justified in relying upon her denial of allergies in prescribing the analgesic. (The question of the liability of the GP even though he did not employ the community nurse is considered in Chapter 24.)

The transfer of confidential information between professionals in the interests of the patient rarely causes problems, but ensuring that confidentiality is not unnecessarily broken becomes more difficult the greater the number of people caring for the patient.

To volunteers

Greater problems arise with the disclosure of information to volunteers – carers, neighbours and others. What confidential information should they be given in the interests of the patient? It might for example be relevant to tell a volunteer who takes out a resident from a community home for those with learning disabilities that she suffers from epilepsy and give some training in what action to take should she have a fit. It would not be appropriate or relevant and would be a breach of confidentiality to inform the volunteer that the resident had an abortion three years before. The key worker/care assistant or the person who is responsible for arranging the assistance of the volunteer should ensure that the volunteer is given sufficient information for both the volunteer and the patient to be safe from reasonably foreseeable harm. If, for example, either the volunteer or the resident is harmed because vital information is not given to the volunteer, there could be liability on the part of those who liaised with the volunteer if it can be shown that the harm would probably not have occurred had the facts been made known to the volunteer (see further Chapter 21).

What, however, if in the situation above of the epileptic patient, the patient had the capacity to refuse to give consent to the transfer of confidential information to the volunteer? It could be argued that disclosure would still be justified in the interests of the safety of the patient, the volunteer or others and the use of the volunteer might be prevented if the patient does not agree to disclosure.

A similar problem arises in the work of the advocate (see glossary). Many community units and homes are encouraging the use of the advocacy system to ensure that patients' needs are made known and to ensure that there is someone who is able to speak up for the residents. However there is still confusion as to what information about a patient such advocates are entitled to receive. They are not appointed as a result of any formal legal process like the *guardian ad litem* (see glossary). They would have no standing in a court of law if there were a dispute as to whether the patient should be given, for example, an operation for sterilisation other than being a witness who may have relevant evidence. They would have no right to access medical records. Yet, unless they are aware of significant facts about patients' past and present physical and mental condition, their work as advocates would be severely impaired. Practice varies across the country as to the extent of information which is given. There are no clear legal guidelines and the question is therefore open to wide variations in practice.

COURT ORDER FOR DISCLOSURE

If a court determines that confidential information about the patient is relevant in any action and should be disclosed then there can be no defence against production on the grounds that the information confidential or the patient has not consented. There are only two exceptions to the right of the court to order the disclosure of relevant information. The one is the right of legal professional privilege where information passing between client and lawyer in connection with litigation is privileged from disclosure; the other is the right to keep information privileged from disclosure on the grounds of public interest. In such cases, the judge may inspect the documents to determine whether that objection to an order for disclosure being made is acceptable.

In any cases involving personal injury or death an order can be made that information relating to the medical history of the patient be disclosed before any action takes place in the case against a person likely to be a party to the proceedings, even before the writ to commence the action has been issued, (Supreme Court Act 1981, section 33(2)). After the writ has been issued disclosure of relevant information can also be made against a party not likely to be a party to the proceedings (section 34).

The Health Service Commissioner has recommended that disclosure of the patient's notes should be made at a much earlier stage in any litigation. This advice is less significant where it is the representative of the patient seeking the information since now the patient has a statutory right of access which is considered in Chapter 6. If, however, the patient's access is blocked on one of the statutory grounds then the right to require disclosure under the Supreme Court Act assumes greater importance.

STATUTORY DUTY TO DISCLOSE

Certain Acts of Parliament require the production of confidential information and these are shown in Figure 5.2.

Figure 5.2 Statutes requiring disclosure of information
- Prevention of Terrorism Acts
- Road Traffic Acts
- Public Health Acts
- Police and Criminal Evidence Act 1984
- Misuse of Drugs Act 1971

Where a health professional is relying upon an Act of Parliament for the justification of disclosure, she must ensure that she is within the requirements of the section. In a recent case in

Cardiff[53] the refusal of a consultant psychiatrist to disclose to the police dates of admission of a patient to hospital was upheld by the Court of Appeal on the grounds that such disclosure did not come within the provisions of the Police and Criminal Evidence Act 1984.

Infectious disease information

Public Health legislation requires the reporting of notifiable diseases. This would normally be by the doctor but a nurse who obtained this information from visiting a patient at home should ensure that it is passed on to the appropriate authorities.

DISCLOSURE IN THE PUBLIC INTEREST

Professional codes of conduct recognise that there are some extreme occasions when the public interest outweighs the rights of the patient in keeping the information confidential. The UKCC in its advisory paper on confidentiality[54] emphasises that there may be occasions when the public interest prevails and it gives guidance to the registered practitioner in such circumstances. This advice is set out in Figure 5.3.

Figure 5.3 UKCC advice on disclosure in the public interest

D 5 In all cases where the practitioner deliberately discloses or withholds information in what he/she believes to be the public interest he/she must be able to justify the decision. These situations can be particularly stressful, especially where vulnerable groups are concerned, as disclosure may mean the involvement of a third party as in the case of children or the mentally handicapped. **Practitioners should always take the opportunity to discuss the matter fully with other practitioners** (not only or necessarily fellow nurses, midwives and health visitors), and if appropriate consult with a professional organisation before making a decision. There will often be ramifications and these are best explored before a final decision as to whether to withhold or disclose information is made.

Once having made a decision the practitioner should write down the reasons within the appropriate record or in a special note that can be kept on file. The practitioner can then justify the action taken should that subsequently become necessary, and can also at a later date review the decision in the light of future developments.

There have been very few court cases on issues relating to confidentiality and it is difficult to establish general principles from these cases since the situations vary so greatly: one concerned the disclosure of an independent medical report on a psychiatric patient who had murdered several people, another involved information about AIDS patients.

Case: *W* v. *Egdell*[55]

W was detained in a secure hospital under sections 37 and 41 of the Mental Health Act 1983 following a conviction for manslaughter on the grounds of diminished responsibility. He had shot dead five people and two others required major surgery. He applied to a Mental Health Review tribunal and obtained an independent medical report from Dr Egdell who formed the view that W was suffering from a paranoid psychosis rather than paranoid schizophrenia. In the light of this report W withdrew the application to the Tribunal. Dr Egdell had assumed that this report would be made available to the hospital and the tribunal. He sought the permission of W to place his report before the hospital and he refused permission. Dr Egdell then sent the report to the managers asking them to forward a copy to the Home Secretary since he considered that his examination had cast new light of the dangerousness of W and it ought to be known to those responsible for his care and for the formulation of any recommendations for discharge.

Subsequently the Home Secretary referred W to a Mental Health Review Tribunal under the rules which require a hearing to be held at least every three years. The Home Secretary sent a copy of Dr Egdell's report to the Tribunal. W then issued writs against Dr Egdell, the hospital board, the Home Secretary and the Secretary of State for Health and the Tribunal, seeking injunctions preventing the defendants from using this material and claiming damages for breach of confidentiality.

The trial judge held that the court had to balance the interest to be served by non-disclosure against the interest served by disclosure. Since W was not an ordinary member of the public but a detained patient in a secure unit, the safety of the public should be the main criterion. Dr Egdell had a duty to the public to place the result of his examination before the proper authorities if in his opinion the public interest so required. The public interest in disclosure outweighed W's private interest.

The Court of Appeal supported this reasoning and stated:

> A consultant psychiatrist who becomes aware, even in the course of a confidential relationship, of information which leads him, in the exercise of what the court considers a sound professional judgment, to fear that such decisions may be made on inadequate information and with a real risk of consequent danger to the public, is entitled to take such steps as are reasonable in

the circumstances to communicate the grounds of his concern to the responsible authorities. (Lord Justice Bingham)

This statement goes hand in hand with the community professional's duty to ensure that steps are taken to inform the relevant professionals if it is feared that the condition of a mentally disordered patient is deteriorating so that the public safety or the patient's own health and safety are endangered. It goes further than this, however, and suggests that even if information were told to a professional in confidence by the patient, this might justify notifying the relevant authorities. It must be remembered, though, that Dr.Egdell was not the patient's doctor but was brought in simply for a medical examination.

Case: *X* v. *Y and Others*[56]

Some employees of a health authority (the plaintiff) obtained information from hospital records and told a reporter (the first defendant) on a national newspaper (the second defendant) about two doctors who were carrying on general practice despite having contracted the disease AIDS. The defendant newspaper company published an article on this and intended publishing the names in a subsequent article. The health authority sought an injunction restraining the defendants from publishing the identity of the two doctors; and seeking disclosure by the defendants of their sources. The defendants pleaded that the public interest justified their publishing and using the information.

The Queens Bench Division held that the public interest in preserving the confidentiality of hospital records identifying actual or potential AIDS sufferers outweighed the public interest in the freedom of the press to publish such information. This was because victims of the disease ought not to be deterred by fear of discovery from going to hospital for treatment, and free and informed public debate about AIDS could still take place without publication of the confidential information acquired by the defendants. The plaintiffs were therefore entitled to a permanent injunction to restrain the defendants from publishing the names. The defendants were not forced to disclose the source of information because the plaintiffs had failed to prove, on a balance of probability, that disclosure was necessary for the prevention of crime within section 10 of the Contempt of Court Act 1981, since the prevention of crime was not the task of the plaintiffs and a criminal investigation would not be the likely consequence if the source were disclosed.

Since this case there have been directions from the Secretary of State on the discovery that health employees are AIDS sufferers or HIV positive. The ruling in this case still, however, stands.

CONCLUSIONS

All those caring for persons in the community should be aware of their duty to the patient to keep information confidential. Where disclosure is justifiable under one of the exceptions discussed above the professional should be familiar with the limitations of that exception and ensure that the specific disclosure is justified. It is also essential that the reasons for the disclosure should be recorded in the client's records so that if there is a subsequent challenge the decision and reasoning behind it can be recalled in detail. The UKCC advice is of value to all professionals, not just registered nurses, health visitors and midwives.

The Department of Health issued a consultation paper[57] in August 1994 on confidentiality and the use and disclosure of personal health information. It defined the basic duty of confidentiality and set out suggestions for defining circumstances in which person health information could legitimately be disclosed without the person's consent. In the meantime a multi-disciplinary professional working party appointed by most health professional bodies has drafted a handbook[58] including a draft bill governing the use and disclosure of personal health information. This is still the subject of discussions and the Department of Health's proposals in response to its consultation exercise are awaited. The final proposals will have to take into account any direction issued by the European Community. A draft directive was issued in 1995[59]. Certainty in this area and the protection of the rights of individuals is essential and urgent because of the introduction of the electronic patient record[60]. The internal market has led to the need for pricing individual patient care and the need for accounts to be audited will require disclosure of personal information. This disclosure must be carefully policed.

CHAPTER 6

Access to health records

As a result of recent legislation, whether a person's health records are held on computer or held in a manual form there is a statutory right of access, subject to specific situations where access can be withheld. In addition there is a right of access to health records completed by the patient's doctor for employment or insurance purposes. There are also rights of access to personal records held by social services and housing departments under the Access to Personal Files Act 1987. These statutory provisions are set out in Figure 6.1.

Figure 6.1 Statutory provisions affording access to health records
- Data Protection Act 1984
- Access to Personal Files Act 1987
- Access to Medical Reports Act 1988
- Access to Health Records Act 1990

This chapter looks at some of the issues relating to access to records which may involve the community health professional and social worker.

DATA PROTECTION ACT 1984

This Act was passed to regulate the use of automatically processed information relating to individuals and the provision of services in respect of such information. It enables the data subject, the individual to whom the personal data relates, to seek compensation through the courts for damage and any associated distress caused by the loss, destruction or unauthorised disclosure of data or by inaccurate data. The individual can also apply to the courts for rectification or erasure of incorrect data and to obtain access to the data about him if this is refused.

Data users must register the personal data they hold, the purposes for which they use it, the sources from which they get it, those to whom they might disclose it and the countries outside the UK to which they might transfer it.

The data protection principles

Basic principles in relation to the holding of personal automated data are set out in Scchedule 1 to the Act and are shown in Figure 6.2.

Figure 6.2   The Date Protection Principles

Part 1 The Principles

1. The information to be contained in personal data shall be obtained, and personal data shall be processed, fairly and lawfully.
2. Personal data shall be held only for one or more specified and lawful purposes.
3. Personal data held for any purpose or purposes shall not be used or disclosed in any manner incompatible with that purpose or those purposes.
4. Personal data held for any purpose or purposes shall be adequate, relevant and not excessive in relation to that purpose or those purposes.
5. Personal data shall be accurate and, where necessary, kept up to date.
6. Personal data held for any purpose or purposes shall not be kept for longer than is necessary for that purpose or those purposes.
7. An individual shall be entitled–

   (a) at reasonable intervals and without undue delay or expense–
       (i) to be informed by any data user whether he holds personal data of which that individual is the subject; and
       (ii) to access to any such data held by a data user; and
   (b) where appropriate, to have such data corrected or erased.

8. Appropriate security measures shall be taken against unauthorised access to, or alteration, disclosure or destruction of, personal data and against accidental loss or destruction of personal data.

[These Principles apply to operators of computer bureaux as well as data users.]

Part 2 of the Schedule provides statutory guidance on the interpretation of the Principles.

Machinery of the Act

The Act created the Data Protection Registrar whose responsibility is to implement the statutory provisions, by:

● establishing the Register of data users and computer bureaux;

- disseminating information on the Act and its operation;
- promoting the observance of the Data Protection Principles;
- encouraging, where appropriate, the development of codes of practice to assist data users in complying with the Principles;
- considering complaints about contravention of the Principles and provisions of the Act.

The Registrar can issue enforcement notices and can remove an entry from the Register. He may also prosecute for non-compliance with notices issued or for other offences.

Data users and computer bureaux can appeal against the Registrar's decisions to a Data Protection Tribunal.

The Principles only apply to automatically processed data but they could equally well be followed in the control and access to manual records. More general practitioner surgeries are arranging for their medical records to be held on computer and it would be usual for the practice manager (if there is such a post) to be the data protection officer for the practice with responsibilities for ensuring compliance with the Data Protection Act. In addition many community health services are arranging for the patient records to be placed on computer and the compliance with data protection requirements would come under the Trust (or directly managed unit) Computer Manager.

Access to data concerning physical or mental health or social work are subject to Orders made by the Secretary of State which modify the provisions of the Act in relation to this kind of data. Data Protection (Subject Access Modification)(Health) Order 1987 No. 1903 which came into force on 11 November 1987 enables access to health records on similar terms to those set out in relation to the Access to Health Records Act 1990 (see below). The same personnel are defined as health professionals. Access can be excluded if serious harm to the physical or mental health of the data subject is likely to be caused or if a third person can be identified who does not wish to be. The 1984 Act and the 1987 Order have no limitation as to the time when the records were made (unlike the Access to Health Records Act 1990 (see below)).

Data Protection (Subject Access Modification) (Social work) Order 1987 No. 1904 covers access to personal data held by a local authority in connection with its social services functions.

It similarly prevents access if serious harm would be caused to the physical or mental health of the data subject *or of any other person*. The words in italics are not present in the order concerning health data.

ACCESSS TO PERSONAL FILES ACT 1987

This Act provides for individuals access to information relating to themselves and allows them to obtain copies and require amendments. It covers information held by a local authority under the Housing Acts in relation to tenancies and also information held by a local social services authority for the purpose of its social services functions.

ACCESS TO MEDICAL REPORTS ACT 1988

This Act gives a right of access to individuals to any medical report from the individual's own doctor relating to that individual which is required for employment or insurance purposes. A medical practitioner is not obliged to give an individual access to any part of a medical report the disclosure of which would in the opinion of the practitioner be likely to cause serious harm to the physical or mental health of the individual or others or which would indicate the intentions of the practitioner in respect of the individual. Nor need any part be disclosed which would be likely to reveal any information about another person or to reveal the identity of another person who has supplied the information to the practitioner about the individual unless that person has consented to the disclosure. This latter exemption does not apply if the third person is a health professional involved in the care of the individual.

If an individual is of the view that these statutory requirements have not been met he can apply to the county court which has the power to make an order for compliance.

ACCESS TO HEALTH RECORDS ACT 1990

The implementation of this Act on 1 November 1991 ended the anomaly of there being a statutory right of access to automated records but not to those held in manual form. The 1990 Act only covers those records which are not held in automated form so there is no overlap between the Access to Health Records Act 1990 and the Data Protection Act 1984. Most of the health records in the community are still held in manual form so for the present time access under this Act will be the most relevant for the majority of patients. The Act also covers non-automated records held by general practitioners.

Health records

'Health record' is defined as in Figure 6.3.

Figure 6.3 Definition of 'health record' under 1990 Act – section 1(1)

In this Act 'health record' means a record which —

(a) consists of information relating to the physical or mental health of an individual who can be identified from that information, or from that and other information in the possession of the holder of the record; and
(b) has been made by or on behalf of a health professional in connection with the care of that individual

but does not include any record which [would be covered by the Data Protection Act 1984].

Health professionals

Health professional is widely defined as seen from Figure 6.4 but it does not include social workers. The records of a social worker are not therefore covered by this legislation but, as we have seen, come under the Access to Personal Files Act 1987. Where, however, social workers are employed by a health authority, such as in the Special Hospitals, then their records might be accessed under this Act if they were written on behalf of a health professional in connection with the care of an individual.

Figure 6.4 Definition of 'health professional' – section 2(1)

In this Act 'health professional' means any of the following, namely —

(a) a registered medical practitioner;
(b) a registered dentist;
(c) a registered optician;
(d) a registered pharmaceutical chemist;
(e) a registered nurse, midwife, or health visitor;
(f) a registered chiropodist, dietician, occupational therapist, orthoptist or physiotherapist;
(g) a clinical psychologist, child psychotherapist or speech therapist;
(h) an art or music therapist employed by a health service body; and
(i) a scientist employed by such a body as head of a department.

Records made by others on behalf of any of the professionals shown in Figure 6.4 will also be covered by the Act. Thus if a nursing assistant completed records on behalf of a registered nurse those records would come under the provisions of the Act. Similarly an occupational therapy assistant would be deemed to be completing records on behalf of a qualified occupational therapist.

Persons who may apply

An application for access may be made by those persons shown in Figure 6.5.

Figure 6.5 Those entitled to apply for access

The following may make the application:

- the patient,
- a person authorised in writing to make the application on the patient's behalf,
- where the patient is a child, a person having parental responsibility (England and Wales)
- where the patient is a pupil, a parent or guardian (Scotland),
- where the patient is incapable of managing his affairs, any person appointed by court to manage those affairs, and
- where the patient has died, the patient's personal representative (see glossary) and any person who may have a claim arising out of the patient's death.

Procedure

The procedure is for the applicant to apply to the holder of the records. Where the records are made by a general practitioner or by a health professional employed by one, the applicant would apply to the general practitioner on whose list the patient is included. If the patient does not have a general practitioner then access would be to the health authority listing the patient's most recent GP. From 1 April 1996 the statutory duties formerly carried out by FHSAs have been the responsibility of the new health authorities which came into being on that date.

Where the records are made by a health professional employed by a health service body, then the holder is the health service body. This would include NHS Trusts and health authorities. The Act applies to health professionals in the service of the Crown.

In all other cases the holder is the health professional by whom or on whose behalf the record is held. Thus in the private sector the holder of the health records would be the health professional providing that private care. All categories of patient are thus covered.

Once the applicant applies to the holder of the records they must be produced within 21 days of the date of the application if none of the records were made more that 40 days before the date of the application; and within 40 days if they relate to records made before that time.

These time limits only commence, however, if there is sufficient information for the holder of the records to identify the patient or be satisfied that the applicant is eligible to apply. If the holder has insufficient information he must request the applicant to furnish the additional information within 14 days of the date of the application.

The only fees which can be charged are those where all the records were made 40 days before the date of the application or where a copy of the record or extract is supplied. In the latter case the cost of the copy and the postage can be charged.

The holder must allow the applicant to have access to the records or a copy unless any of the exclusion provisions apply.

Exclusion provisions

Where the application for access is made by the patient, access can be refused in the circumstances set out in Figure 6.6.

Figure 6.6 Exclusion of the right of access

access shall not be given to any part of a health record —

(a) which, in the opinion of the holder of the record, would disclose —
   (i) information likely to cause serious harm to the physical or mental health of the patient or of any other individual; or
   (ii) information relating to or provided by an individual, other than the patient, who could be identified from that information; or
(b) which was made before the commencement of this Act. (that is 1 November 1991.)

If the individual who can be identified from the records consents to the access then access can be given. Health professionals who has been involved in the care of the patient cannot be protected by this provision.

If the records made before 1 November 1991 are necessary to make intelligible any records to which access is given then they must be disclosed. This obviously becomes less likely as time passes.

There are additional exclusions depending upon the nature of the applicant.

Duty of health service bodies to take advice

Before access is refused under the above provisions, the holder, if a health service body or health authority must take advice from the appropriate health professional before it decides whether, for the purposes of the Act, it is satisfied as to any matter. The appropriate health professional would usually be the medical or dental practitioner currently responsible for the clinical care of the patient.

The Act requires the health service body to take advice: it does not require it to follow the advice it is given and one could therefore imagine some circumstances where the health professional recommends against access but the holder still grants it.

The right of access is not simply confined to seeing or having a copy of the records. The applicant can challenge the accuracy, completeness and meaning of the records. If a person considers that any information contained in a health record, or part of a health record, to which he has been given the statutory right of access, is inaccurate, he may apply to the holder for the necessary correction to be made.

The holder must then make the necessary correction if he is satisfied that the information is inaccurate. If he is not satisfied he must make a note to this effect in the records where the information is alleged to be incorrect. Without charging a fee he must supply the applicant with a copy of the correction or of the note.

Inaccurate means 'incorrect, misleading or incomplete'.

Enforcement provisions

If the holder of the records has failed to comply with any of the statutory provisions, an application can be made to the High Court or a county court. Before such an application can be made the applicant must follow the complaints procedures laid down by the Secretary of State.

The court may require the record to be made available for its own inspection but cannot disclose the record to the applicant until the question of access has been determined.

Situation

A community psychiatric nurse cares for a patient who has a long chronic history of schizophrenia. The patient, whom the nurse suspects is not taking his medication regularly, becomes disturbed and asks to see his medical records. What does the nurse do?

Initially the nurse should notify the patient that he does have a statutory right to see his records but, in certain circumstances, they can be withheld if it is felt that access would cause serious harm to his physical or mental health. She would therefore check the position with the Consultant. (This assumes the patient is still under the care of the Consultant. If not she would consult the general practitioner.) If the appropriate health professional believes that access can be permitted this can be given. Where, however, the health professional is not prepared to agree to access, then the patient should be advised to apply to the holder of the records since that is the person appointed under the Act to deal with applications.

Situation

Taking the facts of the above situation – imagine that one of the reasons the patient wishes to have access is that he wants to know who had earlier informed the health authority that he was back in the district after he had taken absence without leave. As a result of this information being passed on, he was returned to the psychiatric hospital. Now he has been discharged he wishes to know the name of the person who reported him.

The holder of the records should make contact with this person if she can be identified from the records and if she is not prepared to be identified to the patient that part of the records could be withheld from the patient and the rest disclosed.

Case: R v. *Mid Glamorgan Family Health Service and another, ex parte Martin*[61]

It was held that a patient did not have an unconditional right of access at common law to his medical records which existed before the commencement of the Access to Health Records Act 1990.

The facts of this case are given in Chapter 10 on health and safety, page 191. It was argued for the applicant that

the refusal of access involved a denial of the right of the respect for a person's private life and that a patient of sound mind had a right to receive on request all relevant information which he sought . . . If he was entitled, quite irrationally, not to accept treatment which would protect his life he was equally entitled, rationally or not, to require information whatever damage it might do to his health . . . The common law rule was and had been that the confidential relationship between doctor and patient required, subject only to the exception of protecting informants, access as of right to ensure respect for private and family life.

This was not accepted by the High Court Judge who held that there was no right at common law to access any records which pre-existed the 1990 Act.

The Court of Appeal upheld this decision on the grounds that a doctor or health authority was entitled to deny access to the records by the patient on the ground that their disclosure would be detrimental to him. Lord Justice Nourse stated that the doctor's duty and the health authority's duty was to act at all times in the best interests of the patient.

> Those interests would usually require that a patient's medical records should not be disclosed to third parties; conversely that they should be usually handed on from one doctor to the next or should be made available to the patient's legal advisers if they were reasonably required for the purposes of legal proceedings in which he was involved.

GENERAL ISSUES

Relevance of the motives of the patient in seeking access to the records

Situation

A patient has recently been discharged after orthopaedic surgery. The community physiotherapist attends regularly because of post-operative complications. The patient suspects that these complications occurred because he was kept in traction for too long and he is contemplating suing the hospital. He therefore applied for access.

Access cannot be denied in such circumstances unless there would be serious harm to the physical or mental health of the patient or of any other individual or the identification of an individual who did not consent to the identification. The mere fact that the patient would discover information which would assist him in bringing a legal action is not grounds for refusing access. However the physiotherapist would have to check with the consultant in charge of the case his views on disclosure. If he disagreed with access, then the patient should be advised of his legal rights as in the case of the schizophrenic patient described above.

It is important that a distinction is made between access on an informal basis and the statutory right to apply.

Situation

A patient being treated in the community for ulcers to his leg, discovered that he was suffering from diabetes which had not been recognised by the general practitioners who were attending him. He wished to see his records. Could access be withheld?

There would be no justification on these grounds alone to refuse him access. The general practitioner would be both the holder and the appropriate health professional and would have to disclose the records.

Disagreement in the multi-disciplinary team

Situation

A consultant has advised the multi-disciplinary team that a patient should not be notified that the diagnosis is multiple sclerosis since she fears that the patient may wish to harm himself if he knew the diagnosis. In the community the patient is visited by a community nurse, occupational therapist and physiotherapist. When they meet they discuss the patient and discover that the patient asks each one about the diagnosis and prognosis. They do not share the consultant's view about withholding information and sympathise with the patient's anxieties and wishes. What action can they take?

The team work under the clinical authority of the consultant. She determines the clinical needs of the patient. She is, however, unlikely to see the patient as frequently as the other health professionals and in such a case as this the team should advise her of their concerns, suggesting that she should see the patient again and review the situation. If, however, one of the health professionals, against the advice of the consultant, told the patient the diagnosis, and as a result the patient attempted to commit suicide, that professional could be held accountable.

Health records and social services records

It will have been noted that access to these records comes under different legislation. This should be taken into account in any scheme for a unified system of record keeping between NHS provider and social services departments.

Informal disclosure

It must be emphasised that NHS Trusts, directly managed units, GPs, health services and social services departments do not have to wait for a patient or other authorised person to make an application under the relevant statutory provision for access. Some providers have already initiated systems which permit greater patient/client access without requiring statutory applications to be made. Others are emphasising the importance of better communication between professional staff and patients and thus indirectly reducing the number of requests for statutory access. There is nothing in the Act to prevent such access on whatever terms the provider requires, as long as the statutory right is not restricted.

In addition many local charters emphasise the importance of good communications between patients and staff which could include easy access to records.

Patient custody of records

Increasingly health professionals are recognising the value of patients keeping their records. Early pilot schemes with ante-natal records being kept by mothers showed that they were far less likely to be lost and benefits rather than harm resulted. It has long been the practice in the community for nurses to leave at the patient's house the record of their visits, so that each nurse would see easily what her colleagues had done on previous visits. If, however, the community nurses keep a second set of records at the clinic which are not disclosed to the patient, this second set could become the subject of an access application. The definition of health record (see Figure 6.3) is wide and if the patient believes the records he is shown are incomplete then he can request that the full record is made available (subject of course to the exclusion provisions).

The issue of the patient custody of records is considered in Chapter 11.

Benefits from the statutory right of access

Health professionals have tended to be wary about the patient's right of access to his health records seeing it as potentially sinister. However, there are many positive benefits some of which are set out in Figure 6.7.

Figure 6.7 Benefits deriving from access

- The standard of recording keeping should improve. Since the health professional knows the patient may see them there should be

  – less jargon,
  – more meaningful statements,
  – less expression of opinions and more facts,
  – more legible writing,
  – fewer derogatory statements about the patient, and
  – more comprehensive records.

- There should be a greater willingness to discuss the situation more fully with the patient, and less keeping of certain things for the records while telling the patient others.
- There should be an increase in schemes to share record keeping with patients such as allowing the records to remain in the custody of the patient or allowing the patient to add his own words to the records.
- There should be improved monitoring of the standards of record keeping which may lead to training being provided.
- When records are required for complaints, litigation and court hearings those involved should benefit from the higher standard of record keeping.
- Continuity of care should improve as different colleagues caring for the same patient are able to have a better understanding of the earlier treatment and care.
- The development of such initiatives as a single multi-disciplinary combined record for the patient might take place.
- The latter development might encourage greater multi-disciplinary participation in patient care which is often more difficult to achieve in the primary care setting in the community than in hospital care.
- The emphasis in the *Health of the Nation* is on health promotion and the personal involvement of each person in his own health care, and prevention rather than treatment. This personal involvement of the patient can be promoted by greater access and communication by the professionals to the patient so that the latter understands ways of maintaining health and the thinking behind any treatment regime. Greater openness would significantly assist in this development.
- The records may not be lost so frequently. An Audit Commission Report in 1995[62] criticised the standard of record keeping and gave evidence of the high proportion which were lost. It also recommended greater use of patient held records which it considered would raise health awareness of the patient or the parent of a child.

It remains to be seen whether the possible benefits identified above materialise. Certainly greater openness will encourage client/ carer involvement in the assessment process and the determination of priorities in community care. Innovative projects are in place in the patient care of records and in joint record keeping by different professionals. Of interest too is the development of the smart card which contains personal information and which can be accessed at a variety of outlets. Boots the Chemist has recently introduced such a system across its branches which records medication dispensed by its pharmacists. This will clearly come under the Data Protection Act but can perhaps alleviate the risk of misprescription by doctors or deliberate deception and misuse by the patient. Other aspects relating to record keeping are discussed in Chapter 11.

REFERENCES FOR SECTION A

1. *R* v. *Gloucester County Council, ex parte Mahfood, also ex parte Barry, ex parte Grinham and ex parte Dartnell and another* and *R* v. *Islington London Borough Council, ex parte McMillan* Queen's Bench Division Times Law Report June 21 1995
2. *R* v. *Ealing District Health Authority, ex parte Fox* [1993] 3 All ER 170
3. HSG(95)13
4. Select Committee of the House of Commons chaired by Marion Roe *Report* July 1993.
5. *Quality of care: Report of the Residential Staffs Inquiry* Published by the Local Government Management Board on behalf of the National Joint Council of Local Authorities, Administrative, Professional, Technical and Clerical Services 1992.
6. *Home Life: A Code of Practice for Residential Care* Centre for Policy On Ageing, 1984
7. Sue Blennerhassett and Jackie Calder, *Health Direct* November 1992
8. see Mike Fisher's article 'Care management and social work: clients with dementia'. *Practice* Vol. 4 No. 4 page 229–41
9. The Law Commission Consultation Paper No. 119 *Decision Making and the Mentally Incapacitated Adult* HMSO, 1991
10. The Law Commission Consultation Papers Nos. 128, 129 and 130 HMSO, 1993
11. Law Commission Report No. 231 *Mental Incapacity* HMSO, 1995
12. Peter Singh *Community Care: Britain's other Lottery* MENCAP, 1995
13. British Medical Association *Survey on community care reforms* BMA, 1995
14. *Cole* v. *Turner* (1704) 6 Mod Rep 149
15. *Chatterton* v. *Gerson* [1981] 3 WLR 1003
16. *Re W* [1992] 4 All ER 627
17. *Gillick* v. *Wisbech and West Norfolk Area Health Authority* [1985] 3 All ER 402
18. *Re D* [1976] 1 All ER 326
19. *Re B* [1987] 2 All ER 206
20. *Re B* [1981] 1 WLR 1421
21. see White, Carr and Lowe *A Guide to the Children Act 1989* Butterworths, 1991 page 129–135
22. *Re F* also reported as *F* v. *West Berkshire Health Authority* [1989] 2 All ER 545
23. *T* v. *T* [1988] 1 All ER 613
24. *Re T (adult, refusal of treatment)* [1992] 3 WLR 782
25. The Law Commission Consultation Paper No. 129 *Mentally Incapacitated Adults and Decision Making: Medical Treatment and Research* HMSO, 1993
26. Session 1993–4, Volume 1 Report 1994, HMSO paragraphs 181 to 215
27. Law Commission Report No. 231 *Mental Incapacity* HMSO, 1995
28. British Medical Association *Advance Statements about medical treatment: Code of Practice* April 1995
29. *Leigh* v. *Gladstone* (1909) 26 TLR 139
29a. *Re C (adult: refusal of medical treatment)* [1994] 1 FLR 31
30. *F* v. *West Berkshire Health Authority* [1989] 2 All ER 545
31. Law Commission Consultation Paper No. 129 *Mentally Incapacitated Adults and Decision Making: Medical Treatment and Research* HMSO, 1993
32. Law Commission Report No 231 *Mental Incapacity* HMSO 1995
33. *Re T* [1992] 4 All ER 649

34. *Sutton London Borough Council* v. *Davis* [1995] 1 All ER 53
35. *Beckford* v. *R* [1988] AC 130
36. *Palmer* v. *R* [1971] AC 814 Lord Borth-y-Guest at page 832
37. 1979 *Criminal Law Review* at page 310
38. For further information on this see *Blackstone's Criminal Practice* 3rd Edition Blackstone Press, 1993
39. *Sidaway* v. *Bethlem Royal Hospital Governors* [1985] 1 All ER 643
40. B Dimond *Legal Aspects of Child Health Care* Mosby 1996
41. Muir Gray *Health Trends* 1980 Volume 12 pages 72–74
42. Doris Lessing *The Diaries of Jane Somers* Penguin, 1984
43. Law Commission Consultation Paper No. 130 *Mentally Incapacitated and Other Vulnerable Adults: Public Law Protection* (the third paper dealing with Decision Making and the mentally incapacitated adult) HMSO, 1993
44. Law Commission Report No. 231 *Mental Incapacity* HMSO, 1995
45. *D'Souza* v. *Director of Public Prosecutions* [1992] 4 All ER 545
46. Department of Health *Code of Practice: Mental Health Act 1983* HMSO, 1993
47. B. Dimond and F. Barker *Mental Health Law for Nurses* Blackwell Scientific Publications, 1995
48. Royal College of Psychologists *Report* January 1993
49. Department of Health *Legal Powers on the care of mentally ill people in the community: report of the internal review* August 1993
50. Session 1992/93 Fifth report HMSO, June 1993.
51. Law Commission Report No. 231 *Mental Incapacity* HMSO, 1995
52. A. Sixsmith 'Independence and Home in later life' pp. 338–47 from *Dependency and Interdependency in old age – Theoretical perspectives and Policy alternatives* (Eds C. Philipson, M. Bernard and P. Strang) Croom Helm in association with the British Society of Gerontology, London, 1986
53. *R* v. *Cardiff Crown Court* Times Law Report 3 May 1993
54. *Advisory paper on Confidentiality* UKCC April 1987
55. *W* v. *Edgell* [1989] 1 All ER 1089, The Times Nov. 20 1989 Court of Appeal
56. *X* v. *Y and others* [1988] 2 All ER 648
57. Department of Health *Confidentiality, use and disclosure of personal health information* August 1994
58. The Multi-Disciplinary Professional Working Group *An Explanatory Handbook of Guidance Governing Use and Disclosure of Personal Health Information* July 1994 (published with the participation of 12 professional associations and under the observation of the Data Protection Registrar's Office, the MRC and the UKCC)
59. Draft Directive *The protection of individuals with regard to the processing of personal data and on the free movement of such data* 12003/1/94, Rev 1 ECO 291 CODEC 92, Brussels, 3 February 1995
60. See also Anthony Griew and Rosemary Currell *A strategy of security of the electronic patient record* Institute for Health Informatics University of Wales, Aberystwyth.
61. *R* v. *Mid Glamorgan FHSA and another, ex parte Martin* Times Law Report 2 June 1993 QBD upheld by the CA Times Law Report August 16 1994
62. Audit Commission *Putting the record straight* HMSO, 1995

SECTION B

Professionals

At present litigation is more likely to occur as a result of working with the high technology machinery of the district general hospital or in-patient care but there are still dangers and hazards for the professional working in the community. The first part of Section B looks at the field of professional liability in general terms, discussing the principles of negligence, the concept of vicarious liability (that is the liability of the employer for his employees' negligence) and specific situations of negligence. It also considers the law relating to health and safety and the rules relating to medicines. The second part of Section B considers the accountability of each individual profession working in the community and takes examples of areas of concern that are relevant to such professionals.

PART 1

Professional liability

CHAPTER 7

General principles of accountability

ACCOUNTABILITY

In this chapter the topics shown in Figure 7.1 will be considered.

Figure 7.1 Topics covered in this chapter
- Liability in negligence
- Vicarious liability
- The self-employed professional
- Defences to a civil action
- Standards of care and professional accountability
- Freedom of speech

LIABILITY IN NEGLIGENCE

If harm occurs as a result of negligence, an action for compensation may arise. This would usually be an action for negligence, one of the civil wrongs known as 'torts' (see glossary). Other torts include breach of a statutory duty, nuisance, and defamation. The tort of negligence is by far the most common.

The person who has suffered harm, or the representative of that person, must establish the elements shown in Figure 7.2.

Figure 7.2 Elements of an action for negligence
- Duty of care
- Breach of that duty
- Causation
- Reasonably foreseeable harm

Duty of care

In order to succeed in an action for negligence the plaintiff (that is the person bringing the action) must show that a duty of care was owed to him by the defendant. A duty arises as a matter of law where a professional is caring for a client and the existence of that duty would therefore be for the most part self evident. The principles for the determination of whether a duty of care exists were laid down in the case of *Donoghue* v. *Stevenson*[1] where it was held that a duty existed if a person would be so closely and directly affected by one's acts that one ought reasonably to have them in contemplation as being so affected when directing one's mind to the acts or omissions which are called in question. This principle set out by Lord Atkin has become known as the 'neighbour' principle. In an early application of the principle in New Zealand, a duty was held to exist in the case where a doctor disclosed confidential information about a wife to her husband (both were his patients) which could be used against her. The wife won her action against the doctor for breach of his duty of care to her[2].

However it is not always easy to apply. Would it extend, for example, in the case of a district nurse, to taking the prescription of the patient to the pharmacist and returning with the medication? Certainly it would if that task were to be included in the job description, but often that task is specifically excluded. Does this therefore mean that the duty of care recognised by the law of tort excludes it? The answer is that it would depend upon the actual circumstances of the case. There may, for example, be a duty not to cause harm but not necessarily a duty to prevent harm.

Another difficulty is whether the duty of care extends to those who are not actually on the case load of the professional.

Situation

An occupational therapist hears, when visiting her client, that a neighbour, who does not appear to be receiving any support from social services, is extremely immobile and needing urgent help. Does the occupational therapist have a duty recognised by law to visit immediately and assist?

The answer is probably 'no' since for the most part the law does not recognise a failure of omission unless there is a pre-existing duty. However were the occupational therapist to assume the duty and assist the neighbour but in so doing cause her reasonably foreseeable harm through her carelessness, then she would be liable for the breach of duty.

An additional aspect of the situation is whether now, under the provisions for assessment under section 47 of the National Health Service and Community Care Act 1990, the occupational therapist (if employed by the local authority) would be under an obligation to bring to the notice of the local authority the need for an assessment to be carried out. This will be considered on page 396. It hinges on the meaning of the words in the section 'where it appears to the local authority that any person for whom they may provide or arrange for the provision of community care services may be in need of such services . . .'.

Recently the courts have shown reluctance to extend the duty of care owed by public authorities to the wider general public. For example the House of Lords has stated[3] that no duty of care was owed by the police to individual members of the public to identify and apprehend an unknown criminal. This was an action brought by the mother of one of the victims of Peter Sutcliffe, the Yorkshire Ripper. She argued that if the police had done their investigation thoroughly he would have been caught before the attack on her daughter.

In a subsequent case[4] the Court of Appeal held that public policy would not allow a negligence action to be brought against the police for failing to stop a teacher killing a pupil's father and injuring the pupil. In contrast, however, the House of Lords has held that a solicitor who delayed in making a will was liable to the beneficiaries of the intended will[5]. The duty of care which was owed to the client could be extended in law to the intended beneficiary – an identifiable individual was put at risk by the solicitor's delay.

Breach of duty

In order to establish whether there has been a breach of duty it is necessary to determine the standard of care expected of the professional in that set of circumstances.

Situation

A community psychiatric nurse (CPN) visits a patient who was on section 17 leave from the psychiatric hospital (that is leave of absence which the patient's responsible medical officer (RMO) can grant to a detained patient). The patient seems to be excited and talks rapidly, but appears to be coping in the community although he is living on his own. The CPN recommends that the patient should consider attending the consultant's outpatients' department the following week. She does not recommend any more urgent action to be taken. The following day it is discovered that the patient has committed suicide in the night. Would the CPN be held liable?

The issue which arises here is what would any reasonably competent CPN visiting the patient in those circumstances be expected to observe and what action would it be reasonable to expect her to take. If she failed to notice symptoms which would have clearly warned any trained psychiatric nurse to take more care, perhaps ask the GP to visit, or even to recommend to the RMO that the patient should be recalled to hospital, then she would be held to be in breach of the standard of care demanded. If, on the other hand, the suicide was completely unforeseeable and it would be unreasonable to expect any professional to have taken precautions against it then there would be no liability upon the nurse. One difficulty is of course that of proof. The person bringing the court action would have to prove the breach of the duty of care, and this would be extremely difficult in the absence of witnesses and the patient himself, although the standard of proof in a civil claim is on balance of probabilities in contrast to the higher standard in the criminal courts, which is beyond all reasonable doubt.

The test used by the courts to determine what is the standard of care owed by a professional to the client is the Bolam test (see glossary) taken from a case heard in 1957.[6]

In this case which dealt with an allegation of negligence on the the part of doctors administering a certain procedure (in fact electro-convulsive therapy) Mr Justice McNair defined the required standard as follows:

> [W]here you get a situation which involves the use of some special skill or competence, then the test whether there has been negligence or not is not the test of the man on the top of a Clapham omnibus, because he has not got this special skill. The test is the standard of the ordinary skilled man exercising and professing to have that special skill ... [I]n the case of a medical man negligence means failure to act in accordance with the standards of reasonably competent medical men at the time. [But it must be] remembered that there may be one or more perfectly proper standards; and if a medical man conforms with one of those proper standards then he is not negligent.

In the situation above, were a civil action to be brought against the NHS Trust which employed the CPN, evidence would be given as to what would have been the reasonable standard of care which the CPN should have provided and what symptoms a responsible practitioner would reasonably be expected to look for. This would then be compared with the facts of what actually happened.

However the fact that another professional would have acted differently is not fatal to the defence case, if it can be shown that what the defendant did was supported by a responsible body of professional opinion.

Situation

A district nurse was urged by the physician to use a particular product in cleaning the wound and prior to applying the dressing. She used this product, but the client heard that there was criticism of this product in the specialist press and claimed that she had suffered harm as a result of the product being used upon her. In her defence the nurse was able to show that there was a firm body of professional opinion which supported her action and there had been no condemnation of the product she used by the Committee for the Safety of Medicines or any other groups.

In these circumstances she should not be found liable in negligence. The fact that she was obeying the orders of her consultant is not in itself a complete justification. Liability could arise if no reasonable nurse would have obeyed those instructions.

It is possible for there to exist two separate bodies of respected professional opinion which recommend different diagnoses, forms of treatment or advice. In such a situation the House of Lords[7] has held that

> it was not sufficient to establish negligence for the plaintiff to show that there was a body of competent professional opinion that considered the decision was wrong, if there was also a body of equally competent professional opinion that supported the decision as having been reasonable in the circumstances.

Applying this statement to the situation above, the fact that the patient has expert advice which suggests that a particular ointment should not have been used on her wound is not sufficient to show that the nurse has been negligent if the nurse has evidence from a responsible body of professional opinion which supports her use of that ointment in those particular circumstances.

In the case of *Hughes* v. *Waltham Forest Health Authority*[8] damages of £200 000 were awarded against the health authority for breach of the duty of care owed by two specialist surgeons. The authority appealed against this decision and the Court of Appeal allowed the appeal. It held that when considering whether there had been a breach of the standard of care by the surgeons the question to be asked was:

> whether the surgeons in reaching their decision displayed such a lack of clinical judgement that no surgeon exercising proper care and skill would have reached the same decision.

That test had not been applied and the defendant's appeal was allowed.

Clearly there must be evidence of a breach of the duty of care and the burden is on the plaintiff to produce this evidence and satisfy the test on a balance of probabilities.

Case: *Partington v. Wandsworth London Borough Council*[9]

It was held that a local authority was not liable to a person who had received injuries when she had been attacked by an autistic 17 year old who was in their care. The victim had failed to show that the 17 year old was improperly supervised.

Causation

Once it is established that there has been a breach of the duty of care it is necessary to show that it was that breach which caused reasonably foreseeable harm to the patient. This is not easy to do and several cases of compensation have failed because, although a breach of the duty of care could be shown, the causal link between that breach and the harm which occurred could not be proved.

Situation

A district nurse is visiting the home of a patient with very severe ulcers. They are not clearing up and the nurse is told that the patient is very thirsty and feels very weak. The nurse does not realise that the patient may be suffering from diabetes and fails to call the GP in to see the patient or recommend that a urine sample is taken. Eventually the patient is found in a coma and subsequently dies.

The nurse in these circumstances would probably be found to be in breach of the standard of care expected of the reasonable district nurse. Even though nurses are not expected to diagnose conditions they are expected to assess the patient carefully and call in the GP when necessary. However, it might be very difficult for the personal representatives of the client to show that the failure of the nurse actually caused the patient's death. It may be that the patient was so seriously ill that it was only a matter of time before she died. It may be that death was not caused by diabetes. Unless the plaintiff can establish that there was this causal link between the breach of the duty of care and the harm which occurred damages are not payable in the civil courts.

Case: Whooping cough vaccine

In *Loveday* v. *Renton and another*[10] a case was brought against the Wellcome Foundation who made vaccine against whooping cough and against the doctor who administered it seeking compensation for brain damage which was alleged to have been caused by the vaccine. The case failed because the judge held that the plaintiff had not established on a balance of probabilities that the pertussis vaccine had caused the brain damage.

Subsequently however in an Irish case[11] brought against the Wellcome Foundation and others for vaccine damage it has been held that causation as well as breach was established and this enabled the plaintiff in this case to obtain compensation of £2.75 million. The facts were that the High Court had dismissed the plaintiff's claim because of the lack of proof of causation. However the Irish Supreme Court held that the Wellcome Foundation was liable for the negligent manufacture and release of a particular batch of triple vaccine and that the brain damage was caused as a result. It referred the case back to the High Court on the amount of compensation which approved an award of £2.75 million as compensation for the brain damage sustained in September 1969. It should be remembered that compensation is very high in such cases because it includes an estimate of all the costs of future care for the victim.

Harm

Finally in order to succeed in a case of negligence, the plaintiff must prove that harm has been suffered as a result of the breach of the duty of care. A breach may take place but, if the plaintiff does not suffer harm, an action for negligence must fail. Harm can include loss or damage of property as well as personal injury or death.

VICARIOUS LIABILITY

Compensation is usually sought from the employer of the negligent professional rather than from the professional herself. This is possible because of the concept of vicarious liability of the employer for the wrongful acts of an employee whilst acting in course of employment. There are obvious advantages to the claimant since the employer is more likely to be able to pay the compensation. For non-NHS employers, including local authorities, there is compulsory insurance provision under the Employers' Liability (Compulsory Insurance) Act 1969. However, this Act is not binding upon the health service bodies including NHS Trusts. Since 1 January 1990 doctors and dentists have been covered by the concept of Crown indemnity and the employer would therefore assume, under the doctrine of vicarious liability, responsibility for their negligence and other wrongdoing (such as trespass, nuisance) and any compensation which is payable. This does not apply to general practitioners and the other self-employed independent contractors who have contracts for services with the health authorities that took over the functions of the FHSAs in April 1996. These independent contractors would be liable for the compensation themselves or through their insurers.

The elements of vicarious liability are shown in Figure 7.3.

Figure 7.3 Elements of vicarious liability

An employer is vicariously liable for the
- negligence
- of an employee
- acting in course of employment.

Negligence

Negligence has been considered above: each of the four elements shown in Figure 7.2 would have to be proved.

Of an employee

The fact that the negligent person was an employee of the defendant is not usually difficult to establish. There are, however, an increasing number of situations in the community where the status of a person as an employee might not be easy to establish. For example is an agency nurse an employee of the client, an employee of the agency or self-employed? If she is the latter then the agency would not be held vicariously liable for her actions. It might, however, be liable on its own account for sending out an incompetent person. The need for an employment nexus would also *prima facie* mean that voluntary carers sent by an organisation would not be seen as employees of the organisation which would not therefore be vicariously liable for them. However, the courts might well impute the employment relationship to the situation and say that these carers are the equivalent of employees. The point is still to be decided.

Many tasks formerly performed by staff directly employed by local authorities are now carried out by independent agencies who contract with individuals to enter homes to perform services. Thus many firms now provide home care services funded by the local authorities. If the persons sent under contract by the firms into clients' homes are negligent and cause harm, who is liable for the harm? If they are the employees of the firms, the firms will be vicariously responsible. If they are in law self-employed then only they will be accountable. This is further discussed in Chapter 20. At present when GP fund-holders purchase the services of community health professionals from a Trust, the GP would probably not be held vicariously liable for the negligence of the professionals. This issue is discussed in Chapter 24.

Acting in course of employment

Finally it must be shown that the employee was acting in course of employment when the negligent act occurred. Failing to obey orders will not necessarily take the action out of the definition of 'in course of employment'. Even stealing goods of a client might still be attributable to the employer and be regarded as in course of employment for the purposes of holding that a situation of vicarious liability existed.

Situation

A care assistant employed by the local authority on a part time basis was told that she should not take washing home to do in her own home. Because of the dilapidated condition of the client's washing machine, the care assistant ignored these instructions and used to take the washing home. On her way home carrying a heavy load she bumped into a frail elderly lady causing her serious harm. The injured person is now claiming compensation.

Is the local authority liable? Two questions have to be answered: is the employee acting in course of employment when returning home from work and secondly, if the answer to the first question is yes, then does the fact that she is disobeying the employer's instructions mean that she is no longer in course of employment? The answer would probably be that she has ceased to be in course of employment when she leaves the client's house.

What, however, if she returns to the client's house when she is not officially on duty? She may for example wish to check that the client is well. What if harm occurs then? It is likely that the courts would hold that she is there as a result of her duties as a care assistant and therefore the local authority would be liable for her actions. The legal outcome is not, however, certain and much would depend upon the actual circumstances of the case.

In considering a definition of in course of employment the courts have applied it to the situations shown in Figure 7.4.

Figure 7.4 Definition of in course of employment

The following situations have been held to be in course of employment:

- Work where the employee is employed to do a specific activity even though his method of doing it is contrary to instructions.
- Conduct which is within the authorised limits of time and space.
- Conduct which is expressly forbidden but where the acts are still within the scope of employment.
- Acts which are not authorised but are intended to further the employer's interests.
- Deliberate criminal conduct (in certain circumstances) if the act was committed in course of employment.

Right of indemnity

The employee has a duty to his employer to take reasonable care in carrying out his work. If as a result of his negligence, harm is caused to another person or there is loss or damage to property, the employer has a duty to pay compensation to the person who has suffered harm under the concept of vicarious liability discussed above. However, the employer also has the right to seek an indemnity from the employee whose negligence led to the compensation having to be made[12].

It is not the practice to enforce this right of indemnity within the National Health Service. In 1990 the health authorities took from the medical defence organisations financial responsibility for the actions of doctors (other than GPs or other self-employed doctors) and dentists whilst acting in course of their employment. The funding of the compensation claims has still not been resolved for the long term, and there may be a possibility in the future that an NHS employer could exercise this right in exceptional circumstances.

Similarly, the local authority is vicariously liable for all the staff it employs but there is no evidence at present that it would seek to exercise its right of indemnity against an employee whose negligence had led to compensation being paid out.

THE SELF-EMPLOYED PROFESSIONAL

The vast majority of community professionals in this country are employees and would therefore be covered by the employer's vicarious liability, whether NHS, local authority or independent employer, if they had been negligent. However, there is a growing body of independent practitioners who are self-employed and who would have to shoulder the costs of any action for negligence and any compensation payable. In addition there are some professionals who, in addition to being employees, also work for an agency. It is important that all these groups should ensure that they have full insurance cover, not only for liability for causing harm to others but also personal accident cover in case they themselves suffer harm. It is vital that full disclosure of the nature of their work and any inherent risks should be disclosed to the prospective insurance company since a contract for insurance purposes requires a full disclosure of facts within the knowledge of the insured which should be made known to the insurer. If it is subsequently revealed that there has not been a full disclosure of material information then the insurer can refuse to meet the claim.

In addition those seeking personal insurance should ensure the cover is adequate. For example negligence at birth could result in a severely brain damaged child, where compensation of over £1 million may be payable to meet the costs of future care. If an independent midwife only had cover for £500 000 she would have to pay the deficit personally. This would result in her bankruptcy and the victim being inadequately compensated. Most insurance companies adjust the premiums to relate to the maximum cover provided.

Many professionals who work on a self-employed basis have set up their own organisations to represent them. The other legal issues relating to private practice are considered in Chapter 20.

DEFENCES

Should a professional be faced with an allegation of negligence and be sued personally or be in involved in proceedings against the employer for vicarious liability, there are several defences which are available. These are shown in Figure 7.5.

Figure 7.5 Defences to an action for negligence

- Dispute over the facts
- One of the elements of negligence is missing
- Contributory negligence
- Willing assumption of risk
- Limitation of time
- Exemption from liability

Dispute over the facts

Many cases of negligence fail because the defendant denies the facts pleaded by the plaintiff and the plaintiff is unable to show on a balance of probabilities, through her witnesses and other evidence which she brings forward, that she has made out her case. The judge can stop the hearing after the plaintiff has concluded her case and find for the defence on the basis that there is no case for the defendant to answer.

One of the difficulties of working in the community is that many professionals visit homes on their own. They may be alone with a client. If harm occurs, they are vulnerable to false accusations and, should it come to a court hearing, it is their word against that of the client. As indicated above, a court action based on such a false accusation would probably fail for lack of proof but that does not spare the worker from the anxiety that follows from having to defend herself. One way of providing some protection is for professionals and support workers to go in pairs when visiting those clients who are likely to make false accusations against them. (Procedures should also exist for protecting property and taking an inventory when clients who live on their own die.)

Obviously it is essential that the defendant has a high standard of record keeping and statements since comprehensive records can prove invaluable in reminding those involved of the details so that they are able to stand up to cross-examination more effectively.

See Chapter 11 on records and record keeping for further details of standards and uses in court.

One of the elements of negligence missing

The absence of one of the elements of negligence (shown in Figure 7.2) will automatically mean that the plaintiff's case will fail.

Usually whether or not a duty of care exists is clear. However, there may be a dispute as to the standard of care which should have been followed. Professionals need to ensure that through training and regular updating they have an understanding of current practice to protect both themselves and their patients.

Causation is often the most difficult element to establish in health care cases with conflicting expert evidence being proffered to the court.

If the patient has not suffered harm as a result of the breach of the duty of care by the professional then an action for negligence will not succeed.

However, even where the case of negligence fails, the person who is alleged to be at fault may face action through other channels such as disciplinary proceedings by the employer or professional conduct proceedings.

Contributory negligence

If the client is partly to blame for the harm which has occurred then there may still be liability on the part of the professional but the compensation payable might be reduced in proportion to the client's fault. In extreme cases, such a claim may be a complete defence if 100% contributory negligence is shown. In determining the level of contributory negligence, the physical and mental health and the age of the client would be taken into account.

Situation

A prescribing nurse writes a prescription for a cream to be provided for a skin complaint and explains to the client how it should be applied. The client fails to follow the instructions and puts on too much thereby causing a reaction. It is then discovered that the wrong ointment has been prescribed. The nurse is clearly at fault but the client may also be partly to blame for the harm. However account would be taken of the capacity of the client to understand the instructions and whether the harm would have occurred if the nurse had not prescribed the wrong ointment. If, for example, the wrong ointment would still not have caused harm had it not been applied in such quantities, then responsibility would be apportioned between them.

The Law Reform (Contributory Negligence) Act 1945 allows an apportionment of responsibility for the harm which has been caused which may result in a reduction of damages payable. The Court can reduce the damages 'to such extent as it thinks just and equitable having regard to the claimant's share in the responsibility for the damage'. (Section 1(1)).

Willing assumption of risk

Volenti non fit injuria is the Latin tag for the defence that a person willingly undertook the risk of being harmed. It is unlikely to succeed as a defence in an action for professional negligence since the professional cannot contract out of liability where harm occurs as a result of her negligence. See the Unfair Contract Terms Act 1977 which is considered below.

Limitation of Time

Actions for personal injury or death should normally be commenced within three years of the date of the event which gave rise to the harm. There are however some major qualifications to this general principle and these are shown in Figure 7.6.

Figure 7.6 Situations where the limitation of time can be extended,

- Children under 18 years – the time does not start to run until the child is 18 years.
- Those suffering from a disability, for example mental disorder – time runs from recovery (if at all).
- Where the plaintiff did not have actual or constructive knowledge that harm had occurred as a result of negligence – time will run from the time when there was or should have been this knowledge.
- Discretion of the judge – the judge has a statutory power to extend the time within which a plaintiff can bring an action for personal injuries or death, if it is just and equitable to do so.

The implications of the rules relating to limitation of time are that, in those cases which might come under one of the exceptions to the three year time limit, records should be kept and not destroyed. This is particularly important in cases involving children or childbirth. For example in November 1995 a man who was severely brain damaged a month after his birth 33 years ago was awarded £1.25 million damages against the general practitioner who failed to notice that he was becoming seriously unwell from severe dehydration secondary to gastroenteritis[13].

Exemption from liability.

It is possible for a person to exempt himself from liability for harm arising from his negligence but by the Unfair Contract Terms Act 1977 this only applies to loss or damage to property. It must also be shown by the defendant that it is reasonable to rely upon the term or notice which purported to exclude liability. The relevant provisions of the Unfair Contract Terms Act 1977 are shown in Figure 7.8 and see also Figure 34.2.

Figure 7.8 Unfair Contract Terms Act 1977

2(1) A person cannot by reference to any contract term or to a notice given to persons generally or to particular persons exclude or restrict his liability for death or personal injury resulting from negligence.

2(2) In the case of other loss or damage, a person cannot so exclude or restrict his liability for negligence except in so far as the term or notice satisfies the requirement of reasonableness.

11(1) ... the requirement of reasonableness ... is that the term shall have been a fair and reasonable one to be included having regard to the circumstances which were, or ought reasonably to have been, known to or in the contemplation of the parties when the contract was made.

11(5) It is for those claiming that a contract term or notice satisfies the requirements of reasonableness to show that it does.

STANDARDS OF CARE AND PROFESSIONAL ACCOUNTABILITY

Many NHS Trusts now incorporate into the contracts of employment with their staff a term that the employee will observe the standards of professional conduct required by their profession. Where this occurs, it should make less likely the situation where a conflict arises between the employee's duty to obey the codes of professional conduct set by her profession and the duty to obey the reasonable orders of the employer.

The UKCC has suggested that the Council's standards should

be incorporated into the contracts for hospital and community health care services which are agreed between purchaser and provider. To this end a Registrar's letter has been circulated setting out the responsibilities on providers and purchasers. It covers the incorporation of the *Code of Professional Conduct* and the principles of the *Scope of Professional Practice* together with the individual practitioner's right to freedom of speech, the need to ensure post registration education and specific requirements for midwives. The document[14] *Council's Proposed Standards for Incorporation into Contracts for Hospital and Community Health Care Services* was issued in September 1995.

Finally purchasers and providers are asked to ensure that full use should be made of the Council's service to check registration status and to provide effective supervision of support staff.

It is still too early to assess whether these UKCC guidelines are being implemented. The document itself does not have any statutory force nor are there any sanctions which the UKCC can use against those purchasers who fail to incorporate these terms in their NHS agreements. Where these NHS agreements are made between NHS bodies, they are not enforceable in a court of law (see Chapter 23). In addition if such terms are included in an NHS agreement and the provider fails to implement them it is up to the purchaser to impose sanctions or show disapproval of the provider.

FREEDOM OF SPEECH

Professionals can sometimes find that there is a clash between the professional standards which they are expected to maintain as a result of being a registered professional following the professional code issued by their professional body and the requirements of their employers.

In the NHS, the case of Mr Graham Pink illustrated this clash where he maintained that he was dismissed by his employers because he followed the UKCC Code of Professional Practice by drawing attention to unsatisfactory staffing levels in his unit where he was a night nurse for elderly people. This was denied by his employers who said he had been disciplined for breach of confidentiality in reporting a case to the press so that the patient was identified and for failing to report an accident. The subsequent Industrial Tribunal was halted when the health authority offered a settlement to Mr Pink. The health authority said that it was clear that, were the case to continue, then the costs to the health authority would be extremely high and they preferred these moneys to be spent on patient care.

The Secretary of State has issued a circular[15] as part of a process of consultation on freedom of speech. The aim is to ensure that each health authority and NHS Trust has a procedure whereby staff can make known their concerns on patient care without the fear of being victimised. It suggests that a duty should be placed on health service bodies to prepare a local policy for enabling the duty and right of the staff to raise with the employing authority or Trust any matter of concern and to prevent any person who raises such concerns *bona fide* from being penalised for so doing.

If the circular is fully implemented it should be possible for staff to fulfil their professional duties without fearing that they might lose their jobs. It remains to be seen in practice whether the freedom of speech circular is effective, although this aspect of concern has to a certain extent been taken over by the Trade Union Reform and Employment Rights Act 1993 (see Chapter 9), in that an employee now receives protection from unfair dismissal if health and safety issues are brought to the attention of the employer in accordance with the provisions of section 28 and Schedule 5 of that Act.

Similar terms would probably be incorporated into the contract of a person employed by the local authority. If they are concerned about standards of care or hazards at work, they should initially seek redress through the internal management structure making use of the grievance procedure if necessary. If this fails to bring effective action, then the attention of outside persons and organisations could be drawn to the situation.

CONCLUSION

This chapter has sought to identify the nature of accountability for negligence through actions in the civil courts and also to consider the concept of vicarious liability of the employer and possible defences to an action for negligence. In the next chapter we turn to some specific situations which can arise in community care.

CHAPTER 8

Special situations

This chapter continues the discussion of issues relating to professional liability and looks at the specific problems which arise in the situations listed in Figure 8.1.

Figure 8.1 Specific situations
- Negligent advice
- Key worker concept
- Delegation/supervision/instructing others
- Equipment
- Transporting others
- Risk assessment and management
- Communications

NEGLIGENT ADVICE

The giving of advice to clients is as much part of the professional duty of care as the carrying out of treatment and care. Often it will not be easy to separate out advice giving from care giving. However one difficulty faced by the professional in the community is the problem of proving what was said in the event of any dispute arising.

Situation

An occupational therapist gives advice to a client on the use of a hoist. The client totally ignores these instructions and as a result is injured. Is the occupational therapist liable?

She would have to show that her advice was sufficient to enable the client to be safe if it were followed. However, she might have difficulty in establishing what was said. She might also have difficulty in showing that the client had the mental capacity to understand the advice.

One possible precaution which is not often followed is for the professional to give written information to the client, assuming again that there is the capacity to read and understand. In this way the client can refer to the instructions at a later date and the professional can show that reasonable care was taken. Alternatively the professional can confirm a spoken explanation with later instructions in writing.

Situation

A stoma care nurse is questioned by the client about the redness of the skin around the opening. The nurse reassures the client that there is no need for concern. However it then appears that there is a severe infection as a result of which the client has to undergo a further operation. Had the infection been treated earlier with antibiotics it might not have been necessary for the operation to have taken place.

In this case it would appear that the nurse gave negligent advice to her client. In reliance upon this advice the client failed to receive the appropriate treatment and therefore suffered harm. However, the client would have to show that it was reasonable to rely upon this advice and that he did rely upon it. The client would also have to prove that the harm was suffered as a result of his reliance on the careless advice. As we have shown in Chapter 7 dealing with professional liability, to establish causation is very difficult and in a case like this it may be asserted in defence that the second operation would have been necessary anyway as antibiotics given earlier would not have prevented the infection growing.

■ What if the advice is correct but wrongly used?

One difficulty in the giving of advice is proving that it was given appropriately but that subsequently a client has

● failed to read the advice, or
● unknown to the professional, has not understood it but pretended that he did, or
● misread it due to carelessness, or
● ignored it altogether, or

● amended it in the wrong way due to limited knowledge.

Obviously in giving the advice, whether by word of mouth or in writing, professionals have a duty to ensure that clients have understood it. This might mean watching clients undertake a task under supervision. Asking them questions (in a non-hostile way) to see if there is any misunderstanding or ignorance and checking that they are able to read and understand any instructions in writing. If, as a result of a professional's failure to take these precautions, harm occurs to a client then there may well be liability on the professional, but the point made above about causation is relevant.

KEY WORKER CONCEPT

Key workers

Community multi-disciplinary teams have developed a key worker system where, instead of responsibility for one client being divided between many different professionals all of whom visit the client at varying times, one of the team is nominated the key worker and takes on the overall responsibility for the care of that client. The advantages of such a system are obvious:

● the client has to deal in the main with only one professional;
● that professional has the main responsibility so there should not be confusion and gaps over who is taking care of that client;
● one person knows the current situation of the client; and
● the key worker is able to call upon all the specialist skills within and also outside the team as required by the client so that the client's specific needs are met.

There are however dangers.

Situation

The social worker is designated as the key worker for an elderly person with severe mobility problems. She realises that the client is having difficulty bathing herself but considers that with some hand rails the client should be able to get in and out of the bath without requiring either a nurse to attend her or a hoist. The social worker therefore arranges for the rails to be ordered and installed. Unfortunately the client suffers a fall whilst using the bath and is found unconscious. Subsequently the view is expressed that, had an occupational therapist visited the client and carried out an assessment, it is highly unlikely that she would have ordered a bath rail since she would have considered that it would have been unsafe for the client to bath herself.

This situation shows the dangers of the key worker stepping outside her field of competence and failing to bring in the specialist.

The *Scope of Professional Practice*

In nursing the *Scope of Professional Practice* published by the UKCC[16] has recommended the abolition of the concept of the extended role (see glossary) of the nurse. The nurse should not be limited in developing her skills and expertise. Provided that she has the knowledge, skill and competence, can undertake the task safely and follows the principles set out in the document, she should be enabled to undertake a wide variety of activities relating to health care. For convenience a summary of the principles is set out in Figure 8.2.

Figure 8.2 *Scope of Professional Practice* principles

1. The interests of the client/patient must predominate.
2. The practitioner must maintain her knowledge, skill and competence.
3. The practitioner must also acknowledge the limits of her knowledge, skill and competence.
4. The practitioner must not jeopardise standards and must comply with the Code.
5. The practitioner must recognise her direct and personal accountability.
6. The practitioner must avoid inappropriate delegation.

One of the difficulties of this approach is the question of how the practitioner knows whether she is competent. If a specific course of training is not required and if there is no external assessment of her training and competence, it is extremely difficult for the practitioner to know the true picture.

On the other hand the advantages and potential results of this philosophy are that it might lead to a greater mix of professional skills. We might have hybrid community nurse/occupational therapist/social workers where the skills required in very specific situations which are normally provided by several different professionals can, with appropriate training, be acquired by the one professional. Only where there is legislation which places particular duties on specific professionals would there be a legal impediment to the crossing of traditional lines of demarcation between the professionals. If this development were to take place, however, one of the main difficulties may be the organisational boundaries of different statutory authorities.

Legal significance of the team

What becomes even more important in the role of the key worker in knowing her limitations is having a good appreciation of the skills and expertise of other professionals and when their help should be summoned.

Team working, particularly in the community, is becoming a major aspect of inter-professional co-operation. Case conferences are becoming a regular feature of community work and the assessment procedures required by the NHS and Community Care Act 1990 require multi-disciplinary co-operation in making an assessment and the appointment of a key worker. (This is discussed in Chapter 25.) The teams cross the organisational boundaries of the statutory authorities and often include representatives from the voluntary and independent sectors.

■ What is the legal liability if a decision on a particular course of action has been made by a team?

An individual member of that team might disagree with the decision but carry it out because it is the decision of the team. The question arises as to her legal liability if something goes wrong and the client is harmed.

The Court of Appeal has declared that the courts do not recognise legal liability of a team: each individual member of the team is personally accountable for his actions[17].

If, therefore, the team decided that a client should be provided with bath aids which the occupational therapist considered were inappropriate because the client's state of health required her to be visited by a district nurse for home bathing, the occupational therapist would be at fault in carrying out the recommendations of a team which were contrary to her professional opinion.

Similarly, in a totally different and extreme context, if the team decided that a terminally ill client in the community should be allowed to die and death should be hastened by administering a lethal drug, the nurse who administered that drug would be personally and professionally accountable for that action before the UKCC, the criminal and civil courts and could be disciplined by the employers. However if, in addition, it could be established that other members of the team agreed to commit an illegal act, they might be held accountable for conspiracy.

■ What if there is disagreement in the team?

Decisions must be made by those who have the professional competence and training to determine them. There would of course be information sharing and an input by others into the different decisions but ultimately it is the professional whose range of professional activities covers the particular action in question who must determine what is appropriate in the light of the prevailing standards of professional skill, that is those who have the specialist skills and knowledge.

Disputes can arise over the discharge of patients from hospital care to the community. It may be for example that shortage of in-patient facilities leads to premature discharge of a patient.

Situation

As a result of the reduction of in-patient beds, there is pressure to reduce the length of stay of in-patients in the acute psychiatric services. Contrary to the advice of the community psychiatric nurse (CPN), a patient suffering from chronic schizophrenia is discharged to bedsit accommodation. The CPN writes a report advising that in her view the discharge is premature. However her views are ignored by the consultant psychiatrist. The CPN makes all possible arrangements for the support of the patient in the community and visits her every day. One week after her discharge, the CPN visits her only to find that she has died by placing her head in the gas oven. What is the liability of the CPN?

It is not sufficient for the nurse to argue that the decision to discharge was the consultant's and therefore she has no further responsibility. It is still her duty to do all she can to safeguard the health and safety of the patient and any person the patient may harm. If during her visits following discharge it is apparent to her that the patient is becoming more and more depressed then it would be her duty to report this fact to the general practitioner and to the psychiatrist and ensure that all reasonable care was taken of the patient. If necessary this might include recommending the readmission of the patient. If she has done all that but been advised that, because of the shortage of beds the patient cannot be admitted, then it is the responsibility of those in charge of those beds and who determine priorities for those beds. They will have to defend their actions and show that they exercised all reasonable care according to the Bolam test (see glossary).

The issue of the discharge of the chronic mentally ill from hospital accommodation followed by incidents of murder, rape and suicide has attracted considerable media attention and led to claims that the community care programme is in tatters and not working. Following the Ben Silcock incident (see page 77), the Secretary of State set up a committee to investigate the extent to which additional legislation is required. Guidelines on the discharge of patients were also issued. This is discussed in more detail in Chapter 4. In the situation described above it should be pointed out that ultimately the decision to discharge in such circumstances rests with the consultant psychiatrist or her representative (or in the case of a detained patient with the manager of the hospital or the Mental Health Review Tribunal) and that professional would ultimately have to justify the action taken. However the fact that a CPN disagrees with a decision to discharge a patient does not relieve her of the responsibility of providing all the available community support necessary to ensure that the patient will be safe.

DELEGATION/SUPERVISION/INSTRUCTING OTHERS

Unqualified assistants

The skill mix of professionals in the community is changing and there is an increasing use of assistants and unqualified help for most community professionals: nursing assistants or health care assistants support the community nurses, occupational therapy assistants the occupational therapists, and so on. In the past they may have rarely attended a client without being in the company of a registered professional; now they are likely to be making visits on their own.

The same principles of liability apply in this situation as are discussed in Chapter 7 on professional liability.

Situation

A community paediatric physiotherapist asks an unqualified assistant to visit the home of a child with a chronic respiratory problem. The assistant visits and commences drainage and percussion techniques but unfortunately the child chokes and the assistant does not know the remedial action to take. An ambulance is summoned but the child is found to be dead on arrival at the hospital.

In such a situation the physiotherapist in charge of the care of the patient would have to decide:

- what tasks could appropriately be delegated to an assistant;
- what level of supervision would be required; and
- what instructions should be given

to enable both the client and the assistant to be safe.

She has a duty of care to both the client and the assistant in this respect. The standard of care she should follow in carrying out this duty would be determined according to the Bolam test.

Similar principles apply to the situation when the community professional is supervising a student. She should have a good understanding of the student's capabilities and training so far and delegate appropriately, providing the right level of supervision. Some tasks cannot be delegated.

Nurse Prescribing

Nurse prescribing is now permitted under the Medicinal Products (Prescription by Nurses etc.) Act 1992 (see Chapter 12). Initially pilot schemes have been set up in England but, following evaluation, it will extend to the whole country enabling community nurses and health visitors who have received the necessary training to prescribe from a limited list.

Situation

A nurse who is eligible to prescribe visits the home of a client and is accompanied by a student. She decides that the client should be given skin lotion and asks the student to write the prescription form for her to sign. She explains the dose and the product to her. The student completes the prescription. The nurse signs it, failing to notice that the dose was incorrectly written. The prescription is left for the client to take to the chemist who also fails to realise that the dose is wrong. As a result the client suffers a skin reaction.

In this situation the student nurse should not have written out the prescription. Only the nurse is authorised to complete one under the Medicines Act 1968 as amended by the 1992 Act. Even if the clerking by another person is not in contravention of the law, the nurse must take the full responsibility for any errors.

Project 2000 students

Under the new scheme of nurse training, student nurses are no longer part of the work force of the health authority or NHS Trust but are *bona fide* students who receive student bursaries. There would normally be an agreement between the college to which they are attached and the provider unit (either a directly managed unit or NHS Trust) to cover the clinical placements of the students' courses. This agreement should cover the question of liability and indemnity for the injuries caused to students and also harm caused by students during their programme of studies. Normally liability would fall upon the NHS Trust or the employer of those supervising the clinical placement. Thus if there is negligence by the professional/employee who is supervising the student then there may be liability by the provider.

Situation

A student nurse is undertaking her studies on the branch of the Project 2000 course covering those with learning disabilities and is assigned to a community nurse. During the visit to a community home the student is asked to supervise the residents as they are preparing their lunch and unfortunately fails to prevent an accident occurring when boiling water is spilt upon a resident. The student nurse herself is injured.

Significant questions in determining liability in such a situation would be the actual sequence of events, what instruction had been given to the student nurse by the community nurse and the level of understanding of the residents.

Whilst the doctrine of vicarious liability is firmly recognised in relation to the employer it is not held to apply to the situation between individual employees: a senior employee is not vicariously liable for the actions of a junior. The junior would be personally liable herself and the supervisor would be responsible for her own deficiencies only if the junior was given a task which was outside her competence, inadequately supervised, or given insufficient instructions. If the supervisor had delegated appropriately, provided the correct level of supervision, and given adequate instructions, but, in spite of this the student/assistant still acted negligently, there should be no liability on the part of the supervisor.

EQUIPMENT

Many community professionals recommend equipment for home use and some bring equipment with them in the course of caring for someone in the community. Problems can arise in the areas defined in Figure 8.3.

Figure 8.3 Problems arising in relation to equipment

- Supply of equipment and determination of priorities
- Choice of equipment
- Contractual rights against supplier and the Consumer Protection Act
- Installation – by qualified fitter
  - by neighbour/carer
  - by unqualified employee of Social Services
  - by independent contractors paid for by client
- Maintenance
  - duty on Social Services to arrange for it?
  - can it be left to client?
- Exemption notices in supplying equipment
- Insurance cover

All the areas listed in Figure 8.3 cause concern particularly to the community occupational therapist since a large part of her work is concerned with the recommendation, supply, installation, care and use of equipment.

Supply of equipment and determination of priorities

Given the limitation on resources it is inevitable that there is a waiting list for equipment for home use. Even if the equipment is available there might still be a hold-up in arranging installation. This is a major concern to those who have recommended equipment since there may be liability if harm should occur whilst the client is waiting for the equipment.

Determining priorities
However the determination of priorities is part of the duty of care owed by the community professional to the client. If a community professional fails to assess the urgency of a client's need for equipment and harm befalls the client, then there is likely to be an investigation as to the priority which had been attached to that client in comparison with others. In the case of *Deacon* v. *McVicar*[18] the judge ordered the disclosure of the records of the other patients on the ward at the same time as the plaintiff patient in order to assess whether sufficient regard had been made to the needs of the plaintiff patient in comparison with the needs of those others. This is an unusual step but it indicates that the

determination of priorities is a legal duty and can be evidenced from the records.

Priority setting has become even more important since the introduction of a legal duty on social services, in conjunction with health service professionals and others, to assess patients prior to admission to registered homes. It is clear that a thorough assessment will reveal needs not all of which can be immediately met. This will require skilful priority setting both for the care and the facilities which are made available and of priority between different patients. It is essential that the different professional groups working in the community have a major input into the determination of priorities and all levels of decision making. It is also important to ensure that the documentation reflects the reasons upon which the determination of priorities is based (see also Chapter 11).

Refusal to supply equipment
It may be that the decision following a request for equipment is that none should be provided. This is within the scope of the duty of care and the professional who makes that decision should be able to justify it. It is therefore essential that comprehensive records are kept in case the decision is questioned at a much later date. The decision involves the use of professional discretion which can rarely be supplanted by written procedures and policies.

Choice of equipment

The community professional has to make a determination as to the nature of the equipment required by the client, the supplier and any other features in relation to the individual circumstances and physical and mental capabilities of the client. The individual circumstances will also require consideration of the carers and their capacities. Alternatives other than the provision of equipment are also important. For example it may be that there is danger in clients making use of the equipment on their own and additional visits by community staff are necessary instead.

Contractual rights against supplier and the Consumer Protection Act 1987

The provisions of this Act are discussed in Chapter 10. Here the following points should be emphasised. Where a social services authority or health service body supplies equipment for use in the community then that body can become the supplier for the purposes of the Consumer Protection Act. If harm results from a defect in the equipment the appropriate supplier must provide the client with the name and address of the firm from which the equipment was obtained otherwise it will become itself liable for the defects. Records of the source of all equipment are therefore essential in order that clients can be given this information. Since clients are not employees, they cannot use the provisions of the Employer's Liability (Defective Equipment) Act 1969.

If the client is harmed or if there is damage or loss of property, then there may also be a remedy against the manufacturer under the principles of the case of *Donoghue* v. *Stevenson*[19], a leading case in the tort of negligence.

It is essential when equipment is first supplied that the responsibility for it and the rights of action should any defect be discovered are clearly defined. This is discussed below.

Installation

Arrangements for installation vary between authorities. We consider below the liability in a range of different installation systems.

By a qualified fitter

By far the best arrangement, except where the supplier arranges its own fitting of the equipment, is for the equipment to be fitted by a qualified employee of the social services authority which has arranged for the equipment to be supplied. The fitter should be appropriately qualified and liaise with the occupational therapy department which has recommended the provision of the equipment. In this way the height of the fitting can be placed appropriately to the client's needs. The fitter would also be able to judge the thickness of the walls and how the equipment should be attached.

As an employee the fitter would be responsible to the social services authority and thus any harm which occurs through negligence will be its responsibility. Consideration should be given as to which person has the responsibility of instructing the client or carer on the use of the equipment.

By the carer/neighbour

Sometimes the equipment may be supplied by the statutory authority but left to the client to arrange installation. If this is so then there should be comprehensive instructions given on how it should be installed. If, for example, a bath rail comes off having been fitted by a neighbour, liability for the harm would depend upon whether sufficient information was given to the client to ensure that the equipment was safely installed.

If all that could be reasonably done had been done then the client or the person suffering harm would have no right of action against the social services authority.

Unqualified employee of the social services authority

Unfortunately in some districts the installation of equipment is left to the van driver/odd job man of the social services authority. If, as a consequence of a lack of training, the equipment is fitted negligently and harm occurs, the social service authority would be responsible. There might also be some responsibility attached to those community professionals who were aware of the dangers of this practice but failed to bring it to the attention of senior management.

Independent contractor employed by the client

Where the client purchases equipment, or the equipment is supplied by the social services authority but the client undertakes to obtain a contractor to install the equipment, then, providing there has been no negligence by the social services in providing the names of unsuitable contractors, the authority would not be held liable in the event of the equipment being badly installed. The contractor would have to take responsibility.

However, if the harm which occurred was not the result of the faulty installation but the result of negligent advice over what equipment was necessary or suitable, then the contractor is unlikely to be responsible.

Maintenance

Often there is no clarity over who has the responsibility of ensuring that the equipment is regularly checked and if necessary serviced or maintained. It is essential that there should be procedures to determine this when the equipment is first supplied so that the responsibility is clearly defined. Some equipment must by law be regularly serviced, for example lifts. When such equipment is installed, an agreement for the future inspection and servicing should be arranged.

Responsibility for the maintenance would normally reside with the owner of the equipment. If the social services authority remains the owner and the equipment is merely loaned to the client then the authority should set up an appropriate system for inspection and maintenance. Where equipment is transferred into the ownership of clients or clients purchase it themselves, then the clients would usually be responsible for ensuring inspection and maintenance. However the authority would have a responsibility to ensure that all the necessary information was passed on to such a client. Account would also have to be taken of the physical and mental capacity of the client to undertake this. Publicity was given to the situation where a Trust required patients using nebulisers at home to arrange for the servicing of the equipment and pay for it themselves. This was not permitted since the supply of the equipment was regarded as an NHS service and therefore a charge could not be levied. This is not so with equipment and facilities supplied by social services. However, care should be taken before such responsibilities are placed upon the client, since, if the equipment in the ownership of the local authority is not maintained and harm occurs as a result, the local authority may be liable for that harm.

Once the responsibility for ensuring inspection and maintenance is defined then, if harm results from a failure to inspect and maintain, liability should be clear.

Exemption notices in supplying and installing equipment

Some authorities use a form which is signed by the client to exempt themselves from liability should harm occur. An example of such a form is shown in Figure 8.4.

Figure 8.4 Example of notice exempting from liability

I ... acknowledge that the following equipment has been provided to me by the ... Social Services Department:

1 ...
2 ...
3 ...

and I agree to be responsible for the installation and maintenance of this equipment and not to hold the ... Social Services Department responsible for any loss, harm or injury caused by the said equipment.

Signature

Witness

Date

The notice in Figure 8.4 would not be effective in removing liability for personal injury from the Social Services Department if one of their staff had been negligent in carrying out their duties and responsibilities. This is because the provisions of the Unfair Contract Terms Act 1977 prohibits evading liability for negligence resulting in personal injury or death such (see page).

Sometimes, however, the notice is not to exempt from liability but to instruct the client on the use of the equipment and to ensure the client's safety. To provide this kind of written instruction may well be part of the duty of care owed to the client. However, any attempt to use it as an exemption notice will not be effective if personal injury occurs but may be effective in the event of loss or damage to property.

Insurance cover

At the same time that responsibility for the inspection and servicing of the equipment is decided the liability for providing insurance cover should be agreed where this is deemed necessary. It may be that the authority has its own group policy for insurance cover which can be used to protect an individual client.

TRANSPORT AND TRANSPORTING OTHERS

Insurance

As part of their work many community professionals transport other people – clients, carers, colleagues and others. Where this is clearly indicated in the job description then all the necessary measures in terms of appropriate insurance cover should be taken. However, the situation can sometimes arise where an employee is forbidden to give lifts to others and yet feels bound on occasion to disobey these instructions.

Situation

A district nurse is aware that she is not permitted within her job description to give lifts to others. She visits an isolated cottage where the general practitioner has called and left a prescription which the client has not been able to take to a chemists. She realises that the client has no transport and offers to take a carer to the chemist's shop and return with the medication. On the return journey she is involved in an accident. Her insurance company claims that it should not be liable for the injury to the passenger since she had not notified it that she took passengers as part of her job. Her employers claim that she was not acting in course of employment since she was forbidden to transport others and she was employed as a district nurse not as a chauffeur.

In these circumstances the insurance company would probably pay out the compensation due to the passenger (assuming no other person were involved) but then seek an indemnity from the nurse because she was not insured to transport persons during work. The fact that she was forbidden to take passengers will not necessarily take her actions outside the definition of 'in course of employment' (see page 120). However, she is likely to face disciplinary proceedings. In contrast, if she picked up hitch hikers, this would be unlikely to come within the course of employment.

Absolute disclosure is required in any insurance contract and therefore if there is any likelihood that the employee will need to use a car for work this fact and the reasons should be disclosed. Should the driver not inform the insurance company of a significant fact, this omission could invalidate the cover even though it has no relevance to a particular claim. An interesting recent development has been the suggestion that if a driver uses his car for car boot sales without the consent of the insurance company this could invalidate his car insurance. This highlights the importance of ensuring that an insurance company is given full details of every use made of the car.

Innocent third parties have limited protection from the Motor Insurers' Bureau in that compensation for personal injury or death will be paid in the event of the negligent perpetrator having no cover or if the policy is declared invalid by the insurance company.

Where the employee has the use of a crown car, insurance is normally provided through the employer and the crown is exempt from the provisions of the Road Traffic Laws requiring road tax.

■ What if the passenger becomes disturbed?

Situation

A social worker arranges to take an elderly mentally infirm patient home to make an assessment visit. On the journey the client becomes very disturbed and tries to get out of the car and succeeds in opening the back door and falls out. Is the social worker liable?

This situation is of concern to many community workers, particularly occupational therapists. This occurrence is reasonably foreseeable and it could therefore be argued that the social worker should have taken the precaution of arranging 'child locks' on the car so that it could not happen. Alternatively the precautions may have involved taking an assistant with her. Her duty of care to the client would require her to take reasonable precautions against events which are reasonably foreseeable.

■ What if the community professional took passengers on the basis that they were taken 'at their own risk'?

Such an arrangement is prohibited under Road Traffic legislation (Road Traffic Act 1988, section 149) and this device could not be used to exempt the driver from liability for the passenger's safety.

Case: *Eastman* v. *South West Thames Regional Health Authority*[20]
Damages were awarded against the health authority in respect of injuries which the plaintiff sustained when travelling in an ambulance without a seat belt. Although the ambulance driver was acquitted of all blame for the accident it was held that a duty of care was owed to advise passengers to wear a seat belt. The defendants appealed to the Court of Appeal and the appeal was allowed. It was held that adult passengers possessed of their faculties should not need telling what to do. The attendant was under no obligation to point out the existence of a seat belt and a notice recommending their use.

It should be noted that this case refers to the duty of care to adults possessed of their faculties. Where a community professional is transporting a client in her own car and the client is frail or mentally incompetent the courts would probably accept that a duty of care was owed to ensure that the client was reasonably safe. This might in exceptional circumstances require child proof locks.

RISK ASSESSMENT AND MANAGEMENT

It is now recognised that the care of many vulnerable groups particularly the elderly and those with learning disabilities involves the taking of reasonable risks if the clients are to enjoy maximum autonomy, freedom and have a high standard and quality of life. Clearly if persons with learning disabilities spend all their time being watched in institutional surroundings and kept away from traffic and dangers in society, then minimum harm would probably occur. However, the quality of life enjoyed by such clients would be extremely impoverished. Many organisations which care for these vulnerable groups now have policies on risk assessment and risk taking which are designed to balance the protection which the clients require against the risks which occur if opportunities for outings, work, and other activities are provided.

In law the determination of the standard of care required to fulfil the duty of care has for long included a calculation of the balance of the risk involved in any enterprise against the end to be achieved. As Lord Justice Asquith said[21]

> In determining whether a party is negligent, the standard of reasonable care is that which is reasonably demanded in the circumstances. A relevant circumstance to take into account may be the importance of the end to be served by behaving in this way or that. As has often been pointed out, if all the trains in this country were restricted to the speed of five miles an hour, there would be fewer accidents, but our national life would be intolerably slowed down. The purpose to be served, if sufficiently important, justifies the assumption of abnormal risk.

The advantage of a risk assessment policy and procedure is that it enables the community professional or carer to identify the reasonable precautions which should be taken to ensure that the client is safe and at the same time identify which risks it is reasonable to take and which should be avoided. A helpful example of risk assessment in the care of an elderly person suffering from dementia is given by Alison Norman[22]. She shows the advantages and disadvantages of three options in the care of an elderly person suffering from dementia, that is staying at home, moving to live with her daughter or moving to residential care.

Such analysis shows that all reasonably foreseeable risks are taken into account. If such an analysis is clearly documented then the ultimate decision taken in the light of these factors should be defensible in a court of law. Similar analysis should be used to determine, for example:

● Whether a detained patient is given section 17 leave.

● Whether an occupational therapist decides a patient could cope on their own at home.

● The degree of supervision required by clients with learning disabilities who have been transferred from hospital accommodation to a community home.

Another helpful publication is *The Right to take Risks*[23]. It sets out model policies, guidance to staff and training material on restraint and risk taking in residential care and nursing homes for older people.

It is essential that records should be kept of the factors taken into account in any decision making on risks. Evidence from records of the evaluation made in relation to the balancing of the risks of harm against the benefits to the client group in enjoying greater freedom and opportunities would be of significant value if litigation were to be brought following an accident. Each individual client must be assessed separately and decisions made on a personal basis in relation to reasonably justifiable risks.

Further discussion on risk assessment in the context of health and safety is given in Chapter 9.

COMMUNICATIONS

Another area of potential hazard is liabilty for failure to communicate with others according to the reasonable standard of care.

Case: *Chapman* v. *Rix* [24]

A butcher was boning meat when his knife slipped and entered his body. He was seen by Dr Rix who arranged for him to go to the cottage hospital where he examined and probed the wound. The patient then returned home. He was taken ill and seen by a general practitioner. He told the GP that he had been examined and had been told that the wound was superficial. Subsequently the patient died and his widow sued Dr Rix. The House of Lords in a majority decision held that Dr Rix was not liable for failing to communicate appropriately with the GP.

In a note to the case[25] Margaret Puxon states that 'it is difficult to believe that this case would have been decided in this way today'. The case contrasts with the following decision.

Case: *Coles* v. *Reading and District Hospital Management Committee and another* [26]

The patient had a crushed finger and initially attended a cottage hospital to be given first aid. No anti-tetanus injection was given and he was told by the sister to go immediately to another hospital for further examination and treatment. The patient went home where he was seen by his GP. He subsequently died of tetanus.

The court held that the hospital was negligent in failing to communicate properly with the patient by not explaining to him the reasons why he needed to have an anti-tetanus injection and to go to the other hospital. 'Proper communication' was defined as 'that which was reasonably necessary for safeguarding a patient's interests'. It was also held that the GP was negligent in failing to ensure that the patient had received the anti-tetanus injection.

The many different agencies, organisations and individuals involved in the provision of community care make efficient and effective communication vital. The backing up of spoken communications with written confirmation is essential for the proper care of the patient. In addition, the fact that the information has also been communicated by the written word should be an effective defence should litigation result.

CONCLUSIONS

These are only a few of the specific situations which cause concern to professionals working in the community. Other issues are identified in the chapters dealing with individual professional groups in Part 2 of this Section.

CHAPTER 9

Health and safety: 1

These next two chapters look at the health and safety of the person working in the community. This first chapter considers the general issues which are shown in Figure 9.1 and the next chapter looks at additional specialist areas of concern.

Figure 9.1 Topics to be covered in this chapter

- Sources of law relating to health and safety
- Sources of injury and harm
- Sources of compensation
- Common law duty of care of employer
- Statutory health and safety duties
- Management of Health and Safety at Work Regulations
- Manual handling in the community
- Control of Substances Hazardous to Health Regulations
- Risk taking and the rights of clients
- Enforcement provisions
- Food legislation

SOURCES OF LAW RELATING TO HEALTH AND SAFETY

Those professionals who work in the community are vulnerable to injury like their colleagues working in institutions. However, they may not have the same protection from harm nor the same rights to compensation as those who work on the premises occupied by their employer. In addition their legal situation will depend upon whether they are employed by a health service body (health authority, GP fund-holding practice, NHS Trust), by individual general practitioners, by the local authority or in the private sector. Others may be self-employed. Different consequences follow from the nature of the employment. The sources of law which are relevant to the health and safety of employees are shown in Figure 9.2.

149

Figure 9.2 Sources of health and safety law

- Implied term of the contract of employment that the employer will take reasonable care for the employee's health and safety (contractual duty)
- Employer's duty in the law of negligence to fulfil the duty of care
- Health and Safety at Work Act and the regulations made under it
- Employers' Liability (Compulsory Insurance) Act 1969
- Employer's Liability (Defective Equipment) Act 1969
- Occupiers' Liability Acts 1957 and 1984
- Defective Premises Act 1972
- Animals Act 1971
- Criminal Injuries Compensation scheme
- EC legislation and regulations
- Consumer Protection Act 1987
- Fire precautions regulations.

These will be discussed in relation to the different categories of employees.

SOURCES OF INJURY AND HARM

In addition injuries and harm are caused in a wide variety of ways. These are set out in Figure 9.3. Examples will be taken from this list in exploring the legal liability and the chances of the injured person recovering compensation.

Figure 9.3 Examples of injuries/harm which could be suffered in the community

- Being bitten by a dog
- Being assaulted/mugged:
    by a stranger/robber
    by the client/relative
    by a colleague
- Being injured in someone's house:
    where tenant responsible
    where landlord responsible
    which is owner-occupied
- Being injured on premises belonging to the employer
- Catching an infectious disease from a client
- Being injured in a road accident
- Being sexually harassed:
    by a stranger
    by a client/relative
    by a colleague
- Being evicted as a trespasser and then assaulted
- Slipping on the pavement
- Falling on ice
- Suffering verbal abuse
- Receiving poison pen/unwanted attention letters from:
    a stranger
    a client/relative
    a known person

- Injuring one's back
- Being injured by equipment

SOURCES OF COMPENSATION

Whether or not the injured person can obtain compensation will depend upon the law which applies, the nature of the harm which occurred and how it occurred, and the existence of any scheme for compensation. Figure 9.4 shows different ways of obtaining compensation.

Figure 9.4 Methods of obtaining compensation

- Suing the employer for breach of his duty of care
- Suing the employer for breach of a statutory duty
- Suing the local authority for failure to maintain roads, pavements and so on
- Suing the owner/occupier/tenant of property for failure to keep it safe
- Suing an owner of an animal for causing harm
- Claiming compensation through the Criminal Injuries Compensation scheme
- Claiming compensation through the criminal courts following the successful prosecution of an offender
- Claiming on an insurance policy
- Claiming compensation through consumer protection legislation
- Suing the client/relative or other person who has caused harm

COMMON LAW DUTY OF CARE OF EMPLOYER

The employer's and employee's basic duties in relation to health and safety derive from the common law. Common law refers to the law set out by judges as they hear cases and rule upon the law which applies to the dispute in hand. A system of precedents and a clear hierarchy of the courts of law ensure that the judges are aware of which previous decisions are binding upon them and which they can ignore (see glossary).

It is an implied term in every contract of employment that the employer will take reasonable care of the health and safety of the employee. There may also be express terms covering the employer's duty. (In addition to the express and implied duty, specific statutes impose further requirements which are considered later in this chapter.)

'Reasonable'

All employers have this implied duty so health authorities, NHS Trusts, social service authorities and private service providers must all recognise it and make provision accordingly. What is reasonable however will depend upon

- the size of the employer's undertaking,
- the extent of his resources,
- what it would be reasonable for him to provide in the light of the risk to the employee's health and safety,
- the significance of the harm that could arise if he failed to make adequate provision, and
- the cost of removing the risk of harm.

At common law there is not an absolute duty upon the employer to take care for the employee's health and safety: he must do what is reasonable.

Which employees and what type of harm

Does the duty cover all employees? The answer is 'yes' even though an employee has only been with the employer a short time. This is unlike the situation under some employment legislation where the employee is only entitled to certain employment benefits if he has worked continuously for at least two years with 16 or more hours per week, or for five years with 8 or more hours per week (see glossary – continuous period of employment). The employer's common law duty begins as soon as the contract of employment commences or even before. The employer, for example, may have a duty to ascertain from a potential employee any contra-indications against particular features of the work place. It may not, for example, be wise for the employee to be in a smoky atmosphere or to work with certain materials or substances. The employer can be liable for mental harm as well as physical harm to his employees. In a case breaking new ground in 1994 a social services manager with child care responsibilities obtained compensation for the failure of his employer to take reasonable care to prevent him suffering from a second nervous breakdown as a result of pressures at work[27].

Which employer

If the employee is assigned to another employer, questions as to which employer has responsibility for the employee's health and safety (on the basis of the direct liability of the employer) or which is responsible for the negligence of the employee (on the basis of vicarious liability) are decided on the facts of the particular case.

Case: *Mersey Docks and Harbour Board* v. *Coggins and Griffith (Liverpool) Ltd* [28]

This leading case as to which employer is to be vicariously liable involved the hiring out of cranes by the Board together with skilled drivers. The contract stated that the driver was to be the servant of the hirers, but the hirers could not dismiss the driver nor could they tell him how to handle the controls of the crane. The hirers could, however, direct where the crane was to be used. The driver caused injury to a third party as a result of his negligence and the question arose as to which employer was vicariously liable – the Board which was the original employer or the company which hired the crane and the driver. The House of Lords decided that the Board remained vicariously liable for the driver's negligence.

The point may be covered in the contract between the two employers. Where, however, the transferred employee is injured it would usually be a question of fact as to which employer was liable for the injury. This is becoming of increasing significance where staff are seconded between different employers, especially NHS employers and social services employers, for the short term. In such circumstances, it is wise to establish at the outset which employer would be responsible and therefore contractually liable for the safety of the employee and which employer would be vicariously liable for the harm caused by the negligence of the employee, whether to other employees or to clients or others. However, whatever the contract says either employer will remain liable under the general principles of tort for negligent acts or omissions resulting in personal injury to the employee as, by the Unfair Contract Terms Act 1977 (see page 126), such liability cannot be excluded by a contract term. The issue applies at present to the situation of community health professionals whose services may be purchased by GP fund-holders, but who do not actually employ them. They remain the employees of the NHS Trust (see Chapter 24).

Whether an individual is acting as an employee or not is likely to become of increasing importance as the use bank and agency staff and the employment of independent practitioners increases. They will not necessarily be employees of the NHS Trust, or the social services authority or the agency who makes use of their services. This is further discussed in the Chapter 20 relating to the independent practitioner.

Course of employment

To establish liability by the employer for injuries caused to the employee it must be established that the employee was acting in course of employment.

This immediately raises problems in the community since many health professionals working in the community are often asked by clients to undertake tasks which are outside their job description. An occupational therapist might be asked to change a light bulb, a community psychiatric nurse be asked to mend a fuse, someone else may be asked to see about a leaking tap, to take a prescription to the chemists or to purchase a present – all the kinds of tasks that infirm persons living on their own might have difficulties with. Care assistants, in particular, may have their duties laid down by the social services department or by the agency which recruits them but will be placed under considerable pressure by the client to work outside this job description. Reference should be made to the discussion on vicarious liability in Chapter 7.

Injuries whilst acting outside the course of employment

Situation

A social worker is asked by a very infirm client to replace a defunct light bulb. No ladder is available and she uses a chair to stand on. Unfortunately she falls whilst replacing the bulb. Is the employer liable for her safety and therefore liable to pay compensation?

The answer is probably 'no'. In the first place the employee must prove negligence and it would be difficult for the social worker to establish any breach of duty by the employer in such circumstances. In the second place even if it could be established that the employer should have given more guidance to employees on which tasks came within the job description, there is probably a high proportion of contributory negligence by the social worker which led to the harm arising.

Situation

A care worker decides to do some shopping and leaves her regular route, even though she should still be at work, and goes to the Supermarket. On her way there she is involved in an accident. Could the employer be held liable for any harm suffered by someone in the accident?

The answer would depend upon whether the care worker would be seen as still acting in course of employment or whether her going on a shopping spree should be regarded as outside the course of employment, so that the employer was not liable for her actions. This issue only becomes of significance if the care worker has failed to ensure that she has adequate insurance cover. If she is uninsured, the injured person would look to the employer. If the employer denies vicarious liability then the victim would have to seek compensation through the Motor Insurers Bureau scheme for compensating victims for personal injuries caused by uninsured drivers (see page 144). The care worker may be able to show that she went to the shop to purchase items for a client, in which case the employers might find it difficult to dispute that she was acting in course of employment.

If the care worker herself is injured it is unlikely that the employer would be held liable since there has been no negligence on its part and she was probably not acting in course of employment.

Breach of contract by the employer

Since the duty of the employer exists as part of the contract of employment, fundamental failure by the employer is a breach of contract. In this event the employee has a choice:

● she can either see this breach as fundamental and therefore giving her the right to treat the contract as at an end, or

● she can see the contract as continuing and elect to reaffirm the contract and sue for compensation.

Should the employee elect to see the contract as at an end, she should make this choice perfectly clear to the employers and make the decision within a reasonable time of the breach occurring otherwise she will be treated as recognising the continuation of the contract.

To treat the contract as at an end gives the employee, if she is eligible on other grounds (for example two years continuous service of at least 16 hours per week), the right to apply for statutory compensation to an industrial tribunal on the grounds that she has been unfairly dismissed. In this case it would be a question of whether the employer's breach of contract in failing to remedy the safety situation is fundamental and therefore amounts to constructive dismissal.

This course of action is not without peril for the employee who risks the loss of her job without compensation should the industrial tribunal decide that in fact there was a resignation and not a constructive dismissal. In addition the employee may be unable to receive unemployment benefit immediately.

Situation: Constructive dismissal?

A community nurse has a heavy workload nursing and lifting patients who live on their own. She is concerned about the possibilities of harm to her back and, since there are several heavy patients on her case load, she asks for hoists to be provided or for a second nurse to accompany her on her visits to certain patients. Her employers refuse to allow another nurse to accompany her on grounds of cost and staffing shortages. As for the hoists, she is told that these are normally supplied through social services and they have too many requests to meet.

She is also concerned that without assistance or equipment she will be unable to provide the patients with the reasonable standard of care that they are entitled to expect. She gives notice of her concerns to her senior managers and no response is forthcoming. She warns them that unless the situation is improved she will regard their inaction as a fundamental breach of contract and one which will entitle her to treat the contract as terminated by their breach. Still no action takes place and the nurse then leaves the post, alleging that she has been constructively dismissed. Will she win a hearing before the industrial tribunal?

The first issue the tribunal will have to determine is whether there was a resignation or a constructive dismissal. This will involve looking at the circumstances of her leaving work and the employer's conduct – whether that can in all the circumstances be held a fundamental breach of the employment contract such that the employee is entitled to see it as a repudiation by the employer of that contract. The tribunal would look at the events preceding the employee's departure – whether the risk that she faced as a result of the employer's failure to take care of her safety was significant and what else the employee could have done to obtain action but had failed to do. Even if it holds that there was a constructive dismissal it would still ask the question as to whether employer acted reasonably. If it concludes that the employer did not then it could order the payment of compensation and, in theory, reinstatement of the employee.

Legal advice should be obtained by any employee before embarking on this course since failure in the action would result in the employee being held to have resigned and therefore she would be without a job and possibly without unemployment benefit.

An alternative action at civil law where the employee fears for her safety at work is for her to sue the employer for breach of the terms (express or implied) in the contract of employment because of its failure to take reasonable care of her health and safety.

This is unfortunately a slow and costly route and sometimes it is preferable to look for statutory provision which provides either enforcement provisions or compensation such as the Office Shops and Railway Premises Act and other Health and Safety legislation. There are enforcement agencies for these statutes and these can be contacted and the concern expressed to them. This will be considered in the section below.

STATUTORY HEALTH AND SAFETY DUTIES

Many of the common law duties are mirrored more specifically in Acts of Parliament and regulations which prescribe detailed duties to be met by the employer and employee.

The Health and Safety at Work etc. Act 1974

The most important one is the Health and Safety at Work etc. Act 1974 and its subsequent regulations.

Employer's duty
Figure 9.5 sets out the general duty on the employer under the Act.

Figure 9.5 Employer's general duty

Section 2(1) It shall be the duty of every employer to ensure, so far is reasonably practicable, the health, safety and welfare at work of all his employees.

There then follows a detailed list of specific duties which do not, however, limit the comprehensiveness of the general duty.

Nature of the duty
The employer must do what is reasonable to protect the health and safety of the employee in ensuring:

- the employment of competent staff,
- the provision of a safe system of work, and
- safe premises, plant and equipment.

What if the employee is issued with protective clothing? Is this sufficient to fulfil the employer's duty of care?

Case: *Pape* v. *Cumbria County Council*[29]
A part time cleaner was employed to clean lavatories and wash hand basins. She suffered from irritant dermatitis as a result of exposure to the cleaning products. She was issued with protective clothing but it was held that the employers had not only a duty to provide the protective clothing but also a duty to warn the employee of the dangers.

A significant part of the duty placed upon employers by the Health and Safety at Work etc. Act 1974 refers to the maintenance of premises and equipment and does not apply to the community professional who may use no equipment provided by the employer and rarely works in premises owned or occupied by the employer. However the basic duty exists, and if the employee can show that there has been a breach of these statutory duties and the employer fails to remedy the situation there may be justification in drawing this to the attention of the Health and Safety Inspectorate.

Employee's duty
In addition the employee has a duty under this legislation and this is set out in Figure 9.6.

Figure 9.6 Employee's general duty

Section 7 It shall be the duty of every employee while at work —

(a) to take reasonable care for the health and safety of himself and of other persons who may be affected by his acts or omissions at work; and

(b) as regards any duty or requirements imposed on his employer or other person by or under any of the relevant statutory provisions, to co-operate with him so far as is necessary to enable that duty or requirement to be performed or complied with.

Employment protection and health and safety issues

Amendments to the employment protection legislation have given greater job security to an employee who brings to the notice of the employer hazards in relation to the health and safety of himself or his colleagues. The Trade Union Reform and Employment Rights Act 1993 protects the employee against dismissal or other detriment. The circumstances are spelt out in the Act and include situations where the employee is designated to carry out health and safety work by the employer, is a safety representative, a member of the safety committee, or, in the absence of a safety representative or committee,

> he brought to the employer's attention, by reasonable means, circumstances connected with his work which he reasonably believed were harmful or potentially harmful to health and safety.

The employee is also protected under the legislation if he left work because he was exposed to a serious and imminent danger which he could not avert, or took appropriate steps to protect himself or other employees from danger.

The 1993 regulations

From 1 January 1993 new regulations in respect of health and safety at work came into force as a result of a directive from the European Community. They are shown in Figure 9.7.

Figure 9.7 Regulations introduced in 1993

- Provision and use of work equipment Regulations SI 1992/2932
- Manual handling operations Regulations SI 1992/2793
- Workplace (health and safety and welfare) Regulations SI 1992/3004
- Personal Protective Equipment at Work Regulations SI 1992/2966
- Health and Safety (display screen equipment) Regulations SI 1992/2792
- Management of Health and Safety at Work Regulations 1992/2051

These regulations should have a profound effect on the health and safety of people at work since they compel employers and employees to assess together the risks of harm and take appropriate precautions.

THE MANAGEMENT OF HEALTH AND SAFETY AT WORK REGULATIONS 1992

The Management of Health and Safety at Work Regulations are explicitly concerned with the assessment of risk in the work place and cover the topics set out in Figure 9.8.

Figure 9.8 Scope of the Regulations

- Risk assessment (Regulation 3)
- Health and safety arrangements (Regulation 4)
- Health surveillance (Regulation 5)
- Health and safety assistance (Regulation 6)
- Procedures for danger and for danger areas (Regulation 7)
- Information for employees (Regulation 8)
- Co-operation and co-ordination (Regulation 9)
- Self-employed persons (Regulation 10)
- Capabilities and training (Regulation 11)
- Employees' duties (Regulation 12)
- Temporary workers (Regulation 13)
- Exemption certificates (Regulation 14)
- Exclusion of civil liability (Regulation 15)

Figures 9.9 to 9.15 show some of the main themes of the Regulations incorporating where appropriate information from the Code of Practice.

Figure 9.9 Risk Assessment (Regulation 3)

(1) Suitable and sufficient assessment by employers of:
    (a) risks to health and safety of employees
    (b) risks to health and safety of persons on in their employment

This is done by

- identifying significant risks
- familiarity with the literature
- identifying and prioritising measures required
- ensuring such measures relevant to the work in question
- ensuring such measures valid for some time

(2) As above by the self-employed

(3) Review of assessment if
    (a) it may be no longer valid
    (b) there has been significant change

(4) Recording
    (a) significant findings of the assessment
    (b) employees especially at risk

Significant findings may include:

- significant hazards
- the extent to which existing measures are effective

Principles for preventive and protective measures
  (a) if possible avoid a risk altogether
  (b) combat risks at source
  (c) adapt work to the individual
  (d) take advantage of technological and technical progress
  (e) make risk management a part of a coherent policy and approach
  (f) give priority to those measures which protect all
  (g) ensure workers understand what they need to do
  (h) ensure existence of an active health and safety culture

Figure 9.10 Health and safety arrangements (Regulation 4)

Every employer shall

- make and give effect to
- such arrangements as are appropriate, having regard to
- the nature of his activities and
- the size of his undertaking,
- for the effective
      planning,
      organisation,
      control,
      monitoring and
      review
- of the preventive and protective measures.

The exact wording of Regulation 4(1) is split by bullet points for clarity. Regulation 4(2) states that the arrangements must be recorded if there are five or more employees.

Figure 9.11 Health surveillance (Regulation 5)

Employees must be provided with such health surveillance as is appropriate having regard to the risks to their health and safety which are identified by the assessment, especially where:

(a) there is an identifiable disease or adverse health
    condition related to the work concerned
(b) there are valid techniques to detect this
(c) there is a reasonable likelihood of disease and
(d) surveillance likely to further health of employees.

Figure 9.12 Procedures for health surveillance

(a) Inspection of readily detectable conditions
(b) Enquiries about symptoms, inspection and examination by occupational
    health nurse
(c) Medical surveillance
(d) Biological effect monitoring
(e) Biological monitoring

Employees should have opportunity to comment on proposed frequency of such health surveillance procedures.

Figure 9.13 Information for employees (Regulation 8)

Every employer shall provide his employees with comprehensible and relevant information on —

(a) the risks to their health and safety identified by the assessment;
(b) the preventive and protective measures;
(c) the procedures [to be followed in the event of serious and imminent danger];
(d) the identity of those persons nominated [to implement those procedures];
(e) the risks notified to him [by other employers sharing the workplace].

Figure 9.14 Capabilities and training (Regulation 11)

(1) Every employer shall, in entrusting tasks to his employees, take into account their capabilities as regards health and safety.

(2) Every employer shall ensure that his employees are provided with adequate health and safety training —
(a) on their being recruited . . .; and
(b) on their being exposed to new or increased risks because of —
   (i) their being transfered or given a change of responsibilities . . .
   (ii) the introduction of new work equipment or a change [to existing equipment]
   (iii) the introduction of new technology . . . or
   (iv) the introduction of a new system of work . . .

(3) The training . . . shall —
(a) be repeated periodically where appropriate;
(b) be adapted to take account of any new or changed risks to health and safety . . .; and
(c) take place during working hours.

Figure 9.15 Employees' duties (Regulation 12)

(1) Every employee shall use any . . . equipment [and so on] in accordance with both training . . . and instructions . . .

(2) Every employee shall inform his employer . . .
   (a) of any work situation which [he] would reasonably consider represented a serious and immediate danger to health and safety and
   (b) of any matter which [he] would reasonably consider represented a shortcoming in the employer's protection arrangements . . .

MANUAL HANDLING IN THE COMMUNITY

Many community professionals are involved in the lifting of clients and it is therefore essential that they have an understanding of the regulations relating to lifting which came into force on a January 1993 and comply with them (see Figure 9.7). Guidance is contained in a Health and Safety Executive publication on manual handling[30] and in addition the Health and Safety Commission has produced a booklet, *Guidance on Manual Handling of loads in the Health Services*[31].

The booklet covers the following topics:

1. the legal requirements,
2. the need to report injuries,
3. the carrying out of a risk assessment in relation to manual handling,
4. the equipment which may be needed, including mechanical aids and devices,
5. training,
6. staffing levels,
7. investigation of accidents and incidents,
8. monitoring, and
9. health surveillance and staff rehabilitation.

A management checklist and a useful bibliography make this an essential publication for anyone with responsibilities for health and safety in the community.

In relation to staff working in the community, the *Guidance* recommends that a risk assessment should be carried out before the staff begin work in the client's home.

Assessment should be made of the premises, the client's needs, and the capabilities of staff assigned to that client.

It points out that, although the employer's control over client's premises is limited, much can be done to eliminate or reduce the need for manual handling. Hoists should be provided where necessary and, where there is opposition from the client or relatives over such equipment being installed, explanations should be given by a manager to the client and carers. In addition staffing levels should be reviewed as part of risk assessment. Ultimately if the client or carer refuses to accept the necessity of a hoist, the family could be told that the absence of a hoist would present such dangers to the health and safety of the care staff that a service could not be provided. This of course is a last resort but there is a precedent for such extreme action[32], which is further discussed on page 188.

A case study is set out in the Health and Safety Commission's guidelines and is reproduced below:

Situation

An 83 year old patient weighing 13 stone was discharged from hospital at her family's request although she was mentally confused. A bed with cot sides was supplied but its delivery was rejected by the family because it was too high for the patient to get in and out.

Two community nurses attended the patient and found her to be abusive and aggressive. On one occasion while they were helping her out of bed the patient lifted both her feet, placing her full weight on the nurses, who had to lower her to the floor. Both nurses experienced back pain. The strain on resources of providing two nurses for each visit over a long period was considered to be unacceptable and three alternatives were considered:

- To provide a hoist. This was thought to be unsafe because the patient was unco-operative and likely to thrash about.
- To re-admit to hospital. This was strongly opposed by the hospital.
- To provide a bed whose height could be adjusted.

This last alternative was adopted and, after some delay in obtaining an appropriate bed, the problem was solved.

It is essential that a procedure should be drawn up to cover the risk assessment process for each new client referred to the community health services and that this procedure should include looking at the risks in relation to manual handling. This assessment should be regularly revised as the needs of the client change over time and with increasing disability.

■ What if a community professional is lifting with a student?

Case: *Fitzsimmons* v. *Northumberland Health Authority* [32]

In February 1979 the plaintiff was accepted by the defendant health authority as a student nurse on a three year SRN course. Up to April 1982 she had five study blocks of up to 29 days: she received extensive instruction in the principles of lifting and moving patients, and she had practical experience in geriatric, female orthopaedic and spinal wards. In September 1981 the plaintiff left the course and was employed by the defendants as a nursing auxiliary intending to qualify as a SEN. On 6 November 1981, at Hexham General Hospital, she and a student nurse were lifting a male multiple sclerosis patient, weighing about 9 stone, from his bed into a wheel chair. The method of lifting was one in widespread use – each nurse had one arm through the patient's armpit and was blocking the patient's foot and knee sideways. However the patient's legs started buckling, the student nurse was unable to continue to support him, and the plaintiff bore most of the patient's weight as he fell to the floor. The plaintiff suffered a prolapsed disc as a result of the incident. She claimed damages against the defendant alleging negligence in failing to provide a safe system of working.

The judge held that the defendants were liable in negligence because:

1. on the evidence, the defendant knew that the lifting and moving of patients, as a general matter, created risk of injury to its nurses' backs which could range from a minor strain to a serious back injury such as the plaintiff sustained;
2. it was reasonably foreseeable, where a spastic patient was involved, that the patient might behave as this patient had done and that a student nurse of less that two years' experience might withdraw her support;
3. although the plaintiff had not established that the use of a hoist would have been appropriate in the circumstances, the system of work adopted by the defendant was not a reasonably safe system because if a third nurse had been made available the plaintiff's accident would not have happened;
4. it had not been established that the defendant was negligent in failing to use the method of lifting advocated by the plaintiff's expert.

The lessons of this for community staff are considerable since it is very rare that they are able to visit clients in twos let alone threes. However, there is a duty upon the employer to ensure that staff are reasonably safe and this might be necessary. For some very handicapped clients a hoist is not a feasible alternative to increased staffing.

In addition there could be liability on the employer, where one of two employees, as a result of defective lifting technique, injures the other during a joint lifting activity. In such circumstances, the employer would be vicariously liable for the negligence of the one employee, and also possibly directly liable for the injury if it can be established that the employee at fault has not received appropriate training.

Similarly those responsible in management may also be held accountable for failing to set up an appropriate training scheme and to monitor it. Reference should be made to the publication of the Royal College of Nursing on back injuries and manual handling[34].

Case: *Colclough v. Staffordshire County Council*[35]

In this case a local authority was held liable for a back injury suffered by a social worker who attempted with a neighbour to assist a patient in his home back into bed.

She was employed as a social worker in the elderly care team. Her duties consisted largely of assessing clients for residential placement and other needs. She was called out to an elderly man's home after referral from his GP. When she arrived she gained access with a neighbour, only to find the man halfway out of his bed. He was in a very distressed state and she felt it was important for him to be lifted back into the bed as she was worried about him being injured. The neighbour, who had some nursing experience, told the social worker how to lift the man. As both of them attempted to lift the man, who weighed around 15 stone, the social worker sustained a lumber spine injury. She sued on the grounds that the employers had failed to provide her with any training and/or instruction in lifting techniques. The employers denied liability on the ground that it was not a normal part of a social workers' duties to undertake any lifting tasks. The employers alleged that she should have summoned some assistance from the emergency services.

The judge held that it was reasonably foreseeable that the plaintiff would be confronted with emergency situations when working as a social worker in the elderly care team. Although the situation which arose was most unusual, the employers were under a duty to warn her that she should not lift in such circumstances. This duty did not go so far as to impose upon the employer in these circumstances a duty to provide a long training course but certainly to bring to the notice of social workers the risks of lifting. Her claim succeeded without a finding of contributory negligence. The issue as to quantum (that is how much compensation) was adjourned.

Whilst only a county court decision, this case shows that the duty at common law in relation to instruction in lifting or the risks of lifting applies even to staff who do not normally lift as part of their regular work.

The local authority's defence that the post of a social worker did not normally include lifting and therefore there was not a duty to ensure that she was trained in manual handling was not accepted since it should still have ensured that she was aware of the risks of harm.

CONTROL OF SUBSTANCES HAZARDOUS TO HEALTH REGULATIONS 1988

The COSHH Regulations require a full assessment of the health risks in relation to exposure to hazardous substances related to work activities. Whilst hazardous substances are more likely to be found in hospitals, community workers cannot ignore these regulations. Recently a case was reported when a young toddler was able to gain access to a detergent kept in a doctor's surgery and became dangerously ill.

The regulations came into force on 1 January 1992 and state that no work which is liable to expose anyone to substances hazardous to health shall be carried on unless a suitable and sufficient assessment has been made. This is required:

- to evaluate the risks to health arising from work involving substances hazardous to health, and
- to establish what has to be done to meet the requirements of the COSHH Regulations.

The assessment must be reviewed and updated as required.

The duty to make the assessment is placed upon both employers and the self-employed. The duty is owed not only to employees but also to others who may be affected by the work. Thus in the above case the young toddler would be owed a duty under the Regulations.

What substances are covered?

These are defined in the Regulations and in the main cover all substances which have a potential for causing harm to people's health. They do not cover medicines administered to patients, but they do cover the protection of the person administering the drugs. Thus any drugs which are potentially carcinogenic to the person administering them (such as certain cytotoxic drugs) should come under a COSHH assessment.

The list includes substances used in cleaning and maintenance work.

The assessment process

Once potential hazardous substances are identified, it is then necessary to assess if there are particular health risks in relation to individual employees or others. For example, pregnant women may be at greater risk than others. The chance and the nature of any likely exposure must be assessed.

In carrying out this risk assessment, the Health and Safety Executive (HSE) guidelines list the steps set out in Figure 9.16.

Figure 9.16 Steps to be followed in carrying out an assessment under COSHH Regulations

1. Think what hazardous substances might be present in the work place.
2. How can hazardous substances be recognised?
3. How are they hazardous?
4. What effects could they have?
5. Break down the work according to where and how substances may be encountered.
6. Know exactly what is going on.
7. Note any differences between people in a group.
8. Evaluate the risks to health.
9. What is the potential of a substance for causing harm?
10. What is the chance of exposure occurring?
11. Who could be exposed under each of these circumstances?
12. How often is exposure liable to occur?
13. How much are people exposed to and for how long?
14. When might measurements be needed?
15. Has account been taken of reasonably foreseeable changes to working practice?
16. What are the conclusions about the risk?
    - Insignificant at present and in the reasonably foreseeable future.
    - High now and not adequately controlled.
    - Controlled now but could become higher in the future.
    - Nature of hazard known but uncertainty about degree and extent of exposure therefore uncertain about risks.
    - Insufficient information to make an assessment.
17. What action needs to be taken to achieve and sustain control?
18. What should be done to monitor the situation, carry out health surveillance and inform employees?
19. How should the assessment be recorded?
20. When should the assessment be reviewed?

Peripatetic workers

The Health and Safety Executive have prepared a booklet on the *Control of Substances Hazardous to Health Regulations and peripatetic workers*[36]. Within this term 'peripatetic workers' are included many community workers such as the community health care worker, the consultant, the emergency service driver, the general medical practitioner and the home help. They do not have a fixed work place and often work away from direct supervision. The booklet emphasises the need for good communication between employers, their workers and everyone else involved in the work. There should also be good communication between different employers to ensure that information about health risks and the precautions needed can be shared. The booklet identifies the risks from substances already on the premises and substances provided by the employer, and also gives advice about routine work, unusual work and sources of information. It further highlights the importance of training and discusses the use of personal protective equipment.

RISK TAKING AND THE RIGHTS OF CLIENTS

Where clients are incapacitated, balancing the risks of danger to health and safety with the need to ensure that clients have as full a life as they can with the maximum freedom possible is part of the duty of care of any professional or non-professional carer. This was further discussed as a special situation of accountability in Chapter 8. As we have seen risk assessment and risk management is at the heart of statutory health and safety provisions. The same principles apply in relation to assessing the risk to clients.

The NHS Management Executive has provided guidance on risk management[36] across a wide range of areas including:

- Direct patient care risk (standards of care, confidentiality, consent, competence, communication and delays in treatment)
- Indirect patient care risk (security risks, fire, buildings, plant and equipment, waste, and control of infection)
- Health and safety risks
- Organisational risks
- Implementing risk management.

ENFORCEMENT PROVISIONS OF THE HEALTH AND SAFETY AT WORK ETC. ACT 1974

Prior to the passing of the National Health Service (Amendment) Act 1986 health authorities were protected from prosecution under the 1974 Act by the doctrine known as 'crown immunity'. This meant that, although the duties under the Act were binding upon them, they were exempt from facing prosecution or any of the other enforcement provisions through the criminal courts. (They were not, of course, immune from proceedings for civil liability where these could be brought.) The abolition of crown immunity in respect of health service bodies, which has been extended through the NHS and Community Care Act 1990, now means that the Health and Safety Inspectorate is able to prosecute a health service authority for breach of statutory duty.

NHS Trusts, group fund-holding or other general practitioners and social services are not able to claim crown immunity since they are not crown bodies and so they are subject to all the enforcement provisions of this and other legislation (with some exceptions).

The enforcement provisions of the Health and Safety at Work etc. Act are shown in Figure 9.17.

Figure 9.17 Enforcement provisions of Health and Safety at Work etc. Act

- Prosecution
- Enforcement notice
- Prohibition notice
- Powers of entry and inspection
- Disclosure of documents
- Powers to deal with imminent danger

Section 20(2) of the 1974 Act gives to the Health and Safety Inspectors considerable powers to enter onto premises, to inspect, to take measurements and photographs, to take samples of substances and articles, to require any person to answer questions or produce any documents, books and so on for inspection. The subsection concludes with the grant of 'any other power which is necessary for the purpose of exercising any of the above powers'.

In the community, the concerns of the Health and Safety Inspectorate are most likely to centre on health clinics, nursing and residential homes and other community premises. However, if there are reports that defective/dangerous equipment is being supplied to clients' homes, there may well be an investigation by the Inspectorate.

FOOD LEGISLATION

Community homes, day hospitals and centres, meals-on-wheels services and anywhere that food is supplied other than within a family all come under the Food Safety Act 1990 and various food safety and hygiene regulations. Section 54 applies the Act to the crown and came into force in 1994 and so thereafter crown immunity cannot be claimed by any health service body.

The Food Safety Act 1990, which consolidates and extends earlier legislation, applies to a wide definition of food as set out in section 1 and under section 2 applies to the supply of food in circumstances even where there is no sale. Section 2(1) is set out in Figure 9.18.

Figure 9.18 Food Safety Act 1990 – section 2(1)

For the purposes of this Act –

(a) the supply of food, otherwise than on sale, in the course of a business; and

(b) any other thing which is done with respect to food and is specified in an order made by the Ministers,

shall be deemed to be a sale of the food, and references to purchasers and purchasing shall be construed accordingly.

Section 2(2) extends the meaning of sale to include the giving of food as a prize or reward or linked with entertainment to which the public are admitted.

Business is defined in section 1(3) as including 'the undertaking of a canteen, club, school, hospital or institution, whether carried on for profit or not, and any undertaking or activity carried on by a public or local authority'.

Regulations apply whether the food is actually prepared on the premises or just stored and served there.

Any organisation therefore which prepares or supplies food for consumption by others must comply with the regulations relating to hygiene and other food safety requirements. Fuller details of these can be obtained from HMSO or from local environmental inspection officers and trading standards departments, from the Ministry of Agriculture Food and Fisheries, the Institute of Environmental Officers or the Institute of Trading Standards Administrators.

 What about the situation in a small community home (only four residents) for those with learning disabilities?

Situation

Four long term residents from a hospital for the mentally handicapped have been transferred to a community home. They have 24 hour care assistant cover and the task of these assistants is to ensure that the residents take as large a part in the day to day routine of the home as is possible. There is a rota for cooking, serving and washing the dishes. Each resident takes part with the supervision and support of the care assistants. The home was not purpose built but an adaptation of a family bungalow. Not all the facilities for storage are present – in particular there is no freezer or pantry.

- Does the home come under the Food Safety Act and the hygiene regulations?
- Could the residents be prosecuted?
- Is there any liability upon the care assistants?
- The home is managed by a charitable community trust but owned and equipped by a housing association, would either of these bodies be liable under the Food legislation?

It is clear from the definitions of business given above that this community home would be subject to the provisions of the Food Safety Act 1990. Even though the activity is not undertaken for profit, it is part of an undertaking carried on by a public or local authority. If, however, it could be shown that the residents are tenants and they cook for themselves and do not have the assistance of paid employees, then it might be arguable that the food is not supplied in the course of a business and therefore it does not come under the Act.

Enforcement

Food legislation is enforced through environmental health officers and trading standards officers who are employed by local authorities. Powers are set out in the Food Safety Act 1990 and shown in Figure 9.19.

Figure 9.19 Powers given under the Food Safety Act 1990

Section 6(2) Every food authority shall enforce and execute within their area the provisions of this Act with respect to which the duty is not imposed expressly or by necessary implication on some other authority.

Section 6(5) An enforcement authority in England and Wales may institute proceedings under any provisions of this Act or any regulations or orders made under it and, in the case of the Ministers or the Minister, may take over the conduct of any proceedings which have been instituted by some other person.

Section 9 [Inspection and seizure of suspected food]

Section 10 [Improvement notices]

Section 11 [Prohibition orders]

Section 12 [Emergency prohibition notices and orders]

Section 13 [Emergency control orders]

In the past there has been concern that earlier legislation relating to food hygiene has been unevenly enforced across the country and varying standards have been set by different areas. It is now the intention, through nationally produced codes of practice, to ensure greater uniformity. About a dozen codes have already been published and are available from the sources outlined on page 171 above.

Application to registered homes and day centres
A registered home is subject to the enforcement provisions of the food legislation. This is so whether the home is managed by a health authority, an NHS Trust, a social services authority, a charitable trust, a private non-profit making organisation or a private profit making organisation. All are subject to the statutory duties and the enforcement provisions.

Situation

The social services department manage a day centre for the elderly mentally infirm which also carries out clinical assessments on their condition and capacities. In the centre there is a well equipped occupational therapy suite which enables the clients to be bathed, work in a kitchen and carry out other activities for assessment of their capabilities to continue living in their own homes. In order to make the kitchen task more meaningful it was agreed that the meals prepared by clients in the occupational therapy kitchen could be served to the day centre clients.

● Does the preparation and serving of food in such circumstances come under the provisions of the legislation?
● If so, and further equipment and facilities are required but there are no resources for such purchases, would the cooking activity in the occupational therapy suite have to cease?

It is clear that the supply of food in these circumstances would come under the legislation and if new equipment were necessary to comply with the statutory duties this would have to be purchased. The statutory defences do not include lack of resources.

Defences
There are specific statutory defences provided under the Act which are shown in figure 9.20.

Figure 9.20 Defences under the Food Safety Act 1990

Section 20 Offence due to the fault of another person.

Section 21 Defence of due diligence, that is that he took all reasonable precautions and exercised all due diligence to avoid the commission of the offence by himself or by a person under his control.

It would be advisable for any community care provision which involves the supply of food to arrange with the local environmental health officers for an inspection and guidance on the practices which should be followed. It should be noted that the Act includes transport in its definition of premises.

Training

Training is essential for all those who are likely to be involved in the supply, serving or preparation of food for others. In some areas such people may be able to obtain assistance from the local authority. Under section 23(1) of the Act a food authority (the local borough, district or country council) may provide, whether within or outside their area, training courses in food hygiene for persons who are or intend to become involved in food businesses, whether as proprietors or employees or otherwise.

A food authority may contribute towards the expenses incurred under this section by any other such authority, or towards expenses incurred by any other person in providing, such courses as are mentioned in subsection (1) above. At present all food businesses must be registered under the Act though it seems likely that this requirement will be withdrawn.

CONCLUSIONS

This chapter has covered the general principles of the liability of the employer for the employee and others, both at common law and under the health and safety legislation. It has also considered the relevance of the food safety legislation to community care. The next chapter will consider liability in relation to occupation of premises and other areas of health and safety.

CHAPTER 10

Health and safety: 2

This chapter continues the discussion on the law of health and safety in the community and considers the topics shown in Figure 10.1.

Figure 10.1 Topics to be covered in this chapter

- Liability for injuries caused by work in risk areas
- Occupiers' Liability Act 1957
  - visitors
  - notice of dangers
  - independent contractors
  - shared occupation
- Trespassers and Occupiers' Liability Act 1984
- Other problems with trespassing
- Animals
- Violence
- Infectious Diseases
- Documentation and record keeping
- Employers' Liability (Compulsory Insurance) Act 1969
- Employer's Liability (Defective Equipment) Act 1969
- Consumer Protection Act 1987
- Fire Precaution Regulations

LIABILITY FOR INJURIES CAUSED BY WORK IN RISK AREAS

There is both a statutory duty and a common law duty to take care of premises, so that visitors to those premises are not injured. In addition the employers have a duty under the contract of employment for the health and safety of the employee generally and should the employers be the owner or occupier of the premises.

Frequently, however, the professional in the community is entering premises not in the ownership or management of her

175

employer and she is therefore vulnerable to its defects and dangers and cannot necessarily seek compensation from her employer.

■ If she knows that the house in which one of her clients lives is particularly dangerous, could she refuse to enter it?

It is not unknown for example in certain very deprived housing estates with high levels of unemployment for floor boards, staircases, and doors to be used for firewood and the occupants move from joist to joist. Can a community worker refuse to visit clients in such circumstances? If a set of steps leading to a house is known to be dangerous can the community worker insist that she does not have to visit that client?

The answer to these questions is that employers have a duty to take reasonable care for the employee's health and safety and cannot therefore oblige her to take unreasonable risks. What is a reasonable risk will be considered in relation to such dangers as unsafe property, dangerous animals on the premises, threats of violence and verbal abuse and infectious diseases. The basic principle which applies in all these cases is that the employers have, as part of their contractual terms, an implied duty of care to take reasonable care for the employee's health and safety (see page 151). However, only if the employee can show that her injuries have been caused as a result of breach by the employers could she recover compensation from them. In many cases she may find that the employer is not at fault but those who are do not have the funds or insurance cover to provide compensation.

OCCUPIERS' LIABILITY ACT 1957

This Act establishes the occupier's liability for harm caused to visitors who enter onto his property. The occupier is anyone who has control over the land and premises. It could therefore be an owner of the property, a tenant, a manager or any other person who is deemed to have some responsibility for the property such that they could be classified as an occupier.

There might, in fact, be several different occupiers who would be held accountable for different aspects of the safety of the premises. For example a community nurse might visit a home which is rented to a tenant who has certain responsibilities under the lease for internal decoration but the landlord and owner has duties in relation to the structural repairs. In addition there might be contractors on site who are undertaking the internal decoration. If a community professional is injured on the premises she might have a claim against any of these depending upon the cause of her injuries. If she were injured by tripping on a threadbare carpet, this would be the responsibility of the tenant; if she were injured because of the carelessness of the painters in leaving an unsafe ladder in the hallway, the contractors would be liable; if she were injured because the stone steps leading to the house were dangerous, then it would probably be the responsibility of the landlord.

The difficulty which the community professional faces is that it does not necessarily follow that all of these potential defendants would be able to pay any compensation which was due. Unless they had all taken out insurance cover for such an eventuality the professional might have an excellent case yet little chance of recovering compensation. She may of course have her own personal insurance cover for such a risk, but in the absence of this she is unlikely to obtain compensation. Some house insurance contracts include personal accident insurance cover and this type of cover is strongly recommended to all community professionals since serious injury could mean the loss of livelihood. Her employers are unlikely to be held liable since it would have to be established that they failed to take care for her safety. This might be the case if the dangers were known and the risks so great that no reasonable employer would subject employees to such danger, but this would be a very extreme set of circumstances and is unlikely to occur. In any event, the person responsible for the dangerous state of the premises would have to be given warning that a service would cease to be provided if safety measures were not taken.

What has to be established under the Occupiers' Liability Act 1957?

The visitor has to show that the person alleged to be the occupier is in breach of the common duty of care which is owed to all visitors. The Act defines this in section 2(2) as:

> a duty to take such care as in all the circumstances of the case is reasonable to see that the visitor will be reasonably safe in using the premises for the purpose for which he is invited or permitted by the occupier to be there.

Who is a visitor?

The visitor is any one who is invited by the occupier to be on the premises or who would be regarded as a licensee at common law. The latter will include those to whom the occupier has given express permission and also those to whom the occupier has given implied consent. Thus persons such as the milkman and paper boy would be regarded as visitors but the occupier can, of course, bar such visitors by an express prohibition. Whether one is a visitor or not is important since the 1957 Act places a duty on the occupier only to the visitor. If a person does not come into this category then they are defined as a trespasser and a different duty applies which is discussed below. If a visitor refuses to leave, he may become a trespasser. This is also discussed below.

It is only if the visitor stays within the purposes for which he had been permitted to enter the premises that he receives the protection of the Act. If a district nurse visiting a patient in the front room of the downstairs of the house decided to have a look around the rest of the house and was injured she would probably not be protected by the Act unless she had a genuine reason such as needing to have access to a wash hand basin.

Notice of dangers

The occupier can obtain some protection from liability by giving notice of any dangers to the visitor – 'Careful when you go upstairs because the carpet on the third stair is frayed'. If this is sufficient for the visitor to be safe and yet, in spite of the warning, the visitor is injured because she takes inadequate care, then the occupier would probably not be liable.

The exact wording of the section of the 1957 Act is shown in Figure 10.2.

Figure 10.2 Warning by occupier – section 2(4)

(a) in determining whether the occupier of premises has discharged the common duty of care to a visitor, regard is to be had to all the circumstances, so that (for example) where damage is caused to a visitor by a danger of which he had been warned by the occupier, the warning is not to be treated without more as absolving the occupier from liability, unless in all the circumstances it was enough to enable the visitor to be reasonably safe.

In addition an occupier cannot discharge himself of all liability for his negligence by putting up a disclaimer notice – a typical one is shown in Figure 10.3.

Figure 10.3 Typical exemption notice – invalid

The owner accepts no responsibility for any liability for injury or loss or damage to property whilst using these premises.

This is because the Unfair Contracts Terms Act 1977 prevents a person excluding or restricting his liability for negligence where death or personal injury occurs as a result of the negligence.

If the harm which occurs is loss or damage to property liability can be excluded provided it is reasonable so to do. The burden is upon the person seeking to rely upon the contract or notice to show that it is reasonable so to do. Thus in the disclaimer notice shown in Figure 10.3 the occupier could not exempt himself from liability for injuries caused by his negligence but the exemption from liability for property loss or damage might succeed (see further discussion on page 126).

Different categories of visitors

The occupier's duty varies according to the nature of the visitor: greater care would have to be taken for the safety of children and those who cannot take good care of themselves (such as those with learning disabilities). In addition an occupier can expect that any person who enters the premises because of his particular expertise (an electrician, plumber, sweep and so on) will appreciate and guard against any special risks which are ordinarily incident to it, so far as the occupier leaves him free to do so (section 2(3)(b)).

Case: *Neame v. Johnson and another*[38]

The plaintiff, an ambulanceman, was in the defendant's house, in dismal lighting conditions and carrying a chair containing the first defendant, who was unconscious. The plaintiff's colleague, who was also carrying the chair, was walking forwards and the plaintiff was walking backwards. The plaintiff knocked over a pile of books on a landing alongside a wall, trod and slipped on a book and sustained personal injuries. This claim for damages was dismissed by the judge and he appealed to the Court of Appeal, contending *inter alia* (amongst other things) that the judge had erroneously construed section 2(3)(b) of the Occupiers' Liability Act 1957 in concluding that the pile of books composed a special risk that the plaintiff in the exercise of his calling would appreciate and guard against.

The Court of Appeal dismissed the appeal and held that, although the lighting was dismal, the judge had found that the ambulancemen were able to see where they were going; they had shortly before the accident ascended the staircase and crossed the landing; they were trained to look for apparent hazards and the plaintiff's colleague had the ability to give a warning if he perceived a potential hazard. In the circumstances, therefore, it was impossible to say that the pile of books gave rise to a reasonably foreseeable risk of personal injury to the plaintiff. Consequently it was unnecessary to consider the application to the facts of section 2(3)(b) of the Occupier's Liability Act 1957.

Independent contractors

If the harm that arises has been caused by the negligence of contractors who have been brought onto the site, this will normally relieve the occupier of any liability. He must have taken care in selecting them however. The occupier might still be liable if he knows that the contractors are dangerous and slipshod in their methods and as a result harm occurs. In addition the occupier must have taken all steps if any that he reasonably should in order to satisfy himself that the contractor was competent and that the work had been properly done (section 2(4)(b)).

If painters leave out a ladder in a dangerous way which falls and injures a visitor then they will be the only ones liable for that harm unless it could be established that the occupier is also at fault.

Shared premises

It is increasingly common for premises to be shared by different occupiers as community care services and multi-agency teams develop. Thus community nurses and health professionals employed by a NHS Community Trust might work from premises owned by a fund-holding GP practice; the community mental health team might work with social worker colleagues in premises owned by the social services; the NHS Trust might share its premises for community services provision with a variety of associated professionals, some employed by voluntary organisations others by GPs or by social services.

■ If harm should occur in this multi-occupation building who would be liable?

If there is an agreement between the parties over the sharing of premises this may clarify responsibility over liability for maintenance, structural repairs and furnishings and equipment. If personal injury occurs as a result of failure to fulfil one of these responsibilities, then that person or organisation would be liable. Unfortunately such responsibilities are not always defined and in such a case it would be a question of determining liability on the basis of the facts, identifying the person or organisation in control or whose fault caused the harm.

LIABILITY FOR TRESPASSERS

As we have seen, the Occupiers' Liability Act 1957 is only concerned with the duty towards visitors. The Occupiers' Liability Act 1984 was passed to cover the position in relation to trespassers. The Act sets out the rules which determine whether a duty is owed to non-visitors in respect of any risk of their suffering injury on the premises by reason of any danger due to the state of the premises or to things done or omitted to be done on them. It also sets out the nature of the duty.

A duty only arises upon the occupier to those who would not be classified as visitors under the 1957 Act in the circumstances set out in Figure 10.4.

Figure 10.4 The 1984 Act – section 2(3)

An occupier of premises owes a duty to [a trespasser in respect of a danger on the premises] if —

(a) he is aware of the danger or has reasonable grounds to believe that it exists;

(b) he knows or has reasonable grounds to believe that the other is in the vicinity of the danger concerned or that he may come into the vicinity of the danger (in either case, whether the other has lawful authority for being in that vicinity or not); and

(c) the risk is one against which, in all the circumstances of the case, he may reasonably be expected to offer the other some protection.

The primary purpose of the Act was to deal with those tragic circumstances where children had been attracted onto premises by dangerous equipment or activities and as a result were harmed. The issue was to determine what was reasonable in terms of the duty of occupiers in relation to such trespassing and also to provide some protection for such trespassers.

Once it has been determined that a duty arises the nature of the duty upon the occupier is as set out in Figure 10.5

Figure 10.5 Duty of occupier to trespasser – section 2

(4) When [a duty is owed] the duty is to take such care as is reasonable in all the circumstances of the case to see that he does not suffer injury on the premises by reason of the danger concerned.

(5) Any duty owed . . . may be discharged by taking such steps as are reasonable in all the circumstances of the case to give warning of the

danger concerned or to discourage persons from incurring the risk.

(6) No duty is owed . . . to any person in respect of risks willingly accepted as his by that person . . .

No liability arises from this Act for loss or damage caused to property.

Application of the 1984 Act to the community professional worker

For the most part community workers are unlikely to be trespassers as they would normally be classified as visitors under the 1957 Act. However, if they are asked by the occupier to leave and fail to do so, then they would be regarded as trespassers for the purpose of the 1957 Act. The occupier has the right at common law to use reasonable force to evict a trespasser. If a community professional is asked to leave then she has no powers to stay unless she is a social worker or doctor who came to the house in the exercise of her statutory powers under the Mental Health Act 1983 or the National Assistance Act 1948 (see Chapter 4).

Situation

An occupational therapist takes a patient from hospital to her home in order to make a domiciliary assessment. Once the elderly person was back home she refused to return to the hospital and told the occupational therapist to leave. The occupational therapist was very concerned since she felt that the client's physical and mental state was inadequate to cope with living on her own at home. What action can she take?

The occupier is entitled to ask her to leave but she could seek the involvement of relatives and neighbours for the immediate care of the client and arrange for any appropriate social services to be provided for the client. If the client is mentally disordered (see glossary) the occupational therapist could arrange for the client to be visited by two doctors and an approved social worker to consider an admission under the Mental Health Act 1983. She could also initiate the powers under section 47 of the NAA 1948 to remove a person from her home if certain conditions exist. These statutory powers (see Chapter 4) would of course be the last resort and initially the occupational therapist would use all her powers of persuasion to return the client to hospital if that was considered to be in her best interests.

The Court of Appeal considered the 1984 Act in a case in 1996[38a] where it held that an occupier who shot a trespasser through the door of his allotment shed was liable to pay the trespasser compensation.

OTHER PROBLEMS WITH TRESPASSING

Requests by relatives

Often it is not the client who asks the health professional to leave but relatives. This presents additional difficulties since the request effectively prevents the professional from caring for the client who may still want to receive care. In these circumstances the nature of the right of occupation of the relative or carer is vital. If the client is the occupier/owner of the premises then he or she has the right to control admission onto the premises (subject to the statutory rights of authorised persons considered in Chapter 4). If the relatives are the occupiers/owners then they would have the right of control, but in this case their duty of care to the patient (see Chapter 22) might require them to permit the entry of the health professionals and so on who care for the patient. Their refusal to allow such entry might, in extreme circumstances, justify the use of the statutory powers.

General principles

Situation

A social worker is concerned about a client who has not been seen for several days. Neighbours report that they are worried because the client has a history of mental disorder. Receiving no reply to her ring on the door bell but feeling that someone was in the house the social worker went around to the back of the house but found that the garden gate was locked. It was not very high so she started to climb over it when the gate collapsed under her weight and she fell to the ground sustaining serious injuries. It was subsequently revealed that the client was indeed in need of care and attention and was removed to a psychiatric hospital. Could the social worker obtain any compensation?

The answer would appear to be 'no'. There is little doubt that she is trespassing. She would not, therefore, be able to obtain compensation in reliance on the duty placed upon the occupier under the 1957 Act. Nor is it likely that she would receive damages under the 1984 Act since, although the garden gate appears to be dangerous, she was not using it in an appropriate manner and therefore she could not claim that she has been injured as a result of a danger of which the occupier should reasonably have been aware. There is also unlikely to be any claim which she could bring against her employers since there is probably no way in which they have been negligent. She herself is most at fault in failing to follow a reasonable procedure when being concerned about someone in the community such as seeking the assistance of the police (see Chapter 4). Codes of practice should exist for such situations.

ANIMALS

One topic which often worries those who visit homes in the community is the fear of animals and their rights should they be injured by the animals.

- Can I refuse to visit if the client/relative refuses to keep a dog tied up?
- If I am injured by a dog do I have to prove that it is known to be dangerous before I can recover compensation?
- If I do not suffer serious injury but my clothing is damaged can I insist that this is replaced?
- If I live in a rural area and the car is damaged by cows is compensation payable by the farmer?

The situation is governed by the Animals Act 1971 and subsequent legislation. If the animal is defined as dangerous then, in general, any person who is keeper of the animal is liable for any damage or injury caused. 'Dangerous' means either

- of a species which is not commonly domesticated in the British Isles and whose characteristics when fully grown are normally such that they are likely, unless restrained, to cause damage, or that any damage they may cause is likely to be severe, or
- where the animal is not of a dangerous species but the circumstances set out in Figure 10.7 apply to the particular animal in the particular case.

Figure 10.7 Animals Act 1971 – section 2(2)

Where damage is caused by an animal which does not belong to a dangerous species, a keeper of the animal is liable for the damage, except as otherwise provided by this Act, if —

(a) the damage is of a kind which the animal, unless restrained, was likely to cause or which, if caused by the animal, was likely to be severe; and

(b) the likelihood of the damage or of its being severe was due to characteristics of the animal which are not normally found in animals of the same species or are not normally so found except at particular times or in particular circumstances; and

(c) those characteristics were known to that keeper or were at any time known to a person who at that time had charge of the animal as that keeper's servant or, where that keeper is the head of a household, were known to another keeper of the animal who is a member of that household and under the age of sixteen.

[The Act excludes the keeper from liability for

- those who are wholly to blame for the harm;
- those who have voluntarily accepted the risk of damage; and
- those who are trespassing (except in certain specific situations).]

Dogs

In 1975 the Guard Dogs Act was passed. This provided that a person is not allowed to have a guard dog to roam about on his premises unless the dog is under the control of a handler. If he has no handler the dog must be chained up so that it is not at liberty to roam about. If a person contravenes the 1975 Act he can be brought before a magistrate and fined.

Under the Dangerous Dogs Act 1991 there may be liability for failure to keep a dog under proper control (see Figure 10.8).

Figure 10.8 Liability under the Dangerous Dogs Act 1991

Section 3 Keeping dogs under proper control

(1) If a dog is dangerously out of control in a public place —
(a) the owner; and
(b) if different, the person for the time being in charge of the dog,
is guilty of an offence, or, if the dog while so out of control injures any person, an aggravated offence under this subsection.

(2) [Statutory defence for owner if he had reasonably entrusted the control of the dog to another person.]

(3) If the owner or, if different, the person for the time being in charge of a dog allows it to enter a place which is not a public place but where it is not permitted to be and while it is there —
(a) it injures any person; or
(b) there are grounds for reasonable apprehension that it will do so,
he is guilty of an offence, or, if the dog injures any person, an aggravated offence, under this subsection.

Situation

A community psychiatric nurse (CPN) was bitten one night by the terrier dog belonging to the client. There was a large notice on the gate which said 'Beware of the dog'. The dog was not known to be dangerous and was not being kept as a guard dog.

It would seem from these facts that the CPN would be unable to hold the client liable for the bite. Nor would the employer be responsible. However some redress for community health professionals, if an assurance is given by the owner of a dog that it will be kept tied up whilst they visit the premises but it then injures them, is available through the Occupiers' Liability Act 1957 (see above) as the owner is aware of a dangerous situation on his property.

 What if there was known to be a dangerous dog on premises, could the CPN refuse to enter them?

The employer cannot insist that the employee enters into danger. In such circumstances, which would be extreme, the client could be warned that unless steps were taken to tie the dog up the CPN would be unable to visit.

Other measures might be appropriate, for example certain people have a fear of dogs and this phobia might lead to their being more vulnerable – in such circumstances it might be possible for another professional to visit. Similarly, if a dog prevents the admission of a professional to a client's home, then the client could be advised (on the telephone if possible) that a visit cannot be made until it is safe to do so.

Employers should not subject their staff to unreasonable danger and it is a question of fact in each case as to what is reasonable or not.

Animals on the highway

If a health visitor in a rural area has her car damaged by animals straying from unfenced land the person responsible for the animals being on the land is not liable for any harm provided that the land is common land, land where fencing is not customary, or is a town or village green – and he had a right to place the animals on the land. If the animals had broken out through an inadequate fence the landowner responsible for that fence would be liable.

VIOLENCE

Unfortunately the uniform of a health professional is no longer a guarantee of respect and safety (and is in fact less likely to be worn than formerly). Community professionals fear violence not only from total strangers but even from their clients and the relatives of such clients. The needs of drug addicts and their theft of prescription pads means that the recent legislation which enables specified registered nurses and health visitors to prescribe drugs may put them at greater risk.

Violence from strangers

Some of the districts in which community professionals work are extremely dangerous. Policemen would not walk around alone. It is the employers' responsibility to take reasonable care for the safety of their employees and the community staff would be entitled to receive all the reasonable protection which is available. This may include portable two-way radios or mobile telephones. Another possibility is some form of call system or alarm. In some areas it may be important to establish a procedure where staff never visit alone at night and sometimes this rule might have to apply in the day as well.

Situation

A care assistant employed by social services visits a client. She is assaulted by a gang of youths who steal her handbag. She is severely injured and off work for several months. What remedies does she have?

Much would depend upon the reasonableness of the employers sending her out on her own to make a visit in that particular district. Was it a known dangerous area? Had there been similar incidents? If the answer to the questions is affirmative and it is established that her managers took no thought for her safety, then the employers may well be liable to compensate her. If the incident was not reasonably foreseeable, however, or the social services authority had not omitted any action which would have been reasonable, then they would not be liable. The care assistant would therefore have to rely upon compensation through the Criminal Injuries Compensation Scheme or, if the offenders are caught and convicted, compensation ordered by the court.

Applications can be made for compensation from all sources simultaneously since previous awards would be taken into account by each body or court.

In areas where there are problems with drug addiction, every reasonable precaution should be taken to protect staff.

Violence from a client or relative

This is an increasing problem as figures on violence in the community show. If the violence has occurred before and is therefore reasonably foreseeable then the employer must take all reasonable precautions to ensure the staff are safe. Again this may mean that staff only attend in twos or even greater numbers and documentation to this effect is kept. It might also mean that the employer writes to the client warning him of the possibility of the services being withdrawn. Should an incident occur, it should be carefully recorded and reported and notes made of any preventative measures taken. If the employers have failed in their duty, they may be liable to compensate staff injured in this way.

Case: *R* v. *Hillingdon Health Authority, ex parte Wyatt*[39]

Mrs Wyatt suffered from multiple sclerosis, could do nothing for herself and needed nursing assistance. The health authority had the duty to provide a home nursing service under section 25 of the NHS Act 1946 (as amended). The husband, who was also an invalid, abused the nursing staff whenever they visited his wife and was aggressive and threatening. He was asked to give an assurance that he would cease to so behave but he refused. The authority told Mrs Wyatt's solicitors that because of Mr Wyatt's behaviour they could not continue the nursing service. The Wyatts applied to court to enforce the service. However, it was held in the Court of Appeal that the authority was doing all that could reasonably be expected of it and the application was dismissed.

The decision to withdraw services in such circumstances would clearly only be reached after every other solution had been tried. If the patient were mentally disordered and section 135(1) of the Mental Health Act 1983 applied or if the patient came within the provisions of section 47 of the National Assistance Act 1948, then it might be necessary to make use of these statutory provisions to ensure that the patient was removed to a place of safety (see Chapter 4).

Compulsory treatment in the community has been considered as a means of reducing the 'revolving door' phenomenon of mentally disordered patients being constantly admitted, then discharged and then re-admitted to hospital. However it has not yet been approved. There are fears that if such a law were to be passed the community psychiatric nurse or the professional whose duty it was to administer the drugs would be in an extremely vulnerable position (see further discussion on after-care supervision orders and the Mental Health (Patients in the Community) Act 1995 in Chapter 4).

Violence is not however always intentional as the following situation shows:

Situation

A care assistant worked in a community home for four residents with learning disabilities. They had recently been discharged from hospital. One was known to be boisterous and he also suffered from epilepsy which was not under complete control. The care assistant was serving lunch on one occasion when the resident started to have a fit and flayed out with his arms. The care assistant was hit in the chest and the hot soup poured over her arm giving her a serious scald. Can she obtain compensation and from whom?

It does not appear on the facts of this situation that she would have any right to receive compensation from the employer unless she can prove that another employee had caused the harm, that there was not a safe system of work or that the employer had failed to take reasonable care for her safety. Can it be said that hot soup should not have been served? Hardly, though it may depend upon how hot it was. There are risks in community living for those with learning disabilities but those risks have to be balanced against the disadvantages to residents of living in institutional care.

■ Could the care assistant succeed in a claim against the resident?

She would have to show that the resident failed in the duty of care he owed to her. However, that duty of care would be measured according to his own abilities and competence. In addition of course he is unlikely to be able to pay any compensation ordered.

The care assistant could of course seek compensation from the Criminal Injuries Compensation Board but it can only pay out if a crime has occurred and, on the facts, it would be difficult to establish that.

The conclusion is, therefore, that the care assistant is unlikely to be able to recover any compensation and would have to look to social security for benefits unless she has her own personal accident insurance cover.

Violence from residents in residential and nursing homes

This has recently been the focus of attention[40]. Many who would formerly have been in long-stay hospital care are now residents in accommodation under the Registered Homes Act 1984. It is the duty of the owners/managers to undertake a risk assessment of the dangers faced by staff and others from such residents. It is essential that they set up a safe system of work and provide the staffing levels, the training and the equipment to ensure that staff and other residents are reasonably safe from violence. If harm occurs as a result of a failure to take such care, then compensation would be payable by the employers.

Verbal abuse

Verbal abuse can be as distressing as physical violence and makes the professional's task in caring for the client extremely difficult. Often, too, the verbal abuse comes from a carer or relative rather than the client. Similar rules would apply in relation to the need to warn the client of the possibility of withdrawing services as would apply to situations of physical violence. Clear strong support by management is essential for the professional. It is, however, unlikely that compensation could be claimed unless it is shown that the effects of the abuse on the professional are such as to cause an illness. Whether the employers would be accountable to the employee would depend upon their support and whether it would have been reasonable for them to take preventative action at an earlier stage.

Pestering

It sometimes happens that a professional community worker is pursued by a client or relative with unwanted attentions – letters, telephone calls or pestering of one sort or another. This is a police matter and the employer should take all reasonable steps to protect the employee. The employee might need to obtain an unlisted telephone number. In extreme cases, where the employee is personally harassed, it might be necessary to obtain an injunction from the courts prohibiting the harasser from coming in the vicinity of the victim's house. Once an injunction has been obtained it can be enforced by the police. An injunction would not, however, be available against an incapacitated person[41].

Obviously the situation is made even more difficult if the client is suffering from mental disorder but it is essential that the employer and colleagues protect the victim who can be persecuted even when off duty.

Case: *R v. Mid Glamorgan FHSA and another, ex parte Martin*[42]

A former mental patient brought an action against a Family Health Services Authority and Health Authority for their failure to allow him access to his records. He wished to discover the reason why a psychotherapist, who was treating him and with whom he had fallen in love, was taken off his case. He had been haunted by the desire to know why and also to discover the reasons for his detention in 1969 under the Mental Health Act 1959. The Health Authority had said three years before that it would consider disclosure of records but only if it was given an assurance that neither it nor its staff faced legal action. The plaintiff refused to give this assurance. The High Court Judge, Mr Justice Popplewell, refused to allow access. He ruled that the Access to Health Records Act 1990 did not apply since it applied to records after 1 November 1991 and there was no right of access at common law. This decision was upheld on Appeal. (See Chapter 6 on the law relating to access to records.)

PROTECTION FROM DISEASE

The principles covering the duty of the employer in respect of the employee's health and safety also apply to the possibility of the employee being infected with a disease. AIDS and HIV infections are a major concern because as yet there is no cure. However, Hepatitis B and C are also a danger, although this is more likely to be a concern for hospital based employees than for those who work in the community.

The employee is entitled to expect her employer to provide her with all the protective clothing and equipment necessary to ensure that she will be reasonably safe in the work for which she is employed.

Situation

A physiotherapist was caring for a pregnant woman who had a history of drug addiction. Could the physiotherapist insist that the woman was tested for HIV? Could she insist that she be given additional gloves and other protective clothing?

At present there is no right to test a patient compulsorily for HIV infection. This is a good thing since false negatives occur in the early stages of infection and could give a false sense of security. It is, therefore, preferable for the professional to regard every patient as a potential carrier of the HIV infection and ensure a safe system of work is adopted. The employee is entitled to be given the equipment and the clothing which will enable her to be reasonably safe. The physiotherapist could therefore request those facilities from the employer which are necessary to ensure that she would be reasonably safe in her care of the patient.

If the community professional is aware that she is suffering from an infectious disease herself, she would have a responsibility to notify her registration body and her employer. In a recent case, a doctor was imprisoned for failing to disclose that he was suffering from Hepatitis B and because he was fraudulent in his attempts to hide the fact.

Further details of books and guidance relating to the employer's duty in relation to AIDS/HIV transmission are given in Appendix 3.

DOCUMENTATION AND RECORD KEEPING

Whatever the incident, injury or situation it is vital that records are kept and statements made. Employers who set up a system for recording occasions when harm nearly occurs and who monitor these regularly will be also able to set up preventative systems. If an incident occurs it is vital that the staff concerned record the details as soon as possible. Accident forms should be completed and these should, where necessary, be supplemented by statements giving a full account of the incident. Witness reports should also be obtained. The fact that an incident takes place in the community in a client's house does not affect the need for it to be fully documented and reported. Even if the employee feels that compensation is unlikely to be recovered this still should not lead to reports not being submitted. This is further discussed in Chapter 11. Reports which are prepared in contemplation of litigation are protected from compulsory disclosure.

There is a statutory duty to report injuries, diseases and dangerous occurrences under health and safety legislation and employers must ensure not only that these statutory duties are complied with but also that they use the information to ensure that such incidents do not reoccur. This is further considered in the section on risk assessment (see pages 145–7 and 160–2).

EMPLOYERS' LIABILITY (COMPULSORY INSURANCE) ACT 1969

This Act requires employers to arrange insurance cover for employees. However it is one of the few Acts of Parliament (the third party insurance requirements of the Road Traffic Act 1988 is another example) which have survived the abolition of crown immunity and health service bodies including NHS Trusts are not bound by it. It does, of course, apply to general practitioners, non-NHS employers (including local authorities) and owners of private hospitals, nursing and residential homes who would all be obliged to make insurance provision for their employees. The Act requires every employer to insure against liability for bodily injury or disease sustained by his employees and arising out of and in the course of their employment. NHS and NHS Trust staff are covered under the NHS (Injury Benefit) Regulations 1974.

The employer is not responsible for economic loss[43].

EMPLOYER'S LIABILITY (DEFECTIVE EQUIPMENT) ACT 1969

This Act covers the situation where personal injury is caused to an employee in course of his employment as a consequence of a defect in equipment which has been provided by the employer for the purposes of his business and the defect is attributable wholly or partly to the fault of a third party. In such circumstances the employee can seek compensation from the employer since the injury is then deemed to be also attributable to the negligence of the employer. The employer can then recover any compensation from the third party. Its basic purpose is to place upon the employer the burden of establishing fault on the part of the third party and enable the employee to recover compensation more easily. The situation below illustrates the law.

Situation

Martha Jarvis is an occupational therapist and had recommended that a hoist should be provided in the house of her client, Brenda Richards. After it had been delivered by the social services authority employing her she went to Brenda's house to check on the installation and to see if Brenda's daughter understood how it should be used. She attached the sling of the hoist to Brenda to assist her in sitting up in bed and, as she did so, the sling broke and Martha suffered a severe back injury as she attempted to save Brenda from falling.

In these circumstances, if it is shown that the hoist was defective, then Martha could recover compensation from her employer and it would be up to the employer to try to recover that compensation from the firm which supplied the hoist. Martha would have her own right to sue the manufacturers at common law and also to make use of the Consumer Protection Act 1987 (see below). However, there is little point in Martha incurring the expense and time loss in pursuing the case herself when the 1969 Act provides her with an opportunity to obtain compensation relatively quickly.

CONSUMER PROTECTION ACT 1987

This Act came into force on 1 March 1988 and gives a right of compensation against the producers and suppliers of products if a defect in the product causes personal injury, death or loss or damage to property. It is not necessary to show that the defendant was at fault, so it provides a form of strict liability (see glossary). There are, however, significant qualifications to that – for example, the defendant can rely upon the fact that at the time the product was supplied the state of scientific knowledge was such that the defect could not have been discovered. This is known as the 'state of the art' defence. Where a defect in equipment is found to have caused harm the liability is upon the supplier of this equipment. Records should therefore be kept of suppliers or manufacturers so that this information can be given to the injured person. If this information is not known, then the Trust, local authority or GP may be regarded as the supplier for the purposes of this legislation.

A report by the National Consumer Council[44] shows that the Act has been used very little and it offers recommendations on how the process of making civil claims in consumer cases could be improved.

FIRE PRECAUTION REGULATIONS

The health service bodies are no longer immune from the legislation relating to fire precautions. Fire certificates are now obtained from the local authority in respect of specific premises listed in the Fire Precautions Act 1971, as amended by the Fire Safety and Safety of Places of Sport Act 1987.

Certificates must be obtained for all health service premises which are used as shops, offices or factories or are occupied together with such premises in connection with these uses, and meet the criteria for certification.

All designated health service premises exempted from certification are required, under section 9A of the 1971 Act, to be provided with satisfactory means of escape and means for fighting fire in accordance with the guidance contained in the codes of practice[45].

Where health service premises are used as a hotel or boarding house then fire certificates must be obtained under the Fire Precautions (Hotels and Boarding Houses) Order 1972.

One irritant to many who are registered as small home managers and owners is that the fire officers are exacting standards of smoke alarms and door strengths which would not be required for ordinary domestic premises. It is argued that these stipulations are both unnecessary and financially prohibitive. In addition it is found that fire officers in different districts are laying down different standards. There would certainly be a value in uniformity across the country and for there to be a review of the current situation. However, at the present time the home owners and managers have no option other than to comply with the requirements of the fire officer. It is the owner/manager who is liable if there is a fire precautions offence rather than the employee in charge of the day to day running of the institution[46].

CONCLUSIONS

The new Regulations which have resulted from EC rules have placed far more onerous responsibilities upon employers and managers. The monitoring of health and safety provisions in the community places considerable burdens upon employers but community staff are entitled to expect the reasonable standard of care which all employers owe to their employees. These two chapters on health and safety have only been able to touch the surface of the issues. Record keeping in relation to incidents, as well as in relation to the procedures, their implementation and training is extremely important in the field of health and safety and it is this subject to which we now turn.

CHAPTER 11

Record keeping and reports

High standards of record keeping are essential not only because of the possibility of litigation and prosecution but also because records are intrinsic to the care of the client.

The importance is highlighted through the book and simply for convenience various aspects are brought together in this Section on professional liability and health and safety, even though they relate to the professional's care and duties and not merely to the evidential requirements in the event of injuries and harm arising.

This chapter will consider the following topics:

Figure 11.1 Topics to be covered in this chapter

- The principles for record keeping
- The courts and privilege from disclosure
- The preservation of records
- Joint record keeping between social and health services
- Client held records

PRINCIPLES FOR RECORD KEEPING

The UKCC recent advisory paper *Standards for Records and Record Keeping*[46] makes it clear that record keeping is an intrinsic part of caring for the patient or client. The record should 'demonstrate the chronology of events and all significant consultations, assessments, observations, decisions, interventions and outcomes' (Paragraph 14.2). Another useful source of guidance on record keeping is the information provided by the NHS Training Directorate[47].

The UKCC document sets out clearly the purpose of record keeping and its importance, and in Paragraph 13 sets out the essential elements which are shown in Figure 11.2.

Figure 11.2 Essential elements in record keeping

Paragraph 13 of the UKCC document states that record keepers should

13.1 write legibly and indelibly;

13.2 be clear and unambiguous;

13.3 be accurate in each entry as to date and time;

13.4 ensure that alterations are made by scoring out with a single line followed by the initialled, dated and timed correct entry;

13.5 ensure that additions to existing entries are individually dated, timed and signed;

13.6 not include abbreviations, meaningless phrases and offensive subjective statements unrelated to the patient's care and associated observations;

13.7 not allow the use of initials for major entries and, where their use is allowed for other entries, ensure that local arrangements for identifying initials and signatures exist; and

13.8 not include entries made in pencil or blue ink, the former carrying the risk of erasure and the latter (where photocopying is required) of poor quality reproduction.

The advice of the UKCC is of use to all professionals whether or not they are registered with the UKCC. Thus social workers and other professionals employed by the local authorities would find the advice invaluable if applied to their own records.

Importance of records in litigation

All professionals are constantly aware of the need to maintain high standards of record keeping and the importance of records should there be any litigation or court hearings. Reference should be made to the recent report of the Audit Commission on record keeping which highlighted some of the present deficiencies in the standards[48].

Some of the points to follow in record keeping in the community (obtained from community psychiatric nurses based on their experience of errors[49]) are listed in Figure 11.3.

Figure 11.3 Errors identified by community psychiatric nurses

- Failure to include times and dates
- Illegible writing
- Failure to record when an abortive telephone call or visit is made
- Use of ambiguous abbreviations
- Failure to include details of recipient of telephone calls
- Covering errors with tippex
- Omission of signature
- Relevant information on client omitted
- Inaccurate dates
- Omission of dates for medical check up, outpatient/general practitioner's surgery visits, and so on
- Delays in writing up the records after seeing the client and some completed more than 24 hours afterwards

- Allowing another person to complete the records
- Inaccuracies on name, date of birth, address and so on
- Unprofessional terminology
- Meaningless phrases
- Mixing of opinion with facts
- Reliance upon hearsay information without quoting source
- Use of subjective assessments rather than objective ones

Peer review of the standards of record keeping can be helpful in maintaining standards and preventing errors.

THE COURTS AND PRIVILEGE FROM DISCLOSURE

The legal status of records

In one sense records are hearsay evidence. The fact that something has been written down does not necessarily mean that it is proof of the truth of what has been written. Lies, misleading statements, exaggerations can all be recorded. If the records are contemporaneous, then they can be called into evidence and the maker of the records can be cross-examined upon them to ascertain the weight which can properly be attached to them.

Thus a health visitor who is subpoenaed (see glossary) to court with her records can be questioned to ascertain the accuracy of those records and, depending upon her answers and the way in which she withstands the cross-examination, the court will determine how her written evidence should be regarded. If she has failed to cope with the cross-examination and crumples under the questioning, then very little weight will be attached to it.

Disputes between professionals

When litigation arises and the records of all those involved in the case are examined, there may be significant discrepancies between the different accounts.

■ Which does the court accept?

As has been stated, records are not evidence of the accuracy of what is recorded. Where, therefore, there is a conflict of written evidence the judge has to rely on the credibility of the writers of the records and how they withstand cross-examination in order to decide the weight which should be given to the records which each person has kept.

For example in community psychiatry care the CPN may on rare occasions need precautions to protect herself from possible conflict. Whenever she summons a doctor for assistance, she should record the time and the response, the time that the doctor arrives or any second telephone call. If a doctor attends and decides that admission procedures are unnecessary, the CPN should record her own observations of the situation. This defensive system may not augur well for good inter-professional relationships but accurate and full recording may be the CPN's best defence in the event of litigation arising from the failure to admit a patient. In the event of litigation or a dispute more weight will be given to her evidence if she can confirm to the court or professional conduct committee on cross-examination that she habitually makes full and accurate records whether or not potential conflict is in issue.

Privilege

Documents which are prepared in connection with the processing of a legal claim such as communications between client and solicitor are privileged from disclosure in court.

■ Can privileged status be claimed for accident reports?

Case: *Waugh v. British Railways Board*[50]

The plaintiff's husband, an employee of the British Railways Board, was killed in an accident while working on the railways. In accordance with the Board's usual practice a report on the accident, called an internal enquiry report, was prepared by two of the Board's officers two days after the accident. The report was headed 'For the information of the Board's Solicitor'. However, it appeared from an affidavit produced on behalf of the Board that the report was prepared for two purposes: to establish the cause of the accident so that appropriate safety measures could be taken and also to enable the Board's solicitors to advise in the litigation that was almost certain to ensue. The defendant resisted discovery of the document on the grounds that it was protected from disclosure on the basis of legal professional privilege. The master (see glossary) ordered disclosure; the judge reversed the order. The plaintiff appealed to the Court of Appeal which held that a report which came into existence or was obtained for the purpose of anticipated litigation was privileged from production, even though it might serve some other even more important purpose, and dismissed the plaintiff's appeal.

The House of Lords held that the court was faced with two competing principles: namely that all relevant evidence should be made available for the court and that communications between lawyer and client should be allowed to remain confidential and privileged. In reconciling those two principles the public interest was, on balance, best served by rigidly confining within narrow limits the privilege of lawfully withholding material or evidence relevant to litigation. Accordingly, a document was only to be accorded privilege from production on the ground of legal professional privilege if the dominant purpose for which it was prepared was that of submitting it to a legal adviser for advice and use in litigation. Since the purpose of preparing the internal enquiry report for advice and use in anticipated litigation was merely one of the purposes and not the dominant purpose for which it was prepared, the Board's claim of privilege failed and the report would have to be disclosed. The appeal was therefore allowed.

PRESERVATION OF RECORDS

As storage problems increase one concern is how long records must be kept – at what point they can be destroyed. There are two issues:

- the requirements under the Public Records Acts; and
- the minimum time for which they should be kept in anticipation of possible litigation.

Those administrators responsible for the storage and destruction of records should ensure that legal advice is taken.

JOINT RECORD KEEPING

As part of the development of collaborative care it is recommended that, instead of each professional discipline retaining separate records, there should be one set of records for each client. This may be easier to arrange in an institutional context where the patient in a bed on the ward is the focus of attention. It is not so easy to set up in community provision. A further difficulty which arises is where it is intended that there should be a single set of records for both health service personnel and social services personnel as disclosure and access provisions then come under different legislation (see Chapter 6).

The issues which arise have to be resolved at a senior level within both the health authority (or NHS Trust) and the local social services authority, and policies and procedures would have to be developed based upon the following principles:

Confidentiality: both health authority employees and social services employees are bound by this duty to the patient, subject to those exceptions recognised in law. These exceptions should be clearly identified and procedures laid down for appropriate disclosure in such exceptional circumstances (see Chapter 5).

Access to records: health records (those drawn up by health professionals) come under the provisions of the Access to Health Records Act 1990 (see Chapter 6). Social workers do not come under the definition of a health professional. Their records are subject to the similar provisions of the Access to Personal Files Act 1987.

Ownership:

- Health records are owned by the Secretary of State in the case of hospital or health community services and the control is delegated by him to health authorities and NHS Trust Boards.

- GP records are owned by the health authority (which took over the functions of the FHSA from April 1996) and have to be returned to the authority when a patient leaves the GP's list.

- Social services records are owned by the local authority social services.

Security, custody and control: The owner of the records should ensure that the site chosen for central storage is secure in accordance with the duty of confidentiality.

If joint record holding is to be adopted as a policy, this would need to be agreed by senior management in the respective organisations so that the issues of ownership, control and security can be clarified.

CLIENT HELD RECORDS

Many different professionals are increasingly allowing clients to hold their own records. It has, for example, long been the practice in district nursing for the patient records to remain in the home and each visiting nurse completes the record of her care of the patient and leaves the record in the home for the next nurse to read her actions and complete it on her own account. For the most part, this system has worked well and suffered very few problems.

There are some fears associated with the patient acting as custodian of the records.

Situation:

A NHS Trust for community services has adopted a policy that records will be kept in clients' homes so that each professional will have access to them on a house visit without collecting them from a central office. A client was being treated for multiple sclerosis and complained that she was not receiving the appropriate care in terms of visits or specialist help and support. Unfortunately the records for this client were kept in her home and just before the complaint was made they were missing. No duplicate set of records had been kept separately and it was impossible to collate information on

- which health professionals called,
- when, and
- what advice and help they had given.

The fears that this situation could arise could lead to the setting up of a second system of record keeping at a central point. The dangers of this dual system is that neither set might be complete and there might not be consistency on what was recorded in each place.

Many health professionals fear that with the increase in litigation, then records may go missing. For example if there is concern over the standards of the care by a community nurse, the client might deny that she was visited by the community nurse as often as the community nurse claimed that she was seen.

One point which should be borne in mind is that the burden of proof in any civil claim for compensation is upon the plaintiff, that is the person bringing the action. The absence of records would not necessarily work in the favour of the plaintiff but probably rather against the person seeking compensation as opposed to the defendant – particularly where it was the plaintiff who had custody of the records.

Another difficulty which arises from records being kept in patients' homes is that persons other than the patient might have access to them.

Situation

It was the practice in the community nursing services for records to be kept by the client. One client asked if the community trust would safeguard her records, since she did not wish her husband to be aware of the fact that she had had treatment for a venereal disease as a result of which her allergy to a particular antibiotic became known. She knew that if she took the records home, her husband would demand to see them.

In the first place it is unlikely that the records which were being kept for the purpose of a present illness would have the whole history of a client's medical care. Even if they did, there is no reason why special provision could not be made for such a situation. It might also be possible to code the information in such a way that it was not easily understood by an unauthorised person. However, if the client were to seek access any coding system should be explained.

CONCLUSIONS

It should not be forgotten that good standards of record keeping are part of the professional's duty of care to the patient/client and, if this duty is fulfilled, then the professional should be well equipped to face any investigation, court hearing or proceedings.

CHAPTER 12

Medicinal products in the community

The health authorities have the statutory responsibility of ensuring that medicines and other products are available in the community. Through contracts with pharmacists for the supply of services they ensure that there is an even distribution of outlets for the dispensing of prescriptions. In rural areas, general practitioners can be given authority to dispense drugs. Pharmacists require permission from the new health authority (set up in April 1996 replacing the FHSA) to be able to dispense drugs through the NHS in a given area. The authority is responsible for the administration and payment of these services and liaises with the Prescription Pricing Authority (PPA) for information about the sums due.

Since the drugs bill forms a large proportion of NHS costs, the statistics of the PPA are a useful source of information about the levels of prescribing by individual doctors and practices and also of the requirement levels of any particular product. Recent attempts to reduce the increase in expenditure within the NHS on drugs has included the setting up of a limited list which prevents a doctor prescribing specific products through the NHS.

The prescription, supply and administration of drugs in the community can raise difficult legal issues which are being addressed by the Royal Pharmaceutical Society of Great Britain (RPSGB)[51]. As well as the problems of supplying drugs to the confused elderly living on their own, there are now an increasing number of small community homes for those with learning disabilities and others who have been in long-stay institutions. In addition there are many residential and nursing homes where the legal requirements for the supply of drugs are not clear. All of these will be considered in this chapter.

STATUTORY FRAMEWORK

The Medicines Act 1968 provides a statutory framework for the supply and control of medicines. Figure 12.1 shows the basic contents of the Act. The Misuse of Drugs Act 1971 and subsequent legislation regulates the supply of specified controlled drugs which is discussed below.

Figure 12.1 Framework set up by the 1968 Act

- An administrative and licensing system
- to control the sale and supply of medicines to the public,
- retail pharmacies, and
- the packaging and labelling of medicinal products.

CLASSIFICATION OF DRUGS

The statutory classification of drugs is set out in Figure 12.2.

Figure 12.2 Classification of drugs

- General sales list
- Pharmacy only products
- Prescription only list

Any procedure for dealing with medicines in a community home (whether residential care, nursing or mental nursing) should ensure that the specific requirements for these different classes of drugs are met.

The general sales list covers drugs which are sold through a variety of outlets and a registered pharmacist does not have to be present.

Pharmacy only products refers to those drugs which can only be purchased under the supervision of a registered pharmacist or given out by a dispensing doctor (see glossary).

Prescription only drugs can only be obtained from a registered pharmacist. The prescription must be written by a registered doctor or dentist, or a nurse, health visitor or midwife who is eligible to prescribe specified medicines as a result of the recent legislation (see below).

PRESCRIBING DRUGS

Apart from exceptions in relation to the supply of medicinal products in hospitals, prescription only drugs must be requested in writing in the specified form which is presented to a registered pharmacist for dispensing (unless the general practitioner has dispensing rights). The Medicinal Products (Nurse Prescribing etc.) Act 1992 will enable a registered nurse, health visitor or district nurse who has the requisite additional training to prescribe those medicinal products contained in the nursing formulary which is attached to the British National Formulary. (For further details of the legal aspects of nurse prescribing see author's previous works[52].) Section 58 of the Medicines Act 1968 (as amended by the 1992 Act) enables an appropriate practitioner to provide a prescription to be dispensed by the registered pharmacist.

Situation

The care attendant on duty at night in a residential care home was concerned at the condition of one of the residents who appeared to be in considerable pain. She eventually decided to telephone the general practitioner who routinely attended the residents. She told him over the phone the symptoms from which the resident appeared to be suffering. He said that he did not feel that a night visit was necessary and suggested that she should give the resident some paracetamol. The care assistant said that she had already done that and they barely relieved the symptoms but she felt that it was too soon to give another dose. The GP then suggested that she should give to the resident two pain killers from the bottle which he had prescribed for another resident whom he had visited earlier in the week which were prescription only medicines. The care assistant felt that this advice was dubious but she was extremely concerned about the pain the resident was suffering. What should she do?

Unfortunately in this situation an unqualified care assistant is less likely to challenge the advice of a doctor than a registered nurse and one option must be that the care assistant summons the help of a senior manager. In practice the general practitioner's duties in relation to residents in a residential home are the same as those to other individuals on his list who still live in their own homes. The doctor does not have a duty to attend at night whenever he is summoned. He has a duty to provide all reasonable services. It is his judgment whether or not a home visit is justified. The decision can be challenged subsequently in a complaint to health authority (formerly the Family Health Service Authority) with whom the GP contracts his services. However if the GP refuses to come and it is felt that the situation is an emergency, an ambulance can be summoned or the resident taken to the Accident and Emergency Department for immediate attention. The care assistant would probably not be able to organise this herself and she should therefore enlist the help of the senior manager if the situation warrants this.

■ Could she give the resident the drugs prescribed for another resident?

The answer to this is 'No' since a prescription is for a named patient and the product cannot be transferred to another. The drug, in a sense, is the property of the patient named in the prescription. The GP should not have given that advice which would constitute a breach of his terms of service.

DISPENSING

The registered pharmacist who dispenses the prescription is able to give significant advice to the patient/residential home manager/prescriber/carer and many others. The potential for the involvement of the pharmacist in the community care of patients has been recognised by the working party established by the RPSGB[53]. Appendix 3 of their report identifies the role of the Pharmacist in the community and the main points are listed in Figure 12.3.

Figure 12.3 Role of pharmacist in the community

Advising by
- provision of information on medicines
- provision of advice on the handling of medicine in residential homes
- development of local policies
- counselling patients receiving day care in hospital or being discharged
- assisting in patient assessment

Training of
- care staff
- inspection teams

Liaison with
- general practitioners
- social services
- client groups
- voluntary organisations and so on

Special care for the elderly
- Supply of appropriately labelled and packaged medicines and advice on the interpretation of instructions
- Recognition of special client needs such as the blind, those with arthritis, and frail or house bound patients
- Provision of domiciliary pharmaceutical care
- Development of a medicines policy for residential care homes

Legal liability of pharmacist

There is legal authority for the principle that even where the prescription has been written incorrectly in terms of dosage, the pharmacist will take some responsibility for dispensing that drug.

Case: *Dwyer v. Roderick and others*[54]

The facts were that Dr Roderick had prescribed a drug for Mrs Dwyer but on the actual prescription he negligently wrote the number and frequency with which the relevant tablets should be taken so that within a relatively short time the patient had received a dangerous overdose. The trial judge found Dr Roderick, his partner Dr Jackson (who had visited the patient and not spotted the error) and the pharmacist (who dispensed the prescription and should have noticed the error) all liable. The percentages were: Dr Roderick 45%, Dr Jackson 15% and the pharmacist 40%. Damages were agreed at £92 000 for the wife £8000 for the husband.

Although the case was subject to appeal by Dr Jackson (see Chapter 16), the Court's finding as to the principle of apportioning liability between the professionals on a percentage basis was not changed and it was, in fact, the pharmacist's share of liability which was increased by the Court of Appeal when Dr Jackson was exonerated.

Similarly if a pharmacist is unable to decipher a prescription because of the bad handwriting of the doctor, both the pharmacist and the doctor will share the responsibility for any harm that the patient suffers.

Case: *Prendergast v. Sam Dee Ltd and others*[55]

The pharmacist made a mistake in reading Amoxil as Daonil which caused the patient to suffer from severe hypoglycaemia and led to brain damage from oxygen shortage in the blood. The doctor was held 25% liable because of the bad hand writing and the pharmacist 75% liable.

Each case would be considered on its merits. In this case there were many signs which should have indicated to the pharmacist that the patient was not a diabetic, such as the fact that a price was paid for the prescription (whereas diabetes is one of the conditions which exempts sufferers from the requirement to pay prescription charges), the dosage was wrong for daonil, the duration of the course of treatment was much shorter than would have been prescribed for daonil, and the strength of the drug was wrong. Clearly, because there were all these pointers, the liability of the pharmacist was the greater.

There is, therefore, a clear duty of care upon the pharmacist to ensure that the appropriate drug is given to the patient, taking into account other drugs which the pharmacist knows or should reasonably know that the patient is on.

One important area where the pharmacist can advise the patient or carer is on the container in which the drug is kept.

Situation

A man of 50 who lived on his own, returned home after a stroke and was prescribed various medications which were contained in child proof containers. Because of the weakness in his hand he was unable to open the container and hesitated to inform the community nurse who failed to make enquiries. As his condition deteriorated, it was apparent that he was not taking his medication and the pharmacist advised that the medication should be put in wing-cap containers.

Here it could be said that all the professionals involved in the patient's care must accept some responsibility: the doctor because he failed to identify the potential problem when he wrote the prescription, the community nurse because she was slow in realising that the patient was not taking the medication, and the pharmacist who failed to check when dispensing the drug that the patient would be able to handle child proof containers.

One danger in the care of the elderly is that they may be on several drugs which are slow to clear through the kidneys and a patient may develop toxic effects rapidly. The pharmacist would have a responsibility to check the cumulative dosages the patient has been prescribed and the rate that these would clear through the body in the light of the patient's medical condition, and advise the doctor accordingly. If the pharmacist has any concerns with the possible reaction on the patient, he has a duty to contact the prescriber before he dispenses the drug.

ADMINISTRATION OF DRUGS

Nursing homes

Nursing homes have a duty which would be set out in their registration conditions to ensure a specified number of registered nurses are on duty at any one time (see Chapter 30). This means that the administration of the medications can follow the same guidelines as exist in hospitals. The framework set out in the UKCC advisory paper on *Standards for the Administration of Medicines* should be followed[56]. Registered nurses should administer the prescription only medicines according to the doctor's prescription. Additional drugs should only be given with the agreement of the doctor and PRN (as required) medications should only be given according to a clear policy. The policy must ensure that they are regularly reviewed and the dosage and maximum frequency must be written up.

Storage of prescription only medicines should follow the guidelines laid down by the RPSGB[57] and they should be regularly checked and procedures laid down for their disposal when the shelf life has expired. The task of administration of prescription only drugs should not be delegated to non-registered staff, except in very exceptional circumstances when paragraph 34 of the UKCC document should be followed. This covers the situation when the Council's standards in paragraphs 8 to 11 cannot be applied.

Record keeping of the administration of the drugs is essential and again advice is available from the RPSGB.

The RPSGB's working party on community care[58], in defining the role which pharmacists could take in the provision of services in the community, listed the following initiatives to which pharmacists could contribute:

- Involvement with the design of training courses for local care staff
- Personal involvement with the pharmaceutical aspects of training local care staff
- Organising local training programmes for pharmacists in association with GPs
- Assessing the pharmaceutical needs of clients, in collaboration with others, by using suggested criteria
- Developing patient held medication documentation
- Participation in the creation of an environment that will encourage greater awareness of the pharmaceutical role

All community workers, not only those working within the residential or nursing home sector, should be able to count upon the advice of the local community pharmacist in the record keeping, storage, security and disposal of medicines.

Stock drugs

It is often the practice in nursing homes to have standard medications as stock items which can be administered whenever necessary. Prescription only medicines should not be held as stock but prescribed for each patient individually. For pharmacy only items there should be collaboration between doctor and community pharmacist over their storage, use, recording and administration. General sales items should also be subject to similar controls. Stock items are discussed below.

Residential care homes

Although there may be staff employed by the residential care home who are registered nurses they should not be employed as such since patients requiring such services should be in a home which is registered for nursing care. (Where such nurses are employed in a capacity other than that of a registered nurse, the UKCC *Scope of Professional Practice* still expects them to follow the Code of Professional Conduct.) In residential care homes, it is left to care assistants to give out medication. They should receive a basic training so that they understand both the clinical and the legal implications of the tasks they are undertaking. Research suggests that there are some very lax practices in the storage and administration of medications in residential care homes and that more training is essential. The research of Dr Rivers and Dr Poston[58] showed that 467 different household remedies were accumulated in Derbyshire social services residential homes. The ten most common medicines were paracetamol tablets, benylin expectorant, kaolin and morphine mixture, senokot tablets, magnesium trisilicate mixture, dorbanex liquid, optrex eye lotion, milk of magnesia mixture and calamine lotion. The household remedies were secured through FP10 prescription. The doctors were asked to add the household remedies to a resident's repeat prescription (see glossary). The authors also pointed out that

> some prescription only items such as distalgesic and codeine phosphate were used as household remedies. Informal follow up interviews revealed that many staff were unaware of the legal restrictions on the prescribing and the use of these products.

They recommend that the concept of a household remedy formulary should be explored. The formulary should be supplemented with information on dosage and guidelines on use of the products. A suitable method for supplying household remedies should also be specified, including the maximum quantities which may be dispensed. They also suggest that staff should purchase the appropriate medicines with the use of a central fund for that purpose. Alternatively, but this is not the authors' preferred choice, bulk prescriptions could be used. Bulk prescriptions should not be used for prescription only medicines which must be individually prescribed. They also recommend that a district policy should be agreed and enforced between doctors, social workers and pharmacists.

The Council of the Royal Pharmaceutical Society of Great Britain established a working party in 1984 to consider the safe handling and administration of medicines in residential homes.

Self-administration

In order to develop a resident's autonomy and independence many homes now follow a policy of permitting the residents to be responsible for their own medication. This is not possible unless the staff have undertaken an assessment of the individual's ability to care for herself and take the medicines appropriately. In addition staff have to be aware of the possible dangers of other confused residents having access to these medicines and the need to ensure that they are correctly stored (for example in a fridge) and that the resident is monitored to ensure that there is compliance with the instructions.

Small care homes

Many of these homes do not have 24 hour staffing cover but might have a care assistant sleeping in at night in case of emergencies. Here the emphasis is on the development of independence and initiative and a self-medication policy is in place. It is essential to ensure that there is no danger to other patients if medicines are kept in individual lockers, especially with those who have a history of suicide and depression.

Often the home will encourage the resident to attend the doctor's surgery and then, if necessary, take the prescription to the chemist and collect the medicines in the company of a care assistant.

There must also be clear procedures on the control over the storage of the usual household items in these homes, especially those for those with learning disabilities, because of the dangers of misuse and poisoning.

In the patient's own home

Administration and disposal

It is almost impossible to generalise about the administration of drugs in the client's own home since the spectrum of client competence and the availability of carers is so wide. In the care of elderly confused patients, care must be taken to dispense medication that they will be able to administer themselves. Alternatively the pharmacist or community nurse may wish to instruct the carer in the giving of the medicines and what signs to be aware of.

The appropriate disposal of out of date medicines is also vital and the pharmacist can play a role in advising on this and in collecting in unwanted or out of date stock.

Oxygen

An increasing number of clients in the community have oxygen. This may be in the form of an oxygen cylinder or it may be an oxygen concentrator which extracts oxygen from the air. Those professionals who visit such a client should ensure that they are familiar with any dangers associated with the administration of oxygen and that they are able to advise the client on its use and storage. The community pharmacist may be prepared to deliver the cylinders and is an invaluable source of advice. Advice might also be obtained from the oxygen company which installs the oxygen concentrators and will usually have the responsibility of providing a maintenance service for them.

Mechanical aids

The topic of equipment which is provided for those being cared for in the community is considered in Chapter 8.

Other medicinal products/dressings

First Aid boxes should be available in every residential and nursing home and working situation. No medicines should be stored in them, only dressings, plasters and so on.

COSHH regulations

The regulations which are discussed in Chapter 9 also cover such domestic products as disinfectants and gardening products. It is essential that the statutory guidelines are followed in assessing and guarding against the risks involved in such products.

Travelling with drugs

It is preferable, if travelling in the UK, for the prescription to be taken which can be dispensed on holiday rather that for the person to stock up with drugs to take with her.

CONCLUSION

This chapter has endeavoured to show that all community workers would benefit from the advice that a community pharmacist can provide on the storage and administration of medicinal products. The introduction of nurse prescribing, if it shows that it will save funds compared with the existing system, is likely to be extended to other groups of nurse practitioners and cover a wider range of products. This may have far reaching impact upon the relationship of the nurse and doctor to the other community professionals. It may also have significant implications for the respective roles of the practice nurse and district nurse.

REFERENCES FOR SECTION B PART 1

1. *Donoghue* v. *Stevenson* [1932] AC 562
2. *Furniss* v. *Fitchett* [1958] NZLR 396
3. *Hill* v. *Chief Constable of West Yorkshire* Times Law Report 29 April 1988
4. *Osman* v. *Ferguson* The Independent 30 November 1992
5. *White* v. *Jones* [1995] 1 All ER 691
6. *Bolam* v. *Friern Hospital Management Committee* [1957] 2 All ER 118
7. *Maynard* v. *West Midlands Regional Health Authority* [1985] 1 All ER 635
8. *Hughes* v. *Waltham Forest Health Authority* (1991) 2 Med LR, *The Times* 9 November 1990
9. *Partington* v. *Windsworth Borough Council* The Independent 8 November 1989.
10. *Loveday* v. *Renton and another* The Times 31 March 1988
11. *Best* v. *Wellcome Foundation and others* [1994] 5 Med LR page 81 and discussed in *Medico Legal Journal* vol. 61 part 3 1993 page 178
12. See the case of *Lister* v. *Romford Ice and Cold Storage Co. Ltd* [1957] 1 All ER 125
13. Source – Jeremy Laurence, Health Correspondent with *The Times*
14. Registrar's Letter 27/1995 Council's Proposed Standards for Incorporation into Contracts for Hospital and Community Health Care Services
15. DGM (92) 164
16. *Scope of Professional Practice* UKCC 1993
17. *Wilsher* v. *Essex Area Health Authority* [1986] 3 All ER 801 (CA)
18. *Deacon* v. *McVicar and another* 7 January 1984 QBD (available on Lexis)
19. *Donoghue* v. *Stevenson* [1932] AC 562
20. *Eastman* v. *Southwest Thames RHA* Times Law Report 22 July 1991 (CA)
21. *Daborn* v. *Bath Tramways Motor Co Ltd* [1946] 2 All ER 333
22. B. Gearing *et al.* in *Mental Health Problems in Old age* A. Reader (ed.) John Wiley in conjunction with Open University, 1988
23. Counsel and Care, 1992
24. *Chapman* v. *Rix* (Date of judgment 21 December 1960 but reported [1994] 5 Med L.R. 239)
25. Comment by Margaret Puxon 5 Med L.R. page 249
26. *Coles* v. *Reading and District Hospital Management Committee and Another* (1963) 107 S.J. 115
27. *Walker* v. *Northumberland County Council* [1995] 1 All ER 737
28. *Mersey Docks and Harbour Board* v. *Coggins and Griffith (Liverpool) Ltd* [1947] AC 1, [1946] 2 All ER 345
29. *Pape* v. *Cumbria County Council* [1992] 3 All ER 211
30. Health and Safety Executive *Manual Handling: Guidance on Regulations 1992* HMSO, 1993
31. Health Services Advisory Committee Health and Safety Commission *Guidance on Manual Handling of loads in the Health Services* HMSO, 1993
32. *R* v. *Hillingdon Health Authority, ex parte Wyatt* The Times 20 December 1977
33. *Fitzsimons* v. *Northumberland Health Authority* (1990) 1 Modern Law Review page 208
34. Royal College of Nursing *Code of Practice for the Handling of Patients* RCN advisory panel to Back Pain in Nurses No 000126 RCN, 1992
35. *Colclough* v. *Staffordshire County Council* (1994) Current Law No. 208, October 1994

36. Health and Safety Series Booklet HS(G)77, 1992
37. NHSME *Risk Management in the NHS* Department of Health 1993
38. *Neame* v. *Johnson and another* Personal Injuries Quarterly Review, March 1993 page 100
38a. *Revill* v. *Newbery* [1996] 1 All ER 291
39. *R* v. *Hillingdon Health Authority, ex parte Wyatt* The Times 20 December 1977
40. For example item transmitted by HTV West, 1 October 1993 – violence arising because of the different mix of clients.
41. *Wookey* v. *Wookey* [1991] 3 All ER 365
42. *R* v. *Mid Glamorgan FHSA and another, ex parte Martin* Times Law Report 2 June 1993 (QBD), upheld by the Court of Appeal Times Law Report August 16 1994; [1995] 1 WLR 110 (CA)
43. *Reid* v. *Rush and Tompkins Group plc* [1989] 3 All ER 228
44. *Unsafe Products. How the Consumer Protection Act works for Consumers* National Consumer Council, London, November 1995
45. *Fire Safety in Health Care Premises General Fire Precautions* HMSO, 1994; *Fire Precautions in existing hospitals* HMSO, 1994; *Fire Risk assessment in existing hospitals* HMSO, 1994
46. *R* v. *Boal* [1992] 3 All ER 177
47. Advisory Paper, *Standards for Records and Record Keeping* UKCC, April 1993
48. *Keeping the Record Straight* NHS Training Directorate (undated) and *Just for the Record* NHS Training Directorate, 1994
49. Informal personal communications to author in the context of a seminar on this subject
50. *Waugh* v. *British Railways Board* [1979] 2 All ER 1169
51. See the report of the Working Party on Community Care RPSGB, 1992
52. B.C. Dimond *Legal Aspects of Nursing* Prentice Hall, Second edition 1995; B.C. Dimond *Nurse Prescribing* Merck Dermatology and Scutari Press 1995
53. *Report* RPSGB, 1992 and see also *Pharmacy in the Community* Pharmaceutical Services Negotiating Committee, 1993
54. *Dwyer* v. *Roderick and others* The Times 12 November 1983
55. *Prendergast* v. *Sam Dee Ltd and others* Independent 17 March 1988
56. Advisory Paper *Standards for the Administration of Medicines* UKCC, October 1992
57. *Guidelines* RPSGB, 1992
58. *Report* RPSGB, 1992
59. *The Pharmaceutical Journal* May 11 1985, page 590

PART 2

Specific professionals and individuals

In this second part of Section B we consider the individual professional groups who work in the community and study some of the specific problems with which they are faced. This follows on from the general issues discussed in the first part of Section B which are common to all groups. Not every professional can be covered but it is hoped that the issues raised will cover most of the concerns relating to the legal aspects of community care. There are also chapters to cover the volunteer and carer.

CHAPTER 13

Social workers: care managers and key workers

The task of implementing the statutory provisions relating to community care in the National Health Service and Community Care Act 1990 falls mainly on the staff within the local authority social services departments. They will be involved in the statutory duties of:

- preparing and publishing community care plans (see Chapter 25)
- laying down policies and procedures for assessments (see Chapter 25)
- purchasing accommodation in residential and nursing homes (see Section D, especially Chapter 28)
- providing or arranging for the provision of welfare and other services identified through the assessment process (see Chapter 2 on duties and the rest of this chapter)
- providing an inspection service for residential homes and facilities provided for community care (see Chapter 25)

This chapter looks at some of the tasks identified in the white paper which have not been given statutory backing and at some of the changing roles in social services departments. The process of care management will be considered together with the role of the care manager and key worker. Some of the legal issues which arise will then be discussed.

DIRECTOR AND STAFF OF SOCIAL SERVICES DEPARTMENTS

Under section 6 of the Local Authority Social Services Act 1970 each local authority is required to appoint a director of social services and is required to 'secure the provision of adequate staff for assisting him in the exercise of his functions'. Allegations that there has been a failure to fulfil this duty have been the subject of an application for judicial review[1]. It is highly probable that many departments have not had the resources to ensure that additional staff were recruited in order that they could fulfil their new statutory duties.

Transfer of staff from health services

Section 49 of the NHS and Community Care Act 1990 gives to the Secretary of State the power to make regulations with respect to the transfer to employment by a local authority of persons previously employed by a National Health Service body – and back again. The regulations can cover the topics set out in Figure 13.1.

Figure 13.1 Regulations for transfer of staff – section 49

Without prejudice to the generality of subsections (1) and (2) above [powers for the Secretary of State to make regulations], regulations under this section may make provision with respect to—

(a) the terms on which a person is to be employed by a local authority or National Health Service body;
(b) the period and continuity of a person's employment for the purposes of the Employment Protection (Consolidation) Act 1978;
(c) superannuation benefits; and
(d) the circumstances in which, if a person declines an offer of employment made with a view to such a transfer or return as is referred to in subsection (1) or subsection (2) above and then ceases to be employed by a National Health Service body or local authority, he is not to be regarded as entitled to benefits in connection with redundancy. (section 49(3))

Regulations under this section may make different provision with respect to different cases or descriptions of case, including different provision for different areas. (section 49(5))

The purpose behind the provisions set out in Figure 13.1 is to give continuity of service (see glossary) to those who leave health service work in the long-stay institutions as they are closed and go to work for local authority community care services. Without these regulations the person transferring would have no continuity of service for the entitlement to rights under the employment protection legislation such as the right to apply for unfair dismissal, maternity benefits and so on. Conversely, if a person refuses a reasonable offer of transfer she cannot claim to have been made redundant or entitlement to redundancy payment.

Griffiths raised these issues at the outset. The relevant passages of his report are shown in Figure 13.2.

Figure 13.2 The Griffiths report, paragraph 7

7.13 It is important that the skills of staff formerly employed in long stay hospitals are not lost as patients are discharged and responsibility for their care passes to another authority. Such staff are likely to have direct personal knowledge of individual former patients and their needs, as well as a wide range of skills which are equally valuable in a community care setting. There are legislative and other problems which inhibit the smooth transfer of staff between agencies at present, which can delay desirable changes.

7.14 There are a number of options for local action in regard to staff. They may be seconded to the local authority, which has the advantage of being a flexible approach. There can be locally arranged transfers to local authority employment with no redundancy compensation and with the retention of NHS superannuation scheme membership, which can be an important consideration for the staff concerned. Finally the health authority or NHS trust can make the staff redundant followed by engagement of the same staff by the local authority. Each of these options has its own advantages and disadvantages.

Where Social services employ professions supplementary to medicine then directions state that these staff must be registered with the Council for the Professions Supplementary to Medicine. These directions are shown and discussed in Chapter 19.

CARE MANAGEMENT AND CARE MANAGERS

Care management

This is at the heart of the white paper proposals on care in the community. The key part to be played by care management is identified in the *Policy Guidance*[2] and shown in Figure 13.3.

Figure 13.3 Role of care management

The role of care management is to:
- ensure that the resources available (including resources transferred from social security – the funding of residential/nursing home places from April 1993 (see Chapter 28)) are used in the most effective way to meet individual care needs;
- restore and maintain independence by enabling people to live in the community wherever possible;
- work to prevent or to minimise the effects of disability and illness in people of all ages;
- treat those who need services with respect and provide equal opportunities for all;
- promote individual choice and self-determination, and build on existing strengths and care resources; and
- promote partnership between users, carers and service providers in all sectors, together with organisations of and for each group.

The *Guidance* sees the care management process as covering three distinct processes:

- Assessment of the user's circumstances.
- Design of a care package in agreement with users, carers and relevant agencies.
- Implementation and monitoring of the agreed package – including review of the outcome for users and carers and any necessary revision of service provision.

Care managers

In the implementation of the care management system, the care managers play the part of brokers or purchasers. It is not recommended that they should be involved in direct service delivery. The *Guidance* also recommends that they should not 'normally carry managerial responsibility for the services they arrange'. The reason is that this 'removes any possible conflict of interest'. Care managers may come from many different professional backgrounds and can even be appointed from the voluntary sector. The task of assessment is considered in Chapter 25.

Following the assessment the care manager is responsible for the development of a care package agreed with all parties. The order of preference in the *Guidance* is shown in Figure 13.4.

Figure 13.4 Order of preference in the care package

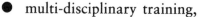

1. Support for the user in his or her own home including day and domiciliary care, respite care, the provision of disability equipment and adaptations to accommodation as necessary.
2. A move to more suitable accommodation, which might be sheltered or very sheltered housing, together with the provision of social services support.
3. Residential care.
4. Nursing home care.
5. Long-stay care.

The importance of training for all those involved in assessment and care management is emphasised in the guidance. The training should include:

- multi-disciplinary training,
- training with staff from other agencies, and
- vocation and professional in-service training.

THE INTERNAL MARKET WITHIN SOCIAL SERVICES

The purchasing and commissioning function of local authority social services departments was identified in the Griffiths Report as a key role. The Department of Health recognised that the development of the purchaser/provider divide within Social Service Departments could only be achieved slowly but by 1993 Departments would be expected to identify purchasing and providing aspects of their work. In addition purchasers would increasingly be looking at the independent sector for the provision of services, but again the Department envisaged 'that this will take several years rather than months to achieve especially in the case of non-residential services'. Some of the legal implications in using the independent sector are considered in Chapter 26.

Guidance is given on the management of the purchasing process in defining the quality of services, service specifications, and the selection of service providers through open tendering, select list tendering, direct negotiation, or setting up new organisations. Advice is also provided on choosing the right type of contract, the length of contract and pricing.

In contrast to the NHS there is not the same statutory basis for an internal market within social services departments. Health authorities and GP fund-holding practices as commissioners can contract with NHS Trusts agreeing section 4 NHS contracts (see Chapter 23). At present in the social services, with a large proportion of direct labour staffed services, purchasers and providers are not necessarily distinct groups and some staff may be operating in both the purchaser and the provider role. Where contracts are made by social services departments with the independent sector, these contracts will not be subject to the same restrictions which operate in relation to NHS agreements (see Chapter 23 and section 4 of the NHS and Community Care Act 1990). This means that they will be subject to the laws of contract and be enforceable in a court of law.

Staff have the following concerns over the implementation of the care programme approach.

- What is the accountability of the care manager in the assessment process?
- What if there is a waiting list for assessments?
- What are the legal implications if the care package cannot be agreed?
- What is the accountability of the care manager in the determination of priorities?

- What is the extent, if any, of the duty of care of the care manager once the service providers assume responsibility?
- Who is responsible for monitoring changes of need?

Accountability and assessment

Clearly if an assessment has been made negligently and harm arises, then there could be an action for compensation in the civil courts by or on behalf of the person harmed.

Situation

A care manager arranges only a level one assessment for a middle aged person living on her own who appeared to be suffering from memory loss. She fails to ensure that a doctor, nurse, or occupational therapist is brought into the assessment team and only minimal help is provided. Subsequently the client is found dead as a result of a fall and it is then ascertained that the client was suffering from multiple sclerosis.

In this case, there could be an action in negligence (considered in Chapter 7). The plaintiff would have to show that

- there was a duty of care owed by the care manager,
- she failed to follow the approved standard of care in not bringing in the appropriate professionals' skills in making the assessment and
- as a reasonably foreseeable consequence of this breach the harm occurred.

The care manager would have a partial defence to show that others also shared responsibility – for example the service providers should have been aware of the dangers to the client or, if the general practitioner was aware of the diagnosis, steps should have been taken to ensure that this information was provided for the assessment.

The *Policy Guidance* states

> In developing care management mechanisms for accessing resources and exercising accountability will have to be clearly defined. All care managers are likely to need training and support. (Paragraph 3.14)

It is essential that training in carrying out the assessments and clear standards of care must be established speedily.

Waiting lists for assessment

Many staff are finding that since the care programme approach was initiated they are having to determine clear priorities in the carrying out of assessments. Certain groups such as those suffering from mental disorder or those awaiting discharge from hospital may be given first priority. The statutory duty under section 117 of the Mental Health Act 1983 to provide after-care for certain formerly detained patients remains as a distinct statutory duty and is not replaced by the care programme approach. It may happen, however, that within different client groups priorities must be set. There could also be complaints made to the social services authority as a result of delays in carrying out the assessment (see Chapter 27).

Situation

Occupational therapists provide an assessment service for independent living and receive referrals from the care managers within the social services, general practitioners and self-referral from potential clients. Because of the volume of requests there is inevitably a waiting list which at the present time stands at three months.

They have a duty of care to ensure that their determination of priorities is reasonable. It is essential that they build within their assessment procedure the ability to deal with emergency assessments straight away. In order to ensure that priorities are determined fairly and accurately it is necessary for them to establish a referral system that gives them sufficient information to make that judgment. This will necessitate requiring general practitioners and self-referrers to provide the necessary information. If they fail to establish a reasonable system and ensure that it is implemented then they could be held accountable if harm befalls a client as a result of a failure to carry out a speedy assessment.

Similar principles apply to the work of the care manager in making her assessments.

Failure to agree the care package

Although there is a needs-led approach to the task of assessment, the *Policy Guidance* emphasises that

> assessment does not take place in a vacuum: account needs to be taken of the local authority's criteria for determining when services should be provided, the types of service they have decided to make available and the overall range of services provided by other agencies, including health authorities.

There are thus likely to be occasions when it is impossible to reach agreement between the care manager, the carer and the client (service user), particularly if other authorities are seen to provide services for which arrangements cannot be made by that particular authority. Should there be disagreement then the points of difference should be recorded. The service user should be advised of his right to make representations and a complaint and be given information on how to proceed.

Accountability in determination of priorities

A care package must be agreed with the service providers or agencies. Once it has been agreed that a service will be provided then it will become the responsibility of the service provider to determine priorities and waiting times. Paragraph 3.26 of the *Guidance* states that

> decisions on service provision should include clear agreement about what is going to be done, by whom and by when, with clearly identified points of access to each of the relevant agencies for the service users, carers and the care manager. No agency's resources should be committed without its prior agreement.

Two situations have to be distinguished:

- where the care manager has inadequate resources to arrange for the purchase of a specific care package;
- where arrangements have been made for the service to be provided, but the service provider has competing priorities.

The former situation is discussed in Chapter 25 on the statutory duties of local authorities and the enforcement provisions in Chapter 27. The latter is a question of the determination of priorities by providers who have to create a waiting list for the services they provide. In each case the determination of priorities in the supply and delivery of care would be subject to the principles of reasonableness.

It may be that the care manager is unable, because of inadequate funding, to agree to the provision of a specific service which a service provider would supply. The client should be informed of this and would have the right to make representations.

Passing on responsibility

In theory provided that the care manager has made the assessment, agreed the care package and arranged for its delivery then liability for the provision of the service should be that of the provider. However, it is essential that there should be a procedure for monitoring the appropriateness of the care package in the light of any changes in the client's situation. Information should be passed from the service providers to the care managers for a reassessment to take place. The key worker responsible for the care of the client would obviously have a major role to play in ensuring that this reassessment was requested.

Monitoring changes of need

As stated above once the care package has been agreed and arrangements made for its delivery, then responsibility would pass to the key worker and the care team to ensure the appropriateness of the services was kept under review. However, in addition the care manager should lay down a system for regular monitoring.

A report on research carried out by MENCAP[3] shows that there is considerable variation between local authorities on the information, accessibility and involvement of clients with learning disabilities in the assessment process and the care programme approach. The report points out that there is no guarantee that large cash injections, even over long periods of time, would fundamentally alter the opportunities for people with learning disabilities. This report is considered in more detail in Chapter 25.

KEY WORKERS AND THE PROVISION OF SERVICES

Assessment and care management is part of the purchasing role and the aim is to secure the separation of the purchasing role from the provision of services. In contrast to care managers, the key worker is the person designated as the main service provider.

Some of the legal issues relating to accountability and the key worker, especially in the field of the extended role (see glossary) are discussed in Chapter 8.

The key worker is the person designated amongst the care team as the one with the main responsibility for the client who will call upon the professional skills of other members of the team as appropriate. Different chapters in this part of the book deal with the specific legal problems which might be encountered by specific professionals.

One area of increasing concern to many is the issue of skill mix and the likelihood that professionally qualified staff are working with a growing number of staff without such qualifications so that the ratio of non-professionals to qualified professionals is increasing all the time. This puts considerable pressure on the skills of professional staff in delegating appropriately and providing the correct level of supervision. The principles of negligence apply in supervision as apply in fulfilling directly the duty of care to the client.

However, the fact that support workers are not registered professionals does not mean that they are untrained. It is essential that support workers who assist registered professionals in carrying out their tasks in the community receive the appropriate training in the areas in which they are to work. It is also vitally important that they are aware of the limitations of their competence.

CONCLUSIONS

The care manager and the key worker are respectively at the heart of the purchasing and provider roles in care in the community. The duty of care which they both owe is, in the main, based in common law rather than statutory definition. Both are likely to be at the sharp end of any complaints or litigation over the supply or quality of service. A full understanding of their roles is essential together with a firm grasp of the principles of record keeping and documentation (see Chapter 11).

CHAPTER 14

Community Nurses

The district or community nurse is central to the health care of persons in the community. Currently the employees of directly managed units or NHS Trusts, they may well in the future become the employees of fund-holding general practitioners. From April 1993 GP fund-holders had the task of purchasing their community health professionals from the appropriate NHS provider, but many are hoping that in the future they will be able to employ their own community health staff. This will give them greater control over the staff and also enable them to avoid the administrative overheads that they currently have to pay. Direct employment of community nurses by general practitioners may lead to changes in the traditional role of the practice nurse (see Chapter 18).

The community nurses act as the liaison between institutional care, the general practitioner, other health professionals, the social services, carers and the clients. Their work has extended as in-patient stay has decreased and as the technology of medicine at home has developed. The earlier discharges and increasing implementation of the 'hospital at home' concept has made them increasingly vulnerable to litigation and increased the pressures upon them. In addition the Patients' Charter and other initiatives have heightened patients' awareness of their rights.

The specific topics which will be considered in this chapter are shown in Figure 14.1.

Figure 14.1 Topics considered in this chapter

- Discharge from hospital
- The *Scope of Professional Practice* and the hospital at home concept
- Priority setting and the caseload
- Keys and the security of clients
- Community nurses and residential care homes
- Nurse prescribing

Other areas are of importance to the community nurse but are covered elsewhere in the book. For example the giving of advice, the key worker concept, delegation and supervision, equipment and transport are considered in Chapter 8 dealing with special situations. The problems of lifting and the dangers for her in carrying out night visits are considered in Chapters 9 and 10 on health and safety.

DISCHARGE FROM HOSPITAL

The time patients stay in hospital has decreased considerably over the last 20 years. They rarely spend any time convalescing in hospital but are discharged as soon as possible after an operation. They no longer remain in hospital until the sutures have been removed. An increasing number of day patients have surgery which might in the past have taken many days recovery as an in-patient, but they are now treated in the community with the community nurse providing the care, attention and treatment formerly provided by the hospital based nurses. This has increased the pressure on the district nurse as well as requiring her to provide greater skills and technical knowledge.

It is essential that the procedure for the discharge of patients from hospital to the community involves the community nurse at every stage and that she is given detailed information on the patient's care to ensure that he will be safe. Many specialties now provide discharge information for the patient and also for the district nurse. The nurse should be given details of the medication prescribed for the patient and also the current treatment which may involve nursing care. She should be given this information directly and should not have to wait for the discharge letter to be sent to the general practitioner. It is preferable if the district nurse can be given information or even see the patient prior to discharge. Many areas have now adopted improved procedures for pre-discharge planning and the district nurse should be involved in this.

It is essential that for every single patient the community nurse has a clear idea of her responsibilities and what instructions the patient also has been given. Errors in this communication could lead to litigation.

Situation

A patient is discharged after a minor operation. She assumes that the sutures will dissolve and do not require removing. The nurse is not asked to dress the wound but calls round to ensure that the patient is looking after herself. The wound becomes infected and eventually the patient needs another operation which is followed by skin grafting. Where does the district nurse stand in law?

Even if the nurse is not given the requisite information by the hospital, there are basic questions she should be asking of the patient to make sure that she is being cared for appropriately. In this case the nurse may well share some of the responsibility for the additional pain and suffering endured by the patient. Much will, of course, depend on the actual facts of the case and the extent of any contributory negligence by the patient. However, the nurse would be required to perform her own individual assessment of the patient's needs and not merely rely upon information from the hospital.

Where there is an absence of a clear procedure for the nurse to be informed of every discharge in her area she should take this issue up with her managers until she is satisfied that the arrangements are sufficient to ensure that patients will be safe.

Department of Health guidance was published in 1989 on the *Discharge of patients from hospital*[4]. It sets out criteria for good practice and procedures on the discharge of all types of people. Research in 1992 carried out on discharge procedures for the elderly showed that many of the guidelines were not then in force[5]. The research showed that intensive care services for old people on their discharge were often patchily provided and seldom able to give comprehensive cover and in no local authority in 1988 was there a fully coherent policy for responding to the new situation in which people were being discharged from hospital 'quicker and sicker'. The report provides useful advice on policy implications and recommendations as a result of the research findings. Further guidance was issued by the Department of Health on a consultation basis in August 1994. This was because of confusion over the respective responsibilities of the NHS and Social Services Departments (see Chapters 23 and 25).

Even where there is the appointment of a discharge organiser, community nurses are likely to have a major role to play in ensuring that the correct services are provided for patients in the community and ensuring that as new situations develop reassessments take place. Central to the after-care planning is the care plan agreed on a multi-disciplinary basis at the time of the assessment of the patient's needs. This is further discussed in Chapter 25.

Often failures in discharge procedures and provisions do not come to the courts as there is little to be gained through litigation. However, complaints over discharge, or over the support of a person following discharge, are often referred to the Health Service Commissioner.

Increasingly there is a transfer of basic activities formerly undertaken by nurses (such as feeding, bathing and personal care) from the community nurse to the care assistant employed or purchased (from a care agency for example) by the social services department. It is, therefore, essential that the areas of work covered by health professionals and those covered by social services are clearly defined.

THE HOSPITAL AT HOME

The work of the community nurse can vary from the basic nursing skills of bathing and feeding to the most specialist forms of high technology medicine. Procedures which were once only performed in hospital may now be taking place in individual homes. Community nurses may be caring for patients on ventilators, being given intravenous injections or oxygen from concentrated oxygen machines or cylinders, patients receiving stomach feeds or nasal gastric feeds and patients requiring many other technical procedures. They need to ensure that they have the training to understand the nature of the procedures and the patients' and their own involvement.

The NHS Management Executive has given guidance in its circular, *Purchasing high-tech health care for patients at home*[6]. In the list of care packages which it suggests that a Trust could provide for care at home are the following:

- continuous ambulatory peritoneal dialysis fluids
- total parenteral nutrition
- alglucerase
- nebulised antibiotics for cystic fibrosis
- intravenous chemotherapy agents for cancer patients
- desferrioxamine for thalassaemia
- intravenous or nebulised anti-infectives for HIV patients.

It is essential that the community nurse has an input into the decision as to which patients could be discharged home when still needing acute care normally carried out in a hospital. In a scheme in Derbyshire[7] criteria for admission to the 'hospital at home' scheme were identified as including the following:

- Patient would otherwise remain in hospital if the 'hospital at home' did not exist.
- Patient must be day four or later post-operation.
- Patient's medical condition must be stable.
- Patient must be orientated in time and place, or at least at pre-admission orientation level.
- Wound must be checked on day of discharge and all drains removed.
- Patient's home must have adequate facilities.
- Patient's home must be geographically accessible in bad weather.
- Patient, relatives, GP and all other staff involved must give consent.
- Re-admission to hospital must be possible at any time if required.

Reference should also be made to the work at Peterborough which first established the concept. The District Nursing Association has published the result of a conference in Peterborough[8] which looked at the 'hospital at home' services from the perspective of both the user (a sufferer from Guillain Barre syndrome) and the provider. Many other districts are now actively developing services to enable patients to be discharged at a much earlier stage in their care, to receive day surgery or not be admitted to hospital at all.

Situation

The nurse is informed that a patient with central line administration of antibiotics and night feeding through a gastrotomy is to be discharged and will be part of her case load. The nurse has never received training in either of these procedures and has no recent knowledge of the intravenous antibiotics which are being used by this patient. She is reluctant to take on the care of this patient but is afraid to voice her concerns to her manager.

The nurse has a professional duty under the code of professional conduct to work within her field of competence. This duty still remains, even though there is a move away from the concept of the extended role of the nurse. The UKCC *Scope of Professional Practice*[9] sets out the guiding principles which nurses should follow in developing their professional expertise. (This is discussed in Chapter 8.) In the situation described here, the nurse should make it absolutely clear to her manager that she has no experience or knowledge of the procedures which the treatment regime of the patient requires. Failure on her part to notify the managers of her ignorance could lead to personal injury or even the death of the patient.

It may be possible for another nurse, experienced in these procedures to be assigned to the patient so that the original nurse could learn under her supervision. It might even be possible for her to be seconded to a hospital ward for a short time to gain understanding and skill. Where any patients who have special needs are due to be discharged it might be possible for the pre-discharge planning to require the appropriate district nurse to be trained at the hospital bedside in those particular procedures.

It is essential that community nurses develop the confidence to assert their training needs and maintain and develop their competence. This will be of particular importance if community nurses are eventually employed by general practitioners.

PRIORITY SETTING AND THE CASE LOAD

It is not usually possible for a community nurse to regulate the pressures upon her by a waiting list system. If a patient is discharged from hospital and requires specific assistance, this cannot be postponed for two weeks until the other patients she is caring for no longer need her help.

She is unlikely to have access to sufficient colleagues to share her load. Failure on her part to provide necessary services could lead to litigation.

■ How does she cope?

If it is clear that her case load is too great for all the necessary work to be done, she needs to assess priorities and analyse the extent to which her clients already have assistance from relatives and friends and the extent to which it is reasonable to rely upon such help. To determine priorities she needs to make visits to her patients to assess their needs and situations. This will involve an assessment of how frequent visits would have to be and the nature and length of each visit. She needs to know which of the specialist nurses (see Chapter 16) would be available to provide services to her clients.

If she cannot meet all the essential demands she will have to discuss with her manager the action which must be taken. It is vitally important that her records reflect the facts upon which her assessment of priorities is based. An unreasonable determination of priorities could be the basis of a claim in negligence against her and her employers (see Chapter 7).

Ideally such an assessment will be undertaken under the provisions of section 47 of the National Health Service and Community Care Act 1990 on a multi-disciplinary basis and where the patient is being discharged from hospital then a hospital professional will be the team leader and initiator of the assessment exercise and the development of a care plan.

Situation

A community nurse is under heavy pressure from a case load with many seriously ill patients requiring skilled care and attention. One patient is receiving intravenous antibiotics through a central line portacath at home given by the nurse, every eight hours. The nurse arrives just after the time due for the transaction and prepares to mix the drugs. Unfortunately in her haste she gives a saline solution at the end instead of the solution of hepsal to keep the vein open. When another nurse comes to the house eight hours later, the vein is blocked and the transfusion cannot be given. It becomes necessary for the patient to have another operation to replace the portacath. The patient blames the nurse when she hears of the mistake and is prepared to seek compensation. Where does the nurse stand in law?

Pressure of work is no defence to an action for negligence. The standard against which the nurse would be judged is the reasonable standard which would be expected of a community nurse. This is known as the Bolam test (see glossary). The nurse owed the patient a duty of care, she is in breach of that duty by failing to follow the accepted approved practice, as a foreseeable consequence of that breach the patient has suffered harm and, therefore, the nurse would be personally liable and her employers vicariously liable for her negligent actions.

The new provisions requiring assessment by local authorities under section 47 of the 1990 Act (see Chapter 25) will involve the community nurse in doing joint assessments where health needs are indicated.

There is a lack of clarity at present as to the extent to which there is a binding duty on local authorities to ensure that, once identified, needs are met. Similarly if health needs are identified in patients who have been discharged from institutions and the district nursing service is, through lack of resources, unable to meet those needs, could the patient successfully sue for breach of statutory duty or negligence? In Chapter 2 it was shown that cases brought alleging breach of statutory duty because a patient had to wait for treatment failed. It remains to be seen how the courts will interpret the recent enactments and the extent to which inadequacy of resources will be a justification for failing to provide a service. This is further discussed in Chapter 23. Enforcement provisions are discussed in Chapter 27.

In carrying out joint assessments with social services staff the community nurse must have a good understanding of the resources which are available to meet patient needs, together with a comprehensive understanding of the input which could be provided by other health professionals (both nursing and non-nursing) and of the legal requirements.

KEYS AND LOCKING THE PATIENT IN

Many patients live on their own. Various devices have been designed to overcome the problem of permitting access by the nurse and ensuring that the patient is secure against unwelcome intruders. The easiest option is for the nurses to be given a spare key to the house and the house to be kept locked against intruders. However, this places upon the community nursing staff the responsibility of ensuring that the key never comes into unauthorised hands and that there is no way in which it could be identified as belonging to a certain house by anyone entering the community headquarters. At the same time the key will be used by many different nurses and it has to be made available to them all as required.

Sometimes the device of securing the key to a piece of string tied to a nail inside the letter box is used. The nurse then opens the letter box, pulls through the key and then opens the door. This method is not recommened since it can be so easily abused. Other practices such as leaving a key under a pot are also extremely dangerous to the patient's safety and it would even be possible for an intruder to precede the nurse into the house.

At other times a key might be left with a neighbour, but this can cause difficulties if the neighbour is out when the nurse visits. It is not recommended that the patient's house is left unlocked for the nurse to enter as necessary, so a safe system must be agreed.

Incidents involving attacks on community nurses have increased and are discussed in the Chapter 10 on health and safety. The nurse must be mindful of the need to take precautions not only for her own safety and that of her colleagues and also for that of her clients who live alone.

COMMUNITY NURSES AND RESIDENTIAL CARE HOMES

Homes which are not registered as nursing homes are unable to care for patients who require extensive nursing input. Such residents should be cared for in registered nursing homes. Where nursing input is required in residential care homes it is provided by the community nurses on the same basis that they provide help to individuals in their own homes.

Situation

A community nurse visits a residential care home to provide injections for insulin and dressings for ulcers. The community nurse is being asked to provide a much more intensive nursing service than she considers reasonable. She is also aware that many of the residents require considerable nursing input and she discovers that there are registered nurse practitioners on the staff who are employed and paid as care assistants. Their nursing skills are, however, being used in the home. What should the nurse do?

In such circumstances, the registration authority, currently the local authority, should be notified that some of the residents are in need of more nursing care than can be provided in a residential care home. In addition the health authority, as registration authority for nursing homes, should be advised that some residents may need to be transferred. In such circumstances it may be that dual registration as both residential care home and nursing home is justified and possible and the owner may wish to investigate this (see also Section D Chapter 29).

Much depends on the facts. It would, for example, be reasonable to care for a terminally ill resident in a residential care home for a short time, with input from the community nursing service, just as such a patient could stay in her own home. However, where it is apparent that services are required for the medium to the long term which are more appropriately provided in a nursing home, the resident should be transferred.

NURSE PRESCRIBING

The community nurse and the health visitor are the two types of registered practitioner who, after appropriate training, will be able to prescribe medicinal products. Pilot schemes are currently in place before the system is introduced throughout the country.

A nurse's formulary listing the products which can be prescribed by approved nurses has been published and can be found in the British National Formulary[10]. Further reference should be made to the works cited in Chapter 12.

CONCLUSIONS

The role of the community nurse practitioner is changing as she cares for levels of infirmity and pre-convalescent patients who ten years ago would still have been in hospital. In addition she is now supported by many specialist nurse practitioners (see Chapter 16) who supplement her services. She should be aware of the nature of their support, if available, and make full use of their specialist services. In addition she should ensure that she maintains strong links with social services workers to provide the maximum support to persons being cared for in the community. In the future she may become the employee of general practitioners. In such a situation she will have a central role in the provision of primary care.

CHAPTER 15

Community psychiatric nurses

In this chapter the term mentally disordered is used to cover two distinct client groups:

- those who suffer from a mental illness and
- those who have learning disabilities.

It is appreciated that these groups have very different needs. However there can be an overlap between the groups since some clients with learning disabilities also suffer from a mental illness. They may both be subject to the statutory provisions of the Mental Health Act 1983. It should be noted however that the definition of mentally disordered in that Act (see Chapter 4 and glossary) does not cover all those with learning disabilities. To be admitted under section 3 of this Act it must be shown that those with learning disabilities have a state of arrested or incomplete development of mind which includes significant impairment of intelligence and social functioning and is associated with abnormally aggressive or seriously irresponsible conduct. The discussion in this chapter covers a wider group than would come under section 3.

For convenience the legal aspects in relation to both groups will be considered here.

Nurses caring for these clients have had an expanding role over the last few years as the closure of institutional beds has gathered momentum. They have found themselves at the centre of the plans for community care of the mentally disordered, often without the resources to care for the patients and concerned that crisis and respite provision is inadequate to meet foreseeable problems.

The topics which will be considered in this chapter are shown in Figure 15.1.

Figure 15.1 Topics considered in this chapter

- Discharge of patients – section 117 of the Mental Health Act and after-care plans for certain detained patients.
- Section 17 of the Mental Health Act – leave of absence
- Care programme approach
- Guardianship
- Compulsory admission
- Learning disabilities and informal patient care

See also Section A, Chapter 4 and Section B, Chapters 9 and 10.

SECTION 117 MENTAL HEALTH ACT 1983

The wording of this is set out in Figure 15.2 broken down with bullet points for clarity.

Figure 15.2 Section 117 of the Mental Health Act 1983

(1) This section applies to persons who are

- detained under section 3 above [admission for treatment], or
- admitted to a hospital in pursuance of a hospital order under section 37 above, or
- transferred to a hospital in pursuance of a transfer direction made under section 47 or 48 above,
- and then cease to be detained and leave the hospital.

(2) It shall be the duty

- of the Health Authority and
- of the local social services authority
- to provide,
- in co-operation with relevant voluntary agencies,
- after-care services for any person to whom the section applies,
- until such time as the Health Authority and the local social services authority
- are satisfied
- that the person concerned
- is no longer in need of such services
- but they shall not be so satisfied if the patient is subject to after-care under supervision [added by the 1995 Act].

[(2A) added by the Mental Health (Patients in the Community) Act 1995 requires the responsible after-care bodies to ensure a patient subject to after-care under supervision is 'at all times' under a section 12 doctor and a supervisor.]

(3) In this section 'the Health Authority' means the Health Authority and 'the local social services authority' means the local social services authority for the area in which the person concerned is resident or to which he is sent on discharge by the hospital in which he was detained.

Joint formulation of after-care plans

The statutory duties under section 117 have existed since 1983 yet many authorities have delayed considerably in the formulation of joint plans for their implementation. There should now be in existence in all districts a joint health authority/local social services authority policy on the implementation of section 117. Some districts have claimed that since the advent of the care programme approach under the community care provisions of the National Health Service and Community Care Act 1990 the specific duties under section 117 can be absorbed within that programme. However, from a legal perspective, it is essential to keep clear records of which patients come under section 117 because of the specific legal requirements which exist in respect of their after-care and also in respect of the legal requirement that a decision that care is no longer required must be specifically made for each individual client.

Further guidance on the formulation of after-care plans and their implementation is given in the revised *Code of Practice: Mental Health Act 1983*[11].

Involvement and responsibilities of the community nurse

The community nurse should be involved in the discharge planning and treatment plan for the patient, preferably from before admission. Increasingly community nurses are sharing accommodation with locality teams set up by social services and mental health teams across the boundaries of the statutory services which are attempting to provide a seamless service for patients. In addition they regularly attend ward rounds, are involved in the care of the patient whilst an in-patient and are central to the multi-disciplinary discussions on after-care arrangements.

Situation

The responsible medical officer (RMO) in considering the future treatment of a patient is mindful of the pressure on beds and patients awaiting urgent admission. He therefore presses for the immediate discharge of a patient who is a chronic schizophrenic, who has a long history of breakdown in the community and who had been admitted under section 3 which had been ended when his condition improved. The community psychiatric nurse is aware of the lack of facilities in the community for this patient and has considerable doubts about his ability to cope if he is discharged.

She warns against the dangers to the patient and to others if the premature discharge is made. The RMO ignores her views and the patient is discharged. A few days later, it is learnt that he has been admitted to the accident and emergency department after an attempted suicide. Where does the nurse stand?

In this situation the RMO has the ultimate responsibility for determining whether a patient should be discharged. If his decision is negligent, then he could face civil proceedings for compensation by the patient, or relatives on behalf of the patient. The nurse is likely to be called to give evidence in the civil court hearing on the condition of the patient before discharge. It is essential that her records are comprehensive and clear to enable her to answer detailed questions (see Chapter 11). The nurse must also be prepared to show that she took all reasonable steps to ensure the safety of the patient once she realised that his condition was deteriorating.

Co-operation with other agencies

Section 117 requires the health authority and the local social services authority to co-operate with relevant voluntary agencies in providing after-care. However, they cannot delegate the statutory duty which remains theirs.

Enforcement of section 117 duty

Case: R v. *Ealing District Health Authority, ex parte Fox*[12]
A restricted patient was given a conditional discharge by a Mental Health Review Tribunal, the discharge being deferred until the Tribunal was satisfied that a consultant psychiatrist was appointed to act as the patient's RMO. Neither the consultant forensic psychiatrist nor the consultant general psychiatrist for the patient's home area were prepared to act as the RMO for the patient. The general manager of the health authority accordingly wrote to the patient. The patient then applied to the court seeking a judicial review of the health authority's failure to provide an RMO. The judge held that the health authority had erred in law in not attempting with all reasonable expedition and diligence to make arrangements so as to enable the patient to comply with the conditions laid down by the Tribunal. The court did not, however,

make an order for mandamus (see glossary) which would have compelled the health authority to provide psychiatric supervision in the community for the patient.

The court clearly recognised that the duties under section 117 are enforceable against both authorities and it is likely that there will be further recourse to this provision if after-care arrangements under section 117 are not planned or provided (see further Chapter 27).

Ending of section 117 duty

The duty comes to an end when the patient dies, or when the health authority and the local social services authority are satisfied that the person concerned is no longer in need of such services. They cannot be so satisfied if the patient is subject to after-care under supervision under the 1995 Act.

To indicate that the person no longer requires such services necessitates a clear decision on the part of officers of both authorities. This should be based on sufficient evidence and clearly recorded.

■ What if the person refuses to receive services – does this discharge the duty owed under the section?

The answer to this must be 'no'. Whilst it is true that after-care services cannot be forced upon the person, the duty still exists as long as a need is considered to exist. Whilst the duty is not enforceable against the person, records should be kept of the person to ensure that he is not lost sight of, since at some later stage his refusal to accept help might change.

Transfer of patients

Where a patient moves from one social services authority to another the section 117 responsibilities are transferred to the new social services authority.

The future

The Mental Health (Patients in the Community) Act 1995 came into force on 1 April 1996. This is discussed in Chapter 4.

SECTION 17 LEAVE OF ABSENCE OF A DETAINED PATIENT

In the situation described above, it might have been preferable if the possibility of giving the patient leave under section 17 of the Mental Health Act 1983 had been considered. However, the need to create an empty bed is not a justification for section 17 leave.

The grant of section 17 leave

Section 17 enables the RMO to grant any patient who is for the time being liable to be detained in a hospital leave to be absent from the hospital subject to such conditions (if any) as that officer considers necessary in the interests of the patient or for the protection of other persons.

Leave can be granted for the remainder of the period of detention or on specified occasions or for any specified period which can be extended up to the time of the detention.

Leave does not necessarily mean freedom for the detained patient, since it could simply be leave to go to another institution where the patient would still be kept in custody. This provision has been used by the special hospitals and regional secure units to enable a patient to stay in less secure accommodation. It should not be used as a substitute for discharge from the section.

Where leave is granted under the section it should be in writing and signed by the RMO (this is not a statutory requirement but would be good practice) and good practice should allow the community nurse to have a copy of the section 17 approval form. She should, in any case, have been involved in the discussions which led to section 17 leave being granted. Where the leave permits the detained patient to remain in the community with the family or in other non-secure accommodation, the nurse should ensure that she monitors the situation and when necessary alerts the RMO and the ward.

Situation

A patient is given section 17 leave on condition that he lives with his parents and continues to receive his injections which are given every two weeks by the community nurse. On one visit she is told by the patient that he is well and no longer requires the medication. She explains that he feels better because of the medication but he needs to continue to take it. He does not accept this and is supported by his parents. Where does she stand?

There are no powers for her to enforce his taking of the medication. Even if he is subject to a second medical recommendation under section 58 of the Act (which means that medication can be given against his will) she could not compulsorily force him to have the medication in the community. Since the refusal of medication is likely to lead to a decline in the patient's condition it is her duty to inform the RMO who could if he wishes exercise the powers of recall under section 17(4). Reference should be made to the revised *Code of Practice* for guidance on the use of section 17.

Recall of patient from section 17 leave

Section 17(4) is set out in Figure 15.3.

Figure 15.3 Recall of patient

17(4) In any case where a patient is absent from a hospital in pursuance of leave of absence granted under this section, and it appears to the responsible medical officer that it is necessary so to do in the interests of the patient's health or safety or for the protection of other persons, that officer may, subject to subsection (5) below, by notice in writing given to the patient or to the person for the time being in charge of the patient, revoke the leave of absence and recall the patient to the hospital.

■ What if the patient does not keep to the conditions of the leave of absence?

This may be grounds for recalling the patient under section 17(4) but the requirements of that subsection would have to be satisfied as shown in Figure 15.3.

It is not possible to use the power to recall if the patient has ceased to be liable to be detained. Nor can this power be used if the intention is not that the patient should return to hospital but so that the section could be renewed. This was the ruling in the case of *R* v. *Hallstrom*[13]. An after-care supervision order which enables a patient to be subject to review, but not recall, has been available since April 1996 (see Chapter 4).

CARE PROGRAMME APPROACH

This initiative under the NHS and Community Care Act 1990 incorporates a much wider group of clients than the narrow group of detained patients covered by section 117. Further details of the scheme and the responsibilities of social services are given in Chapter 25.

Just as in the discussions under section 117, the community nurse for the mentally ill and those with learning disabilities should be working closely with the social services authority, with other health professionals and with the voluntary sector and private sector.

Section 47 of the 1990 Act requires an assessment to be made and for many mentally disordered persons a joint health/social services assessment would be required to identify their needs. This should be more than a paper exercise: not only is it essential to determine the needs and the extent to which they can be met for each individual client, it is also part of the strategic planning. As a result of the assessments it should be possible to identify priorities and also deficiencies in service provision. For example it may be possible to show that if more day places were available and more respite beds it could be possible for more mentally ill persons to live outside institutional accommodation or not require any form of in-patient care.

GUARDIANSHIP

Whilst some social service authorities have made good use of guardianship there has in general been little use of the powers under these provisions of the Mental Health Act 1983. One reason is said to be the lack of effective power of a guardian under the Act. The statutory powers are shown in Figure 15.4.

Figure 15.4 Powers of a guardian – section 8(1) of the Mental Health Act 1983

(a) the power to require the patient to reside at a place specified by the authority or person named as guardian;
(b) the power to require the patient to attend at places and times so specified for the purpose of medical treatment, occupation, education or training;
(c) the power to require access to the patient to be given, at any place where the patient is residing, to any registered medical practitioner, approved social worker or other person so specified.

These powers are limited and, apart from the right to return the patient to the specified place under section 18(3), unenforceable. The provisions of section 18(3) are set out in Figure 15.5.

Figure 15.6 Section 18(3) of the Mental Health Act 1983

Where a patient who is for the time being subject to guardianship under this Part of this Act absents himself without the leave of the guardian from the place at which he is required by the guardian to reside, he may, subject to the provisions of this section, be taken into custody and returned to that place by any constable, or by any person authorised in writing by the guardian or a local social services authority.

The community nurse for the mentally disordered is likely to have a key role in the care of patients under guardianship. She may well be required to visit them to administer medication as well as carry out assessments, provide advice, liaise with other officers and so on.

COMPULSORY ADMISSION

Less than 10 per cent of those patients who are treated for mental disorder in hospital are admitted under a compulsory section. The emphasis of the Mental Health Act 1983 is to enable patients to remain in the community or, if admission as an inpatient is necessary, it should be on the basis of informal admission. Only in exceptional circumstances should admission under section be used. It is therefore a rare occurrence for a community nurse for the mentally disordered to be involved in compulsory admission of a patient but it could happen. This presents the nurse with considerable problems. She is likely to be extremely rusty on the procedures which are necessary yet she may have to act in an emergency where there is less opportunity to seek advice. She therefore needs to keep up to date on the law and the procedures which should be followed[14].

She should be aware of the provisions of the main sections for admission, she should have a copy of the revised *Code of Practice* published by the Department of Health and she should attend refresher courses. The main admission provisions are shown in Chapter 4.

Her regular contact with clients, especially those with chronic conditions, may make it possible to foresee the deterioration of their conditions and enable her to take early action which could lead to informal admission or involve the consultant psychiatrist at an early stage. In addition, her regular contact with the psychiatric wards and a good infrastructure of community/day care support may enable some compulsory admissions to be avoided.

Whilst the community nurse for the mentally disordered has no statutory part to play in the compulsory admission of the patient, she may well play a key role in bringing in the relevant disciplines at the appropriate time and will probably be the first community professional to be aware of the need for action. She should ensure that she maintains contact with the relevant approved social workers if they are not organised on the same locality grouping as the health care professionals as described above. She should also be aware of the definition of nearest relative under the Mental Health Act 1983 and who would be regarded as this person for her clients. The statutory definition is set out in Figures 4.14 and 4.15 in Chapter 4 and the powers of the nearest relative set out in Figure 4.16 of the same chapter. She may also be appointed as the supervisor of a patient subject to after-care under supervision.

LEARNING DISABILITIES AND INFORMAL PATIENT CARE

The community nurse for those with learning disabilities has a diverse role and increasingly there is a tendency for the care of those with learning disabilities to be seen as not requiring nursing skills. Those appointed to work in community homes for those with learning disabilities frequently do not have nursing qualifications. There is a danger that the skills which were developed by registered nurses for those with learning disabilities whilst these clients were cared for in institutions will be lost. Whilst it is true that these clients are not 'ill', their care requires considerable skills and understanding and staff are not necessarily receiving the training for this at present.

At the present time there is a public debate[15] on the future educational needs for these professionals. A paper putting forward five options was presented by David Simes at a consensus conference. The Department of Health responded by a statement given in a press release which supported the option of a two stage assimilation of the pre-qualifying nurse training programme for mental handicap nursing within the child, adult and mental health branches of Project 2000 and within the revised post-qualifying framework.

The choice of this option has not met with unconditional support. It is vital however that an early decision should be made on the skills required to care for this group of clients since, as the number of community homes for those with learning disabilities increases, there is a danger that there will not be sufficient professional staff with the skills required to maintain a high standard of living for the clients. Community care puts considerable pressures upon the staff who do not have the supporting services which they were accustomed to have in the institutions. The legal responsibility for the provision of properly qualified staff would rest with the owners and managers of the homes and, if harm occurs to residents or to others as a result of negligence in this respect, litigation could commence in the civil courts.

Community homes for those with learning disabilities

Very few of these homes will be caring for clients who are detained under the Mental Health Act 1983. However they face problems in relation to the control of those with challenging behaviour and there is a possibility that restraint, seclusion and other devices might be used against these clients illegally.

Informal patients cannot be detained against their will, or be given treatment by force – apart from very exceptional circumstances when the common law recognises that action out of necessity can be taken. The powers which were described by the House of Lords in *Re F* (see glossary and Chapter 3) apply essentially when the client is not competent to make a decision and the professional would be authorised to act in the best interests of the client following the Bolam test (see glossary and Chapter 7). However there is no consensus that such powers could be used against an unwilling incompetent patient except in an emergency. For example if a client with learning disabilities was about to run out of the house onto a dangerous road, it would be lawful for the carer to save the client from an accident by returning him to the home. However, if detention were required for any significant period it is essential that statutory powers should be called upon. Helpful advice on the management of the informal patient is given in paragraph 18.27 of the revised *Code of Practice: Mental Health Act 1983*[16].

This same principle applies to the locking of doors and the use of other forms of restraint. It is preferable, if adequate staffing levels are provided, to ensure maximum supervision of the clients rather than the use of restraint belts, locks, and other sinister forms of control.

Similar rules apply to the use of seclusion. Used against an informal patient/client (that is one who is not detained under the Act) it may be an unlawful form of false imprisonment. Any home which had to resort to such methods should radically review its clientele and consider whether protection of the clients under the Act should be provided.

At present there is a vacuum in the law relating to the giving of consent to treatment or research by the mentally incompetent adult. Thus if a person with learning disabilities required dental surgery there is no-one eligible to give consent on his behalf. The professional would have to act out of necessity in the best interests of the client and follow the Bolam test (see Chapter 3). This is further discussed in the Chapter 4 where the consultation document of the Law Commission[17] is considered.

CHAPTER 16

Specialist nurses

There are a growing number of nurses providing nursing care in highly specialist areas. They include stoma care nurses, diabetic nurses, breast care nurses, paediatric nurses, continence adviser nurses, nurses for the care of the terminally ill, palliative care nurses and wound care advisers. This chapter will consider some of the specific legal issues which specialists encounter. The general information in the other chapters will also be relevant to them. Reference must also be made to specific law works which cover their duties and responsibilities[18].

Specialist nurses have an important role to play in the multi-disciplinary team providing community care. Because of their services many patients who would have required continuing hospital care are able to be discharged earlier and enjoy the benefits of being at home whilst continuing to receive specialist help. Problems can arise however in a number of areas and these are set out in Figure 16.1.

Figure 16.1 Issues covered in this chapter

- The role of the carer/client *vis-à-vis* the specialist
- Training and role definition
- External pressures
- Equipment issues
- Resources
- Care of the dying and pain relief

ROLE OF THE CARER/CLIENT *VIS-À-VIS* THE SPECIALIST

There is a growing development of giving highly specialist tasks to the carers or clients themselves to perform following some instruction by hospital or community staff. This however can give rise to legal issues.

Liability for errors

Situation

A child with a chronic chest condition was discharged from hospital on the understanding that the mother would administer the intravenous antibiotics. She was given some instruction at the hospital and told that the community paediatric nurse would visit her to ensure that she was undertaking it correctly. She was not given any instructions in writing.

The mother proceeded to give the medicines at home, mixing the antibiotics with the saline or water solution as appropriate. The community pediatric nurse attended and failed to notice that the mother had been told to give the wrong dosage of one antibiotic – 2 grams rather than 1/2 gram. The community nurse did not ask to see the patient's copy of the prescribed medication. She checked that the mother was following a sterile technique and said she would call back in a few days to see the progress of the child. The child developed a rash and initially the mother assumed that it was something she had eaten and did not take her into hospital and make enquiries. However the child then became seriously ill and was admitted to hospital where the type and level of antibiotics were queried and the mistake then noticed. Where does the community paediatric nurse stand?

In a situation such as this analysing the respective responsibilities of community as opposed to hospital staff can be difficult if this has not been defined in advance. Where clients, parents or other carers are given tasks which the professional staff would normally have carried out it is essential that the carers/clients are given sufficient information to enable the clients to be safe. In this situation there has clearly been an error by the doctor in writing a prescription for an excessive dose and by the pharmacist in either dispensing the wrong medication or in failing to notice the error by the doctor.

■ Should the community nurse have spotted the overdose?

The answer would depend upon

● the age of the child;
● how clear it was that the dose was excessive;
● whether the nurse should routinely look at the client's copy of the prescription; and (if so)

● whether she would have spotted the error (judged by the approved standard of her profession).

Some assistance is given by the case of *Dwyer* v. *Roderick* which is discussed in Chapter 12 and below.

The other failure which this situation highlights is the weakness of communication between the professionals and the carer, both at hospital and in the community, and between the professionals themselves. The procedure to be followed by the mother should have been put in writing as well as being explained to her by word of mouth. The explanation should have included warnings about adverse signs to look for and what action should be taken. The hospital should have ensured that she was told of the rash and its significance. The community nurse should also not have assumed that the mother knew the significance of such signs as a rash appearing. Failure to communicate effectively can be as much a breach of the duty of care as an action which causes harm.

 What if the mother has signed an exclusion clause as is shown in Figure 16.2?

Figure 16.2 Exclusion clause

I . . . . . being the parent of . . . . . do agree that I have received instruction on the administration of intravenous antibiotics at home. I hereby willingly agree that I am prepared to administer the drugs and not to hold the . . . . . NHS trust its employees servants or agents responsible for any harm which arises.

Signed . . . . .   Date . . . . .

Such a form would only be effective if there has been no negligence by the NHS Trust staff. If there has been negligence (as when they failed to warn her to look for any adverse signs or prescribed an overdose of the drug) then the effect of the Unfair Contract Terms Act is to prevent the exclusion of liability where it results in personal injury or death. This Act is discussed in Chapter 9. Good practice should ensure that a note to that effect is written upon the form the carer is asked to sign so that she is not misled. It could also be pointed out that the form does not affect any statutory or common law rights of the patient.

Where there is uncertainty by the community professional as to what information the client or carer has been given then there would be a duty on her part to discover any gaps in the patient's understanding.

Instructing others

In delegating to the client or carer tasks which would normally be carried out by others, it is essential that note is taken of the capacity of the carer or client to follow the instructions accurately and to understand the dangers of harm occurring. If the view is formed by the community specialist that the carer or client is incapable of undertaking these tasks safely then alternative provision must be made.

Situation

Kate is an elderly lady who has suffered from diabetes for many years. She attends the clinic at the hospital and is also visited by the diabetic nurse. On one visit the nurse noticed that Kate's sugar count is up and she seems to be in a volatile mood. She questions her about taking the injections and suspects that Kate has been neglecting herself and has failed to give herself the appropriate injections.

In a situation such as this the nurse would probably arrange for Kate to be seen by the doctor and might well suggest that a nurse should call regularly to administer the injections to Kate. If she ignores the situation and trusts to luck that Kate is coping and if Kate eventually suffers harm, then the nurse may well be held liable for failing to take the appropriate action to protect her.

Conflicting advice

One aspect which can cause concern to clients is where there is conflicting advice from professionals, and especially where one professional openly disagrees with advice that another has given and advises the client to ignore it.

Situation

A wound care specialist visited a client recently discharged after major surgery where the wound had not completely healed. The client was able to undertake her own dressings and the wound care adviser recommended that the wound should be dressed in a particular way using a particular solution. The patient was subsequently visited by a community nurse who, on hearing of the advice by the wound specialist, told the client that the particular procedure recommended was not necessary and suggested that the client should dress the wound in a different way. The client took the advice of the community nurse. When the wound specialist visited the client some time later, she was concerned to discover that her advice had been overruled, especially as the wound had still not healed. What is the legal situation?

This situation does, of course, reveal extremely poor practice in professional relationships. No professional should contradict the advice given by another unless it is clearly wrong and likely to cause harm to the client. In this case it would have been preferable for the community nurse, knowing that the client had been visited by a specialist in wound management, to have made a point of seeking out that specialist and discussing with her the treatment if she was sure that the wrong advice had been given. This would enable the wound specialist to visit the patient again and advise her accordingly.

Only if there were immediate danger to the client should the community nurse halt the treatment recommended by another professional. Such a situation might arise if, unknown to the wound adviser, the patient was allergic to a particular substance, or if the patient was diabetic and the wound adviser did not take this into account in her advice.

■ What is the legal situation should the patient suffer harm as a result of following the advice of the community nurse rather that staying with the instructions of the specialist?

If the community nurse had failed to follow the responsible professional practice in the advice she gave the client then she may well be held liable if her instructions had led to harm. Her employers would be vicariously liable for the harm which had been caused.

On the other hand, if the wound specialist had given the wrong advice and for the client to follow those instructions would be dangerous, then the failure of the nurse to take appropriate steps could lead to her being liable. It would have to be established by the plaintiff that any reasonable nurse following the accepted professional standard would have taken immediate action and also that it would have been reasonable for her to have spotted the mistake.

In such cases of multi-disciplinary involvement in patient care it is essential to designate who is responsible for the care of the patient and to what extent (see below).

The liability of a second doctor who visited a patient who had been given the wrong medication was canvassed in the case of *Dwyer* v. *Roderick and Others* (see Chapter 12, page 209). It was held on appeal that, on the facts of this particular case, the second doctor was not liable for failing to realise the mistake in the prescription, but 15% of the liability had been attributed to him by the trial judge and there was a strong dissenting judgment in the Court of Appeal.

Case: *Dwyer* v. *Roderick and others* (on appeal)

The facts, given in Chapter 12, concerned negligently prescribed medication. The trial judge found all the professionals involved liable. The percentages were: Dr Roderick (the prescribing doctor) 45%, Dr Jackson (the second doctor who had visited the patient) 15% and the pharmacist 40%. Dr Jackson appealed against this decision and his share of the £100 000 damages. The Court of Appeal allowed his appeal by a majority decision. It was not established that there was a bottle of Migril tablets by the side of the patient's bed and Dr Jackson's evidence that it was his normal practice to ask the patient what drugs she was on could not be rejected.

The dissenting judge (Lord Justice Dillon), however, put the issues very clearly:

1. Either the bottle was on the table or it was not on the table.
2. If it was on the table, Dr Jackson was negligent in overlooking it and not reading the label. If it was not on the table, Dr Jackson ought to have asked Mrs Dwyer whether she was taking any other drugs, and he was negligent if he did not ask her.
3. If Dr Jackson had asked her whether she was taking any other drugs she would either have answered 'Yes' or 'No'. On the general evidence of Dr Jackson as to his visit to her, there was no question of her answering incoherently or being unable to answer at all. If she had answered that she was taking other drugs, Dr Jackson was negligent in that he did not find out what the other drugs were.

This view was not accepted by the majority and therefore Dr Jackson was found not to be negligent.

One difficulty of the case was that the facts took place in November 1973 but the hearing of the High Court was not held till 10 February 1982. Witnesses, the defendants and the plaintiff were therefore being questioned about facts which took place more than eight years before.

Lord Justice May complained of the delay and said:

> After the passage of so many years the task of witnesses, and that of the court, is extremely difficult. After so long the memories of witnesses are bound to have faded; even the most honest human recollection may be rendered inaccurate, may be distorted by natural and understandable rationalisation or by subsequent experiences, or indeed by both. After so long it is almost inevitable that, however truthful a witness may be trying to be, at least part of his evidence will be inaccurate.

The lesson for every professional entering the home of a client who is being visited by other professionals is that there is a duty of care owed to the patient by all of them and if it is reasonable that they should be aware of errors in the care given then there could be liability. This does not turn each professional into a watchdog for others, but it does mean that there must be communication between those who visit the client. Fortunately the development of community teams and the identification of key workers should assist in ensuring that the clients receive a service where there is maximum communication between all different community professionals.

TRAINING AND ROLE DEFINITION

The *Scope of Professional Practice* enables practitioners to develop their skills and competencies on the basis of the six key principles set out in Figure 8.2. There is, however, a personal liability upon the practitioner to ensure that she has the knowledge, skill and competence to undertake the tasks which she is called upon to perform. Most of those nurses who undertake specialist roles in the community do so on the basis of an approved course of instruction. However, there is a danger that some nurses, especially those employed by general practitioners or by health service bodies who give a low priority to training, may find that they are asked to carry out functions for which they are ill-equipped.

Situation

An out-patient nurse, who worked on the surgical clinic and assisted patients who came to Out Patients for stoma examination, was asked to work in the community visiting former patients to reduce the need for them to have hospital care. She had received no specific training in stoma care and was concerned that she would not be able to perform the task appropriately. She was reassured by the doctor who told her that there was nothing to it and she could carry out the work on the basis of what she already knew. Where does she stand if she makes a mistake in advising the client?

One of the difficulties which confront practitioners as a result of the UKCC paper on the *Scope of Professional Practice* is how, without certification, does the nurse know when she is competent – as in the situation above. Clearly in that case the nurse needs to ask those already practising as stoma nurses about the instruction they have received and the areas which they have covered in order to determine whether her own experience in the Out Patient Clinic has fitted her for work in the community in this field. She could, for example, before accepting the doctor's assurances that she is competent, ask for leave to spend time with stoma care practitioners visiting their clients and also check with the training schools the content of specialist courses. If she continues to have doubts over her knowledge, skill and competence to undertake the work safely then she should refuse to carry it out until she has received the appropriate training.

If she should take on the new role and, through ignorance and inexperience, gives the wrong advice or treatment to the patient then she will be personally and professionally accountable for the harm which results.

Nurses who work for individual general practitioners are particularly vulnerable to the pressure to work outside their field of competence and, if they have not completed the necessary length of continuous service, may face the possibility of dismissal without any right to apply to an industrial tribunal. If sufficient notice has been given to them, they cannot take an action in the civil court for wrongful dismissal. It would, however, be theoretically possible for the nurse to have written into her contract at the outset terms covering the GP's responsibility in connection with training.

Communications between the general practitioner and the specialist nurse can sometimes cause difficulties. The latter might be the employee of the general practitioner(s) or she might be employed by an NHS Trust or directly managed unit. The following situation typifies the problems which can arise.

Situation

A wound care specialist found that a wound was healing particularly slowly and thought that the client might be suffering from a protein deficiency. She suggested to the general practitioner that the client should have a blood test to check protein levels but the general practitioner decided that this should not be done. The specialist would have liked to recommend protein supplements if it was found that there was a deficiency. These would have to be prescribed by the doctor who was unwilling also to do this. What is the legal situation?

A community professional would care for patients who come under the direct responsibility of either a general practitioner or a consultant. If there is a conflict between a health professional and the doctor who has clinical responsibility for the client/patient, it is essential that the community professional puts her concerns clearly to the doctor and, if the doctor does not accept her recommendations, she should record these recommendations in writing. Registered Nurse practitioners have the UKCC advice in *Exercising Accountability*[19] to guide them. Professions supplementary to medicine would follow similar advice.

In the above situation, if the patient were to suffer harm as a result of the doctor's failure to identify protein deficiency, the fact that the wound specialist advised a blood test to be taken and protein supplements to be given would probably relieve her of legal liability. It would clearly be essential for the wound specialist to put her recommendations in writing and to use all possible means to persuade the doctor to arrange for the necessary tests to be taken.

This situation is discussed on the basis that only the general practitioner can request blood samples to be taken and analyzed. If this is not the case, then the wound specialist could make her own arrangements for the tests to be made and for the results to be shown to the doctor.

WHAT IF THE NURSE IS SUBJECT TO EXTERNAL PRESSURES?

Other pressures can be applied to the nurse and this is so particularly where the nurse is paid by a pharmaceutical company to provide a certain specialist service in a particular locality.

Situation

A nurse specialising in continence advice was appointed by a Community Trust from funds given by manufacturers of an enuretic alarm. Her job description required her to visit families where children suffered from incontinence and give advice on how to solve it. The clients were referred to her from the general practitioners or health visitors. Many were fairly wealthy and the firm who provided the funds expected the nurse to recommend their products for purchase by the parents. There were a few alarms which were available from the Community Trust without payment, but these were in short supply. The nurse discovered that unfortunately there appeared to be a defect in the products sold by the firm which required costly maintenance and repairs and she felt that she could not recommend them. She ceased to hand out the leaflets relating to the firm's products and instead, if she was asked to recommend an alarm, she named a rival firm. Her employers are now threatening to sack her.

Not surprising one may think, but where does the nurse's duty lie? Does she have a greater professional duty to her client than the duty to the firm which is providing funds for her employment? The situation is complicated by the fact that her employers are the Community Trust, not the manufacturers. Her job security rests on the nature of the contract which she has with the NHS Trust. It may be that her job was meant to continue even when that source of funds failed. There is no doubt, however, that she has a professional duty towards the patient/client which would take precedence over the duty owed to the employer and the firm.

If, for example, the alarm actually caused harm to a child and the nurse knew that there was this possibility because of the defect, then, if she continued to recommend it, she could be held liable for negligence in the civil courts (though in practice her employer would be held vicariously liable) and guilty of professional misconduct (that is conduct unworthy of a nurse) before the

Professional Conduct Committee of the UKCC. She may also be liable as a supplier under the Consumer Protection Act (see Chapter 10) and would have to pass on to the client the name and details of the manufacturer of the equipment.

There may be other occasions when there is a clash because the purchasers of a nurse's services expect particular actions from her or for her to give specific advice. In such cases the nurse has to ensure that her duty of care to the patient is paramount even though she personally stands to lose her job. For example clinic nurses may find that the manufacturers of baby foods and so on expect them to promote their products in the baby clinics. They might even encourage this process by leaving gifts, providing refreshments, and other benefits. Giving in to such pressures is clearly contrary to the *Code of Professional Conduct* of the UKCC. Reference should also be made to official advice on the requirement that Trusts should notify purchasers of sponsorship of clinical staff by any independent company which is a significant provider of goods and services to the NHS[20].

Another difficulty in this area is the situation where free supplies are given by manufacturers to practitioners who are then expected to give them out to clients. For the most part this is harmless, but there are dangers. Are the practitioners thereby warranting that the products are recommended? If there are defects in them the practitioner may be regarded as the supplier for the purposes of consumer protection legislation. For example it is alleged that some fruit and herbal drinks which are given to babies can cause tooth decay. If mothers have received such products from nurses in their clinics, could the nurses be held accountable? The answer is probably 'yes', unless the nurse has given explicit instructions on how tooth decay should be avoided (for example, never giving the drink undiluted in a comforter).

EQUIPMENT ISSUES

Keeping track of equipment

The specialist nurse in the community might be providing clients with equipment, which in some cases is costly, for use in their homes. Such equipment remains the property of the health services and responsibilities for maintenance and care should be clearly defined. It should be returned to the health service body when the patient no longer requires it.

Situation

Macmillan nurses were caring for a young man who was terminally ill at home. He died shortly after three o'clock one morning and they were called in. After laying out the body, they collected up all the property which had been lent to the family, including the lambs wool blanket, the lambs wool ankle protectors, the drip stand, the nebuliser and the fan. The family subsequently protested that they had removed equipment which had been purchased by the family for the patient's use and did not belong to the health service.

The removal of equipment in such circumstances must be undertaken with extreme sensitivity, the timing, the method and the means of identification of what belongs to whom are important factors in ensuring minimum upset. Records should be maintained to identify which property has been loaned by the health service, social services or other agency and the equipment should be marked to prevent any mistakes arising. It is distressing for the family to cope with the death without having a battle to recover property which should never have been removed from the house.

Maintenance of equipment

Where property is lent by the health or social services or any other body it is essential to clarify responsibilities in respect of inspection and maintenance (see further Chapter 8).

Situation

A nebuliser was lent to a family where the wife suffered from a chronic lung condition. She received prescriptions for the drugs for nebulising from her general practitioner. She regularly cleaned the equipment. One day she received an electric shock from the equipment and, following enquiries, it was learnt that the nebuliser had not been serviced in the eight years she had been using it. The general practitioner who prescribed the drugs assumed that the hospital who owned the property was maintaining it; the hospital had assumed that she had ceased to use it and had no record that the equipment was still in use at her home.

This is not an unusual situation even though it might not take as long as eight years to track down the equipment. The liability would probably rest with the hospital whose equipment it was to keep a check on its use and ensure that it was regularly serviced and inspected. Figure 16.3 sets out the *minimum* information which should be kept relating to equipment on loan to patients.

Figure 16.3 Equipment on loan

- The identity of the equipment – make, number, manufacturer and any distinguishing features
- Date of loan
- Name and address of borrower
- Dates of inspections and records of action taken
- Date return requested
- Department and name of individual who authorised its loan

Further discussion on the legal issues relating to equipment for home use can be found in Chapter 8.

RESOURCES

Specialist practitioners in the community face the same problems in relation to staffing levels and other resources as their colleagues working in institutions. They are under the same professional duty to 'report to an appropriate person or authority, having regard to the physical, psychological and social effects on patients and clients, any circumstances in the environment of care which could jeopardise standards of practice'. (Rule 11 *Code of Professional Conduct* UKCC.) A similar duty exists in Rules 12 and 13.

One problem which confronts the practitioner who points out inadequacies to the managers is what action she can take if there is no positive response from the managers to her report. This topic is discussed in Chapter 7 in relation to freedom of speech.

CARE OF THE DYING AND PAIN RELIEF

Those practitioners who specialise in the care of the dying may be employed by health service bodies such as health authorities or NHS Trusts, a charity or voluntary group, or a private trust. They face particular problems in relation to the level of medication for pain relief and working with other disciplines. Often, for example, the general practitioner may be happy to leave the day to day contact with the client with the specialist nurse relying upon the latter to let him know when his intervention is necessary or when another prescription is required. The decisions on the quantity of pain relieving drugs to be given is left to the discretion of the practitioner on a PRN basis within the maximum which has been prescribed by the doctor.

Provided that the purpose of the drug is the alleviation of pain, the fact that it might incidentally shorten life will not be grounds for prosecution if death occurs. However if the intention is to cause the death of the patient and put an end to the suffering then, if the patient dies as a result of the drug, a prosecution for causing the death of the patient may succeed.

Case: *R* v. *Cox*[21]

The case of Dr Nigel Cox illustrates the law on this issue. He was prosecuted for causing the death of a patient by giving her potassium chloride. His defence was that this terminally ill patient was in so much pain that, with the agreement of her children, he wished to relieve her of her suffering. He was convicted and given a suspended sentence. His case was also heard by the General Medical Council who did not strike him from the register but recommended that he should receive further training, especially in pain relief. His employers, the Wessex Regional Health Authority held disciplinary proceedings but did not dismiss him from his post. Thus he was held accountable in three different forums.

Subsequently the House of Lords Select Committee on Medical Ethics has confirmed that there should be no change in the law relating to euthanasia and mercy killing should not be recognised in law[22]. This is further discussed in Chapter 3. The practitioner in this area needs to be aware of the legal context within which she works and the fact that, should she be asked by a client to assist in her death, to do so would be a criminal act of aiding and abetting a suicide. On the other hand a mentally competent person has the right in law to refuse even life-saving treatment. This also is further discussed in Chapter 3.

Pain relief and palliative care

It is debateable whether a person has a legal right to enforce the services necessary to be free of pain. This may not be scientifically possible and, even when it is, there is no absolute right to obtain health service care immediately. Many chronic pain sufferers are dependent upon the services of community staff. Increasingly however NHS Trusts are setting up specialist clinics to provide diagnosis and relief. It is essential that the community practitioner is aware of the services and specialisms which are available locally and that she ensures that the client and carer also receives all possible support. Knowledge, too, of the social security benefits which are payable to those who are sick or disabled or terminally ill is also important (see Chapter 33).

CONCLUSION

Not all the specialist health tasks in the community can be discussed in this chapter. The general principles of accountability set out in Chapters 7 and 8 apply to them all.

CHAPTER 17

Health visitors

The issues to be covered in this chapter are set out in Figure 17.1.

Figure 17.1   Issues covered in this chapter
- Court appearances/statements and record keeping
- Statutory duty to visit
- Prevention and health education role
- Liability for negligent advice
- Protecting the elderly from abuse
- Prescribing

COURT APPEARANCES/STATEMENTS AND RECORD KEEPING

Of those professionals who work in the community the health visitor is the most likely to be involved with the police and the courts. She needs to be prepared to be cross-examined on her work and her clients and to ensure that her records and the statements she makes not only are the best in terms of client care, but also provide her with the necessary protection should the occasion arise.

Being subpoenaed

In the past health visitors have taken the view that they will not voluntarily offer information to the courts and the police against their clients. If their evidence was required in court then they would wait for the subpoena (see glossary) to be served upon them. In this way they were able to preserve the relationship of trust which they had developed with the client. However this view is changing. The Children Act 1989 makes the welfare of the child of paramount consideration and this may mean volunteering evidence before the court. The client is after all the child and the health visitor must act in the best interests of the child.

Suspicions of child abuse

If they fear that a child under their care is a victim of non-accidental circumstances, they have a professional and legal duty to report any suspicions of abuse in accordance with the provisions of the Children Act and the procedures laid down by the Area Protection Committee[23].

As soon as such suspicions arise it is essential that they keep very comprehensive records of all actions they take. This will include making a full record of any telephone calls they make and receive – the date, the caller, the contents and the outcome. Such information is essential if there is ever a subsequent enquiry or court case and even when there are no further court proceedings there is a professional duty to maintain high standards of record keeping.

The records of visits must be detailed and meaningful. It is essential that the health visitor does all she can to ensure that the child is reasonably safe. She must work with the social services in taking advantage of the provisions of the Children Act 1989. Further reference can be made to the Chapter 11 on record keeping. The health visitor will be expected to contribute to case conferences with social services and other professionals. The procedure is often now to include the parents of the child and clear records must be kept of these discussions and the agreed action.

Statements

■ Can the health visitor refuse to make a statement?

If the police are investigating the abuse of a child the health visitor should co-operate in their investigations. It is highly desirable for her to make a statement as soon as possible and she should seek help in the compiling of the statement from her senior manager or the solicitor to her employer. She should read through her notes and make sure that the statement is factually correct and there is no inconsistency with her records. She should make sure that she reads it over and asks for changes to be made until she is absolutely 100 per cent satisfied with it and is prepared to sign it.

This is essential, since not only herself, but also the prosecution lawyers in a criminal case, are likely to be heavily dependent upon this statement in any court hearing. The health visitor would wish to feel confident of its accuracy or completeness. She will be extremely vulnerable in any cross-examination if there are any flaws in the statement or inconsistencies between her records and the statement.

A contemporaneous statement can be used in court as an aid to memory, although it can be looked at by the other side. She can also take her case notes into court.

In other cases where she is asked to provide a statement, such as in disciplinary proceedings against a colleague, she should take advice about the appropriateness of providing one and, if it is considered that a statement is advisable, she should seek assistance in compiling it.

■ Whose side is the health visitor on?

When the health visitor is summoned to court as a witness of fact, she should not see herself as partisan. She must give her evidence truthfully and fully without feeling that she is letting down one side or the other. She is not there to secure a conviction nor is she there to defend a client. She is in court to give an unbiased, detached, truthful and professional account of the events which are the subject of the hearing. If she adopts this approach she is likely to feel less tense about the giving of evidence.

■ What preparation should she make for court hearings?

The health visitor should if possible discuss with a solicitor before she gives evidence the questions she is likely to be asked and the procedure which would be followed by the court. If it is not possible to speak to the solicitor she should discuss the court hearing and her role with a senior manager.

If she has the time it is advisable to attend a different court hearing a few days before she is due to appear, as a member of the public. In this way she can get the feel of the proceedings and the order and the formalities without herself being emotionally involved.

She should ensure that she knows the entries in the case notes and that they are in the correct order.

DUTY TO VISIT

The health visitor has the responsibility of visiting young babies and children after the midwife has ceased to be responsible. Increasingly, however, routine visiting is being replaced by special emphasis upon those mothers and babies who need extra support. Similarly, in the care of the aged, the health visitor is expected to use her discretion to decide the frequency of visits (if any).

This calls for skills of analysis, and diagnosis of indicators as to whether the visits should be more or less frequent. It also requires comprehensive clear record keeping in case the health visitor is called upon to justify the decisions she made in relation to the priorities of the patient.

PREVENTION AND HEALTH EDUCATION ROLE

Much of the focus on the recent strategic planning in health care is on the prevention of disease and health education. The *Health of the Nation* strategy published by the Department of Health[24] and the *Strategic Intent and Direction Initiative* issued by the Welsh Office[25] give priority in planning for prevention. Health gain areas have been identified and these are the foundation of the local strategies to be followed by health commissioners and GP fund-holding practices in purchasing health care.

The health visitor has always played a significant health education and preventive role. Increasingly now this work is being enlarged as the strategy for health care moves to health gain areas and targets of health gain are identified. The new GP contracts which commenced in 1990 give GPs incentives to provide vaccinations and other public health preventative measures. In addition there are incentives to provide yearly assessments for those of 75 years and over. It is likely that many of these assessments will be carried out by health visitors. It is essential that they receive the appropriate training to be able to do this successfully. Failure to detect ill-health problems could lead to an action for negligence.

In its discussion paper[26] on the way forward in health visiting as part of a strategy for nursing, the Welsh Office following a conference identified the following key issues:

- Maximising the skills and knowledge of staff and fully utilising them in the new arena of health and social care
- Focusing health visiting practice on health needs assessment health gain and health outcome
- Use and interpretation of data
- Contribution to primary health care
- Contribution to community health care
- Contribution to commissioning
- Leadership
- Education and training
- Research

LIABILITY FOR NEGLIGENCE ADVICE

Part of the function of the health visitor is the giving of advice to clients. There can be liability for negligent advice.

Situation

A health visitor is asked by the mother of a four month baby about the wisdom of the child receiving a vaccination against whooping cough and other disorders. The health visitor stresses that every child should receive these inoculations, since the risk of being harmed is far less than the dangers of suffering from the actual diseases. The health visitor fails to appreciate that the child has a history of convulsions when she was only a few weeks old and is therefore in the category where such inoculations should only be given with great caution and after a small test. The child receives the full dose of vaccine and subsequently suffers brain damage. There is a chance that this has resulted from the inoculations. Where does the health visitor stand?

She was clearly negligent in failing to check whether the general advice which she was giving was appropriate to that particular patient. She had a duty of care to the patient and was in breach of that duty by failing to follow the approved accepted practice of her profession. The mother could sue the employer of the health visitor (Trust or health service body) and claim compensation for the vicarious liability for the negligence of the health visitor. In this way she is likely to recover more compensation than she would be entitled to receive under the Vaccine Damage Payments Act 1979. The maximum compensation payable under that scheme is £30 000. However, in claiming under the statutory scheme she would not have to prove fault, simply that the brain damage has resulted from the vaccine (see also Chapter 7).

There may also be liability by the general practitioner if he should have been aware of the contra-indications to the vaccine being given. The liability of a group fund-holding practice in relation to a health visitor's negligence is discussed in Chapter 24.

PROTECTING THE ELDERLY FROM ABUSE

The work of the health visitor means that they are often the first professionals in the community to realise that an elderly person is subject to abuse. Recent research reveals that abuse of the elderly is on a greater scale than was previously appreciated. The report by the Social Services Inspectorate of the Department of Health[27] produced the following findings based on the two London boroughs which participated in the fieldwork in 1990.

- Most of the abused people were female and over half were aged 81 years or more.
- Frequently the abuse came from a close member of the family.
- In most cases the abuser was the principal carer of the elderly person.
- Physical abuse was by far the most frequently mentioned form of abuse, but half the cases involved more than one type of abuse.
- Most of the abused people were already known to the social services department – half the cases came to the attention of the social services departments through contact with social workers or other direct service providers.
- The rate of 'self-disclosure' of abuse was low.
- Requests for help were often 'masked' rather than direct.
- In a high proportion of cases abuse was long standing.

As regards the field staff dealing with the problem, the report indicated as follows:

- Policies for the management of elderly abuse had not been developed.
- Field staff were working without departmental guidelines for the management of cases of elderly abuse.
- They felt unsupported and indicated that they would appreciate a structure within which to work.
- They also said they would appreciate training
  (a) in defining elder abuse,
  (b) in skills to confront the abuse, and
  (c) in strategies for intervention.

Concerning existing strategies the research showed that:

- The first goal of intervention was to maintain the abused person at home with increased health or social services.
- Although a high proportion of the abused people were eventually moved into long term institutional care, this was not a preferred option.

- In some cases, intervention was difficult because of a refusal to take up the services offered or because of denial of abuse by the elderly person.

'Granny bashing' has only recently been recognised as a significant problem and guidelines were issued in 1993 by the Government to local authorities to identify and take appropriate action. Elderly people are often reluctant to report abuse because of the probability that they would be removed to residential care. At a conference of the Royal College of Psychiatrists in May 1993 Dr Jonathan Fisk of Airedale General Hospital, Keighley made the following points:

- The physical abuse of elderly people was more widespread that had been thought and took many forms.
- Those at high risk are thought to be female, aged over 75 years, physically frail, mentally incompetent, socially isolated and more ready to adopt a sick role.
- Abusers appear more likely to be aged less than 50 years, living with the victim, very commonly sons or husbands, in poor mental health and with a history of alcohol abuse.
- Abuse took the form of verbal, sexual or physical assault or it could be negative – the removal of food, warmth, affection, security or money.
- Victims may fear revenge if they talk or may know that the abuser represents their only chance of remaining in their own home.

No Longer Afraid: the Safeguard of older people in domestic settings produced by the Social Services Inspectorate of the Department of Health[28] gives practical guidelines where abuse of elderly people in domestic settings is suspected, alleged or confirmed. It recommends that local authorities should have a policy statement relating to older people which includes a policy on the management of abuse to older people including financial abuse. Social services departments, housing departments, legal departments, the police, the health authorities (both purchasers and providers) and the voluntary and private sector should all co-operate in the formulation of policies and the development of a strategy for implementation.

An important part of the strategy has to be the recognition of the stress under which carers are working and this is further discussed in Chapter 22 on carers.

A new protective agency called 'Action on Elder Abuse' is being set up by the Government in the wake of growing evidence of an increase in abuse. The group is to be established at the

Age Concern headquarters in London under the auspices of the National Council on Ageing.

Situation

Dora Barnes, a health visitor has been asked by a general practitioner to carry out an assessment on elderly persons over 75 years in the district. Dora met Gwen Taylor an elderly person of 80 who lives with her daughter and son-in-law. She noticed some bruising to Gwen's face and questioned her but Gwen said she fell against the door and it was nothing to worry about. On a subsequent visit she noticed further bruising to her arm and leg. Again Gwen gave an explanation which did not ring true to Dora. Dora is sure that Gwen is subject to abuse but does not know how to deal with the situation.

There should be in existence a policy for the elderly comparable to the non-accidental injury policy in respect of children. This would give guidelines on how the health visitor should proceed. The difficulty which arises is that often the elderly person is dependent for their daily care upon those who abuse them. Sometimes the fear of being sent to a residential or nursing home is such that they submit to abuse, denying even that there is any abuse, because of the fear of being sent away. In such circumstances it may be very difficult for a prosecution to succeed since the victim is unlikely to give evidence.

One possibility is for the health visitor to arrange with the social services for the elderly person to attend at a day centre. This would relieve the stress at home and reduce the contact. It might also be possible for the health visitor and the social worker to show that there are some benefits from living in a home if they consider that this may be in the interests of the elderly person.

Ultimately the health visitor has a duty of care to such elderly people. If she feels that they are at risk, she may have to make arrangements for them to be removed from the family home and for alternative accommodation to be arranged. Confrontation with the abusers might be necessary, but she should have support before she undertakes this task, possibly enlisting the help of the police.

The health visitor may be called to give evidence before the courts and it is therefore essential that her records are complete and clear.

The Law Commission recommendations on the decision making by the mentally incompetent adult[29] are still being debated (see Chapter 3) but they should lead to the implementation of procedures to clarify powers and responsibilities in relation to the protection of all mentally incapacitated adults, including the elderly, from physical (including sexual) and financial abuse.

PRESCRIBING

Health visitors were one of the specialisms within nursing to be given the powers of prescribing. Initially the powers have been used in eight demonstration areas. It remains to be seen how this affects the role of the health visitor (see further Chapters 12 and 14).

CONCLUSION

The health visitor is more likely to be directly involved in legal proceedings than any of the other community professionals. She should therefore ensure that she is familiar with her legal duty and is always prepared for this eventuality. Chapter 7 on professional accountability and Chapter 11 record keeping are particularly relevant to her.

CHAPTER 18

Practice nurses

The issues which are particular concern to the practice nurse and which will be covered in this chapter are set out in Figure 18.1.

Figure 18.1 Issues covered in this chapter
- Vulnerability
- Scope of professional practice
- Training
- Relationship with general practitioners and employment issues
- Health and safety

VULNERABILITY

The vast majority of practice nurses are employed either by single handed general practitioners or by group practices. A few are employed by health authorities and some facilitators are employed by the health authorities that have taken over the functions of the former Family Health Services Authorities. Many are extremely vulnerable. They may be the only practice nurses with any particular practice and, unlike their counterparts working in the community services for a health service body, they would not have a group of colleagues from whom they can seek advice, support and comradeship. Nor would there be a management hierarchy above them of similar professionals. Frequently they work on their own, accountable to themselves and their patients and their general practitioners, and sometimes with no sounding board for assistance.

There are of course advantages in this. Some practice nurses like the autonomy which working in a small business can bring. They enjoy the independence which the lack of a management hierarchy above them implies. After all many of them made a positive choice to work outside a large organisation like a NHS Trust or a health authority.

The Welsh Office Nursing and Midwifery Committee[30] published a report on *Practice Nursing* in August 1992. It concluded that 'There is inadequate support to individual practitioners on a day to day basis' and recommended 'the appointment of a nurse adviser post within each FHSA to meet the needs of this developing area of practice'. This advice has been implemented and most authorities taking over the functions of the FHSAs now have a facilitator or nurse adviser.

In the past the isolation of practice nurses had meant that it was more difficult to ensure quality standards were maintained. This is, however, changing.

Recent years have seen an increase in the advice and help available to practice nurses. The Royal College of Nursing has improved the supply of information and support. The UKCC has published advice for them[31]. The facilitators have worked to develop standards and protocols for their use and the emphasis on primary health care, the appointment of fund-holding general practices and the developments in community care have all given to the individual practice nurse an increased role and reduced her sense of isolation.

SCOPE OF PROFESSIONAL PRACTICE

Competence

One of the major concerns of practice nurses has always been in defining their role and competence. Some help has been given by the UKCC in issuing its document on the *Scope of Professional Practice* which recommended abolishing both the concept of the extended role and the use of certificates to define and illustrate competence. However, the concerns remain about undertaking new activities that were formerly the exclusive province of doctors.

Situation

A practice nurse is asked by her general practitioner to take blood samples from a patient suffering from a viral infection for analysis in the Haematology laboratory. She has noticed the doctors performing these tasks though she has never performed it herself. Unfortunately in inserting the needle she caused damage to a nerve and the patient lost sensitivity in her arm.

In this situation, there could be liability on the part of the practice nurse for carrying out a task which she was not competent to perform, there would also be liability on the part of the doctor, both indirectly as her employer (vicarious liability) and also directly for failing to make sure that the blood was taken by someone who was trained and competent to do so.

■ How does the nurse ensure that she is competent?

She must make sure that she has had a minimum training and has undertaken the task under the supervision of someone who is competent. The length of the training and the supervision will obviously vary with the complexity of the task.

Situation

The following is correspondence taken from the *Practice Nurse Journal*[32].

I was recently asked to give a series of injections to a patient receiving treatment for infertility at a private clinic. The injections were required during the preparation period before *in vitro* fertilisation, and it was inconvenient for the patient to travel daily to the London clinic. The GP for whom I worked was advised by the Medical Defence Union not to administer this treatment in a very specialised field of medicine not fully understood by most GPs. I got around the problem by teaching the patient to give the injections herself, as I was anxious not to appear uncooperative and uncaring. How would I stand in law if things went wrong?

The reply (given by the author) was as follows:

A nurse is legally bound to follow the approved, accepted practice of her profession in providing care to the patient unless there are reasonable acceptable grounds for deviating from the accepted practice in particular circumstances. In addition she should work within her field of competence, training and experience unless an emergency situation arises where greater harm would befall the patient if she failed to act than if she did act.

In the situation given here, a specialized procedure was required which the general practitioner, advised by the MDU, adjudged himself incompetent to perform. It is also apparent that the nurse herself had not received specific training in this procedure and would therefore be incompetent to perform it. In instructing the patient to perform a task that she herself would be incompetent to perform she is running clear risks. Does she know all the instructions that should be given to the patient? Does she know exactly the timing, site, method, and other factors relating to the injection? Are there specific instructions in case something goes wrong? Are there any contra-indications? And so on.

If the nurse in ignorance of some of these basic facts instructs the patient negligently, and the patient suffers reasonably foreseeable harm, then the nurse could be liable to the patient for that harm. (In practice, of course, it would be the general practitioner who would be sued, being vicariously liable for the practice nurse.)

Perhaps a better solution on the particular facts of the case would be for the patient to have been taught to carry out the injections by those who initiated and supervised the course of treatment. They should have the knowledge of all the factors described above and they could ensure that the patient was given the appropriate instruction and information to prevent any foreseeable harm arising. Alternatively, in the long term and if it was deemed necessary, the general practitioner and practice nurse could receive appropriate instructions for carrying out the procedure.

Unfortunately it seems in this situation that the GP has abdicated all responsibilities as an employer: 'I refuse to have anything to do with this patient, nurse. However, if you do be it on your own head.' (The general practitioner cannot, of course, in law do this, being vicariously liable for harm caused by the negligence of employees acting in course of employment.)

Situation: 'flu vaccinations

Another query sent into the same journal[33] is as follows:

My main area of concern is the administration of 'flu and tetanus injections without written consent from a GP. These injections are usually given while I am screening patients during a well-person clinic. If I establish that there are no contra-indications, I offer tetanus and 'flu injections as appropriate. The doctors are aware that I am doing this, but I do not consult them about each patient before giving the injections. My role as a nurse has also been extended to giving 'flu and tetanus injections in the home, as well as venepuncture and ear syringing. I am also involved in the dispensing of drugs.

I should be grateful if you would clarify the legal aspects concerning these areas of extended role.

The answer referred to the then current guidelines on extended role in relation to the appropriate delegation of tasks to those who were competent and willing where they had received adequate and appropriate training, and the task had been agreed by both the employer and by the professional body as being appropriate to be performed by a nurse.

Since then the *Scope of Professional Practice* has been issued and note must now be taken of the six principles set out in the document which should ensure that practice develops safety in the interests of the professional and client (see Chapter 8).

The practitioner must, as well as ensuring that those six principles are followed, also ensure that she keeps within the law. This means that she should not be prescribing drugs contrary to section 58 of the Medicines Act 1968 unless she is a recognised nurse prescriber with the appropriate training and she stays within the specified nursing formulary (see Chapter 12). In the UKCC advisory paper on the *Administration of Medicines*[34] it is suggested that local protocols should be devised which cover the situations described above. The practice nurse should be particularly on her guard if she is asked to administer medicines, vaccines and other preparations where there is no signed prescription and the GP signs it retrospectively.

In the above situation, it would appear that the practice nurse has not developed the necessary skill, competence or knowledge to carry out the tasks safely for the patients and she should be prepared to refuse to undertake them until she has. In addition she should not infringe the statutory provisions of the Medicines Act.

Nurse prescribing

At present it is not the intention that the practice nurse should be eligible to prescribe (see Chapter 12). Unless she has a district nurse or health visitor training she is not covered by the new legislation on nurse prescribing. However, if the initial pilot schemes on nurse prescribing succeed, then the provisions may be extended to cover prescribing by practice nurses.

The practice nurse is often expected to take a major role in the work of immunisation against infectious diseases. She should be aware of the publication *Immunisation against infectious disease* produced by the Department of Health, Welsh Office and Scottish Home and Health Department[35]. This gives an account of the different diseases with a useful introductory section on general topics such as consent to treatment and children, contra-indications, special risk groups, HIV positive persons and adverse reaction spotting. It also discusses immunisation procedures and the role of the nurse. The advice is that if each of three conditions are satisfied, and the nurse carries out the immunisation in accordance with accepted District Health Authority policy, then the authority will accept responsibility for immunisation by nurses. The three conditions are:

- the nurse is willing to be professionally accountable for this work,
- she has received training and is competent in all aspects of immunisation including the contra-indications to specific vaccines, and
- adequate training has been given in the recognition and treatment of anaphylaxis.

UKCC guidance

In 1990 the UKCC published a statement[36] on practice nurses and aspects of the new GP contract which had come into force on 1 April 1990. The UKCC was concerned to ensure that standards are established and improved at a time of change. It emphasised that 'it is essential that Practice Nurses ascertain which fee-attracting services require the services to be provided by the GP personally and which could be provided by other members of the practice staff'. It was concerned to ensure that nurses were fully prepared in order to practice competently and recommended the following to ensure that the interests of patients are best served:

- that sound policies for practice are developed and made known to all doctors and nurses concerned;
- that any forms of medication, under current prescribing arrangements, are individually prescribed in advance by medical practitioners or are the subject of a local protocol approved by all the medical practitioners concerned and which is acceptable to the nurses involved; and
- that informed consent is overtly sought from or on behalf of patients and clients and obtained, wherever appropriate, consistently with the Council's position.

An example of one area fraught with difficulties is that of breast and cervical screening. Increasingly practices are setting up 'well-woman' clinics and health promotion clinics. The practice nurse may well be expected to carry out these clinics and it is essential that she has sufficient training and experience to undertake them on her own, and that she has a clear understanding of her limitations. It is equally important that she does not give any false impression of her competence to the clients. In a recent case in Birmingham many patients had to be recalled for cervical screening after a locum doctor discovered that the practice nurse was using the wrong technique in carrying out the procedure. It was said that she had been taught the procedure by her general practitioner.

The new GP contracts introduced in 1990 gave a higher capitation fee for patients aged 75 years and above provided that a skilled assessment resulting from an annual visit to the patient's home is offered. Practice nurses may well be asked to carry out these assessments and the UKCC in its statement emphasised that

> it is essential that the practitioner conducting the assessment possesses the necessary skills to perform it competently. An assessment of the type required is complex and requires a high level of skill.

The UKCC statement expects that all employers will require, as an integral basis of employment and practice, adherence to the Council's *Code of Professional Conduct* to which all nurses, midwives and health visitors are subject. If the GP practice in which a practice nurse works accepts the *Code* it should be easier for the nurse in question to refuse to carry out an assessment which she is incompetent to do. However, even where the *Code* has not been incorporated in her contract of employment, the nurse should still ensure that she does not take on tasks for which she lacks the training or experience.

TRAINING

Training is in the main the employer's obligations and its importance in risk assessment and management has been re-emphasised by the new health and safety regulations (see Chapter 9). The practice nurse, however, has a duty to remind the GP employer of her needs and ensure that she personally remains up to date. The report on PREP (Post Registration Education and Practice) by the UKCC was accepted by the Department of Health and legislation passed to implement it in April 1995. It is recognised that at the present time it is unrealistic to expect that there should be huge funds allocated for its implementation. However, the practitioner herself is responsible for maintaining her own competence and post-registration education.

Under the PREP provisions the practitioner has to undergo at least five days study time every three years to be able to renew her registration. There is an implied duty on the part of employers that they will ensure that their employees are competent. If the employer is in breach of this obligation and as a result the practice nurse is unable to maintain her competence then she could claim that the employer is in fundamental breach of the contract of employment. However, unless she has the continuous service requirement (see glossary) to maintain an action for unfair dismissal, she runs the risk of losing her job without compensation, except through a civil court action which would be much less straightforward than an industrial tribunal claim.

RELATIONSHIPS WITH GENERAL PRACTITIONERS

Isolation

It was noted at the beginning of this chapter that the practice nurse is particularly vulnerable and isolated. The standard of general practitioners varies considerably and the support they provide for their staff extremely disparate. The Welsh Office report cited earlier recommends that a nurse adviser post should be made within each health authority (formerly the FHSA) to provide the necessary support for practice nurses and this is now being undertaken. The greater number of practice nurses being appointed and the meetings which they now regularly hold may facilitate mutual support and an exchange of information across a district so that the nurses are not so isolated.

The employment contract

At the heart of the relationship of practice nurse/GP is, of course, the contract of employment. All employees are entitled to receive a statement in writing of the main terms of their contract and any changes must be notified to the employee at the earliest opportunity and, in any event, not later that one month after the change (see Figure 18.2).

Figure 18.2 Written Statement of the main terms and conditions of employment

1. Names of employer and employee
2. Date the employment began
3. Whether any employment with a previous employer counts as part of the employee's continuous period of employment and if so the date on which the period of continuous employment began
4. Scale or rate of remuneration or method of calculating remuneration
5. Intervals at which remuneration is paid
6. Any terms and conditions relating to hours of work

7. Any terms and conditions relating to:
   — holidays and holiday pay
   — incapacity for work
   — pensions and pension schemes
   — length of notice the employee must give or receive
8. Title of the job
9. Disciplinary and grievance procedures (where there are over 19 employees)

This written statement must be given to the employee within two months after commencing employment.

The basics of a contract are set out in Chapter 20. An employee who has served for the relevant period of continuous employment (see glossary) is entitled to the employee benefits set out in the employment legislation. Some of these are shown in Figure 18.3. (Some benefits require no continuous service.)

Figure 18.3 Employment benefits

1. Guarantee payments
2. Suspension on medical grounds under health and safety regulations
3. Rights on the insolvency of an employer
4. Redundancy payments
5. Time off: to seek job or training in a redundancy situation
            to attend for public duties, acting as a JP, as a local
            councillor, on a health service body and so on
6. Written statement of terms and conditions of employment
7. Itemized pay statement
8. Right to notice and reasons for dismissal
9. To apply to an industrial tribunal for unfair dismissal
10. Rights in relation to trade union membership and activities
11. Right to be protected against unjustifiable discipline by a trade union

Situation

Mavis worked as the receptionist at the surgery and helped out with first aid tasks and gradually took on more work of a clinical nature. Patients tended to call her 'nurse'. The single handed GP for whom she worked also referred to her in front of the patients as 'the nurse'. One day she tried to syringe the ear of a patient and perforated the ear drum. Where does she stand?

It is illegal for anyone to give the impression that they are a state registered nurse and they can be prosecuted for such an offence. Does allowing someone to call one nurse imply that one is state registered? The answer is probably 'no', since many nursing auxiliaries who are not state registered are called nurse and they do not hold themselves out as being state registered.

In this situation the GP is clearly at fault in allowing a receptionist to undertake tasks which are outside her competence and training. The receptionist is also liable personally for embarking on a task she should not have undertaken. The GP will be both directly liable for the harm to the patient since he should not have allowed the receptionist to perform it and he will also be vicariously liable as the employer for the negligence of the receptionist.

Situation

A practice nurse works for a group of general practitioners who decide that they will apply for fund-holding status. They are successful in their application and then ask the practice nurse if she would change her conditions of service: they want her to work for more hours per day (she is part time) but they are not prepared to increase her salary accordingly. She is a single parent, needs the income and does not want to lose her job. What are her rights?

The terms of a contract cannot be changed unilaterally. The general practitioners cannot therefore make her accept these changed conditions. However, if she were to be dismissed for refusing the new terms and does not have the necessary continuous period of employment (see glossary) she cannot apply to an industrial tribunal for unfair dismissal. She could sue for breach of contract, but the employers could avoid a hearing by giving her the notice of termination of contract to which she is entitled or pay her in lieu of notice.

HEALTH AND SAFETY

The practice nurse like all employees has a duty under the Health and Safety at Work Act 1974 to carry out the employers' instructions in relation to the health and safety policy (see Chapter 9). She has a duty both in relation to her colleagues, to her clients and other visitors and to herself. Her employer also has a statutory duty to protect the health and safety of his employees and others who may be affected by his work.

Situation

A practice nurse was using an old sterilising boiler in the surgery. Instruments were placed in the boiler and left for half and hour until they were considered to be sterile. The practice nurse had approached the GPs about the possibility of using the local CSSD service, but they had refused on the grounds of cost and the possibility of lost instruments. She knows that the present method is unsafe and was condemned in a report many years before, but the GPs are adamant that they will not change the practice. Where does she stand?

In this difficult situation, it is preferable for the practice nurse to make out a reasoned case for changing the existing system of sterilising, pointing out clearly and rationally the dangers. If the GPs ignore this statement and if the dangers from such a system are great the practice nurse should enlist outside help. This could include a nurse adviser if such a person has been appointed by the health authority. She could also seek advice from the senior officers of the health authority since there is a possibility that the GPs are in breach of their contract for services to it. The Local Medical Committee may provide advice and support for her and she might also consult the UKCC. Ultimately, in exceptional circumstances, there is the possibility of calling in the health and safety inspectorate whose powers are discussed in Chapter 9.

CONCLUSION

Only a few of the areas of law relevant to the practice nurse have been considered here. The role of the practice nurse is likely to develop as more general practitioners are accepted for group fund-holding status and practice nurses should ensure that they are aware of the implications of these changes for their professional development. The new health authorities set up on 1 April 1996 have the task of ensuring a greater emphasis on primary rather than secondary care. The practice nurse will therefore be increasingly at the centre of provision and some GPs are already considering the possibility of employing their own community health staff and reviewing the respective roles of practice nurse and district nurse.

CHAPTER 19

Professions supplementary to medicine

Over the past ten years health professionals traditionally associated with in-patient care have been increasingly employed in the provision of care in the community. Some have had an entirely community focus others have covered both spheres. The professions covered by the Council to the Professions Supplementary to Medicine (CPSM) include the following:

- chiropodists,
- dietitians,
- medical laboratory technicians,
- occupational therapists,
- physiotherapists,
- radiographers, and
- orthoptists.

Speech therapists, pharmacists and psychologists are not covered by the Council to the Professions Supplementary to Medicine, but have their own professional bodies responsible for training, admission to professional status and professional conduct.

Each of the professions covered by the Professions Supplementary to Medicine Act 1960 has a Board which is a body corporate with perpetual succession and a common seal. The Boards have the general function of promoting high standards of professional education and professional conduct among the members of the relevant professions. With the approval of the Council a Board may appoint committees to carry out on the Board's behalf such of its functions as it may determine and are not required to be carried out by an investigating or disciplinary committee. It may also make standing orders for regulating its proceedings (including a quorum) or those of a committee. It can appoint teaching and other staff in connection with courses of training and examinations conducted under arrangements made by it.

Each Board must set up investigation and disciplinary committees. The former has the duty of conducting a preliminary investigation into any case where it is alleged that a person registered by the Board is liable to have his name removed and of deciding whether the case should be referred to the disciplinary committee. The latter has the duty of considering and determining any case referred to it by the investigating committee and any case where an application is made for the restoration of a person's name to the register.

The Boards may also make regulations for membership of the committees, meetings and quorums, all in consultation with the Council for Professions Supplementary to Medicine.

It is an offence for an individual falsely to claim registered status.

This chapter deals with the issues which are of particular relevance to these professions as shown in Figure 19.1.

Figure 19.1 Issues dealt with in this chapter
- Clinical relationships
- Community role
- Isolation
- Delegation to patients or carers
- Patients rights: consent and confidentiality
- Employment
- Purchasing and provider strategies

CLINICAL RELATIONSHIPS

As the group name of these professions suggests, their original role was seen as a support to the medical professional. Originally they waited for a referral from the appropriate medical specialist. For example until the early 1980s a physiotherapist had to have patients referred by a doctor who would tell the physiotherapist the nature of the physiotherapy treatment to be provided. As physiotherapists' expertise grew it was clear that the referral was not necessarily appropriate and the treatment specified by doctors not necessarily in the best interests of the patients. It was, therefore, established that following a referral the physiotherapist could determine the appropriate treatment to be given in the light of the symptoms and medical history. Others, apart from doctors, can now refer patients and some may feel that the title Professions Supplementary to Medicine is now a misnomer.

However the freedom for the professionals to determine the treatment which they should give the client rather than have it specified by a doctor does raise issues in relation to clinical accountability. If a professional works under the umbrella of a medical practitioner, then ultimately the medical practitioner has the right to determine the treatment and outcome for the patient. Clearly multi-disciplinary views would be taken into account but in the final analysis the medical practitioner has the last word. Yet in areas where there have been considerable developments this may not be appropriate.

This issue has developed in its significance with the agreement of contracts for the purchase of professional services. Where the purchaser is a GP fund-holder it is essential that he has a full understanding of the role and services which the professional supplementary to medicine can provide in the community. Likewise, those contracting with the Health Commissioner for community services should receive from these professionals full details of their potential services and role in the community. The implication of this is that the professionals supplementary to medicine must, in the new culture of the internal market, be prepared to identify and market the skills which they have and the benefit which they can bring to the care of patients (see final section of this chapter below).

COMMUNITY ROLE

The growth of small community centres/hospitals has meant that many of these professionals now work in a multi-disciplinary team in the community with links to the larger in-patient institutions. From these bases they provide a service to clients in their own homes as well as seeing them in an out-patient setting or in the small community homes/hospitals/day centres.

The advantages which come from this integrated, seamless care are undoubted and make carrying out assessments and training for independent living more meaningful. However, there can be problems. One is the blurring of the traditional roles of the individual professions and there is likely to be a continued development in this area. The distinction between the role of the community nurse, the social worker and these professions supplementary to medicine is also likely to grow less distinct.

ISOLATION

One danger of the community professional who works from an institution without being part of a supportive team is that she could become isolated and find herself taking decisions which are not within her competence.

Situation

A paediatric physiotherapist who worked solely in the community found that she was expected to provide all the home equipment out of her very small budget. There was increasing use of nebulisers, lung function testing equipment and oxygen therapy at home and her clients were suffering because she was unable to provide this equipment. As a result children were admitted to the paediatric ward unnecessarily. The ward refused to permit more of its equipment to be used at home because they needed to keep a minimum supply because of emergency admissions. Would the community paediatric physiotherapist be liable if harm befell a client because of this failure to provide equipment?

The physiotherapist has a duty of care to the client. It is her responsibility to follow the approved accepted practice of her profession according to the Bolam test (see glossary). She should therefore ensure that the patient does not suffer harm because the necessary equipment is not provided. This may mean admission to hospital so that the patient can use the equipment. In the long run the physiotherapist should be able to produce figures to show that if her budget were expanded she could actually save the health service body/NHS Trust funds. (For discussion on the issue of maintenance and loan of equipment see Chapter 8.)

Another danger of working in isolation is that standards of practice are not developed and the community professional therefore needs to take steps herself to keep abreast of research and developments within her profession. Clarification of the role of management and the development of policies and training strategy is also essential.

DELEGATION TO PATIENTS OR CARERS

The awareness that many tasks associated with high technology can not only be carried out in a patient's home but also be taught to the carer or the client himself has meant that patients who a few years ago would never have left an institution are now being cared for in their own homes, often adapted for that purpose. Thus tetraplegic and paraplegic patients, others on life support systems and persons in a vegetative state are now being moved into the community if a carer is available and able to take over the responsibilities.

Before the move to the community can take place equipment has to be provided, adaptations to the house made and changes to the electricity supply or an emergency generator may have to be supplied. In addition it is essential that the carer receives the necessary instruction to ensure the patient will be safe and, if appropriate, also receives the additional supplementary staffing support. Such an alternative may not necessarily be cheaper than institutional care, but the quality of life that the patient enjoys should be higher.

There should also be a clear determination of responsibilities of those professionals who provide a supporting role and clarification as to which of them the carer should contact in the event of any emergency.

Other tasks are now routinely delegated to carers and the clients such as the testing and injections for diabetes and intravenous medication in chronic conditions. Chapters 21 and 22 on volunteers and carers look at some of the legal implications of the delegation of these highly technical tasks to a carer or volunteer.

Sometimes a decision must be made that following the assessment the family are unable to cope with caring for the patient at home and that admission to a nursing home is the only alternative. The family might object to this, particularly as the cost of long term care is increasingly provided on a means-tested basis. However, if it is clear that the patient needs more support than can be provided in the family, admission to a nursing or residential home must be arranged.

PATIENTS' RIGHTS – CONSENT AND CONFIDENTIALITY

Exactly the same principles in relation to the rights of the patient/client apply in the community as in hospital. However, it is more difficult to monitor the situation when care is provided in hundreds of homes rather than in a few institutions. There are dangers that abuse of the patient could take place without protective action being taken and there are dangers that the patient's autonomy will be overruled (not necessarily in the patient's best interests). The Law Commission Consultation Paper No. 119 and the subsequent Papers Nos. 128, 129 and 130 on *Decision making and the mentally incapacitated adult* point out some of the dangers in the present situation. The Law Commission has made firm proposals and drafted legislation[37] (see Chapter 3).

Situation

A chiropodist visited the home of an elderly patient every six months to attend to her feet. She was finding the patient increasingly difficult to cope with as her mental state deteriorated. On her last visit she found that the patient was tied to an armchair. The daughter explained that she had become such a wanderer it was the only way of keeping her away from the open fire and in the room safely. The daughter said it would be easier for the chiropodist to care for her feet if she remained tied up. The chiropodist did not like the situation but carried out a foot inspection and treatment whilst the patient remained tied up. Was the chiropodist right to accept the situation?

What the chiropodist observed was false imprisonment and illegal restraint. Yet what action should she take? Clearly she should ensure that the social services are informed of the situation and visit the family to check if there is any other abuse of the elderly woman. In addition she should ensure that the community nurses are also aware of the situation. If there is in existence a policy for abuse in the elderly she should ensure that she takes all the appropriate steps. She should also ensure that the family are obtaining all the possible support required to deal with a very difficult situation. Reference should be made to the discussion in Chapter 17 on elderly abuse and the health visitor.

As far as the practice of her profession is concerned the chiropodist would be wiser to seek the voluntary co-operation of the patient/client rather than take advantage of her false imprisonment. If this fails there is ultimately the common law power of the professional to act in the best interests of the patient who is mentally incompetent under the ruling in *Re F* (see glossary and Chapter 3). However, treatment against a person's will should only be given in exceptional circumstances.

EMPLOYMENT OF PROFESSIONS SUPPLEMENTARY TO MEDICINE BY LOCAL AUTHORITIES

Formerly most professionals supplementary to medicine were employed within the National Health Service to work in hospitals and increasingly in the community. The Griffiths Report envisaged that many staff formerly employed within the NHS would be transferred into local authority employment. Directions relating to such employment have been issued.

The Secretary of State for Health in exercise of powers conferred on him by section 7A of the Local Authority Social Services Act 1970, as inserted by section 50 of the National Health Service and Community Care Act, see Figure 27.1, has directed that, of the persons covered by the Professions Supplementary to Medicine Act 1960 (that is, chiropodists, dietitians, medical laboratory scientific officers, occupational therapists, orthoptists, physiotherapists and radiographers), a local authority shall only employ people in that capacity who are on a register maintained by the appropriate Board in accordance with the 1960 Act (as amended). It is also not permitted for the local authority to make arrangements to employ such unregistered persons through an agent.

This direction raises some interesting points since it prohibits the employment of unregistered professionals in such a capacity. It does not seem to cover the case where a registered occupational therapist acquires skills normally undertaken by a registered physiotherapist. Nor does it appear to cover the situation where a care assistant is employed as a care assistant but undertakes work which would normally be undertaken by one of the professions listed above.

This is discussed further in the section on key workers in Chapter 8.

PURCHASING AND PROVIDER STRATEGIES

Each of the professions supplementary to medicine has had to take on board a community orientated perspective in addition to the role which they traditionally played in the hospital. This, together with the context of the internal market, has meant that each such profession has had to develop an awareness of its intrinsic value in the health and social care of the individual and develop with purchasers the identification of needs which can be met by the particular professional group. They also have to prepare a strategy for meeting those needs.

Space does not permit a detailed examination of all professions but, as an example of the process of change, the work of the chiropodist will be examined.

In 1994 a joint report of the Department of Health and Task Force of Chiropodists was published, appropriately called *Feet First*[38]. Maintaining mobility of individuals who live alone can be the key to their continued stay in non-residential/nursing home accommodation. The report recognised the 'central role' played by this small professional group in helping to keep the growing elderly population mobile, independent, and active for longer in the community, thus improving the quality of life of the individual. The report identified seven general principles to commissioning foot care. These are set out in Figure 19.2.

Figure 19.2 General Principles to commissioning foot care

1. Need to take a strategic view – at least 5 year forward look including the need to link it with other strategies (in particular the shift from secondary to primary care).
2. There should be robust contracts – these should specify volume, quality and price.
3. Decisions should be based on knowledge and research.
4. There should be responsiveness to local people.
5. Purchasers should develop mature relations with providers and should take account of the benefits of chiropodists working in teams or departments and the specialisms which are taking place within the profession.
6. Purchasers should look to working with both NHS and private sector chiropodists and social services and voluntary agencies to improve needs assessment and joint purchasing.
7. Purchasers should follow the following stages:
   - assessment of need
   - prioritisation and resource allocation
   - specification of the services required
   - contractual agreement with providers
   - monitoring and review.

Both the general principles and the stages set out in Principle 7 probably apply to all professions supplementary to medicine. What is clear from the development of the GP fund-holding system is that unless each individual profession makes clear the benefits it can bring to clients and identifies both the cost and the value, they will find that their services are not taken up and the GP fund-holders will be purchasing alternative care which may be cheaper. One example is the tendency for GP fund-holders to employ nurse counsellors. In many cases these can provide an appropriate service to clients. However, there is a danger to clinical psychologists that unless they can establish both the necessity and the value of their service to specific clients both in the short term and the long term, their services will not be purchased. Each individual profession has to identify its role in this way. They also need to ensure that the clients as well as the purchasers are aware of the benefits which they can give. Although clients do not have a legally enforceable right to obtain a particular service, if the clients know the benefits which can be given, they are more likely to be able to influence the GP fund-holder in his purchasing strategy.

Generally, for legal problems faced by these professionals reference should be made to the general principles of law discussed in the chapters of the first part of Section B of this book.

THE FUTURE

A review of the Professions Supplementary to Medicine Act 1960 has been undertaken by JM Consulting Ltd under a steering group chaired by Professor Sheila McLean. A consultation document was issued in October 1995 and the report published in July 1996[38a].

After discussing the weaknesses of the 1960 Act and significant changes since that date the report makes many major recommendations. These include the following:

- The establishment of a new statutory body (the Council for Health Professions (CHP)) with new, more effective and more flexible powers.
- Legislation to protect the public and allow for growth in the number of professions represented.
- Cover of a profession to be based on the potential for harm from invasive procedures or from the impact of the professional's unsupervised judgment on client health or welfare.
- The professions included to be the seven existing ones under the CPSM, plus arts therapy, prosthetics and orthotics.
- Other professional groups to be potentially eligible.
- Common title for the regulated professions to be protected.
- The government, through the Secretary of State or the Privy Council, to continue to provide oversight and the ultimate forum of appeal, but with reduced involvement in policy and administrative matters.
- The normal costs of the regulatory body to be funded by registration fees.
- The CHP to delegate much of its work to Statutory Committees (such as Preliminary Proceedings, Professional Conduct, Health, and Education).
- A Panel of Professional Advisers appointed by the CHP to provide the resources and expertise to carry out much of the detailed work in education, and so on.
- The Panel to provide members for working parties, committees and course validation panels and also to provide a source of consultation on specific issues.
- The present professional boards to no longer exist.

The Government's response to these recommendations, which will require new legislation, is awaited.

CHAPTER 20

Private practitioners

A growing number of professionals work as self-employed independent contractors and there is every likelihood that this number will grow as NHS Trusts, fund-holding general practitioners, other health service bodies, social services authorities and groups such as charitable organisations and private health care providers have the capacity to contract with self-employed individuals for services. Figure 20.1 shows some of the differing contracting partners for the independent contractors.

Figure 20.1 Contracts and the private practitioner

- with private patients
- with NHS Trusts
- with health authorities
- with fund-holding general practitioners
- with residential and nursing homes
- with private hospitals
- with agencies
- with local authorities
- with charities
- with solicitors

Many health professionals who provide a private practice service have their own organisations and hold conferences and seminars.

SIGNIFICANCE OF SELF-EMPLOYMENT

Most of the areas of law covered in this book will be of relevance to the private practitioner but in addition they will also be concerned with business law, since as self-employed professionals they will be running a business organisation sometimes also being employers themselves.

'Contractor' not 'employee'

As self-employed professionals they do not have an employer who will be vicariously liable for their actions and therefore pay out compensation arising from their negligence. Some of the differences are shown in Figure 20.2.

Figure 20.2 Contract for services – not a contract of employment
- No vicarious liability if proved negligent
- No employee rights
- No indemnity by another
- Personal liability for health and safety of self and others
- Liable for breach of contract

The relationship between the independent contractor and the contracting party is not a contract of employment but a contract for services. All the benefits which the employment legislation gives to employees such as time off work for specific purposes, protection against unfair dismissal and redundancy and guaranteed payments are not there for the self-employed. Since they have to pay personally any compensation arising out of their negligence, they have to ensure that they are adequately insured in respect of public liability. In addition they cannot look to an employer for protection in relation to health and safety but should take out their own personal accident cover. In this respect they are like those professionals who are employees but whose employer would rarely be liable for their health and safety in other people's homes (see Chapter 10). Moreover, if they are employers themselves they must ensure that they recognise the employment rights of their employees.

Running the business

In running a business they should seek professional help on the areas shown in Figure 20.3.

Figure 20.3 The private practitioner and business law
- Inland Revenue (income tax for self and PAYE for employees)
- National Insurance (self and others)
- Customs and Excise (VAT)
- Insurance and Indemnity
- Health and Safety Regulations:
    - Employer's Liability (Defective Equipment) Act 1969
    - Personal accident cover
    - Employers' Liability (Compulsory Insurance) Act 1969
- Contracts for supplies and services
- Development and Training (self and others)
- Employment law
- Data protection registration
- Pensions and sickness

● Formation of business
    (a) Type: sole trader/partnership/limited company/co-operative
    (b) Name
    (c) Protection through patents/registered designs
    (d) Premises:
            planning permission
            building regulations
            the lease
            special trades
    (e) Trading laws:
            Supply of Goods and Services Act 1982
            Trade Descriptions Act 1968
            Unfair Contract Terms Act 1977 and so on
    (f) Taxation and starting up: capital allowances/deciding on tax year

In determining the type of arrangement the independent practitioner should have if working with one or more other people, it is essential that she takes legal advice. For example, it may seem preferable to set up a partnership so that the profits and overheads can be shared. However, each partner would be responsible for the debts of the partnership even if she has not personally incurred them.

Accountability and the private practitioner

Figure 20.4 illustrates the arenas of accountability for the private practitioner. For the most part they are equivalent to those of the professional who works as an employee.

Figure 20.4 Accountability and the private practitioner

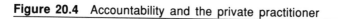

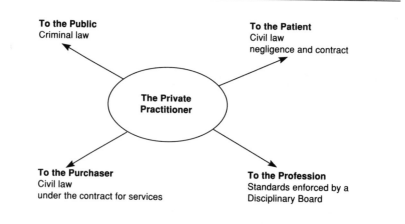

To the Public
Criminal law

To the Patient
Civil law
negligence and contract

The Private Practitioner

To the Purchaser
Civil law
under the contract for services

To the Profession
Standards enforced by a
Disciplinary Board

CONTRACT LAW

Instead of being accountable to an employer the private practitioner has a contract for services with a purchaser (see Figure 20.1). If there is a breach of contract then the referral is not to the industrial tribunal but to the civil courts. The private practitioner must therefore have a good understanding of the law of contract. Some of the essential features of contract law are shown in Figure 20.5.

Figure 20.5 Elements of contract law

- Formation: invitation to treat (see glossary)/offer/acceptance
- Contents: fundamental terms and warranties (see glossary)
  implied and express terms
- Performance
- Breach: remedies for breach – termination and/or damages
  right of election
- Termination: by performance
  by breach
  by agreement
  by notice
  by frustration

Formation of the contract

There may often be a lengthy period of negotiations before a contract is formed. There may, for example, be an 'invitation to treat' (see glossary) by the one party which is on very different terms to those eventually arrived at. The contract is eventually reached where one party can be said to have made an offer which the other party accepts. If an offer is made and the other party responds by offering alternative conditions, this is a counter offer which, if accepted by the other party, constitutes the agreement and therefore the contract. The contract may not be entirely in writing. It may be partly in writing and partly oral (by word of mouth). It is a question of interpretation if, following a dispute, one party argues that additional terms discussed during negotiations became part of the contract and are therefore binding even though not in writing.

The three essential elements to make a contract binding are:

- an agreement;
- consideration; and
- an intention to create legal relations.

Consideration need not necessarily be payment of money in return for the performance of the agreement by the other side. It could be a benefit in kind. It could be an agreement not to do something which the party would otherwise have a duty to do. It need not necessarily equate with what the other is prepared to do – in other words, consideration does not have to equal what is offered by the other party, it merely has to exist. For example, a physiotherapist who has a private practice may agree that, because a client is extremely short of funds but has suffered a sports injury, she will forego any payment on the understanding that she will be given two tickets for her son and a friend to attend the next international rugby match at Cardiff Arms Park; on that basis the agreement is made and she provides the physiotherapy. If the client then goes back on that agreement he is in breach of contract. If he never had the power to obtain those tickets he would be guilty of obtaining a pecuniary advantage by deception. The physiotherapist has the right to seek damages for breach of contract in the civil courts. In practice she may prefer not to attract the publicity which such an action would bring.

In commercial contracts the intention to create legal relations would normally be presumed. In domestic matters, there is a presumption that this is not the intention. Where a practitioner is carrying out private work it is essential for her to make it absolutely clear that it is intended to create a binding agreement in order to be able to enforce the contract through the courts.

Where possible the private practitioner should ensure that all the terms of the contract are put in writing to protect herself in the event of a dispute.

Breach of contract

If it is claimed that one party is in fundamental breach of the contract then the innocent party has the right of election, that is, she can either elect to see the contract as at an end with her own obligations terminating from that date and seek damages for breach of the contract or she can elect to treat the contract as continuing but seek compensation for it being otherwise than had originally been agreed. It is important that the innocent party makes it clear how she elects, since if she delays and appears to carry on regarding the contract as subsisting it could be said that by her conduct she has treated the contract as continuing and has therefore lost the right of election.

Termination of contract

It is advisable to consider at the beginning of the contract how it should end.

- Is it for a specific number of treatments?
- Is it for a certain length of time?
- Is it until a specified number of weeks after the birth of a baby?
- Can it be ended on notice by one party to the other?
- How long should that notice be?

In the absence of notice provisions in an employment contract the courts will imply a reasonable notice provision into the contract and there are statutory minimum periods. However, these do not exist for contracts for services and it would be more difficult to determine what is reasonable notice.

'Frustration' of contract arises when as event takes place which is right outside the contemplation of the parties when the contract was made.

Situation

An occupational therapist agreed to provide occupational therapy services to a client in the community. Her main task was to carry out an assessment of the aids and assistance the client would need to live on his own. She had almost completely carried out this task and compiled a suggested list of equipment and suppliers when the client informed her that his widowed brother was coming to live with him and he would not therefore require any aids and help from the occupational therapist. The occupational therapist claimed the money due to her for the work she had already done. The client refused to pay on the grounds that he no longer required her help.

In this case the client or occupational therapist could argue that the contract had been frustrated by the unforeseen event of the brother's arrival. However the occupational therapist should be able to recover for the work she had already undertaken. As a result of the Law Reform (Frustrated Contracts) Act 1943

- all sums paid before the contract was frustrated are repayable,
- any money due to be paid but not paid before frustration ceases to be payable,
- any expenses reasonably incurred can be recovered or retained out of the money already received, and

● (where one party has received a benefit) the court can allow the party conferring this benefit
    (a) to recover a reasonable sum by way of compensation or
    (b) to retain such sum out of money already received.

This Act does not apply where the contract itself makes provision for any frustrating event and it would, therefore, be possible for the private practitioner to include in the agreement provision defining what rights exist if a frustrating event occurs.

What if the client refuses to pay?

Payment is the passing of consideration from the one party to the contract in return for the provision of some service. Time of payment is not normally a fundamental term unless the contract clearly makes it so. It is, therefore, advisable for the professional to include in the contract a term in relation to when the fee should be paid – in advance, in instalments at each session, after each session, monthly and so on. When she is negotiating with a health service body or NHS Trust there might not be much choice for her, but it is essential that she should agree this so it is clear when there has been a breach of contract and she can commence action for recovery.

Situation

A physiotherapist contracted with NHS Trust for physiotherapy services to be provided for four sessions a week on the basis that payment would be made every month in arrears on completion and submission of a return certified by the unit manager. The physiotherapist duly performed the services and submitted the return but several months later was still without payment. Should she cease to work?

Looking back at the section on breach of contract, it will be recalled that failure to pay could be regarded as breach of a fundamental clause of the contract giving the innocent party the right of election. The physiotherapist could therefore treat the contract as at an end, stop work and sue for the outstanding payment and damages for the breach of contract. However, if there is every likelihood that she would eventually be paid, she might well prefer to elect to see the contract as continuing and continue to perform her sessions meanwhile chasing them for the outstanding payments. Should she eventually be forced into taking legal action she could, depending upon the amount outstanding, take the case to the small claims court (up to £3000), to the County Court (up to £50 000) or to the High Court (over £50 000). With the contract in writing and evidence of the sessions she has carried out she should obtain her payments with no valid defence being available against her.

THE PRACTITIONER AND HEALTH AND SAFETY

Whilst there exists no employer who is responsible for the self-employed practitioner, she may be an employer herself and therefore have responsibilities to her employees. The duty to take reasonable care of the health and safety of the employee exists whether the employee is full or part time. She also has a duty under the health and safety legislation to take care of the safety of others who may be effected by her work. Examples of issues in relation to health and safety are seen in Chapter 9.

The Management of Health and Safety at Work Regulations 1992 refer specifically to the self-employed in Regulation 3(2) (see Figure 9.9). The requirement is for self-employed persons to make 'suitable and sufficient' assessments of the risks to their own health and safety as well as to that of others arising in connection with their work.

Situation

An occupational therapist works as a self-employed practitioner and has a case load of clients for whom she provides services. One client is extremely demanding and is very anxious to obtain a chair lift from the social services. The occupational therapist forms the view that a lift is neither appropriate nor practicable and, in fact, given the client's particular circumstances could be dangerous. The occupational therapist is told by the client that unless she is prepared to support her claim their contract for services will be ended. What should the occupational therapist do?

The answer should be clear: she must abide by her professional standards and not be demand-led by the client into recommending equipment which is entirely unsuitable. The difference between the employee status and the self-employed status, however, is apparent. If employees refuse to agree with clients on professional grounds, their employment should not be endangered. If it is the employer who is putting pressure on them to act unprofessionally then, provided they have the continuous service requirement (see glossary), they could claim constructive dismissal in the industrial tribunal. However, the self-employed professional has no such protection. If she sticks to her professional standards then she might lose that client and suffer economically. There is, however, no alternative if she wishes to remain a registered professional.

Not everyone is content with health care developments outside the National Health Service. There may for example be some fund-holding general practitioners who refuse to contract with private practitioners. What action can the private practitioners take? The fund-holders have the statutory freedom to buy services from those providers that they consider would be best for their patients. They cannot be forced to go outside the NHS nor can they be forced to stay within it. If a GP practice refuses to use the services of the private sector there is no action which can be taken other than to hope that they eventually realise that in terms of quality and price the private service can offer a service equivalent to those within the NHS.

COMPENSATION CLAIMS: EXPERT WITNESS AND WITNESS OF FACT

Expert witness

An increasing part of the practitioner's work is the provision of expert reports for those who have been involved in litigation and are seeking compensation. The practitioner might be asked by the plaintiff's solicitor or the defendant's solicitor for an expert report on the situation and the prognosis in order to assess the amount of compensation (known as quantum). One useful rule for the practitioner to follow is to give an honest reasoned opinion whichever side call her. She must not be partisan, nor should she exaggerate or belittle the amount of compensation. Given the rules on legal costs if a reasonable offer of settlement is refused, she would be doing those who instruct her a disservice if (in the false hope of being able to persuade the judge on their behalf) she 'beefs up' her report to the extent that they believe their claim is worth more than it actually is.

If she always gives an honest and professional view, she will be respected by solicitors who will know that they can trust her to withstand cross-examination and that she is reliable. She must not see the court battle as involving her personally and thus whichever side wins, she should be able to feel that she has given an honest report. Solicitors will always be keeping an eye open for good experts in any field and a good job done, even for the losing side, might lead to recommendations or work from any of the lawyers involved.

Witness of fact

She may also be called as a witness of fact. In this situation she is required to give direct evidence of a matter with which she has been involved. Again she should ensure that she keeps to the facts and does not, for example, magnify the extent of the disability and the poor prognosis in order to obtain more compensation for the client. The practitioner has to ensure that her professional standards are maintained and she tells the client honestly the nature of the prognosis as she sees it. She may need guidance and training in how to withstand cross-examination. It is vital that she does not express views outside her competence.

COMPLAINTS AND UNPROFESSIONAL CONDUCT BY OTHERS

Because the private practitioner often works on her own, she is more vulnerable in pointing out low standards of care provided by other professionals. She lacks a management hierarchy and does not belong to a large organisation (other than her own professional association) to be able to take action effectively without herself becoming a scapegoat or losing out financially.

Situation

An occupational therapist provides services at a residential care home. She is horrified to discover that the residents have a very low standard of care. There appear to be only two sessions a week when they receive any occupational activities and for the most part they sit around the walls of the room with very little to do, despite the fact that many of them have active minds and are capable of undertaking a variety of activities. She tried to point this out discreetly to the manager, but unfortunately the manager reacts badly at the implied criticism, suggests she is merely touting for more sessions and says the funds do not exist for more activities to be undertaken and that the staff are too busy as it is.

There are several options open to the occupational therapist:

- She could report the situation to the owners or senior management.
- She could complain to the Registration Authority under the Registered Homes Act (see Chapter 29) who would have to investigate her complaint. This would be the local authority.
- In extremely serious cases where it would appear that criminal activities are taking place, she could report the situation to the police.
- She could report the situation to the Social Services Inspectorate of the Department of Health.

However, all are likely to end her association with the home.

■ What if the unsound or unsafe practice she witnesses, is by another professional?

Situation

A chiropodist visits an elderly person who lives alone and is always profusely grateful for the help and attention she receives. She notices that on the dresser the client keeps a few notes of money. She questions her about the advisability of keeping money in the house and on the dresser. The client explains that she always gives the ambulance driver £5 after each visit to the day hospital. The chiropodist fears that the ambulance man might be exploiting the old lady. What action, if any, should she take?

One course would be to explain to the client that the service provided by the ambulance is free and no payment need be made. If the client says that the ambulance men expect it, what does the chiropodist do then? One possibility is for her to take up the complaint to the director of the ambulance service. This would be preferable to writing an anonymous letter or complaining indirectly, but she may find that she becomes a scapegoat.

It is essential, however, that she takes appropriate action and does not ignore the dangers to the client. She has a duty of care to the client and, if harm were eventually to befall the client and it were ascertained that the professional had been aware of the situation but had taken no action, she could face professional misconduct proceedings.

CONCLUSION

There is likely to be an increase in professionals who are self-employed offering their services in the community. As well as those registered under the Council to the Professions Supplementary to Medicine, there are a growing number of complementary medicine therapists whose services are being increasingly purchased from health service bodies within the NHS and by individuals privately. The diversity of care which they can offer brings new challenges to traditional medicine. However, it is essential that clear protocols are established for the safety of clients and that training of the therapists themselves, and also of other professionals in the way in which traditional medicine can be complemented, takes place on a validated basis.

CHAPTER 21

Volunteers

Part of the philosophy of the 1990 NHS and Community Care Act is that the statutory services (whether health or social services) should work in association with voluntary groups, carers and the private sector in providing care to those in need. The voluntary sector is not homogeneous: it embraces those large national organisations such as MIND, MENCAP and Age Concern which are registered charities and have many full time paid staff working for them as well as hundreds of unpaid voluntary helpers, voluntary groups which have no paid staff and finally those carers (who may or may not be part of a recognised organisation) who provide day to day care for many elderly and physically and mentally disabled persons.

This chapter is concerned with the liability for those volunteer workers should they be injured as a result of volunteering their help and also with the issue as to who is responsible if, during their voluntary work, they cause injury or loss or damage to property. In addition the question of the duty of the organisation which appoints volunteers and trains them shall be considered. The next chapter looks at legal issues in relation to the carer.

INJURY CAUSED TO THE VOLUNTEER

It does not follow that because the helper has volunteered his services he therefore takes on the risks of any possible harm befalling him. If he has been appointed and allocated to a client by an organisation which failed to inform him of certain facts, which would have enabled him to be safer had he known them, it could be said that the organisation was in breach of the duty of care that was owed to the volunteer.

Duty to pass on information

Situation

An organisation for the after-care of patients who have received hospital care for the mentally disordered recruit volunteers for visiting the clients and maintaining contact with them. One volunteer develops contact with one client but is not told by the organisation that this client has a history of sexual offences against children. The volunteer invites the client back to his house to meet his family including his three young grandchildren. In ignorance of the client's history he permits the client to take the children to a local play ground where an offence takes place. He claims that he should have known of the client's history before he was introduced to him.

There is no decided case on the point but, working from basic legal principles, it could be argued that the organisation which linked up volunteers with clients should have passed on to the volunteer sufficient information to ensure that the client and the volunteer would be safe. In Chapter 5 on confidentiality the example is used of a justifiable exception to the rule of confidentiality in the public interest in ensuring that volunteers would be safe (see page 88). The organisation might not of course have the requisite information. If, however, they do and if this would ensure that appropriate precautions could be taken then it could be argued that a duty would be recognised in law.

Of course it could be said that the volunteer grandfather was himself at fault since it was extremely irresponsible to allow his grandchildren to be looked after by someone he barely knew.

Another point which arises is the liability of those who referred the client to the voluntary group. Does the referral agent have a duty to pass on relevant information relating to the client's previous offences and previous mental and physical history? If so, might there be a danger that clients will never be able to start a new life? Legislation for a register of paedophiles is to be introduced. (Government announcement, June 1996)

Volenti non fit injuria

This means that 'to the willing there is no wrong' and is a valid defence when injuries occur during high risk activities which have been voluntarily undertaken by the injured person (see Chapter 7).

For example the possibility of being injured during a boxing match or a rugby game is high and, provided these injuries occurred whilst the person who caused them was following the rules of the game, there could not be a successful claim for the damage suffered.

However, this principle does not exonerate the organisers of the game or activity from all responsibility. In a recent case a 17 year old rugby player was awarded damages because the referee of a schoolboy match had failed to keep tight control over the game and it cannot be said that the volunteer automatically takes upon himself the risks of being injured if the referral organisation has been negligent. Nor would a clause attempting to place all responsibility upon the volunteer necessarily be effective.

Situation

A person volunteers his services to assist in a community club. Before he starts he is asked to sign a document which reads as follows:

I agree that if I am injured in anyway whatsoever I shall not hold the organisers, their helpers and their clients responsible.

The volunteer signs the document and starts to work, but is unfortunately injured when a tea urn which is not properly fixed is knocked over and he is scalded. Is he able to seek compensation in spite of the notice?

Such a clause would be covered by the Unfair Contracts Terms Act 1977 which prevents the evasion of liability for negligence where the negligence causes personal injury or death. The volunteer would have to show that a duty of care was owed to him by those responsible for the community hall, that there was a breach of this duty by the failure to fix the tea urn properly and that as a result of that breach he has suffered harm.

Were it only loss or damage to property that occurs as a result of negligence, then such an exemption notice might be effective if it is reasonable to rely upon it. The provisions of the Unfair Contract Terms Act in relation to such notices are shown in Figure 34.2.

■ What however of those circumstances where the volunteer has not been selected and sent to the client by an organisation but has made contact with the client by some other means?

Situation

A neighbour discovers that the person next door is living on her own and has just been discharged from hospital. She helps her by taking in food and by doing her shopping. One day however she discovers the patient in a very distressed state and when she tries to help her is severely punched in the stomach and suffers internal damage.

In these circumstances she has no remedy against any organisation. She might be able to claim criminal injuries compensation or, if there is a prosecution of the patient, the neighbour may be awarded compensation in the criminal court. Although in theory it would be possible for the neighbour to bring a civil action for battery it is unlikely that she would do so or that the patient would have the funds to pay compensation. In such circumstances volunteers take the risk upon themselves.

■ What is the position if the volunteer is injured when using equipment in the home of the client?

Situation

A good neighbour scheme arranges links between those in need and those with time to help. As a result of joining this scheme, Bob Brown used to help an elderly person who lived on his own to have a bath, since he preferred to bath more frequently than the once a week offered by the district nurse service. Bob was assisting the client into the hoist to be lowered into the bath when the strap broke and Bob took the full weight of the old man. Bob subsequently discovered that he had sustained a severe injury to his back. Can he claim compensation?

In a situation like this, it is difficult to find an obvious defendant who would be liable to pay compensation. If the hoist had been newly installed then, depending on the cause of the accident, it may be possible to claim against the manufacturers either on the basis of their liability under the Consumer Protection Act or on the basis of their liability under the tort of negligence. However, if the hoist had been installed for some time and there was no maintenance agreement with the manufacturers they are unlikely to be liable. If the client should have maintained the hoist in good repair then he may be liable but it might be difficult to establish fault, and even if this were possible he may be unable to pay compensation. There may be household insurance which might cover such risks. There is unlikely to be any liability on the part of the network organisation which arranged the links, since they are unlikely to have inspected the equipment. If, when occupational therapists or other community workers visited the premises, they should have noticed the state of the equipment and advised an inspection or maintenance agreement, then there may be liability on the part of the social services or health departments, but this may be difficult to establish. It is little help to the volunteer to discover that he was breaking the regulations relating to manual handling (see Chapter 9). Where a voluntary organisation is sending helpers to assist with community care it is essential that they provide the volunteers with a basic training in the assessment of risks and manual handling.

The best protection for the volunteer is to ensure that he has personal accident cover which would cover such events wherever they occur. Some network organisations who make use of volunteers may take out insurance cover for them.

■ What if the volunteer is actually paid a small sum in recompense by the client, would this affect the liability position?

If an employment situation exists between client and carer, then the employer/client would have a duty to take reasonable care to ensure the health and safety of the employee. This is covered in Chapter 9. However, it is emphasised that the question is one of reasonableness. What elderly people can be expected to do, living on their own, to safeguard the safety of the employee is very different to what can be expected from a large employing organisation.

INJURY CAUSED BY THE VOLUNTEER

Let us look at the reverse situation where it is the volunteer who causes injury to the client or to a third party.

■ Can the injured person recover compensation?

Transport and insurance cover

Situation

A voluntary group organise transport and sitting services for those in need. The volunteers are paid a fee for petrol but otherwise provide their services free. The volunteer agreed to transport an elderly woman to the day hospital and to collect her later. On the way the volunteer drove carelessly and was involved in a collision with another vehicle and the client was injured. It was then discovered that the volunteer did not have any insurance cover.

In such a situation, the Motor Insurers' Bureau would arrange for the payment of compensation in respect of personal injury or death, so the client should be able to recover some compensation. The volunteer was acting illegally and could be prosecuted for driving without insurance cover and also for driving without due care and attention.

■ Would the organisation which arranged the link also be liable?

It could be argued that if it were arranging transport for those in need in the community then it should have been on the basis that the drivers it sent to clients had valid insurance cover. It had a duty of care to take precautions to ensure that the clients would be reasonably safe with the volunteers. However, this has not been argued in court and it remains to be seen whether such a duty of care would be recognised. Much would depend on the terms of the agreement between the networking organisation and the clients taking up the service. It is not sufficient for the voluntary organisation to check the insurance cover initially. Regular checking would have to take place as appropriate.

Vetting volunteers

A similar problem arises in relation to the character and criminal history/propensities of the volunteers. For example it might be that the volunteer has a criminal history of theft and uses the network as a means of entering the property of elderly people or it could be that the volunteer has a history of indecent assault against children and uses the network to give himself a cloak of respectability. The organisation has a responsibility for vetting the volunteers whom it takes on its rotas in order to protect clients. It could be argued that known facts which made the volunteer prima facie unsuitable could not be ignored by the organisation. The voluntary organisation could not exempt itself from liability for its own negligence in failing to vet the suitability of volunteers because of the effect of the Unfair Contract Terms Act 1977 (see above page 126 and Chapters 7 and 34). Where an organisation is an unincorporated body, individual members could be sued.

The standard of care expected of the volunteer

There is one reported case involving a volunteer working for the St John's Ambulance Brigade.

Case: *Cattley v. St. John's Ambulance Brigade*[39]

The St John's Ambulance Brigade were sued by the person helped by two of their members on the grounds that they had caused the victim further harm. The person claiming compensation was 15 at the time of the accident. He had been competing in a motor cycle scramble for school boys. He came off his bike and was treated at the track by two brigade members. He suffered from cracked ribs and also compression fractures of the sixth and seventh dorsal vertebrae which had damaged the spinal cord and caused incomplete paraplegia. He claimed that the spinal injury was aggravated by the negligent examination and treatment offered him by the St John's Ambulance personnel in the period immediately after the fall. It was alleged that he had been lifted to his feet causing further damage to his already injured spinal cord.

The question arose was there a duty of care owed and if so what was the standard? The Judge found no difficulty in holding that there was a duty of care and he held that the standard should be an adaptation of the Bolam test (see glossary and Chapter 7). Did the first aider act in accordance with the standards of the ordinary skilled first aider exercising and professing to have the special skills of a first aider?

In applying this test the judge in this case rejected the evidence of the boy and his father and held that all the evidence pointed to the fact that at all times the first aiders had acted in accordance with the ordinary skill to be expected of a properly trained first aider. The claim was therefore rejected.

Applying this ruling to the situation where a nurse volunteers help in an emergency, the standard which would be applied to her would be the standard of the reasonable professional exercising and professing to have those special skills. The courts would, of course, take into account the circumstances of the case and the facilities which were or were not available in the emergency situation.

In ordinary day to day care by non-professional volunteers, the courts would probably apply the standard of the ordinary volunteer without professional training using reasonable common sense. Where the volunteer has received a professional training then the courts would apply the standard of a person of that profession, whether or not they are being used in that capacity. The UKCC document the *Scope of Professional Practice* states

> Registered nurses who are employed in this sector [personal social services and residential care], whether in homes or in the provision of other services, remain accountable to the Council and subject to the Council's code of Professional Conduct, even if their posts do not require nursing qualifications.

There is no reason why similar principles could not apply even though the registered nurse is offering her unpaid services and other professions might follow the same principles. It does not necessarily follow that the courts would apply the same standard as the professions, but they may well expect a higher standard of care from a person with professional qualifications than a person without.

Training and selection of volunteers

The larger the organisation, the more likely it is that it should arrange for those chosen to assist in the community in clients homes or in community homes to be trained for the tasks expected of them even though they receive no payment for carrying out the tasks.

It is advisable that those organisations using voluntary help should make use of the following precautions.

Interviews: Vital information can be obtained from a face to face interview including questions on the motivation of the volunteer. This personal contact is essential to ensure that suitable persons are recruited. Clearly, however, much depends upon the skill and training of the interviewer herself.

Application form: This should be completed so that full information can be obtained and the consent of the volunteer be obtained to check on driving licence, health record and with the police where appropriate.

References: Should be requested and taken up to ensure that the person is identified and there is nothing which would detract from his suitability.

Training: If volunteers are taken on then training might be essential, depending upon their experience and knowledge.

Support and supervision: This might also be necessary to check out the volunteer's competence in the early stages.

All these procedures must be handled sensitively since there is sometimes a feeling that since volunteers will not be paid, then there should be no hurdles to their offering help and that the organisation should be grateful to all individuals who do volunteer.

Management of volunteers

There is a necessity, especially where large numbers of volunteers are recruited, for them to be managed: this would involve monitoring of their work and identifying any training needs and safeguarding the health and safety and welfare of the clients.

Prior to their active involvement, essential information should be given to the volunteers. This would probably cover the topics listed in Figure 21.1.

Figure 21.1 Essential information for volunteers

- Brief description of the organisation (which might be statutory or charitable) which is arranging the voluntary help. This might include the description of the structure with names and addresses and telephone numbers of relevant officers and contacts.
- Emergency help and telephone numbers.
- Names and telephone numbers of contacts in voluntary agencies.
- Description of opportunities for volunteer help
- Advice on the limits to the volunteers' activities and initiatives.
- Instructions on dealing with crises – epileptic attacks, heart attacks, diabetic comas, aggression/tantrums, and so on.
- Personal confidential information about the client which would be essential for the safety of the volunteer and the client. Some of this could be given by word of mouth. The confidential nature of some of the information should be stressed and the volunteer warned of the repercussions of a breach of confidentiality.
- The position on insurance cover. The volunteer should be advised as to whether the organisation had arranged personal accident and liability insurance cover for its volunteers and what action should be taken if this had not been provided.

If the organisation takes these actions it is unlikely to be held liable for any harm caused by or to the volunteer.

Government guidelines

A circular[40] from the NHS Management Executive in 1992 provided guidelines on voluntary work in hospitals and many of the earlier circulars were replaced. It emphasises that

Voluntary work help has an important place in NHS hospitals. Properly used, it can benefit the patient, the volunteer and NHS management, and should complement the work of paid staff not supplant it. Volunteers should not be used as a substitute for paid staff. Where they are used, it is important that their role is understood and accepted by staff who will be working alongside them.

The circular states that provider units may:

- Make payments to voluntary bodies to enable them to provide services for hospitals. Such payments may be made from trust funds, provided the payments are within the terms of the trusts, or from statutory funds under section 64 of the Health Services and Public Health Act 1968.
- Provide voluntary organisations with facilities or equipment needed to enable them to carry out work for the hospital.
- Reimburse volunteers' travelling expenses and other expenses that arise in the course of their work for the hospital.

Providers are advised to:

- define clearly the scope and limits of the volunteers' activities, and accept liability for the results of such activities; and
- treat voluntary workers in the same way as paid staff for liability purposes.

This circular replaces most of the earlier circulars covering the use of volunteers in hospitals. Although it only addresses the use of volunteer help in hospitals, there is no reason why the same principles should not apply to the use of voluntary help in the community and an NHS Trust which provides community services should be able to make use of voluntary help, accept liability and pay expenses on the same basis as a Trust providing hospital services.

CHAPTER 22

Carers

This chapter is concerned with the legal issues relating to carers, defined here as the unpaid carer looking after his or her relative who is living at home. The legal issues which arise for the carer will be considered against the background of the numbers undertaking a caring role and the problems which they face.

THE BACKGROUND

What is the number of carers?

The Carers National Association has estimated that there are six million carers looking after those with a wide variety of conditions and handicaps.

A survey conducted for the Cancer Relief and Macmillan Fund by MORI in 1992 found as follows:

- Cancer sufferers receive inadequate home care and many relied upon the good nature of friends and relatives.
- Carers spend an average of 12 hours a day helping cancer sufferers and a fifth devote 24 hours a day.
- The regional nurse adviser of the East Anglia Health Region said that too many people are falling through the net.
- There are good voluntary groups but this is patchy.
- Hopes were placed on the forthcoming implementation of the community care aspects of the 1990 Act that these needs would be identified.
- Sixty percent of the carers became ill because of the enormous pressures.

What is the cost to the carers?

A survey by the Alzheimer's Disease Society in 1993 showed that:

● Forty per cent of carers for people with dementia are having to use private savings or arrange loans to meet the cost of the care.

● More than 25 per cent are paying over £100 a month and 20 per cent aged over 80 are spending more than £200 per month.

The Society concluded that the NHS was turning its back on long term help for the old and sick, transferring the burden to their families and causing financial hardship and emotional stress. The Society stated the many of the increased costs for carers are caused by the introduction of charges following the implementation of the community care provisions of the 1990 Act in April 1993. One carer cited that the annual cost of looking after her relative had risen by almost £2000 since her local authority started charging £230 a week for respite care – taken eight weeks a year to give her a break – and for meals in the day centre the relative attends. The Society estimated that long term NHS beds for the elderly have been cut by almost a fifth since 1986 to 45 000, at a time of rapid growth in the elderly population, and that less than a third of the carers surveyed had access to them. Two thirds said that there was no sitting service, with trained volunteers providing relief care, in their local area.

Who are the carers?

Women and elderly men

Research studies have shown that a disproportionate burden of caring falls upon women. In 1980 a survey carried out by the Equal Opportunities Commission reported that 75 per cent of carers were women and see also other references quoted by Mike Fisher in his article, 'Care Management and Social Work: Working with carers'[43]. The general household survey carried out in 1985 estimated that there were 6 million carers of which some 3.5 million were women and 76 per cent of carers were caring for someone over 65. The survey, however, also brought out that a higher proportion of men in the over 65 age group are carers compared with women over that age and that a considerable number of them are caring for a spouse.

Elderly parents

A survey by the North West Thames region in 1992 showed a population of 2400 mentally handicapped people with an average age of 30 who are living at home. Almost half of their parents are aged over 60 years and it was calculated that 50 to 60 sets of parents in the region will die every year so their children will need providing for.

Employees

Employers do not recognise the needs of their employees who are also carers. A survey in 1989 by the Institute of Personnel Management found that of 500 firms contacted in the private sector none offered terms or conditions to help carers and that only a few of public sector employers gave help. A survey by the Department of Employment and the Office of Population Censuses and Surveys showed that half of women carers felt they were prevented from going to work mostly because of problems in getting time off. The Institute of Personnel Management suggested that companies should offer employees advice on caring, flexible work patterns and consultations comparable to some firms in America.

Young carers

Recently Carers National Association has drawn attention to the number of young people, many of school age and some below 10, who are the main carer in the family. Clearly their needs as well as the client for whom they care must be taken into account in assessing the needs and the services which should be provided under community care legislation. In some situations, action under the Children Act 1989 may also be required to ensure that the child receives appropriate protection.

Granny dumping

Because of the pressure upon carers it is suggested that granny dumping might start in this country. 'Granny dumping' is a phenomena so far only evidenced in the United States where an elderly dependent is left at an institution or hospital, sometimes in a wheel chair with a label around the neck saying 'please look after granny'[44]. The American College of Emergency Physicians had estimated that up to 70 000 elderly people were being dumped every year in America. Dr Harper's study showed that in a small survey of 100 elderly people and their families only 25 per cent of the elderly had the kind of extended family necessary for providing long term care. A further 25 per cent had no family near by so were looked after by the social services.

The most disadvantaged group was the remainder, those who had one family member near by who bore the entire burden of caring. Typically this might mean that a daughter in her sixties was looking after a mother in her eighties fulltime, with little outside support. Overstretched social services departments concentrated resources on the elderly with no relation near by, leaving the single carers unsupported. (Refer also to Chapter 17 on elder abuse and the health visitor.)

LIABILITIES OF THE CARER

What is the legal situation in relation to carers – do they have a duty to care? How does this duty arise?

Is there a duty to care?

Many carers find themselves in the situation of being the main carer by accident rather than design. A study of daughters showed it was not a question of carers actively deciding to care, it was rather a drift into a caring relationship[45].

- What is the legal duty of carers? Could they refuse to have a father or sister back home after the relative has been in hospital?
- What if they tire of the onerous duties of caring? Can they refuse to carry on and arrange for others to take over?
- Is there any legal burden on a carer if they perform their task inadequately? Would they be legally liable if the standard of care they provided fell below that which could reasonably have been expected?

Statutory provisions

There is some statutory guidance on the legal responsibility of the carer.

A parent is responsible for the care of his child up to the age of 18 years. This applies even though some other person subsequently acquires parental responsibility for the child (Children Act 1989 Section 2(5)). Parental responsibility can only be lost before the child reaches 18 through adoption or death. It is defined as 'all the rights, duties, powers, responsibilities and authority which by law a parent of a child has in relation to the child and his property' (Section 3(1) Children Act 1989).

People who care for mentally disordered patients commit an offence under the Mental Health Act 1983 section 127 if they ill-treat or wilfully neglect a mentally disordered person in their care. See Figure 22.1 for the actual words of the section.

Figure 22.1 Mental Health Act 1983, section 127(2)

It shall be an offence for any individual to ill-treat or wilfully to neglect a mentally disordered patient who is for the time being subject to his guardianship under this Act or otherwise in his custody or care (whether by virtue of legal or moral obligation or otherwise).

The Law Commission in its second consultation paper on decision making and the mentally incapacitated adult[46] has suggested that this offence should be extended to include all incapacitated persons. In its final report *Mental Incapacity*[47] it sets out a draft Bill and clause 32 is shown below:

> It is an offence for any person to whom this section applies to ill-treat or wilfully neglect a person in relation to whom he has powers by virtue of this part of the Act.

The persons covered by this clause are shown in Figure 22.2.

Figure 22.2 Persons covered by clause 32 of the Bill on Mental Incapacity

(a) any person having care of, or in the lawful control of property of the person concerned;
(b) any donee of a continuing power of attorney granted by him;
(c) any person appointed by the court to be his manager

The Government at the time of writing has not indicated its intentions in relation to the Law Commission report, apart from setting up a working party to look at the proposals in relation to advance refusals of treatment.

The question of whether carers who have an existing duty to care can legally discharge the duty of caring for another person or have it set aside is not however considered.

Criminal sanctions
It can be a criminal offence if there is failure to care for an infirm person. For example a conviction for manslaughter can be based on reckless breach of the duty to care for the victim.

Case: *R* v. *Stone, R* v. *Dobinson*[48]

A partially deaf and almost blind man of low average intelligence and no appreciable sense of smell and his mistress, who was ineffectual and inadequate, (the appellants) lived together in his house with his mentally handicapped son. The man's sister came to live at the house as a lodger in one room without ventilation, toilet or washing facilities except a polythene bucket. She was morbidly anxious not to put on weight, denied herself proper meals, spent days at a time in the room and within three years became helplessly infirm so that she did not leave her bed. She did not, however, complain. The mistress (who took the sister such food as she required) attempted to wash her with the aid of a neighbour, who advised the mistress to go to social services. The licensee of a public house which the appellants used to visit advised also the mistress to obtain a doctor. The sister had refused to give the appellants the name of her doctor, whom they had unsuccessfully tried to find. An attempt by the man to obtain his own doctor for her was unsuccessful, but the couple did no more to enlist outside professional help. They did not mention anything to the social worker who used to visit the son. Some three weeks after the attempt to wash the sister she died from toxaemia spreading from infected bed sores, prolonged immobilisation and lack of food. If she had received medical care in the intervening period she would probably have survived.

The couple were charged with manslaughter. The jury were directed to consider the circumstances in relation to each of the couple according to their individual knowledge of the sister's condition and their appreciation of the need to act and the consequence of inaction in view of procurable facilities, and to determine whether the prosecution had established a gross neglect of a duty of care amounting to reckless disregard of the sister's health and well-being. They were convicted and appealed against their conviction. The appeal was dismissed on the ground that on the facts the jury were entitled to find that the couple had assumed a duty to care for the sister and were obliged to summon help or care for the sister themselves when she became helplessly infirm.

Since they had undertaken the duty of caring for the sister who was incapable of caring for herself, the breach of duty which had to be established was a reckless disregard of danger to her health and welfare by indifference to an obvious risk of injury to health – actually foreseeing the risk and determining nevertheless to run it. Mere inadvertence was insufficient. However, since the jury had been directed in accordance with the principles applicable, the appeal failed. It must be emphasised that this was a criminal case where it was duties in relation to the criminal law which were the subject of the prosecution.

Thus there is both statutory provision and a recognition at common law in the criminal law that there is a duty to care in specific circumstances. However these circumstances are not clearly identified and it would appear that, unless the relationship is parent/child or the carer lives with the relative who needs caring, the law would not recognise a duty to care in the criminal law.

Civil sanction

The situation in relation to the duty of care in the civil law is unclear. On the one hand there is clear judicial recognition of the fact that there is no duty in the civil law to volunteer assistance if there is not a pre-existing duty. On the other hand it is possible that by volunteering assistance initially, a person is deemed to take on a duty of care.

Situation

Frank lives in a house which is rented by several different tenants who live in separate rooms but share a kitchen and bathroom. They all have separate tenancy contracts with the landlord. They mix very little but Frank becomes aware that a tenant on the same floor as himself seems to leave her room very little and never seems to be in the kitchen preparing food. He knew that she had a history of mental illness and hospitalisation. He decided not to interfere and it was several days before she was eventually discovered to be at the point of death from starvation. An inquest was held and Frank was called to give evidence.

In this case it is unlikely that Frank would be prosecuted under the Mental Health Act section 127 since the girl was not under his care and control. However, if he had started to take her food or in other ways show care the section could be interpreted as applying to him. If Frank were, in fact, the resident landlord and the relatives of the dead tenant were to bring a civil action against him they would have to prove that he owed a duty of care to his tenant beyond that set out in any tenancy agreement and it is submitted that this might be difficult to establish.

If the Law Commission draft Bill quoted above is enacted, it may lead to a clarification of both civil and criminal responsibility in relation to identifying who is regarded as having a legal duty as carer.

Effect of assuming duty of care

■ What if carers decide that they cannot undertake the burden any longer and leave the person in need – can they be prosecuted?

The statutory provisions and the cases quoted earlier show that once the carer has assumed the duty of care, then it cannot be relinquished unless alternative arrangements are made to ensure that the client will be reasonably safe. This would also apply to the arrangements in respect of decision making by the mentally incapacitated set out in the Law Commission Report No. 231 cited above.

Financial responsibility

Financial responsibility is more clearly defined in the Social Security Regulations. Thus a husband and wife are each liable to maintain the other. Under section 106 of the Social Security Administration Act 1992 the Secretary of State has power to attempt to recover expenditure on income support from a person liable for maintenance. Where one spouse becomes a resident in residential care or a nursing home, the couple's finances are treated separately. The resident's income and capital alone is taken into account in determining income support, but the other non-resident spouse might be liable to contribute (see Chapter 33). The local authority also has power under section 42 of the National Assistance Act 1948 to recover maintenance from a spouse or former spouse.

It has been suggested[49] that the wider family and not the state should be responsible for providing financial help to impoverished relatives what ever the nature of the relationship: thus parents, grandparents, uncles, aunts, children should be sent the bill for state support to their impoverished relatives. It must be emphasised however that this is not yet so in law and no legal duty exists on this wider family to provide financial support.

ASSESSMENT AND SUPPORT FOR CARERS

Discussion in relation to the abuse of the elderly can be found in Chapter 17. It is now recognised that some abuse might result from the stress to which the carer is subjected and therefore one of the key elements in the strategy to prevent elder abuse is the assessment of the needs of carers in their own right. Guidance from the Social Services Inspectorate[50] confirms that 'while a separate assessment may not always be appropriate, carers' needs should always be assessed as part of the overall process'. The strategy identifies different types of service for different situations which may reduce carer stress. Figure 22.3 shows the list of services suggested in the report which is based on information from Patricia Riley, former Divisional Director Leeds SSD.

Figure 22.3 Support for carers and alleviation of elder abuse

Relief of carer stress	Making environment less abusive
● Health information	● Advocacy and empowerment
● Respite care	● Refuges
● Day care	● Preventive health screening
● Home care	● Legal interventions
● Nursing support	● Family placement (long term)
● Continence advice and aids	● Institutional care
● Welfare rights services	● Police involvement
● Aids/adaptations	● Counselling of abuser
● Carer support groups	● Removal of abuser
● Adult placement schemes (short term)	● Re-housing

An Act was passed in 1995 which placed a duty upon the local authority to carry out an assessment of the carers. The Carers (Recognition and Services) Act 1995 aims at providing for the assessment of the ability of carers to provide care. The provisions of the Act are set out in Figure 22.4.

Figure 22.4 Carers (Recognition and Services) Act 1995 – section 1

Assessment of carer under 1990 Act assessment

(1) Subject to subsection (3) below, in any case where —

(a) a local authority carry out an assessment under section 47(1)(a) of the National Health Service and Community Care Act 1990 of the needs of a person ('the relevant person') for community care services, and

(b) an individual ('the carer') provides or intends to provide a substantial amount of care on a regular basis for the relevant person,

the carer may request the local authority, before they make their decision as to whether the needs of the relevant person call for the provision of any services, to carry out an assessment of his ability to provide and to continue to provide care for the relevant person; and if he makes such a request, the local authority shall carry out such an assessment and shall take into account the results of that assessment in making that decision.

(2) [Identical provisions in relation to assessment of disabled children under Part III of the Children Act 1989 or section 2 of the Chronically Sick and Disabled Persons Act 1970]

(3) No request may be made under subsection (1) or (2) above by an individual who provides or will provide the care in question —

(a) by virtue of a contract of employment or other contract with any person; or

(b) as a volunteer for a voluntary organisation.

The Secretary of State is empowered by the Act to give directions as to the manner in which an assessment is to be carried out or the form it is to take and, subject to these directions, the local authority shall carry out the assessment in such manner and take such form as it considers appropriate. The Act also makes financial provision: there shall be paid out of money provided by Parliament any increase attributable to this Act in the sums payable out of money so provided under any other enactment. The Act came into force on 1 April 1996. Separate provisions apply to Scotland and the Act does not apply to Northern Ireland.

The Act is likely to have limited effect unless resources are provided to implement both the requirement to assess the carer, if a request is made, and also to provide the necessary additional services required to both carer and client which are indicated by that assessment.

In addition the Act only requires the request for the assessment to be made by the carer rather than requiring an automatic assessment of the carer when the assessment of the client is made. Logically one would have considered that both should go hand in hand without a specific request having to be made. It remains to be seen what directions, if any, are issued on the nature of the assessment.

DOES THE CARER HAVE ANY RIGHTS?

■ How many of the services listed in Figure 22.3 are available to the carer by statutory right?

There are no statutory provisions which set out any rights of the carer. Of course should they, as frequently happens, become ill themselves as a result of the pressure and stress of caring, they would have their own entitlements to care as a client. In addition the capabilities of the carer should be taken into account in the assessment of the client under section 47 of the 1990 Act. As we have seen, however, if this assessment leads to a recognition of needs which cannot be resourced because of inadequate allocation there is little that the carer or client can do in law other than complain through the complaints procedure. Reference should be made to Chapter 2 on the rights of the client and to Chapter 27 on enforcement provisions.

Situation

Doris, a daughter aged 65, had been caring for her 87 year old mother who had been suffering from Alzheimer's disease for many years. She herself suffered from arthritis and looked forward to a two week respite break she had each year when her mother was taken into the assessment ward for the elderly mentally infirm. She was informed that because of the pressure upon beds and the demand for respite they would not be able to allocate her mother a place in the hospital. The only alternative was for her to be sent to a private nursing home but in this case she would have to pay several hundred pounds for the two week stay. Neither Doris nor her mother had such funds and contacted the social services who from 1 April 1993 had become responsible for purchasing places in the private sector for persons in need of residential and nursing home accommodation. Doris was told that, although she had a very good case, she could not be given priority, since in view of the shortage of funds priority had to be given to those who needed permanent residential/nursing home care. What are Doris' legal rights?

There appears to be no simple way in which Doris can enforce the provision of respite care. Firstly, there is no clear legal right to such claims, and it is apparent that over the country some social service departments and health authorities have far more generous provision for respite than others. Secondly, even if there were such a right the legal means of enforcement are slow expensive and uncertain as can be seen from Chapter 27.

The irony is that if Doris, through pressure and stress, becomes so ill that she herself has to be admitted to hospital, the social services department would then have a clear duty in law to arrange for the institutional or alternative care of Doris' mother.

Similarly the carer appears to have no legal right to support, night care services, and other assistance. Where the client requires this help, the carer could apply to the providers on behalf of the client. In addition carers should take a major part in the assessment process and their views be taken into account in assessing needs and priorities.

With the uncertainties of local authority social services provision it is inevitable that many carers and clients have become dependent upon the support and services provided in the voluntary sector by such organisations as the Alzheimer's Disease Society, Age Concern and many others.

It is too early to assess what effects the community provisions of the 1990 Act have had upon the carers – whether more information has been given to them and whether they have been given a meaningful role in the assessment process – although as seen above[51] the charging provisions have caused increased financial hardship.

Many of the voluntary organisations call for the recognition of rights for the carers. The Alzheimer's Disease Society for example have called for urgent action for the following needs of carers and sufferers to be recognised:

- early assessment and support;
- co-operation (especially between health and social services departments in planning and support services, and in the discharge procedures);
- adequate financial support;
- regular breaks and respite care provision;
- a full range of domiciliary and residential care services funded by health and social services in every district and
- reliable support from flexible generic home care workers, properly paid and trained.

A new initiative chaired by the Princess Royal has been set up to recognise the work of carers and to provide support and protection for them.

The Carers National Association is one of several charities which have sought legal advice on the duties of assessment and meeting the needs of clients under the provisions of the NHS and Community Care Act 1990 (see Chapter 25) and will test the new statutory provisions by supporting individuals in bringing cases to court.

WHAT RIGHT DOES THE CARER HAVE TO SPEAK ON BEHALF OF THE CLIENT?

Those sections of the Disabled Persons (Services, Consultation and Representation) Act 1986 which would enable a representative to be appointed to speak for the client have not been implemented. This is further discussed in Chapters 2 and 25.

Therefore, at present the carers are in an anomalous position. They are often asked to give consent on behalf of a mentally incapacitated adult; their views might be sought over resuscitation, over operative procedures and also in non-health areas such as living accommodation, finances, education and training. Yet they have no legal status in the giving of such advice. The law does not give them a right to speak on behalf of the incapacitated adult. This anomaly is being considered by the Law Commission in the series of consultation papers which are discussed in Chapter 3 and have led to final recommendations with draft legislation.

It is essential that the recommendations of the Law Commission on the decision making on behalf of the mentally incapacitated adult are implemented as soon as possible since the present situation of the carer in relation to decision making is far from satisfactory. They are frequently exploited because of their ignorance of the legal situation in relation to responsibilities for caring, financial responsibilities, decision making on treatment and care. They often breach confidentiality, or are asked to give consent when there is no legal power to do so. Many carers believe that they are guardians of those in their care, but this is not the legal situation. Where the client is mentally incapacitated there is a legal duty and power on the part of the professional to take decisions on the basis of the decision in the case of *Re F* (see Chapter 3 and glossary)

The decisions of carers can be overridden where they are not made in the best interests of the client but the procedure for so doing is not clearly established and the Law Commission's proposals are vital in this respect.

CONCLUSION

Carer support networks are vital and some useful addresses can be found in Appendix 7. The Carers National Association in particular provides information and campaigns for their needs and rights to be recognised. Many carers are isolated. Many do not have the basic information of what services are available and how they can be accessed. Nevertheless, through the networks they can receive practical help and occasionally the legal advice necessary to support any claim for assistance for themselves or their relatives.

REFERENCES FOR SECTION B PART 2

1. Smith & Bailey *The Modern English Legal System* (eds S. H. Bailey & M. J. Gunn) Sweet & Maxwell, 1991, Chapter 17
2. Department of Health *Caring for People: Community Care in the next decade and beyond – Policy Guidance* HMSO, 1990
3. Peter Singh *Community Care: Britain's other Lottery* MENCAP, 1995
4. Department of Health *Discharge of Patients from Hospital* DoH, 1989
5. June Neill and Jenny Williams *Leaving Hospital: Elderly people and their discharge to community care* National Institute for Social Work Research Unit, HMSO, 1992
6. Department of Health Circular EL (95) 5 *Purchasing high-tech health care for patients at home.* NHSME, 1995
7. Pauline Roberts *Hospital at Home* Nursing Times Vol. 88 No. 44 28 October 1992
8. Edited by Ann Mackenzie *Hospital at Home: the District Nurse as a key worker – four different viewpoints.* District Nursing Association, Edinburgh, 1991
9. Advisory Paper *Scope of Professional Practice* UKCC, 1992
10. *British National Formulary* RPSGB
11. Department of Health *Code of Practice: Mental Health Act 1983* HMSO, 1993
12. *R v. Ealing District Health Authority, ex parte Fox* [1993] 2 All ER 170
13. *R v. Hallstrom, ex parte W; R v. Gardner, ex parte L* [1986] 2 WLR 883; [1986] 2 All ER 306
14. B. Dimond and F. Barker *Mental Health Law for Nurses* Blackwell Science 1995
15. David Simes *Opportunities for Change – A New Direction for Nursing for People with learning disabilities* reported in BJN and see Mark Jukes BJN 1993 Vol. 2 No. 10, May/June 1993
16. Department of Health *Code of Practice: Mental Health Act 1983* HMSO, 1993
17. Law Commission Report No. 231 *Mental Incapacity* HMSO 1995
18. For example B. Dimond *Legal Aspects of Child Health Care* Mosby, 1995
19. Advisory Paper *Exercising Accountability* UKCC, March 1989
20. *Standards for business and conduct for NHS staff* HSG(93)5
21. *R v. Cox* [1993] All ER 19
22. Session 1993–1994 HMSO, 1994
23. B. Dimond *Legal Aspects of Child Health Care* Mosby, 1995
24. Department of Health *The Health of the Nation* HMSO, 1993
25. Welsh Office *Strategic Intent and Direction Initiative* HMSO, 1989
26. Welsh Office *Strategy for Nursing – Health Visiting* Circulated under cover of Chief Nursing Officer letter CNO(93) 10
27. HMSO 1992
28. SSI *No longer afraid: the safeguard of older people in domestic settings* HMSO, 1993
29. Law Commission Consultation Papers No. 119, HMSO, 1991; and Nos. 128, 129 and 130 HMSO, 1993; and Report No. 231 HMSO 1995
30. Chaired by Mr Monty Graham: Welsh Office, 1992
31. Registrar's letter on Practice Nurses, UKCC, 1993
32. *Practice nurse journal* March 1989, Vol. 1, No. 8, page 392
33. *Practice nurse journal* September 1989, Vol. 2, No. 4, page 150
34. Advisory Paper *Standards for the Administration of Medicines* UKCC, October 1992

35. Department of Health *Immunization Against Infections Diseases* HMSO, 1990
36. Registrar's letter on Practice Nurses, UKCC, 1993
37. Law Commission Report No. 231 *Mental Incapacity* HMSO 1995
38. Department of Health *Feet First: Report of the Department of Health and NHS Chiropody Task Force* NHS Executive 1994 (see EL (94) 69)
38a. JM Consulting Ltd (1996) *The Regulation of Health Professions: Report of a review of the Professions Supplementary to Medicine Act (1960) with recommendations for new legislation* Conducted and Published by JM Consulting Ltd
39. *Cattley* v. *St John's Ambulance Brigade* QBD 25 November 1989 unreported but see article by Gerwyn Griffiths in *Modern Law Review* 1990 Vol. 53, page 255
40. HSG(92) 15
41. reported at the time in the national press
42. reported at the time in the national press
43. Mike Fisher 'Care Management and Social Work: Working with Carers' *Practice* Vol. 4, No. 4, pages 242–52
44. Sarah Harper, Royal Holloway and Beford College, speaking at the Institute of British Geographers, 9 January 1992
45. J. Lewis and B. Meredith *Daughters who care* London, Routledge and Kegan Paul, 1988
46. Law Commission Consultation Paper No 12 *A New jurisdiction* HMSO, 1993
47. Law Commission Report No. 231 *Mental Incapacity* HMSO, 1995
48. *R* v. *Stone, R* v. *Dobinson* [1977] QB 354
49. Digby Anderson Sunday Times 7 January 1990
50. *Confronting Elder Abuse* SSI, 1992 and *Different Types of Service for different situations* SSI, 1993
51. The Alzheimer's Disease Society survey 1993

SECTION C

The Statutory Authorities and other organisations

The purpose of this Section is to look at those organisations through which care in the community is purchased and delivered and to consider the changes effected by recent legislation. The first chapter deals with the statutory duties of health authorities and NHS Trusts. The next chapter looks at the statutory duties of health authorities in relation to primary care and the role of the General Practitioner fund-holders. A consideration of the role of local authorities then follows and then there is a chapter which considers the independent sector. Finally there is a look at the ways in which the duties of these statutory bodies can be enforced.

CHAPTER 23

Health Authorities and Trusts

STATUTORY DUTIES IN THE NATIONAL HEALTH SERVICE

The main statutes outlining the duties of health service bodies to provide community care are set out in Figure 23.1.

Figure 23.1 Statutes covering the duty to provide health and community care

- National Health Service Act 1977 (based on the National Health Service Act 1946)
- Health and Social Services and Social Security Adjudication Act 1983
- Mental Health Act 1983
- National Health Service and Community Care Act 1990

Other relevant legislation will be covered in the appropriate chapter. The emphasis in this chapter will be upon the changes brought about by the recent legislation.

HEALTH SERVICES

The National Health Service Act 1977 (re-enacting the provisions with amendments of the National Health Service Act 1946) places the duty shown in Figure 23.2 on the Secretary of State.

Figure 23.2 The National Health Service Act 1977 – Section 1(1)

It is the Secretary of State's duty to continue the promotion in England and Wales of a comprehensive health service designed to secure improvement —

(a) in the physical and mental health of the people of those countries, and
(b) in the prevention, diagnosis and treatment of illness,

and for the purpose to provide or secure the effective provision of services in accordance with this Act.

Section 2 gives the Secretary of State a general power as shown in Figure 23.3.

Figure 23.3 National Health Service Act 1977 – section 2

Without prejudice [see glossary] to the Secretary of State's powers apart from this section, he has power —

(a) to provide such services as he considers appropriate for the purpose of discharging any duty imposed on him by this Act; and
(b) to do any other thing whatsoever which is calculated to facilitate, or is conducive or incidental to, the discharge of such a duty.

This section is subject to section 3(3) below.

It should also be noted that the list of powers given in Figure 23.3 does not cut down the general power shown in Figure 23.2 or other powers given in other sections.

Section 3 sets out in more detail the specific provisions which the Secretary of State has a duty to make (see Figure 23.4).

Figure 23.4 Specific services to be provided – section 3(3)

It is the Secretary of State's duty to provide throughout England and Wales, *to such extent as he considers necessary to meet all reasonable requirements* [author's emphasis] —

(a) hospital accommodation;
(b) other accommodation for the purpose of any service provided under this Act;
(c) medical, dental, nursing and ambulance services;
(d) such other facilities for the care of expectant and nursing mothers and young children as he considers are appropriate as part of the health service;
(e) such facilities for the prevention of illness, the care of persons suffering from illness and the after-care of persons who have suffered from illness as he considers are appropriate as part of the health service;
(f) such other services as are required for the diagnosis and treatment of illness.

Some of the other specific powers set out in the 1977 Act are shown in Figure 23.5.

Figure 23.5 Additional powers of the Secretary of State

Section 5(1)(a): school health and dental inspections treatment and education

Section 5(1)(b): contraceptive advice and supplies

Section 5(2)(a): provision of invalid carriages

Section 5(2)(b): accommodation outside Great Britain for those suffering from respiratory tuberculosis

Section 5(2)(c): a microbiological service for which charges can be made (2A)

Section 5(2)(d): research into causation, prevention, diagnosis or treatment of illness

Duties, powers and enforcement

It should be noted that whilst sections 1 and 3 are framed as duties, sections 2 and section 5 give him powers. A duty means that there is an obligation upon the Secretary of State to ensure that provision of a service is made. In contrast, he has a complete discretion over whether a power should be exercised. However, even when a duty is set down within the section it is not necessarily absolute. Section 3 shows clearly that the Secretary of State is given a discretion in determining how this duty is to be performed as can be seen from the emphasised phrase in Figure 23.4. In addition, the reported cases where individuals have attempted to force the Secretary of State and health service bodies into providing hospital care have all failed. The courts have held that it is not their task to determine the allocation of resources and, providing that the task is undertaken reasonably and that there is no breach of the public duty, the court would not interfere[1]. For discussion on the enforceability of these statutory duties see Chapter 27.

CO-OPERATION BETWEEN HEALTH SERVICES AND LOCAL AUTHORITY SERVICES

There are several ways in which the statutory provisions ensure that there is co-operation between the health and social services authorities. The following will be discussed below:

- A statutory duty to co-operate
- The establishment of Joint Consultative Committees
- Sharing of duties by the authorities
- Sharing of staff
- Joint funding of projects
- Transfer of health services funds for social services, voluntary and other services.

A statutory duty to co-operate

Co-operation between health and local authorities is a requirement under section 22(1) of the 1977 Act as shown in Figure 23.6.

Figure 23.6 The NHS Act 1977 – section 22(1)

In exercising their respective functions health authorities and local authorities shall co-operate with one another in order to secure and advance the health and welfare of the people of England and Wales

Other legislation places a duty on the two authorities to co-operate in specific circumstances, such as section 117 of the Mental Health Act 1983 which requires the health authority and the local authority to work together with voluntary organisations in the planning and provision of after-care services for certain formally detained patients once they have left hospital.

The establishment of Joint Consultative Committees (JCCs)

These are the bodies which are set up between health authorities, and the relevant local authorities, together with other organisations in the area, to consider the joint planning of health and social services. They must be set up under section 22(2) of the 1977 Act which states that the joint consultative committees shall advise bodies represented on them on performance of their duty to co-operate under section 22(1), and on the planning and operation of services of common concern to those authorities.

Sharing of duties by the authorities

Schedule 8 of the National Health Service Act 1977 enables the local authority to carry out some of the duties placed upon the Secretary of State for Health and is as set out in Figure 23.7. Note, however, that the right of the authority to make payments to individuals is limited by Paragraph 2(2).

Figure 23.7 Schedule 8 – Local Social Services Authorities

Care of mothers and young children (Paragraph 1)

1. (1) A local social service authority may, with the Secretary of State's approval, and to such extent as he may direct shall, make arrangements for the care of expectant and nursing mothers other than for the provision of residential accommodation for them and of children who have not attained the age of five years and are not attending primary schools maintained by a local education authority.

Prevention, care and after-care (Paragraph 2)

2. (1) A local social services authority may, with the Secretary of State's approval, and to such extent as he may direct shall, make arrangements for the purpose of the prevention of illness and for the care of persons suffering from illness and for the after-care of persons who have been so suffering and in particular for —

[(a) provision of residential accommodation – repealed]

(b) the provision, for persons whose care is undertaken with a view to preventing them from becoming ill, persons suffering from illness and persons who have been so suffering, of centres or other facilities for training them or keeping them suitably occupied and the equipment and maintenance of such centres;

(c) the provision, for the benefit of such persons as are mentioned in paragraph (b) above, of ancillary or supplemental services; and

(d) for the exercise of the functions of the authority in respect of persons suffering from mental disorder who are received into guardianship under Part II or Part III of the Mental Health Act 1983 (whether the guardianship of the local social service authority or other persons).

Such an authority shall neither have the power nor be subject to a duty to make under this paragraph arrangements to provide facilities for any of the purposes mentioned in section 15(1) of the Disabled Persons (Employment) Act 1944.

(2) No arrangements under this paragraph shall provide for the payment of money to persons for whose benefit they are made except —

(a) in so far as they may provide for the remuneration of such persons engaged in suitable work in accordance with the arrangements; or

(b) to persons who —
  (i) are, or have been, suffering from mental disorder within the meaning of the Mental Health Act 1983,
  (ii) are under the age of 16 years, and
  (iii) are resident in accommodation provided under the arrangements,

  of such amounts as the local social service authority think fit in respect of their occasional personal expenses where it appears to that authority that no such payment would otherwise be made.

(3) The Secretary of State may make regulations as to the conduct of premises in which, in pursuance of arrangements made under this paragraph, are provided for persons whose care is undertaken with a view to preventing them from becoming sufferers from mental disorder with the meaning of that Act of 1983 or who are, or have been, so suffering, facilities for training them or keeping them suitably occupied.

. . .

(4AA) No authority is authorised or may be required under this paragraph to provide residential accommodation for any person. [A restriction inserted by the NHS and Community Care Act 1990.]
[The provision or purchase of residential places in accommodation by local authorities comes under another Act (see Section D)]

Home help and laundry facilities (Paragraph 3)

(1) It is the duty of every local social services authority to provide on such a scale as is adequate for the needs of their area, or to arrange for the provision on such a scale as is so adequate, of home help for households where such help is required owing to the presence of —

(a) a person who is suffering from illness, lying-in, an expectant mother, aged, handicapped as a result of having suffered from illness or by congenital deformity, or

(b) a child who has not attained the age which, for the purposes of the Education Act 1944 is, in his case, the upper limit for compulsory school age,

and every such authority has power to provide or arrange for the provision of laundry facilities for households for which home help is being, or can be, provided under this sub-paragraph.

Research (Paragraph 4)
[Added by the Health and Social Services and Social Security Adjudications Act 1983]

4. Without prejudice to any powers conferred on them by any other Act, a local social services authority may conduct or assist other persons in conducting research into matters relating to the functions of local social services authorities under this Schedule.

Sharing of staff

Section 28 as amended by the Health and Medicines Act 1988 section 19 and the NHS and Community Care Act 1990 enables the local social services authority staff to assist in the provision of health services. It is set out in Figure 23.8.

Figure 23.8 Section 28 – Supply of Goods and Services by local authorities

(3) Every local authority shall make available to health authorities and NHS trusts acting in the area of the local authority the services of persons employed by the local authority for the purposes of the local authority's functions under the Local Authorities Social Services Act 1970 so far as is reasonably necessary and practicable to enable health authorities and NHS trusts to discharge their functions under this Act and the National Health Service and Community Care Act 1990.

Joint funding of projects and transfer of funds

The provisions of the new section 28A and Schedule 8 of the NHS Act 1977 as amended enabled the transfer of funds from the health services to local social services to make provision for persons who would otherwise be retained in hospital accommodation because of a lack of resources in the community. The Act also enables payments to be made to voluntary organisations but there is a requirement that such payments should be recommended and be in accord with the advice given by the Joint Consultative Committee.

Details of the powers are set out in Figure 23.9.

Figure 23.9 Section 28A – Power to make payments towards
expenditure on community services

(1) This section applies to the following authorities —

(a) a Health Authority; and
(b) a special teaching health authority established for a London Post-
Graduate Teaching Hospital.

(2) An authority to whom this section applies may, if they think fit, make
payments —

(a) to a local social services authority towards expenditure incurred or to
be incurred by them in connection with [various functions]
(b) to a district council, towards expenditure incurred or to be incurred by
them in connection with their functions [in connection with residential
homes and meals and recreation for old people];
(c) to an authority who are a local education authority for the purposes of
the Education Acts 1944 to 1981, towards expenditure incurred or to
be incurred by them in connection with their functions for the benefit
of disabled persons;
(d) to an authority who are a local authority for the purposes of the
Housing Act 1957, towards expenditure incurred or to be incurred by
them in connection with their functions [for provision of housing
accommodation]; and
(e) to [various] bodies, in respect of expenditure incurred or to be incurred
by them in connection with the provision of housing accommodation —
[housing associations, new towns and so on].

(3) A payment under this section may be made in respect of expenditure
of a capital or of a revenue nature or in respect of both kinds of
expenditure.

(4) No payment shall be made under this section in respect of any
expenditure unless the expenditure has been recommended for a payment
under this section by a joint consultative committee on which the authority
proposing to make the payment are represented.

(5) The Secretary of State may by directions prescribe conditions relating
to payments under this section.

(6) The power to give such directions may be exercised so as to make,
as respects the cases in relation to which it is exercised, the same
provision for all cases, or different provision for different cases or different
classes of case, or different provision as respects the same case or class
of case for different purposes.

(7) Without prejudice to the generality of subsection (5) above, the power
may be exercised —

(a) so as to make different provision for England and Wales and different
provision for different districts in either; and
(b) so as to require, in such circumstances as may be specified —
   (i) repayment of the whole or any part of a payment under this
   section;
   (ii) payment, in respect of property acquired with money paid under
   this section, of an amount representing the whole or part of an
   increase in the value of the property which has occurred since its
   acquisition.

(8) No payment shall be made under this section in respect of any expenditure unless the conditions relating to it —

(a) accord with the advice given by the joint consultative committee in making the recommendation for a payment under this section in respect of the expenditure in question; and

(b) conform with the conditions prescribed for payments of that description under subsection (5) above.

(9) Where expenditure which has been recommended by a joint consultative committee for a payment under this section is expenditure in connection with services to be provided by a voluntary organisation —

(a) the authority who are to make the payment may make payments to the voluntary organisation towards the expenditure incurred or to be incurred by the organisation in connection with the provision of those services, instead of or in addition to making payments under subsection (2) above; and

(b) an authority of one of the descriptions specified in paragraph (a) (b) (c) or (d) of subsection (2) above and who have received payments under that subsection may make out of the sums paid to them payments to the voluntary organisation towards expenditure incurred or to be incurred by the organisation in connection with the provision of those services,

but no payment shall be made under this subsection except subject to conditions —

(i) which conform with the conditions prescribed for payments of that description under subsection (5) above; and

(ii) which accord with the advice given by the joint consultative committee in recommending the expenditure for a payment under this section.

[Section 28B gives powers to the Secretary of State to make payments towards expenditure on community services in Wales.]

Comments on co-operation between health and social services
The possibility of jointly funding projects and transferring funds between the authorities has underpinned the rapid development of care in the community, with funds from the closure of in-patient wards being used for the provision of community accommodation, whether provided by the local authority or by the voluntary sector, and for building up the infrastructure of community support which is essential if re-admission to institutional care is to be avoided.

It should also be noted that the Joint Consultative Committees have a major role to play in agreeing to projects and transfer of funds, and in setting guidance for their establishment.

Charges – a limitation on co-operation
One important feature of the National Health Service legislation is that the service was initially given free at the point of use. Charges were not exacted for hospital and health care (see Figure 23.10).

Figure 23.10 The NHS Act 1977 – section 1(2)

The services so provided shall be free of charge except in so far as the making and recovery of charges is expressly provided for by or under any enactment, whenever passed.

Prescription charges were introduced very soon after the NHS was set up and there are now charges for dental services and many other services. However, unless there is express authority, charging is illegal and recently hospitals which had charged patients for the home use of nebulisers or expected patients to pay the maintenance costs had to withdraw such charges.

This contrasts with local authority social services which are provided under the National Assistance Act and subsequent legislation and can be means-tested. Local authority social services have never been subject to the concept of being free at the point of use.

THE ADMINISTRATIVE FRAMEWORK

The Secretary of State exercises the powers and duties discussed above through the National Health Service Management Executive and Regional NHSMEs which oversee Health Authorities and GPs and so on as primarily purchasers on the one hand and NHS Trusts as the main providers on the other (although, of course, the internal market is not that simple and one body can function as both purchaser and provider in different circumstances). There are also Special Health Authorities such as the Mental Health Act Commission responsible directly in the Department of Health. The administrative structure of the NHS in England in 1996 is shown in Figure 23.11.

The 1995 changes

From 1995 the enlarged Regional Health Authorities were replaced by regional offices of the NHS Management Executive. The details are set out in the document *Managing the New NHS* issued by the Secretary of State in October 1993. From 1 April 1996 District Health Authorities and FHSAs were replaced by single health authorities at local level accountable to the Secretary of State through the NHS Management Executive regional offices.

The functions of the new health authorities include:

- responsibility for the implementing national health policy;
- assessing health care needs of the local population;
- developing integrated strategies for meeting those needs across primary and secondary care boundaries;

Figure 23.11 Structure of the health service in England in1996

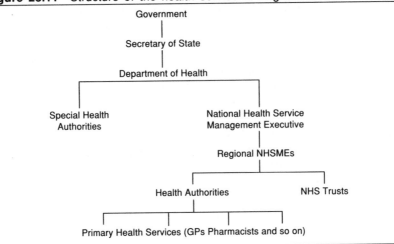

- forging constructive partnership with GPs;
- purchasing services outside the GP fund-holding schemes;
- discharging public health functions;
- advice to GPs and support for their primary care and fund-holding functions.

The internal market

The National Health Service and Community Care Act 1990 introduced into the health service the concept of the internal market by the establishment of purchasers (in the Act known as 'acquirers') and providers. In addition it created fund-holding practices of doctors and new health service bodies known as NHS Trusts.

The NHS Trust

The NHS Trust is a statutory body approved by the Secretary of State with the power to set its own terms and conditions for employees. It is defined in the NHS and Community Care Act 1990 as shown in Figure 23.12.

Figure 23.12 Section 5(1) – definition of NHS Trust

[T]he Secretary of State may establish bodies . . . —
(a) to assume responsibility, in accordance with this Act, for the ownership and management of hospitals or other establishments or facilities which were previously managed or provided by Regional, District or Special Health Authorities; or
(b) to provide and manage hospitals or other establishments or facilities.

By section 5(2) consultation is required with Community Health Councils and other persons or bodies. It was held to be solely for the Secretary of State for Health and not for the local health authorities, to consider the results of consultation under this section[2].

The basis of the NHS Trust itself is as set out in Figure 23.13.

Figure 23.13   Section 5(5) and (6) – status of an NHS Trust

(5) Every NHS trust —

(a) shall be a body corporate having a board of directors consisting of a chairman appointed by the Secretary of State and, subject to paragraph 5(2) of Schedule 2 to this Act, executive and non-executive directors (that is to say, directors who, subject to subsection (7) below, respectively are and are not employees of the trust); and

(b) shall have the functions conferred on it by an order under subsection (1) above and by Schedule 2 to this Act.

(6) The functions specified [by the Secretary of State] shall include such functions as [he] considers appropriate in relation to the provision of services by the trust for one or more health authorities.

Regulations have been made under section 5(7) for the qualifications and tenure of office of the chairman and directors, appointment of directors, maximum and minimum numbers, proceedings for dealing with vacancies, and the appointment, constitution, and exercise of functions by committees and sub-committees.

The initial (known as first wave) NHS Trusts came into being in April 1991. The chairman and the non-executive directors of the Trust are appointed by the Secretary of State and they can make arrangements with health service bodies and other organisation for the provision of services. Several Trusts provide small hospital and community health services and are called 'community trusts'. Others may combine acute in-patient care and community health services or mental health services with community health services. Great diversity has emerged in relation to the pattern of trust activity and the organisation of the provision of services.

Transfer of staff and rights, duties and so on

Section 6 covers the law relating to the transfer of employees and the rights, powers, duties and liabilities of the health authority to the Trust.

Section 7 provides additional provisions for staff transferred and covers the situation where staff work partly for a Trust and partly for an authority.

Section 8 enables the Secretary of State to make an order transferring property, rights and liabilities of a health authority which need to be transferred to the Trust for the purpose of enabling it to carry out its functions. The order may create or impose such new rights or liabilities in respect of what is transferred or what is retained by a health authority or the Secretary of State as appear to him to be necessary or expedient.

Sections 9 and 10 cover the financial obligations of the Trust.

Section 11 deals with the appointment of trustees for the holding and administration of funds held on trust.

Schedule 2, Part II sets out the duties, powers and status of the NHS Trust in more detail and it is specified that the NHS Trust's functions are to be carried out 'effectively, efficiently and economically' – 'the three Es'.

Purchaser or provider

It is a misunderstanding to see the divide between provider and purchaser as absolute. At the present time health authorities may be both purchasers and providers; similarly the Trusts may be providers for some services but purchasers of others. However, in future years it is likely that the vast proportion of health services previously provided through health authorities will come under an NHS Trust.

The NHS contract

At the heart of the relationship of the health authority and the NHS Trust is an NHS agreement or 'contract'. Section 4 sets out the basic arrangements for the provision and purchase of services (see Figure 23.14).

Figure 23.14 Section 4(1) – The NHS contract

In this Act the expression 'NHS contract' means an arrangement under which one health service body ('the acquirer') arranges for the provision to it by another health service body ('the provider') of goods or services which it reasonably requires for the purposes of its functions.

It is explicitly stated however that this NHS contract does not give rise to contractual rights and liabilities (see Figure 23.15).

Figure 23.15 Section 4(3) – Nature of an NHS contract

Whether or not an arrangement which constitutes an NHS contract would, apart from this subsection, be a contract in law, it shall not be regarded for any purpose as giving rise to contractual rights and liabilities, but if any dispute arises with respect to such an arrangement, either party may refer the matter to the Secretary of State for determination under the following provisions of this section.

Reference to the Secretary of state

The requirement to refer to the Secretary of State also includes disputes over the agreement leading to the NHS contract (see Figure 23.6).

Figure 23.16 Section 4(4) – Advance reference to the Secretary of State

If, in the course of negotiations intending to lead to an arrangement which will be an NHS contract, it appears to a health service body —

(a) that the terms proposed by another health service body are unfair by reason that the other is seeking to take advantage of its position as the only, or the only practicable, provider of the goods or services concerned or by reason of any other unequal bargaining position as between the prospective parties to the proposed arrangement, or

(b) that for any other reason arising out of the relative bargaining positions of the prospective parties any of the terms of the proposed arrangement cannot be agreed,

that health service body may refer the terms of the proposed arrangement to the Secretary of State for determination under the following provisions of this section.

It is assumed that the general right to refer to the Secretary of State given in subsection (3) is not limited to the more specific right given in subsection (4) since the subsection (4) arrangements apply only to those which arise during the course of the negotiations and not once the agreement has been concluded.

Dispute resolution

Situation

An NHS Community Trust agrees with a health authority that they will provide 20 beds for geriatric patients. Unfortunately because of subsidence under the building the wards had to be closed and the NHS Trust could not take geriatric patients. The health authority claimed a breach of contract and required a reduction in the financial allocation. The Trust refused to agree this since they had not been able to make staff redundant as it was hoped that the ward would eventually be re-opened. What action can the health authority take?

If the matter could not be resolved locally between Trust and health authority, the health authority would have to refer the issue to the Secretary of State under section 4(3). The Secretary of State could either determine the issue himself or he might appoint an adjudicator.

If, on the other hand, the dispute had been between the health authority and a private hospital, then the health authority could take the private hospital owners or company to court alleging breach of contract and the court would determine the outcome.

The effect of excluding jurisdiction of the courts

The fact that section 4 operates to exclude the courts from hearing disputes over NHS contracts may mean that much of the law of contract will not be automatically incorporated into the NHS agreement. Rules relating to the formation of contract, remedies for breach of contract and the way contracts are terminated (including the law of frustration (see glossary)) may not become part of the working relationship between providers and purchasers. It remains to be seen.

'Health service body'

The term health service body used in section 4(1) to describe the parties to an NHS contract is defined as shown in Figure 23.17.

Figure 23.17 Section 4(2) – Definition of health service body

In this section 'health service body' means any of the following, namely, —

(a) a health authority;
(b) a health board;
(c) the Common Services Agency for the Scottish Health Service;
(d) a Family Health Services Authority [merged with the DHAs in April 1996];
(e) an NHS trust;
(f) a recognised fund-holding practice [created by section 14 – see next chapter];
(g) the Dental Practice Board or the Scottish Dental Practice Board;
(h) the Public Health Laboratory Service Board; and
(i) the Secretary of State.

DISTINCTION BETWEEN HEALTH AND SOCIAL SERVICES

One major issue which has arisen as a result of the new framework is the definition of health as opposed to social services. The definition has grown in significance as the local authorities charge for their services. Thus nursing services provided by the health authority cannot be charged for. However, if these same services are provided by the local authority, then the client can be means-tested and required to pay or contribute.

■ How is the distinction between what should be provided under the NHS legislation and what can be provided by social services departments drawn?

Historical background

In some ways it is primarily historical and based on the initial legislation. Changes were made in the 1973 reorganisation when services such as the ambulance and community health services were transferred from the province of the local authorities to that of the health authorities, and medical social workers who had been employees of the health authorities were transferred to the local social services authorities.

The situation became more complex in 1977 with the joint funding of projects between health and social services and the transfer of health authority funds to social services. Formerly services provided by the NHS in relation to the care of mothers and children, prevention care and after-care and home help and laundry services were, under section 21 of the NHS Act 1977, described as functions exercisable by local social services authorities, (see below page 387).

The work of the Joint Consultation Committees set up between health authorities and social services authorities enabled the development of many jointly financed projects to be undertaken.

The effect of the 1990 Act

This issue has, however, become more important with the introduction of the NHS and Community Care Act 1990, since one of the main aims of the legislation is to provide for a seamless service and create greater flexibility in the provision of services between health providers and social services. The definition as to what can properly be described as an NHS duty and what is defined as a local authority social services function is significant because of the inability of the NHS to make charges and a local authority's power to charge.

Definition problems

The problems of definition are seen in:
● the reports of the Health Service Commissioner (the Ombudsman);

- reports of ambulance services refusing to transport clients to a nursing home unless they were paid;
- Welsh Office and Department of Health guidance; and
- a recent case on social security payments discussed below.

Reports of the Ombudsman

Several cases have come before the Health Service Commissioner relating to the legal responsibilities of health authorities. For example he has criticized the Winchester Health Authority for ward closures resulting in a patient being discharged with inadequate medical cover and against the consultant's advice.

In his annual report for 1990/1991 he drew attention to three cases where there was a clash between carers/patients and the health authorities over the extent of the latter's duties.

Case

In one case[3] a man suffering from dementia was admitted to a private nursing home on the advice of a consultant geriatrician who could not offer him a NHS bed. The man's daughter tried to secure her father's admission to hospital, or financial assistance with the nursing home charges. The DHA told her that her father would certainly be admitted if a bed became available, but said that they were not empowered to help her with the nursing home costs, and that there were others waiting for a NHS bed whose need was greater.

Following a letter from a minister at the Department of Health and Social Services to a national charity, which implied that the NHS had an absolute duty to provide services in such a case as this, the HSC took up the issue with the Chief Executive of the NHS Management Executive and was told that provision of care was qualified by the resources available and that payments intended to 'top-up' social security payments were not possible. The HSC accepted that, where demand exceeded available resources, there might be some individuals whose clinical priority was such that their needs could not be met under the NHS. Eventually in this case, the DHA agreed to make a suitable *ex gratia* (see glossary) payment to the daughter in recognition of the distress she had been caused.

Case

Another case in the same report[4] dealt with the issue of health service responsibilities in respect of long-term care for a victim of head injuries. In this case the patient had spent 18 months in a NHS neurosurgical unit before being discharged to a private nursing home. The son complained that the DHA had not met their responsibility to provide for his mother's needs, and that undue pressure had been put on the family to move their mother to a nursing home.

The HSC formed the view, in the light of the discussion in the case above, that NHS care should be provided without charge if in a doctor's professional judgment it was required, and concluded that the DHA had a duty to continue providing the care the woman required. He upheld the complaint. The DHA agreed to meet the ongoing nursing home costs in respect of the woman's care and treatment which it was the function of the NHS to provide.

Case

In another case, where the complaint was not upheld, a patient who was suffering from a chronic debilitating condition required in-patient care. Since no hospital beds were available he was transferred to a private nursing home where he stayed for nine months when a long-stay hospital place was provided.

The wife's complaint that a place should have been offered before then was not upheld. The consultant geriatricians concerned had exercised their clinical judgment over the priority to be given to patients and matters of clinical judgment are outside the remit of the HSC. The HSC stated that he believed that the DHA had a duty to provide some level of care for people in the husband's condition, but he found that the allocation of resources for that purpose was a discretionary decision, proper to the DHA. Such matters are not open to question by the HSC unless there is evidence of maladministration in the decision making process and there was none in this case. The DHA had developed, and kept under review, policies which they believed made the best use of resources.

Ambulance transport

Ambulance officers in the South East were reported on 4 October 1993 as refusing to transport a person to a nursing home unless the transport was paid for. It was not until the social services had agreed to the payment that the person was transported, some four hours later.

The Welsh Office Circular

In the Welsh Office circular[5] on continuing care, *Boundaries between health and social services*, it is stated that:

> There can be no rigidly defined boundary between health and social care, but this Circular sets out Local Authority and NHS responsibilities in relevant key areas including:
> a. Local authority contracts for residential or nursing home care: NHS related aspects.
> b. District Health Authority consent to people entering Nursing Homes with Local Authority financial support.
> c. Supply of incontinence aids for people living in community care.

It states in the background to the paper that:

> At the margins there is in practice a degree of substitutability of health and social care and rigid delimitation is not possible; different balances and different patterns of health and social services care have, quite understandably, developed in different parts of Wales.

This makes the answer in relation to the enforceability of obligations extremely difficult. It could arise, for example, that neither social services nor health authority provider supplies a service required by someone living in the community and the uncertainty over who has the duty to supply it means that the legal responsibilities are equally unclear.

A useful example of the problem is given by the topic of the supply of incontinence aids to people living in the community[6]. The guidance considered the situation of someone in a nursing home compared to other residential accommodation.

Clients in nursing homes. The guidance states that where the client is in a nursing home, then the provision of the general nursing care is the responsibility of the home and this responsibility would include the cost of those aids. The fees could be regarded as covering this. So where a health authority or NHS Trust agrees to supply routine incontinence aids to a nursing home, it is proper to charge the home for those supplies (under the income generation powers conferred by section 7 of the Health and Medicines Act 1988 which gives the Secretary of State powers to make more income available for improving the health service).

Clients in residential homes or in their own homes. Residential homes are not permitted to supply nursing services beyond what would be given by a caring relative, otherwise they would have to be registered as nursing homes. NHS Trusts and health authorities have no statutory duty to supply incontinence aids but could do so at their discretion. Where they do so, or where they supply clients in their own homes, the service must be provided free at the point of use and eligibility should be decided on the basis of the needs of individuals, irrespective of the type of accommodation.

The Department of Health executive letter
In a Department of Health executive letter[7] guidance is given on NHS and local authority collaboration. It states that the principles set down under the 1974 collaboration arrangements (HRC(74)19) still apply, that is health authorities are still responsible for ensuring health service support is provided to local authorities, including payment for general medical services provided to local authorities, and their contracts with provider units should reflect this. Local authorities, are still responsible for providing social work support to the NHS, including NHS Trusts. No changes to the services provided should be made without prior consultation.

The level of provision of health service support and of health-related social workers (HRSWs) by local authorities should be discussed by the relevant bodies in the context of Community Care Plans and plans for services for children, for example in relation to child protection and services for children with disabilities. In addition, local authorities will need to discuss arrangements for the provision of health services and of HRSWs with NHS provider units.

Local authorities continue to be responsible for the provision of HRSWs under current arrangements. However, the Department is aware that in some places NHS provider units are funding, and sometimes also providing, one or more HRSWs in addition to the HRSWs funded and provided by the local authority.

> There is no reason why provider units should not fund an additional post(s) where they consider it improves the service they can provide for their patients. Where this occurs, this could be done through the local authority.

The Department is considering further national advice in this area[8]. (See below)

At present it appears that an NHS trust or health authority would not have the statutory power to appoint an approved social worker for the purposes of the Mental Health Act 1983.

The case on social security payments

These matters came to the fore in a decision of the Court of Appeal which stated that the Department of Social Security was not liable to make payments to residents in nursing homes because they were the responsibility of the National Health Service[9]. In this Court of Appeal case it was decided that income support from the Department of Social Security was not payable at the higher level to residents in nursing homes before 1 April 1993 since nursing homes are effectively hospitals or similar institutions and therefore the cost must fall on the NHS.

Case: *White v. Department of Social Security*

Percival White was one of 14 residents in a nursing home in East Sussex and had been discharged from hospital care before 1 April 1993. He applied for social security income support at the higher level to help towards the fees. However he was turned down on the grounds that he was receiving nursing care and therefore was still the responsibility of the Mid-Downs District Health Authority. The effect of this decision was that he was not entitled to the income support paid at the higher levels to those who were in residential and nursing home accommodation before 1 April 1993, when the regulations changed.

There is concern at the lack of uniformity between different health authorities and commissioning purchasers in defining the NHS duties in relation to long term nursing care. Some Trusts are providing such care under the NHS; others are passing that duty on to the non-NHS sector and to social services. Since the latter is means-tested, the financial implications for clients and their families are considerable.

The 1995 guidance on long term health care

Recent further guidance has been issued by the Department of Health and the Welsh Office clarifying responsibilities for long term health care[10]. It emphasises that:

The NHS is responsible for arranging and funding a range of

services to meet the needs of people who require continuing physical or mental health care.

Such care may include, where appropriate the services shown in Figure 23.18.

Figure 23.18 NHS responsibilities for securing continuing health care

- specialist medical and nursing assessment
- rehabilitation and recovery
- palliative health care
- continuing in-patient care under specialist supervision in hospital or in a nursing home
- respite health care
- specialist health care support to people in nursing homes or residential care homes or the community
- community health services to people at home or in residential care homes
- primary health care
- specialist transport services

Local policies and eligibility criteria
Health authorities, GP fund-holders and social services authorities are required to agree local policies on meeting the continuing health care needs and in agreeing their respective responsibilities for continuing care. They must also produce local policies and eligibility criteria for continuing health care. Annex A to the circular sets out the conditions for local policies and eligibility criteria for continuing health care for the services covered in Figure 23.18.

Reviewing decisions
Guidance on this matter, *Discharge from NHS Inpatient care of people with continuing health or social care needs: Arrangements for reviewing decisions on eligibility for NHS Continuing Care,* has been issued by the Department of Health (HSG(95)39; LAC(95)17). It sets out the procedure for reviewing decisions on eligibility for NHS continuing care. Appendix 1 provides a table of the overall process for review procedure and Appendix 2 gives a checklist of issues to be considered before referring a case to a panel.

The full text of this guidance is included in Appendix 4. Only time will show the extent to which these arrangements work and the extent to which the consumer accepts the boundaries currently drawn around NHS responsibilities and those of the local authority.

The Guidance also covers collaboration with local authorities and implementation and monitoring.

The authorities involved should take into account the changes in the pattern of services following the introduction of the new community care arrangements.

RESIDENCE CRITERIA

The main criterion for determining the obligation of the health authority to purchase care, whether hospital or community care, is residence within the catchment area. The NHS Management Executive has issued guidance on *Establishing the District of Residence*[12] for the purpose of contracting services. It emphasises that:

> the underlying principle is that there should be no 'gaps' in responsibility; nobody should fail to be cared for because of uncertainty or ambiguity as to who is responsible for them.

The main test is the usual residence of the person, which can normally be obtained from the patient who will say where she usually lives. This excludes holiday or second homes. Where a patient is registered with a GP is not important with regard to determining district of residence. Temporary residents are to be regarded as resident at the address they give to the person or body providing them with treatment[13]. Long-stay mental illness patients and patients with learning disabilities (see glossary) should be treated either as residents at the address at which they were usually resident before they became an in-patient or, if the previous address cannot be determined, at the address of the hospital in which they are in-patients. However if they have been in-patients since 1 January 1970 (learning disabilities) or 1 January 1971 (mentally ill) then they are treated as residents of where they are at present[14].

For determination of residence in relation to community care assessments see Chapter 25.

NHS INVOLVEMENT IN COMMUNITY CARE UNDER THE 1990 ACT

Community care plans

Under section 46(2)(a) a local authority must consult any health authority which has all or part of its area within the local authority boundaries in preparing and publishing plans for the provision of community care services. The duty to prepare plans and the consultation process are the subject of directions given by the Secretary of State. The preparation of community care plans is discussed in Chapter 25 (see Figure 25.9).

Assessments

In carrying out its duty under section 47(1) of the NHS and Community Care Act 1990, a local authority must notify the health authority and invite it to assist in the making of the assessment of needs (Section 47(3)). This duty to notify arises if 'it appears to a local authority ... that there may be a need for the provision to that person by such Health Authority as may be determined in accordance with regulations of any services under the National Health Service Act 1977'.

One weakness of this section is that if the local authority does not think that health services are likely to be required then the health authority might not be notified of the need to make a joint assessment. The local authority has to take into account any services which are likely to be made available for the client by that health authority in deciding whether to notify the authority. It is essential, therefore, that it has full information on the health authority services available.

The health authority must give its consent before the local authority can make provision for accommodation for a client in a nursing home. See Chapter 25 for further details of the assessment process. Section 42 of the NHS and Community Care Act 1990 amends section 26 of the National Assistance Act 1948. The local authority cannot make arrangements for the provision of residential accommodation where nursing care is provided without the consent of the health authority. This does not apply to the making of temporary arrangements for the accommodation of any person as a matter of urgency, but, as soon as practicable after any such temporary arrangements have been made, the authority must seek the consent required above.

CONCLUSIONS

The introduction of the internal market into the administration of the health services has probably had a more significant effect that any of the organisational changes which have been taking place since the NHS was established in 1948. The basic duties laid upon the Secretary of State by the 1946 Act and incorporated into the 1977 Act still, however, remain virtually unchanged. Health services for the most part are still provided free at the point of delivery and this distinction from local authority services will place considerable barriers to achieving the seamless service between health and local authority hospital and community provision. It remains to be seen how far the delegation to local policies of the criteria for eligibility for NHS care leads to a neglect or reduction in the scope and performance of statutory duties under the NHS legislation. This is particularly so in the context of increasing numbers of GP fund-holders as purchasers.

CHAPTER 24

GP Fund-holding practices

General practitioners, dentists, and pharmacists who work within the NHS have since 1948 (apart from those appointed within the hospital service) been independent practitioners holding contracts initially with the Executive Council, then with the Family Practitioner Committees and subsequently with the Family Health Services Authorities. From 1 April 1996 they held their contracts with the new health authorities. They are not employees but contract to provide services and are obliged to follow the nationally set terms and conditions of service. Note should be made of the changes (discussed in the last chapter) in the administrative structure of the NHS and the amalgamation of the FHSAs and DHAs into new Commissioning Authorities effected in April 1996. The following discussion is based on the fact that the duty to organise primary health services is placed on the health authorities.

The development of the primary health care services has been central to the initiatives in community care and general practitioners and the other professions have been expected to contribute to the planning and development of community services.

Although marginalised by the extent to which dentists have to charge contributions for their work, dental services are an integral part of the NHS. Dentists working within the NHS are accountable to and in contract with the new health authorities (the FHSAs before April 1996) as are doctors and community pharmacists (the role of the latter in the community being considered in some detail in Chapter 12). However, it is the central position of the GP, and in particular the GP fund-holder, which is dealt with in this chapter.

The statutory basis of GP services

Section 29 of the NHS Act 1977 places a duty upon the health authority

in accordance with the regulations, to arrange as respects their locality with medical practitioners to provide personal medical services for all person in the locality who wish to take advantage of the arrangements.

These are known as 'general medical services'. Section 29(2), (3) and (5) enable regulations to be drawn up to provide for the preparation and publication of the medical list and the payment for services.

Each health authority is obliged to keep a list of general practitioners who practice in its area which is known as 'the medical list'. The National Health Service (General Medical Services) Regulations 1992 SI No. 635 set out the rules relating to the medical list and additions and withdrawals to and from the list. Under Part IV of the Regulations the health authority must also keep a list of patients in its locality accepted by or assigned to the doctor.

Schedule 2 of the regulations lays down the terms of service for doctors, including the definition of a patient, the transfer of responsibility for patients, deputising services and arrangements of practices. Paragraph 12 which is shown in Figure 24.1 sets out the basic duty of the general practitioner.

Figure 24.1 Paragraph 12 of Schedule 2 to the 1992 Regulations

(1) Subject to paragraphs 3, 13, and 44, a doctor shall render to his patients all necessary and appropriate personal medical services of the type usually provided by general medical practitioners.

(2) The services which a doctor is required by sub-paragraph (1) to render shall include the following —

(a) giving advice, where appropriate, to a patient in connection with the patient's general health, and in particular about the significance of diet, exercise, the use of tobacco, the consumption of alcohol and the misuse of drugs or solvents;

(b) offering to patients consultations and, where appropriate, physical examinations for the purpose of identifying, or reducing the risk of disease or injury;

(c) offering to patients, where appropriate, vaccination or immunisation against measles, mumps, rubella, pertussis, poliomyelitis, diphtheria and tetanus;

(d) arranging for the referral of patients, as appropriate, for the provision of any other services under the Act; and

(e) giving advice, as appropriate, to enable patients to avail themselves of services provided by a local social services authority.

(3) A doctor is not required by sub-paragraph (1) or (2)

(a) to provide to any person child health surveillance services, contraceptive services, minor surgery services nor, except in an emergency, maternity medical services, unless he has previously undertaken to the health authority to provide such services to that person; or

(b) where he is a restricted services principal, to provide any category of general medical services which he has not undertaken to provide.

FUND-HOLDING GENERAL PRACTITIONERS

Described as 'the jokers in the pack' the fund-holding general practitioners set up under the 1990 Act have introduced an element of unpredictability into the purchaser/provider divide created by those reforms. Following the acceptance of an application to become a fund-holding practice, the practice is given a budget for the purchase of health services for patients registered with it. The practice still has to perform those duties set down in the Regulations for its registered patients, like any non-fundholding practice.

After the first two years it became evident that the difficulties in setting budgets for the first year of the second wave fundholdings and the second year of the first wave had led to possible over-allocation. The savings which resulted from this and from a more efficient management of resources led to the practices spending moneys on such matters as improvements for the surgery and so on. At least one district general manager (Andrew Wall, Bath) complained that the holding back on expenditure was depriving NHS hospitals of funds for secondary care of patients.

● To what extent did the regional health authorities have the power to claw the savings back?

● How could these savings be used?

● Would they be taxed on the savings?

These were the questions which arose for debate[16].

From 1993 the purchasing of some of the community health services also became the responsibility of the fund-holding general practitioners with consequential uncertainty for providers over how and where these funds would be spent. Planning of services for community NHS Trusts or for DHA purchasers and directly managed community units also became more difficult and fragmented since they were now compelled to negotiate with many different organisations who were not always prepared to negotiate jointly or form consortia for planning purposes.

The following issues will be considered:

- the statutory basis of the fund-holding practice;
- the criteria required to make an application;
- the services which such practices can purchase and provide;
- the significance of the contractual relationships;
- the provision of community care; and
- the relationship with the individual patient.

STATUTORY BASIS OF FUND-HOLDING PRACTICES

Sections 14 to 19 of the NHS and Community Care Act 1990 set out the provisions for the establishment of fund-holding practices. It should be emphasised that fund-holding system relates to the purchasing of services by those who have been accepted as fund-holders. Such general practitioners still have a contract for services with the health authority and they are still bound by the terms of service discussed above.

Section 14 of the 1990 Act enables medical practitioners providing general medical services to apply to the regional health authorities for recognition as a fund-holding practice (in Wales the application is to be made to the Welsh Office). See Figure 24.2.

Figure 24.2 Fund-holding practices – section 14(1)

Any one or more medical practitioners who are providing general medical services in accordance with arrangements under section 29 of the [1977] Act may apply to the relevant Regional Health Authority for recognition as a fund-holding practice.

Section 14 also enables regulations to be made covering those issues set out in Figure 24.3.

Figure 24.3 Regulations – section 14(6)

Regulations may make provision with respect to —

(a) the making of applications under subsection (1) above;
(b) the granting and refusal of recognition as a fund-holding practice;
(c) the conditions to be fulfilled for obtaining and continuing to be entitled to such recognition;
(d) appeals against any refusal of such recognition;
(e) withdrawing from, or becoming a member of, an existing recognised fund-holding practice;
(f) the continuity or otherwise of a recognised fund-holding practice in the event of the death or withdrawal of a member or the addition of a new member; and
(g) the operation of this section in a case where one or more of the medical practitioners wishing to make an application under subsection (1) is also on the medical list of a health board . . .

Under the power given by this section the following regulations have been drawn up: SI 1990 No. 1753, SI 1991 No. 636, SI 1992 No. 582, and SI 1996 No. 706. This last statutory instrument which consolidates and amends previous SIs is summarised in Appendix 6.

The Audit Commission has produced a digest of information about practices during the first five years – *Fundholding Fact* published by the HMSO in 1996.

CRITERIA FOR BECOMING ACCEPTED AS A FUND-HOLDING PRACTICE

The criteria set initially have been broadened and at the present time there are both criteria set in relation to the year prior to the commencement of fund-holding status and criteria which are used to assess the practice's suitability during the preparatory year.

Prior to the preparatory year

This is set out in SI 1996 No. 706. The criteria cover the following areas:

- Minimum list size (This could be on the basis of a group of practices but if practices do join for such purposes it must be shown that they have arrangements for joint working together.)
- Partnership commitment (*All* partners must evidence their commitment by signing the application form.)
- Managerial support
- Computing support.

Criteria during the preparatory year

These cover
- Contracting capability
- Effectiveness in collecting data over the period
- The development plan.

Advice is given on the data collection and the other information required for making an application by the *Guide to GP Fundholding* produced and updated by the South Western Regional Health Authority.

Expansion of the options

An announcement was made by the Secretary of State in October 1994 that the criteria for applications was being widened to enable more GP practices to apply to become fund-holders and also that the services which they would be able to purchase would also be extended. Executive letter EL(94)79 dated 20 October 1994 *Developing NHS purchasing and GP Fund-holding* sets out proposals for a major expansion of the options for GP fund-holding, which remains voluntary, in which three types of fund-holding are envisaged.

Community fund-holding This will be a new option for small practices with 3000 or more patients or for those who are not ready to take on standard fund-holding. This option will include staff, drugs, diagnostic tests and most of the community health services in the standard scheme (excluding mental illness and learning disability services). It will exclude all acute hospital treatments (including out-patient attendance).

Standard fund-holding This is an expanded and more coherent version of the existing scheme. In addition to existing services this option will include specialist nursing services (for example diabetic and stoma care) and virtually all elective surgery and out-patients (with a few very high cost exceptions, for example heart transplants). The minimum list size requirement for standard fund-holding is reduced from 7000 to 5000 patients.

Total purchasing This is where GPs in a locality purchase all hospital and community health service care for their patients. Pilot projects are under way.

● Maternity services will be piloted in six sites with both standard and total purchasing.

● Osteopathy, chiropractic and patient transport services will be piloted within standard fund-holding practices.

● Medical in-patients, mental illness and other long-stay treatments will be piloted for possible inclusion at a later stage.

The regulations are consolidated in the NHS (Fund-holding Practices) Regulations 1996 (see Appendix 6).

An example of the benefits of total fund-holding is given in an article in *GP Fundholding*[17] which describes the primary health care team's involvement in the treatment and after-care of cancer patients. The total fund-holding practice is planning to appoint a surgery-based specialist cancer nurse to act as a linchpin for a reorganisation of oncology services.

Composition and constitution of fund-holding practices

Certain anxieties have arisen which are discussed below.

The legal effects of forming a consortium

There is nothing to prevent sets of fund-holders joining together as a planning group and joint purchasing/provider group. Each individual member of the group would, however, have to meet and comply with the legal requirements separately. If a joint fund-holding group is formed, it would be advisable to seek legal advice on the terminology to be used and the contents of any agreement. For example if the group calls itself a partnership significant legal implications arise which may not be wanted by the fund-holders. An agreement drawn up between the separate fund-holding practices should cover the topics listed below:

- Names of parties
- Commencement date
- Duration of agreement
- Head office
- Nature of co-operation between the parties
- Scope of the agreement
- How decisions are to be made
- Financial arrangements
- Holding of assets
- Names of relevant advisers, for example solicitors, accountants, bankers, and insurers.

Payment to fund-holders

This is authorised by section 15 of the 1990 Act which enables the health authority to pay to the members of each recognised fund-holding practice 'a sum determined in such manner and by reference to such factors as the Secretary of State may direct'. The sum is known as the 'allotted sum'. Provisions exist for part or all of the allotted sum to be in the form of meeting the liabilities of the practice to any other person (in particular liabilities under NHS contracts). There are also provisions for recovering the moneys paid from other HAs if some of the patients in the practice are in another region.

Section 15 also enables regulations to be drawn up covering the issues listed in Figure 24.4.

Figure 24.4 Regulations on the allotted sums – section 15(7)

Such regulations:

- require payment out of allotted sums to the Health Authority for the basic cost of drugs, medicines and listed appliances;
- specify a list of approved goods and services other than general medical services on which the allotted sum can be spent; and
- impose a limit on the amount which may be spent out of an allotted sum on the provision of goods and services for any one individual, being a limit above which the cost of any goods and services for that individual in the financial year will fall to be met by the Health Authority.

The regulations drawn up under section 15 are currently enacted in the National Health Service (Fund-holding Practices) Regulations 1996, SI 1996 No. 706 (see Appendix 6).

Monitoring of the fund-holding practice

Under section 15(9) the relevant health authority shall monitor the expenditure of the members of a recognised fund-holding practice and may institute an audit and review in any case where it is considered necessary to do so.

Renunciation and removal of recognition as a fund-holding practice and the withholding of funds

Section 16 enables regulations to be drawn up covering these areas. In addition section 16(4) enables regulations to be drawn up covering the areas listed in Figure 24.5.

Figure 24.5 Regulations under section 16(4)

(a) may provide for the transfer of rights and obligations from the members of the fund-holding practice to one or more Health Authorities determined in accordance with the regulations;

(b) may provide for the recovery of sums from the members of the practice; and

(c) may require the members to furnish such information as may reasonably be required by the Secretary of State.

The Secretary of State is not obliged to continue to recognise the status of the fund-holding practice while an appeal against removal of recognition takes place and is not required to make payments (section 16(5)).

Regulations can make provision for the recovery of parts of the allotted sum spent on purposes other than those specified in the regulations (section 16(6)).

Regulations covering areas specified in section 16 are to be found in SI 1996 No. 706 summarised in Appendix 6.

If during the year of its operation a group fund-holding practice ceases to meet the eligibility criteria for being accepted as a group fund-holding practice. It will continue to operate to the end of the financial year, the future situation being determined at the appropriate time.

Transfer of functions relating to fund-holding practices
Section 17 enables the Secretary of State to make regulations to transfer some of the functions set out in sections 14 to 16 from himself to the new health authorities.

Regulations made under this section are also to be found in SI 1996 No. 706 summarised in Appendix 6.

SERVICES THEY CAN PURCHASE AND PROVIDE

The fund-holding practice has a wide discretion over possible providers it may secure a purchasing agreement with. These include:

- NHS Trusts
- Directly Managed Units
- Public Health Laboratories
- Ministry of Defence Hospitals
- Special Health Authorities
- Private clinics, hospitals and laboratories
- Voluntary organisations
- Any other provider of health care services.

At present there is a financial limit on the services which the GP fund-holder is expected to purchase in respect of any one patient, and over that limit the cost falls on the health authority as commissioner. This means that such treatments as heart lung transplants and other high technology treatments fall outside the GP fund-holders' capabilities. However, the experiments in total purchasing (see above) may eventually lead to GP fund-holders generally being responsible for the entire budget.

Could the GPFH purchase services from abroad?
At present the Government has declared it illegal for a fund-holding practice to send patients abroad for treatment in order to avoid long waiting times, stating that this would contravene the National Health Service Act 1964 (NHSME letter 16 September 1991). However, it is being debated whether this infringes the EC laws relating to the freedom of movement of goods and services in the Community.

THE SIGNIFICANCE OF THE CONTRACTUAL RELATIONSHIP

The contractual significance of any agreement is greatly dependant on which party agrees to provide services to the GPFH. This is discussed below.

Contracts

If the agreement to purchase services is between a GP fund-holder and a directly managed unit or an NHS Trust, then this is an NHS contract and is subject to section 4 of the 1990 Act.

This is discussed in the previous chapter but for convenience the section is set out in Figure 24.6.

Figure 24.6 NHS contract – section 4

In this Act the expression 'NHS contract' means an arrangement under which one health service body ('the acquirer') arranges for the provision to it by another health service body ('the provider') of goods and services which it reasonably requires for the purposes of its functions.

The definition of health service body includes a recognised fund-holding practice, NHS Trusts, health authorities and so on (see Figure 23.18).

Exclusion of the jurisdiction of the courts

Much concern has been centred on the meaning of this section and its contractual and other legal consequences. Section 4(3) makes it clear that the agreement does not give rise to contractual rights and liabilities if it is between health service bodies (see Figure 23.15). Thus any court action for breach of contract in relation to an NHS contract is effectively prevented. Section 4(3) might not, however, prevent an action for judicial review. To obtain a judicial review it would be necessary to show that the principles of natural justice were not followed or that the decision made was irrational, unreasonable or perverse (the *Wednesbury* principle – see glossary) and should not be allowed to stand (see Chapter 27).

The section provides an answer to the following worries of fund-holders.

■ Can the fund-holder insist on documentary evidence being provided of service provision before he arranges for payment?

The answer is that if the contract is between the fund-holder and an NHS provider then any term within the agreement is not legally enforceable. The fund-holder cannot refuse to pay nor seek court action to force observance of the terms of the agreement.

However, if the agreement is with a private hospital or voluntary body, then it would be a binding contract in law and would be subject to all the contractual rules relating to formation, performance, enforcement, breach and termination. (These are considered in Chapter 20 in relation to the contracting power of the private practitioner.)

■ Could the Secretary of State claw back funds which have not been spent by the fund-holder?

Since the fund-holder is undertaking the provision of services which are the prime duty of the Secretary of State and the health authority, there is probably no legal reason why excess funds could not be recovered. The NHS contract is not in itself legally binding and the fund-holder cannot, therefore, take the authority to court over any clawback. Some authorities have sought a way out of this dilemma by coming to agreements with fund-holders that any savings will be channelled back to provider units, but the fund-holders should have a say over what the money should be used for.

■ If the NHS contract is not legally enforceable what sanctions are available for breach?

Section 4 provides a remedy for dispute by setting up a system of appeal to the Secretary of State who can refer the dispute to a person appointed for that task (see Chapter 23).

The most important sanction is, however, the possibility that the purchaser will buy elsewhere for the forthcoming year. This does depend upon availability of an alternative supply, but it would probably be easier for a fund-holder to make alternative arrangements for supply than for a health authority to do so. However, we are likely to see a fragmentation of these agreements as contracts for certain services are removed from one provider and placed with another. This would give more choice to the purchasers but make planning of services more difficult for individual providers, especially as these NHS contracts last only for one year.

■ What is the legal position if a fund-holding practice makes an agreement with a consultant to provide out-patient services within the health centre?

One way of providing a far more efficient service for their patients is for fund-holders to arrange for consultants to provide a service to the patients within the health centre/practice premises. Advice on the contracts to be drawn up by fund-holders is given in the journal, *GP Fundholding*, (Vol 1 No. 12, 21 May 1992) and it is suggested that they should cover:

- the names and addresses of the parties;
- the exact nature and scope of the contract;
- the duration of the contract;
- any payment to be made – its frequency and method of payment;
- the location, frequency and time at which the clinics or duties are to be carried out; and
- arrangements by which the contract may be renewed.

If the contract is made with a consultant acting as a private practitioner, it would appear that this does not form an NHS contract for the purposes of section 4, since the consultant does not come within the definition of health service body for the purpose of that section. This would mean that there is no reason why the contract could not be enforceable in a court of law unless there was a stipulation to the contrary within the contract.

The Department of Health has stated that where full-time consultants undertake such a contract, then the services must come from out of the 10% permitted for private work. On the other hand, if the contract is with the NHS Trust as employer of the consultants, then the contract would come under the definition of NHS contract for the purposes of section 4, it would not be legally enforceable and the consultants could carry out any services which form part of the agreement as part of their NHS work.

■ Are there any specific rules which must be followed if the fund-holders contract with an organisation which is outside the NHS?

In these circumstances SI 1996 No. 706 sets down guidelines which include the following requirements:

- that fund-holders should ensure that the professional staff providing care are suitably qualified;
- that the care provided falls within the regional strategic framework in terms of being effective, appropriate, accessible to the patient, timely and socially acceptable; and
- that the provider uses suitable audit mechanisms to address effectiveness and social acceptability.

■ What if a partner in the GPFH has a financial interest in the non-NHS provider? Could the GPFH still make the contract?

There is a duty for this fact to be disclosed and written approval must be obtained from the health authority before the contract is made.

FUND-HOLDERS AND COMMUNITY SERVICES

Extension of the original scheme

The scope of purchasing by fund-holding practices has gradually been extended and from April 1993 they were able to purchase community health services. At this stage they are restricted to buying in the services of community health staff such as health visitors and community nurses from the health authority, or the NHS Trust which covers community health services. Many fund-holding practices hope, however, that they will in due course be empowered to employ their own community health staff.

Guidance on the extension of the hospital and community health services elements of the GP fund-holding scheme from 1 April 1993 is given in EL (92) 48 which is supplemented by HSG(92)53 published by the NHS Management Executive.

Contracting for such services

From 1993 fund-holders thus had a duty to place contracts for community nursing services, but these need not necessarily be with the provider who has given those services in the past, nor with simply one provider. The fund-holders can choose. The basis of the allocation of funding for such purchasers is to be determined by the HA on the basis of the current level of services provided to each fund-holding practice.

The range of services which can be provided as set out by the NHS Management Executive is shown in Figure 24.7.

Figure 24.7 Range of services under Hospital and Community Health Services (HCHS)

- district nursing
- health visiting
- chiropody
- dietetics
- all community and out-patient mental health services
- mental health counselling
- health services for people with a learning disability
- referrals made by health visitors, district nurses and community mental handicap nurses.

Model forms of agreement for the purchase of these services are set out in the Annex to EL(92)48.

Expenditure in excess of £5000 for any one individual patient can be recovered from the health authority as under section 15(7). However, where the fund-holders are paying for services on a fixed price non-attributable basis, this limit does not apply.

The contract for services, apart from chiropody and dietetics, does not have to be placed with an NHS provider. Since funding for these will be based on the previous year's expenditure, where these are shortage specialities, the funding is low. Virement (the transfer of funds from one budget head to another) can take place, however, from other services and the GPs could employ their own direct staff.

Self-referrals are at present omitted from the scheme.

The specimen contract

In the further guidance given by HSG(92)53 a checklist of negotiating issues for GP fund-holders, community nursing services, chiropody and dietetics, and community psychiatric nursing services is provided. A specimen contract for community nursing services is also given and covers the topics shown in Figure 24.8. It is emphasised that it is only intended to be a guide and form a basis for discussion.

Figure 24.8 Sample guidance on community nursing services contract

1. Contract definition
2. Contract scope
3. Community nursing services:
   (a) district nursing services
   (b) health visiting services
   (c) excluded services
4. Staff included:
   (a) current staffing
   (b) cover for short term absences
   (c) future staffing
   (d) community practice teachers
   (e) new staff
5. Managerial and support services
6. Quality issues:
   (a) service specific
   (b) information gathering
   (c) protocols
7. Information exchange
8. Primary health care team relationships
9. Costings and billing
10. Aids and appliances
11. Monitoring
12. Assignment and sub-contracting

13. Patients' complaints
14. Variation of contract
15. Non-performance
16. Arbitration
17. Right to get out of contract
18. Public availability and confidentiality
19. Duration and re-negotiation.

■ What is the legal position if the fund-holding practice fails to purchase the necessary services?

Under the terms of the service contract with the health authority, the general practitioner has a contractual duty to perform specified services for patients on his list and also to non-residents and others in an emergency. If he is unable to provide the services personally, then he may use deputising services, but there are strict controls over these. As a member of a fund-holding practice, he has a duty as purchaser to ensure that specified services are available for his patients.

If he fails to purchase these services and harm befalls the patient, then he may well be sued in the civil courts for breach of his duty of care.

For example, under the new community health service provision regulations a fund-holding practice has a duty to purchase health visiting services from an NHS provider, if the fund-holding practice failed to purchase these and, as a consequence of the lack of health visiting services, duties under the Children Act were not implemented in that practice area, consequential harm befalling any children could be regarded as the basis of an action for negligence against the practice.

The supplementary guidance to fund-holders (HSG(92)53) makes this clear. The relevant paragraphs are set out in Figure 24.9, although the references to DHAs are now out of date.

Figure 24.9 Failure to provide cover

Paragraph 21: Some fundholders have asked whether they could leave responsibility for purchasing services to be added to the scheme with the DHA. There is no scope to do so within the legislation: once a service has been added to the list of goods and services which fundholders purchase, it becomes their purchasing responsibility and the DHA has no jurisdiction to purchase these services on behalf of fundholders' patients.

Paragraph 36: The question has been raised as to liability in the event of a child death following a lack of effective intervention by the responsible health visitor. . . .

Paragraph 37: . . . If it could be shown that there had been a failure to purchase an adequate level of service or the right type of service, the fundholder could possibly be held to be liable as could the DHA in comparable circumstances. This could apply where the fundholder had been funded for three health visiting posts and had contracted for only one (though the Region would then withhold its consent to the contract). This could also apply where a fundholder had in some way prevented the health visitor from adequately managing her under-5s case load . . .

Paragraph 38: In these circumstances, the fundholder could either also be a defendant in the case or could be joined as a third party by the health visitor and employer.

The circular also points out the difference between the duty to purchase and to provide.

> If the fundholder were unable to purchase appropriate services because, for example, they were not available, the fundholder would not be liable.

The situation on legal liability is complicated by the fact that at present the fund-holding practice does not employ its own community health staff but buys that provision in from the NHS Trust or from the directly managed unit. It cannot at present employ its own staff. This raises the issue as to who is liable if these staff are negligent. The basic rule of law is that the employer is vicariously liable for the negligence of the employee whilst the latter is acting in course of employment (see Chapter 7). If a community health worker is negligent whilst performing duties purchased from her employers, does the original employer remain liable for her negligence or has she been contracted to the fund-holders who give her instructions and therefore the fund-holders become vicariously liable for her. Much will depend upon the nature of the agreement under which the fund-holder purchases the community services.

Situation

A client claims that a health visitor whose services were being purchased by a GP fund-holding practice failed to arrange for the admission of a seriously ill baby, who subsequently died. Who is liable?

If the health visitor is the employee of the community health trust, then the community health trust as employer would usually be vicariously liable. However, there may also be direct liability of the GP fund-holders for failure to visit the patient or for inappropriately sending the health visitor to see the patient.

It is also possible for the contracting arrangements (when the community services are purchased by the GP fund-holder) to provide that the latter accept responsibility for the health and safety and also the negligence of those individuals who provide the services.

Savings
The fund-holders can only use savings to purchase services which are authorised by the Secretary of State.

The rules governing a GP fund-holder's use of savings have been extended from April 1995 (see EL(94)79) to include clinical audit, research and development, and training (subject to prior approval by the health authority).

If savings arise when a GP fund-holder ceases to be a fund-holder, those savings are still subject to the GP fund-holder scheme and, once all liabilities have been settled, they could be used for the approved purposes.

Range of services which can be provided by the fund-holders
There is a statutory duty for fund-holders to provide those duties set out in the statutory instruments identified above, but they may like to provide other services for their patients

■ Can fund-holders provide pharmaceutical services?

There are strict rules relating to the provision of pharmaceutical services which are paid for by the new health authorities. Approval must be obtained from the authority for the supply of pharmaceutical services in a district. General practitioners may provide these services with the consent of the authority but only where it is adjudged to be a rural practice which warrants a dispensing permit.

These provisions only apply to the supply of prescription only medicines and products or those which must be sold under the supervision of a registered pharmacist. There would appear to be nothing to prevent a fund-holding practice selling to the patients other medicinal products and items such as dressings and over-the-counter medicines which do not require the supervision of a registered pharmacist.

■ What about the purchase of pathology laboratory tests?

It is reported that one fund-holding practice has established a contract with a hospital for pathology tests to be carried out in private residential homes[18]. They had found it difficult to get blood samples tested in the past and therefore entered this agreement whereby the hospital arranged for the collection of the blood samples from the residents and provided screening tests on each. They found that of the 130 patients tested in eight residential homes 25% required following up.

■ What about GP referrals to special hospitals?

One area of secondary care which at present the GP fund-holding practice does not have to finance is the care of their patients in special health authorities. These include the care and treatment of patients in the special hospitals for mental disorder (Broadmoor, Rampton and Ashworth) as well as the care provided by Great Ormond Street, the National Hospital for Nervous Diseases, Moorfields Eye Hospital, Bethlem Royal Hospital, the Royal Brompton National Heart and Lung Hospital, the Royal Marsden and Hammersmith and Queen Charlotte's Hospital.

Patients leaving or joining a practice
Even though a referral for treatment and care has been arranged by the previous fund-holding practice to which the patient was once attached, the new practice to which the patient moves will have the responsibility of meeting the cost of that care. Thus if a patient moves to a new practice that practice meets the cost of the care unless the treatment is carried out before the patient changed practices.

RELATIONSHIPS WITH INDIVIDUAL PATIENTS

It must be emphasised that GP fund-holders retain all the responsibilities as the direct providers of the general medical services for the patients on their lists, as well as becoming the purchasers of their secondary and community care. A concern raised in the media and elsewhere is the danger that GPs will remove patients from their lists because they are considered to be too expensive[19]. At present a GP does not have to give reasons for asking for a patient to be removed from his list. The health authority would have a duty to arrange for that patient to be transferred to another GP. The patient has no right to appeal against a decision to remove him from his doctor's list. A survey by the National Association of Community Health Councils estimated that doctors removed 30 000 patients from their lists in 1993[20].

At the time of writing there is still uncertainty as to the effect of potential tensions in the duty of the GP as the professional responsible for the medical care of each patient on his list and the role of the GP as budget holder and purchaser.

PROBLEMS FOR THE FUTURE

One of the major issues for the future is on the question of resources and the legal liability if insufficient resources are provided for the GPFH to purchase sufficient care for the patients on their lists.

■ Could the patient sue the GPFH or any other body?

Cases which are discussed in Chapter 27 show that patients who have been placed on waiting lists have not succeeded in bringing a successful action against their health authority or the Secretary of State. The courts are reluctant to intervene if the issue relates to the allocation of resources provided there is no gross unreasonableness.

However, in community care, resources cannot always be rationed by means of a waiting list. If services are not available, harm could befall a patient who is already in the community or the patient may not be able to be discharged from hospital if provision is not made for support. Alternatively the patient may have to be transferred to hospital if community services are not provided.

These issues of inadequate funding in relation to demand and the rights of the patient to enforce community care provision are further discussed in Chapter 27.

CONCLUSION

The general practitioner, whether fund-holder or not, can be seen as the linchpin of the success of community care. As more long-stay beds in institutions are closed, as length of stay in acute hospitals declines and more treatments are provided on a day-patient or out-patient basis, so the general practitioner takes an increasingly significant role in treatments and care which would formerly have come under secondary care. More general practitioner beds in GP managed units and minor surgery facilities will speed this development. In addition, the care of the chronic mentally ill and the elderly will increasingly be the responsibility of the GP rather than the hospital consultant as the in-patient NHS facilities close. The GP will be central to the assessment of medical and nursing needs in the community and will have a major part to play in the determination of needs in community service provision.

Prescribed conditions have been laid down which must be met before a practice is deemed to be eligible for fund-holding status. The earlier conditions have been widened to enable more practices to apply.

There were initially only a few practices applying for fund-holding status. The fund-holding practices are becoming more sophisticated in their policies and strategies and it was reported in the *Times* 10 November 1992 that groups of fund-holding practices have combined together. It was the intention of the Conservative Government in introducing the system that eventually all general practitioners should be working within the fund-holding arrangements, but the voluntary nature of the process was stressed. Certainly the changes announced in October 1994 and discussed above should lead to many more practices putting in applications for fund-holding status. Evaluations of the shadow fund-holding in Scotland have now been undertaken[21] and it is clear that it had a major impact upon the pattern of hospital referrals, prescribing patterns and clinical care.

As well as the digest of information referred to on page 362 the Audit Commission has published a study of GP fund-holders in England and Wales (*What the Doctor Ordered*, HMSO 1996) which shows the wide variation in the achievements of fund-holding practices. It makes strong recommendations in relation to the benefits for patients, the management of fund-holding, the management of the scheme itself and arrangements with NHS Trusts. It remains to be seen if these recommendations are implemented and if fund-holding survives any political changes.

CHAPTER 25

Local authorities

In Chapter 2 the statutory definition of community care is given with reference to specific statutory powers and duties. The purpose of this chapter is to look at those duties and powers which are relevant to the role of the local authorities.

The legislation shown in Figure 25.1 will be considered.

Figure 25.1 Legislation considered in this chapter

- Section 29, National Assistance Act 1948 (Sections 21, 24 and 26 covering powers and duties in relation to accommodation are discussed in Section D of this book)
- Section 45, Health Service and Public Health Act 1968
- Sections 1 and 2, Chronically Sick and Disabled Persons Act 1970
- Disabled Persons (Services, Consultation and Representation) Act 1986
- Sections 21, 22 and 28 and Schedule 8, National Health Service Act 1977
- Section 117, Mental Health Act 1983
- Part III National Health Service and Community Care Act 1990

It must be emphasised that the services provided for the disabled are outside the definition of community care for the purposes of the National Health Service and Community Care Act 1990 but this book covers a wider scope than the provisions of that Act.

This chapter covers first some preliminary points and the need for consolidating legislation. Pre-1990 statutory provisions that are still relevant are then considered, particularly those relating to the care of the disabled. Finally we look at Part III of the 1990 Act and the obligations it places on local authorities to set out community care plans, to make assessments of those seen to require services and to provide an inspection service for various facilities.

378

PRELIMINARY POINTS

Powers of Secretary of State as respects social services functions of local authorities

Section 50 of the 1990 Act gives powers to the Secretary of State to give directions as to the exercise of social services functions and to require local authorities to establish a complaints procedure (see Chapter 27). This is done by adding new sections to the Local Authority Social Services Act 1970 (see figure 27.1).

Reference will also be made to the Circulars giving guidance for the implementation of the duties or powers set out in the statutes.

Statutory provisions relating to accommodation are discussed in the Section D of the book, Chapters 28 to 32.

Need for a consolidating Act

It would have been considerably easier for clients, professionals and lawyers alike if, in the 1990 Act, the opportunity had been taken to consolidate the existing legislation and to clarify the legal position of the local authority in relation to its new and existing duties. The opportunity, however, was not taken and instead progress was made by amendments and additions to various statutes dating back to the National Assistance Act 1948. Before some of the amendments have even come into force amendments of the amendments were made by the 1992 Act. In addition many of the sections do not have force in themselves but rely upon ministerial directions to give a mandatory duty to local authorities to perform specific functions.

There is also substantial ministerial and NHS Management Executive guidance which does not have statutory force but which, like the *Highway Code* or the *Code of Practice: the Mental Health Act 1983*, has persuasive authority and could usually be relied upon by judges to show evidence of a failure to perform statutory functions appropriately should the question arise.

The result is a jigsaw where even the basic questions cannot be answered with ease or certainty. It is inevitable, given the way in which the new legislation has been drafted, that there will follow, as the users and their support organisations attempt to get to grips with the legal situation, many cases for judicial review, possibly as much with the aim of clarifying the legal situation as to enforce the provisions of community care. The result will be a gold mine for lawyers but a hardship and burden to those of already inadequate means who seek an understanding of their legal entitlements. It will also be a drain on public funds. (This is further discussed in Chapter 27.)

The situation is also complicated by the transfer of the funding of certain persons in residential or nursing care from social security to local authority. These provisions only affect those admitted into such accommodation after 1 April 1993. Those already in such accommodation on that date and entitled to the receipt of income support at the higher level have preserved rights of entitlement which will continue for the foreseeable future. There has been concern from directors of social services that the funding is not sufficient to meet the basic community care needs of those already identified as requiring such services. The provision of accommodation and its funding is discussed in Section D of this book and the shortfall in meeting assessed needs on pages 401–3 of this chapter.

STATUTORY DUTIES

Section 29, National Assistance Act 1948

Figure 25.2   The National Assistance Act 1948 – section 29(1)

A local authority may, with the approval of the Secretary of State, and to such extent as he may direct in relation to person ordinarily resident in the area of the local authority shall, make arrangements for promoting the welfare of persons to whom this section applies, that is to say persons aged eighteen or over who are blind, deaf or dumb or who suffer from mental disorder of any description, and other persons aged eighteen or over who are substantially and permanently handicapped by illness, injury or congenital deformity or such other disabilities as may be prescribed by the Minister.

The section also enables arrangements to be made for informing persons of the services which are available and giving such persons instruction in their own homes or elsewhere in methods of overcoming the effects of their disabilities, for providing workshops and (under section 29(4)(f)) 'for providing such persons with recreational facilities in their own homes or elsewhere'.

This section has been given mandatory force by Directions from the Secretary of State which are contained in LAC(93)10 which also gives guidance on identifying those to whom the section applies. (See Appendix 1 and also below.)

Section 29 of the National Assistance Act is the basis of many subsequent statutory powers and duties for providing welfare services.

Approvals and directions under section 29 National Assistance Act 1948

LAC(93)10 consolidates the existing approvals and directions of the Secretary of State and Appendix 2 covers the approval and directions given under Section 29 of the 1948 Act and, although other extracts are reproduced in Appendix 1 of this book, Appendix 2 of LAC(93)10 is shown in Figure 25.3.

Figure 25.3 LAC(93)10, Appendix 2

Powers and duties to make welfare arrangements

2(1) The Secretary of State hereby *approves* the making by Local Authorities of arrangements under section 29(1) of the Act for all persons who whom that subsection applies and *directs* Local Authorities to make arrangements under section 29(1) of the Act in relation to persons who are ordinarily resident in their area for all or any of the following purposes —

(a) to provide a social work service and such advice and support as may be needed for people in their own homes or elsewhere;
(b) to provide, whether at centres or elsewhere, facilities for social rehabilitation and adjustment to disability including assistance in overcoming limitations of mobility or communication;
(c) to provide, whether at centres or elsewhere, facilities for occupational, social, cultural and recreational activities and, where appropriate, the making of payments to persons for work undertaken by them; (see section 29(4)(d) and 29(6)(a) of 1948 Act);

2(2) The Secretary of State hereby *directs* Local Authorities to make the arrangements referred to in section 29(4)(g) of the Act (compiling and maintaining registers) in relation to persons who are ordinarily resident in their area.

2(3) The Secretary of State hereby *approves* the making by Local Authorities of arrangements under section 29(1) of the Act for all persons to whom that subsection applies for the following purposes —

(a) to provide holiday homes;
(b) to provide free or subsidised travel for all or any persons who do not otherwise qualify for travel concessions, but only in respect of travel arrangements for which concessions are available;
(c) to assist a person in finding accommodation which will enable him to take advantage of any arrangements made under section 29(1) of the Act;
(d) to contribute to the cost of employing a warden on welfare functions in warden assisted housing schemes;
(e) to provide warden services for occupiers of private housing.

2(4) Save as is otherwise provided for under this paragraph, the Secretary of State hereby *approves* the making by Local Authorities of all or any of the arrangements referred to in section 29(4) of the Act (amended by Employment and Training Act 1973 and section 44(7) of the NHS and Community Care Act 1990) (Welfare arrangements etc) for all persons to whom section 29(1) applies.

Welfare arrangements with another Local Authority

3. The Secretary of State hereby *approves* the making by Local Authorities of arrangements under section 29(1) of the Act, where appropriate, with another Local Authority for the provision of any of the services referred to in these Approvals and Directions.

Welfare arrangements with vouluntary organisations and otherwise

4. For the avoidance of doubt, these Approvals and Directions are without prejudice [see glossary] to the powers conferred on Local Authorities by section 30(1) of the Act (Voluntary organisations for disabled persons' welfare) (Amended by Local Government Act 1972 and by section 42(6) of the NHS and Community Care Act 1990).

[author's emphasis of 'approves'/'directs']

Appendix 4 to LAC(93)10 gives guidance on the keeping of registers necessary under section 29 of the National Assistance Act 1948. The form of the registers is not prescribed and

'the Department hopes that this will enable authorities to keep registers in whatever form and by whatever method will most readily meet their operational requirements'.

It is also stated that, once it is established that a person comes within the scope of section 29, the giving of assistance under that section, as extended by section 2 of the Chronically Sick and Disabled Persons Act 1970, is not dependent on formal registration – that is, registration is not a prerequisite to giving assistance. It is therefore possible for a person to ask for their name not to be registered but still be entitled to receive assistance.

Coming within the scope of section 29
LAC(93)10 gives guidance on the meaning of the terms used to define which people come within the scope of section 29. Explanations are given of the following terms:

- visually impaired people
- hearing impaired people
- handicapped people in the general classes.

LAC(93)10 offers guidance on statutory provision for persons suffering from a mental disorder within the meaning of the Mental Health Act 1983, and states that, although they should be regarded as coming within the general class of handicapped persons, where they are registered they should be separately identified (Paragraphs 13 and 14).

Annex 2 to Appendix 4 of LAC(93)10 gives guidance on the definitions of deaf and hard of hearing following the Young Husband Report.

Section 29 of the National Assistance Act 1948 and the accompanying directions provide the basis of local authority powers and duties in relation to welfare services. The distinction should be noted as to when the Secretary of State 'directs' and when the Secretary of State 'approves'. Thus there is a direction to provide social work services, facilities for rehabilitation and occupational activities and the making of a register. There is no direction in relation to arrangements for holiday homes, free or subsidised travel and the other services.

Section 45, Health Services and Public Health Act 1968

This section makes provision for services for the elderly and is shown in Figure 25.4.

Figure 25.4   Health Services and Public Health Act 1968 – section 45

(1) A local authority may with the approval of the Secretary of State and to such extent as he may direct shall, make arrangements for promoting the welfare of old people.

(2) [repealed]

(3) A local authority may employ as their agent for the purposes of this section any voluntary organisation *or any person carrying on, professionally or by way of trade or business, activities which consist of or include the provision of services for old people, being an organisation or person appearing to the authority to be capable of promoting the welfare of old people.* [words in italics added by section 42(7) of the National Health Service and Community Care Act 1990.]

(4) No arrangements under this section shall provide —

(a) for the payment of money to old people except in so far as the arrangements may provide for the remuneration of old people engaged in suitable work in accordance with the arrangements;
(b) for making available any accommodation or services required to be provided under the National Health Service Act 1977

This section must be read in conjunction with Circular LAC(93)10 which gives directions on its implementation and can be found in Appendix 1.

Provisions for chronically sick and disabled persons

Every local authority is under a duty to ascertain the number of chronically sick and disabled persons in its area and to publicise the services provided for them. This is imposed by section 1 of the Chronically Sick and Disabled Persons Act 1970 which is set out in Figure 25.5.

Figure 25.5   Chronically Sick and Disabled Persons Act 1970 – section 1

(1) It shall be the duty of every local authority having functions under section 29 of the National Assistance Act 1948 to inform themselves of

the number of persons to whom that section applies within their area and of the need for the making by the authority of arrangements under that section for such persons.

(2) Every such authority —

(a) shall cause to be published from time to time at such times and in such manner as they consider appropriate general information as to the services provided under arrangements made by the authority under the said section 29 which are for the time being available in their area; and

(b) shall ensure that any such person as aforesaid who uses any of those services is informed of any other *service provided by the authority (whether under any such arrangements or not)* which in the opinion of the authority is relevant to his needs *and of any service provided by any other authority or organisation which in the opinion of the authority is so relevant and of which particulars are in the authority's possession.*

[words in italics introduced by the 1986 Act (see below).]

Section 2 of the 1970 Act lists the provisions that the local authority has a duty to make once it has identified persons in its area to whom section 29 of the National Assistance Act 1948 applies. Details are given in Figure 2.3.

The right to enforce provision under section 2 is being considered by the House of Lords in a recent case[22] where disabled persons applied for judicial review of the decision by Gloucester County Council to cut social services for the disabled. The High Court held that the County Council should re-assess when making cuts but was entitled to take its resources into account. The CA reversed this principle, but that decision has such far-reaching implications for LAs that it is likely to be overtuned by the House of Lords or legislated upon (see also Chapter 27, pages 441–3).

Disabled Persons (Services, etc.) Act 1986

One of the major deficiencies of the 1970 Act was the failure to introduce provision for the assessment of persons who were potentially under its jurisdiction. The Disabled Persons (Services, Consultation and Representation) Act 1986, introduced by Tom Clarke MP, aimed at meeting this and other deficiencies of the 1970 Act. The Act provided for the improvement of the effectiveness and co-ordination of services for the mentally and physically handicapped and the mentally ill, and established new procedures for the assessment of the needs of the disabled.

However whilst it received the Royal Assent in July 1986 its sections were due to be implemented at dates to be appointed. Resource implications have delayed the coming into force of some of the crucial parts of the Act. In particular at the present time sections 1, 2, and 3 on the

- appointment of representatives,
- the rights of an authorised representative and
- assessment by local authorities of the needs of disabled persons

are not in force and there is no clear statement from the Government of when, or indeed if, they will be implemented.

Appointment of authorised representatives
It was a weakness of the 1970 Act that those most in need of assistance were often those incapable through their disabilities of claiming entitlements and services. A system for such disadvantaged persons to be represented was essential to ensure that their needs were assessed and that the appropriate services were provided. Section 1 of the 1986 Act, therefore, was proposed to set up a system for the appointment of an authorised representative in relation to any disabled person. However, this and the supplementary sections have not been brought into force.

Assessment of the needs of disabled persons
The provisions for the assessment are set out under section 3 of the Act which is referred to in the 1990 legislation (see below) even though it has not come into force, and probably will not, having been largely over taken by the 1990 Act.

Duty of local authority to consider the needs of disabled persons
Section 4 of the Act was implemented in 1987 and requires the local authority to consider the needs of the disabled person. It is set out in Figure 25.6.

Figure 25.6 Disabled Persons (Services etc.) Act 1986 – section 4

When requested to do so by —

(a) a disabled person
(b) his authorised representative [not yet in force]
(c) any person who provides care for him in the circumstances mentioned in section 8

a local authority shall decide whether the needs of the disabled person call for the provision by the authority of any services in accordance with section 2(1) of the 1970 Act (provision of welfare services).

The services referred to are those set out in Figure 2.3.

The circumstances mentioned in Section 8 are set out in Figure 25.7.

Figure 25.7 Disabled persons (Services, etc.) Act 1986 – section 8

(1) Where

(a) a disabled person is living at home and receiving a substantial amount of care on a regular basis from another person (who is not a person employed to provide such care by any body in the exercise of its functions under any enactment) and

(b) it falls to a local authority to decide whether the disabled person's needs call for the provision by them of any services for him under any of the welfare enactments,

the local authority shall, in deciding that question, have regard to the ability of that other person to continue to provide such care on a regular basis.

Section 8(1), the duty of the local authority to have regard to the ability of the carer to provide such care on a regular basis, came into force on 1 April 1987. However those authorities following the best practice would already have had regard to this necessity since it could be argued that, unless this assessment of the care being received was made, it would be difficult for a local authority to carry out its duties under section 2 of the 1970 Act.

The 1986 Act provides no definition of substantial care and thus it is open to each local authority to determine the yardsticks to be used in determining what is substantial until such time as there is judicial determination of the definition. It would presumably require some element of significance in quantity but what may be seen subjectively by some clients as substantial may be seen as meagre by others.

Note that subsections 8(2) and (3) have not yet been brought into force. These concern the more onerous duties of providing incapacitated carers with services, for example signing interpreters, to enable them to communicate with the authority (section 8(2)) and taking views of the representative appointed by section 1 of the Act, also not in force.

Information
Section 9 has widened the duty of the local authority under section 1 of the 1970 Act in publishing the services provided (see Figure 25.5). Since 1 April 1987 a local authority must ensure that any disabled person who uses the services is informed about not only those services provided by the authority itself but also any service provided by any other authority or organisation which, in the opinion of the authority, is relevant and of which particulars are in the authority's possession. It could, therefore, be argued that if a voluntary group sends in to the local authority, or to one of its officers, details concerning its services, then those details would be deemed to be in the possession of the authority

and, if relevant, should be made available to any disabled person. Improved communication between officers and departments of the authority is, therefore, essential in the implementation of this duty.

Consultation
Under section 10 which came into force on 1 April 1987, the organisations of disabled persons must be consulted before the appointment or co-option of any person to a council, committee or body on which members with a special knowledge of disabled persons are statutorily required. Section 15 of the 1970 Act, for example, requires the local authority, when exercising the powers of co-opting onto a committee concerned with the special needs of the chronically sick or disabled, to consider appointing people with relevant experience, and to consider whether someone actually chronically sick or disabled should be appointed.

There have been some applications seeking judicial review or remedies for breach of statutory duty on the basis of duties laid down in the 1970 and 1986 Acts and these are discussed in Chapter 27.

National Health Service Act 1977, section 21 and Schedule 8

Section 21 and Schedule 8 of the National Health Service Act 1977 cover:

- the provision of services for the care of mothers and young children;
- prevention, care and after-care;
- home help and laundry facilities.

Section 21 describes these services as functions exercisable by a local social services authority.

Section 21 is set out in Figure 25.8 and Schedule 8 can be found in Figure 23.7.

Figure 25.8 The 1977 Act – section 21

(1) Subject to paragraphs (d) and (e) of section 3(1) above, [the extent to which such services are considered appropriate as part of the health service] the services described in Schedule 8 to this Act in relation to

(a) care of mothers and young children,
(b) prevention, care and after-care,
(c) home help and laundry facilities,

are functions exercisable by local social services authorities, and that Schedule has effect accordingly.

(2) A local social services authority who provide premises, furniture or equipment for any of the purposes of this Act may permit the use of premises, furniture or equipment —

(a) by any other local social services authority, or
(b) by any of the bodies constituted under this Act, or
(c) by a local education authority.

This permission may be on such terms (including terms with respect to the services of any staff employed by the authority giving permission) as may be agreed.

[Subsection 3 enables the local social services authority to provide, improve or furnish residential accommodation for their own officers or for those belonging to a voluntary organisation carrying out functions under section 21 or Schedule 8.]

Approval and Directions were consolidated in LAC(93)10 (see Appendix 1 of this book). Appendix 3 of this circular relates to the powers under Schedule 8 of National Health Service Act 1977 under the following headings:

● Services for expectant and nursing mothers
● Services for the purpose of prevention of illness etc.
● Services made available by another local authority etc.

Section 117, Mental Health Act 1983

Section 117 (see pages 242–5) applies to the following patients:

● patients detained under section 3,
● patients admitted under section 37,
● patients transferred under sections 47 or 48.

The duty consists in the two authorities (health and local social services) co-operating with voluntary agencies to provide after-care services for any person under this section and lasts until the both authorities are satisfied that the person concerned is no longer in need of such services and is not subject to after-care under supervision.

It is highly desirable that after-care planning should begin as soon as possible, perhaps even before the patient's admission. *The Code of Practice: the Mental Health Act 1983* issued by the Department of Health (see Chapter 4) gives guidance on the procedures to be followed and the staff who should be involved in the discussions. In a recent case the court has held that there is a statutory duty upon the authorities to comply with the requirements of section 117 and this is enforceable by an individual patient.

Case: *R. v. Ealing District Health Authority, ex parte Fox*

Mr. Fox sought judicial review of the refusal by Ealing Health Authority to make the necessary arrangements for after-care as required under section 117 (see above page 244). The Oxford Mental Health Review Tribunal had ordered a conditional discharge to come into effect when appropriate arrangements for after-care could be made. Following such an order, the health authority had a duty to make practical arrangements to enable the patient to fulfil any discharge conditions. In this case it was the appointment of a consultant psychiatrist for the patient.

It should be noted that, under section 7E of the Local Authority Social Services Act 1970 (which was introduced by section 50 of the NHS and Community Care Act 1990) the Secretary of State may, with the approval of the Treasury, make grants out of money provided by Parliament towards any expenses of local authorities incurred in exercising their social services functions in relation to persons suffering from mental illness.

NATIONAL HEALTH SERVICE AND COMMUNITY CARE ACT 1990 – PART III

Community Care Plans

The duty
Section 46 of the 1990 Act requires each local authority to prepare and publish a plan for the provision of community care in their area.

The section also requires the local authority to keep the plan and any further plans prepared by them under this section under review and empowers the Secretary of State to direct the intervals at which the local authority must prepare and publish modifications to the current plan or a new plan.

The sections came into force following a direction issued by the Secretary of State for Health in 1991 shown in Figure 25.9.

Figure 25.9 *Community Care Plans Direction 1991*

The Secretary of State for Health in exercise of the powers conferred upon him by paragraphs (a) and (c) of section 46(1) of the National Health Service and Community Care Act 1990 hereby gives the following directions:

1. Each local authority shall

(a) prepare and publish a plan for the provision of community care services in their area within a period of one year after the date appointed for the coming into force of section 46 of the National Health Service and Community Care Act 1990 [this date was 1 April 1991]; and

(b) thereafter prepare and publish modifications to the current plan or, if the case requires, a new plan at intervals of not more than one year. (see Circular LAC(91)16)

The consultation

There are statutory duties under section 46(2) for the local authority to consult the organisations shown in Figure 25.10.

Figure 25.10 Duty to consult under section 46(2)

In carrying out any of their functions [set out in Figure 25.9], a local authority shall consult —
(a) any Health Authority the whole or any part of whose area lies within the area of the local authority;
(b) [reference to FHSA – repealed by the 1995 Act]
(c) in so far as any proposed plan, review or modifications of a plan may affect or be affected by the provision or availability of housing and the local authority is not itself a local housing authority ... every local housing authority [in its area];
(d) such voluntary organisations as appear to the authority to represent the interests of persons who use or are likely to use any community care services within the area of the authority or the interests of private carers who, within that area, provide care to persons for whom, in the exercise of their social services functions, the local authority have a power or a duty to provide a service;
(e) such voluntary housing agencies and other bodies as appear to the local authority to provide housing or community care services in their area; and
(f) such other persons as the Secretary of State may direct.

Definitions of each of these terms are given and 'private carer' is defined as a person who is not employed to provide the care in question by any body in the exercise of its functions under any enactment.

Directions on Consultation were issued by the Secretary of State for Health in 1993 and are shown in Figure 25.11.

Figure 25.11 Community Care Plans (Consultation) Directions 1993

Article 2 Each local authority shall, in carrying out any of their functions under section 46(1) of the National Health Service and Community Care Act 1990 (community care plans), consult any representative organisation (including any incorporated or unincorporated body of persons) which represents providers in the authority's area with whom the authority may arrange to provide community care services as defined in section 46 of the National Health Service and Community Care Act 1990 where that organisation notifies the local authority in writing of their wish to be consulted in respect of the authority's community care plans.

Article 3 Each local authority shall include in the plan which they prepare and publish for the provision of community care services in their area pursuant to section 46 of the National Health Services Act 1990 details of how they propose to consult those persons specified in

(a) section 46(2) of the 1990 Act [see Figure 25.10], and
(b) article 2 of these Directions.

The explanatory note states that the Directions are intended to ensure that there is full and proper consultation between local authorities and independent sector providers on community care plans by requiring local authorities to consult with organisations which have declared themselves as representing such providers.

The Directions extend the consultation requirement to representatives of independent sector providers. The guidance gives justification for the need to consult with the independent sector.

> It already provides two thirds of the long term residential and nursing home care for elderly people in England. Independent day and domiciliary care is also growing. Local Authorities will need to make contact with independent sector providers in their area in planning and developing purchasing strategies for those people for whom they have a responsibility to arrange domiciliary, day, residential and nursing home care. This is particularly so for the 110 000 new clients who would have entered residential and nursing home care in 1993–4 and been supported by DSS benefits.

The guidance makes it clear that the nature and style of the consultation will be a matter for each authority to decide, but suggests the following basic principles:

- Views must be invited on proposals, not the final document.
- Reasonable time must be allowed.
- Views must be taken into consideration.
- It may be sufficient to hold meetings but, if the proposals are placed on the agenda of a regular forum, care needs to be taken to ensure that those who need to be consulted are properly informed.

Initial policy guidance on the preparation of community care plans was given in 1990 by the Department of Health in *Caring for People: Community Care in the Next Decade and Beyond; Policy Guidance*. This advised local authorities on:

- the statutory requirements on them to consult in the planning process;
- the statutory requirements for publishing plans;

- the arrangements for monitoring plans; and
- the scope and content of SSDs' plans.

Purchasing non-residential care from the independent sector
In 1994 Directions were issued requiring local authorities to include in their plans such proposals as they have for making arrangements to purchase non-residential care from independent sector providers[23]. Directions were issued under section 7A of the Local Authority Social Services Act 1970 and came into force on 1 June 1994. The Direction states that

> each local authority shall include in the plan which they prepare and publish for the provision of community care services in their area details of such proposals as they may have for making arrangements to purchase non-residential services from independent sector providers of such services as part of the local authority's overall provision for community care services in their area.

Definitions of 'independent sector' and 'non-residential' are shown in Figure 25.12.

Figure 25.12 Definitions of independent sector and non-residential

Independent sector providers are defined as any providers of non-residential services other than:

(a) individuals employed by a local authority under a contract of service; or
(b) organisations which are owned or controlled or managed by a local authority or by more than one local authority.

Non-residential services means community care services other than:

(a) arrangements for providing residential accommodation made under section 21 of the NAA 1948;
(b) hostel arrangements made under section 29(4)(c) of NAA 1948;
(c) holiday arrangements made under section 2(1)(f) of Chronically Sick and Disabled Persons Act 1970; or
(d) accommodation arrangements made by a local authority as an after-care service under section 117 of the Mental Health Act 1983.

In the guidance notes on these directions it is pointed out that the independent (voluntary and private) sector has a vital role to play in the mixed economy of care if users and carers are to reap the benefits of choice and quality that result from diversity of provision.

Social services departments have been encouraged to provide for the purchasing of residential and nursing home care[24].

Comment on duty to provide community care plans
The Parliamentary Under-Secretary for the Department of Social Security, Lord Henley, described[25] these plans as:

> a cornerstone of our policy. They are designed to enable local authorities to set out and publish the needs of the community they serve, their objectives for the arrangement of services to meet those needs within the resources available to them, and to set out targets which they are setting themselves to develop and improve the services available in their areas. We shall also require local authorities in drawing up their care plans to consult local statutory, voluntary and other agencies to ensure that the approach to community care becomes much more user driven rather that fitting clients into existing services ... It may well be that as authorities develop their plans over time they may wish publicly to state the standards and specifications which they may require from service providers, including their own directly managed provision.

Speeches in both House of Commons and Lords emphasised the 'seamless service' which must be provided, and referred to the guidance for local authorities in planning with health authorities to identify and meet needs within the totality of the resources available. Circular LAC (89)7 with its booklet *The discharge of patients from hospital* is discussed in Chapter 14.

Assessment of needs and provision of services

The statutory duty
Section 47 of the 1990 Act places upon the local authority the duty both to carry out assessments and then to decide on the provision of services. This double duty is shown in Figure 25.13

Figure 25.13 The 1990 Act – section 47(1)

[W]here it appears to a local authority that any person for whom they may provide or arrange for the provision of community care services may be in need of any services, the authority —

(a) *shall* carry out an assessment of his needs for those services; *and*
(b) having regard to the results of that assessment, *shall* then decide whether his needs call for the provision by them of any such services.

[author's emphasis]

Disabled persons and assessments

Section 47(2) makes specific provision for assessment of disabled persons and, as shown in Figure 25.14, automatically applies section 4 of the Disabled Persons (Services, Consultation and Representation) Act 1986. Section 4 of the 1986 Act is set out in Figure 25.6.

Figure 25.14 The 1990 Act – section 47(2)

If at any time during the assessment of the needs of any person under subsection (1)(a) above it appears to the local authority that he is a disabled person, the authority —

(a) shall proceed to make such a decision as to the services he requires as is mentioned in section 4 of the Disabled Persons (Services, Consultation and Representation) Act 1986 without his requesting them to do so under that section; and

(b) shall inform him that they will be doing so and of this rights under that Act.

Subsection (7) states that section 47 is without prejudice (see glossary) to section 3 of the Disabled Persons (Services, Consultation and Representation) Act 1986. This means that it does not affect the provisions of the 1986 Act which exist in parallel with the provisions for giving information under the 1990 Act. If should, however, be noted that section 3 of the 1986 Act is not yet in force.

'Disabled person' has the same meaning as that used in the 1986 Act.

Involvement with other authorities

Section 47(3) requires the local authority to involve the health authority and the local housing authority if there appears to be a need of services from these organisations.

In such circumstances the local authority must notify the health authority or housing authority and invite them to assist, to such extent as is reasonable in the circumstances, in the making of the assessment; and in making their decision as to the provision of the services needed for the person in question, the local authority shall take into account any services which are likely to be made available for him by the health authority or local housing authority.

Directions on assessments

Subsection (4) gives power to the Secretary of State to give directions as to how an assessment is to be carried out or the form it is to take with the proviso that, subject to any such directions and to the parallel duties under the Disabled Persons

(Services, etc.) Act 1986, it shall be carried out in such manner and take such form as the local authority consider appropriate. Directions have been not yet been given and the relevant section of the 1986 Act is not yet in force so local authorities have a free hand which makes enforcement difficult (see Chapter 27).

Policy guidance has, however, been issued (*Caring for People: Community Care in the next decade and beyond; Policy guidance* pages 21–34). In addition the social services inspectorate has prepared several handbooks of guidance on care management and assessment for managers and practitioners (see Appendix 3(B) and discussion above on pages 223–4 and below on page 398). Note that section 7 of the Local Government Social Services Act 1970 requires a local authority to act under the guidance of the Secretary of State in exercising its social services functions.

Urgent situations

The duty shown in Figure 25.13 is subject to subsections (5) and (6) shown in Figure 25.15.

Figure 25.15   The 1990 Act – section 47(5) and (6)

(5) Nothing in this section shall prevent a local authority from temporarily providing or arranging for the provision of community care services for any person without carrying out a prior assessment of his needs in accordance with the preceding provisions of this section if, in the opinion of the authority, the condition of that person is such that he requires those services as a matter of urgency.

(6) If, by virtue of subsection (5) above, community care services have been provided temporarily for any person as a matter of urgency, then, as soon as practicable thereafter, an assessment of his needs shall be made in accordance with the preceding provisions of this section.

[See discussion of this in Chapter 13]

Comments on section 47

This section has not been without its critics: Richard Gordon in an article in the *Times*[26] described the 1990 Act as vaguely and sloppily drafted and as having the effect of transferring responsibility to the courts. He points out the uncertainties in relation to entitlement to an assessment and also to the way in which an assessment should be carried out[27].

Entitlement to assessment

Entitlement is not defined in the section other than in terms of eligibility for service provision.

■ How should need for assessment be brought to the attention of the local authority?

Section 47(1) is very loosely worded. 'Where it appears to a local authority that any person for whom they may provide or arrange for the provision of community care services may be in need of any such service' is by no means clear. It would, however, certainly suggest that, if there is any reasonable doubt about whether a service is needed, then the presumption should be in favour of an assessment being made.

'Appears to a local authority' would include not only information which was gained from their own officers but also information received from a wide variety of unlimited sources such as general practitioners, health professionals, carers, potential clients, concerned persons from the voluntary or private sector or other branches of the public sector such as social security. If any information from any of these sources given to a local authority suggests that a person may be in need, then the duty under section 47 to carry out an assessment arises.

An example would be of a health professional, say an occupational therapist, becoming aware as a neighbour that a person appears to be in need of community services. It is uncertain from the drafting of the section whether there is a duty upon this health professional to convey this information to the local authority and whether this knowledge should therefore be imputed to the local authority.

The only limitation on the duty to assess is to whom it is owed. It is owed to those for whom the local authority may provide or arrange for the provision of community care services. It is thus restricted to those in its catchment area through residence (see below).

■ Could it be argued that if the local authority does not provide specific services then the assessment for those services need not be carried out?

Situation:

The General Practitioner notified the local authority that one of his patients required facilities for a chair lift up the stairs and suggested that an assessment should be carried out. Since that specific local authority did not provide facilities for enabling chair lifts to be installed it decided not to carry out the assessment. Would this refusal be lawful?

The answer is probably that it would be unlawful and a breach of section 47(1)(a). The term 'any person for whom they may provide or arrange for the provision of community care services' covers all those services specified in section 46(3) which defines what is meant by community care services. The fact that the local authority does not supply all the services the client may require cannot be a justification for not carrying out the assessment. After all it could be argued that until the assessment has been carried out it cannot be certain which services the client would require.

Ordinary residence
Richard Gordon points out that many community care services are tied to the legal and somewhat artificial notion of ordinary residence. There may thus be attempts by local authorities to divest themselves of responsibilities to local authorities many miles away. He states that this dilutes still further the obviously immediate connection that there should be between client need and a responsive provision of community care. In addition there is the possibility of disputes between local authorities over liability for assessment and meeting needs.

Guidance on the possibility of making arrangements with other local authorities does, however, stress the need to take into account the desirability of providing services in the locality. Where patients from long-stay accommodation are to be resettled and they do not come originally from the district in which the hospital is located there may be humanitarian reasons why they should be resettled in the local area, even though the authority in which they originally lived will be responsible for purchasing the accommodation.

Where the health authority is brought into the assessment process under section 47(3), its responsibility is determined on the basis of residence[28]. Where the local authority place someone in residential care or nursing home outside the district of his usual residence then, if this placement is temporary, the district of usual residence remains responsible. If the move is permanent, the responsible health authority is that in which the nursing or residential care home is situated. Residency as a criteria is considered in detail in Chapter 28.

Carrying out the assessment

There are no statutory directions stating how the assessment should be carried out. Since the assessment relates directly to the services which should be provided there could be great variations in practice across the country.

Stages of assessment

Whilst directions have not yet been issued on the carrying out of assessments guidance has been given to local authorities for assessment in several publications (see Appendix 3(B)).

In addition the summary of practice guidance included in both the *Managers' Guide* and the *Practitioners' Guide* sets out the stages which should be followed in implementing the care management and assessment process. These stages are shown in Figure 25.16.

Figure 25.16 Care management and assessment process

Stage 1 Information is given to carers and prospective clients on needs for which the agencies accept responsibilities and the range of services currently available.

Stage 2 The level of the assessment required is decided.

Stage 3 A practitioner is allocated to assess the needs of the individual and of any carers.

Stage 4 The resources available from statutory, voluntary, private or community sources that best meet the individual's requirements are considered. The role of the practitioner is to assist the user in making choices from these resources, and to put together an individual care plan.

Stage 5 The implementation of the plan, that is securing the necessary financial or other identified resources.

Stage 6 Monitoring implementation of the care plan.

Stage 7 Review of the care plan with the user, carers and service providers to ensure that services remain relevant to needs and, secondly, to evaluate services as part of the continuing quest for improvement.

Levels of assessment

The care management and assessment *Practitioners' Guide* suggests that Stage One requires an initial identification of the need to determine the level of assessment required in the light of the need identified. For example it sets out six possible levels of assessment:

- **level one**   simple assessment
- **level two**   limited assessment
- **level three**   multiple assessment
- **level four**   specialist assessment either simple or complex
- **level five**   complex assessment
- **level six**   comprehensive assessment.

An example of an outcome from level one is a bus pass or disabled car badge. An example of an outcome from a level six could be family therapy, substitute care or intensive domiciliary support.

The assessment of need is described in the *Practitioners' Guide* as being undertaken

> to understand an individual's needs; to relate them to agency policies and priorities, and to agree the objectives for any intervention.

The practitioner is required by the guidance

> to define, as precisely as possible, the cause of any difficulty.

It recognises that need is unlikely to be perceived and defined in the same way by users, their carers, and any other care agencies involved. It suggests that

> the practitioner must, therefore, aim for a degree of consensus but, so long as they are competent, the users' views should carry the most weight. Where it is impossible to reconcile different perceptions, these differences should be acknowledged and recorded.

The High Court has emphasised[29] that a local authority should not depart without good reason from the policy guidance issued by the Secretary of State.

Who carries out the assessment?

There is an emphasis on a multi-disciplinary approach to the task of assessment with local authorities bringing in relevant professionals where necessary. The white paper on *Caring for people: Community care in the next decade and beyond* suggests:

> **3.25**   All agencies and professions involved with the individual and his or her problems should be brought into the assessment procedure when necessary. These may include social workers, GPs, community nurses, hospital staff such as consultants in geriatric medicine, psychiatry, rehabilitation and other hospital specialties, nurses, physiotherapists, occupational therapists, speech therapists, continence advisers, community psychiatric nurses, staff involved with vision and hearing impairment, housing officers, the Employment Department's Settlement Officers and its Employment Rehabilitation Service, home helps, home care assistants and voluntary workers.

> **3.26**   Assessments should take account of the wishes of the individual and his or her carer, and of the carer's ability to continue to provide care, and where possible should include their active participation. Effort should be made to

offer flexible services which enable individuals and carers to make choices.

Where the client is in hospital then the lead agency for carrying out the assessment will be the health service; where the client is in the community or in residential accommodation then the lead agency for carrying out the assessment will be the local authority.

What if the client refuses to co-operate in the assessment?
It would seem that there is a duty under section 47(1)(a) of the 1990 Act for the assessment to be made even if the client refuses. Clearly, however, this may lead to a less than satisfactory assessment and any later objection by such clients to their assessment would take account of their lack of co-operation. Where the client is incapable of assisting in the assessment, for example as a result of mental disability, the co-operation of relatives, carers or other representatives should be sought. The Law Commission's recommendations on decision making on behalf of the mentally incapacitated adult should, when implemented, fill this vacuum (see Chapter 4).

MENCAP research
In an analysis by a mixture of desk and field research[30], which involved interviews and questionnaires with clients with learning disabilities and officers in six local authority areas, MENCAP came to the conclusion that 'the concept of a needs led community care assessment is yet to be realised'. Some of its main conclusions and recommendations are shown in Figure 25.17.

Figure 25.17 Mencap conclusions

- Local authorities are failing to produce and disseminate accessible information. As a result, most people with learning disabilities do not know what assessment and care management is.
- Service users have to wait too long between assessment, referral and service provision.
- Assessment procedures and subsequent care plans often fail to take a full account of all needs – particularly the long term aspirations of people with learning disabilities and the needs of carers.
- Few people take an active part in their own assessment.
- Many care plans still concentrate on services rather than needs.
- Information collated about each individual is neither fully analysed nor adequately used.
- Monitoring and review procedures are rarely carried out to set timescales and in some cases not at all.

MENCAP points out that its findings are supported by other research and it comes to the conclusion that

The extent to which the needs and aspirations of a person with learning disability are met may be determined by where that person lives.

Future litigation
It is likely that gradually, as interest groups take up test cases, a body of law interpreting these statutory provisions will emerge. (A case brought against Gloucester County Council on the assessment of the needs of the disabled and resources is considered in Chapter 27 on enforcement provisions.) There are likely to be precedents which would clarify.

● who is entitled to be assessed;

● in what circumstances would it be justifiable for an assessment to be refused;

● what procedures should be followed by local authorities in undertaking the assessment (which might include whether or not the client can be represented and whether the local authority is bound to accept medical evidence); and

● what a reasonable time would be within which an assessment should be carried out.

Owners and managers of registered homes complained in the early months of the implementation of the assessment provisions that places were not filled in the homes because of delays in carrying out assessments even though they were aware of potential clients requiring residential or nursing home accommodation.

There is also likely to be a wide variety in the standard of assessment across the country. For example in some areas multi-disciplinary co-operation may be excellent. In others shortages of key disciplines such as occupational therapists or a lack of interest by general practitioners might make effective multi-disciplinary assessment extremely difficult to organise.

An article in *Community Care*[31] by Mike George discusses the possibility of judicial review being used by clients and their pressure groups. He points out that in the early 1980s there were about 500 applications for judicial review per year and in 1992 there were 2439. He suggests that there are likely to be many cases over the assessment of needs and unmet needs.

Should assessment include needs which there are no resources to meet?
Most commentators on the Act are agreed that the fact that the local authority is under pressure in relation to resourcing will

not justify either a failure to carry out an assessment under section 47(1) or a failure to record needs which cannot be met.

Original instructions from the Department (known as 'the Laming letter'[32] from the SSI Chief Inspector Herbert Laming) were interpreted as meaning that social services departments did not have to disclose needs which they did not intend to meet to the clients. This approach would suggest that assessment is made within the context of the available services. However in the article from *Community Care* quoted above Mike George states that Alan Moses QC has given an opinion to eight charities that, in the light of section 47, both the official guidance and the public statement of the Minister of Health at the time, Timothy Yeo, are not supportable in law. It is clear that social service departments are not all following the Laming advice. In a survey carried out by Community Care[33] eight out of ten Directors of Social Services Departments which responded to the survey said that they would not accept this approach and would record unmet need, even though they feared this could lead to legal challenge from clients. Some 80 per cent of respondents feared legal challenge. It should be noted, however, that the respondents might arguably be those more responsible authorities and it may well be that the actual proportion acting strictly in accordance with the Laming advice is higher.

The problem of the gap between the assessed needs and the resources to meet them should not be underestimated. In research carried out by the University of Bath on behalf of Gloucester County Council[34] it was estimated that to meet the needs for community care services would cost in the region of £100 million and the County Council had allocated only £40 million. The result would be more people having to be moved into residential care which, of course, from 1 April 1993 has to be met from the budgets of Social Services Departments.

The Social Services research and development unit at the University of Bath has developed a computerised model which on the one hand provides information about people who have potential needs and on the other allows for the matching of money and resources to meet the needs. The model is flexible in that it can be updated as information becomes available through referral, assessment and the care management process.

Duty to decide on the services to be provided
It does not, however, follow that, because an assessment reveals that a particular service is required, this service must therefore be provided. The implication of section 47(1)(b) being a distinct duty is that local authorities are entitled to determine priorities

within the available resources, and this will inevitably mean that some assessed needs are not met. Provided the local authority can show that the assessment and the consequential determination of priorities has been carried out fairly, openly and reasonably it is probable that an action for breach of statutory duty or for judicial review will not succeed (see Chapter 27).

A Court of Appeal decision in a case brought against Gloucester County Council suggests that there is an absolute duty under section 2 of the 1970 Act to provide services, irrespective of the resources. However, this is contrary to the view of the High Court that such assessment could take into account the overall level of resources available and the CA decision is likely to be reviewed by the House of Lords (see Chapter 27, page 441).

It was repeated in the Parliamentary debates that the local authorities were not obliged to meet all the needs which were assessed and that priorities and available resources would have to be taken into account. Essentially the philosophy behind the provision of community care is that there should be a needs-led approach rather than fitting the individual into the services which are available. In practice, however, the resources which are available will determine which needs can be met and there are dangers that realistic assessments will become resource-led.

Procedure following assessment

The Act does not cover the practical issues of how quickly decisions should be made and whether reasons must be given for a particular assessment or service provision decision. The guidance from the Social Services Inspectorate suggests that the client should be given a copy of the assessment. There is no statutory duty to provide this, but access could be claimed under the provisions of the Access to Personal Files (Social Services) Regulations 1987 (see Chapter 6). In addition it will be possible to use the complaints procedure, which the local authority has a statutory duty to provide, to complain about any delays in carrying out assessments and thereby speed up the process. (For the complaints procedure see Chapter 27.)

Assessment and charges

Social services departments can charge for personal social services under statutory arrangements based on section 22 of the National Assistance Act 1948 (residential and nursing home care) and under the discretionary provisions of section 17 of the Health and Social Services Adjudication and Social Security Adjudications Act 1983 (welfare services).

Community Care in the Next Decade and Beyond: Policy Guidance makes it clear that the provision of services, whether or not the local authority is under a statutory duty to make provision, should not be related to the ability of the user of their families to meet the costs ... The assessment of financial means should, therefore, follow the assessment of need and decisions about service provision.

In the absence of uniformity between local authorities, where they have a discretion over charges extremes exist. One local authority may, for example, charge a fee of £18 for a person to attend a day centre and another less than £5. There is a danger that, even where on the basis of a needs assessment certain services are considered essential, charges might limit the take up.

Conclusions

The publications which preceded the Bill and the Act do not address all these issues. They speak optimistically about the level of service provision and meeting the individual needs of clients. They are, however, aware of resource constraints. Whilst the assessment itself is legally enforceable, the provision of services is not always so. However, this depends on the individual section within each statutory provision, some like section 117 duties under the Mental Health Act are enforceable at the insistence of the individual (see above pages 244 and 389) others are not. It is clear that the lawyers will have a field-day whilst the uncertainties and ambiguities are challenged in the courts.

INSPECTION OF PREMISES USED FOR THE PROVISION OF COMMUNITY CARE SERVICES

A power to inspect is given under section 48 subsection 1 which is set out in Figure 25.18.

Figure 25.18 Section 48 – Inspections and powers

(1) Any person authorised by the Secretary of State may at any reasonable time enter and inspect any premises (other than premises in respect of which any person is registered under the Registered Homes Act 1984) in which community care services are or are proposed to be provided by a local authority, whether directly or under arrangements made with another person.

(2) Any person inspecting any premises under this section may—

(a) make such examination into the state and management of the premises and the facilities and services provided therein as he thinks fit;

(b) inspect any records (in whatever form they are held) relating to the premises, or any person for whom community care services have been or are to be provided there; and

(c) require the owner of, or any person employed in, the premises to furnish him with such information as he may request.

(3) Any [such] person—

(a) Shall be entitled at any reasonable time to have access to, and inspect and check the operation of, any computer and any associated apparatus or material which is or has been in use in connection with the records in question; and

(b) may require [the person in charge of the computer or on whose behalf it has been used] to give him such reasonable assistance as he may require.

(4) Any person inspecting any premises under this section—

(a) may interview any person residing there in private—
  (i) for the purpose of investigating any complaint as to those premises or the community care services provided there, or
  (ii) if he has reason to believe that the community care services being provided there for that person are not satisfactory; and

(b) may examine any such person in private.

(5) [Only a person who is registered as a medical practitioner can exercise the power to inspect medical records or interview a resident in private.]

(6) Any [inspector] shall if so required, produce some duly authenticated document showing his authority to do so.

(7) Any person who intentionally obstructs another in the exercise of that power shall be guilty of an offence . . .

Comment

The purpose of giving these powers to the Secretary of State is to ensure that premises not covered by the Registered Homes Act 1984 but where community services are provided can be inspected. The persons to inspect would be appointed by the Secretary of State and would include Department of Health and Welsh office social service inspectors, nurses and doctors.

A government Whip, Baroness Blatch, stated in the House of Lords[35] that:

> The purpose of the power is to enable the authorised persons to inspect both the services provided and the way the local authority is exercising its community care functions. We would expect such inspections to form part of the investigation of serious complaints and other major irregularities. They may also be used in conjunction with monitoring of local authorities' performance. In any event we do not expect that it will be necessary to make a great deal of use of them. The main inspection and monitoring function in respect of private and voluntary facilities with which local authorities have made arrangements will fall to

the authorities themselves. They do not need special legislative provision for this and will be expected to include in contracts the arrangements for access and inspection. It may happen, especially in small homes, that the residents' doctors may decide to keep case notes on the premises. Medical records held on other premises, such as day centres, may contain details of care or treatment provided elsewhere. Given the general purpose of these provisions, we do not feel that it would be right for such records to be open to inspection, nor do we see any need for them to be.

Inspection units
Inspection Units Directions were issued in 1990 and came into force on 1 April 1991. Under these directions every local authority is required to establish as inspection unit. This inspection unit has an obligation to inspect:

- residential accommodation provided by the local authority under sections 21 and 26 of Part III of the National Assistance Act 1948 and under Schedule 8 to the National Health Service Act 1977, and

- residential accommodation within the area of the local authority which is required to be registered under Part I of the Registered Homes Act 1984, and any records kept pursuant to that Act (see Chapter 29).

In addition every local authority is required to establish an advisory committee to advise on the operation of the inspection unit. Membership of the advisory committee shall be determined by the local authority.

Policy guidance on the community care implementation was issued under the Secretary of State's powers in Section 7(1) of the Local Authority Social Services Act 1970 – *Community Care in the Next Decade and Beyond: Policy Guidance*, (pages 45–57). This required local authorities to carry out such inspections in a consistent and even-handed manner in respect of services in local authority, private and voluntary sectors.

Guidance was also issued in terms of the structure, accountability, staffing, collaboration with Health Authorities, and working practices. The Directions do not preclude the possibility of the use of agency arrangements. (Section 101 of the Local Government Act 1972 permits a local authority to arrange for its statutory functions to be discharged on its behalf by another local authority. However, as the circular LAC(90)13 points out, the making of agency arrangements will not release any local authority from its responsibility to comply with the directions.)

The Social Service Inspectorate of the Department of Health was, in the *Caring for People* policy guidance, given the task of monitoring the progress of inspection units and in particular to

> examine the operational framework of the unit and its role and functions within the SSD; the links between the unit and other agencies; recruitment practices; the consultative arrangements; the working methods and standards applied and the follow up arrangements made.

The inspectorate will also seek to measure the adequacy of the response made by authorities to reports on their own directly provided homes.

The 1993 report

The first report of the Social Services Inspectorate Division was published by the HMSO in 1993. Ten social services departments were chosen by means of a weighted random selection process. The inspection team examined written material, interviewed key SSD staff, service users and service providers and invited written comments from other interested parties. An overview of the Inspection was published in addition to individual reports on each SSD.

Its findings were assessed against the following criteria:

- policy,
- management,
- workload and resources,
- service standards,
- conduct of inspections,
- efficiency and effectiveness,
- inspection reports,
- inspection follow-up, and
- collaboration.

It reached the following conclusions:

- The inspection units had concentrated their energies in setting up a sound structural and professional foundation for future operations which meant that targets for inspections and not always been met.
- They had applied standards with equal force in relation to both local authority and independent sector services.
- However, there was a need for some SSDs to set up procedures to ensure that action be taken to consider and act upon the unit inspector's recommendations as actively in the public sector as in relation to the independent sector.
- Collaboration with other agencies and organisations varied and there was some adverse comment from the private sector.

● Liaison with other parts of the SSDs was not well organised in some instances, particularly with regard to inspection follow up.

The directions issued by the Secretary of State under cover of LAC(90)13 have since been replaced by Directions issued under LAC(94)16 in order to ensure consistency with contemporary policy guidance and they have been extended to apply to community homes and registered children's homes within the meaning of the Children Act 1989. Their essential requirements otherwise remain the same.

Charter principles

Further steps are being taken in line with the Citizen's Charter to ensure independence, openness and lay involvement of the inspectorate in accordance with the principles described below.

Inspection of nursing homes. The charter principles are to be extended to the registration and inspection of nursing homes undertaken by the health authorities.

The role of lay assessors. Lay assessors will complement the work done by professional inspectors. They will have independent status and play a full role in inspections, with their views incorporated in the inspection reports.

Inspection advisory panels. These were originally recommended but left to the local authority to determine. The requirement now is that the number of places given to lay people is at least equal to the number of places given to service providers, including the officers mainly or wholly concerned with the provision of services. It is not intended that these advisory panels should have executive powers and the guidance states that where these advisory committees have been set up as sub-committees under section 4 of the Local Authority Social Services Act 1970 or section 102 of the Local Government Act 1972 they should be reconstituted on less formal lines. They should choose their own chairmen, the appointment should be for a fixed term, and made from among the provider, lay or consumer members of the group. The panel should meet at least twice a year.

Inspection Reports. These should be clear, objective and accurate; avoid jargon and wherever possible contain a succinct summary of findings and recommendations. The inspection advisory panel should be given the opportunity to comment on the unit's annual report before that report is presented to the Social Services Committee.

Follow up of inspection reports. Local authorities should have in place policy guidelines which explain how recommendations made in inspection reports on directly provided care homes will be acted upon. The policy statement should set out:

(a) who will be responsible for following up the reports to ensure that any required action is taken on the recommendations;

(b) the time limits for follow-up action which will be set; and

(c) how the adequacy of the response to the reports will be monitored.

Chief Executive's annual report. This must contain an assessment covering the work of the inspection unit and of the social services department's response to inspection reports on the services which it manages[36].

Local authority and information technology
Supplementary credit approvals for information technology support in the implementation of *Caring for People* has been made available to be used to develop IT systems, including the purchase of software. Close collaboration with health authorities was urged upon local authorities and the circular suggests that, when drawing up their information strategies, they should consult and work closely together. (LAC(93)5)

Transfer of staff – section 49

Section 49 gives to the Secretary of State the power to make regulations with respect to the transfer to employment by a local authority of persons previously employed by a National Health Service body and this is discussed in Chapter 23.

Complaints

Section 50 adds section 7B to the 1970 Act and enables the Secretary of State to require local authorities to establish a complaints procedure. This is discussed in Chapter 27. The existence of a complaints mechanism should enable many grievances in relation to assessments and service provision and priority determination to be aired and settled without recourse to the courts. This was the hope when the provisions were discussed in Parliament (see further in Chapter 27).

Monitoring implementation of community care

The Audit Commission regularly monitors the implementation of community care in England focusing on local authorities as lead agencies and on financial issues. In its latest report – *Balancing the Care Equation: Progress with Community Care* published by the HMSO in March 1996 – it highlights the problems faced in keeping financial commitments within the funds available. It points out the significant variation in the proportion of people assessed, the eligibility criteria local authorities apply and the local arrangements in place to implement changes. The bulletin stresses the key role played by good information.

CONCLUSIONS

A lost opportunity

An opportunity was lost to clarify the legal responsibilities of social services authorities, both those under earlier legislation and those introduced by the NHS and Community Care Act 1990, by drafting consolidating legislation. The jigsaw which has emerged is patchy and unclear, and implementation may depend greatly upon the individual commitment of authorities to the philosophy of community care rather than on the clarity of the law. As will be seen in the Chapter 27 there are numerous difficulties in ensuring the implementation of the statutory duties through the courts of law.

A future review

On 22 September 1995 the Department of Health and the Welsh Office launched a major review[37] of the regulation and inspection of social services. It is intended to lead to a wide and constructive debate and will probably result in significant changes to the current system of regulation and inspection.

CHAPTER 26

The independent sector

One of the key objectives of the white paper *Caring for People* was 'to promote the development of a flourishing independent sector alongside good quality public services'. The statutory mechanism to enable this development to take place for both health authorities and local social services authorities is contained in section 23 and sections 28, 28A and 28B of the National Health Service Act 1977 and in sections 21, 22 and 30 of the National Assistance Act 1948 and subsequent legislation.

STATUTORY POWERS AND DUTIES

The powers of the local authority to employ certain voluntary organisations as their agents for the provision of welfare services for disabled persons under section 30 of the National Assistance Act 1948 was extended by section 42(6) of the National Health Service and Community Care Act 1990 to include the persons shown in Figure 26.1.

Figure 26.1   Extension of section 30 NAA 1948 – powers to appoint agents

[As well as registered voluntary organisations the local authority, for the provision of welfare services for the disabled, may appoint as their agents] any person carrying on, professionally or by way of trade or business, activities which consist of or include the provision of services for any of the persons to whom section 29 above applies, being an organisation or person appearing to the authority to be capable of providing the service to which the arrangements apply.

Similarly Section 45(3) of the Health Services and Public Health Act 1968 under which a local authority may employ certain voluntary organisations as their agents for promoting the welfare of old people was extended as shown in Figure 25.4.

411

We have noted in Chapter 25 the Directions under section 46(2) of the NHS and Community Care Act 1990 relating to the consultation on community plans and the requirement to consult with the representatives of the independent sector providers in the preparation and review of the plans. The guidance noted that two thirds of the providers of long term care for nursing homes and residential care for the elderly are from the independent sector. Independent day care and domiciliary support is also growing. There is every likelihood that this development will continue. The decision by the Court of Appeal in the case brought by Mr Beckwith against Wandsworth London Borough Council[38] (see Chapter 28) will enable total independent sector provision of residential accommodation to take place in satisfaction of the local authority's statutory duties.

THE NATURE OF THE INDEPENDENT SECTOR

The purpose of this chapter is to look at some of the legal issues which arise in the use of the independent sector to support the statutory duties and powers of the public sector.

The independent sector is not of course homogeneous. There are large voluntary/charitable organisations which may receive some public funds, small groups which depend heavily on grants and allocations from the public sector and other charitable groups which have minimal or no public funding. The term also includes the work of private profit making organisations.

Co-operation between these non-statutory organisations and the statutory bodies is central to the philosophy of community care. Various statutes require the statutory bodies to co-operate, consult, plan with and share in the provision of services through the non-statutory sector. Section 46(2) of the 1990 Act has been covered in the previous chapter. Section 117 of the Mental Health Act 1983 requires local authorities and health authorities to co-operate similarly with voluntary organisations in the planning and provision of after-care.

However, the independent sector does not have to comply with statutory duties though there may well be contracts agreed between them and the statutory organisations for the provision of services.

Many charitable organisations play an essential role in the provision of community services and receive only a small proportion of their funds from the government purse. MIND, for example, out of a total income for 1992 of £2 709 618 received £434 728 as a grant from the Department of Health and £81 775 from local authorities, health authorities and the Welsh Office. Almost half of its expenditure came from appeals. In contrast,

Bridges, a small charity for working together with people with learning disabilities, had a total income for 1992 of £13 054 of which £5000 was a Department of Health section 64 grant.

It is impossible in a work of this kind to do justice to the variety and significance of the work which is performed by the independent sector in the provision of community services. The addresses of some of the main organisations can be found in Appendix 7.

The statutory obligation to co-operate with the independent sector has been encouraged by the requirement that 85% of the funding by local authorities for residential/nursing home accommodation must be spent in the independent sector. The legal requirements on the provision of accommodation are considered in Section D of this book.

The liability and rights of volunteers who work in the non-statutory sector are considered in Chapter 21 and those of carers in Chapter 22. Here we touch upon the duty of care owed by the volunteers and the local authority, considered in more detail in Chapter 21, and cover the issues arising out of the contractual relationship of the local authority employing outside agents to fulfil its statutory duties.

THE VOLUNTEER'S DUTY OF CARE

A feature developing over the last few decades is the increase in the number of non-statutory organisations which are providing support to individuals who live in their own homes (rented or privately owned) or with families. This trend is likely to continue as local social services departments are able to contract with such groups to pay for the provision of services. In addition, since local social services are means-tested, as contributions from clients increase, so there is greater incentive for clients to purchase these services from organisations not part of the local authority, whether profit making, charitable or voluntary.

Improvements in both the level of contributions from social security and also the range of clients covered, to those who require invalidity support, disability living allowance and attendance allowance, have also enabled more clients to purchase services. British Red Cross, for example, provides a service for those being discharged home from hospital. It will provide volunteers, all trained members of the British Red Cross, who undertake the following:

● preparing the home
● lighting the fire

- companionship
- help with mobility
- help to prepare meals
- collecting prescriptions
- accompanying on visits
- shopping
- supporting carers
- writing letters.

The legal issues which can arise in the use of such volunteers are considered in Chapter 21 but in summary there is a duty of care upon the independent agent and its volunteers. Even though the assumption of the duty was voluntary in that there is no statutory obligation upon that organisation and even no payment, once the duty is assumed, then all reasonable care has to be used in fulfilling it and it cannot be abandoned without appropriate arrangements being made.

In contrast Crossroads employs staff to undertake such tasks and there is, therefore, also a contractual duty placed upon the care assistant which can be enforced by the employer.

THE LOCAL AUTHORITY'S DUTY OF CARE

One concern of staff who work with the statutory authorities is that, if they use as agents for the fulfilment of their statutory responsibilities persons and organisations from the independent sector and those persons/organisations let the client down and do not fulfil those responsibilities, where does the statutory authority stand? Could they be liable for the defaults of the independent person/organisation?

Situation

An assessment may be made that an elderly person living on her own requires daily visits to assist her in getting up and making drinks and meals, and putting her to bed at night. There is a charitable organisation comprising a group of volunteers who undertake to visit and care for the elderly person. Arrangements are then made with that organisation. A few weeks later, the client is found dead in her home and it is then discovered that she had never been visited and had probably been dead for some time. Where does liability, if any, lie?

It can be seen from Figures 26.1 and 25.4 that in making arrangements with agents the local authority has a duty to ensure that the person or organisation is 'capable' of either providing the service for the disabled (26.1) or promoting the welfare of old people (25.4). This means that the local authority has a responsibility to check that the persons or organisations are reasonably able to provide the required service. This would involve the social services in a vetting procedure, monitoring and review, the legal implications of which are considered in detail in Chapter 21.

In addition, where funds are transferred between local authority and the agent for the purpose of providing the service, then there would be a contract for services (see glossary), which, if the agent is not a health service body as defined in section 4(2) of the 1990 Act (see Chapter 23), would be enforceable in a court of law. Section D of this book covering accommodation looks at the rights of the local authority as both inspector and purchaser of residential care and purchaser of nursing home accommodation. Here attention will be given to the work of the independent sector in providing domiciliary support.

CONTRACTING OUT DOMICILIARY CARE ASSISTANCE

One example of an organisation providing domiciliary support is DayBreak (Wales) which was launched by Bishop John Poole-Hughes in 1985 and operates as a not-for-profit organisation providing home care and support for people in their own homes. Amongst the range of services it provides are home care, home convalescence, social care and carer support. These can include:

- personal care
- washing and dressing
- overnight care
- home care
- meal preparation
- shopping
- companionship
- social outings
- respite and holiday relief for carers.

Unlike the British Red Cross it does not use volunteers but directs to the clients care assistants who are usually paid directly by the clients.

The service can be provided both for the short or long term and can be provided for up to 24 hours a day. It is personally tailored to meet each client's individual requirements. It operates to the standards required by the United Kingdom Homecare Association (UKHCA) set out in their Code of Practice.

The following are some of the legal issues which arise and which will be discussed below:

- What is the nature of the relationship between care agency, care assistant and client?

- Who is responsible if the care assistant sent by the agency causes harm to the client? What is the liability of the agency if the care assistant assaults the client or commits a criminal offence whilst in the client's house?

- Who is responsible if the care assistant is injured in the client's home?

- What if the client fails to reimburse the care assistant?

- What is the role of the UKHCA in quality assurance and in handling complaints?

- What is the nature of the relationship between the social services department and the agency?

Relationship between care agency, care assistant and client

The care agency does not necessarily act as the employer of the care assistants. Often it merely acts as an introduction network and the contractual relationship exists between the client and the care assistant who is introduced to the client by the agency. The agency might claim a fee from the client for this service. This fee would go towards the administrative costs and perhaps the training of the care assistants. However, it would be the client who employs the care assistant and who would be responsible, if appropriate for paying national insurance contributions. Alternatively, the care assistant could be self-employed and hire out her services, on a fee for service basis, being responsible for the payment of her own national insurance contributions and income tax as a self-employed person.

Where the agency employs the care assistant and hires her out to the clients, it is a question of the interpretation of the contracts between the parties (care assistant/agency and client/agency) as to the nature of the relationship and the liability of the agency for any negligence of or harm caused by the care assistant.

The nature of this relationship is crucial to the financial position of the agency since, if the agency is seen as an employer of care assistants, then VAT is payable on the whole cost to the client and also the agency becomes responsible for national insurance employer's contributions and has to administer the employee's tax. This can add high overheads to the cost of the agency and therefore the charges which they would have to make to the clients. If, on the other hand, the agency is not seen as an employer, then VAT is only payable on the agency fees and tax and national insurance are the responsibility of the care assistant or, possibly, the client.

An already complex situation has become more so since April 1993 and the introduction of the community care provisions. Some local authorities are now contracting with the agencies for the provision of care assistants. The contractual and financial situation is not always clear: the local authority might pay the agency for its assistance (claiming moneys from the clients on a means-tested basis) and the agency will then pass the money to the care assistants. Alternatively the care assistant might be reimbursed by the client to the extent of her means-tested contribution and receive any shortfall in hourly payment from the local authority. Where the care assistant is self-employed the main contract is still between the care assistant and the client. However, if the client has a nil contribution the contract would probably exist between the care assistant and the local authority or the care assistant and the agency. It might appear that such minutiae are insignificant and of concern only to the lawyer but this is not the case as the following example illustrates.

Situation

A care assistant works under a home care agency who arranges work placements for her. She is then usually paid directly by the client for her hours of work and the client also pays a small fee to the agency. The local authority agree with the agency that funds will be made available to the agency for home care services to supplement the contributions paid directly by the client to the care assistant calculated by means-testing. In this way, more clients will be able to have the benefit of home services and the local authority will be making use of the private sector (in accordance with government policy) rather than only using direct labour services. The contract between the agency and the local authority sets out the work which the care assistants are to undertake. This contract does not include the care assistant taking the client outside the home.

The care assistant, who receives from the client her means-tested contribution and receives the shortfall of her hourly rate from the agency, is asked by the client to take her shopping since, although she is very unstable on her feet, she was anxious to get out of the house. The care assistant is aware of the list of duties contained in the agreement between local authority and her agency and knows that this particular request is not on the list. However, since the client specifically requested this and she sympathised with her wishes, she agreed. Unfortunately as they were walking through the shopping arcade the client stumbled. In an effort to keep her upright the care assistant ricked her back and the client fell to the ground fracturing her pelvis. Can either the client or the care assistant claim compensation and from whom?

The first question which would have to be resolved is whether either the local authority or the agency are the employer of the care assistant. If the answer is 'yes', then the fact that the care assistant is doing a non-agreed task will not necessarily take her actions outside 'the course of employment' and therefore the employer could be liable for the care assistant's negligence in causing harm to the client. Clearly there will be a large element of contributory negligence if the client should have realised that it was unsafe for her to go walking outside the home.

Can the care assistant obtain compensation? The care assistant would only be able to claim compensation for her own injuries if she can show that she is an employee and that there is some negligence on the part of her employer. For example if she has not had appropriate training. To determine whether or not there is liability by the employer, would require an examination of the agreements between the various parties and in particular the manner of paying the shortfall in the hourly rate to the care assistant.

If it is established that neither the social services nor the agency is the employer of the care assistant, then the only way the client could obtain compensation would be to sue the care assistant personally and there would be little point if the care assistant was not insured or did not have any assets.

It is essential, as the number of agreements between agencies and local authorities for the provision of home care services grows, for the contractual relationships to be agreed between all parties including the client and the care assistant and for the implications of such arrangements to be made clear.

What if the care assistant injures the client?

Situation

Relatives of an elderly person living alone at home arrange with an agency for a care assistant to be sent to the home. The care assistant in making a lunch scalds the client who is severely injured. The relatives of the client wish to obtain compensation for her pain and suffering. Is the agency, the care assistant or both liable?

If the agency is the employer of the care assistant then it would be liable for the negligence of the care assistant under the concept of vicarious liability discussed in Chapter 7. If it can be shown that a duty of care was owed and the care assistant in the course of her employment was in breach of that duty and caused harm to the client, then the agency could be liable.

If the agency had not held itself out as the employer of the care assistant it would be more difficult to establish the principle of vicarious liability. However, the relatives may be able to show that the agency owed a duty to take reasonable care in ensuring that the care assistants whom it recommended were competent. In this case it would have to be shown that the agency failed to take basic steps to assure itself of the competence of the care assistant and that had they taken those steps it would have discovered that that care assistant should not have been recommended. Whilst such agencies have the duty and power to check on the criminal convictions of those who are to be employed with children they do not have the power to check on any record for those being employed with other clients, except in relation to registered homes.

Many agencies, however, have public liability insurance cover which would include cover for negligent acts of the care assistants they recommend which lead to personal injury of the client or damage and loss of property. In this case the care assistant may be asked to contribute to the cost of this insurance.

What if the care assistant is injured?

If the agency is not the employer of the care assistant then it would probably have no liability for harm caused to her whilst working for a client. What, however, if the agency should have known that it was sending the care assistant into possible danger?

Situation

A request was made to a care agency by a former patient from a psychiatric hospital for assistance. A care assistant was sent along who agreed terms of service with the client. Neither the agency nor the client mentioned to the care assistant that there was a history of psychiatric disorder. Some weeks later the client became verbally abusive to the care assistant, who reciprocated and, eventually, the care assistant was injured by the client. It was then discovered that the care assistant had no knowledge of the client's mental condition nor any understanding or training in how to deal with such situations. Can the care assistant obtain compensation for the injuries and from whom?

If the care agency were the employer, it would be clear (see Chapter 9) that the agency would have a duty to its employees to ensure that they were reasonably safe in the work which they were set. This would include training, where appropriate, in dealing with mentally disordered persons. If the employer had failed to take reasonable steps in this respect then it would be directly liable for the harm to the care assistant.

Where there is no such employment relationship between the agency and the care assistant it would then be a matter of the construction of each agreement between care assistant and agency over the nature of the duty owed by the latter to the former in relation to health and safety. Certainly, where the agency offers the care assistant training, then it could be implied that this training would be sufficient to ensure that the care assistant is reasonably safe at work.

Risk assessment

The health and safety laws are considered in detail in Chapters 9 and 10.

Where there is an agency which arranges for self-employed care assistants to contract with clients it is essential that the responsibility of carrying out of a health and safety at work risk assessment is clarified. It could be argued that this should be the responsibility of the agency. Where the local authority arranges an agreement with the agency for the supply of domiciliary services, then again it is necessary to ensure that this agreement makes it clear whether it is the agency the local authority or the care assistant who undertakes the risk assessment as required under health and safety legislation.

What if the client fails to pay the care assistant?

Where the client is the employer of the care assistant or has hired the care assistant on a self-employed basis, then the client would have the duty of paying the care assistant direct, and that debt is enforceable through the courts as in any other case of breach of contract. The care assistant would need to establish the existence of the agreement and the hours she had worked and could then take the case to the small claims court or the county court. Difficulties can arise where the relatives of the client have made arrangements for the care assistant to be employed and have expressed a wish that the client was not made aware of this arrangement. In such circumstances it is essential that the care assistant obtains the agreement with the relatives in writing.

Where the agency employs the care assistant it would, of course, be liable to pay the care assistant whether or not it obtains the fees from the clients. In this situation the care assistant would have all the benefits of any employee under the employment protection legislation, subject to the hours of service per week and the length of service.

Where the local authority is subsidising the services from public funds there may be a variety of means of payment as discussed above. Where the client pays the means-tested contribution direct to the care assistant, there may be different sources which the care assistant would have to pursue to obtain payment.

There appears to be no uniform system of means-testing or charges across the local authorities. At present clients in certain areas may obtain specific services free, whereas other areas means-test for these same services. Nor is the calculation of means-testing the same across the country.

Quality assurance and the UKHCA

By setting out minimum standards of service the United Kingdom Homecare Association aims to identify and promote the highest standards of home care. The Code of Practice emphasises the rights of the client, the operation of the service, the responsibilities of care workers and the legal and financial responsibilities of its member organisations.

However, since care assistants are not always the employees of organisations which are members of UKHCA, it is not easy for the association to enforce recognition and implementation of the Code of Practice on all assistants. Nor is there any law to prevent individuals setting themselves up as care assistants and offering their services to clients without working with an umbrella organisation which is a member of the UKHCA. Such individuals can undercut the charges and fees which organisations attached to the UKHCA charge. Sometimes these individuals might have been recommended to clients by a care agency but decide, when their reputation is known, to work outside the remit of the agency. Should this occur, there is little the agency can do given the fact that the care assistant is not an employee. Even if there were a restraint of trade covenant (see glossary) in place, it might not be worthwhile or financially realistic to enforce it.

Ultimately the way towards higher standards is in the professional training and development of those providing the care. This could be coupled with a registration system for home care assistants which would give the clients greater protection and ensure that high standards were set and monitored. However, this is likely to lead to requests for higher levels of remuneration for care assistants which clients are unable to afford and social services with limited budgets are unwilling and/or unable to fund.

Handling complaints

Clients can complain to the care assistant with whom they have a contract for services or employment. However, this is not likely to lead to effective action other than the care assistant refusing to work for that client. The client could complain to the agency which referred the care assistant and that agency could strike that individual off its books, but there is nothing to prevent that individual setting up on her own account and working without any agency support. The UKHCA has a complaints procedure whereby any complaint against one of its member organisations will be investigated and considered by the Executive Committee.

Complaints could also be made to the Social Services Department. This might be effective where there is a contract between an agency administering home care services and the local authority. However, in the absence of such a contract, there is little that the local authority can do. Even where the agency responds to the criticism and removes the care assistant who is at fault from its books, there are no further sanctions which are available and it would be up to the complainant to seek whatever legal action is available and appropriate.

What is the nature of the relationship between the social services department and the agency?

There should be ideally close co-operation to ensure that the potential clients are informed of the existence of the agency and to ensure that they are able to obtain home care services. In some areas social services are able to contribute to the overheads of the agency in advance to enable them to assist in the assessment of the clients and the local authority employ care managers who supervise the work of the care assistants. There is potential with the implementation of the community care provisions of the 1990 Act for much greater liaison and co-operation between social services departments and home care organisations.

ISSUES FOR THE FUTURE

Comparative costs of home care/residential care

It is clear that, if a client requires more than four hours of assistance per day, then it is cheaper for that person to be transferred to residential accommodation than to remain in their own home. This is contrary to the basic philosophy of the care in the community principles and the threshold at which residential care is necessary should be reviewed.

Financial support for agencies

The overheads of home care organisations and agencies including selection of care assistants, training, and supervision of their work should be recognised as requiring support from public funds. Otherwise there will be an incentive for individuals to undercut such organisations and clients will not be able to rely upon a high quality of service.

Registration

The possibility of introducing a system of registration for individual home care assistants has been floated and the idea could be developed and implemented. There is a registration system for child minders and, even taking into account the greater complexities of home care services for a wider range of clientèle, it should be possible to develop such a system to protect the individual client.

An alternative suggestion is the introduction of registration of each home care agency. This was the proposal in the Bill introduced into Parliament in April 1993 by David Hinchcliffe MP. Only one MP voted against it but it failed to complete all its stages. The Bill contained proposals to require all agencies in the private, voluntary and public sector to be registered and inspected by local authority registration and inspection units. At present it is possible for anyone to set up a home care agency with no form of regulation to protect vulnerable people who live in their own homes. The junior health minister (Mr Tim Yeo) stated that self-regulation was the best way of developing the private domiciliary sector. The MP who voted against the Bill did so on the basis that registering care agencies would create an unnecessary bureaucracy and would be counter-productive. It would not lead to better care or value for money, but would add hurdles and handicaps to the system. These arguments are similar to the reasons behind the present consultation paper on the deregulation of the registered homes (see Chapter 31).

In a debate in the House of Lords on January 17 1995 Baroness Cumberlege for the Government claimed that regulation would hinder the development of domiciliary care agencies. In a letter to the *Times* 22 January 1995 the president of the United Kingdom Homecare Association claimed that the opposite was the case and set out the arguments in favour of a properly thought out national scheme to set minimum acceptable standards and which all local authorities would recognise (so that any agency would only have to go through the registration process once), which would be less administratively cumbersome and less expensive.

Registration of the agencies would not, of course, have any effect on the quality and training of individual home care assistants who do not work through an agency.

A watchdog/protection agency

Such a body to ensure the protection of persons relying on home care assistants is required to prevent the exploitation of this vulnerable group of clients.

Local authorities are able to monitor the work of the agencies with whom they place contracts, but many agencies do not receive funding from local authorities and are, therefore, outside their control.

CHAPTER 27

Enforcement of statutory duties

This is one of the most complex areas of law in relation to health and social services and the situation has been further complicated by the additional powers given to the Secretary of State under the National Health Service and Community Care Act 1990.

This chapter will attempt to draw together some of the ways in which powers and duties set up under the different statutes, regulations, directions, and guidance can be enforced.

PUBLIC LAW/PRIVATE LAW

First the distinction should be noted between public and private law. Certain statutes and parts of the common law create rights and duties which are enforceable through the public laws, other laws create rights and duties of individuals or bodies which are actionable through private law remedies. Public law would include such areas as criminal law, laws relating to welfare and health, and revenue law. Private law comprises the law of contract, the law of tort (see glossary) and the law relating to property, trusts and wills.

Different remedies and powers of enforcement exist in public law compared with private law, but there are overlaps which will be pointed out. It was declared in 1982[39] that where it is sought to protect a right conferred by public law, as opposed to private law, then the appropriate relief should be claimed in an application for judicial review rather than in an ordinary action[40].

Before considering these remedies it would perhaps be useful to identify the different forms of law and guidance which relate to the NHS and local authorities.

Statutes

Acts of Parliament can impose powers or duties. These would take precedence over any other form of law, even over the decisions made by judges in a court of law. Following our admission into the European Community, European laws take precedence over the laws of this country since the effect of section 2(1) of the European Communities Act 1972 is that whenever there is a conflict between the European Community law and domestic law the former is directly applicable.

The interpretation of statutes has become more of an art than a science, though the courts do have rules for interpretation when ambiguities, uncertainties and inconsistencies are present.

A commencement date may be contained within the Act itself or the Act, or sections of the Act, can be brought into force on separate dates by statutory instrument (see below). For example in the Disabled Persons (Services, Consultation and Representation) Act 1986 sections were brought in at different dates and some are still not in force.

Regulations

These are made as a result of powers given in an Act of Parliament which enable a Minister of the Crown to enact regulations in the form of statutory instruments. They are known as delegated legislation. They must be placed before both Houses of Parliament before being issued: some need to be confirmed by simple resolution of both Houses of Parliament; others become law simply by being laid before Parliament for a specific time. The contents of the Statutory Instrument must not go outside the scope given in the enabling Act of Parliament otherwise they can be challenged in the courts on the basis of being *ultra vires* (see glossary).

Other delegated legislation

Other examples of delegated legislation include by-laws made by local authorities under enabling statutes such as the Local Government Act 1972 or Public Health Act 1936.

Directions

A feature of recent legislation is the empowerment of a Minister to make directions requiring other bodies to carry out specific duties. Section 50 of the NHS and Community Care Act 1990 inserts new sections into section 7 of the Local Authority Social Services Act 1970. Section 7A enables the Secretary of State to issue directions and is set out in Figure 27.1.

Figure 27.1 Local Authority Social Services Act 1970 – Section 7A

Without prejudice [see glossary] to section 7 of this Act [local authorities to exercise social services functions under the general guidance of the Secretary of State], every local authority shall exercise their social services functions in accordance with such directions as may be given to them under this section by the Secretary of State.

(2) Directions under this section—

(a) shall be given in writing; and
(b) may be given to a particular authority, or to authorities of a particular class, or to authorities generally.

The operation of section 50 of the 1990 Act in introducing a new section 7E of the Local Authorities Social Services Act 1970 (enabling the Secretary of State to provide grants to local authorities to meet expenses incurred in connection with the provision of services for persons suffering from mental illness) was considered in the case of *R. v Secretary of State for Health, ex parte Alcohol Recovery Project*[41] which is discussed below.

In the Parliamentary debates preceding the enactment of the 1990 Act it was not thought that the power to issue directions would be used regularly but many directions have already been issued including:

● Complaints Procedure Directions 1990

● Community Care Plans Direction 1991

● Inspection Units Directions 1990

● Payment to Voluntary Organisations (Alcohol or Drug Misusers) Directions 1990

● Employment of Professions under the Professions Supplementary to Medicine Act 1960 Directions 1991

● Secretary of State's Directions under paragraph 2 of Schedule 8 to National Health Service Act 1977 Directions 1991

● Secretary of State's Directions under section 21(1) of the National Assistance Act 1948 Directions 1991.

Some of these are discussed in the relevant chapters.

Like statutory instruments the directions can be challenged if they are outside the enabling powers of the Act of Parliament authorising their making. They must be distinguished from circulars which are discussed below.

General directions can be given to all authorities (within the scope of the enabling legislation) but specific directions can also be given to individual authorities if they are failing to follow the ministerial guidance. Powers to make general directions are given by section 21 and 29 of the National Assistance Act 1948 and under section 45 of the Health Services and Public Health Act 1968, see Figure 27.2.

Figure 27.2 Health Services and Public Health Act 1968 – section 45 (summarised)

(1) A local authority *may*, with the approval of the Minister of Health and *to such extent as he may direct, shall*, make arrangements for promoting the welfare of old people.
[author's emphasis]

Note the distinction that the local authority has the overall discretion to make arrangements for the welfare of old people with the Minister's approval but when he makes directions the duty becomes obligatory.

Guidance

Section 7 of the Local Authority Social Services Act 1970 requires the authority exercising social services functions to act under the general guidance of the Secretary of State. Unlike the issue of Directions, there are no stipulations under this Act as to the form in which the guidance should be given.

One of the significant features of the community care provisions under the 1990 Act has been the extent to which circulars, publications and other guidance material has been made available by various government departments to those organisations working in the field. Unless the circular contains directions or contains the wording of the statute or statutory instrument it does not in itself have the force of law, but it is expected that it would be followed.

One difficulty in interpreting the weight to be given to guidance material is that some preceded the legislation and may have been overtaken by the detailed enactments subsequently passed. In addition, as the *Beckwith* case shows[42], the guidance may not be correct.

The extract of LAC(93)10 is an example of the guidance material and can be found in Appendix 1. Other material has been quoted and referred to throughout this book.

The *Code of Practice on the Mental Health Act 1983* published by the Department of Health is an example of guidance material which, whilst it does not have the force of law, would be used in any litigation as the basis of good practice which should usually be followed.

Guidance material must be taken into consideration in making decisions and so on, but directions must be followed to the letter. Both, however, could be subject to judicial review by the courts.

ENFORCEMENT PROVISIONS

The activities of local authorities can be challenged in many ways but the rights of an individual to take the local authority to court for failure to fulfil its statutory duties are limited.

Remedies (listed in Figure 27.3) which may be available include the following private law remedies:

- an action for damages for breach of statutory duty;
- an action for breach of the duty of care owed in the law of negligence;
- an action for an injunction to stop a public body carrying out a particular activity;
- an order for specific performance (for example of a contract); and/or
- an action for a declaration.

Decisions on public law matters can be challenged by way of a judicial review. This can result in orders known as prerogative orders being granted. These are available against ministers, public bodies and courts and are considered below. They include actions for certiorari, prohibition and mandamus (see glossary and below).

Reliance upon the Secretary of State's powers to compel compliance with statutory duties through default powers, setting up an inquiry or using any powers to issue directions given to him in the statute may be more important than individual rights of legal action. This is considered below.

Figure 27.3 Enforcement measures

- Action for breach of statutory duty
- Claim of negligence
- Injunction
- Order for specific performance
- Declaration

- Judicial review: orders of certiorari, prohibition and mandamus
- Use of default powers
- An Inquiry
- Issue of Directions
- Representations and complaints machinery
- Ombudsmen: Health Service Commissioner/Local Authority Commissioner

ACTION FOR BREACH OF STATUTORY DUTY

There exists in the law of tort (a group of civil wrongs which an individual can use as the basis of a court case – see glossary) an action known as an action for damages for breach of statutory duty. Not all statutes would be regarded as conferring this right of action and much depends upon how the court interprets the duties set by the statute. Where the statute itself provides other remedies of enforcement, such as default powers given to the Secretary of State (see below), the court might decide that this specific remedy removes the right to sue for breach of a statutory duty.

In addition the plaintiff (that is the person bringing the action) must establish:

- that the statutory duty is placed on the defendant;
- that this duty is owed to the plaintiff as an ascertainable member of a distinct group of people rather than to the public in general;
- that the interest which he wishes to protect is within the scope of the statute;
- that the statute protects his interests by way of an action in tort.

Cases on health service provision

Actions for breach of statutory duty have not succeeded against the Secretary of State in the enforcement of his duty to provide a National Health Service.

Case: *R* v. *Secretary of State for Social Services and others, ex parte Hincks*[43]

In this case orthopaedic patients who had waited for treatment longer that was medically advisable brought an action against the Secretary of State, the regional health authority and the area health authority seeking a declaration that the defendants were in breach of statutory duty under the 1977 National Health Service Act.

It was held that the court could only interfere with the actions of the Secretary of State if the Secretary of State acted so as to frustrate the policy of the Act or as no reasonable Minster could have acted. No such breach was found on the facts before it. The court could not grant mandamus, an order requiring performance of a public legal duty (see glossary), or a declaration against the area or regional health authorities since specific remedies against them were available by section 85 and Part V of the National Health Service Act 1977 (see below). The application was therefore dismissed.

Case: *Re Walker's application*[44]

In a more recent case the court applied the same reasoning. It therefore refused an application by a mother of a child who required a heart operation. A date had been fixed for the operation but it had to be postponed. The Court of Appeal held that it was not for the court to substitute its own judgment for that of those responsible for the allocation of resources. It would only interfere if there had been a failure to allocate funds in a way which was unreasonable or where there had been breaches of public duties.

Case: *Wyatt v. London Borough of Hillingdon*[45]

An example of an unsuccessful attempt to obtain damages for breach of statutory duty can be seen in the Wyatt case. The plaintiff suffered from disseminated sclerosis and was registered with the local authority as a disabled person under the Chronically Sick and Disabled Persons Act 1970. By writ of 15 September 1977 the plaintiff and her husband claimed damages against the local authority for negligence and/or breach of statutory duty under section 2 of the Act of 1970 in that they failed to meet the plaintiff's need for adequate home help or to provide practical assistance to her in her home. Specifically it was alleged that the local authority had failed to provide a particular sort of invalid bed at a cost of more than £200. (Note that this was before 1978. The equivalent price in 1995 would be over £600.) The action was struck out by the Master (see glossary) as disclosing no cause of action and his decision was confirmed by the High Court judge. The Court of Appeal confirmed the decision of the High Court and dismissed the plaintiff's appeal.

The Court held that the local authority's duty to the plaintiff arose solely under the 1970 Act read together with section 29 of the National Assistance Act 1948 and that, since the remedy for breach of statute was provided by the Minister's default powers under section 36 of the National Assistance Act 1948, her statement of claim had been rightly struck out as disclosing no cause of action. The remedy given by section 36 of the 1948 Act was appropriate and an action for damages was inappropriate for a claim for breach of a statute providing for the welfare of the sick and disabled.

Lord Justice Geoffrey Lane stated:

It seems to me that a statute such as this which is dealing with the distribution of benefits – or, to put it perhaps more accurately, comforts to the sick and disabled – does not in its very nature give rise to an action by the disappointed sick person. It seems to me quite extraordinary that if the local authority, as is alleged here, provided, for example, two hours less home help than the sick person considered herself entitled to that that can amount to a breach of statutory duty which will permit the sick person to claim a sum of monetary damages by way of breach of statutory duty. It seems to me that eminently that is the sort of situation where precisely the remedy provided by section 36 of the Act is appropriate and an action in damages is not appropriate.

Later he stated:

With regard to the further suggestion that in some way an action in negligence can be established against a local authority quite apart from the breach of statutory duty, I confess that does not impress me. It seems to me that in this case the duty, such as it is, arises if at all from the statute and from the statute only. It is not the sort of situation where the home help has acted negligently – if, for example, she had dropped the plaintiff and injured her, or that the bed provided by the local authority has proved to be a defective bed which has collapsed and injured the plaintiff. It seems to me that this is a case where the duty starts and ends with the statute.

The Wyatt case was distinguished (see glossary) in the case of R v. *Department of Health and Social Security and others, ex parte Bruce*[46] which is discussed below page 440).

House of Lords guidance

In a recent House of Lords decision guidance has been given on when an action for breach of statutory duty is and is not appropriate[48]. The rulings relate to a number of different actions brought against several Councils in relation to their duties in respect of child care and the education of children. The basic principles set down are as follows:

1. A breach of statutory duty did not, by itself, give rise to any private law cause of action, but such a cause would arise if it could be shown, as a matter of construction of the statute, that the statutory duty was imposed for the protection of a limited class of the public and that Parliament intended to confer on members of that class a private right of action for breach of duty.

2. If the statute provides some other means of enforcing the duty, that would normally indicate that the statutory right was intended to be enforceable by those means and not by private right of action.

3. In order to found a cause of action flowing from the careless exercise of statutory powers or duties, the plaintiff had to show that the circumstances were such as to raise a duty of care at common law (see below). The mere assertion of the careless exercise of a statutory power or duty was not sufficient. A broad distinction had to be drawn between

(a) cases in which it was alleged that the authority owed a duty of care in the manner in which it exercised a statutory discretion and

(b) cases in which a duty of care was alleged to arise from the manner in which the statutory duty had been implemented in practice.

4. Where Parliament had conferred a statutory discreation on a public authority, it was for the authority, not for the courts, to exercise the discretion. Nothing which the authority did within the ambit of the discretion could be actionable at common law. (Note that judicial review (see below) only succeeds when the local authority's action is well outside the normal ambit of the discretion allowed to it.)

5. Where the decision complained of fell outside the statutory discretion, it could give rise to common law liability but, where the factors relevant to the exercise of the discretion included matters of policy, the court could not adjudicate on such policy matters and therefore could not reach the conclusion that the decision was outside the ambit of the statutory discretion. *Therefore, a common law duty of care in relation to the taking of decisions involving policy matters could not exist.* (author's emphasis)

6. It was not just and reasonable to superimpose a common law duty of care on the local authority in relation to the performance of its statutory duties to protect children. That would cut across the whole statutory system, which was an inter-disciplinary system, set up for the protection of children at risk.

The House of Lords has thus shown its unwillingness to extend further the concept of the duty of care at common law by confirming that negligence could not arise from the exercise or not of a statutory duty where there was a discretion involving policy considerations, nor where the acts were within the ambit of the local authority's discretion.

It does not follow, however, that the door is closed to civil action in relation to the practical implementation of the statutory duties – a case could still be brought on the basis of the authority's vicarious liability for the negligence of its employees whilst acting in the course of their employment.

CLAIM OF NEGLIGENCE

Prerequisites of a claim

An action in negligence for breach of the duty of care at common law can be brought against an authority in respect of its statutory duties if it can be shown that:

- a duty of care was owed to the person bringing the action (the plaintiff) and
- the authority was in breach of this duty of care and
- harm has occurred which
- was a reasonably foreseeable result of the breach of duty.

Vicarious liability

Where one of the employees of the authority has been in breach of the duty of care thereby causing harm the employing authority can be joined in the action as if it were itself responsible.

This is known as the vicarious liability of the employer and is discussed in Chapter 7. As can be seen in the statements of the courts in the Wyatt case (see above) and from the House of Lords guidance, the failure to provide a service will not usually be actionable in negligence if there are other provisions for enforcement contained in the Act. However, a negligence claim may be possible, where, as a result of performing the body's statutory duty, an employee of the statutory body has, in breach of her duty of care (see Chapter 7), caused harm to the plaintiff.

The effect of assessment under the 1990 Act

Under the provision of section 47(1) of the NHS and Community Care Act 1990 it might be that, if an assessment has been made and it is decided that a specific service should be provided for a client and then the provider of that service fails to make the service available and as a result of that failure the client suffers harm, there could then be an action for either breach of statutory duty or breach of the duty owed at common law to the client.

A case on this point has yet to be decided, but one of the first is an action being brought by Christopher Clunis, a chronic schizophrenic who was convicted of manslaughter in June 1993. It is reported[50] that writs have been issued against North Thames and South Thames Regional Health Authorities claiming a lack of supervision and care in discharging him into the community with the result that he killed Jonathan Zito. The official inquiry chaired by Jean Richie QC[51] criticised doctors, social workers and police. The case, if it is eventually heard, will set an important precedent in relation to the availability of an action for negligence in such circumstances. It will of course be decided in the light of the House of Lords ruling set out above.

INJUNCTION

This action is available against a public authority if it is alleged that it is acting outside its powers (*ultra vires* – see glossary) or if it is acting contrary to natural justice (see below).

The injunction is a court order obliging the defendant either to do some specific act or, more usually, to refrain from doing it (see the case of the Broadmoor patient, page 50). It is most commonly sought to prevent the destruction of property or the removal of assets but it could be used in conjunction with an action for breach of statutory duty to restrain the authority from acting contrary to that duty or to oblige it to fulfil it.

SPECIFIC PERFORMANCE

This is a particular type of injunction which requires the defendant to carry out a specific duty but only lies if there is a contractual obligation on the part of the defendant to perform that duty. It might be possible for this remedy to be used where, for example, a contract is agreed between a local authority and a private residential home for the sale of land and the local authority fails to convey the property. However, if the payment of damages is a realistic alternative remedy specific performance will not be ordered.

DECLARATION

This is a useful private law remedy to challenge the actions of a public authority without at the same time requesting any other relief. It has been used in a variety of situations such as:

- challenging or confirming the validity of an administrative or judicial decision;
- challenging the validity of delegated legislation and the legality of the exercise of delegated legislative powers;
- clarifying the rights of public employees; or
- securing the recognition of a right, which is being denied, to engage in a particular occupation or activity.

Nowadays, if a private citizen wishes to obtain a declaration against a public body, the preferred route is to make an application for judicial review under Order 53 of the Rules of the Supreme Court. This is discussed below.

JUDICIAL REVIEW AND THE PREROGATIVE ORDERS

There have existed since medieval times orders, originally known as prerogative writs, which enabled the king to bring an action against his officials to ensure that they exercised their functions properly and did not abuse their powers. In 1938 these became known as the 'prerogative orders' and can be brought against both public authorities and private citizens.

An application for judicial review can result in one of the three prerogative orders being awarded (certiorari, prohibition, or mandamus) as well as the non-prerogative orders such as a declaration, injunction or damages.

Judicial review

This is an application to the court to consider the validity of a decision made by an administrative or judicial body. Richard Gordon has suggested that 'the principle means of challenge [to decisions under the community care legislation] will be by judicial review'[52].

The procedures relating to the application for judicial review are set out in Order 53 of the Rules of the Supreme Court. Order 53, rule 1(2) is set out in Figure 27.4.

Figure 27.4 Order 53, rule 1(2)

... the Court may grant the declaration or injunction claimed if it considers that, having regard to —

(a) the nature of the matters in respect of which relief may be granted by way of an order of mandamus, prohibition or certiorari,
(b) the nature of the persons and bodies against whom the relief may be granted by way of such an order, and
(c) all the circumstances of the case,

it would be just and convenient for the declaration or injunction to be granted on an application for judicial review.

No application for judicial review can be made unless leave of the court has been obtained in accordance with Order 53, rule 3. The application for leave to apply must be made promptly and in any event within three months from the date when the grounds for the application first arose, unless the Court considers that there is good reason for granting an extension (rule 4).

■ Who can apply for judicial review?

The applicant must have 'sufficient interest in the matter to which the application relates' (Supreme Court Act 1981, section 31(3) and Order 53, rule 3(7)).

■ Against whom is it available?

It is available against an inferior court or tribunal and any persons or bodies which perform public duties or functions whether in a judicial or administrative capacity.

■ Can damages be awarded?

In certain circumstances, specified in rule 7, the Court may award damages to the applicant for judicial review.

■ Can it be combined with another claim?

Another point which should be noted about judicial review is that the application can be brought at the same time as an action for a breach of statutory duty and, even if the latter were to fail, the application for judicial review could still succeed. Bringing an action on more than one basis like this is known as 'pleading in the alternative' (see glossary).

■ Does an alternative remedy have any effect?

An application for judicial review will not normally be granted where there is the existence of an alternative remedy.

> It is a cardinal principle that, save in the most exceptional circumstances, [the jurisdiction to grant judicial review] will not be exercised where other remedies were available and have not been used.[53]

In a recent case, however, the existence of an alternative statutory remedy did not prevent an application for judicial review succeeding.

Case: *R* v. *Devon Council, ex parte Baker and another; R* v. *Durham County Council, ex parte Broxson and another*[54]

For the facts in this case see Chapter 31, pages 522–3.

It was suggested that judicial review should not be granted because of the alternative remedy of applying to the Secretary of State under section 7D of the Local Authority Social Services Act 1970, as inserted by section 50 of the NHS and Community Care Act 1990. However the Court of Appeal stated that it was not clear whether the duty to consult in the present context was itself a social services function for the purposes of section 7D. Because of this uncertainty and

> as the issue was entirely one in law in a developing field which was peculiarly appropriate for decision by the courts rather than the Secretary of State, the appellants were not precluded from making their applications for judicial review by the availability of another remedy.

The appeal was therefore allowed.

Illustrative cases

An example of a case where a judicial review was granted, although no damages were awarded and the 'wrong' was not set right, is Mr Leaman's action against the London Borough of Ealing[55].

Case: *Leaman* v. *London Borough of Ealing*

Mr Leaman was a disabled person confined to a wheel chair. In May 1982 he had the opportunity of taking a holiday. It was not a holiday sponsored by the London Borough: it was a private holiday. He sought assistance from the Borough towards the cost of the holiday under the Chronically Sick and Disabled Persons Act 1970. Section 2(1)(f) of this Act enables an authority to facilitate the taking of holidays by a disabled person (see Figure 2.3 for full section).

Ealing Borough responded to Mr Leaman's request by refusing it (by reason of financial constraints the authority did not make grants towards the cost of private holidays and confirmed this in writing).

> Due to financial cut-backs, Ealing do not currently provide grants, but will sponsor applicants for council organised holidays for handicapped people.

Mr Leaman then sought the intervention of the Secretary of State by reason of the default powers contained in section 36 of the National Assistance Act 1948 which enables the Minister, 'after such inquiry as he may think fit make an order declaring the authority to be in default' (the full section is set out below in Figure 27.5)

The Department of Health and Social Security eventually replied to him saying that, on the evidence, it appeared that the Ealing Borough was not in breach of their duty under section 2(1)(f) of the 1970 Act:

> It is for the local authority to determine an individual's needs, and to make arrangements for meeting those needs in accordance with the Act. You question whether need was adequately assessed in your case. The Act does not, however, specify how a need should be assessed. This is entirely a matter for the local authority and one which should be taken up direct with them. If you have continuing needs which you consider should be assessed by the local authority, I would suggest that you advise them of your circumstances so that an assessment may be made of those needs.

The judge disagreed with the view that there had been no breach of statutory duty by the local authority. He held that:

> The London Borough were wrong in declining to consider any application which the Applicant might have made for assistance

with his private holiday. Whether, having regard to a proper consideration of a person's needs, those needs required the making of a grant to a private holiday is an entirely different question. It is a question wholly within the province of the local authority. However it was quite wrong for them to deprive themselves of the opportunity of asking that question.

Since the claim for damages had been abandoned and an application for certiorari (an order for the legality of a decision to be examined – see below) was not pursued, the judge decided that the justice of the case would be met by a declaration that the London Borough were wrong in declining to consider an application for grant towards a private holiday.

Case: *R* v. *Secretary of State, ex parte Alcohol Recovery Project*[56]

In a contrasting case, an application for a judicial review on the allocation of a specific grant for alcohol and drugs funding was refused. Whilst the judge held that the Alcohol Recovery Project had sufficient interest to bring judicial review proceedings, it was not established that it had a legitimate expectation of consultation before the Secretary of State changed her mind on the issue of specific grant funding.

Case: *R* v. *Department of Health and Social Security and others, ex parte Bruce*[57]

In this case the applicant claimed judicial review of the fact that the local authority had not properly catered to his needs under the National Assistance Act section 29 and the Chronically Sick and Disabled Persons Act 1970 section 2(1). He also alleged that the Department had not properly exercised its default powers under section 36(1) of the NAA 1948. He also claimed that there had been insufficient revelation to him of pertinent documents.

The judge (Mr Justice Simon Brown) distinguished the *Wyatt* case (see above page 431) on the grounds that the *Wyatt* case was concerned with a claim for damages and

it is of no relevance to this application which is for judicial review, a wholly different proceeding. There can certainly be no doubt that an applicant may properly bring before the court an application for judicial review in regard to an alleged breach of statutory duty by an authority notwithstanding that there is within the relevant legislation a ministerial default power. That is plain from a variety of cases arising out of various statutes.

However it was held that the applicant had failed:

- firstly, to identify with precision the specific need for which arrangements should be made;
- secondly, to specify the actual arrangements which were required to meet that need;
- thirdly to make an express request to the relevant local authority to meet that identified need by making those particularised arrangements; and
- fourthly, to show a clear failure by the local authority to satisfy that request.

It would still be necessary for the applicant to show that the refusal to meet the identified or contended for need was irrational within the accepted sense of that term in this jurisdiction. In other words, he would have to show that no local authority, properly discharging their duty and having regard to the facts before them, would have declined that request.

The applicant's claim therefore failed and in respect of his request for documents it appears that the Department had provided copies of its own documents and the applicant was required to make a specific request for copies of the inter-authority correspondence.

There is a more recent case where a judicial review was sought of the County Council's failure to implement section 2 of the Chronically Sick and Disabled Persons Act 1970

Case: *R v. Gloucester County Council ex parte Mahfood*[58]

Disabled persons complained when services had been curtailed following withdrawal of a government grant upon which the County Council's plans had been based and the Council gave greater priority to the more seriously disabled. They had not reassessed in the light of the cut backs but had simply sent out a standard letter withdrawing services. The court held that it was right, when making an assessment of a disabled person's needs and the arrangements required to meet them, for the local authority to take account of resources available to it; but, once it had decided that arrangements were necessary, it was under an absolute duty to make them and the resources were no longer relevant.

The court held that a local authority faced an impossible task unless it could have regard to the size of the 'cake of resources' so that it could know how fairest and best to cut it. There would be situations where a reasonable authority could only conclude that some arrangements were necessary to meet the needs of a particular person, and in which it could not reasonably conclude that a lack of resources provided an answer.

Certain persons would be at severe physical risk if they were unable to have some practical assistance in their homes. In those situations the judge could not conceive that an authority would be held to have acted reasonably if it used shortage of resources as a reason for not being satisfied that some arrangement should be made to meet those person's needs. Section 2(1) of the 1970 Act was needs-led by reference to the particular need of a particular disabled person.

A balancing exercise had to be carried out assessing the particular needs of that person in the context of the needs of others and the resources available but, if no reasonable authority could conclude other than that some practical help was necessary, that would have to be its decision. Furthermore once it had decided that it was necessary to make the arrangements, it was under an absolute duty to make them. That was a duty owed to a specific individual and not a target duty. No term was to be implied that the local authority was obliged to comply with the duty only if it had the revenue to do so. Once under that duty resources did not come into it. The failure of Gloucester to reassess once the cuts became known amounted to treating the cut in resources as the sole factor to be taken into account and that was unlawful.

The Court of Appeal has now ruled that even in making the original assessment resources should not be considered. Care must be provided whether or not the Council have sufficient funding.

At the same time the court heard an application by Mr McMillan for judicial review of the decision of Islington Borough Council not to provide him with home help cover, when his carers were ill or away. This application failed on the grounds that the Council had conducted a proper balancing exercise taking into account resources and the comparative needs of the disabled in its area. It held that the Council was not in breach of the duty which it owed to the applicant.

The decision at first instance eased the pressure on Councils in meeting their statutory duties under Community Care legislation and other Acts on the provision of services in that the resources available could legitimately be taken into account in making the assessment. The Council would have to meet the needs absolutely necessary and lack of resources could not be used as an answer for not providing them but in assessing other needs it would be reasonable to balance priorities.

The outcome of the appeal brought by Mr. Barry (one of Mr. Mahfood's co-applicants) was enthusiastically greeted by those representing the disabled since it has the effect that *all* needs, once identified, have to be met irrespective of resources and services cut through budget reductions will have to be restored. However, it has severe implications for local authority funding and the Council have indicated their intention to appeal to the House of Lords. It is most probable that the Lords will reinstate the judgment of the lower court and if they do not legislation is likely to be forthcoming restore the position.

The prerogative orders

The three prerogative remedies which are available following an action for judicial review are certiorari, prohibition and mandamus.

Certiorari

This latin term is short for *certiorari volumus* – we wish to make certain – and enables an action to be brought before the courts to challenge the decision of a lower court, a public authority or government minister. If the decision is found to be invalid it will be quashed (that is, struck out). Whilst certiorari is not available against the crown it is available against individual ministers of the crown.

A decision could be found to be invalid on the grounds that it was not within the powers of that body (*ultra vires* – see glossary), that it was contrary to natural justice or that it was made in error of law.

Ultra vires   Decisions/actions can be challenged and found invalid on the basis that they were ultra vires (that is, outside the powers of the authority/court). The court would look at the enabling powers and determine whether they authorised the specific action complained of.

Natural justice   Certiorari can also be used where it is alleged that the principles of natural justice have not been followed. The rules of natural justice require that justice be done and be seen to be done. Thus if a decision is made in the absence of the case of the opposing party being heard or considered this would be a violation of natural justice (*audi alteram partem* – hear the other party). The rules require the decision maker to act fairly. If someone making the decision which is in question has interests in the case then this can be challenged (*nemo judex in causa sua potest* – no one can be a judge in his own cause). There is also a rule against bias.

Error of law   A decision can be challenged through the certiorari procedure if there is an error of law on the face of the record.

Prohibition

This order often goes hand in hand with certiorari and an application is made to the High Court for both orders to be given. Prohibition will be requested where the wish is to stop an authority exceeding its jurisdiction. It can be used both against courts and also increasingly against any public body or person exercising a public duty. Certiorari is concerned with past activities; prohibition with future activities. To succeed in an application for prohibition, similar grounds to those required for an application of certiorari must be shown.

Mandamus

This means 'we command' and is used when what is sought is an order or command requiring a body to carry out a specific act. It can be used to enforce a discretion as well as to carry out a legal duty. It will not be ordered:

- if there is an alternative remedy;
- if it is impracticable to order it; or
- where the applicant has delayed in applying for it.

It is not available against the crown but may be available against individual ministers if they owe a legal duty to a member of the public. It has been granted in many cases against local authorities:

- to command performance of public duties owed by local authorities;
- to ensure that a local authority abides by its own standing orders[59].

Anyone who is acting in obedience to an order of mandamus is protected from any legal action. (Order 53, rule 10 RSC)

Judicial review and the 1990 Act

In relation to the duties under section 47 to assess and to make a decision about what services, if any, to provide, judicial review may be available in the following situations (not exhaustive):

● failure to assess, where the client fulfils the eligibility criteria;

● failure to make an adequate assessment;

● failure to make an assessment within a reasonable time;

● failure to notify the client of the results of the assessment.

It should also be noted that it would be available where a health authority or a housing authority were called in to assist in the assessment under the provisions of section 47(3) and refused to co-operate.

DEFAULT POWERS

Some legislation has built in enforcement provisions such as the default powers of the Secretary of State under section 7D added to 1970 Local Authority Social Services Act by section 50 of the NHS and Community Care Act 1990 (see Figure 27.6).

In addition the 1990 Act gives power to the local authorities to set up complaints procedures (see below).

The National Assistance Act 1948

Default powers are given to the Secretary of State under section 36 of the National Assistance Act 1948. These are set out in Figure 27.5 which gives the precise words of the statute but is broken down into bullet points for clarity.

Figure 27.5 National Assistance Act 1948 – section 36

● Where the minister is of the opinion . . .
● that a local authority
● has failed to discharge
● any of their functions under this Part of this Act . . .
● he may after such inquiry as he may think fit
● make an order
● declaring the authority to be in default.

Local Authority Social Services Act 1970

Section 50 of the National Health Service and Community Care Act 1990 introduces section 7D into the Local Authority Social Services Act 1970 and is shown in Figure 27.6, likewise broken down by the author into bullet points.

Figure 27.6 The Local Authority Social Services Act 1970 – section 7D

(1) If the Secretary of State is satisfied

- that any local authority
- have failed, without reasonable excuse,
- to comply with any of their duties
- which are social services functions (other than a duty imposed by or under the Children Act 1989),
- he may make an order
- declaring that authority to be in default
- with respect to the duty in question.

(2) An order under subsection (1) may contain such directions for the purpose of ensuring that the duty is complied with within such period as may be specified in the order as appear to the Secretary of State to be necessary.

(3) Any such direction shall, on the application of the Secretary of State, be enforceable by mandamus.

The National Health Service Act 1977

Under the National Health Service Act 1977 the Secretary of State has the power to act in default under section 85. This, as amended by the Health Authorities Act 1995, is set out in Figure 27.7.

Figure 27.7 NHS Act 1977 – section 85

(1) Where the Secretary of State is of the opinion, on complaint or otherwise, that —

- (a) any Health Authority;
- (b) any Special Health Authority;
- (c) an NHS trust;
- (d) the Medical Practices Committee; or
- (e) the Dental Estimates Board;
- have failed to carry out any functions conferred or imposed on them by or under this Act or Part I of the National Health Service and Community Care Act 1990, or
- have in carrying out those functions
- failed to comply with any regulations or directions relating to those functions,
- he may after such inquiry as he may think fit
- make an order declaring them to be in default.

[Bullet points inserted by author]

The effect of a default order issued under section 85(1) is shown in Figure 27.8 and can be very draconian.

Figure 27.8 Effect of default order – section 85(2) and (5)

(2) The members of the body in default shall forthwith vacate their office, and the order —

(a) shall provide for the appointment, in accordance with the provisions of this Act, of new members of the body; and

(b) may contain such provisions as seem to the Secretary of State expedient for authorising any person to act in the place of the body in question pending the appointment of new members.

(5) An order made under this section may contain such supplementary and incidental provisions as appear to the Secretary of State to be necessary or expedient, including —

(a) provision for the transfer to the Secretary of State of property and liabilities of the body in default; and

(b) where any such order is varied or revoked by a subsequent order, provision in the revoking order or a subsequent order for the transfer to the body in default of any property or liabilities acquired or incurred by the Secretary of State in discharging any of the functions transferred to him.

Inquiries

The Secretary of State has the power to set up an inquiry under section 7C of the 1970 Local Authority Social Services Act, added by section 50 of the 1990 Act, and also under the National Health Service Act 1977 section 84. An Inquiry will usually precede the use of default powers and is often sufficient to make the body concerned conform.

The powers given to the Secretary of State under section 84 of the NHS Act 1977 (as updated) are shown in Figure 27.9.

Figure 27.9 Inquiry and the NHS – section 84

(1) The Secretary of State may cause an inquiry to be held in any case where he deems it advisable to do so in connection with any matter arising under this Act or Part I of the National Health Service and Community Care Act 1990.

(2) For the purpose of any such inquiry (but subject to subsection (3) below) the person appointed to hold the inquiry —

(a) may by summons require any person to attend, at a time and place stated in the summons, to give evidence or to produce any documents in his custody or under his control which relate to any matter in question at the inquiry; and

(b) may take evidence on oath, and for that purpose administer oaths, or may, instead of administering an oath, require the person examined to make a solemn affirmation.

(3) [Payment of witness expenses]

(4) Any person who refuses or deliberately fails to attend in obedience to a summons under this section, or to give evidence, or who deliberately

alters, suppresses, conceals, destroys, or refuses to produce any book or other document which he is required or is liable to be required to produce for the purposes of this section, shall be liable on summary conviction to a fine ... or imprisonment ..., or to both.

(5) Where the Secretary of State causes an inquiry to be held under this section —

(a) the costs incurred by him in relation to the inquiry (including such reasonable sum not exceeding £30 a day as he may determine for the services of any officer engaged in the inquiry) shall be paid by such local authority or party to the inquiry as he may direct, and

(b) he may cause the amount of the costs so incurred to be certified, and any amount so certified and directed to be paid by any authority or person shall be recoverable from that authority or person by the Secretary of State summarily as a civil debt.

(6) Where the Secretary of State causes an inquiry to be held under this section he may make orders —

(a) as to the costs of the parties at the inquiry, and
(b) as to the parties by whom the costs are to be paid,

and every such order may be made a rule of the High Court on the application of any party named in the order.

An inquiry held under section 84 will be subject to the Tribunals and Inquiries Act 1971.

The National Health Service Act and Community Care Act 1990 section 50 has added section 7C to the Local Authority and Social Services Act 1970 and gives to the Secretary of State the power to hold an inquiry. The section is set out in Figure 27.10.

Figure 27.10 The Local Authority Social Services Act 1970 – section 7C

(1) The Secretary of State may cause an inquiry to be held in any case where, whether on representations made to him or otherwise, he considers it advisable to do so in connection with the exercise by any local authority of any of their social services functions (except in so far as those functions relate to persons under the age of eighteen).

(2) Subsections (2) to (5) of section 250 of the Local Government Act 1972 (powers in relation to local inquiries) shall apply in relation to an inquiry under this section as they apply in relation to an inquiry under that section.

Directions and emergency powers

Section 86 of the NHS Act 1977 gives emergency powers to the Secretary of State and these are shown in Figure 27.11.

Figure 27.11 Emergency powers – section 86, NHS Act 1977

(1) If the Secretary of State —

(a) considers that by reason of an emergency it is necessary, in order to ensure that a service falling to be provided in pursuance of this Act or Part I of the National Health Service and Community Care Act 1990 is provided, to direct that during the period specified by the directions a function conferred on any body or person by virtue of this Act or that Part shall to the exclusion of or concurrently with that body or person be performed by another body or person, then

(b) he may give directions accordingly and it shall be the duty of the bodies or persons in question to comply with the directions.

The powers conferred on the Secretary of State by this section are in addition to any other powers exercisable by him.

Commentary

Where there are default powers the court, as can be seen above, is reluctant to give any direct remedy to an aggrieved person. Lord Denning[60] said

> Seeing that section 36 is the remedy given by the statute, I do not think there is any other remedy available. The case falls within the principle that: 'where an Act creates an obligation, and enforces the obligation in a specified manner, we take it to be the general rule that performance cannot be enforced in any other manner'.

Baroness Hooper (Parliamentary Under-Secretary of State for the Department of Health) explained how these default procedures would work during the debates in the House of Lords.

> We expect the default procedures in this [section] to work in the following way. The first stage will be when it comes to the Secretary of State's attention that an authority is failing to discharge its functions. This may come from a number of directions – the work of the social services inspectorate, information received from organisations representing disabled people or by direct representations to the Secretary of State by users of services. The first thing the Secretary of State needs to do is to satisfy himself that the authority has failed without reasonable excuse to exercise its functions. This will entail some form of further investigation or inquiry and may, if the Secretary of State feels it would be useful, include using the general powers of direction to direct the authority to exercise its functions in a particular way.
>
> It will be only after these processes have been exhausted and work with the authorities through the Social Services Inspectorate has failed to secure any improvement in the situation

that the use of the default powers will be considered . . . When these powers are used the Secretary of State first has to issue an order then, if it is not complied with, he can seek an order from the court to enforce it.

It remains to be seen, in the operation of the 1990 Act, what the effect of these sections relating to the setting up of inquiries and the default powers is and whether they are effective in ensuring that the duties set out in the community care legislation are kept.

To what extent, for example, will lack of resources be regarded as a reasonable excuse for failing to carry out a comprehensive assessment and therefore the use of the default powers or directions by the Secretary of State be refused in such circumstances? Will lack of resources justify a failure to set up a procedure for reviewing complaints and representations and again the use of default powers and powers of direction be refused?

As we have seen in cases before the courts on judicial review, the courts have taken the line that they will not interfere with the decision if it is a question of resources (see above and the discussion of the *Hincks* case page 430). Will this same argument be applied by the Secretary of State when an application is made for him to exercise his powers of direction or default?

Other outstanding issues are:

- Who will be recognised by the Secretary of State as having the right to bring an action for default?
- How wide a definition will he permit of those who are allowed to make representations?
- How will the courts review his decisions on such matters if application is made to them by way of judicial review of the Secretary of State's decisions and actions?

REPRESENTATIONS AND COMPLAINTS

Both health service bodies, including NHS trusts, and local authorities have a duty to establish complaints procedures and give a complainant the right to make representations to the authority. The statutory basis is however different.

Local authority community services

The first stage in requiring action or remedial action to be taken is a representation and/or complaint to the relevant authority and the National Health Service and Community Care Act 1990 makes an important feature of the right to make representations about social services provision.

Under the 1990 Act section 50 added section 7B to the Local Authority Social Services Act 1970 which enables the Secretary of State to require the local authority to set up a procedure to hear representations and complaints. The section is set out in Figure 27.12.

Figure 27.12 Local Authorities Social Services Act 1970 – section 7B

(1) The Secretary of State may by order

- require local authorities
- to establish a procedure
- for considering any representations (including complaints)
- which are made to them
- by a qualifying individual,
- or anyone acting on his behalf,
- in relation to the discharge of, or any failure to discharge,
- any of their social services functions in respect of that individual.

(2) In relation to a particular local authority, an individual is a qualifying individual for the purposes of section (1) above if —

(a) the authority have a power or a duty to provide, or to secure the provision of, a service for him; and
(b) his need or possible need for such a service has (by whatever means) come to the attention of the authority.

(3) A local authority shall comply with any directions given by the Secretary of State as to the procedure to be adopted in considering representations made as mentioned in subsection (1) above and as to the taking of such action as may be necessary in consequence of such representations.

(4) Local authorities shall give such publicity to any procedure established pursuant to this section as they consider appropriate.

Directions for complaints procedures were issued by the Secretary of State in 1990 and they cover representations and their consideration, the monitoring of the operation of the procedures and other general aspects.

The guidance issued in *Caring for People: Community Care in the next decade and beyond* covers the objectives of complaints procedures and the need to ensure that they are developed after consultation. It defines the essential requirements of a complaints procedure as being:

- The designation of an officer to co-ordinate the consideration of complaints;
- The key stages being identified together with staff responsibilities;

- Members and staff of the authority being familiar with the arrangements, responsibilities and key stages;
- Every registered complaint being considered and responded to within 28 days of receipt and, if that is not possible, an explanation being given followed by a full response within three months;
- Response to the complainant and advice on further options for the complainant;
- The review panel meeting within 28 days of the complainant's request;
- The review panel's decision being recorded within 24 hours of the completion of their deliberations and sent formally to the authority, complainant and anybody acting on his behalf;
- The authority deciding on its reaction to the review recommendation within 28 days of the receipt of the recommendation, with appropriate notification to specified persons; and
- Keeping a record of all complaints received and the outcome in each case, identifying separately those cases where the time limits imposed by the directions have been breached.

The policy guidance also covers:

- The operation of the procedure in terms of staffing
- The form of complaint
- The response to complaints
- The review stage
- Monitoring
- Publicity
- Support for complainants
- Assessment decisions
- Special cases
- Voluntary and private sector provision
- Nursing homes
- Collaborative assessments
- Elected members
- The role of the Mental Health Act Commission
- The Children Act 1989 and the Disabled Persons (Services, Consultation and Representation) Act 1986
- Training.

An Annex gives details of the setting up and role of the review panels.

The right to make representations or complaints under section 7B is narrow and at first sight it gives no power for bodies or advocates to make representations on behalf of individuals who lack the competence to apply in their own right. Although Baroness Blatch in the House of Lords stated that organisations and carers should be able to make representations on behalf of other service users, a specific legal right for them to do so has not been given. The courts will ultimately have to determine who are qualifying individuals under this section and it is hoped that they do not take too narrow a view. The guidance requires that the final stage in the hearing of complaints and representations should be before an independent person/panel.

If the procedure operates effectively it is likely to reduce the extent of litigation before the courts over assessments and the provision of services.

Complaints relating to health services

There is a statutory duty under the Hospital Complaints Act 1985 for each health authority to establish a complaints procedure. Guidance requires authorities to establish a procedure in relation to community health services as well.

In addition, as part of the Patient's Charter initiative, local charters covering the handling of complaints are also required of providers. Such requirements may be included in NHS contracts between health authority purchasers and providers.

NHS Trusts and complaints

Where an NHS Trust has been established, the Health Authority which previously had responsibility for a hospital which has become a Trust will remain formally responsible for the investigation of any complaint which refers to services provided before the Trust was set up. It will liaise in any subsequent investigation with the Health Service Commissioner. This includes responding formally to the Commissioner's initial summary of the complaint, providing all background papers, nominating a liaison officer and making arrangements for local interviews.

Complaints relating to services provided after the Trust was set up will be the responsibility of the Trust according to the procedure set down under the Hospital Complaints Procedures Act 1985.

Where a complaint spans the time before and after the establishment of the Trust, since it would be unreasonable to expect the complainant to deal with two separate NHS bodies, the Trust should take the lead in investigating such complaints, keeping the Authority fully informed of the investigation and any action taken.

Following the review committee chaired by Professor Alan Wilson into the handling of hospital complaints, a consultation document was published[61]. The Department of Health has indicated that it accepts the principal recommendations of the Wilson Report and in 1996 issued details of the scheme to be implemented by NHS Trusts and health service authorities.

The previous hospital complaints procedure has been subject to judicial review.

Case: R v. *Canterbury and Thanet DHA and another, ex parte F and W*[62]

Complaints were made by eight families that a doctor employed by the first defendants and seconded to the second defendants either diagnosed sexual abuse when it should not have been diagnosed or delayed in telling the parents of the diagnosis. A legal aid certificate was obtained by one of the complainants. The doctor withdrew her co-operation in view of the possibility of legal proceedings. The defendants subsequently considered that an inquiry was inappropriate. The complainants applied for judicial review contending, *inter alia*, that there was a duty to review their complaints. The court held that the complaints procedure was not appropriate where litigation was likely because

(a) the purpose of the inquiry was either to obtain a second opinion and a change of diagnosis or to enable the health authority to change its procedures in the light of matters brought to its attention during the investigation; and
(b) the procedure depends on the co-operation of the doctor concerned which obviously would not be forthcoming if legal proceedings were likely.

The issues raised in the above case will not be resolved by the implementation of the Wilson Report. To require a complainant to agree not to bring legal proceedings whatever the outcome of the investigation would appear to be unjust and may mean that some complainants may not make use of the complaints system. Thus the possiblity of resolving the issues without recourse to litigation will be lost.

Complaints and the Community Health Councils

It is recognised that the Community Health Council has greater responsiblities in representing the people in its area following the reorganisation of health authorities on 1 April 1996. This is because the larger commissioning authorities will be too large to be effective in representing the localities. Each Community Health Council will therefore have a significant role to play both in the representation of its community at large and in facilitating complaints by individuals.

OMBUDSMEN

If a complainant is not satisfied with the response of the authority to a complaint, he can apply to the Ombudsman for further investigation. This is the Health Service Commissioner in respect of complaints about the National Health Service and the Local Authority Commissioner in respect of complaints about local authority services. Following the Wilson recommendation the jurisdiction of the Health Services Commissioner has been extended to include complaints on the exercise of clinical judgment and the actions of general practitioners.

CONCLUSIONS

There are thus a variety of measures for ensuring that there is compliance with statutory powers and duties. The framework is shown in Figure 27.12 but it must be emphasised that different remedies might be sought concurrently and the steps shown are not necessarily consecutive.

If, during this process, the complainant considers there are good reasons for taking individual court action then there could be:

- an application for judicial review and/or
- an action for breach of statutory duty or
- an application for one of the orders cited above or
- an action based on negligence (less likely).

It remains to be seen how responsive the local authorities and health authorities are to the guidance and directions issued by the Secretary of State and the frequency of applications for judicial review.

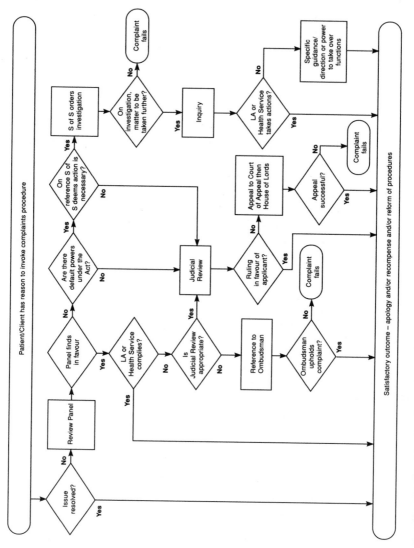

Figure 27.12 Mechanisms for redress

REFERENCES FOR SECTION C

1. *Re Walker* The Times, 26 November 1981 and *R* v. *Secretary of State and others, ex parte Hinks* (1979) Solicitors' Journal, 29 June 1979 page 436
2. Rochdale Metropolitan Borough Council failed in its application for judicial review of the decision by Rochdale Health Authority not to provide further financial information. (*The Times* 17 February 1992).
3. W.194/89–90, pages 27–39 of House of Commons 482
4. W.478/89, on pages 80–90 of House of Commons 482
5. 27/93 Welsh health circular *Boundaries between health and social services* (93)23, Welsh health circular (FP)(93)13
6. This is the subject of guidance given in Annex C of the Welsh Office circular, (27/93)
7. EL(91)122 also issued as LAC(91)14
8. Circular LAC(91)14 and EL(91)122
9. *White* v. *Department of Social Security* Independent 22 July 1993; *White* v. *Chief Adjudication Officer* The Times 2 August 1993
10. HSG(95)8; LAC(95)5; WHC(95)7; WOC 16/95
11. HSG(95)39, LAC(95)17
12. NHSME, *Establishing the District of Residence* Department of Health, date not given
13. Regulation 2(5)(a) of the *NHS Functions (Directions to Authorities and Administrative Arrangements) Regulations 1991*, SI 1991/554
14. EL(91)45
15. HMSO, 1994
16. see 'Help line' pages in *GP Fundholding*
17. Kathryn Godfrey 'Taking cancer care into the community' *GP Fundholding* Vol. 4 No. 12 June 21 1995 pages 16–18
18. *GP Fundholding* Vol. 1 No. 21 October 21 1992 Dr Bulger and Dr Aswani, fund-holders in East London
19. Report of British Medical Association reported by Lois Rogers in *The Sunday Times* 16 October 1994
20. See reference 3
21. J.G.R. Howie *Summary of key findings of research of General practice fundholding Shadow project – an evaluation* University of Edinburgh, 1995
22. *R* v. *Gloucester County Council, ex parte Mahfood (et al)* Times Law Report June 21, 1995 (QBD); Times Law Report July 12, 1996 (CA)
23. *Community Care Plans (Independent Sector Non-Residential Care) Directions* 1994 LAC(94)12
24. CI(92)30; EL(92)65
25. Hansard HL Vol. 518, cols 1477–8 quoted in *Encyclopedia for Social Services Law and Practice*, Sweet & Maxwell
26. *The Times* 13 April 1993
27. See also Richard Gordon *Community Care Assessments* Longman, 1993
28. *Residential Accommodation (Determination of District Health Authority) Regulations 1992* SI 1992/3183
29. *R* v. *Islington LBC, ex parte Rixon* Times Law Report April 17 1996 (QBD)
30. Peter Singh *Community Care: Britain's other Lottery* MENCAP 1995
31. Mike George *Community Care* 29 April, 1993, pages 18–9
32. Circular CI(92)34
33. *Community Care* 1 April 1993
34. Judy Wright *et al*, University of Bath, The Social Services research and development unit (personal communication)
35. Hansard HL Vol. 519, cols 41–2 quoted in *Encyclopedia of Social Services*

Law and Practice, Sweet & Maxwell

36. Inspection Unit Directions 1994 Annex A to circular LAC(94)16
37. Department of Health and Welsh Office *Moving Forward: a Consultation Document on the Regulation and Inspection of Social Services* HMSO, 1995
38. *R v. Wandsworth London Borough Council, ex parte Beckwith* Times Law Report 29 June 1995 (CA) and [1996] All ER 129 (HL)
39. *O'Reilly v. Mackman* [1982] 3 All ER 1124
40. See Terence Ingman *The English Legal Process* Blackstone Press, 1991, page 284
41. *R v. Secretary of State for Health, ex parte Alcohol Recovery Project* [1993] Crown Office Digest 344
42. *R v. Wandsworth London Borough Council, ex parte Beckwith* Times Law Report 29 June 1995 (CA) and 15 December 1995 (HL)
43. *R v. Secretary of State for Social Services and other, ex parte Hinks* Solicitor's Journal 29 June 1979 436
44. *Re: Walker's application* The Times, 26 November 1987
45. *Wyatt v. Hillingdon London Borough* 76 LGR 1978 (CA) 727
46. *R v. DHSS and others, ex parte Bruce* QBD *The Times* 8 February 1986
47. *Saunders v. Holborn District Board of Works* (1895) 1 QB 64.
48. *X (minor) v. Bedfordshire County Council; M (a minor) and another v. Newham London Borough Council and others; E (a minor) v. Dorset County Council; Christmas v. Hampshire County Council; Keating v. Bromley London Borough Council* [1995] 3 All ER 353
49. J. Butler and G. Wood 'Newham and Bedfordshire: negligence in residential care' *New Law Journal* 8 December 1995, pages 826–7
50. Announced by Susan Allison in a report in *The Sunday Times* 13 November 1994
51. HMSO 1994
52. Richard Gordon *Community Care Assessments* Longman, 1993 page 3 and 55–65
53. *R v. Epping and Harlow General Commissioners, ex parte Goldstraw* [1983] 3 All ER 257 (Sir John Donaldson at page 267)
54. *R v. Devon County Council, ex parte Baker and another; R v. Durham County Council, ex parte Broxson and another* [1995] 1 All ER 73
55. *R v. the London Borough of Ealing, ex parte Leaman* QBD *The Times* 10 February 1984
56. *R v. Secretary of State for Health, ex parte Alcohol Recovery Project,* [1993] Crown Office Digest 344
57. *R v. Department of Health and Social Security and others, ex parte Bruce* QBD *The Times* 8 February 1986
58. *R v. Gloucester County Council, ex parte Mahfood, also ex parte Barry, ex parte Grinham and ex parte Dartnell and another* and *R v. Islington London Borough Council, ex parte McMillan* QBD Times Law Report June 21 1995
59. See Terence Ingman *The English Legal Process*, Blackstone Press for examples of the cases and uses of these prerogative powers.
60. *Southwark London Borough Council v. Williams* [1971] 2 WLR 467
61. *Being Heard. The Report of a review committee on NHS complaints procedures.* Department of Health 1994
62. *R v. Canterbury and Thanet District Health Authority and South East Thames Regional Health Authority, ex parte F and W* (CA) [1994] 5 Med L.R. 132

Section D

Accommodation and community care

This Section of the book looks at the changes brought about by the National Health Service and Community Care Act 1990 in the duties of the local authority to provide accommodation in the community for those discharged from hospitals. Chapters also deal with the law relating to registered homes (nursing homes and residential care homes) and also consider the function and procedures relating to registered homes tribunals. Finally the Section covers the work of the Housing Corporations and Housing Associations in the provision of accommodation for special needs. There is other legislation relating to the provision of housing for homeless persons and the function of local authority housing departments but these topics are not included in this book.

CHAPTER 28

Local authorities and the provision of accommodation

In this chapter the role of the local authority in the provision of accommodation will be considered. The following issues are covered:

● Power and duty to provide accommodation
● Determination of residency
● Choice of accommodation
● Management of premises and standards of accommodation
● Voluntary organisations and agency arrangements
● Co-operation between the local authority and NHS
● Exclusion of powers to accommodate
● Contractual responsibilities.

Provisions in relation to charging for the accommodation and recovery of sums due are discussed in Section E, Chapter 33.

The present powers and duties of local authorities in relation to the provision of accommodation date from the implementation of the National Assistance Act 1948 (the NAA 1948) which, together with other legislation, saw the ending of the poor law régime and the introduction of a welfare state on the foundation of the concepts and thinking contained in the Beveridge Report.

Sections 21 to 26 of the NAA set out the main provisions relating to the provision of accommodation by the local authorities. The National Health Service and Community Care Act 1990 has amended these sections to enable those recommendations of the white paper, *Community Care in the next decade and beyond*, to be implemented. The result, unfortunately, is a more confusing situation in law than if a new consolidating act had

461

been passed. In the discussion which follows the original sections of the 1948 Act will be shown as amended by the 1990 Act and subsequent legislation. The sections will be shown in figures outside the main body of text, so that the reader who does not wish to have the details of the law can omit them.

The effects of the NHS Community Care Act 1990 on the NAA 1948 is shown in summary form in Figure 28.1.

Figure 28.1 Provisions of the 1990 Act relating to accommodation and charging

Section 42:

- amends Section 21 of the NAA 1948 in the definition of those for whom local authorities have a duty to provide accommodation and makes changes to the agency arrangements which local authorities can make (additional amendments are made in Schedule 9),
- amends section 30 of the NAA 1948 and extends the nature of the organisations with which the local authority may make arrangements for accommodation; and
- amends section 45(3) of the Health Services and Public Health Act 1968 and extends the organisations and persons with which the local authority can make arrangements for promoting the welfare of old people.

Section 43 of the 1990 Act excludes certain persons from the powers of local authorities to provide accommodation by amending section 26 of the NAA 1948.

Section 44:

- amends the provisions of section 22 of the NAA 1948 under which local authorities can charge for the accommodation provided; and
- amends section 29 of the NAA 1948 under which arrangements can be made for the provision of hostel accommodation for those in receipt of welfare services.

Section 45 amends sections 21, 22, 23 and 24 of the Health and Social Services and Social Security Adjudication Act 1983 under which the local authority can recover sums due to it where persons in residential accommodation have disposed of assets and gives powers to the Secretary of State to make directions [discussed in Section E, Chapter 33].

These sections and amendments shown in Figure 28.1 are considered in detail below. The financial changes are discussed in the next Section of the book.

POWER AND DUTY OF THE LOCAL AUTHORITY TO PROVIDE ACCOMMODATION FOR CERTAIN PERSONS

This duty is specified in section 21 of the National Assistance Act 1948 and has been amended as illustrated in Figure 28.2.

(Words in italics indicate the changes which have been made by the 1990 Act.)

Figure 28.2 The National Assistance Act 1948 – section 21

(1) Subject to and in accordance with the provisions of this Part of this Act, a local authority may with the approval of the Secretary of State, and to such extent as he may direct shall, make arrangements for providing —

(a) residential accommodation for persons aged eighteen or over who by reason of age, *illness, disability,* or any other circumstances are in need of care and attention which is not otherwise available to them; and

(aa) *residential accommodation for expectant and nursing mothers who are in need of care and attention which is not otherwise available to them.*

(b) [repealed]

(2) In making such arrangements a local authority shall have regard to the welfare of all persons for whom accommodation is provided, and in particular to the need for providing accommodation of different descriptions suited to different descriptions of such persons as are mentioned in the last foregoing subsection.

(3) [repealed by the Local Government Act 1972]

(4) *Subject to the provisions of section 26 of this Act,* accommodation provided by a local authority in the exercise of their functions under this section shall be provided in premises managed by the authority or, to such extent as may be determined in accordance with the arrangements under this section, in such premises managed by another local authority as may be agreed between the two authorities and on such terms, including terms as to the reimbursement of expenditure incurred by the said other authority, as may be so agreed.

(5) References in this Act to accommodation provided under this Part thereof shall be construed as references to accommodation provided in accordance with this and the five next following sections, and as including references to board and other services, amenities and requisites provided in connection with the accommodation except where in the opinion of the authority managing the premises their provision is unnecessary.

(6) References in this Act to a local authority providing accommodation shall be construed, in any case where a local authority agree with another local authority for the provision of accommodation in premises managed by the said other authority, as references to the first-mentioned local authority.

(7) Without prejudice [see glossary] to the generality of the foregoing provisions of this section, a local authority may —

(a) provide, in such cases as they may consider appropriate, for the conveyance of persons to and from premises in which accommodation is provided for them under this Part of the Act;

(b) *make arrangements for the provision on the premises in which the accommodation is being provided of such other services as appear to the authority to be required.*

(8) Nothing in this section shall authorise or require a local authority to make any provision authorised or required to be made (whether by that or

by any other authority) by or under any enactment not contained in this
Part of this Act *or authorised or required to be provided under the
National Health Service Act 1977.*

The effect of these changes has continued to widen the scope of
the persons for whom the local authority may or must provide
accommodation. It will be noticed that whilst the local authority has a power under section 21(1) to provide accommodation,
it does not have a duty unless a direction is made by the Secretary of State.

Directions under this provision

A Direction has been issued under the amended section 21 and,
together with other directions and approvals, is consolidated in
LAC(93)10 extracts of which can be found in Appendix 1 to
this book.

Appendix 1 to Circular LAC(93)10 gives the Approvals and
Directions under section 21(1) of the 1948 Act. They come into
force on 1 April 1993 and apply only to England and Wales.
They cover the following topics:
A. Residential accommodation for persons in need of care and
   attention.
B. Residential accomodation for expectant and nursing mothers.
C. Arrangements to provide services for residents.
D. Arrangements for the conveyance of residents.
E. Duties in respect of residents in transferred accommodation.
E. Powers to make arrangements with other local authorities and
   voluntary organisations, etc.

Discussion

The following points should be noted about the provisions set
out in Figure 28.2 and Directions in Appendix 1 to circular
LAC(93)10:

● The distinction between the direction of the Secretary of State
  to provide accommodation and the approval of arrangements
  for the provision of a service. The former gives the local
  authority no freedom to determine whether the service will
  be provided.

● The words 'illness and disability' replacing 'infirmity' extend
  the duty of the local authority.

● The duty is also extended to cover the provision of residential accommodation for expectant mothers and nursing mothers

who are 'in need of care and attention'. However, this duty only arises when appropriate accommodation 'is not otherwise available to them'.

- There is no duty on the local authority to provide accommodation which is part of the statutory duty of the National Health Service.

- The powers to contract for other agencies to provide accommodation, as permitted by the amended section 26 of the NAA Act (see below), are not restricted by this section.

Section 21 of the National Assistance Act 1948 as amended by the National Health Service and Community Care Act 1990 has come under judicial scrutiny.

Case: R v. Wandsworth Borough Council, ex parte Beckwith

Mr. Beckwith applied for judicial review of the decision of Wandsworth Borough Council to close George Potter House in which he lived, to sell its remaining residential care homes for elderly people to the private sector and to cease to be a provider of residential care for elderly people. The Council argued that there was nothing in the amended 1948 Act which required it to keep on managed premises for each of the classes of person cited in section 21 and that it was open to it to dispose of all its residential care homes provided it still kept places for people with learning disabilities or people with mental health problems. Mr Beckwith, in contrast, maintained that the Council was bound to retain at least one of its homes designated for residential care. The judge held[1] that the provisions of section 21(1) of the 1948 Act did envisage different classes of person to whom the duty was owed and for whom different provisions needed to be made. In addition he considered that the Council had been wrongly advised that there was an oversupply of residential care for elderly people in the borough. It had therefore decided to close all residential care homes without considering the issues of what it should do if it was not in law allowed to dispose of all its residential homes. The judge therefore quashed the whole of the council's decision and submitted the matter to it for reconsideration.

The council appealed against the decision and the Court of Appeal, later confirmed by the House of Lords, overruled the judge's decision[2].

The Court of Appeal held that the council had accepted that it had a duty to make some direct provision of accommodation under section 21 of the National Assistance Act 1948 as a result of the views of the Department of Health in its circular[3] to the effect that section 42 of the 1990 Act will require authorities to make some direct provision for residential care under section 21 of the 1948 Act. The Court of Appeal held that that view was not correct and sections 21 and 26 of the 1948 Act, as amended by the 1990 Act, enabled the local authority to cease altogether to be a direct provider of residential care for the elderly.

The Court of Appeal refused leave to appeal to the House of Lords but the applicants petitioned the House of Lords direct for leave to appeal. The Council, however, vacated and closed the Home, which had become uneconomic to run, without awaiting the outcome of the petition to the House of Lords, whose ruling in fact confirmed the judgment of the Court of Appeal.

This decision sets the scene for local authorities to cease to be direct providers of residential accommodation for any of the classes of persons set out in section 21 of the 1948 Act. It also highlights the danger of relying absolutely upon Department of Health guidance on the interpretation of the statutory provisions.

DETERMINATION OF RESIDENCY AND RESPONSIBILITY OF THE LOCAL AUTHORITY

Section 24 of the National Assistance Act 1948 clarifies the persons for whom the local authority is responsible and has been amended by the 1990 Act to take into account the responsibility for persons who are patients in hospital. The full section, together with the amendments, is shown in Figure 28.3.

Figure 28.3 The NAA – section 24

(1) The local authority empowered under this Part of this Act to provide residential accommodation for any person shall subject to the following provisions of this Part of this Act be the authority in whose area the person is ordinarily resident.

(2) [repealed by Housing (Homeless Persons) Act 1977 s.20(4)]

(3) Where a person in the area of a local authority —

(a) is a person with no settled residence, or
(b) not being ordinarily resident in the area of the local authority, is in urgent need of residential accommodation under this Part of this Act,

the authority shall have the like power to provided residential accommodation for him as if he were ordinarily resident in their area.

(4) Subject to and in accordance with the arrangements under section

twenty-one of this Act, a local authority shall have power, as respects a person ordinarily resident in the area of another local authority, with the consent of that other authority to provide residential accommodation for him in any case where the authority would have a duty to provide such accommodation if he were ordinarily resident in their area.

(5) Where a person is provided with residential accommodation under this Part of this Act, he shall be deemed for the purposes of this Act to continue to be ordinarily resident in the area in which he was ordinarily resident immediately before the residential accommodation was provided for him.

(6) *For the purposes of the provision of residential accommodation under this Part of this Act, a patient in a hospital vested in the Secretary of State or an NHS trust shall be deemed to be ordinarily resident in the area, if any, in which he was ordinarily resident immediately before he was admitted as a patient to the hospital, whether or not he in fact continues to be ordinarily resident in that area.*

(7) *In subsection (6) above 'NHS trust' means a National Health Service trust established under Part I of the National Health Service and Community Care Act 1990 or under the National Health Service (Scotland) Act 1978.*

This section, and particularly the last two subsections in italics for emphasis clarifies which local authority is responsible for those long-stay patients who may have lost all contact with their previous residence, especially where their relatives have moved away. The situation is that it is the local authority in which the patient was ordinarily resident before he moved to hospital which is respon-sible for providing the appropriate accommodation. For a dis-cussion on establishing the district of residence in relation to the purchasing function of the health authority see Chapter 23.

CHOICE OF ACCOMMODATION

It is important for the rights of individuals that they are not transferred against their will to accommodation over which they have had no choice. The assessment process should take into account the views as well as the needs of clients and the right of the client to choose has been the subject of formal directions.

Choice of Accommodation Directions

When a local authority decides to make arrangements for resi-dential accommodation for someone with preserved rights the National Assistance Act 1948 (Choice of Accommodation) Dir-ections 1992 permit the resident choice of a home. However the choice is subject to the regulations and these directions could not be used by a resident to require the local authority to make a placement in the same home from which he is threatened with eviction. The text of part of the directions is shown in Figure 28.4.

Figure 28.4 National Assistance Act 1948 (Choice of Accommodation) Directions 1992

Local authorities to provide preferred accommodation

2. Where a local authority have assessed a person under section 47 of the National Health Service and Community Care Act 1990 (assessment) and have decided that accommodation should be provided pursuant to section 21 of the National Assistance Act 1948 (provision of residential accommodation), the local authority shall, subject to paragraph 3 of these Directions, make arrangements for accommodation pursuant to section 21 for that person at the place of his choice within *England and Wales* [note the Directions extend only to England] (in these Directions called 'preferred accommodation') if he has indicated that he wishes to be accommodated in preferred accommodation.

Conditions for provision of preferred accommodation

3. Subject to paragraph 4 of these Directions the local authority shall only be required to make or continue to make arrangements for a person to be accommodated in his preferred accommodation if —

(a) the preferred accommodation appears to the authority to be suitable in relation to his needs as assessed by them;

(b) the cost of making arrangements for him at his preferred accommodation would not require the authority to pay more than they would usually expect to pay having regard to his assessed needs;

(c) the preferred accommodation is available;

(d) the persons in charge of the preferred accommodation provide it subject to the authority's usual terms and conditions, having regard to the nature of the accommodation, for providing accommodation for such a person under Part III of the National Assistance Act 1948.

Preferred Accommodation outside local authority's usual limit

4(1) [the cost restriction paragraph 3(b) above does not apply if a third party's contribution makes up the amount required]

(2) [paragraph 3(b) does apply if the third party's contributions are made by a spouse or parent]

(3) Nothing in these Directions shall prevent a local authority from making or continuing to make arrangements for a person to be accommodated in his preferred accommodation where the cost of making such arrangements is more that the local authority would usually expect to pay having regard to the person's assessed needs.

Guidance accompanying the directions[4] makes it clear that the purpose behind the Directions is to ensure that when social services make placements in residential care and nursing homes people are able to exercise a genuine choice over where they live. The guidance covers the suitability of the accommodation, the cost, the availability, the conditions and the possibility of more expensive accommodation where a third party is paying. The guidance also suggests that, where prospective residents are unable to express a preference for themselves, it would be reasonable to expect authorities to act on the preferences expressed by their carers in the same way that they would on the resident's own wishes (unless exceptionally that would be against the best interests of the resident).

Case: R v. Avon Country Council, ex parte M[5]

The decision of the local authority on choice of accommodation was challenged in a recent case when a 22 year old man with Down's syndrome sought judicial review of Avon County Council's decision that he be placed in a particular residential home. He preferred to live in a different home and his preference had been supported by the authority's independently chaired review panel. He satisfied the requirements under the National Assistance Act 1948 (Choice of Accommodation) Directions 1992 (that is, it was suitable to his needs, the cost was not over the limit of what the local authority would usually expect to pay, and the preferred accommodation was available). The Court held that, in determining what his current needs were, this included his psychological needs – as the panel had correctly identified. The expert evidence showed that his determined aversion to the authority's proposed placement was not simply a whim, but an aspect of his psychological needs, contributed to by his Down's syndrome. Therefore, to place him in his preferred choice of accommodation would not be to satisfy a mere whim but, in fact, be to fulfil his needs. The authority could not overrule the panel's recommendation without a substantial reason. It appeared to have given the recommendation insufficient weight and its decision was quashed.

The independent panel is part of the complaints mechanism which each local authority is statutorily obliged to set up (see Chapter 27). This case shows that the local authority must have very good reasons before it is justified in going against the recommendations of its independent panel.

Case: *R v. North Yorkshire County Council, ex parte Hargreaves*[6]

In another challenge to a local authority which failed to take into account the preference expressed in relation to the location of respite care the court allowed the application for judicial review of the decision. The facts were that the applicant sought judicial review of the decision by the County Council which offered placements for respite care which did not accord with the choices of his sister, who suffered from physical and mental handicap. The court held that the Council had assumed that the preferences of the client were the same as those of the applicant, which the Council was not entitled to do. There might be circumstances in which it was quite impossible to ascertain the preferences of the user and/or carer, for example, if there was a wilful lack of co-operation or if the user or carer suffered from a disability which prevented communication. That was not, however, the case here, where the sister had her own views.

Choice of accommodation and the mentally incapacitated adult

Pending the implementation of the Law Commission's recommendations on decision making on behalf of the mentally incapacitated adult[7] there is at present no person who has the legal right to determine in which accommodation an incapacitated adult should be housed. Reference would usually be made to relatives and in some circumstances they may agree to top up the payments. It could happen, as in a guardianship order or order for detention under the Mental Health Act 1983, that persons are directed to live in particular establishments to which they have been unable to give a valid consent and yet they must contribute to the fees levied.

MANAGEMENT OF PREMISES AND STANDARDS OF ACCOMMODATION

Section 23 of the National Assistance Act 1948 is unchanged by the 1990 Act and is shown in Figure 28.5.

Figure 28.5 The National Assistance Act 1948 – section 23

(1) Subject to the provisions of this Part of this Act, a local authority may make rules as to the conduct of premises under their management in which accommodation is provided under this Part of this Act and as to the preservation of order in the premises.

(2) Rules under this section may provide that where by reason of any change in a person's circumstances he is no longer qualified to receive accommodation under this Part of this Act or where a person has otherwise become unsuitable therefor, he may be required by the local authority managing the premises to leave the premises in which the accommodation is provided.

(3) Rules under this section may provide for the waiving of part of the payment due under the last foregoing section [charges to be made for accommodation] where in compliance with the rules persons for whom accommodation is provided assist in the running of the premises.

Where a person is evicted from one home it may still be the local authority's responsibility to find accommodation elsewhere (see below in discussion on home closure) and in extreme cases the provisions for the homeless (not covered by this book) come into play.

VOLUNTARY ORGANISATIONS AND AGENCY ARRANGEMENTS

One of the main philosophies in the introduction of community care was to enable local authorities to purchase accommodation from a wider range of organisations than was previously possible.

Section 26 of the National Assistance Act 1948 enabled the provision of accommodation in premises maintained by voluntary organisations. Section 26(1) has been amended by the 1990 Act which in turn is amended by the Community Care (Residential Accommodation) Act 1992. The amended section is shown in Figure 28.6.

Figure 28.6 National Assistance Act 1948 – section 26 (as amended)

(1) Subject to subsection (1A) and (1B) of this section, arrangements under section 21 of this Act may include arrangements with a voluntary organisation or with any other person who is not a local authority where —

(a) that organisation or person manages premises which provide for reward accommodation falling within subsection (1)(a) or (aa) of that section, and
(b) the arrangements are for the provision of such accommodation in those premises.

(1A) Subject to subsection (1B) below, arrangements made with any voluntary organisation or other person by virtue of this section must, if they are for the provision of residential accommodation with both board and personal care for such persons as are mentioned in section 1(1) of the Registered Homes Act 1984 (requirement for registration), be arrangements for the provision of such accommodation in a residential care home which is managed by the organisation or person in question, being such a home in respect of which that organisation or person —

(a) is registered under Part I of that Act, or

(b) is not required to be so registered by virtue of section 1(4)(a) or (b) of that Act (certain small homes) or by virtue of the home being managed or provided by an exempt body;

and for this purpose 'personal care' and 'residential care home' have the same meaning as in that Part of that Act.

(1B) Arrangements made with any voluntary organisation or other person by virtue of this section must, if they are for the provision of residential accommodation where nursing care is provided, be arrangements for the provision of such accommodation in premises which are managed by the organisation or person in question, being premises —

(a) in respect of which that organisation or person is registered under Part II of the Registered Homes Act 1984, or

(b) which, by reason only of being maintained or controlled by an exempt body, do not fall within the definition of a nursing home in section 21 of that Act.

[subsections (1C) and (1D) are discussed below]

The effect of the provisions shown in Figure 28.6 is that the flexibility of the local authority to make appropriate arrangements for residential care which had been inadvertently curtailed by the amending provisions in section 42(2) of the 1990 Act has been restored. The original provisions required the local authority to provide accommodation which came under the Registered Homes Act 1984 (or were exempt). This prevented the social services departments making arrangements for accommodation such as that provided by the Abbeyfield Society which did not provide personal care.

Local authorities now possess a general power to make arrangements with the independent sector for the provision of accommodation. Where the arrangements include the provision of personal care or nursing care then the premises must be registered under the Registered Homes Act 1984 (see Chapter 29) unless they are exempt under that Act.

Guidance to local social services departments on the purchasing of residential and nursing home care was given in 1992[8].

The powers of the local authority in relation to contracting for places with the independent sector under section 26(1) of the National Assistance Act 1948 as amended by section 42 of the 1990 Act have come under judicial scrutiny.

Case: R v. *Cleveland County Council, ex parte Ward*[9]

A decision by a local authority not to fund a placement in a nursing home, came under scrutiny in an application for judicial review brought against Cleveland County Council. Mrs Ward was 72 years and had been admitted to South Cleveland hospital with two fractured vertebrae. When she was about to be discharged she was assessed by the Council as being in need of nursing care. She decided that she would prefer to go to accommodation at Elton Hall on her discharge. The owner of the home failed to provide full information to the Council on his accounts and was told that until the full audited accounts were submitted Elton Hall would not be placed on the approved list of providers being compiled by the local authority. As a result he would not be able to contract with them for the provision of care services. Thus Mrs Ward was informed that she could not go to Elton Hall as the proprietor did not have a contract with Cleveland County Council. She was, however, admitted to Elton Hall but the County Council was not paying for her accommodation. The action was brought by Mrs Ward to seek judicial review of the Council's refusal to fund the place.

The judge held that, in taking the course it did, the local authority was not acting *ultra vires* the Act (see glossary), and he was satisfied that it was entitled to require the proprietor to supply full accounts for Elton Hall when he submitted his tender. Nor was the Council acting unreasonably in the *Wednesbury* sense (see glossary). Mrs Ward's application was therefore refused.

Case: *R* v. *Newcastle upon Tyne City Council, ex parte Dixon*[10]
The second case was brought against Newcastle upon Tyne City Council. The Council was the registration authority under the 1984 Act and, with the aid of a substantial government grant, provided by arrangement with the operators of those homes a large number of residential and nursing home care places. The Council negotiated individually with the operator of each registered residential care home a suitable placement for each person the Council wished to provide with residential or nursing care. It established a list of residential care home operators registered under the 1984 Act with whom it was prepared to contract for the provision of such accommodation. The applicants, who were operators of homes registered under the 1984 Act, wished to be included on the list. The form of contract insisted on by the Council required the home to be and to remain registered under the Act and imposed on the operator obligations additional to those imposed on him by virtue of the registration. The applicants'

concern was that the contract should not conflict with the detailed and precise provisions of the 1984 Act, which they maintained it did by the mixing of statutory standards and contractual requirements in the standard form, and that it should not be uncertain as to the respective operation of, and relationship between, the two.

The court held that the contractual arrangements did not affect the operation to the 1984 Act or curtail the rights it gave to those registered under it. There was no public law duty on councils to the home owners with whom they made arrangements to provide such services; the contracts were ones for public works within the meaning of section 17 of the Local Government Act 1988 into which the councils were obliged to enter on a commercial basis. There was no reason, in law, why an authority should not impose a stricter contractual régime on operators through which it fulfils its community care duties under the 1948 Act than that provided by the 1948 Act for purpose. The requirements were neither *ultra vires* the power of the local authority (see glossary) nor were they contrary to the principles of reasonableness as set out in the *Wednesbury* case[11] (see glossary).

CO-OPERATION BETWEEN LOCAL AUTHORITY AND NHS AUTHORITIES

There is a statutory requirement for the health authority to be involved in the assessment before a person can be transferred to nursing home accommodation (section 26(1C) of the National Assistance Act 1948 as amended) unless an urgent situation exists (section 26(1D)) in which case the assessment must follow soon after. These are set out in Figure 28.7.

Figure 28.7 The National Assistance Act 1948 – section 26(1C) and (1D) (as amended).

(1C) Subject to subsection (1D) below, no such arrangements as are mentioned in subsection (1B) above may be made by an authority for the accommodation of any person without the consent of such Health Authority as may be determined in accordance with regulations.

(1D) Subsection (1C) above does not apply to the making by an authority of temporary arrangements for the accommodation of any person as a matter of urgency; but, as soon as practicable after any such temporary arrangements have been made, the authority shall seek the consent required by subsection (1C) above to the making of appropriate arrangements for the accommodation of the person concerned.

Co-operation between health authority and local authority in the making of arrangements for persons to enter nursing homes is secured by these provisions. (See Chapters 23 and 25 for comparable obligations to co-operate on assessments for care in the community.) A health authority must give its consent before a person may be placed in a nursing home with local authority financial support. The regulations referred to in section 1C follow the current purchasing/contracting line, that is the health authority responsible is the one where the person is usually resident. If there is doubt about where a person is usually resident, a person is treated as usually resident in one of the following places:

- the address which he gives as being that at which he usually resides;
- where he gives no such address, the address which he gives as his most recent address;
- where his address cannot be determined under the above, the region or district in which he is at present.

Circular LAC(92)22 suggests what local arrangements should be put in place to ensure that the health authority gives consent for a person to go into a nursing home. Although provider unit staff will probably have been involved in the assessment of the individual, the consent is required from the purchaser. The health authority consent is not required in advance of a local authority making urgent temporary arrangements to place a person in a nursing home. However once the placement has been made, such consent needs to be sought as soon as practicable thereafter.

As discussed above, the local authority is required to give a person a choice about the nursing home into which he goes and the guidance points out that

> Except in exceptional circumstances, where the choice of care was thought by the DHA [since 1 April 1996 the Health Authority] not to be appropriate to a person's assessed needs, a DHA would be expected not to interfere with an individual's choice.

Some concern has been expressed about this provision since in the absence of directions relating to assessment, there is no statutory requirement for the local authority to involve the health authority in the assessment of a person in the community where no nursing care is contemplated. (If the provision of health services is contemplated, the health authority must be involved in the assessment under section 47(3) of the 1990 Act – see Chapter 23). Owners fear that an inadequate assessment may be carried out and nursing accommodation not recommended because of the absence of a nurse in the assessment process. Clearly there could also be a financial saving to the authority since a place in a nursing home would be more costly. (For further discussion on the statutory duty to make assessments see Chapter 25.)

EXCLUSION OF POWERS TO ACCOMMODATE

Section 26A of the National Assistance Act 1948 as amended by the National Health Service and Community Care Act 1990 prohibits the local authority from making residential accommodation arrangements for people who, on 31 March 1993, were in residential care or nursing homes registered under the Registered Homes Act 1984, or in homes exempt from registration because they are managed or provided by an exempt body – 'relevant premises'. The effect of this provision is that such persons continue to be entitled to receive social security higher level income support, subject to financial eligibility, and will continue to do so under the aegis of the DSS until they die or leave residential/ nursing home accommodation. The rights that they thereby acquired through such occupation are known as 'preserved rights' and will remain with them to death unless they come within the categories described below.

Whilst the basic principle appears fairly clear, there are many categories of individuals who do not fall neatly into this picture and the Act enabled regulations to be drawn up to identify the anomalous situations where the responsibilities remain with the DSS and where they are taken over by the local authority. For example a person who was temporarily absent (defined in detail in the regulations) from the home on 31 March 1993 is still to be treated as ordinarily resident there on the date and therefore entitled to preserved rights.

Some of the questions raised by this change are considered below, but see the Regulations[12] for the details and see also Chapter 33.

■ What about people without preserved rights or who lose their preserved rights?

The example given of this category of client are those in small residential care homes (for less than four people) who have not satisfied the current criteria for the higher levels of income support. Strictly, they would encounter difficulties if they need to seek local authority support at some future stage, for instance to enter a different home because their care needs have altered, but Regulation 5 enables a local authority to make the appropriate arrangements.

■ What if clients are in homes owned or managed by close relatives?

Before 31 March 1993 these people were not entitled to income support at the higher rate. Local authorities can now make residential accommodation arrangements for such persons in homes of a close relative under Regulation 5. This is, however, subject to the provisions of section 21 of the National Assistance Act 1948 which permits the local authority to provide accommodation only in specific circumstances and accommodation with close relatives might not meet these requirements. Should such persons move to another registered home or the home was taken over by a non-relative then the individual would then have entitlement to higher level income support and the local authority would not be able to make arrangements for residential accommodation.

■ What if people over pensionable age in independent sector residential care homes move, or face home closure or eviction?

Regulations 8 and 9 provide that local authorities will be able to make arrangements for the above categories. If it were not for this provision, such groups would be prevented from benefiting from local authorities' arrangements as a result of section 26A.

Once a local authority has made arrangements for a person to be placed in residential accommodation Regulation 9(1) enables the local authority to make arrangements for the person to be placed in a nursing home, if necessary. If, following placement in a nursing home, they are evicted the local authority can only make further arrangements in accommodation which is not owned or managed by the person or organisation which owns or manages the home (Regulation 9(2)). This rule is to prevent undue pressure being placed upon local authorities to provide funding for residents with preserved rights. This does not apply where the home closes.

Closure of nursing home or eviction of resident

The Department's view generally is that the onus is on the following to find alternative accommodation:

● the health authority where the health authority has purchased the nursing home place;

● the resident or their relatives, with help from the home owner.

From 1 April 1993 local authorities were able to assist nursing home residents in such circumstances to find alternative accommodation using their preserved rights and any other resources available to them.

It is recommended that local authorities should draw up with health authorities plans and protocols in the event that a nursing home is closed or a resident is evicted.

CONTRACTUAL RESPONSIBILITIES OF LOCAL AUTHORITIES

Where the local authority assists a person with preserved rights its obligations are the same as those that would apply if a place were being arranged for that person for the first time. This means that an assessment must be carried out unless the provisions for urgent cases apply. The advice suggests that when making a placement in an independent sector home, the authority should contract for the full cost of the accommodation even though the amount of income support it will be able to recover through charging will be higher than for other people because of the preserved rights.

Methods of payment

Section 26(3A) enables residents for whom authorities are responsible in independent sector homes to pay their assessed contributions, as calculated by the local authority, direct to the proprietor of the home. The proprietor, the authority and the resident must all agree to this method of payment. Should the resident fail to pay the appropriate amount, the local authority would have to pay the full amount.

Person with convictions under the Registered Homes Act

Section 42 of the 1990 Act as amended by the Community Care (Residential Accommodation) Act 1992 inserts subsection (1E) into section 26A of the National Assistance Act 1948 which precludes contractual relations under the section with those who have been convicted of an offence under:

● the Registered Homes Act 1984 or equivalent legislation; or

● regulations under that Act.

Community Care plans

Each local authority has a statutory responsibility to prepare a community care plan in conjunction with health authorities and following consultation with a wide variety of organisations. The full details of this statutory responsibility are set out in Chapter 25 but it should be noted that this community care plan should also include the necessity to purchase places in residential care homes and nursing homes. Shortfalls in current purchasing plans for accommodation should be identified and included in the revised plan for the next year. All staff involved in the assessments for community care should ensure that they feed information into the discussions on revision for the following year.

CONCLUSIONS

It is inevitable that there will be some fine tuning of the rules relating to the provision of accommodation and in determining the actual duties of local authorities. Already there is some concern that there is abuse of the fact that local authorities are purchasing places for people to look after their own relatives at home.

CHAPTER 29

Registered homes 1: residential homes

The 1980s have witnessed a rapid increase in the number of registered homes, nursing and residential. The increase in the numbers of elderly as a proportion of the population and the closure of long-stay beds in the National Health Service have increased the demand for residential and nursing home accommodation in the community. Prior to 1 April 1993 this development was encouraged by the fact that, provided that a resident was eligible on financial criteria to receive higher level income support payments from the department of social security and a place was available, no further assessment was required. As a result the availability of social security provision provided an incentive in favour of residential or nursing home accommodation, even when support in the community for clients in their own homes might have been preferable.

LOCAL AUTHORITY FUNCTIONS UNDER THE 1990 ACT

One of the main purposes of the National Health Service and Community Care Act 1990 was to destroy this incentive by placing responsibility for the state funding of places in registered care and nursing homes after 31 March 1993 upon local authorities. This, together with the statutory duty to make an assessment of the client prior to admission to a home, should ensure that all the alternative options to residential or nursing home accommodation are reviewed before the client is transferred to a home. The development of more services within the community should enable clients to stay in their own homes. The assessment process should determine both the individual needs of the client

480

and also the existence of services to meet those needs. The local authority can means-test the client to determine the contribution (if any) the client must make towards the cost.

The local authority has the following functions:

- It has a statutory duty to assess the client (together with the health services where this is indicated). This duty is discussed in Chapter 25.

- It has a power or duty to provide, either by direct provision or through purchase, places in residential or nursing home accommodation (see Chapter 28).

- It has a duty to register and inspect residential accommodation under the Registered Homes Act 1984.

This last duty is the subject of this chapter. The registration of nursing homes and mental nursing homes is considered in Chapter 30 and the Registered Homes Tribunal, offences under the 1984 Act and duties in relation to inspection and quality control are discussed in Chapter 31.

The relevant statutes

Under the National Assistance Act 1948 section 21 (as amended by the 1990 Act) the local authority may or shall according to the directions of the Secretary of State provide accommodation as set out in Figure 28.2.

The Community Care (Residential Accommodation) Act 1992 amended the amended section 26 of the National Assistance Act 1948 to enable provision to be made even when personal care was not required, thus protecting the Abbeyfield Society (see page 472).

The Registered Homes Act 1984 and its subsequent regulations sets the framework for the control and inspection of residential homes. This chapter looks at the provisions of Part I of the Registered Homes Act 1984 and covers the topics shown in Figure 29.1.

Figure 29.1 Topics covered in this chapter

The registration process
- Definition of residential care home
- Registration provisions
- Procedure for registration
- Certificate of registration and publicity

Administrative matters
- Death of person registered
- Inspection of registers
- Powers of registration authority

Refusal and cancellation of registration
- Refusal by authority to register
- Cancellation of registration
- Urgent cancellation provisions

Representations and appeals
- Right to make representations
- Appeals and appeals procedure

Regulations and inspection
- Regulations by Secretary of State
- Inspection of residential care homes

Small residential care homes

Residential care homes, community care and the future

THE REGISTRATION PROCESS

Definition of residential care homes

For the purposes of the 1984 Act a residential care home is

> any establishment which provides or is intended to provide, whether for reward or not, residential accommodation with both board and personal care for persons in need of personal care by reason of old age, disablement, past or present dependence on alcohol or drugs, or past or present mental disorder. (section 1(1))

Under the Registered Homes Act 1984 any such establishment was required to register unless the number of persons provided with both board and personal care is less than four. The number four excludes those who manage the home or who are employed there and their relatives (section 1(4)). However, in 1991 an Amendment Act was passed to provide a modified form of regulatory control for homes with fewer than four residents (see below page 492).

Registration provisions

Unless excluded under section 1(5) (specific exclusions such as hospitals and universities) any such establishment with four or more persons must be registered. To carry on a residential care home without registration is an offence (section 2). (Note that establishments with fewer than four residents are subject to the 1991 Act (see below page 492).)

■ What if the owner is separate from the person in control?

Registration is personal as well as of the premises and section 3 provides that where the manager or intended manager of a residential care home is not in control of it (whether as owner or otherwise) both the manager or intended manager and the person in control are to be treated as carrying on or intending to carry on the home and accordingly are required to be registered under the Act.

Procedure for registration

1. The applicant should apply to the registration authority, which is the social services authority, with the approved fee.
2. The authority can then register the applicant in respect of the home named in the application.
3. A certificate of registration is then issued.
4. The registration can be for a specific number of residents and on conditions imposed by the authority.

Section 12 sets out further procedures which are shown in Figure 29.2.

Figure 29.2 Procedures in registration – section 12 (summarised)

- Where a person applies for registration and the authority intend to grant the application, the authority shall give him written notice of their proposal and of the conditions subject to which they propose to grant his application.
- This requirement for the notice of the proposal does not apply if the only conditions have either been specified by the applicant in the application or have been subsequently agreed between applicant and authority.
- The authority must give notice of a proposal to refuse the application.
- Notice must be given to any person registered in respect of a residential care home of a proposal to
  (a) cancel the registration;
  (b) vary any condition; or
  (c) impose any additional condition.
  This does not apply where the authority applies to a justice of the peace under section 11 (see below)
- Any notice must give the authority's reasons for the proposal.

Certificate of registration and publicity

The certificate of registration must be fixed in a conspicuous place in the home (section 5(6)).

ADMINISTRATIVE MATTERS

Death of person registered

If only one person is registered in respect of the residential care home and that person dies, the personal representatives or widow or any other relative can carry on the home without being registered for a period not exceeding four weeks from his death. The authority has the power to sanction a longer period (section 6).

Inspection of registers

The registers kept by the authority shall be kept available for inspection at all reasonable times. Any person inspecting any register shall be entitled to make copies of entries in the register on payment of such reasonable fee as the registration authority may determine.

Powers of registration authority

The registration authority has the following powers:

- To register on conditions
- To refuse to register (section 9)
- To cancel a registration (section 10)
- To cancel the registration with immediate effect (section 11)
- To inspect (section 17).

REFUSAL AND CANCELLATION OF REGISTRATION

Refusal of authority to register

The authority can refuse to register if they are satisfied of the conditions shown in Figure 29.3.

Figure 29.3 Grounds for refusing to register – section 9

The registration authority may refuse to register an applicant for registration in respect of a residential care home if they are satisfied —

(a) that he or any other person concerned or intended to be concerned in carrying on the home is not a fit person to be concerned in carrying on a residential care home;

(b) that for reasons connected with their situation, construction, state of repair, accommodation, staffing, or equipment, the premises used or intended to be used for the purpose of the home, or any other premises used or intended to be used in connection with it, are not fit to be so used; or

(c) that the way in which it is intended to carry on the home is such as not to provide services or facilities reasonably required.

This section has been interpreted in an unrestrictive way as can be seen in the following case.

Case: *Isle of Wight County Council* v. *Humphreys*[13]

In this case the certificate of registration permitted the provision of residential accommodation for nine residents. It was subsequently varied on two occasions so that the number of residents that could be cared for was increased to 16. The proprietors then applied to vary the registration and increase the number to 23. The Council refused the application because they considered that there was no need for increased residential care provisions in the area. The proprietors appealed under section 5 of the Registered Homes Act 1984. The Registered Homes Tribunal decided that the Council had erred in law and should only have regard to the matters listed in section 9 of the Registered Homes Act 1984. The Council appealed.

The Queens Bench Division allowed the appeal on the grounds that section 9 of the Act provided the reasons for refusing an application for registration as a residential care home; but, where the application for registration was accepted, the Act made no provision as to the criteria to be applied when imposing conditions. The power to vary conditions was subject to as wide a discretion as the power to impose conditions on registration, and accordingly a registration authority, in considering whether to vary a condition of registration, was not bound to base their decision on criteria provided for in section 9 of the Act.

Cancellation of registration

The grounds for the cancellation of registration are shown in Figure 29.4.

Figure 29.4 Cancellation of registration – section 10

The registration authority may cancel the registration of a person in respect of a residential care home —

(a) On any ground which would entitle them to refuse an application for his registration in respect of it;

(b) on the ground that the annual fee in respect of the home has not been paid on or before the due date; or

(c) on the ground —
  (i) that he has been convicted of an offence under this Part of this Act or any regulations made under it in respect of that or any other residential care home;

(ii) that any other person has been convicted of such an offence in respect of that home; or

(iii) that any condition for the time being in force in respect of the home by virtue of this Part of this Act has not been complied with.

The ground for the cancellation of registration was discussed in the following case.

Case: *Harrison v. Cornwall County Council*[14]

The registration conditions for the residential accommodation provided by Mrs Harrison was that the number of persons for whom residential accommodation with both board and personal care was provided in the home at any one time was not to exceed eight. The county council made a proposal to cancel the registration on the ground that she had persistently disregarded the condition of registration concerning the number of residents and that she was not a fit person to be concerned in the carrying on of a residential care home. Mrs Harrison appealed to a Registered Homes Tribunal.

The tribunal held that personal care as defined in section 29(1) of the 1984 Act was not restricted to the provision of assistance with bodily functions but embraced emotional and psychiatric as well as physical care and the two of the residents in question were in need of and provided with personal care. The cancellation of the registration was upheld.

Mrs Harrison appealed to the Queens Bench Division and her appeal was allowed. The High Court held that the tribunal's interpretation of the definition of personal care was wrong. Personal care was defined in terms of assistance with bodily functions; if that was not provided, the establishment was not providing personal care within the meaning of the Act.

The Council appealed to the Court of Appeal which allowed the appeal. The Court of Appeal held that the definition of personal care was not exhaustive and was not confined to the requirement or provision of assistance with bodily functions and, accordingly, the tribunal was correct in its construction of the section. Nor did the Court of Appeal hold that the tribunal was obliged to keep her registration on foot on the ground that cancelling it would inevitably result in disruption of the lives of the residents. The decision of the tribunal was restored.

Urgent cancellation provisions

In extreme circumstances the authority can apply to a justice of the peace for an order cancelling the registration, or varying or imposing conditions on the registration. If the justice of the peace grants the order it comes into effect from the date the order is made. The justice of the peace must be satisfied 'that there will be a serious risk to the life, health or well-being of the residents of the home unless the order is made' (section 11).

The section has been the subject of judicial consideration.

Case: *Hillingdon London Borough Council* v. *McClean*[15]

The Borough Council had registered the property in February 1987 subject to a condition that there should be in the home no more that 17 elderly people who should not be severely elderly, handicapped or confused. On 1 May 1987 the registration authority applied for the cancellation of the registration under section 11(1)(a) of the Registered Homes Act 1984 following a warning from the fire department that insufficient staff supervision meant that the fire hazard presented a serious risk. The justices cancelled the registration on the ground that there was a serious risk to the life, health or well-being of the residents in the home. The proprietor appealed to the Tribunal who found in her favour on the grounds that although there was a risk of fire that amounted to a serious risk it was not a serious risk such as to justify the closure of the home. The registration authority appealed to the High Court on the grounds that the Tribunal had erred in law. The High Court upheld the decision of the Tribunal on the following grounds:

> The question to be decided was not whether there was a serious risk, but whether the risk that there was, was such as to justify cancellation of the registration and thereby the closure of the home, that being the standard by which to decide whether there was a serious risk as defined in the Act; and that if the risk justified closure of the home then it was axiomatic that it was a serious risk in the terms of the Act.

The procedure for making an application under section 11 is that it should be supported by a written statement of the registration authority's reasons for making the application.

The order of the justice of the peace must be in writing (section 11(3)) and the registration authority must, as soon as practicable after the making of the order, serve the following documents on any person registered in respect of the home:

- the notice of the making of the order and its terms; and
- a copy of the statement of the authority's reasons which supported their application (section 11(4)).

REPRESENTATIONS AND APPEALS

Right to make representations

The applicant or registered person can make representations where he has been served with a notice under section 12 above. The notice must state that within 14 days of the service of the notice any person on whom it is served may in writing require the registration authority to give him an opportunity to make representations to them concerning the matter.

If a section 12 notice has been served the authority cannot conclude the matter until either

- any person on whom the notice was served has made representations concerning the matter; or
- the period given to any such person for him to require an opportunity to make representations has elapsed without such a request being made; or
- having requested an opportunity to make representations, the person concerned has failed to do so within the reasonable time allowed to him for that purpose by the registration authority.

Representations can be made either orally or in writing at the option of the person making them (section 13(4)). If he wishes to make them orally he should be given an opportunity of appearing before and of being heard by a committee or subcommittee of the registration authority (section 13(5)).

Appeals and appeal procedure

When decisions take effect

If the authority decides to grant the application where the conditions (if any) are agreed or refuses an application for registration, the decision will take immediate effect. In other cases the decision of the authority does not take effect until,

- if no appeal is brought, the expiration of the period of 28 days for making the appeal, or
- if an appeal is brought, it is determined or abandoned (section 14(3)).

Procedure for appeals
These can be made to a Registered Homes Tribunal against a decision of a registration authority or an order made by a justice of the peace under section 11 (section 15). The details are set out in Figure 29.5.

Figure 29.5 Regulations relating to appeals

1. An appeal shall be brought by notice in writing to the registration authority.
2. It must be brought within 28 days after the service of the notice of the decision or order.
3. The tribunal can confirm the decision of an authority or direct that it shall not have effect.
4. The tribunal can confirm the order of a justice of the peace or direct that it shall cease to have effect.
5. The tribunal can also:
   (a) vary any conditions for the time being in force in respect of the home to which the appeal relates;
   (b) direct that any such condition shall cease to have effect; or
   (c) direct that any condition as it thinks fit shall have effect in respect of the home.

Subject to judicial review on a point of law the registration authority must comply with any direction given by a tribunal under this section (section 15).

The scope of this procedure is limited to cases where the authority takes away a pre-existing entitlement to registration by cancellation or the imposition or variation of conditions.

Case: *Coomb and another* v. *Hertfordshire County Council*[16]

The proprietors of a home had had their application to increase the certificate from 11 permitted residents to 12 turned down. They appealed under section 15(2) to the Registered Homes Tribunal which said that it had no jurisdiction to hear the appeal. The proprietors appealed to the High Court who dismissed the appeal on the ground that there was no provision in the Act for an appeal against the registration authority's refusal to vary the conditions where the proposal to vary had been made by the proprietor rather that by the registration authority.

Appeal also lies to the Queens Bench Division of the High Court by way of a judicial review of the decisions of the registration authority. An example of a case heard in the Queens Bench Division is given below.

Case: *R v. Humberside County Council, ex parte Bogdal*[17]

In this case a residential care home had been registered under the Registered Homes Act 1984 because its running was entrusted to the management of a company regarded as a fit person for the purposes of the Act. The Company was called Care by Design and it specialised in running care homes. Registration had been agreed for the home on the understanding that the applicant would play only a subsidiary and background role in the running of the home which was to be the responsibility of the company acting through a manager and an assistant. Following a disagreement the company ceased to act as managers and the applicant was informed by notice under section 12(4)(a) of the Act that registration was cancelled as she was no longer a fit person. The notice set out her right to make written and oral representations. This she did in September 1989, the issue being that nothing had occurred, since her acceptance on registration, to render her no longer fit. Arrangements were made for her to appear before the subcommittee on 4 January 1990, rearranged on 15 January 1990, adjourned at her request and refixed for 9 February 1990.

In the meantime she applied for judicial review. The applicant's barrister argued that section 9(a) concerning fitness of a person, section 9(b) fitness of the premises and section 9(c) the way intended to carry on the home, were quite separate. This view was not accepted by the court who held that it could well be that the way that it was intended to carry on a home under section 9(c) might influence the way an authority decided fitness of a person under section 9(a). The departure of the managing company from the home could justify the authority in cancelling the registration. The applicant therefore lost her appeal.

REGULATIONS AND INSPECTION

Regulations by the Secretary of State

Under section 16 the Secretary of State has the power to make regulations on all the matters set out in Figure 29.6.

Figure 29.6 Regulations under section 16

The Secretary of State may make regulations as to the conduct of residential care homes, and in particular —

(a) as to the facilities and services to be provided in such homes;
(b) as to the number and qualifications of staff to be employed in such homes;

(c) as to the numbers of suitably qualified and competent staff to be on duty in such homes;

(d) as to the records to be kept and notices to be given in respect of persons received in such homes;

(e) as to the notification of events occurring in such homes;

(f) as to the giving of notice by a person of a description specified in the regulations of periods during which any person of a description so specified proposes to be absent from a home;

(g) as to the information to be supplied in such a notice;

(h) making provision for children under the age of 18 years who are resident in such homes to receive a religious upbringing appropriate to the religious persuasion to which they belong;

(j) as to the form of registers to be kept by registration authorities for the purposes of this Part of this Act and the particulars to be contained in them; and

(k) as to the information to be supplied on an application for registration.

Regulations have been issued covering all these points.

Inspection of residential care homes

This is an extremely important weapon of the registration authority in maintaining standards and compliance with the conditions of registration and the rules relating to inspections are found in section 17 (see Figure 29.7).

Figure 29.7 Inspections by authorities – section 17

(1) Any person authorised in that behalf by the Secretary of State may at all times enter and inspect any premises which are used, or which that person has reasonable cause to believe to be used, for the purposes of a residential home.

(2) Any person authorised in that behalf by a registration authority may at all times enter and inspect any premises in the area of the authority which are used, or which that person has reasonable cause to believe are to be used, for those purposes.

(3) The powers of inspection conferred by subsections (1) and (2) above shall include the power to inspect any records required to be kept in accordance with regulations under this Part of this Act. [see Chapter 30]

(4) The Secretary of State may by regulations require that residential care homes shall be inspected on such occasions or at such intervals as the regulations may prescribe.

(5) Any person proposing to exercise any power of entry or inspection under this section shall if so required produce some duly authenticated document showing his authority to exercise the power.

(6) Any person who obstructs the exercise of any such power shall be guilty of an offence.

SMALL RESIDENTIAL CARE HOMES

Under the Registered Homes Act 1984, private and voluntary residential care homes with less than four residents (as defined above) were exempt from registration. This exemption was removed by the Registered Homes (Amendment) Act 1991. New regulations modifying existing ones in their application to homes with less than four residents, excluding staff and their relatives, came into force on 1 April 1993. It is now an offence to operate an unregistered small residential care home which is not exempt from the requirement to register.

Guidance covers the following topics:

- registration and de-registration
- the 'lighter touch' for small homes
- staffing
- waiver or subsidy of fees
- fees on expansion to cater for four or more residents
- inspection and annual returns
- local authority registers and certification of registration
- adult placement, respite care and similar schemes
- members of religious communities
- occasional provision of care
- dual registration – nursing homes
- categories of residents catered for
- medicines
- application of other legislation to small homes
- publicity
- inspection

In summary the Registered Homes (Amendment) Act 1991 requires registration of almost all homes but the local authority can waive part or all of the registration fee, the certificate of registration need not be on public display, and registration may only be refused if a person involved in the running of the home is not a fit person to do so. There is provision for an annual return to be required by the Secretary of State to be sent to the local authority and failure to do so could lead to the cancellation of registration.

RESIDENTIAL CARE HOMES, COMMUNITY CARE AND THE FUTURE

One of the effects of the community care legislation is that the local authority has a dual role in relation to residential care homes. On the one hand it is the registration authority and therefore exercises all the powers and duties set out above. On the other hand, it is the purchaser of places in both residential care homes and nursing homes. As its contractual role expands standards are being developed for the basis of purchasing agreements which may well exceed those stipulated by the authority in its capacity as registration authority. This is justifiable. (See page 473 and the case of *Dixon*.) Proprietors and managers might protest, particularly if demands are increased without recognising the financial implications and enhancing the payments made by the authorities.

At the same time there is a government-led initiative to reduce the regulations to which such homes are subject. A paper for consultation was issued by the Department of Health in August 1994 putting forward proposals to improve the regulatory process. These proposals have been drafted in the light of responses from home owners, national organisations of care providers and the regulatory authorities[18].

The purposes of the amendments are:

- a reduction in paperwork;
- promoting local definition and consultation on standards and procedures, and hence fewer unwelcome surprises for providers;
- taking fuller account of other regulatory and monitoring pressures on providers;
- distinguishing more clearly between basic standards proper to statutory regulation and advice on other issues where change is optional;
- considering more carefully the degrees of attention justified for individual homes;
- promoting closer working between health and local authorities in the regulation of homes dually registered with both.

When finalised the new regulations will be issued under section 7(1) of the Local Authority Social Services Act 1970. It is intended to complement LAC(94)16 which strengthens the regulatory system by introducing lay assessors and enhancing the effectiveness and independence of inspectors.

Concern was expressed by Age Concern and other organisations at the suggestions for deregulating the registered homes in order to reduce the bureaucracy[19]. The extent to which the requirements under the statutory registration provisions can be simplified without at the same time endangering the standards of care provided for the residents will continue to be monitored very closely.

The consultation exercise was followed by NHS Management Executive Guidelines (HSG(95)41) published in September 1995, *Regulation of Nursing Homes and Independent Hospitals*. The circular aimed

> to promote sensible regulation of nursing homes and independent hospitals, without any loss of necessary safeguards for patients.

This is to be done mainly by:

- a reduction in paperwork,
- consistency of enforcement in practice within and between health authorities,
- transparency of arrangements so that home owners know what is expected of them and what enforcement action can be taken by the regulators, and
- targeting of enforcement action and co-ordination between the agencies.

It is not anticipated that new legislation will be required, but the Department of Health will continue to review the areas discussed in the circular.

The circular is reproduced as Appendix 5 to this book.

CHAPTER 30

Registered homes 2: nursing and mental nursing homes

One of the major effects of the National Health Service and Community Care Act 1990 is the reduction in NHS accommodation for long-stay chronically sick, mentally infirm and elderly persons and the care of such persons in non-NHS accommodation. The implications of this are that the patients (and/or their spouses) are means-tested towards the cost of the accommodation and will have to use their revenue and capital funds towards the cost of upkeep, subject to the eligibility for income support at the lower level. The general public are slowly waking to the fact that increasingly the cost of care is falling upon the individual client and not borne by the state through the NHS.

The picture is confusing because of the inconsistency between health purchasers over the extent to which they are purchasing long-stay NHS accommodation. In some areas arrangements are made for patients discharged from long-stay NHS accommodation to be accommodated in smaller community homes which remain NHS funded and therefore the residents are not required to make any contribution to the revenue costs; in other districts there is a paucity of such accommodation provided as part of the NHS but it is provided by the private or voluntary sector and, under the arrangements set up after 1 April 1993, local authorities hold the budget for purchasing places for those who are unable to pay for them fully from their own resources.

One successful NHS scheme was the three experimental homes projects funded by the Government which were opened in the early eighties to create a more positive environment for those who require publicly funded constant nursing care. One of these was the Jubilee House in Cosham, Portsmouth in Hampshire for 25 residents. Many of these have suffered strokes and are severely handicapped. However, they live in a domestic environment with maximum freedom and decision making. It is feared, however, that such projects have not been followed as the closure of long-stay beds and failure to provide more NHS homes is shifting financial responsibility for the elderly from the public sector to individuals and their families[20].

There had been a mushrooming of private nursing homes and mental nursing homes through the 1980s encouraged by the fact that prior to 1 April 1993 fees were automatically supported at the higher level income support rates (subject to means-testing) from social security without the necessity for an assessment as to the appropriateness of the client's need for such accommodation.

This growth has been pointed out in consecutive biennial reports of the Mental Health Act Commission which has suffered difficulties in that there is no obligation upon a registration authority to notify the Commission of a new registration of a home able to take detained patients, even though the Commission has a statutory duty to visit patients detained in such a home. The biennial reports discuss the problems in relation to mental nursing homes which are registered to take detained patients.

The registration authority for nursing homes is the health authority and the functions specified in the Act to be carried out by the Secretary of State are delegated to that health authority.

This chapter looks at the provisions of Part II of the Registered Homes Act 1984 which covers the registration provisions for nursing and mental nursing homes and also looks at some of the practical legal problems which have arisen with regard to the detention of patients in mental nursing homes. The topics set out in Figure 30.1 relating to registration under the 1989 Act will be considered in the first part of the chapter, then the matters relating specifically to mental nursing homes covered by the 1983 Act and finally the linked responsibilities of health and local authorities.

Figure 30.1 Topics to be covered in this chapter

Definitions
- Definition of nursing home and exclusions from that definition
- Definition of mental nursing home

The registration process
- The necessity for registration
- Procedure for registration
- Criminal convictions
- Refusal by the authority to register

Regulations and inspection
- Regulations
- Numbers in the home
- Inspection

Cancellation of registration
- Grounds for cancellation
- Urgent procedure for cancellation
- Non-urgent cancellations

Notice and representations
- Notice of registration and conditions
- Representations
- Notice of decision by Secretary of State

Appeals
- Powers of the tribunal

Miscellaneous points
- Death in a home
- Cancellation of registration or death of registered person
- Christian Science Homes
- Dual registration

DEFINITIONS

Definition of nursing home and exclusions from that definition

A nursing home is defined in section 21 (see Figure 30.2).

Figure 30.2 Definition of a nursing home – section 21

(a) any premises used, or intended to be used, for the reception of, and the provision of nursing for, persons suffering from any sickness, injury or infirmity;

(b) any premises used, or intended to be used, for the reception of pregnant women, or of women immediately after childbirth . . . [that is a maternity home]; and

(c) any premises not falling within either of the preceding paragraphs which are used, or intended to be used for the provision of all or any of the following services, namely —
  (i) the carrying out of surgical procedures under anaesthesia;
  (ii) the termination of pregnancies;
  (iii) endoscopy;
  (iv) haemodialysis or peritoneal dialysis;
  (vi) treatment by specially controlled techniques.

By section 21(4) and (5) the Secretary of State may issue regulations to make any technique of medicine or surgery (including cosmetic surgery) subject to control if he is satisfied that its use may create a hazard for persons treated or for staff at premises where the technique is used, and he can also define a technique by reference to any criteria he considers appropriate. Treatment includes diagnosis.

Exclusions from the definition of nursing home

These are set out in section 21(3) and exclude mental nursing homes and premises controlled by a government department or local authority or any other authority which has been instituted by special Act of Parliament or incorporated by Royal Charter. There is no, and never has been any, exclusion for small nursing homes which once existed in the case of small residential homes.

Definition of mental nursing home

This means any premises used, or intended to be used, for the reception of one or more mentally disordered patients (meaning persons suffering, or appearing to suffer, from mental disorder (see glossary)), and for the provision of nursing or other medical treatment (including care, habilitation and rehabilitation under medical supervision) for such persons whether exclusively or in common with others (section 22(1)).

The definition does not however include any hospital within the meaning of the NHS Act 1977 on any accommodation provided by a local authority and used as a hospital by or on behalf of the Secretary of State (section 22(2)).

THE REGISTRATION PROCESS

The necessity for registration

Any person who carries on a nursing home or a mental nursing home without being registered under Part II of the Act shall be guilty of an offence (section 23).

Registration under Part II of the Act does not affect the need to register under Part I.

Procedure for registration

1. The applicant must apply to the Secretary of State with the prescribed fee and, in the case of a mental nursing home, specify whether or not it is proposed to receive in the home patients who are liable to be detained under the provisions of the Mental Health Act 1983 (section 23(3)).
2. The Secretary of State shall register the applicant in respect of the home named in the application and shall issue a certificate of registration.
3. Where it is the intention to receive patients detained under the Mental Health Act, then that fact shall be specified in the certificate of registration and the particulars of registration shall be entered by the Secretary of State in a separate part of the register.

Publication of certificate

The certificate of registration shall be affixed in a conspicuous place in the home and, if default is made in complying with this subsection, the person carrying on the home shall be guilty of an offence (section 23(6)).

It is also an offence to indicate that a nursing or maternity or mental nursing home is such unless it has been registered (section 24).

Criminal convictions

The Nursing Homes and Mental Nursing Homes (Amendment) Regulations 1991 require applicants seeking registration of a private hospital, clinic, or nursing home under Part II of the Registered Homes Act 1984 to declare any criminal convictions and to produce proof of identity on request (subject to the restrictions of the Human Fertilisation and Embryology Act 1990).

A scheme has been set up by the Department of Health and the Home Office which allows health authority registration units to check with the police whether applicants have criminal records. These arrangements are described in circular HC(91)16 and the regulations set out in HSG(91)27.

Refusal by the authority to register

The Secretary of State can refuse to register an application for a nursing or mental nursing home if he is satisfied of the facts shown in Figure 30.3.

Figure 30.3 The principal grounds for refusing to register – section 25(1)

(a) that the applicant, or any person employed or proposed to be employed by the applicant at the home, is not a fit person (whether by reason of age or otherwise) to carry on or be employed at a home of such a description as that named in the application; or

(b) that, for reasons connected with situation, construction, state of repair, accommodation, staffing or equipment, the home is not, or any premises used in connection with the home are not, fit to be used for such a home; or

(c) that the home is, or any premises used in connection with the home are, used, or proposed to be used, for purposes which are in any way improper or undesirable in the case of such a home; or

. . .

(f) that the home is not, or will not be, in the charge of a person who is either a registered medical practitioner or a qualified nurse or, in the case of a maternity home, a registered midwife; or

(g) that the condition mentioned in subsection (3) below [specification by the Secretary of State of the number and qualifications of nursing staff required to be on duty at specified times] is not, or will not be, fulfilled in relation to the home.

REGULATIONS AND INSPECTION

Regulations

Power is given by section 26 for the Secretary of State to make regulations as to the conduct of nursing homes and mental nursing homes and these may cover the areas set out in Figure 30.4.

Figure 30.4 Regulations – section 26

[These may]
(a) make provision as to the facilities and services to be provided;
(b) make provision as to the giving of notice by a person registered in respect of such a home of periods during which he or, if he is not in charge of the home, the person who is in charge of it, proposes to be absent from the home;
(c) specify the information to be supplied in such a notice;
(d) provide for the making of adequate arrangements for the running of such a home during a period when the person in charge of it is absent from it;
(e) provide that a contravention of or failure to comply with any specified provision of the regulations shall be an offence against the regulations.

Additional regulations can cover the areas set out in Figure 30.5.

Figure 30.5 Additional regulations – section 27

[These may be made]
(a) with respect to the registration of persons under this Part of this Act in respect of nursing homes and mental nursing homes and in particular with respect to —
(i) the making of applications for registration; and
(ii) the refusal and cancellation of registration;
(b) with respect to the keeping of records relating to nursing homes and mental nursing homes, including records relating to the detention and treatment of persons detained under the Mental Health Act 1983 in a mental nursing home;
(c) with respect to the notification of events occurring in nursing homes and mental nursing homes;
(d) with respect to entry into and the inspection of premises used or reasonably believed to be used as a nursing home;
(e) requiring persons registered under this Part of this Act to pay an annual fee [as specified];
(f) specifying when the fee is to be paid;
(g) providing that contravention of or failure to comply with any specified provision of the regulations shall be an offence against the regulations.

Regulations covering all these matters have been issued and have the force of law.

Numbers in the home

Section 29 provides that it shall be a condition of the registration of any person in respect of a nursing home or mental nursing home that the number of persons kept at any one time in the home (excluding persons managing or employed in the home, together with their families) does not exceed such number as may be specified in the certificate of registration. In addition the Secretary of State can specify the age, sex or other category of persons who may be received in the home in question. These conditions will be specified in the certificate of registration (section 29(2)).

The Secretary of State may also make regulations varying the conditions and imposing additional conditions (section 29(3)).

Inspection – section 35

Any person authorised by the Secretary of State may at any time produce if asked to do so some duly authenticated document showing that he is so authorised, and enter and inspect any premises which are used, or which he has reasonable cause to believe are used, for the purposes of a mental nursing home. He may also inspect any records kept in pursuance of section 27.

The authorised person may visit and interview in private any patient residing in the home who is, or appears to be, suffering from mental disorder

- for the purpose of investigating any complaint as to his treatment made by or on behalf of the patient; or
- in any case where the person so authorised has reasonable cause to believe that the patient is not receiving proper care.

Where the authorised person is a medical practitioner, he may examine the patient in private and may inspect any medical records relating to the patient's treatment in that home requiring their production if necessary (section 35(2)).

Any person who refuses to allow the inspection of any premises or, without reasonable cause, refuses to allow such visits interviews or examination, or refuses to produce any document or record or is otherwise obstructive is guilty of an offence. It is also an offence to refuse to withdraw when requested to do so by a person authorised to interview and examine a person in private (section 35(6)).

CANCELLATION OF REGISTRATION

Grounds for cancellation

The Secretary of State may at any time cancel the registration of a person in respect of a (mental) nursing home on the grounds shown in Figure 30.6.

Figure 30.6 Grounds for cancellation of registration – section 28

(a) on any ground which would entitle him to refuse an application for the registration of that person in respect of that home;

(b) on the ground that that person has been convicted of an offence against the provisions of this Part of this Act relating to nursing homes or mental nursing homes or on the ground that any other person has been convicted of such an offence in respect of that home;

(c) on the ground that any condition for the time being in force in respect of the home by virtue of this Part of this Act has not been complied with;

(d) on the ground that that person has been convicted of an offence against regulations made under section 26 or 27 [see above];

(e) on the ground that the annual fee in respect of the home has not been paid on or before the due date.

Urgent procedure for cancellation

Section 30 provides for an urgent cancellation of registration following an application to a justice of the peace. The application by the Secretary of State could be for the cancellation of registration, the varying of any conditions or the imposing of additional conditions. It must appear to the justice of the peace that:

> there will be a serious risk to the life, health or well-being of the patients in the home unless the order is made.

The cancellation, variation or imposition has effect from the date on which the order is made.

The application must be accompanied by a written statement of the Secretary of State's reasons for making the application. The order must be in writing.

As soon as practicable after it is made the order must be served on any person registered in respect of the home, as must notice of the making of the order and details of its terms. A copy of the statement of the Secretary of State's reasons which supported his application for the order must also be served.

Case: *Martine* v. *South East Kent Health Authority*[21]

The South East Kent Health Authority was challenged by Mrs Martine when, under section 30 of the Act, it applied to cancel the registration of her nursing home. The proprietor alleged that the health authority owed a duty of care in carrying out the investigations which led to the application for cancellation. The Court of Appeal dismissed an appeal brought by Martine against the decision of the High Court judge which struck out two paragraphs of her statement of claim alleging a breach of the duty of care. Lord Justice Dillon said that section 30 of the 1984 Act was intended to provide an urgent procedure in cases where the area health authority believed there was a serious risk to the life, health or welfare of patients in a registered nursing home. The justice of the peace had the duty to ask for more information or reject the case. These were the checks and balances provided in the Act. Lord Keith said that if an area health authority, in deciding whether it was appropriate to invoke the urgent procedure under section 30 was looking over its shoulder to see whether it was exposing itself to a claim for damages at the suit of a registered proprietor of a nursing home, it might be that an application which was in truth warranted would not be made until it was too late.

Non-urgent cancellation – section 31

Where the urgent provisions do not apply the Secretary of State shall give any person registered in respect of a nursing home or mental nursing home notice of any proposal:

- to cancel the registration;
- to vary any condition for the time being in force in respect of the home; or
- to impose any additional condition.

The notice must include the reasons for his proposal.

NOTICES AND REPRESENTATIONS

Notice of registration and conditions

Where an application has been made for registration and the Secretary of State proposes to grant the application, section 31 provides that the applicant must be given written notice of the proposal and of the conditions subject to which it is proposed that his application be granted.

If the application is refused written notice must be given under section 31(2).

Representations

Representations can be made against a section 31 notice. (This includes both the conditions for registration or refusal of registration as well as a proposal to cancel, vary or impose additional conditions). The detailed provisions relating to representations are in almost identical terms to those in relation to the registration of residential homes (see Chapter 29).

If the person indicates to the Secretary of State that he wishes to make oral representations, the Secretary of State shall give him an opportunity of appearing before and of being heard by a person appointed by the Secretary of State (section 32(5)).

Notice of decision by Secretary of State

If the Secretary of State decides to adopt the proposal he shall serve notice in writing of his decision on any person on whom he was required to serve notice of the proposal.

A notice shall be accompanied by a note explaining the right of appeal conferred by section 34.

The decision of the Secretary of State shall not take effect until either the time for appealing (28 days) has elapsed, or if an appeal has been brought, it has been determined or abandoned (section 33(3)). This does not apply where the decision is one of granting an application for registration subject to conditions which have been agreed between the Secretary of State and the applicant or a decision to refuse an application.

APPEALS

An appeal against a decision of the Secretary of State or an order made by a justice of the peace can be made to the Registered Homes Tribunal (section 34).

The appeal must be brought by notice in writing given to the Secretary of State within 28 days after service of the notice of the decision or order.

Powers of the tribunal

The tribunal can confirm the decision of the Secretary of State or direct that it shall not have effect.

The tribunal can confirm the order made by the justice of the peace or direct that it shall cease to have effect.

The tribunal also has the powers set out in Figure 30.8.

Figure 30.8 Powers of tribunal – section 34(6)

(a) to vary any condition for the time being in force in respect of the home to which the appeal relates . . .;
(b) to direct that any such condition shall cease to have effect;
(c) to direct that any such condition as it thinks fit shall have effect in respect of the home.

The Secretary of State must comply with any directions given by a tribunal (section 34(7)).

The next chapter covers the procedure and constitution of the tribunal.

MISCELLANEOUS POINTS

Death in a home

The health authority, as the registration authority for a nursing home or mental nursing home, requires the home to notify the authority of any death in the home. In addition the local authority as the purchaser of places in a home will require notification of the death of one of the residents whose place is supported by local authority funding. The manager of the home will have to ensure that both authorities are appropriately notified. In addition the local authority might require notification of a resident whose place is likely to become vacant.

Cancellation of registration or death of registered person

If the cancellation of the registration of a mental nursing home takes place and any patient is liable to be detained in the home under the provisions of the Mental Health Act 1983, by virtue of section 36 the registration shall continue in force until the expiry of the period of two months beginning with the date of the cancellation or until every such patient has ceased to be so liable, whichever occurs first.

If the registered person dies, then the registration can continue in force until the expiry of two months beginning with the death, until every such patient has ceased to be so liable, or until a person other than the deceased has been registered in respect of the home, whichever occurs first.

Christian Science homes

The Secretary of State has the power by section 37 to exempt from the provisions of the Part II of the Act any nursing or mental nursing home which he is satisfied is being or will be carried on in accordance with the practice and principles of the body known as the Church of Christ Scientist.

DUAL REGISTRATION

This is permitted under the 1984 Registered Homes Act and makes for greater flexibility in the running of homes that function as both a residential and a nursing home. Frequently joint working parties have been organised by the local authority and health authority to ensure that there is agreement on the guidelines for dual registration. As far as the law is concerned each authority remains separately liable for the registration and inspection of the residential care homes and the nursing homes respectively.

Some particular issues have, however, arisen.

- How is the distinction between nursing and residential care maintained?
- At what point does a residential care home require registration as a nursing home?
- How flexible can the different kinds of accommodation be to meet both needs?
- Are applications for nursing registration for a residential home frequently refused?
- When does a residential client become a nursing client?
- How temporary is temporary nursing care for a residential client?
- Are local authorities being too relaxed over the definition of nursing needs?
- If there is dual registration does the proportion of nursing: residential clients have to remain the same?
- How can it be ensured that the appropriate staffing mix is available if the ratios change?
- Are disputes possible between health authority registration officers and the local authority if the latter allows nursing cases to be kept in residential accommodation?

Many of these issues are resolved by seeing the premises as two separate ones: the one for residential care and the other for nursing home care. The respective numbers of places for each have to be agreed with the relevant registration authority as do the required numbers of qualified staff. Undoubtedly many problems can be dealt with by joint inspections by the two authorities. What has become a greater issue for both residential and nursing home proprietors and managers is the fact that places in their homes can be brought by different local authorities, each of which have their own contractual standards that the home must comply with.

MENTAL NURSING HOMES

The distinction between those homes which are registered to take patients suffering from mental disorder and those which in addition are registered to take detained patients is not always appreciated by home owners and managers yet in law the distinction is important.

Duties of managers

If the home is able to take detained patients then it is essential that the managers of the home understand their statutory duties under the Mental Health Act 1983. They are shown in Figure 30.9.

Figure 30.9 Duties of the managers under Mental Health Act 1983

- To accept a patient and record admission on Form 14 (regulation 4(3)).
- To give information to detained patients (section 132).
- To give information to the nearest relative unless the patient requests otherwise (section 132(4)).
- To give information to the nearest relative of the discharge of the patient unless the patient requests otherwise (section 133(1)).
- To inform the nearest relative of the continued detention of the patient after a report from the responsible medical officer has been received (section 25(2)).
- To discharge the patient if appropriate (section 23(2)(b)).
- To refer the patient to a mental health review tribunal (section 68(1) and (2)).
- To transfer a patient (section 19(3) and 19(1A), regulation 7(2) and (3)).
- To scrutinise and oversee the documentation and consider whether to give consent to rectification.
- To oversee generally the care and treatment of the detained patient.
- To monitor the handling of complaints.

Managers' conflict of interest on discharge

The Mental Health Act 1983 defines the manager in relation to a mental nursing home registered under the Registered Homes

Act 1984 as 'the person or persons registered in respect of the home' (section 145 Mental Health Act 1983 (as amended)). This can create a conflict of interest in that the managers are on the one hand concerned with the financial viability of the home and on the other hand will be receiving applications to admit patients under section and also receiving applications from patients for discharge and against renewal of the section. The Mental Health Act Commission[22] has commended the practice whereby alternate directors are appointed who do not have any financial interest for the purpose of admissions and renewals.

Alternatively it is possible to appoint three independent persons with an interest in health from the locality. This is possible because, as well as being exercisable by the managers, the statutory duties in relation to the discharge of patients under section 23 can be exercised by any three or more of members of the health authority, or by three or more members of a committee or subcommittee authorised by them for that purpose (section 23(4)).

Responsible medical officer

Any mental nursing home registered to take detained patients must identify a responsible medical officer or officers who will legally be the registered medical practitioner in relation to any patients. Under section 5(2) it is only the registered medical practitioner in charge of the treatment of the patient (or his nominee) who can detain an informal patient. Section 5(3) enables the registered medical practitioner to nominate one (but not more than one) other registered medical practitioner on the staff of that hospital to act for him under section 5(2) in his absence. Note that section 34 construes references to a hospital as also including references to a mental nursing home which is registered to take detained patients.

Nurse's holding power

Section 5(4) enables a prescribed nurse (that is, one qualified in the treatment of the mentally ill or mentally handicapped) in certain circumstances to detain for up to six hours, or until the earlier arrival of the registered medical practitioner, any in-patient who is being treated for mental disorder. It is the view of the Mental Health Act Commission that this power should only be used in the case of mental nursing homes by those which are registered to take detained patients[23]. In the case of a home which is not so registered an immediate application for admission to a mental hospital would be the most appropriate course.

Section 17 leave

Section 17 of the Mental Health Act 1983 enables the responsible medical officer to give leave of absence to a detained patient. Section 17 applies to mental nursing homes in two ways:

- on the one hand a mental nursing home may be used to receive section 17 patients on leave from another institution;
- on the other hand the responsible medical officer in a mental nursing home registered to take detained patients can allow his own patients to take section 17 leave.

Section 17 patients from another institution

The use of mental nursing homes for accommodation for detained patients on leave of absence from psychiatric hospitals is not uncommon as a planned move to less secure accommodation. However, there is often ignorance around the implications of this for the mental nursing home:

- A mental nursing home does not have to be registered to take detained patients in order to provide accommodation for a detained patient on section 17 leave.
- The responsible medical officer at the hospital or original mental nursing home where the patient was detained remains responsible for his care and treatment and alone can sign the consent forms required under Part IV of the Mental Health Act 1983.
- The managers of that hospital or mental nursing home remain the managers for the purpose of the Act and any application for discharge or renewal of detention must be heard by them.

The responsible medical officer can exercise his powers to recall the patient from section 17 leave under section 17(4). The revocation must be in writing and be given to the patient or to the person for the time being in charge of the patient. The grounds for recall are where 'it appears to the responsible medical officer that it is necessary so to do in the interests of the patient's health or safety or for the protection of other persons'.

Section 17 leave for patients from that home

The responsible medical officer for a detained patient in a mental nursing home registered to take detained patients can grant leave of absence to the patient under section 17. He will remain clinically responsible for the patient and the managers of the mental nursing home will remain as managers for the purposes of the Act. Homes should ensure that there is a clearly written policy governing the use of section 17 supported by documentation signed by the responsible medical officer detailing the nature of the leave permitted. Section 17 does not require the leave to be granted in writing by the responsible medical officer, but there are clear reasons in practice why this is strongly recommended. See also the Mental Health Act *Code of Practice.*

Guardianship

Some Social services departments have used mental nursing homes as the specified place for a patient subject to guardianship under the Mental Health Act 1983. Section 18 would enable the patient to be returned to the nursing home should he abscond. However there is no express power in the Act to enable the patient to be taken compulsorily to the specified place. The use of mental nursing homes in this way was criticised by the Mental Health Act Commission in its Second Biennial Report[24] on the grounds that

- guardianship was intended to be less restrictive than hospital detention and to detain the patient in a mental nursing home is contrary to the intention of the Act, and
- the patient does not have the protection which Part IV gives to detained patients over consent to treatment.

Training

If a home is registered to take detained patients it is essential that there should be regular training on the Act and Code of Practice for both staff and managers. Reference should also be made to Chapter 15 on the community psychiatric nurse.

Fees and the detained patient in a mental nursing home

Problems can arise when a mental nursing home is used for detained patients in that, although the patients are not in the home by choice, they must still contribute to the fees. Indeed the full cost could be payable. Also, unlike the patient on income support detained in NHS accommodation who has six weeks before income support is ended, in a mental nursing home the income support received is immediately taken into account in assessing the patient's contribution to fees. There is justification for ensuring that the NHS fund detained patients in mental nursing homes.

RESPONSIBILITIES OF HEALTH AUTHORITIES AND LOCAL AUTHORITIES

Demarcation between health authorities and local authorities in relation to residential care

One of the aims of the philosophy of care in the community is the provision of a seamless service where support and care is provided to the individual on the basis of that individual's assessed need's irrespective of the authority, organisation or individual providing that support or service. This continuity can, however, lead to difficulties in determining which authority or organisation is undertaking which, if any, services and whether or not they are means-tested. One particular difficulty which has arisen for example is determining the responsibility for the provision of aids and health services into residential homes.

Guidance and circulars

Guidance on the responsibilities of health authorities and local authorities for funding community health services for residents of residential care and nursing homes who have been placed in those homes by local authorities is given in a circular from the NHS Management Executive HSG(92)50 and LAC(92)24.

It requires the health authorities to discuss and agree with local authorities the arrangements for supplying specialist nursing (primarily continence advice and stoma care, but also other specialist nursing such as diabetic liaison) and other community health services (primarily physiotherapy, speech and language therapy and chiropody) to be provided to residents placed in nursing homes by local authorities.

Contractual arrangements

Health authorities must also ensure that their contracts with provider units continue to cover the provision of community health services for residents of residential care homes and reflect the arrangements agreed with local authorities for provision of services to local authority supported residents of nursing homes.

A local authority's contracts for independent sector residential care should not include provision of any service which it is the responsibility of the NHS to provide. The NHS has the responsibility to provide where necessary community health services to residents of local authority and independent residential care homes on the same basis as to people in their own homes. These services include the provision of district nursing and other specialist nursing services (such as incontinence advice) as well as provision, where necessary, of incontinence and nursing aids, physiotherapy, speech and language therapy and chiropody. Where such services are provided they must be free of charge to people in independent sector residential care homes as well as to residents of local authority Part III homes.

The 1993 changes

From 1993, the implementation of the *Caring for People* white paper meant that local authorities have the responsibility for purchasing nursing home care for the great majority of people who need it and require public support. After 1993, if a local authority placed a person in a nursing home following joint local authority/health authority assessment, the local authority was responsible for purchasing services to meet the general nursing care needs of that person, including the cost of incontinence services (such as laundry) and those incontinence and nursing supplies which were not available on prescription. Health authorities were responsible for purchasing (within the resources available and in line with their priorities) physiotherapy, chiropody and speech and language therapy (with appropriate equipment) and for the provision of specialist nursing advice (such as continence advice and stoma care) for those people placed in nursing homes by local authorities with the consent of a health authority. Health authorities can opt to purchase these services through directly managed units, NHS Trusts or other providers including the nursing home concerned. Where the patient belongs to a fund-holding practice, the fund-holders have the responsibility of purchasing these community health services.

It is suggested that the responsibility for occupational health services should be agreed at a local level between health and local authorities.

Inspection procedures

Nursing homes and mental nursing homes are not only answerable to the health authority as the registration body and the inspectorate but also answerable to the local social services authorities as purchasers of care. It is essential that there should be agreement between health authority and local authority over the standards of care required.

Department of health consultation

In its consultation document[25] the Department of Health sought to reduce the regulatory burdens including compliance and enforcement of costs where ever possible. Its suggestions cover:

- the review of the inspection procedures by health authorities,
- the review of administrative arrangements associated with registration and inspection,
- the frequency and duration of inspection.

It also gives advice on the inspection standards but emphasises that contracting and inspection are two separate processes. It recognises the importance of joint working between health authorities and local authorities but states that alternatives to dual registration will be examined.

Following this consultation HSG(95)41 *Regulation of Nursing Homes and Independent Hospitals* was published in September 1995 (see page 494 and Appendix 5).

The UKCC and RCN reports

Any change to the inspection and registration procedures should take account of recent criticisms of professional standards in certain nursing homes. The UKCC issued a report in 1994[26] which has been circulated by the NHS Management Executive[27] asking health authorities to draw the attention of owners of nursing homes in their locality to the report. The report covers issues relating to the staffing, training and treatment of residents, and managerial and clinical supervision and the conduct of practitioners. The role of the health authority as registration authority in assisting to maintain and improve standards is emphasised.

The Royal College of Nursing has published a report on the inspection of nursing homes[28] which gives the results of a survey across its membership on the regulation of independent nursing homes and private hospitals. It shows the variation in practice across the country and a 'worrying lack of scrutiny and audit'. This is against a background of confusion on the responsibility for the funding of care which it does not consider that the Government's consultation paper on guidelines for discharge (see page 354) will resolve. The RCN calls for a national audit of the regulation of private nursing homes and hospitals with agreed national standards and protocols for their registration, with training and agreed national standards for the registration inspectors. Standards and quality assurance in Registered Homes are discussed in the next chapter.

CHAPTER 31

Registered Homes 3: tribunals and complaints

The aim of this chapter is to consider the procedures and rules relating to the holding of a Registered Homes Tribunal, offences under the Registered Homes Act and to look at other issues relating to residents' rights and quality assurance. The topics covered are set out in Figure 31.1.

Figure 31.1 Topics covered in this chapter

Registered Homes Tribunals
- Jurisdiction
- Appointment of panels
- Constitution
- Regulations
- Procedure

Offences under the 1984 Act

Other spheres of accountability

Enforcing quality
- Standards of care
- Patients' rights
- Codes of practice

REGISTERED HOMES TRIBUNALS

The detailed rules relating to Registered Homes Tribunals 1984 are set out in Statutory Instrument 1984 No. 1346.

Jurisdiction

The Registered Homes Tribunals have jurisdiction over appeals in relation to the Children Act 1989 and Parts I and II of the Registered Homes Act 1984.

514

Appointment of panels

There is a panel of Chairmen (known as the legal panel) appointed by the Lord Chancellor and a panel of experts appointed by the Lord President of the Council.

Nobody is qualified to be a member of the legal panel unless they possess such qualifications as the Lord Chancellor considers suitable; nobody can be appointed to the panel of experts unless they have had experience in social work, medicine, nursing or midwifery, or such other experience as the Lord President of the Council considers suitable.

No officer of a government department can be appointed to either panel.

Constitution

Each Registered Homes Tribunal consists of a chairman and two other members, the chair being a member of the legal panel appointed to the tribunal by the Lord Chancellor. The other two members are appointed to the Tribunal from the panel of experts by the Lord President of the Council.

A Registered Homes Tribunal hearing an appeal relating solely to registration under Part II of the 1984 Act must include a registered medical practitioner (section 42). If the appeal relates to the registration of a maternity home the panel must include a registered midwife; in any other case the panel must include a registered nurse (section 42(2)).

Regulations

The Secretary of State may by section 43 make regulations covering the constitution and proceedings of tribunals including:

- the particulars to be supplied of matters relevant to the determination of an appeal;
- enabling two or more appeals to be heard together; and
- as to representation before a tribunal, by counsel or a solicitor or otherwise.

This he has done by S1 1984 No. 1346 referred to above.

The Secretary of State has the power to assign staff for the Registered Homes Tribunals. He may also allow fees and allowances to be paid to the members and defray the expenses of such tribunals up to such amount as he may determine with the consent of the Treasury.

Procedure

Whilst the aim of the tribunal system for hearing disputes was intended to create a speedy, less costly and more informal process it is inevitable that the formality of the hearings has increased. Decided cases by other tribunals are not precedents (see glossary) but they are often referred to as persuasive authority.

The Secretariat is provided by the Department of Health (see address in Appendix 7) and makes the arrangements for holding a hearing. It can advise on procedure but not on the law.

The person appealing against the decision of a registration authority must send the appeal to that authority but it is suggested that, in the interests of speed, a copy is also sent to the Secretariat.

The registration authority must send a copy of their reasons for the decision at least 30 days before the hearing. The appellant must send four copies of the statement giving reasons for the appeal to the Secretariat at least 21 days before the hearing.

The parties can request the subpoena (see glossary) of witnesses to the hearing and must apply for the subpoena to the Crown Office, Royal Courts of Justice well in advance of the hearing giving details of the date of the hearing and the witness required.

OFFENCES

As has been noted, several offences are created by the Act and Part IV sets out the penalties and nature of the offence including the following:

● Failure to register (breach of section 2 or section 23(1))
● Failure to display the certificate of registration (breach of section 5(6) or section 23(6))
● Breach of conditions as to registration, that is breach of section 5(5) or section 29(4)
● Contravention of regulations (breach of section 16(2) or section 26 and 27)
● Falsely holding out premises as a nursing home and so on (breach of section 24)
● Obstruction in the exercise of any power (section 17(6))
● Refusing to allow an inspection (section 35(5) or 35(6)).

Bodies corporate and their officers

Where an offence under the Act and its regulations has been committed by a body corporate and is proved to have been committed with the consent or connivance of (or to be attributable to any neglect on the part of) any director, manager, secretary or other similar officer of the body corporate, or any person purporting to act in any such capacity, he as well as the body corporate shall be deemed to be guilty of that offence and shall be liable to be proceeded against and punished accordingly.

Proceedings

It is necessary to obtain the written consent of the Attorney General if any person, other than a party aggrieved or the Secretary of State, wishes to bring proceedings under section 23(1) and (6) (registration and display of certificate of registration).

The local social services authority may institute proceedings under section 35(5) and (6) (refusal to allow inspection and so on or to withdraw when requested to do so).

Statutory defences

There are certain defences provided in the Act, for example that set out in Figure 31.2.

Figure 31.2 Defences to prosecution under Part I – section 18

(1) In any proceedings for an offence under this Part of this Act ... it shall be a defence for the person charged to prove—

(a) that the commission of the offence was due to a mistake or to reliance on information supplied to him or to the act or default of another person, an accident or some other cause beyond his control; and
(b) he took all reasonable precautions and exercised all due diligence to avoid the commission of such an offence by himself or any person under his control.

Statutory defences can be subject to procedural requirements. Where the person charged relies on the defence that the commission of the offence was due to the act or default by another person, he is not entitled to rely upon this defence unless, within a period ending seven clear days before the hearing, he served notice in writing on the prosecutor giving such information to identify or assist in the identification of that other person as he then had. The court has, however, the discretion to allow reliance on this defence without the serving of such a notice.

OTHER SPHERES OF ACCOUNTABILITY

A breach of the regulations may also lead to proceedings in the civil courts if negligence has led to the personal injury or death of a patient. It might also lead to professional conduct proceedings. Registered practitioners with the UKCC should note that, even though a registered practitioner is not employed as such and is working in a residential care home, she is still expected to comply with the code of professional conduct. She could thus face professional proceedings for misconduct even though she is employed as a care assistant and not as a registered nurse[29].

Situation

The following case is an example of a professional conduct case heard by the UKCC and reported in the *Times* 23 April 1992.

A nurse had tied senile patients to chairs with bandages and rugs and barricaded others in their rooms and beds using poles or chairs. She force fed one woman with a syringe cutting her lip and causing her mouth to bleed. Other examples of cruelty were cited in the professional conduct proceedings which not surprisingly led to her being struck off the register. What is surprising is that her defence counsel said that

> She is 72 years old and trained many years ago and, in my conversations with her, she told me that she thought her actions were always in the best interests of the patients.

The matron of the nursing home told the hearing that she was not aware of the nurse's methods on the night shift.

> At the time I did not realise what was going on, otherwise I would have stopped it immediately.

ENFORCING QUALITY

Standards of care

Despite the statutory powers of registration and inspection there has been considerable criticism of the standards of care and the quality of service provided in residential homes. For example in the report *The Quality of Care* (Inquiry chaired by Lady Howe)[30] it was recommended that local authorities should draw up codes of rights for residents which include clear methods by which residents can make their views known to managers and elected members. The Inquiry believed that a code of rights for residents is fundamental to the delivery of a quality service. Each authority should draw up its own code. In the meantime the Inquiry asked the Department of Health to gather together appropriate bodies to discuss a national minimum code.

The British Medical Association also called for an investigation into the unacceptable standards in some of Britain's residential homes and psychogeriatric institutions[31]. The BMA working party, chaired by Sir Douglas Black, was concerned at the erosion of inspection powers for treatment of the mentally-ill in Britain's prisons, secure hospitals and residential centres. The present trend towards small, more isolated psychiatric units, and transferring mentally-ill patients into the community, also provides a greater potential for abuse. Dr Fisher of the BMA, introducing the report, said that 'Doctors must bear the responsibility of blowing the whistle on human rights abuses where they are aware that they are occurring'. The report also looked at the need for doctors to be given training in spotting the physical and psychological signs of torture.

Reports by the UKCC and the RCN are discussed in the previous chapter.

The Social Services Inspectorate of the Department of Health issued *Caring for Quality* which is guidance on standards for residential homes for elderly people[32]. The guide includes advice on setting standards, beliefs and values, standards for homes, the quality of life, the quality of care and the quality of management – and using the standards. Useful appendices provide detailed advice.

Patients' rights

In Chapter 2 references were made to the works which suggested that there should be a recognition of the rights of those who live in registered homes whether nursing or residential. This section sets out some of these ideas and explores the legal implications.

A code of practice
As long ago as 1984 *Home Life: a code of practice for residential care* was published. It was the report of a working party sponsored by the Department of Health and Social Security and convened by the Centre for Policy on Aging[33]. It set out basic rights including:

- fulfilment
- dignity
- autonomy
- individuality
- esteem
- quality of experience
- emotional needs being met
- risk and choice.

It shows how, through a code of practice which covers

- admission procedures
- terms and conditions of residence
- general administration
- security of tenure
- financial procedures
- health care
- the physical features of the home and
- the care of specific client groups

it should be possible to ensure that these rights are protected. It clearly identifies the role of the registration authorities in ensuring that the rights are protected.

Unfortunately it is apparent that, at the time Lady Howe's working party undertook its review, many homes were failing to implement this recommended code of practice.

Identifying standards
Homes are for Living in published by the Department of Health Social Services Inspectorate in 1990 (HMSO) identifies the following values which should be respected:

- privacy
- dignity
- independence
- choice
- rights
- fulfilment

It sees these as fundamental to good residential care practice for elderly people and to the quality of life of those who receive the service. It defines these terms and suggests yardsticks for each.

Inspecting for Quality: Standards for the residential care of elderly people with mental disorders[34] takes these values and identifies the standards of practice which are required to be implemented. The document is written primarily for those who purchase, register, inspect or manage the provision of residential services but it is thought that it will also be useful to staff who work in residential homes. Section 4 sets out the values and rights in relation to decision making, risk taking, restraint, the environment, health care, relatives and friends and equal opportunities. For each section it takes the criteria used to identify whether the standards are met and the evidence which should be looked for. It provides a useful summary for quality assurance in the residential sector.

Is a Charter the answer?

Ron Walton questions[35] whether a statutory code of residents' rights would be the most effective way of improving the quality of life for residents. He details the most common forms of violation of residents' dignity as:

- opening and screening of mail and restricted communication;
- rules and regulations imposed by staff and agencies which restrict the liberty of residents to go out, have control over their money and so on;
- punishments, which may be unfair or undignified, imposed by staff;
- non-involvement in decision making affecting key aspects of the residents' lives;
- absence of any properly constituted appeal procedure if a resident feels that he has been treated unfairly;
- compulsory or secure detention without adequate recourse to appeals procedures.

He shows that problems are not automatically solved by a Charter of Rights:

the danger is that the achievement of a Charter for Residents might be seen as an end rather than a beginning.

He suggests, however, that a dialogue could be commenced by management and staff on issues relating to the rights of residents.

Not all conflicts would be resolved by this approach, but they would be set in a climate of greater trust and constructive effort.

Quality assurance and audit

Guidance on undertaking an audit on the quality of nursing homes is provided by the *Nursing Home Monitor*[36]. It provides guidelines for an audit covering:

- home profile,
- home management,
- patient welfare,
- nursing care,
- patient dependency,
- workloads, and
- guidelines for the appropriate placement of individuals.

An audit for locally specified criteria is also included.

Closure of a home

No discussion on residents' rights would be complete without looking at the issue of what rights residents have when a home is to be closed. The issue was considered in the following cases heard together in the Court of Appeal.

Case: *R* v. *Devon County Council, ex parte Baker and another, R v. Durham County Council, ex parte Broxson and another*[37]

In the first case, Helen May Baker and Nellie Edith Johns applied for judicial review of the decision of Devon County Council on October 24 1991 to close Tory Brook and to phase out Ingleside residential homes. The judge refused the application and they appealed to the Court of Appeal who dismissed their appeal. The homes had been established by the council under section 21 of the National Assistance Act 1948. It was not challenged that the local authority had the power in appropriate circumstances to close the homes. The applicants contended, however, that the council owed a duty in law to consult the permanent residents of a home over any proposed closure of that home and not merely over what was to happen to the residents after it was closed.

In Devon the Chairman of the Council's Social Services committee had given specific promises of consultation. The Court considered that support committees in respect of the residents had and took ample opportunity to publicise their cause and put the grounds of their objections to closure before the councillors and they were not prevented from so doing. The residents knew that their homes were under threat well before the final decision to close was made and that the council was making a comprehensive survey and assessment of all its residential homes. There was ample time to make representations and the Council's officers were scrupulously fair in putting all such representations before councillors. The Court held that each individual resident did not have an individual right to be consulted face to face by permanent officers or groups of councillors. Consultation could perfectly well be achieved by meetings held by Council officers with the residents generally at a particular home or by views expressed through the support groups.

In the Durham case Elizabeth Jane Broxson and Mabel Curtis appealed against the dismissal of their application for judicial review of the decision by Durham County Council to close Ridgeway House residential home. The Court of Appeal held that the closure of this home did not have the long drawn out history that the question of closures had in Devon. Council officials were aware that there would be opposition from residents to any closure of homes. Nothing was done about consultation with residents except a letter sent by hand to each home five days before the meeting of the Council's Social Services Committee that approved the closure of the home.

The Court of Appeal considered that the letter did not give the residents sufficiently clear notice that closure of the home was under consideration, nor did it give them long enough time to make representations to the Council about closure. Therefore the case of procedural unfairness was made out.

It was also suggested that judicial review should not be granted because of the availability of an alternative remedy and this aspect of the case (which did not succeed) is discussed in Chapter 27, page 438.

CONCLUSIONS

At present there is a conflict between those who would like to see the current regulation of residential care and nursing homes simplified and made less onerous and those who consider that the present regulations are not efficient in ensuring that the quality of care for the residents is maintained. The debate is on-going but at present it appears that any changes to the Registered Homes Act 1984 are low on the Government's list of priorities.

CHAPTER 32

Housing corporations and associations and planning concerns

A wide variety of organisations have sprung up as a result of government, voluntary, private sector and personal initiatives in ensuring that there is available in the community accommodation and support for those who could be discharged from institutional care. This chapter will look at the role of the Housing Corporation, Housing for Wales, the housing associations and the housing groups managing care. It will also briefly consider the issues relating to planning permission for accommodation for those transferred from institutional care.

THE HOUSING CORPORATION AND HOUSING FOR WALES

The Government uses the Housing Corporation as the agency through which the capital funds for generating the provision of accommodation is supplied. The Housing Corporation has the responsibility of monitoring the expenditure of the grants and is able to threaten to block further advances of grant if its rules are not followed. It is governed by the rules laid down in the Housing Associations Act 1985 (as amended by the Housing Act 1988 and other legislation). The different parts of the United Kingdom come under different organisations.

● In Scotland, for housing associations registered in Scotland, the Corporation means 'Scottish Homes'

● In Wales, for housing associations or charities registered in Wales, the Corporation means 'Housing for Wales'

● In England the Corporation means the Housing Corporation.

The constitution of the Housing Corporation

The constitution of the Housing Corporation is set out in Schedule 6 to the Housing Association Act 1985. The main points are shown in Figure 32.1.

Figure 32.1 Constitution of the Housing Corporation – Schedule 6 to Housing Association Act 1985

- It is a body corporate and a public body for the purposes of the Prevention of Corruption Acts 1889 to 1916.
- It is not regarded as the servant or agent of the Crown or as enjoying any status, immunity or privilege of the Crown or exempt from any tax, duty, rate or levy.
- The members of the Housing Corporation, of which there must not be more than 15, are appointed by the Secretary of State, who has a duty before making an appointment to satisfy himself that the member will have no financial or other interest likely to affect prejudicially the exercise of his functions as a member. The Secretary of State has powers to check periodically on the lack of financial and other interest of members and also to remove members.
- A chairman and deputy chairman are appointed by the Secretary of State from amongst the members and the office continues only so long as the holder continues to be a member.
- There is power for the Secretary of State to pay the chairman, deputy chairman and members remuneration, allowances and pensions.

Further rules are laid down about its procedures, quorum, disclosure of interest and so on.

In Wales, registered housing associations were funded and supervised by the Housing Corporation through its Welsh Regional Office. On 1 April 1989 Tai Cymru, Housing for Wales commenced its activities. Set up under the amendments to the Housing Associations Act 1985 made by the Housing Act 1988, it is responsible for the funding and monitoring the provision of affordable homes by housing associations in Wales. It is a non-departmental public body, which is controlled by a board of eight members, appointed by the Secretary of State for Wales. Its mission statement reads as follows:

> To increase the supply of well managed, good quality housing for those unable to meet their housing needs through purchase or rental at open market prices.

Registration

Each corporation has the duty to maintain a register of housing associations which is to be open to inspection at the head office of the Corporation at all reasonable times. Conditions for the eligibility for registration are set out in Figure 31.2.

Figure 31.2 Conditions for registration with the Housing Corporation

Section 4 – Housing Associations Act 1985

(1) A housing association is eligible for registration if it is:—

(a) a registered charity; or

(b) a society registered under the Industrial and Provident Societies Act 1965 which fulfils the following conditions.

(2) The conditions are that the association does not trade for profit and is established for the purpose of, or has among its objects or powers, the provision, construction, improvement or management of—

(a) houses to be kept available for letting; or

(b) houses for occupation by members of the association, where the rules of the association restrict membership to persons entitled or prospectively entitled (as tenants or otherwise) to occupy a house provided or managed by the association, or

(c) hostels,

and that any additional purposes or objects are among the following.

(3) The permissible additional purposes or objects are—

(a) providing land, amenities or services or providing, constructing, repairing, or improving buildings, for the benefit of the association's residents, either exclusively or together with other persons;

(b) acquiring, or repairing and improving, or creating by the conversion of houses or other property, houses to be disposed of on sale, on lease or on shared ownership terms;

(c) constructing houses to be disposed of on shared ownership terms;

(d) managing houses which are held on leases or other lettings (not being houses falling within subsections (2)(a) or (b)) or blocks of flats;

(e) providing services of any description for owners or occupiers of houses in arranging or carrying out works of maintenance, repair or improvement, or encouraging or facilitating the carrying out of such works;

(f) encouraging and giving advice on the formation of other housing associations or providing services for, and giving advice on the running of, such associations and other voluntary organisations concerned with housing, or matters connected with housing.

(4) A housing association shall not be ineligible for registration by reason only that its powers include the power—

(a) to acquire commercial premises or businesses as an incidental part of a project or series of projects undertaken for purposes or objects falling within subsections (2) or (3);

(b) to repair, improve or convert any commercial premises acquired as mentioned in paragraph (a) or to carry on, for a limited period, any business so acquired;

(c) to repair or improve houses, or buildings in which houses are situated, after the tenants have exercised, or claimed to exercise, acquisition rights;

(d) to acquire houses to be disposed of at a discount to tenants to whom section 58 of the Housing Act 1988 applies (tenants of charitable housing associations etc.)

Additional criteria for registration
Under section 5 of the Housing Associations Act 1985 (as amended) the Corporation may register any housing association which is eligible for registration but each Housing Corporation is required to establish criteria which should be satisfied by a housing association seeking registration and shall consider whether a housing association meets these criteria in deciding whether to register it. The Corporations are not required to establish the same criteria. The Corporation must give notice to the Charity Commissioners or the Industrial and Provident Society as appropriate.

Removal from the register
This can only take place in accordance with the provisions of section 6 of the 1985 Act. If it appears to the Corporation that a body which is on the register is no longer a housing association eligible for registration, or has ceased to exist or does not operate, then it can, after giving the body at least 14 days notice, remove it from the register.

Appeal against removal from the register
Section 7 enables an aggrieved body to appeal against the intention to remove from the register. The Corporation cannot remove the name until the appeal is heard.

Statutory powers of the Housing Corporation

In addition to registration and removal from the register the Housing Corporation has various powers under the Act in connection with dealing with the dissolution of housing associations, the issue of guidance and overseeing their management. It can initiate an inquiry (section 28) and, if it transpires that there has been 'misconduct or mismanagement', it can take various steps to redeem the situation and remove or suspend those responsible.

The Corporation's powers in relation to a charity are limited by section 31 which only enables the right of inquiry or audit to take place where the body has received a grant or loan under specified statutes.

Section 32 gives the power to the Corporation to direct the transfer of land if it is satisfied that there has been misconduct or mismanagement, but this power can only be exercised with the consent of the Secretary of State.

The general functions of the Corporation are set out in section 75 of the Housing Associations Act 1985 and shown in Figure 32.3.

Figure 32.3 General functions – section 75

(1) The Corporation has the following general functions—

(a) to promote and assist the development of registered housing associations and unregistered self-build societies;

(b) to facilitate the proper performance of the functions, and to publicise the aims and principles, of registered housing associations and unregistered self-build societies;

(c) to maintain the register of housing associations referred to in section 3 and to exercise supervision and control over registered housing associations;

(d) [repealed]

(e) to undertake, to such extent as the Corporation considers necessary, the provision (by construction, acquisition, conversion, improvement or otherwise) of dwellings for letting or for sale and of hostels, and the management of dwellings or hostels so provided.

(2) The Corporation shall exercise its general functions subject to and in accordance with the provisions of this Act.

(3) Subsection (1) is without prejudice [see glossary] to specific functions conferred on the Corporation by or under this Act.

(4) The Corporation may do such things and enter into such transactions as are incidental to or conductive to the exercise of any of its functions, general or specific under this Act.

Power of Secretary of State to give directions

Under Section 76 the Secretary of State has the power to give directions to the Corporation as to the exercise of its functions. These directions may be of a general or particular character and may be varied or revoked by subsequent directions. Non-compliance with the directions does not invalidate a transaction between a person and the Corporation unless the person had actual notice of the direction.

Advisory service

Section 77 permits the Corporation to provide an advisory service for the purpose of giving advice on legal, architectural and other technical matters to housing associations (whether registered or unregistered) and to persons who are forming a housing association or are interested in the possibility of doing so.

Annual reports

The Corporation must provide an annual report as soon as possible after the end of each financial year and make a report to the Secretary of State on the exercise of its function during the year. The Secretary of State must lay a copy of the annual report before each House of Parliament.

Financing
Powers to lend, guarantee loans and indemnify certain lenders are given in sections 79, 83 and 84 respectively.

Performance review

Each Housing Corporation is required to monitor the performance of the registered housing associations.

The Housing Corporation revised its regulatory role in 1990 and new arrangements were introduced from 1 April 1991. These aimed to distance the regulatory process from involvement in the every day business of housing associations, while making it more focused and rigorous. The Corporation's Registration and Supervision Division took responsibility for the full range of the Corporation's regulatory activities including those financial aspects previously carried out by other parts of the Corporation. Regional Directors took line management responsibility for their local performance audit teams, which previously reported directly to the Registration and Supervision Division at the Housing Corporation.

The criteria used by the Housing Corporation against which the housing associations were graded on visits are:

- Committees and accountability
- Management Control
- Finance
- Race equality and equal opportunities
- Access to housing
- Housing management service
- Maintenance
- Development.

Of the 595 visits paid in 1990–92 the functions where weaknesses were most frequently found were management control, finance, access, and race and equal opportunities.

In Wales Housing for Wales has published a copy of a performance audit annual report. The report for 1991–2 analyses the visits undertaken by Housing for Wales. It reviews performance against the following expectations:

- Meeting housing need
- Design and maintenance
- Access to housing
- Housing management service

- Equal opportunities
- Committee and association accountability
- Management control
- Finance
- Housing for people with special needs.

The latter expectation reads as follows:

> Associations should ensure that tenants with special needs receive the support they require to achieve their maximum levels of independence and have opportunities to become valued members of the community.

Housing corporations and special needs

The Housing Corporation Report for 1991–92 states that the need for people with disabilities to gain access to specialised housing had been very much on the Corporation agenda that year. A major review by the Corporations's research section, carried out with input from a range of specialist housing associations from around the country, looked at the needs of disabled people and the supply of housing for them.

The work showed that the housing needs of disabled people – particularly wheelchair users – were not matched by the supply of wheelchair housing, the Corporation was now working with local authorities and housing associations to achieve better provision. The annual report cited the following projects as examples of innovative schemes for people with disabilities funded by the Corporation:

Croydon Churches Housing Association: Speakers Court, the rehabilitation of a former church to provide homes for elderly people and a new build scheme for the disabled managed by the Spastics Society.

Look Ahead Housing Association: Castle Lane, a 20-unit registered home providing move-on accommodation to residents of an adjacent hostel. The scheme caters for people with special needs such as deafness, blindness and learning difficulties.

Wandsworth: a scheme which linked Servite Houses, South Thames Regional Health Authority, Wandsworth Health Authority and Wandsworth borough council, at a cost of £10.2 million, to provide a housing-with-care scheme providing homes for over 100 elderly Londoners – many of whom were frail, confused or mentally ill.

The Corporation report cites as an example of the need to integrate disabled people fully into the community, the grant to the Hyde Housing Association project in Southampton which combines homes for one or two parent families with a number of special disability units.

In Wales about 10% of the funding is spent on special needs accommodation. Clearly however the funds available for capital development are determined by the availability of revenue support funding. Before any approval is given to capital expenditure on special needs accommodation, the revenue funding must be demonstrated.

The Housing for Wales report on *Investment policies and plans 1992/93* states that Wales is moving to an emphasis on the integration of special needs provision within existing schemes. Previously the majority of schemes for special needs were provided by the acquisition and conversion of existing houses (many of them very large). Increasingly, in each new development associations are including one or more dwellings for special needs provision.

> Schemes for people with learning difficulties have typically accounted for half of all developments for people with special needs in recent years. Housing for Wales and the Social Care Division of the Welsh Office met with each Social Services Department to discuss the proposals for new housing developments contained in the County Plan.... These discussions have enabled Housing for Wales to make judgements concerning the level of allocation to each County based on the likely revenue availability and relative priority of particular developments. In the current year this has led to resources being targeted to facilitate hospital closures, enabling the capital and revenue tied up in these services to be released. (*Investment Policies and Plans 1992/93* Tai Cymru)

The present target is between 330 and 350 bed spaces per year.

Special needs management allowance

There are two capital allowances, special projects promotional allowance (SPPA) and furniture allowance, which are each paid before schemes come into management. There is also one revenue allowance, special needs management allowance (SNMA). The SNMA is allocated by the Housing Corporations in recognition of the housing management support people with special needs require (for example about benefits, understanding their tenancy agreement and so on). It replaced the allowance known as hostel deficit grant and is given to the housing associations for each place allocated in the homes. This has had a significant effect in sufficient income being raised to cover the housing related costs of schemes. It is not known how long this payment will continue to be made, but it is clearly of great significance in the balancing of the books for the housing associations.

In Wales about £6–7 million revenue funding from the Housing Corporation is given to housing associations for special needs.

HOUSING ASSOCIATIONS

Purpose and number

A housing association is an organisation whose purpose is the provision of homes for people who cannot afford to buy or rent a home on the open market. They have had an increasing part to play in the discharge of long-term patients from institutional care, as well as people with special needs already living in the community, and have enabled homes to be built and provided through a variety of complex financial arrangements.

It is impossible to generalise about their size or function.

In England 2314 housing associations were on the Register for 1991. £1.585 billion was spent with new homes exceeding 27 000 and approvals for new homes totalling 51 000. The annual report does not quote the numbers of homes for special needs separately.

In Wales associations manage more than 29 000 homes with this number increasing by over 3300 every year. There are approximately 100 associations registered with Housing for Wales. Some associations cover the whole of Wales, others are concerned with only one area.

Funding

Housing associations registered as Friendly Societies register with the Housing Corporation and receive housing association grants (HAGs) to build accommodation to meet specific needs. Often partnerships are made with potential care organisations or providers to ensure that specialist services are available.

In Wales 65% of the income for housing associations comes from Housing for Wales. The rest comes from loans taken out with banks and building societies. Local authorities also transfer funds to enable new homes to be built.

All schemes funded through HAGs are eligible for SNMA which is an important element in the calculation of income.

Health authority funding

Section 28A of the 1977 National Health Service Act enabled health authorities to contract with voluntary groups including Housing Associations for the provision of services of patients (see Figure 23.9).

A health authority can fund places provided by a Housing Association using the moneys it would have had to pay for patients originally accommodated in long-stay hospital accommodation. Against this agreement the Housing Association may borrow 100% of the capital required to build the accommodation and loan repayment is built in to the calculation of rental cost.

Local authority funding

As a result of the community care provisions each individual is assessed and if some form of community/residential/nursing home accommodation is required then the local authority's co-ordinator will arrange an agreement for a suitable place. One of the aims of the new assessment procedures introduced in April 1993 is that residential accommodation should only be provided if it is not possible, with domiciliary support, for patients to remain in their own homes.

Following the assessment, a contract will be agreed between the local authority and the provider of the accommodation and care. A Housing Association can often provide the accommodation and sometimes elements of the care as well.

CARE MANAGER ORGANISATIONS

Sometimes organisations have been established with the purpose of working in partnership with housing associations to provide the support staff and care for the tenants. It is difficult to generalise about the care associations – some may be linked with national charities, others may be local groups.

Many such organisations are not involved in the capital acquisition and concentrate solely on the management of the care. In other cases the Housing Associations not only provide the accommodation but also provide the support organisation for the tenants. There may be advantages to the tenants in having two separate organisations but further research is necessary into this.

Financial provisions

This is further considered in Section E, Chapter 33. At present there is a wide variety in the financial basis on which someone might be residing in accommodation.

- They could be paying for themselves in a private nursing/residential home, meeting the full costs on their own account or with the assistance of relatives.
- They could be in a private nursing home where the health authority has purchased places for patients formerly in hospital accommodation. They would not be eligible for continuing income support.
- They could be in a private nursing/residential home admitted before 1 April 1993 where they receive higher income support (for which they have preserved rights) which is used to meet the fees. Any deficit in the fees over the income support available would have to be met by relatives or charitable associations.
- They could be in a private nursing/residential home admitted after 31 March 1993 where the local authority has purchased places. The local authority would charge residents according to their means; the residents might be eligible to receive income support at the lower rate, which would be taken into account in the charges levied by the local authority. The residents would be entitled to claim their personal allowance of £13.75 per week (figure for 1996).
- They could be tenants in accommodation secured by a housing association where it or another care group acts as the caring agency. Special needs management allowance would be paid to subsidise the costs. They would be entitled to income support at the lower level for admissions after 31 March 1993 and income support at the higher level for admissions before 1 April 1993. In the former case the local authority still would be responsible for purchasing places.
- They could be tenants of associations which were not registered with the Housing Corporation and were not therefore entitled to SNMA.

These distinctions are important since they affect the nature of the organisations who have responsibilities over the accommodation and therefore the nature of the powers of inspection and control. It may well be that a review of the registered homes provisions will be required together with a review of the protection of tenants in unregistered accommodation who lack the capacity to protect themselves.

If tenants are in unregistered homes, they are eligible for disability allowances for their own use and to claim income support and housing benefit at the ceiling agreed with rent officers. Additional funding for the support services could also be available for the local authorities. For a typical scheme for four tenants the SNMA funding in 1993 was about £18 788 per annum.

Assessment of revenue support

There are considerable difficulties in making the assessment of the revenue funds required in support. It is difficult to assess the level of support required compared with institutional care. There are also difficulties in determining the quality of life which should be resourced. For example, it is infinitely preferable if the residents do not spend all their time in the accommodation but are able to take part in the community activities and go on outings and trips. This will often require transport and the costs will depend upon the frequency of such activities and the mobility of the clients. Recreational activities are an essential part of the quality of non-institutional life but in rural areas where the expense of transport is much greater it is difficult to estimate costs. It is desirable, too, for tenants to go out on an individual basis rather than in a minibus and this is clearly more expensive.

A key focus of community activities is to help people develop friendships within that community. Tenants must be treated as individuals and costs are therefore likely to be higher.

In the exodus from institutional care there was a danger that the initial inclination was to discharge those with higher levels of skills so that the costs of accommodating the last to leave the institution are considerably higher than for the earlier discharges. There are also problems of wheelchair users or people with challenging behaviour being grouped together on their own, which do not help in the assimilation of people into the community.

The future funding

The provisions of the 1990 Act have placed considerable uncertainties over the operation of accommodation provided by housing associations. Those residents in place on the 31 March 1993 have preserved rights in relation to the higher levels of income support. From 1 April 1993 funding of new tenants is from the social services who will contract for individual places.

A situation could arise where a tenant with preserved rights dies or leaves his accommodation and the local authority do not agree to pay for another tenant to join the home. This could therefore mean that a four bedroomed house is only occupied by three tenants and the care manager organisation whose costs are based on full accommodation is running at a loss. The housing associations charge a cost per bed space and would therefore still require the same income from the company. Difficulties could arise in meeting management charges.

Competition

Competition with the private sector is growing as the latter increases the number of homes. In one county for example there are 38 private schemes for those with special needs and only 10 voluntary schemes. In the past the private sector has been handicapped by its lack of entitlement to SNMA.

Unmet needs

Another concern resulting from the new provisions is the possibility that, even after a potential tenant has been assessed as requiring accommodation, these needs may not be met. The assessment problems are discussed in Chapter 25. There is also a difficulty over representation of the client since the provisions for representatives to be appointed under the 1986 Act have not been brought into force. There is a danger that the person doing the assessment will be the care manager who is also the purchaser of services for the local authority and therefore financial considerations may prevail over meeting the identified needs of the client.

Security of tenure

The right of the tenant to remain in the accommodation whilst subject to a tenancy agreement could be in jeopardy in the following circumstances:

● If the tenant is no longer supported by the agency which placed him in that accommodation (if the agency, perhaps, goes into liquidation) or if the local authority are not able to support him with the social services he requires (for example, because they have inadequate funding to do so) and the tenant insists on a right of tenure, what is the legal situation?

● If the tenant is unable to care for himself in the accommodation to which he was originally transferred, could he be removed? Will his rights of occupancy be overridden by other legal rights to oust him?

● If he fails to receive those support services which he is assessed as requiring and is therefore unable to continue to live in the accommodation, could he be evicted?

Clearly in some cases the tenancy agreement will clarify the rights of occupation of the client, in others there may be no clear answer to these questions. Many of the residents in residential and nursing homes do not have any security of tenure and their rights of occupation are therefore uncertain.

Quality standards

It is clear that whilst there are many bodies concerned with the setting of standards (including the Housing Corporations, the housing associations, the care organisations, the registration authorities, the purchasers – whether NHS or Social Services Departments or other contractors – and those groups which represent the clients) there is no uniformity in the standards required.

Conflicting requirements

There can be a tension between the statutory requirements and the institutional perspective possessed by some of the enforcement authorities and the attempt of the organisation which manages care to create a homely domestic environment.

For example fire officers routinely require an integrated fire alarm system and fire doors for a small home when all that would have been required in domestic accommodation to ensure safety would have been smoke alarms. There is a clash between the Fire Regulations and the Building Controls. For example the Fire Protection measures require half hour fire check doors upstairs and down stairs, whereas building control regulations only require such doors down stairs.

In respect of design requirements Housing for Wales requires that where a scheme is to be registered under the Registered Homes Act 1984, associations must take account of the requirements of the Registration Officer in preparing the design. In the case of small scale ordinary housing projects where these requirements exceed those which would be incorporated by a responsible householder, the association must ask the Registration Officer to reconsider the requirements in light of the aspirations of the scheme.

Any reform to the Registered Homes Act 1984 needs to take into account these concerns.

Conflicting rights
Registration of the home appears to present an anomaly as it creates a 'person in control' (PIC). The responsibilities of the PIC in exercising control over the dwelling may appear to conflict with the rights of the tenant as expressed in the tenancy and Tenants' Guarantee. Registration also gives to any person authorised by the Secretary of State the right at all times to enter and inspect premises which raises similar questions about the right of the occupiers to refuse access.

CONCLUSIONS

There are still many uncertainties to be resolved in the accommodation of those from institutional care into the community. Many of these relate to the funding of not only the capital but also the revenue costs, other issues relate to the rights of the tenants, residents and clients. The capacity of the local community to absorb and treat on an equal footing those with special needs is varied and uncertain and it is likely that the fragile toleration which exists in certain areas may be broken if the new residents fail to maintain high standards of behaviour.

COMMUNITY CARE AND PLANNING ISSUES

Space does not permit a detailed review of the laws relating to planning permissions and community care but mention must be made of some of the difficulties which have arisen with the transfer of patients from institutions into the community in relation to obtaining planning consent.

As accommodation has been sought for people in institutions to move into the community concern has arisen[38], particularly in relation to the provision of community homes for those with learning disabilities, over issues in relation to planning applications.

Town and Country Planning (Use Classes) order 1987

Differences of opinion have emerged over the seeking of planning consent for a residential home: some authorities are taking the view that, provided that there are six or less residents, planning permission is not necessary, others say that if 24 hour care is necessary then planning permission is required.

The Department of the Environment, in a letter from the Development Control Policy Division in December 1990, has given an informal view to the effect that property is exempt from planning control

- where the same use or class of property is envisaged,
- where there are not more than six residents, and
- where care is provided by resident staff who are counted as one of the residents.

Where staff are not resident, it is not necessary to obtain planning consent.

Alleged detriment to the area

A planning application by the Richmond Fellowship Scotland to turn a detached house into a home for eight people with mental health problems was rejected by the Kilarnock and Loudon district planning committee[39]. The grounds of rejection were that the home would be detrimental to the character and residential amenity of the area. The locals had protested vigorously, concerned for their children because they were afraid the patients (who may have schizophrenia) could be violent.

In contrast in the case of *Brown and others* v. *Heathlands Mental Health Trust*[40] the Chancery Division of the High Court refused an injuction or damages to those holding the benefit of restrictive covenants when the Trust acquired a property to be used for five adults suffering from mental disorder. It was held that private rights restricting the use of land could not be enforced against a statutory body which had the power in law to acquire and hold land to fulfil its statutory purposes under section 5 of the NHS and Community Care Act 1990.

The importance of the planning issues in community care is highlighted by the report[41] that insurance companies are refusing to insure housing associations planning to set up care in the community projects. They are refusing to give restrictive covenant indemnity insurance. Restrictive covenants usually prohibit commercial activity from being carried out in certain neighbourhoods and have been used successfully by 'not-in-my-back-yard' campaigners to block projects in the past. Without the insurance housing associations are ineligible to receive grants from the Housing Corporations.

Eventually legislation will be required to resolve this issue of the conflicting interests of those wishing to return to the community from institutions and those who wish to live in areas free from such persons.

REFERENCES FOR SECTION D

1. *R* v. *Wandsworth Borough Council, ex parte Beckwith* Times Law Report 4 May 1995; [1996] 1 All ER 129 (HL)
2. *R* v. *Wandsworth London Borough Council, ex parte Beckwith* Times Law Report 29 June 1995 (CA) and [1996] 1 All ER 129 (HL)
3. LAC (91)12 Community Care
4. LAC (92)27
5. *R* v. *Avon County Council, ex parte M* QBD [1994] 2 FLR 1006
6. *R* v. *North Yorkshire County Council, ex parte Hargreaves* Times Law Report 9 November 1994
7. Law Commission Consultation Papers No. 119, 1991, HMSO; and Nos. 128, 129 and 130, 1993, HMSO
8. CI (92)30/EL(92)65 Department of Health
9. *R* v. *Cleveland County Council, ex parte Ward* QBD (transcript from Lexis)
10. *R* v. *Newcastle upon Tyne City Council, ex parte Dixon* Times Law Report 26 October 1993
11. *Associated Provincial Picture House Ltd.* v. *Wednesbury Corporation* [1948] 1 KB 223
12. Residential Accommodation (Relevant Premises, Ordinary Residence and Exemption) Regulations 1993 SI No. 477
13. *Isle of Wight County Council* v. *Humphreys* QBD (1991) 90 LGR 186
14. *Harrison* v. *Cornwall County Council* CA (1991) 90 LGR 81
15. *Hillingdon London Borough Council* v. *McClean* (1988) 88 LGR 49
16. *Coomb and another* v. *Hertfordshire County Council* (1991) 89 LGR 774
17. *R* v. *Humberside County Council, ex parte Bogdal* Times Law Report 1 June 1992
18. Department of Health *Regulation of Residential Care and Nursing Homes and Independent Hospitals* 5 August 1994 (enclosing draft circulars on the regulation of residential care homes and the registration and inspection of nursing homes and independent hospitals)
19. see *The Times* 8 September 1993 and 'Today', Radio 4, 7 September 1993
20. See Kings Fund Institute Report 1992 and article by Alison Roberts *The Times* 25 August 1992
21. *Martine* v. *South East Kent Area Health Authority* Times Law Report 8 March 1993 CA
22. see *Second Biennial Report 1985–7* paragraph 19.3, HMSO, 1988
23. see *Second Biennial Report 1985–7* paragraph 19.2, HMSO, 1988
24. 1985–87, HMSO, 1988
25. Department of Health 5 August, 1994 *Regulation of Residential Care and Nursing Homes and Independent Hospitals*, Annex 2 sets out a draft circular on Registration and Inspection of Nursing Homes and Independent Hospitals
26. Registrar's letter No. 12 1994 *Standards of Nursing in Nursing Homes*
27. EL (94)67 *Professional Conduct: Occasional report of standards of nursing in nursing homes.* NHSME
28. *An Inspector Calls* Royal College of Nursing, August 1994
29. See *Scope of Professional Practice* UKCC, 1992
30. *The Quality of Care:* a report of the residential homes Inquiry chaired by Lady Howe and published by the Local Government Management Board on behalf of the National Joint Council of Local Authorities Administration, Professional, Technical and Clerical Services, 1992.
31. see *The Times* 30 June 1992 and *Medicine Betrayed* BMA 1992
32. *Caring for Quality* HMSO, 1990

33. *Home Life: a code of practice for residential care* the Centre for policy on Ageing, 1984

34. *Inspecting for Quality: Standards for the residential care of elderly people with mental disorders*

35. Chapter 20 'A Charter of Rights: the end or the beginning?' from *Residential care – a Reader theory and practice* (eds Ronald G. Walton and Doreen Elliott) Pergamon Press, 1980, page 239–41

36. Written by J. Morton, L.A. Goldstone, A. Turner, S. Harrison and R. Morgan it is published by the Gale Centre Publications. 1991. (Gale Centre Publications Whitakers Way Loughton Essex, IG10 1SQ. Tel 081 508 9344.)

37. 21 January 1993 Times Law Reports.

38. I am grateful for a personal communication with Bill Mcloughlin, Development Director Walsingham Community Homes, on 12 July 1993 on this issue.

39. Report by Stuart Watt *Care Weekly* 2 September 1993 Vol. 289

40. *Brown and others* v. *Heathlands Mental Health NHS Trust* [1996] All ER 133

41. Report by Stuart Watt *Care Weekly* 2 September 1993 Vol. 289

SECTION E

Finances and the client

There are two distinct aspects of community care finances and the client. One is the charges which are levied and the income entitlements, mainly the benefits, payable by the Department of Social Security; the other is the management of the resident's finances within the community or a residential/nursing home. The first chapter will be concerned with charges and income and the next will look at the management of client's property.

CHAPTER 33

Charges and income

The topics which will be covered in this chapter are shown in Figure 33.1.

Figure 33.1 Topics covered in this chapter

- Charges for community services
- Charges for accommodation – general
- Local authority charges for accommodation
- Means-testing by Social Services Departments
- Assessment of capital – including property
- Social Security Benefits
  Social fund
  Independent living fund
  Disability living allowance
  Attendance allowance
  Invalid care allowance
  Income support

An excellent guide to the rights and benefits which are available is provided annually by the Benefits Agency. This provides far more detail that can be given in this chapter which gives only a basic outline of the general principles.

CHARGES FOR COMMUNITY SERVICES

Where community services are provided within the National Health Service there can be no charges. Health services which are provided in the community such as district nurses or general practitioner services are all provided without means-testing unless the client opts for private health care.

However, local authority services provided under the statutory duties outlined in Chapter 25 are means-tested. There are no nationally agreed charges for these local authority social services:

thus what the clients pay for home helps, day hospital, respite care, night sitter charges and so on vary widely across the country.

CHARGES FOR ACCOMMODATION

Where accommodation is provided two systems currently prevail depending upon whether a client has 'preserved rights' (see also Chapter 28).

One of the most important changes brought about by the NHS and Community Care legislation was in the nature of funding for residential and nursing home places. From April 1993 the local authority social services has the responsibility of funding these places for clients admitted on or after that date and who meet the eligibility requirements (see Chapter 28). Clients who were in such accommodation on 31 March 1993 continue to receive funding at higher levels of income support (on a means-tested basis) from the Department of Social Security as before. They therefore have what are known as 'preserved rights' which, it is envisaged at present, will continue indefinitely. There are thus two parallel systems of funding: the old system for those in homes on 31 March 1993 and the new for those who entered such accommodation on 1 April 1993 or later.

DSS responsibility

Those residents in a home before 1 April 1993 will continue to claim income support at the higher level from the Department of Social Security. They will be means-tested according to the Social Security rules. Social security income support is not available to those who are patients in hospital accommodation. The decision of the Court of Appeal in *White* v. *Department of Social Security* (see page 354) has caused some uncertainty in relation to the definition of hospital since it was held that the nursing home accommodation in which Mr White was resident was a hospital for the purposes of the social security legislation and he was not therefore entitled to receive income support.

Local authority responsibility

For those who take up residence in residential care or nursing home accommodation after 31 March 1993 the local social services department is responsible for purchasing accommodation. It has a legal duty to charge the full cost to the authority of providing that accommodation subject to means-testing (see below). The client is entitled to claim income support but only at the levels at which he could claim were he living at home, not at the higher level which can be claimed by those with preserved rights. The contributions required by local authorities will take into account the income support payments. This means-testing by local authorities is subject to national rules set down in the annual National (Assessment of Resources) Regulations. The details relating to the charges for residential accommodation (known as CRAG) are set out in a guide issued by the Department of Health which publishes amendment notices from time to time[1]. Residents who come under the local authority means-testing are also entitled to a weekly personal allowance[2]. The means-testing of clients should ensure that each client is left with this minimum level of personal allowance. This is prescribed in Regulations made under section 22(4) and (4A) of the National Assistance Act 1948. The amount allowed for personal expenses in the local authority charging assessment is now the same as the amount awarded in the Income Support assessment for residents in residential accommodation who have preserved rights, and is the same for residents whether they are placed in a local authority or independent sector home. Those with preserved rights and who therefore have higher levels of income support – instead of receiving local authority support – will receive their personal expenses from the Benefits Agency. There has been concern that some home managers take account of this guaranteed income and set their level of fees accordingly.

LOCAL AUTHORITY CHARGES FOR ACCOMMODATION

Provision is made in section 22 of the National Assistance Act 1948 for charges to be levied by local authorities for accommodation. Amendments are made to this section by section 44 of the 1990 Act and the amended section is shown in Figure 33.2.

Figure 33.2 National Assistance Act 1948 – section 22

(1) *Subject to section 26 of this Act, where a person is provided with accommodation under this Part of this Act the local authority providing the accommodation shall recover from him the amount of the payment which he is liable to make* in accordance with the following provisions of this section.

(2) Subject to the following provisions of this section, the payment *which a person is liable to make* for any such accommodation shall be in accordance with a standard rate fixed for that accommodation by the authority managing the premises in which it is provided *and the standard rate shall represent the full cost to the authority of providing that accommodation.*

(3) Where a person for whom the accommodation in premises managed by any local authority is provided, or proposed to be provided, under this Part of this Act satisfies the local authority that he is unable to pay therefor at the standard rate, the authority shall assess his ability to pay, and accordingly determine at what lower rate he shall be liable to pay for the accommodation.

(4) In assessing for the purposes of the last foregoing subsection a person's ability to pay, a local authority shall assume that he will need for his personal requirements such sum per week as may be prescribed by the Minister, or such other sum as in special circumstances the authority may consider appropriate.

(4A) Regulations made for the purposes of subsection 4 of this section may prescribe different sums for different circumstances.

(5) In assessing as aforesaid a person's ability to pay, a local authority shall give effect to regulations made by the Secretary of State for the purposes of this subsection except until the first such regulations come into force, a local authority shall give effect to Part III of Schedule 1 to the Supplementary Benefits Act 1976, as it had effect immediately before the amendments made by Schedule 2 of the Social Security Act 1980.

(5A) If they think fit, an authority managing premises in which accommodation is provided for a person shall have power on each occasion when they provide accommodation for him, irrespective of his means, to limit to *such amount as appears to them reasonable for him to pay* [instead of 'the minimum weekly rate prescribed under subsection (3) above'] the payments required from him for his accommodation during a period commencing when they begin to provide the accommodation for him and ending not more than eight weeks after that.

(6) [repealed by Housing (Homeless Persons) Act 1977]

(7) [Repealed by 1990 Act]

(8) Where accommodation is provided by a local authority in premises managed by another local authority, the payment therefor under this section shall be made to the authority managing the premises and not to the authority providing accommodation, but the authority managing the premises shall account for the payment to the authority providing the accommodation.

Comment on section 22

The amended section 22 covers two main provisions:

- the right to charge a cost for accommodation which represents the full cost of the accommodation, based on a standard national figure, and
- the assessment of the individual's contributions on a means-tested/ability to pay basis.

This has the result that national charges are laid down and the local authority is entitled to recover the full cost from each resident. Means-testing is also subject to national criteria. This system is in contrast to the provisions under section 17 of the Health and Social Services and Social Security Adjudication Act 1983 (which is discussed below) whereby contributions can be levied for other welfare services provided by the local authority and where there is no standard basis across the country of either the charge or the means-testing.

Regulations made under section 22(3) and (4), section 35(1) and section 64(1) of the National Assistance Act set charges and are updated from time to time.

Effect of other social security benefits

Whether or not residents have preserved rights, if they are not paying the full cost of the accommodation the care element of any disability living allowance which they are claiming is taken into account in assessing the level of support (see below). In contrast those who are in accommodation for which they pay themselves are entitled to the full levels of attendance allowance and the disability living allowance.

Topping up

By a third party
A third party can offer to 'top up' the payment for accommodation so that the client is placed in accommodation which is more costly than that for which the local authority would normally pay for a person with those needs. If the third party is also liable to support the client (that is a spouse or a parent) the topping up must come after that liability is taken into account. The client can himself top up out of moneys which are disregarded for the purpose of income support.

By a local authority
Section 26A National Assistance Act 1948 prevents the local authority from funding a person entitled to preserved rights unless the situation comes under the *Residential Accommodation (Relevant Premises, Ordinary Residence and Exemptions) Regulations 1993 SI No. 477* These are discussed briefly in Chapter 28 and principally cover transitional arrangements, rectifying some of the anomalies that gave rise to injustice on the strict implementation of the change.

Married couples

Where a person is in receipt of an occupational pension the social services departments can take this into account in assessing the contribution towards the fees of residential/nursing home accommodation, even though the pension is shared with a spouse who may or may not have her own separate income. The result of this may be that the occupational pension is used up entirely for the fees and the spouse remaining at home is dependent upon state benefits. This applies even though after the death of the resident who is entitled to the occupational pension the widow or widower will be entitled to a proportion of the occupational pension for life. Age Concern had suggested that there should be an amendment to the Pensions Bill, now the Pensions Act 1995, to allow the spouse who remains at home the right to half of the partner's occupational pension. This would certainly have alleviated some of the hardship suffered by such a spouse especially where, as in the case of many wives, they do not have entitlement to an occupational pension in their own right. The suggestion was not, however, accepted.

Once one of the couple becomes a resident, for the purpose of income support both are considered separately. However the non-resident partner may be liable to contribute to the fees of accommodation.

MEANS-TESTING BY SOCIAL SERVICES DEPARTMENTS

A local authority is able to charge for specific welfare services on the basis of the National Assistance Act 1948 and the Health and Social Services and Social Security Adjudication Act 1983. Figure 33.3 sets out section 17 of that Act in relation to charges.

Figure 33.3 The 1983 Act – section 17

(1) Subject to subsection (3) below, an authority providing a service to which this section applies may recover such charge (if any) for it as they consider reasonable.

(2) This section applies to services provided under the following enactments —

(a) section 29 of the National Assistance Act 1948 (Welfare arrangements for blind, deaf, dumb and crippled person etc) [see Figure 2.2]
(b) section 45(1) of the Health Services and Public Health Act 1968 (welfare of old people)
(c) [repealed]
(d) section 8 of the Residential Homes Act 1980 (meals and recreation for old people); and
(e) paragraph 1 of Part II of Schedule 9 to this Act *other than the provision of services for which payment may be required under section 22 or 26 of the National Assistance Act 1948* [words italicized added

by to the 1990 Act and came into force on 1 April 1993]

(3) If a person

(a) avails himself of a service to which this section applies, and

(b) satisfies the authority providing the service that his means are insufficient for it to be reasonably practicable for him to pay for the service the amount which he would otherwise be obliged to pay for it,

the authority shall not require him to pay more for it than it appears to them that it is reasonably practicable for him to pay.

As stated above, there is no uniformity across the country in respect of either the charges made or the criteria for means-testing.

ASSESSMENT OF CAPITAL INCLUDING PROPERTY

Where an individual's capital exceeds a specified amount he would have to pay the full charges of any accommodation or other non-NHS welfare service provided. There is a sliding scale for means-testing where the capital is between a lower limit below which no contribution is required and the specified amount above which the resident pays full changes. If there is evidence that an individual has deprived himself of capital in order that he is not eligible to pay for the charges, there can be an assessment of that capital and a consequential reduction of the financial support given (see below).

Where spouses and close relatives live together and one has to be admitted to residential/nursing home accommodation, the value of the house is not taken into account in calculating the client's capital for the purposes of assessing his contribution to the fees. There is no statutory obligation on the person remaining in the house to sell the house or move into a smaller one to be able to contribute to the fees.

However where individuals who live on their own are transferred to residential/nursing home accommodation it is possible for the local authority to recover the sums due where assets are disposed of. There is, therefore, clearly an incentive, because of the nature of this means-testing, for an individual who has to seek residential/nursing home accommodation to attempt to save his assets for his family and to avoid any capital being utilised towards the costs of the accommodation. Such attempts were potentially blocked by the passing of section 21 of the Health and Social Services and Social Security Adjudication Act 1983 although this was not brought into force until 12 April 1993 (SI 1992/2974). Any beneficiary from the transfer of capital is now liable to repay the funds. This section is shown in Figure 33.4.

Figure 33.4   The 1983 Act – section 21

(1) Subject to the following provisions of this section, where –

(a) a person avails himself of Part III accommodation; and

(b) that person knowingly and with the intention of avoiding charges for the accommodation –

   (i) has transferred any asset to which this section applies to some other person or persons not more than six months before the date on which he begins to reside in such accommodation; or

   (ii) transfers any such asset to some other person or persons while residing in the accommodation; and

(c) either

   (i) the consideration of the transfer is less than the value of the asset; or

   (ii) there is not consideration for the transfer,

the person or persons to whom the asset is transferred by the person availing himself of the accommodation shall be liable to pay the local authority providing the accommodation or arranging for its provision the difference between the amount assessed as due to be paid for the accommodation by the person availing himself of it and the amount which the local authority receive from him for it.

(2) This section applies to cash and any other asset which falls to be taken into account for the purpose of assessing under section 22 of the National Assistance Act 1948 the ability to pay for the accommodation of the person availing himself of it.

(3) Subsection (1) above shall have effect in relation to a transfer by a person who leaves Part III accommodation and subsequently resumes residence in such accommodation as if the period mentioned in paragraph (b)(i) were a period of six months before the date on which he resumed residence in such accommodation.

(3A) If the Secretary of State so directs, subsection (1) above shall not apply in such cases as may be specified in the direction. [Underlined words added by section 45(1) of the NHS and Community Care Act 1990 and brought into force on 12 April 1993]

(4) Where a person has transferred an asset to which this section applies to more than one person, the liability of each of the persons to whom it was transferred shall be in proportion to the benefit accruing to him from the transfer.

(5) A person's liability under this section shall not exceed the benefit accruing to him from the trade.

(6) Subject to subsection (7) below, the value of any asset to which this section applies, other than cash, which has been transferred shall be taken to be the amount of the consideration which would have been realised for it if it had been sold on the open market by a willing seller at the time of the transfer.

(7) For the purpose of calculating the value of an asset under subsection (6) above there shall be deducted from the amount of the consideration –

(a) the amount of any incumbrance on the asset; and

(b) a reasonable amount in respect of the expenses of the sale.

Up to 1 July 1992 no order had been made under section 32(2) bringing this section into force. However a commencement order (SI 1992/2974) brought sections 21 to 24 of the 1983 Act into force on 12 April 1993 when it could be co-ordinated with the changes made by the NHS and Community Care Act 1990.

Charge on land to cover debts due

Section 22 of the 1983 Act enables the local authority to create a charge on the interest in the land (see glossary) of any person who fails to pay any sum assessed as due to be paid by him for accommodation provided under Part III of the National Assistance Act 1948 but the 1990 Act introduced an amendment enabling the Secretary of State to issue directions curtailing the discretion of the local authority in determining whether to exercise this power.

Interest on the debt for accommodation secured by such a charge runs from the day after that on which the person for whom the local authority provided the accommodation dies (section 24(1) of the 1983 Act). This means that a resident is not faced with interest charges increasing the burden of debt due for accommodation but there is an incentive on the personal representatives (see glossary) to deal promptly with the estate after the resident's death.

SOCIAL SECURITY BENEFITS

The social fund

This was set up to meet one-off payments and covers two forms of payment, repayable and non-repayable loans. The Social Fund is budget limited and is separated into two divisions: one budget covering budgeting and crisis loans, the other covering community care grants. Applications will be priority rated. Guidance on priorities is given in the leaflets. The fund covers the following payments:

- budgeting loan
- crisis loan
- community care grant
- maternity payments
- funeral payments
- cold weather payments.

Budgeting loan:
This is interest free but repayable, and it is allotted on three priority levels.

It covers as a high priority:

- essential items of furniture or household equipment including bed clothes;
- removal expenses for a move deemed to be essential;
- fuel meter installation and reconnection charges; and
- non-mains fuel costs such as central heating oil, solid fuel or bottled gas.

Medium priority covers:

- non-essential items of furniture and household equipment;
- redecoration;
- hire purchase and other debts;
- clothing where what one has is inadequate or insufficient.

Low priority items (which with budget pressures are unlikely to be met):

- rent in advance;
- removal costs;
- leisure items.

The rating of the applications in terms of priority is in the discretion of the Social Fund Officer. The granting of the application will depend upon the priority rating and if there is enough money left in the Social Fund budget.

Excluded expenses: Certain expenditures are excluded:

- maternity expenses, funeral expenses and cold weather payments (which are available from other social fund payments);
- medical services (NHS services are free to any one on income support);
- needs outside the UK;
- repairs to a council house/flat;
- educational or training needs;
- distinctive school clothing;
- travelling expenses to and from school;
- school meals;
- expenses due to a court appearance;
- removal charges if being permanently rehoused;
- domestic assistance or respite care;
- a returnable deposit for accommodation;

- any expense connected with looking for or getting work;
- debts to Government departments;
- investments;
- mains fuel consumption;
- housing costs.

Conditions of eligibility: Any funds over £500 will reduce the loan pound for pound. The loan will normally be for a minimum of £30 and a maximum of £1000. The amount lent will depend upon the ability to repay. In calculating the weekly repayment figure (which must be agreed with the recipient) account will be taken of other debts and income of the recipient. There are three repayment rates:

- 15% of weekly income support;
- 10% of weekly income support; and
- 5% of weekly income support.

The loans must normally be repaid over a maximum of 78 weeks.

Payment is usually in one lump sum to the recipient but it can in certain circumstances be made payable to someone else.

Those in residential/nursing homes: The recipients will be expected to repay the loan out of the personal allowance which they have.

Crisis loans
These are interest free and are similarly repayable.

They cover the costs arising from an emergency or crisis where no other help is immediately available and there is a serious risk to the health or safety of applicants or their family. A crisis loan can cover:

- a disaster causing damage, loss or destruction of possessions or property;
- loss of money following a burglary;
- the days waiting for payment of income support;
- emergency travel expenses for someone stranded away from home;
- other crises which in the discretion of the Social Fund Officer merit payment and where there are funds in the budget.

Excluded items: These are all those expenses listed under the exclusions to a budgeting loan and in addition:

- installation, rental and call charges for a telephone;
- holidays;
- a television or radio, or a licence, aerial or rental charges for these items;
- costs connected with running a vehicle.

Eligibility: The applicant does not have to be in receipt of income support but the following are excluded from receiving a crisis loan:

- someone aged under 18 years;
- a resident of a nursing or residential home or anyone in Part III accommodation;
- anyone detained by law;
- anyone who is a member of a religious order and provided for by the order;
- a hospital in-patient;
- a person treated as in full-time education.

The Social Fund Officer will take into account resources including savings, earnings and cash in hand, and other sources of help including employers, relatives, charities and benevolent funds.

There is no minimum amount. The maximum amount for living expenses is 75% of the income support which would be appropriate for the circumstances of the recipient. For other needs the maximum will be the lower of the full cost of repair or the full cost of purchasing an item or service.

The time of repayment and period over which it is to be paid will be agreed with the Social Fund Officer.

Funeral payments
These are repayable from the estate of the dead person. The loan covers

- the cost within the UK of bringing the body home to the UK if the person died abroad;
- travel to arrange the funeral;
- death certificate and the cost of other necessary documentation;
- an ordinary coffin;
- a car for the coffin and bearers and one other car;
- flowers from the person arranging the funeral;
- fees for the undertaker, chaplain and organist for a simple burial;

- cemetery or crematorium fees;
- up to £75 extra costs because of the religion of the dead person.

The amount granted will take into account the resources of the applicant and funds available from the estate. Apart from that, the sums payable are fixed and not at the discretion of the Social Fund Officer.

Community care grant

The aim of this grant, which is not repayable, is to provide help for people to lead independent lives in the community. It can be paid to those leaving institutional care and also those who need assistance to help them remain in the community.

Excluded items: Those exclusions listed under budget loans and crisis loans are also excluded from a community care grant.

Eligibility: This depends upon whether the applicant is in receipt of income support and will be reduced pound for pound by any funds over £500. Priority groups include the following:

- elderly people;
- mentally handicapped;
- mentally ill;
- physically disabled people, including those with impaired hearing, sight or speech;
- chronically sick people, especially the terminally ill;
- people who have misused alcohol or drugs;
- ex-offenders who need resettlement;
- people with no settled way of life;
- families under stress;
- young people leaving council care.

Those leaving institutional or residential care: Such people may be able to obtain a grant if they are setting up home in the community and will be responsible for their own rent and furniture. The grant could cover:

- items of furniture, furnishings, household equipment or bedding
- clothing
- removal expenses
- travel costs
- connection charges.

The grant can also be paid to someone who is moving house in order to look after someone who is leaving residential or institutional care.

Help to stay in the community: A community grant is available to improve living conditions or to help the applicant move to more suitable accommodation.

The grant can also be paid to those who:

- are moving to be nearer to relatives;
- are moving to look after a vulnerable person;
- are moving into the community for the first time.

If help is needed to stay in the existing situation it can be used to cover:

- internal redecoration
- bedding or extra warmth
- fuel costs
- laundry
- special furniture
- clothing
- moving expenses
- travel costs
- connection or reconnection charges
- essential items of furniture, household equipment or bedding.

Families under stress: This priority group includes families where there is

- someone suffering from a disability or chronic sickness;
- a breakdown of relationships;
- a deterioration in the accommodation.

The payments can cover:

- clothing
- decoration
- security items
- installation of meters
- moving costs
- minor structural repairs
- reconnection charges
- travelling expenses
- accommodation.

The Social Fund Officer will take into account the means of the applicant including savings. Any amount over £500 will be reduced pound for pound.

Maternity payments

These are paid as an entitlement to those who are eligible on a means-tested basis and who meet the other eligibility requirements. It is paid to those who are getting either income support or family credit. It can be applied for after the 29th week of pregnancy and until the child is three months old. It is not repayable.

Cold weather payments

These are intended to help towards the extra heating costs during very cold weather. They are paid from the Social Fund as lump sums and are not repayable. The applicant (or partner) must be over 60 or disabled or long-term sick and in receipt of income support.

The payment is made when the average daily temperature in the area is freezing or colder over a continuous period of seven days.

Challenges to the decisions of Social Fund Officers

There is a right of appeal to an independent Social Security Appeals tribunal. The appeal must be made within three months of the decision being made.

A request can also be made for the decision to be reviewed. This would apply where:

- the decision was made without the Social Fund Officer being aware of all the facts; or
- a factual mistake was made; or
- the law was applied wrongly; or
- the applicant's circumstances have changed since the decision was made.

The review decision can be appealed against.

Independent living fund

This fund set up by the Government and the Disablement Income Group enables additional payments to be made to those with severe disabilities living in the community. In April 1993 two separate funds were set up:

- the Independent Living (Extension) Fund which continued to provide assistance to those who were in receipt of payments from the old ILF; and
- the Independent Living (1993) Fund which provides help to the severely disabled who had not received help from the old ILF.

The new rules are more restrictive than those under the original ILF and further details of each of the funds can be obtained from Nottingham (see address in Appendix 7).

Disability living allowance

The disability living allowance is a non-means tested benefit which consists of two separate parts, the care component and the mobility component. A person may be eligible for both of these, either of these or neither. The provisions are set out in the Social Security Contributions and Benefits Act 1992. The main provisions are given below. For further details refer to the *Disability Rights Handbook*[3] and the Benefits Agency publication.

Care component
A person will be entitled if:

- he is so severely disabled physically or mentally that he requires in connection with his bodily functions attention from another person for a significant portion of the day (whether during a single period or a number of periods), or he cannot prepare a cooked main meal for himself if he has the ingredients; or
- he is so severely disabled physically or mentally that, by day, he requires from another person frequent attention throughout the day in connection with his bodily functions, or continual supervision throughout the day in order to avoid substantial danger to himself or others; or
- he is so severely disabled physically or mentally that, at night, he requires from another person prolonged or repeated attention in connection with his bodily functions, or in order to avoid substantial danger to himself or others he requires another person to be awake for a prolonged period or at frequent intervals for the purpose of watching over him.

There are three weekly rates for the care component. It is normally payable only to those under 65 years (for those over 65 see attendance allowance below) and specific provisions apply to the terminally ill and those under 16 years.

The care component is not payable to those living in the following accommodation:

- residential care homes (unless the resident has preserved rights); and
- nursing home accommodation paid for out of public or local funds as a result of legislation (unless the resident has preserved rights).

Stays under 28 days do not count, unless there has been an admission in the previous 28 days.

Mobility component
This is available to a person over five years if:

- he is suffering from physical disablement such that he is either unable to walk or virtually unable to do so; or
- he is both blind and deaf and he satisfies such other conditions as may be prescribed; or
- he is able to walk but is so severely disabled physically or mentally that, disregarding any ability he may have to use routes which are familiar to him on his own, he cannot take advantage of the faculty out of doors without guidance or supervision from another person most of the time.

There are two levels of payment. It is also payable to the terminally ill.

Attendance allowance

Attendance allowance is payable to those of 65 and over and who are severely physically or mentally disabled. It is not means-tested.

There are two levels of payment – the middle and the higher rates of the care component of the disability living allowance allocated according to the level of care needed.

Invalid care allowance

This is a non-means tested benefit payable to people of working age who regularly spend at least 35 hours a week caring for a severely disabled person. It is payable to the person who is caring for a person who is in receipt of attendance allowance or the care component of disability living allowance at the middle or higher level.

Income support

This is a means-tested benefit which is available to those who are out of work and whose income is lower than the sum calculated and specified by the regulations as the minimum income (known as 'the applicable amount'). Payment is calculated as the difference between the actual income and the applicable amount, taking into account those whom the individual is liable to maintain. A person is liable in law to maintain his or her spouse.

A parent is liable to maintain children up to the age of 16 years and children of 16, 17 and 18 if they are in full time education or if another person is obtaining income support in respect of that child.

If a patient is admitted into NHS accommodation, his entitlement to income support ceases after six weeks of hospitalisation.

CONCLUSION

The view is gradually emerging that radical changes must eventually be made to the funding of social services and social security payments since, with the growing proportion of those over 75 and 85 in the population, it will be impossible to meet their needs from public expenditure on the same basis as at present. One move towards this change is the shifting of expenditure on long-term care from the NHS to social services on a means-tested basis. Interestingly, this development has not led to any major savings in the NHS budget since the new developments in acute and high technology medicine have more than swallowed any transfer of long-term and geriatric care to the social services budget.

Groups such as Help the Aged and Age Concern recognise that there may have to be major changes to funding of long-term care. In a report *Coming Clean on Costs*[4] Help the Aged suggests that a scheme set up in Germany should be the model for a new compulsory scheme to finance long-term care of elderly people. The scheme is funded by contribution from employers and members of the work force who pay an extra 1 per cent on eligible earnings with a maximum monthly contribution of about £24. Other suggestions which are being examined by Government[5] include:

- tax breaks to encourage new-style private residential and nursing homes, where residents could buy a lease;
- creating a tax-privileged 'care bond' to encourage saving for old age;

- changing the tax system to encourage the growth of care insurance for the elderly; and

- allowing an elderly person, on entering residential care, to invest the capital from the sale of his house in a trust, pay the fees from the income and be able to leave the trust for family to inherit.

The latter suggestion is to meet the criticism that inheritance hopes are dashed when property is sold to meet fees.

In May 1996 the Government issued a Consultation Paper *A New Partnership for Care in Old Age* which aimed to encourage people to make provision for their own long term needs and to stimulate the financial services industry to offer attractive, reliable products which will enable people to make provision easily and affordably. One suggestion is the promotion of a partnership scheme whereby there would be disregards of capital for sums paid for insurance benefit, to provide protection against means-testing.

Subject to the responses to the Consultation Paper, legislation is to be introduced in time for schemes to be marketed in 1997.

Undoubtedly more suggestions will come forth on the issue of the funding, not only of accomodation, but also of all health care costs for the growing numbers of elderly in society.

CHAPTER 34

The management of finances and handling client's property

Care staff are often extremely concerned about the property of their clients. Some residents may have considerable funds in their hands and some may buy expensive equipment.

● What is the duty of the care staff and other professionals in connection with such items, whether cash or property?

● What systems should be established to ensure that the property is taken care of appropriately?

● What is the liability of the care staff if equipment or cash goes missing?

● How can the care staff protect themselves against charges of fraud or theft or obtaining property by deception?

This chapter seeks to provide an answer to these questions. The topics set out in Figure 34.1 will be considered.

Figure 34.1 Topics covered in this chapter

● Nature of the duty of care
● Liability for financial and other advice
● Exemption from liability
● Bailment principles
● Cash on the premises
● System for recording expenditure
● Duty to prevent clients exploiting each other
● Valuable equipment
● Risk taking and property
● Gifts to staff
● Incompetent clients:
    Agency and powers of attorney
    Social security appointees
    Guardianship

Court of Protection
● Accumulated savings
● Making of wills

NATURE OF THE DUTY OF CARE

Those who care for the vulnerable in society have a duty to care not only for their health and safety but also for their property. In certain circumstances, the duty to look after property can be excluded – for example in a general hospital patients would be invited to hand over any valuable property to the safety of the staff and warned that any other property they wish to keep with them will be at their own risk. However where clients clearly do not have the mental or physical capacity to look after their own property safely, then the duty will fall upon care staff.

■ What standards would be applied to this duty?

Care staff would be expected to take reasonable precautions to safeguard property against reasonably foreseeable events according to the accepted approved standard of practice at the time. Guidance on what this would include can be found in such publications as *Other People's Money* produced by Age Concern in conjunction with other charities[6].

LIABILITY FOR FINANCIAL AND OTHER ADVICE

Staff may sometimes be asked for advice by residents on their entitlement, expenditure and other financial problems. If advice is given negligently and is wrong (for example the client is wrongly told that he is not eligible to claim a particular benefit and as a result the client loses the opportunity of receiving certain funds) then the person giving that advice could be held liable, and the employer held vicariously liable if the advice was given in course of employment. In these circumstances the staff should be instructed on who is the most appropriate person to give such advice. Some districts have set up liaison officers between social services and social security who would be able to provide advice when necessary.

EXEMPTION FROM LIABILITY

It is possible to exclude liability for negligence in relation to property. The Unfair Contract Terms Act 1977 allows for liability for negligence to be excluded where property is lost or damaged, but only if it is reasonable to rely upon that exclusion clause.

The definition of reasonable in section 11 of the Act is set out in Figure 34.2.

Figure 34.2 Unfair Contract Terms Act 1977 – section 11

(3) In relation to a notice (not being a notice having contractual effect), the requirement of reasonableness under this Act is that it should be fair and reasonable to allow reliance on it, having regard to all the circumstances obtaining when the liability arose or (but for the notice) would have arisen.

(4) Where by a reference to a contract term or notice a person seeks to restrict liability to a specified sum of money, and the question arises (under this or any other Act) whether the term or notice satisfies the requirement of reasonableness, regard shall be had in particular . . . to —

(a) the resources which he could expect to be available to him for the purpose of meeting the liability should it arise; and
(b) how far it was open to him to cover himself by insurance.

(5) It is for those claiming that a contract term or notice satisfies the requirement of reasonableness to show that it does.

BAILMENT PRINCIPLES

If property is entrusted to a member of staff then the principles of the law of bailment apply. The person who is given the property to look after is known as the bailee and she has a duty to take all reasonable precautions to safeguard the property and to return it to the bailor (the person who entrusted the property for the bailee's safekeeping) when requested to do so or according to the agreement. Should the property be lost or damaged, then the burden is on the bailee to show that she was not negligent in taking care of the property, thus reversing the usual burden of proof.

CASH ON THE PREMISES

Holding large sums of cash on the premises should be avoided for both internal and external reasons. The responsibility of controlling those funds in relation to the clients themselves becomes more difficult and, if it becomes known outside that sums of cash are kept on the premises, there is a greater danger of burglaries. If holding cash on the premises is temporarily unavoidable steps should be taken to ensure that reasonable precautions are taken and these would include the use of a safe.

SYSTEM FOR RECORDING EXPENDITURE

One of the requirements under the Residential Care Homes (Amendment) Regulations 1988 issued under the Registered Homes Act 1984 is that

> the person registered shall compile the records specified in Schedule 2 to the regulations and shall keep them in the home at all times available for inspection by any person authorised in that behalf by the registration authority or, as the case may be, the Secretary of State[7].

Schedule 2 (as amended) provides for records for each individual resident of any money or other valuables received on his behalf and how it has been spent or disposed of by the registered person.

Even where the Registered Homes Act does not apply, there are considerable advantages for the carer to keep an account of the expenditure of the client's money where the latter is too incapacitated to spend it himself. This also applies whenever the carer assists the client in shopping or buys purchases on his behalf. A clear system of accounting should be set up in the home. It should include account of sums given out to the client for him to spend and it should also include details of all transactions on behalf of the client, with receipts indicating the expenditure and with a witness to show that the expenditure was incurred on the client's behalf. (A receipt on its own merely indicates that a payment has been made – it does not show who has obtained the benefit.)

The same principles apply to the handing out of the pocket moneys to clients, and their expenditure.

VALUABLE EQUIPMENT

It is not unusual for valuable equipment to be brought onto the premises of residential homes and care accommodation.

■ What responsibilities do the managers and staff have in relation to the protection of such equipment?

In most hospitals there is now a procedure for patients to be offered the facility of handing over their property for safekeeping to the hospital managers and, if they fail to do so, then they accept that they are responsible for it and the hospital is not liable for its loss or damage. This is entirely appropriate where there is a short length of stay. However, where the residential home, hostel or accommodation is the client's home for the immediate future, it is not always appropriate.

Care staff would have a responsibility to ensure that all reasonable precautions were taken in relation to the safety of residents' property and to ensure that residents are given proper advice over its care. The staff would obviously have to take into account the capacity of each client to take precautions and to take simple steps for protection of property. Suitable advice might include advice on insurance cover or enabling clients to have secure cupboards or locks to their bedrooms.

DUTY TO PREVENT CLIENTS EXPLOITING EACH OTHER

Many of the clients who are the subject of community care are vulnerable to exploitation by others. These others may include not only fellow residents in residential accommodation but also staff and relatives. Difficulties arise particularly for some clients who are especially generous and wish to share any property or cash they have with others. In some cases the level of competence of the client is so low that they do not appreciate that they are being exploited.

■ At what stage do staff have a duty to step in and prevent exploitation?

Where those doing the exploiting are other clients, then the carer or staff should ensure that the exploited client receives training over the care of his money and the use which can be made of it. Where relatives are exploiting the client difficulties arise. If relatives are the appointees of rights of entitlement from social security, it is difficult for staff to ensure that the funds are always spent wisely and in the best interests of the client. They can however ask relevant questions to put the appointees on guard that the situation is being noted. Certain benefits will cease after the client has been in NHS accommodation for more than four weeks. In residential accommodation social security benefits such as income support would be allocated toward the costs of the accommodation. Clients should have their personal allowance of £13.75 (in 1996) but this may be managed on their behalf. Recommendations have been made that the supervision of appointees should be tightened up.

Where persons are being cared for at home, it is more difficult to ensure that the income they receive from social security is used for their benefit and there is at present no system for the financial arrangements to be monitored. This is the subject of the Law Commission's consultation paper Number 128. The Department of Social Security enable an appointee to be named to be the recipient of income on behalf of a beneficiary (see discussion below). However, whilst there would be checks on records kept in residential care homes of the client's finances and thus controls when the person registered under the Registered Homes Act 1984 is the appointee, in the domestic situation there is no system for checks and regular controls, or even for records to be kept. The Law Commission in its final report on mental incapacity[8] has drafted legislation which provides for the court, after a declaration that an individual lacks the capacity to make a particular decision or decisions, could make specific decisions on that person's behalf or appoint a manager.

RISK TAKING AND PROPERTY

In a residential home where other residents are exploiting the good nature of a particular resident, staff have to draw a distinction between allowing the resident to make his own choices on how he wishes to spend his money and stepping in to protect him when such exploitation amounts to theft.

This is part of the risk taking which is necessary for the care of persons in the community. To enable clients to have responsibility for their own property and income means that certain risks have to be taken. These can be assessed and reasonable precautions taken if necessary. The protection of the vulnerable by staff could also consist of attempts to reason with the exploiter and prevent the abuse occurring. (See the discussion on risk taking in relation to professional accountability in Chapter 7 and in relation to health and safety in Chapter 9.)

One of the biggest difficulties for care staff is knowing at which point, they should step in to protect residents or clients against themselves. At one extreme this may simply be a question of preventing a client spending all his pocket money on ice creams and making himself ill. Much of course depends upon the capacity of the client to understand cause and effect and to learn lessons in relation to the spending of money inappropriately and the subsequent discomfort. If there is no such capacity, then it could be argued that the staff have a duty in law to prevent the client harming himself through the purchases he makes. If there is capacity to understand then it could be argued that such a lesson may mean that the client will not spend in such a way on a subsequent occasion.

At the other extreme it could be the question of the use of credit cards by a manic depressive person.

Situation

A person who has suffered from manic depression for many years suffers from bouts of illness when he spends widely and extravagantly, incurring considerable debts. During such a bout care staff in the hostel where he was living suggested to him that he should give them his credit cards to avoid incurring debts which he could not repay. He refused to surrender the cards and went off to the shops. The staff knew that he would spend wildly. They also knew that he would regret this as soon as that episode of the illness was over. They considered whether they should contact the credit card company to inform it of the circumstances, so that the company could withdraw the card. What is their legal position?

On the one hand it could be argued that the carers have a duty to protect the client and therefore this would justify and include the duty to report the situation to the credit company. Indeed, in so doing it might be what the client in his right mind would wish of them. Failure to report the client would therefore be a breach of the duty of care which is owed to the client.

On the other hand it could be argued that to report the client is to step outside the boundaries of the duty required of care staff. The client might challenge their actions when he is recovered and in fact that reporting might lead to long-term effects, perhaps depriving the client of the possibility of obtaining credit at a later time when it was necessary and he was capable of handling it competently.

There has been no court case to determine the issue but it could be argued that the House of Lords decision in *Re F* (see glossary) applies to this situation as well as to the context of personal care and treatment. This case is discussed in Chapter 3. The House of Lords held that if a professional acted in the best interests of an incapacitated patient out of necessity according to the Bolam test (see glossary) he would not be acting unlawfully. There is judicial authority[9] for acting in an emergency to save property. These authorities are cited in the Law Commission's consultation paper on a new jurisdiction for *Decision Making and the Mentally Incapacitated Adult*[10]. The Law Commission states that

> where the owner is incapable of consenting the defence of necessity may be available if, in an emergency for example, interference is reasonably necessary to protect the property.

It will not apply in other circumstances, even where the person interfering has acted in good faith.

Unfortunately the Court of Protection as at present constituted does not have the powers to deal with the situation where the incapacitated person has no property, only the potential to obtain credit and incur debts. The possibility of alternative decision making procedures which would include financial decision making is the subject of this second consultation by the Law Commission[11]. The Law Commission has produced firm proposals including draft legislation for decision making on behalf of the mentally incapacitated adult. At the time of writing these are awaiting Government response[12].

GIFTS TO STAFF

There should be a policy which sets out the owners'/social services policy on gifts. In addition professional staff will be bound by their codes of professional conduct. The clearest policy is that no gifts are acceptable between clients and staff. However this is not entirely realistic and could be upsetting to clients who wish to show their affection to staff, especially on birthdays and at Christmas.

One alternative approach is to allow communal gifts for the benefit of all staff or personal gifts which do not cost money but represent the craft or work of the client. Where there is no blanket policy against the receipt of gifts, it is essential for staff always to notify their manager of any gift which they have been given, and to check if it is acceptable and ensure that the receipt is recorded. Care must be taken to ensure that there is no favouritism as a result of the receipt of gifts.

Paragraph 15 of the revised *Code of Conduct* issued by the UKCC in June 1992 is as follows:

> Refuse any gift, favour, or hospitality from patients or clients currently in your care which might be interpreted as seeking to exert influence to obtain preferential consideration.

These guidelines would be appropriate for all staff whether or not they are registered practitioners.

Exactly the same principles apply to gifts from relatives and others.

There is also a danger that, if the gift is not reported and subsequently the client changes his mind or forgets that he has made the person a gift, the recipient could be charged with theft.

In the absence of a witness or a report and discussion with a senior manager it would be very difficult for the recipient to prove that there was actually a gift and not a theft[13].

INCOMPETENT CLIENTS

The basic presumption is in support of the client being responsible for his own finances. In residential accommodation this principle should also apply[14]. Where, however, the client is incapable of such control and responsibility other controls must be used.

There are various devices for protecting the property of those who are mentally incompetent or for other reasons are unable to handle their own financial affairs. The entire topic is the subject of review by the Law Commission which has initiated consultation on decision making by the mentally incompetent adult. Consultation paper No. 119[15] explored the background to the problem and set out the general issues and possible changes to the law. Following the response to the consultation, Papers Nos. 128, 129 and 130 were issued on specific aspects of decision making by the mentally incompetent adult. Subsequently the Law Commission has issued Report No. 231 which contains draft legislation covering the area. The Government response to this is currently being analysed and legislation is anticipated shortly.

Below is a summary of various ways currently available of appointing agents of for handling property and finances on behalf of another.

Agency and powers of attorney

It has always been possible for a person to appoint another to act as his or her agent, providing the appointer has the capacity to do so. A 'power of attorney' can be set up which gives specific powers for an individual to act on behalf of another. However, if the appointer became mentally incompetent, the power ended by law. This was often, of course, the very time that another person would be required to act as agent, so the Enduring Powers of Attorney Act 1985 was passed which would enable those powers to still be exercised when the appointer became mentally incompetent.

There are strict formalities relating to the setting up of an enduring power of attorney and the appointee must work within the powers given to him. These can be very wide or narrowly defined. A significant safeguard is that the enduring power has to be registered when the appointer becomes mentally incapable and this registration has to be notified to the appointer and his or her nearest relatives.

Powers of attorney can only relate to financial and property matters. It is considered that they do not extend to decision making in relation to medical treatment.

Social security appointees

If a social security beneficiary is unable to manage his affairs, the Secretary of State for Social Security may appoint someone else to exercise on behalf of the beneficiary the right to make claims for and receive payment on his behalf. If the beneficiary is in residential care accommodation a close relative who regularly visits the client may be appointed. As a last resort the person registered under the Registered Homes Act 1984 may be appointed. The records which must be kept by the registered person in relation to client's moneys will show how the DSS moneys are accounted for.

Where the appointee in respect of a claim for income support is the registered person under the 1984 Act, the DSS local offices then have a duty to inform the local social services authority with whom the person running the home is registered of all existing and future appointments. On their inspections the local authority social services must inspect the statutory records. If the authority suspect that the income is being misused, then it should inform the local social security office. The DSS can take any necessary action, including the revocation of the appointeeship. For further details of this system see LAC (88)15 and LAC(89)8 and Appendix 1 to that circular[16]. The Alzheimer's Disease Society has also published a useful information sheet.

Sometimes the carer will be the appointee for the receipt of benefits from the Department of Social Security. The appointee has a duty to use these benefits in the best interests of the client. However, there is at present little monitoring of expenditure by appointees on the client's behalf and the Law Commission is suggesting that there could be a tightening up of this system.

Guardianship

Guardianship of an adult is only available when a person is mentally disordered within the definition of the Mental Health Act 1983. There are only limited powers – none in relation to property (see Chapter 4).

Court of Protection

Where the client has significant property but through mental disorder is unable to care for it, then an application can be made to the Court of Protection for the court to appoint a receiver. Specialist books and pamphlets are recommended on this.

Part VII of the Mental Health Act 1983 covers the law relating to the functions of a judge of the Court of Protection over the property and affairs of a mentally disordered person and the appointment of a receiver. There has been criticism that the system is too slow and costly for small funds and the short procedure which has been introduced does not meet all the criticisms. In addition, legal aid is not available for help with the costs charged by the Court of Protection or legal fees in making the application. Further information can, however, be obtained from the Public Trustee Office.

The role of the Court of Protection is also the subject of review within the Law Commission's Consultation on decision making and the mentally incapacitated adult[17].

ACCUMULATED SAVINGS

When the mentally disordered and elderly were living in long stay institutional accommodation, large sums of savings grew and became a concern to hospital managers. Mersey Regional Health Authority prepared a paper setting out guidelines on the use of these funds[18]. The legal justification for using these funds for the benefit of all patients rather than just the individual's benefit is of doubtful origin and legal advice should be sought before these funds are used for purposes other than for the individual benefit of the patient.

This problem is less likely to arise in the community, where the encouragement of and opportunity for clients to purchase for their own benefit is likely to reduce the tendency for savings to accumulate. However, where for one reason or another large sums do accumulate and the client lacks the competence to determine how they should be spent, it is necessary to have recourse to the Court of Protection.

MAKING OF WILLS

Clients may sometimes wish to make a will of property to the home in which they are living. In such cases it is essential to ensure that the client receives independent advice and that a solicitor draws up the will. There is a rule that a beneficiary cannot benefit from a will which he has witnessed. It is essential, therefore, that no-one in the home should be a witness in such cases. The mental capacity of the testator to make a will must also be verified.

To be valid a will must comply with the statutory requirements shown in figure 34.3.

Figure 34.3 Legal requirements for a valid will

- The testator must have the mental capacity to make a will.
- The testator is not under the influence of any one.
- Testator is 18 or over.
- The will is in writing.
- It is signed by the testator, or by some other person under his direction, and such signature is witnessed.
- Two witnesses sign the will as witnesses in the presence of the testator.

Capacity of the testator

To be recognised as a valid will, the person making the will must have the required mental capacity. The person making the will must understand the nature of the transaction which she is undertaking and the likely effects and purposes of it and intend to make those dispositions. In other words, the individual must understand what a will is, what will happen and intend the particular gifts after death.

Where a carer or professional is aware that a person wishes to make a will and there is doubt as to her mental capacity to do so, it would be wise to ensure that a doctor was called to determine the capacity and in any case for legal advice to be sought. (See Alzheimer's Disease Society information sheet no. 5 on making a will.)

A will can be challenged on the grounds that it was made by someone who lacked the necessary testamentary capacity, or who was under the undue influence at the time it was made so that it does not reflect his real wishes. It can be challenged on the grounds that it was not validly executed.

Where there is reasonable doubt as to the competence of an individual to make a will, it may be necessary to call in the assistance of the Court of Protection which can arrange for a judge to draw up a will on behalf of a person who is mentally disordered. Section 96(1)(e) of the Mental Health Act 1983 gives power to a judge to make orders relating to

> the execution for the patient of a will making any provision (whether by way of disposing of property or exercising a power or otherwise) which could be made by a will executed by the patient if he were not mentally disordered.

Section 97 sets out the formalities which must be followed in the execution of such a will to ensure that it is valid.

CONCLUSIONS

The highest standards of practice are required in the care of another person's property. Community professionals need to ensure that not only do they take reasonable care for the protection of the property of the clients, but that they also follow the procedures necessary to ensure that they themselves are above reproach and beyond suspicion. Where clients lack the requisite capacity to take care of their own property themselves duties in relation to that property are placed upon community professionals and carers.

REFERENCES FOR SECTION E

1. At the time of writing the latest amendment is LAC(95)8 Manuscript amendment to *Charging for Residential Accommodation* (CRAG)
2. *National Assistance (Sums for Personal Requirements) Regulations* 1996, SI No. 391
3. Disability Rights Handbook, Disability Alliance ERA (annual)
4. Martin Kohler *Coming Clean on Costs* Help the Aged, 1995
5. Michael Prescott 'Major throws a lifeline to families caring for the elderly,' *Sunday Times* 23 April 1995
5a. Consultation Paper *A New Partnership for Care in Old Age* HMSO, 1996
6. *Other People's Money* Age Concern 1992
7. *Residential Care Homes (Amendment) Regulations 1988* Paragraph 6(1)
8. Law Commission Report No 231 Mental Incapacity HMSO 1995
9. *Kirk* v. *Gregory* 1876 1 Ex.D 55 and *Rigby* v. *Chief Constable of North* [1985] 1 WLR 1242 at 1254
10. Paragraph 2.5 Law Commission Consultation Paper No. 128 *A new jurisdiction* HMSO, 1993
11. see Consultation Paper No. 128 *Mentally Incapacitated Adults and Decision Making: a new jurisdiction* HMSO, 1993
12. Law Commission Report No. 231 *Mental Incapacity* HMSO, 1995
13. see HC(62)21
14. *Home Life: A Code of Practice for Residential Care* Centre for the Policy on Ageing 1984
15. issued in 1991 HMSO
16. DHSS Circular No. LAC(88)15 paragraph 12
17. Law Commission Report No. 231 *Mental Incapacity* HMSO, 1995
18. Mersey Regional Health Authority *A precious resource: guidelines for the use of money held by health authorities on behalf of long stay patients.* Revised edition January 1991.

CHAPTER 35

The future

Writing on the law of community care is like sitting at the sea-side, trying to draw the sea at a particular moment. The tide is moving too quickly for it to be accurate for more than one tiny moment of time. Between putting aside the word processor and the date of publication of this book, there are likely to be more developments in policy, practice and the law – each of significance. However, this hopefully does not destroy the need for such a book as this.

It is inevitable that there will be further fine tuning of the statutory basis of the laws relating to community care and further directions from the Department of Health can be expected as problems which cannot be resolved locally emerge. Recent court decisions have shown that the courts are ambivalent in intervening over resourcing issues and are unwilling to recognise individual applications to the courts for breach of statutory duties. Discontent therefore with assessment regimes and the allocation of resources will have to resort to political remedies rather than judicial resolution.

The Department of Health and the Audit Commission have kept under close review the implementation of the community care reforms and are likely to continue to do so, but the dilemma between additional central control and a *laissez faire* approach devolving responsibility to the new local unitary authorities and health authorities will always remain as long as Ministers are answerable to Parliament for the minutiae of community care activities and omissions.

Further developments will be seen in the following areas:

Primary health care. The health authorities set up in April 1996 are obliged to have a primary health care focus. The significance and meaning of this remains to be seen and much will depend upon the willingness of general practitioners to play a full role in community care provision. New responsibilities are being placed upon them through the impact of day surgery and a shorter length of stay for acute care, but the full implications of the loss of long-stay continuing care beds provided by the NHS are still to be realised.

Secondary care. If primary care focus does take place, there are likely to be further reductions in the number of acute beds and even of District General Hospitals and very little long-stay accommodation will be provided by the NHS. More manpower will be shifted from secondary care to primary and community care.

GP fund-holding. This, subject to a change of Government, will expand until the vast majority of health care purchasing will be in the hands of the GPs. The issues surrounding the accountability of the GP fund-holder to the Health Commissioners or Department of Health are still to be resolved and the conflict between the GP's duty of care to the individual patient and his or her duty as a budget holder is likely to arise in court actions brought by aggrieved patients.

Legislation may be issued to cover the following areas:

- A new Mental Health Act which unlike the current 1983 Act is focused on the community rather than institutional care.
- The implementation of the Law Commission's proposals for a statutory framework for decision making on behalf of the mentally incapacitated adult including protection for the elderly who are subject to abuse.
- Legislation to clarify and consolidate all community care statutory provision. (Possibly the author's wishful thinking!)

Inevitably as the proportion of elderly in our population increases, any Government will be faced with the funding issues of community care, both NHS and social services. Both major political parties now recognise that private individuals must be required to contribute to schemes which will fund the cost of pensions and their care in old age. The Adam Smith Institute has put forward ideas for privatising the £90 billion welfare budget (*The Times*, 5 January 1996) which the labour party are currently studying. The main charities caring for the elderly have recognised that the future costs are likely to be too great to be met entirely by central funds.

In the long term it is likely that there will be major organisational changes to the administrative structure of the health and social services. The split between purchasing and providing, the new local government unitary authorities established in April 1996 and the health authorities which combine functions formally exercised by FHSAs and DHAs will facilitate the move towards combined health and social services commissioning organisations, perhaps close to the model in Northern Ireland. Social services may be removed from local authority controls and health authority boards be abolished and both come under the direct control of the NHS Management Executive, regional tier.

This is for the future. The implications for the individual professional working in the community are clear. They must be constantly vigilant to the new ideas, directions, policies, and legal changes which take place. Even though after each report of violence by a former patient of an institution, there are calls for the progress toward community care to be reversed, this is unlikely to occur. The effect of the after-care supervision order will determine the extent to which community care provision is sufficient to protect the public and the patient.

The community professional has an important part to play in supporting the family (which has always played the most significant role in providing community care) to shoulder the burden of an increasingly older population and caring for the physically and mentally impaired and ill. To undertake this task successfully, the community professional requires to have a thorough detailed knowledge of the clients' rights and also a clear understanding of her or his statutory responsibilities, duties and rights and must ensure that this knowledge is regularly updated.

Inevitably the success or failure of care in the community rests upon the extent to which each member of society is prepared to recognise and support the right of each individual to live outside the institutions and within the community.

The members of a community participate in one another's nature: we appreciate what others do as things we might have done but which they do for us, and what we do is similarly done for them.

John Rowls
A Theory of Justice
Oxford University Press, 1973 page 565

APPENDIX 1

Extract from LAC(93)10

LOCAL AUTHORITY CIRCULAR   **LAC(93)10**

DEPARTMENT OF HEALTH

March 1993

APPROVALS AND DIRECTIONS FOR ARRANGEMENTS FROM 1 APRIL 1993 MADE UNDER SCHEDULE 8 TO THE NATIONAL HEALTH SERVICE ACT 1977 AND SECTIONS 21 AND 29 OF THE NATIONAL ASSISTANCE ACT 1948

SUMMARY

This circular contains guidance on the consolidated approvals and directions made by the Secretary of State for Health on local authorities continuing responsibilities, from 1 April 1993, to provide residential accommodation and welfare services, insofar as they are provided under sections 21 and 29 of the National Assistance Act, 1948 and paragraphs 1 and 2 of Schedule 8 of the NHS Act, 1977.

ACTION

1.   This circular contains approvals and directions made by the Secretary of State in exercise of the powers conferred by sections 21 (1) and 29 (1) of the National Assistance Act 1948 and paragraphs 1 and 2 of Schedule 8 to the National Health Service Act 1977.

2.   It consolidates the existing approvals and directions contained in LAC13/74, LAC19/74, LAC(74)28 and Annexes 1 and 2 of LAC(91)12. This circular does not of itself create any additional responsibilities which have not previously been expected of local services authorities. This circular also updates existing guidance on registration practice and related statistics.

BACKGROUND

3.   Social service authorities' powers under sections 21 and 29 of the 1948 Act and under Schedule 8 to the 1977 Act are subject to the requirement to act with the approval and under the direction of the Secretary of State. The relevant information is at:

— Appendix 1 = Approvals and Directions under section 21(1) of the 1948 Act.
— Appendix 2 = Approvals and Directions under section 29(1) of the 1948 Act.
— Appendix 3 = Approvals and Directions under paras 1 and 2 of Schedule 8 of the 1977 Act.

4.   The approvals and directions contained in this circular take account of the amendments made to Part III of the 1948 Act and Schedule 8 of the 1977 Act by the Mental Health Act 1983, the Children Act 1989, the National Health Service and Community Care Act 1990 and the Community Care (Residential Accommodation) Act 1992.

It is the view of the Department that the amendments introduced into the 1948 Act by section 1 of the Community Care (Residential Accommodation) Act 1992 will require authorities to make some direct provision for residential care under Part III of the 1948 Act.

5.   From 1 April 1993, when section 43 of the 1990 Act comes into force, authorities will not be able to provide accommodation to people ordinarily resident in independent homes immediately before that date with preserved rights to the higher levels of Income Support. The new section 26A(3) of the 1948 Act, inserted by section 43 of the 1990 Act, gives the Secretary of State power to make exceptions. These are set out in LAC(93)6 together with SI 1993 No 477.

6.   Paragraphs 1 and 2 of the Schedule 8 to the National Health Service Act 1977 will remain in force after 1 April 1993, but they will be amended so that local authorities will no longer be able to provide residential accommodation under them. For convenience, the approvals and directions previously contained in Circulars 19/74 and 74/28, which related to services other than the provision of accommodation have been included in this Circular.

7.   The opportunity has been taken to consolidate and update circulars 25/61, 17/74, (74)37 and (78)20 concerning registration practice and statistics. Appendix 4 refers.

WHITE PAPER AND POLICY GUIDANCE

8.   It will be the responsibility of Social Services Departments to make maximum possible use of private and voluntary providers and so increase the available range of options and widen consumer choice (paragraph 1.11 of the White Paper 'Caring for People' (Cm 849)). The Government welcomes the action being taken by authorities to review the range of services they are currently providing, as part of a comprehensive review of the needs and services available in their area. Social services authorities will continue to play a valuable role in the provision of services, but in those cases where they are currently the main or sole providers of services, they will be expected to take all reasonable steps to secure diversity of provision (paragraph 3.4.1). Regarding the circumstances in which direct provision may be needed the White Paper said (paragraph 3.4.11) that the Government will expect local authorities to retain the ability to act as direct service providers, if other forms of service provision are unforthcoming or unsuitable. This is likely to be particularly important in services for people with high levels of dependency, or particularly challenging patterns of behaviour, whose care it is essential to safeguard.

9.   The role of housing and social services authorities in relation to housing and community care is set out in the joint circular from the Departments of Health (LAC(92)12) and the environment (10/92). This circular has also been issued to housing associations by the Housing Corporation.

10.   By virtue of Section 2 of the Chronically Sick and Disabled Persons Act 1970 the matters dealt with in subsection (1) of that section do not need to be included in the arrangements contained in Appendix 2.

11.   It is not necessary for the arrangements contained in this circular to cover the provision by local authorities of sheltered employment as this is provided under powers deriving from the Disabled Persons (Employment) Acts 1944 and 1958.

12.   The Secretary of State hopes that authorities will keep in mind the needs of individuals, families and groups to ensure that the services provided are administered flexibly and in accordance with changing needs. For the purpose of any of these arrangements, where no express statutory power exists for authorities to use outside service providers, the Secretary of State has also approved the use by authorities of suitable accommodation, services or facilities made available by another authority, voluntary body or person on such conditions as may be agreed. Thus, for example, authorities may continue to make use on a repayment basis of suitable residential or training places made available by other authorities, though they are asked nevertheless to bear in mind the importance of such services being provided as near to the person's home place as is practicable.

13.   Social services authorities' powers to prevent mental disorder or provide care for those who are or have been suffering from mental disorder are embraced in their wider powers under paragraph 2 of Schedule 8 to the 1977 Act to prevent illness and provide care for those

who are or have been suffering from it. In addition, if authorities wish to provide services other than accommodation specifically for persons who are alcoholic or drug-dependent, the Secretary of State has approved them so doing. Because authorities' powers to provide accommodation under paragraph 2 of Schedule 8 are being repealed, the approvals and directions in relation to the provision of accommodation for the prevention of mental disorder or for persons who are or who have been suffering from mental disorder, or specifically for persons who are alcoholic or drug-dependent, have all been transferred to section 21(1) of the 1948 Act. Further guidance on the provision of alcohol and drug services within community care is contained in LAC(93)2.

EFFECTIVE DATE

14.   The Approvals and Directions are effective from 1 April 1993.

CANCELLATION OF CIRCULARS

15.   This circular cancels LAC13/74, LAC19/74, LAC(74)28, LAC17/74, LAC(74)37 and LAC(78)20. It also cancels Annexes 1 and 2 of LAC(91)12. Authorities should note however the saving provision contained in paragraph 6(3) of Appendix 1 to this circular in relation to the directions contained in Annexes 1 and 2 of Circular LAC(91)12.

ENQUIRIES

16.   Enquiries about this circular should be made to CS1 Division, Department of Health on 071 972 4237.

SECRETARY OF STATE'S APPROVALS AND DIRECTIONS UNDER SECTION 21(1) OF THE NATIONAL ASSISTANCE ACT 1948	**LAC(93)10 Appendix 1**

The Secretary of State for Health, in exercise of the powers conferred on her by section 21(1) of the National Assistance Act 1948(a), hereby makes the following Approvals and Directions: –

Residential accommodation for persons in need of care and attention

2.–(1)   The Secretary of State hereby–

(a) approves the making by local authorities of arrangements under section 21(1)(a) of the Act in relation to persons with no settled residence and, to such extent as the authority may consider desirable, in relation to persons who are ordinarily resident in the area of another local authority, with the consent of that other authority; and

(b) directs local authorities to make arrangements under section 21(1)(a) of the Act in relation to persons who are ordinarily resident in their area and other persons who are in urgent need thereof, to provide residential accommodation for persons aged 18 or over who by reason of age, illness, disability or any other circumstance are in need of care and attention not otherwise available to them.

(2)   Without prejudice to the generality of sub-paragraph (1), the Secretary of State hereby directs local authorities to make arrangements under section 21(1)(a) of the Act to provide temporary accommodation for persons who are in urgent need thereof in circumstances where the need for that accommodation could not reasonably have been foreseen.

(3)   Without prejudice to the generality of sub-paragraph (1), the Secretary of State hereby directs local authorities to make arrangements under section 21(1)(a) of the Act to provide accommodation–

> (a) in relation to persons who are or have been suffering from mental disorder, or
>
> (b) for the purpose of the prevention of mental disorder,

for persons who are ordinarily resident in their area and for persons with no settled residence who are in the authority's area.

(4)   Without prejudice to the generality of sub-paragraph (1) and subject to section 24(4) of the Act, the Secretary of State hereby approves the making by local authorities of arrangements under section 21(1)(a) of the Act to provide residential accommodation–

> (a) in relation to persons who are or have been suffering from mental disorder; or
>
> (b) for the purposes of the prevention of mental disorder,

for persons who are ordinarily resident in the area of another local authority but who following discharge from hospital have become resident in the authority's area;

(5)   Without prejudice to the generality of sub-paragraph (1), the Secretary of State hereby approves the making by local authorities of arrangements under section 21(1)(a) of the Act to provide accommodation to meet the needs of persons for–

> (a) the prevention of illness;
>
> (b) the care of those suffering from illness; and
>
> (c) the aftercare of those so suffering.

(6)   Without prejudice to the generality of sub-paragraph (1), the Secretary of State hereby approves the making by local authorities of arrangements under section 21(1)(a) of the Act specifically for persons who are alcoholic or drug-dependent.

Residential accommodation for expectant and nursing mothers

3.   The Secretary of State hereby approves the making by local authorities of arrangements under section 21(1)(aa) of the Act to provide residential accommodation (in particular mother and baby homes) for expectant and nursing mothers (of any age) who are in need of care and attention which is not otherwise available to them.

Arrangements to provide services for residents

4.   The Secretary of State hereby directs local authorities to make arrangements in relation to persons provided with accommodation under section 21(1) of the Act for all or any of the following purposes–

> (a) for the welfare of all persons for whom accommodation is provided;
>
> (b) for the supervision of the hygiene of the accommodation so provided;

(c) to enable persons for whom accommodation is provided to obtain–
  (i) medical attention,
  (ii) nursing attention during illnesses of a kind which are ordinarily nursed at home, and
  (iii) the benefit of any services provided by the National Health Service of which they may from time to time be in need,
  but nothing in this paragraph shall require a local authority to make any provision authorised or required to be provided under the National Health Service Act 1977;
(d) for the provision of board and such other services, amenities and requisites provided in connection with the accommodation, except where in the opinion of the authority managing the premises their provision is unnecessary;
(e) to review regularly the provision made under the arrangements and to make such improvements as the authority considers necessary.

Arrangements for the conveyance of residents

5.　　The Secretary of State hereby approves the making by local authorities of arrangements under section 21(1) of the Act to provide, in such cases as the authority considers appropriate, for the conveyance of persons to and from premises in which accommodation is provided for them under Part III of the Act.

Duties in respect of residents in transferred accommodation

6.–(1)　　Where a person is provided with accommodation pursuant to section 21(1) of the Act, and–
(a) the residential accommodation is local authority accommodation provided pursuant to section 21(4) of the 1948 Act (a);
(b) the local authority transfer the management of the residential accommodation to a voluntary organisation who–
  (i) manages it as a residential care home within the meaning of Part I of the Registered Homes Act 1984, and
  (ii) is registered under that Part or is not required to be so registered by virtue of being an exempt body; and
(c) the person is accommodated in the residential accommodation immediately before and after the transfer,
while that person remains accommodated in that residential accommodation, the local authority shall remain under a duty to make arrangements to provide accommodation for him after any transfer to which paragraph (b) of this sub-paragraph refers.

(2)　　For the purposes of paragraph (c) of sub-paragraph (1), a person shall be regarded as accommodated in residential accommodation if–
(a) he is temporarily absent from such accommodation (including circumstances in which he is in hospital or on holiday);
(b) before 1st April 1993, that accommodation was provided under paragraph 2(1) of Schedule 8 to the National Health Service Act 1977.

(3)   Where immediately before these Approvals and Directions come into force a local authority was under a duty to provide a person with accommodation by virtue of–

(a) the Secretary of States's former Directions under Section 21(1) of the National Assistance Act 1948 contained in Annex 1 of Department of Health Circular LAC(91)12; or

(b) The Secretary of State's former Directions under paragraph 2 of the Schedule 8 to the National Health Service Act 1977 contained in Annex 2 of Department of Health Circular LAC(91)12,

while that person remains accommodated in that residential accommodation, the local authority shall remain under a duty to make arrangements to provide that person with accommodation from the date on which these Directions come into force.

Powers to make arrangements with other local authorities and voluntary organisations etc.

7.   For the avoidance of doubt, these Approvals and Directions are without prejudice to any of the powers conferred on local authorities by section 21(4) and section 26(1) of the Act (arrangements with voluntary organisations etc.).

[LAC(93)10 Appendix 2 – see Figure 25.3, page 381]

SECRETARY OF STATE'S APPROVALS AND   **LAC(93)10**
DIRECTIONS UNDER PARAGRAPHS 1 AND 2   **Appendix 3**
OF SCHEDULE 8 TO THE NATIONAL HEALTH
SERVICE ACT 1977

The Secretary of State for Health, in exercise of the powers conferred on her by paragraph 1(1) and 2(1) of Schedule 8 to the National Health Service Act 1977, hereby makes the following Approvals and Directions:–

Services for expectant and nursing mothers

2.   The Secretary of State hereby approves the making of arrangements under paragraph 1(1) of Schedule 8 to the Act for the care of expectant and nursing mothers (of any age) other than the provision of residential accommodation for them.

Services for the purpose of the prevention of illness etc.

3.–(1)   The Secretary of State hereby approves the making by local authorities of arrangements under paragraph 2(1) of Schedule 8 to the Act for the purpose of the prevention of illness, and the care of persons suffering from illness and for the aftercare of persons who have been so suffering and in particular for–

(a) the provision, for persons whose care is undertaken with a view to preventing them becoming ill, persons suffering from illness and persons who have been so suffering, of centres or other facilities for training them or keeping them suitably occupied and the equipment and maintenance of such centres;

(b) the provision, for the benefit of such persons as are mentioned in paragraph (a) above, of ancillary or supplemental services.

(2)   The Secretary of State hereby directs local authorities to make arrangements under paragraph 2(1) of Schedule 8 to the Act for the purposes of the prevention of mental disorder, or in relation to persons who are or who have been suffering from mental disorder–

    (a) for the provision of centres (including training centres and day centres) or other facilities (including domiciliary facilities), whether in premises managed by the local authority or otherwise, for training or occupation of such persons;

    (b) for the appointment of sufficient social workers in their area to act as approved social workers for the purposes of the Mental Health Act 1983;

    (c) for the exercise of the functions of the authority in respect of persons suffering from mental disorder who are received into guardianship under Part II or III of the Mental Health Act 1983 (whether the guardianship of the local social services authority or of other persons);

    (d) for the provision of social work and related services to help in the identification, diagnosis, assessment and social treatment of mental disorder and to provide social work support and other domiciliary and care services to people living in their homes and elsewhere.

(3)   Without prejudice to the generality of sub-paragraph (1), the Secretary of State hereby approves the making by local authorities of arrangements under paragraph 2(1) of Schedule 8 to the Act for the provision of–

    (a) meals to be served at the centres or other facilities referred to in sub-paragraphs (1)(a) and (2)(a) above and meals-on-wheels for house-bound people not provided for–
       (i) under section 45(1) of the Health Services and Public Health Act 1968, or
       (ii) by a district council under paragraph 1 of Part II of Schedule 9 to the Health and Social Services and Social Security Adjudications Act 1983;

    (b) remuneration for persons engaged in suitable work at the centres or other facilities referred to in sub-paragraphs (1)(a) and (2)(a) above, subject to paragraph 2(2)(a) of Schedule 8 to the Act;

    (c) social services (including advice and support) for the purposes of preventing the impairment of physical or mental health of adults in families where such impairment is likely, and for the purposes of preventing the break-up of such families, or for assisting in their rehabilitation;

    (d) night-sitter services;

    (e) recuperative holidays;

    (f) facilities for social and recreational activities;

    (g) services specifically for persons who are alcoholic or drug-dependent.

Services made available by another local authority etc.

4.   For the purposes of any arrangements made under these Approvals and Directions, the Secretary of State hereby approves the use by local authorities of services or facilities made available by another authority,

voluntary body or person on such conditions as may be agreed, but in making such arrangements, a local authority shall have regard to the importance of services being provided as near to a person's home as is practicable.

[Appendix 4, Section 29 of the NAA 1948 – Registration Practice and Related Statistics, is not reproduced here. It incorporates as Annex 1 an extract from the report *Handicapped and Impaired in Great Britain* and as Annex 2 the Ministry of Health Circular 25/61 *NAA 1948 – Welfare Services for the Deaf*]

Consent Form: Treatment by health professionals (not doctors or dentists)

NOTES TO:

Health Professionals, other than doctors or dentists

A patient has a legal right to grant or withhold consent prior to examination or treatment. Patients should be given sufficient information, in a way they can understand, about the proposed treatment and the possible alternatives. Patients must be allowed to decide whether they will agree to the treatment and they may refuse or withdraw consent to treatment at any time. The patient's consent to treatment should be recorded on this form (further guidance is given in HC(90)22 *(A Guide to Consent for Examination or Treatment.)*

Patients

■ The health professional named on this form is here to help you. He or she will explain the proposed treatment and what the alternatives are. You can ask any questions and seek further information. You can refuse the treatment.

■ You may ask for a relative, or friend, or another member of staff to be present.

■ Training health professionals is essential to the continuation of the health service and improving the quality of care. Your treatment may provide an important opportunity for such training, where necessary under the careful supervision of a fully qualified health professional. You may refuse any involvement in a formal training programme without this adversely affecting your care and treatment.

591

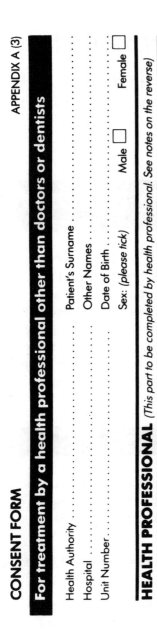

APPENDIX A (3)

CONSENT FORM

For treatment by a health professional other than doctors or dentists

Health Authority ....

Hospital ....

Unit Number. ....

Patient's Surname ....

Other Names ....

Date of Birth ....

Sex: *(please tick)*   Male ☐   Female ☐

HEALTH PROFESSIONAL *(This part to be completed by health professional. See notes on the reverse)*

TYPE OF TREATMENT PROPOSED

Complete this part of the form

I confirm that I have explained the treatment proposed and such appropriate options as are available to the patient in terms which in my judgement are suited to the understanding of the patient and/or to one of the parents or guardians of the patient.

Signature. . . . . Date. . . . / . . . / . . . . . .

Name of health professional. . . . .

Job title of health professional. . . . .

PATIENT/PARENT/GUARDIAN

1. Please read this form and the notes overleaf very carefully.

2. If there is anything that you don't understand about the explanation, or if you want more information, you should ask the health professional who has explained the treatment proposed.

3. Please check that all the information on the form is correct. If it is, and you understand the treatment proposed, then sign the form.

I am the patient/parent/guardian *(delete as necessary)*

I agree ■ to what is proposed which has been explained to me by the health professional named on this form.

Signature . . . .

Name . . . .

Address . . . .

(if not the patient) . . . .

NHS *Management Executive*

Consent Form: Patient unable to consent because of mental disorder

Medical or dental treatment of a patient who is unable to consent because of mental disorder

Health Authority ....

Hospital ....

Unit Number. ....

Patient's Surname ....

Other Names ....

Date of Birth ....

Sex: *(please tick)*   Male ☐   Female ☐

NOTE

If there is any doubt about the ability of a mentally disordered patient to give consent to treatment, the Registered Medical Practitioner in charge of the patient should be asked to interview the patient. If, in his or her opinion, the patient is able to give valid consent to medical, dental or surgical treatment, he or she should be asked to do so and no-one further need be involved.

If the patient is considered unable to give valid consent it is considered good practice to discuss any proposed treatment with the next of kin.

For surgical or dental operations the form should also be signed by the Registered Medical or Dental Practitioner who carries out the treatment.

DOCTORS/DENTISTS

Describe investigation, operation or treatment proposed.

(Complete this part of the form)

In my opinion . . . . is not capable of giving consent to treatment. In my opinion the treatment proposed is in his/her best interests and should be given.

The patient's next of kin have/have not been so informed. *(delete as necessary)*

Date: . . . .

Signature . . . . Signature

Name of Registered Medical Practitioner
in charge of the patient:

. . . . Name of Second Registered Medical/Dental
Practitioner who is providing treatment:

. . . .

NHS *Management Executive*

APPENDIX 3

Specialist Bibliographies

HEALTH AND SAFETY AND HIV/AIDS

Guidance for health care worker's protection against infection with HIV and Hepatitis from the Committee of expert Advisory Group on AIDS (HMSO 1994)

Immunisation against infectious disease produced by the Department of Health, Welsh Office and Scottish Home and Health Department (HMSO 1990)

Management of Health and Safety at work approved code of practice Health and Safety Commission (HMSO 1992)

Manual Handling Regulations approved code of practice Health and Safety Commission (HMSO 1992)

Guidelines on Manual Handling in the Health Services Health and Safety Commission (HMSO 1992)

UKCC report on Professional Conduct hearings and registered nursing homes

GENERAL COMMUNITY CARE AND ASSESSMENT

The Audit Commission Report *Making a Reality of Community Care*, HMSO, December 1986

Sir Roy Griffiths *Community Care: Agenda for Action*, DoH, February 1988

White paper: *Caring for People; Community Care in the next decade and beyond*, Cmnd 849, HMSO, November 1989

Report of the Select Committee of the House of Commons chaired by Marion Roe, July 1993, HMSO, 1993

Caring for People in the Next Decade and Beyond: Policy Guidance, HMSO, 1990

Caring for People: Training for the Future, Department of Health, 1993

Care Management and Assessment: Manager's Guide, HMSO, 1991

Care Management and Assessment: Practitioner's Guide, HMSO, 1990

Care Management and Assessment: Summary of Practice Guidance, HMSO, 1991

Getting the Message Across: A guide to Developing and Communicating Policies, Principles and Procedure on Assessment, HMSO, 1991

Circular CI(92) 34 ('the Laming Letter')

Taking Care: Progress with care in the community, Audit Commission, December 1993

Richard Gordon *Community Care Assessments: A practical legal Framework*, Longmans, 1993

June Neill and Jenny Williams *Leaving Hospital: Elderly people and their discharge to community care*, National Institute for Social Work Research Unit, HMSO, 1992

596

APPENDIX 4

HSG(95)39

Covering: HSG(95)39
                   LAC(95)17

To: DHA Chief Executives
        FHSA Chief Executives,
        Directors of Social Services
        Chief Executives of NHS Trusts
        Chief Executives of Special Health Authorities

Copies: Regional Directors
            Chief Executives of Local Authorities
            Chief Officers of Community Health Councils

Dear Colleague

DISCHARGE FROM NHS INPATIENT CARE OF PEOPLE WITH CONTINUING HEALTH OR SOCIAL CARE NEEDS: ARRANGEMENTS FOR REVIEWING DECISIONS ON ELIGIBILITY FOR NHS CONTINUING INPATIENT CARE

As promised in HSG(95)8/LAC(95)5, 'NHS Responsibilities for Meeting Continuing Health Care Needs', we enclose with this letter guidance on the arrangements to be put in place for reviewing decisions on eligibility for NHS continuing inpatient care.

The guidance sets the review procedure firmly in the context of high quality discharge policies which centre on proper assessment, provision of all relevant information, and sensitivity to the needs and concerns of patients and their families. It outlines the scope and purpose of the procedure and the steps which must be taken before a case is referred to an independent panel for consideration. Finally it sets out what health authorities, in conjunction with all interested parties, must do to establish the panels; how the panels should operate; and the information to be made available on the outcome of requests for a review.

Introduction

1.   The guidance issued to health authorities, local authorities and other agencies in February 1995 on 'NHS responsibilities for meeting continuing health care needs'. HSG(95)8/LAC(95)5, outlined arrangements for reviewing decisions on eligibility for NHS continuing inpatient care. Further guidance was promised for health authorities and other agencies on the details of the procedure and in particular on the establishment and operation of the independent panels.

Summary of action

2.   In the light of this guidance:

a)   **Health authorities** must in consultation with local authorities, GP Fundholders and other relevant parties

— ensure a clear action plan is in place for the introduction of the review procedure

— review arrangements for handling disputes with local authorities about their respective responsibilities for funding care in individual cases (paragraph 10)

— ensure that the overall process for the review procedure is established and, where necessary, properly reflected in 1996/7 contracts (paragraph 12)

— put in place the necessary arrangements to secure independent clinical advice (paragraph 30)

— appoint a designated officer to be responsible for the operation of the review procedure (paragraph 16)

— select and appoint a Chairman and members of the panel including, on the nomination of the relevant local authority/ies, the LA representative (paragraphs 20–24)

— ensure other arrangements are in place to enable a smooth start to full operation of the panels from 1 April 1996.

b)   NHS Trusts and other hospitals and social services departments must:

— review arrangements for discharge of patients with continuing health or social care needs (paragraph 3)

— review procedures for supplying appropriate information to patients and their families and any carers (paragraphs 3, 9, Appendix 2)

— ensure appropriate front line staff are fully conversant with the review procedure as outlined in this guidance, and with eligibility criteria.

Scope and purpose of the review procedure

3.   It is of crucial importance that the review procedure is seen in the context of high quality discharge policies as outlined in our Hospital Discharge Workbook (A Manual on Hospital Discharge Practice) and in Section C of HSG(95)8. The main stages leading to decisions on discharge are:

— a decision has been taken that a patient no longer needs NHS inpatient care:

— a patient who is likely to have continuing health or social care needs has received an appropriate multi-disciplinary assessment which has included, where necessary, specialists with expertise in continuing care:

— in making decisions on the need for NHS continuing inpatient care those responsible have had regard to all aspects of the criteria, including whether the patient is likely to die in the very near future and discharge from NHS care would be inappropriate:

— the need for rehabilitation and/or time for recovery have been considered, with adequate allowance for the special needs of older people who may need a longer period to reach their full potential for recovery:

— where appropriate, the different options for care in the future have been explained and discussed with the patient, his or her family and any carer, and the potential impact of these on family members and carers have been acknowledged:

— the patient and his or her family and any relevant carer have been consulted and kept fully informed at all stages, and have received a written continuing care plan clearly setting out the care and services to be provided following discharge from NHS inpatient care.

4.   The review procedure is intended as an additional safeguard for patients assessed as ready for discharge from NHS inpatient care who require ongoing continuing support from health and/or social services, and who consider that the health authority's eligibility criteria for NHS continuing inpatient care (whether in a hospital or in some other setting such as a nursing home) have not been correctly applied in their case.

5. The review procedure applies to all patients who have been receiving NHS inpatient care, whether in a hospital, or arranged and funded by the NHS in a hospice, nursing home, or elsewhere, and to all client groups covered in local eligibility criteria.

6. The scope of the review procedure is therefore:

— to check that proper procedures have been followed in reaching decisions about the need for NHS continuing inpatient care:

— to ensure that the health authority's eligibility criteria for NHS continuing inpatient care are properly and consistently applied.

7. It is important that all concerned should appreciate that the review procedure is **not** a formal appeals mechanism or a complaints procedure, and does not affect patients' rights under existing NHS and local authority complaints procedures.

8. The review procedure does **not** apply where patients or their families and any carer wish to challenge:

— the content, rather than the application, of the health authority's eligibility criteria:

— the type and location of any offer NHS-funded continuing inpatient care:

— the content of any alternative care package which they have been offered:

— their treatment or any other aspect of their stay in hospital.

9. Such patient should be advised of the appropriate route by which to pursue their grievance. In particular, information on NHS and local authority complaints procedures, and any other relevant information, should be made freely available.

10. The review procedure should **not** be used to resolve disputes between health and local authorities about their responsibility for funding care in individual cases, and should be clearly separate from agreements which health and local authorities must have in place for resolving disputes about responsibility for meeting continuing care needs in individual cases. Authorities should ensure that appropriate arrangements are in place for handling disputes of this kind.

11. The procedure applies to patients of those GP Fundholders who are participating in total purchasing pilots. Health authorities are expected to administer the review procedure on behalf of total purchasers. The outcome of reviews may impact upon GPs and GP Fundholders and it is therefore important to ensure that all GPs are consulted fully from the outset on the operation of the procedure. Consultation should of course have taken place at an earlier stage on the health authority's continuing care policies and eligibility criteria, as required in HSG(95)8.

Review procedure

12. **Appendix 1** describes the various stages of the review procedure. It will be clear from this that both the health authority and the relevant provider unit have important responsibilities in their respective areas. These should be underpinned by contractual arrangements and backed up by effective liaison in order for the process to run smoothly.

13. Patients should be given a written continuing care plan which includes the name of somebody, usually a member of the multi-disciplinary team, who they can talk to if they or their family or any carer wish to discuss the result of the assessment or are unhappy with the arrangements for their discharge from NHS inpatient care. The person identified should be someone who can discuss the relevant decisions clearly and impartially while being sensitive to the concerns of patients, their families and any carers.

14. Patients should be given clear information about the review procedure, the situations it does and does not cover and how it operates locally. It may be helpful to have a standard leaflet for this purpose. The possibility that a patient may require an advocate should be kept in view, and the nominated individual should confirm that a patient who needs this help has had the opportunity and assistance they may need to secure someone suitable. Sources of such help will be well known locally and will normally include the Community Health Council and Citizens' Advice Bureau in addition to local advocacy schemes.

15. Every effort should be made to address the concerns of patients and their families at this initial stage. The checklist of the issues which should be properly examined is given at **Appendix 2**. If, after all reasonable efforts, agreement cannot be reached, the patient, his or her family or any carer is entitled to ask the health authority where the patient is normally resident to review the decision that the patient's needs do not meet the eligibility criteria for NHS continuing inpatient care. The normal expectation is that a health authority in reaching a view will seek advice from an independent panel. Before doing so it should ensure that:

— on the basis of the checklist (Appendix 2) all reasonable action has been taken to resolve the case informally:

— the issues raised by the patient relate to the application of the eligibility criteria.

16. Within each health authority there should be a designated officer who is responsible for the review procedure. He or she will be responsible for:

— the efficient operation of the procedure:

— checking, in liaison with the provider, that all appropriate steps have been taken to resolve the case informally:

— collection of information for the panel including interviewing patients, family members and any relevant carer(s).

17.　Once it has received a request from a patient, his or her family or any relevant carer the health authority should aim to ensure that the review procedure is completed within two weeks. This period starts once any action to resolve the case informally has been completed. It may be extended if there are exceptional circumstances – for example, if unforeseen difficulties arise over the provision of clinical advice or in convening the panel, or public holidays have made adherence to this timescale impossible.

18.　While the review procedure is being conducted patients should remain NHS funded accommodation.

19.　The health authority does have the right to decide in any individual case not to convene a panel. It is expected that such decisions will be confined to those cases where the patient falls well outside the eligibility criteria, or where the case is very clearly not appropriate for the panel to consider (see para 8). Before taking a decision the authority should seek the advice of the chairman of the panel. In all cases where a decision not to convene a panel is made, the health authority should give the patient, his or her family or carer a full written explanation of the basis of its decision, together with a reminder of their rights under the NHS complaints procedure.

Establishment and operation of review panels

20.　To ensure consistency of approach and to develop knowledge and expertise the health authority should maintain a standing panel. The panel should comprise an independent chairman and single representatives from the health authority and local authority/ies.

21.　The independent chairman should be selected following an open advertisement and his or her appointment should be made by the health authority. The person selected must:

— have a sound grasp of the remit of the panel and of the pivotal role of the chairman:

— be seen to be free of bias towards either party:

— have the capacity to determine, on the basis of appropriate advice, whether eligibility criteria have been properly applied in individual cases:

— be capable of applying impartial judgement, while taking a sympathetic view of the concerns of patients and their families:

— have the personal confidence to make difficult decisions in this highly sensitive area without being swayed by the inevitable pressures the role will entail.

22. Selection of the right person as Chairman, who is capable of securing the confidence of all parties, will be a crucial factor in the success of the procedure. Current non-executive Directors of health authorities or LA members should not be considered, but people who have formerly held such a position are eligible for consideration. Health authorities are strongly advised to involve lay people (for example, representatives of CHCs) in the selection process.

23. The appointment of representatives of the health authority and appropriate local authority will be on the basis of the nomination of those authorities. They should take account of the professional and other skills which will be relevant to the work of the panel.

24. Authorities may wish to appoint an alternative Chairman and members to cover absences, or to make a reciprocal arrangement for cover with a neighbouring authority. It is open to authorities with the same eligibility criteria to operate a single panel.

25. The chairman and members should receive reasonable expenses.

26. All members of panels must receive appropriate training for their role. The Department of Health intend to issue training material in the autumn.

27. The designated health authority officer (paragraph 16) is responsible for preparing information for the panel. The panel should have access to any existing documentation which is relevant, including the record of assessment. They should also have access to the views of the key parties involved in the case including the patient, his or her family and, if appropriate, carer, health and social services staff, and any other relevant bodies or individuals. It will be open to the key parties to put their views in writing or to request an interview with the health authority officer, or in exceptional circumstances with another person nominated by the panel.

28. The panel must retain patient confidentiality at all times.

29. When interviewed by the health authority's officer, or other person nominated by the panel, a patient may have a representative present to speak on his or her behalf where they wish, or are unable to present their own views. The health authority must aim to ensure that the views of patients who are unable to speak for themselves, for whatever reason, are appropriately represented. This may be done by a relative or carer, but the health authority will need to ensure that it is not any person whose interests or wishes might conflict with those of the patient.

30. The panel will require access to independent clinical advice which should take account of the range of medical, nursing and therapy needs involved in each case. There should be standing arrangements to provide this, which are reflected in contracts between the provider unit which employs the adviser(s) and the appropriate authority, to ensure consistency of advice. Such arrangements should not involve any providers with whom the authority most commonly contracts for services.

31. The role of the clinical advisers is to advise the panel on the original clinical judgements and on how those judgements relate to the health authority's eligibility criteria. It is **not** to provide a second opinion on the clinical diagnosis, management or prognosis of the patient.

32. The members of the panel should meet to consider individual cases. They may wish to invite the clinical adviser(s) and the health authority officer, or if appropriate the person they have nominated to take the views of the parties concerned, to attend their meetings. This should ensure that the panel has access to all the information it will require and to the views of all parties. It is not proposed that anyone else should attend the panel's meetings.

33. The role of the panel is advisory. However, while its decisions will not be formally binding, the expectation is that its recommendations will be accepted in all but very exceptional circumstances. If a health authority decides to reject a panel's recommendation in an individual case it must put in writing to the patient and to the chairman of the panel its reasons for doing so.

34. In all cases the health authority must communicate in writing to the patient the outcome of the review, with reasons. The relevant hospital, consultant or GP should also receive this information.

Public information

35. Information on the review procedure should be made publicly available on an annual basis in a report to the health authority. The information likely to be required is:

— number of patients requesting a review;

— number of cases referred to the panel;

— number of cases upheld;

— number of cases upheld by the panel but rejected by the health authority.

36. At a national level the NHS Executive will monitor the numbers and results of the panels held by individual authorities, and will review the operation of the review procedure in the light of this information.

APPENDIX 1

Overall process for review procedure

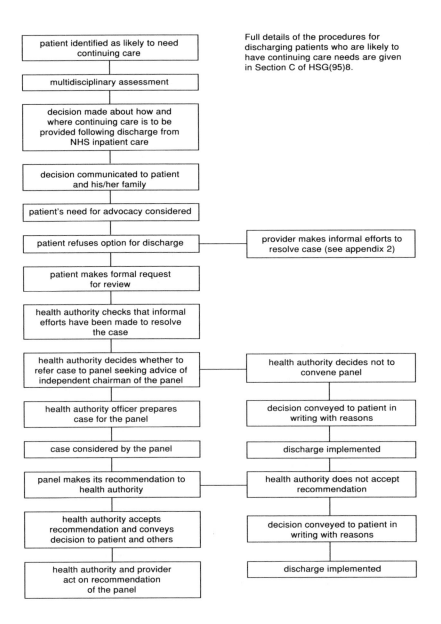

Full details of the procedures for discharging patients who are likely to have continuing care needs are given in Section C of HSG(95)8.

APPENDIX 2

Checklist of issues to be considered before referring a case to a panel

Assessment of need

1. Has there been an appropriate assessment of the patient's needs? Has this included appropriate specialists with expertise in continuing care needs? Has the need for a second clinical opinion been considered?

2. Have all the criteria in the health authority's published eligibility criteria been considered by the multi-disciplinary team?

3. Has proper account been taken of the patient's clinical prognosis – is the patient likely to die in the very near future so that discharge from NHS care may be inappropriate?

4. Were the patient's needs for a period of rehabilitation or recovery properly considered, bearing in mind that older people may need longer to reach their full potential for recovery?

5. Does the multi-disciplinary team agree that the patient does not meet the eligibility criteria for NHS continuing inpatient care?

6. Has the multi-disciplinary team reviewed its decision?

Information for the patient, his or her family and any carer

7. Have the patient, his or her family and any carer been made fully aware of the eligibility criteria?

8. Have the patient, his/her family or carer received the following:

— clear written information about how hospital discharge procedures will operate, and what will happen if continuing care is needed?

— the necessary information, where appropriate in writing, to enable them to take any decisions about continuing care?

— written details of the likely cost of any option which they have been asked to consider by social services (including where possible and appropriate the availability of social security benefits and financial assistance from LA social services)?

— a written continuing care plan including a clear statement of which aspects of care will be arranged and funded by the NHS?

9. Have the views of the patient, his or her family and any carer been take into consideration as part of the assessment process? Has the possibility that the patient might need an advocate been considered?

Alternative care options

10. Has the possibility of an ECR been considered if the patient met the eligibility criteria but contracted provision for NHS continuing inpatient care was full?

11. Have alternative options for care (eg a package at home) been discussed with the patient and his or her family?

APPENDIX 5

HSG(95)41

Health Service
Guidelines

Executive

HSG(95)41

September 1995

REGULATION OF NURSING HOMES AND INDEPENDENT HOSPITALS

Executive Summary

1.   This circular gives guidance on improving the way in which the Registered Homes Act 1984 is applied and enforced in nursing homes and independent hospitals. Its purpose is to promote sensible regulation of nursing homes and independent hospitals, without any loss of necessary safeguards for patients, mainly by:

— a reduction in paperwork

— *consistency* of enforcement practice within and between health authorities

— *transparency* of arrangements so that home owners know what is expected of them and what enforcement action can be taken by the regulators

— *targeting* of enforcement action and co-ordination between the agencies

2.   The circular also announces the intention to amend regulations concerning 'mother and baby' homes and the notification of deaths in hospices (paragraphs 36 and 37 refer).

Introduction

3.   As part of the Government's general review of regulations affecting business, nursing home and independent hospital owners and managers were asked to put forward their thoughts on the operation of the regulatory system for these establishments. As a result of consultation on these proposals with the regulatory, provider and user interests there is no intention to dismantle the regulatory system. The primary objectives of the registration and inspection system are to protect patients and maintain

standards. These objectives are unchanged. Owners, managers and regulatory interests have however raised a number of practical issues to improve and streamline the regulatory system.

4.   Many matters raised by owners and managers can be addressed by an improved local dialogue between the regulators and owners and managers of independent hospitals and nursing homes so that each has a better appreciation of what the registration and inspection process is trying to achieve and how it works in practice in the homes. It should be the aim of authorities to reduce to the necessary minimum the administrative requirements made of those running homes by the registration and inspection processes. Authorities should re-examine these arrangements to ensure that they are efficient and not unnecessarily onerous. The circular sets out a framework for local problem solving.

5.   Separate and similar guidance is being issued to local authorities responsible for the regulation of residential care homes.

Codes of Practice

6.   Home owners and managers accept the need for regulation. In general, those matters they have raised have been about the way in which the regulations are enforced. In accordance with principles set out in the Citizen's Charter, homeowners and managers are entitled to know what the regulatory regime is about and how it will be applied. That knowledge will make it easier to comply with the law to the benefit of the homes, patients and the public.

7.   All health authorities should now take action to produce a code of practice for nursing homes and independent hospitals following the principles set out in 'Working with Business: A code for enforcement agencies'. This guide, obtainable from the Department of Trade and Industry has already been commended to local authorities who were asked to adopt the principles. As regulators of a large and growing business sector health authorities should also have transparent arrangements.

8.   Health authorities need to satisfy themselves that their codes of practice reflect their policies and that their registration and inspecting officers work within those policies. Insufficient weight is being given by some registration officers to the series of guidelines published by the National Association of Health Authorities and Trusts (NAHAT).

Local Business Partnerships

9.   Local Business Partnerships were launched by the Department of Trade and Industry in 1992 and the scheme has been widely promoted. The aim of the scheme is to encourage regulatory authorities and their local businesses to work together to streamline the regulation process and to make it work without fuss. The schemes help business to understand regulations and to make it easier to comply. Information and advice is provided on the level of service from the authority, the regulatory responsibilities, enforcement procedures and appeals about an enforcement decision. Schemes also provide a forum for discussing how regulation works in practice and how the system can be improved. DTI guidance says that the residential home sector should be included in the prescribed arrangements and this is happening in a few areas. Similarly

health authorities, for the reason set out in paragraph 7, should now take steps to ensure that where local business partnerships exist, the nursing home sector is encouraged to be fully involved.

Standard Setting

10.	In drawing up or revising local standards many authorities already consult owners and managers of independent hospitals and nursing homes, and service users. All authorities should now take steps to do this. As part of the Citizen's Charter initiative to provide customers with more and better information these standards should be readily available to all owners and managers, and should be made public. The published standards should make clear the distinction between those which are required to meet legal requirements and any good practice advice which may be given additionally. Consultation on and publication of standards will avoid any difficulty which might arise if home owners were faced with unannounced changes in standards or the opinions of different inspectors.

Reducing Inconsistencies in Standards

11.	Some differences between the standards adopted by different health authorities are inevitable given the flexibility which the legislation deliberately allows. Such variations can however, be particularly frustrating for organisations and others with homes or hospitals in a number of different health authority areas. There is a need for greater consistency so that, without attempting to impose an unnecessary and inflexible uniformity, the procedures used by different authorities and the standards asked of proprietors do not differ significantly between authorities. Where such differences are drawn to their attention, authorities should re-examine the justification for their different requirements and should be prepared to modify these where appropriate.

12.	A number of models exist in other sectors such as food safety and trading standards under which neighbouring authorities run voluntary agreements to provide unified standards throughout their areas. Networking between authorities should be helpful in identifying such variations and assisting discussion of ways of minimising them. Authorities should consider common standards with their neighbouring authorities and joint training initiatives. Health authorities should also ensure that registration officers are trained and adequately supported for their role, and that their work is properly monitored. Many owners and managers of independent hospitals and nursing homes appear to be unaware that registration officers are accountable to their health authorities for their actions.

13.	Individual homes should not be faced with differing requirements depending on which individual inspector from their health authority conducts an inspection. Particularly if they receive complaints about this, authorities should review their training, guidance and supervision arrangements for inspectors to avoid this situation.

14.	Recent amalgamations of registration units have provided benefits of scale by reducing the variation of standards required by adjoining authorities prior to mergers. The tendency has been to adopt the highest standards within the units amalgamated, resulting in increased standards being imposed on many independent hospitals and nursing homes. Health authorities will wish to consider whether the imposition of higher standards in these circumstances can always be justified.

15.   Planning authorities may occasionally seek advice from health authorities about the design of new buildings. Authorities should ensure that when advice is given by health authority staff on planning applications the advice is consistent with the standards that will be applied at the registration stage.

16.   Homeowners and regulators both raised the possibility of national standards. This will be best considered as part of the review of social services regulation and inspection which, as Ministers have already announced, will begin later this year.

Inspection and Other Agencies

17.   The statutory duty for registering and inspecting nursing homes and independent hospitals under the Registered Homes Act 1984 lies with the health authority. The health authority will continue to be the lead agency responsible for ensuring that the total environment of nursing homes and independent hospitals is safe, healthy and appropriate to the patients' needs. However, in practice, registration and inspection officers will need to call in other agencies to advise them on specialist areas such as fire or food and health and safety issues. Health authority staff should deal only with matters within their professional competence and should not normally substitute their judgement for the expert advice of other specialist agencies. Close liaison between all the relevant agencies on local policy and standards will also ensure that conflicting requirements are avoided.

18.   Health authority inspection units are only one of a number of regulatory agencies with which homeowners have to deal. Inspection by other agencies is not however specified in the way that it is for nursing homes and independent hospitals. Fire authorities only visit homes at the request of the homeowner or registration authority. Frequency of inspection by the Health and Safety Executive and environmental health officers is determined by risk assessment.

19.   It is, however, important that nursing homes and patients are not disrupted by the uncoordinated attentions of all these agencies. As the lead agency for nursing homes and independent hospitals, health authorities should seek to co-ordinate visiting by regulatory agencies so that there are reasonable intervals between visits.

Joint Working with Local Authorities and Dual Registration

20.   Close collaboration between health and local authorities is particularly important. Local authorities have already been asked to co-operate with health authorities when dealing with dually registered homes (see HC(84)21, LAC(84)15 and LASSL(92)10). Some authorities have set up joint inspection units and others are planning such arrangements. All authorities should now ensure that where they have dually registered homes the arrangements for collaboration with the local authorities are effective and designed to remove duplication of procedures eg forms and visits.

21.   At present some homes must be registered with both the health authority and local authority if the home is to provide both nursing and personal care. It is recognised that people in each sort of home will have

both health and social care needs. The distinction between the sorts of care provided in each setting is not as clear in many cases as it may have been, with the result that dual registration imposes an unnecessary regulatory burden in some cases. This issue will be examined further and any implications for the Registered Homes Act 1984 will be considered.

Frequency of and Duration of Inspection

22.   The frequency of inspection visits is prescribed in regulations which state that 'the registration authority may inspect any home on such occasions and at such intervals as it may decide but shall in any case do so not less than twice in every period of 12 months'. It is advisable that one of the visits should be made unannounced. The Department does not consider that there is at present a case to alter this but will review the matter from time to time.

23.   It is important that the regulatory burden on providers should be kept to the minimum consistent with the need to ensure adequate protection for patients and that the overall efficiency of registration and inspection activity should be kept under constant scrutiny. It should not be necessary for registration units *routinely* to carry out additional visits in excess of the minimum prescribed by legislation. More frequent inspections will only be necessary where there is a specific reason for them.

24.   In making a judgement about whether particular homes need to be inspected more than the statutory minimum, authorities will wish to satisfy themselves that such visits are necessary to ensure the protection of vulnerable patients, eg because of notified changes since the previous visit, or because patients, relatives or others have brought concerns to light. There may well be other occasions when an informal visit agreed between inspector and owners or managers of independent hospitals or nursing homes can be beneficial and supportive. This will enable resources to be concentrated in a more efficient way.

25.   The purpose of the inspection visit is to ensure that the home or hospital is meeting the standards required by the regulations to obtain and maintain registration. Authorites are reminded that it is their responsibility delegated by Secretary of State to carry out this important public duty and to inspect *all* registered nursing homes twice a year. Inspection in accordance with the law is a standard which all patients are entitled to expect. The duration of each inspection visit for that purpose is a matter for the authority to decide. Authorities should however keep in mind that not every home or hospital may require the same intensity of inspection or visits above the minimum frequency. Authorities should take account in any particular case of matters such as:

— the different needs of different client groups in each home or hospital

— whether a home or hospital has a good record with stable standards and there is no other reason to be concerned for example about a change of owner or manager

— whether a home or hospital is a member of an association which sets and adequately monitors the standards of its members

— whether a home or hospital runs a quality assurance scheme which in the opinion of the authority provides a significant degree of protection. Such schemes may for example be those which are properly accredited or have quality assurance panels involving outsiders.

Fees for Registration and Inspection

26.   The fees for registration and inspection which authorities must charge owners of independent hospitals and nursing homes are intended to cover the reasonable costs of carrying out their regulatory functions. Clearly, the cost of inspection activity and, hence, the fee levels which that activity implies is dependent on the amount of effort each authority puts into inspection. Authorities, however, have a responsibility to ensure the most cost-effective use of the resources available to them so that fees charged are no higher than necessary.

27.   The Department is unconvinced that the current fees are insufficient to enable authorities to carry out their statutory functions to ensure the standards required in the regulations are being met. This circular has drawn attention to the need for authorities to review their inspection activity to ensure that it is concentrated on its central purpose and carried out as efficiently as possible. Unnecessary inspection activity above this level merely increases the likelihood of inspection costs outstripping the level of income from fees, which impacts directly on resources available for patient care.

Payment of Fees

28.   Responses from the consultation exercise suggest that some owners and managers of independent hospitals and nursing homes do not fully understand the circumstances in which fees may be charged. Authorities are also reminded that there is no obstacle in law to the payment of fees by instalments, provided payment is completed by the due date. Authorities should ensure that these points are included in their codes of practice on regulation and inspection.

Administrative Arrangements Associated with Registration and Inspection

29.   Authorities should re-examine the registration and inspection process to ensure that they are efficient and not unnecessarily onerous for owners and managers of independent hospitals and nursing homes. In reviewing their arrangements authorities should consult the local providers specifically to consider the scope for improving the way in which regulation is applied and enforced locally. There might then be periodic reviews.

Pre-inspection Questionnaires

30.   Pre-inspection questionnaires can be a useful tool to help health authorities decide whether to make an inspection above the minimum required by the Registered Homes Act. It is important however that the questionnaire is user friendly, as short as possible and relevant. The same applies to any other documentation required from providers. Authorities should not insist on completion of a questionnaire before each

visit if the circumstances of the home are known or thought to be unchanged since completion of the previous form. Forms should be designed to facilitate 'no change' responses to specific questions. Further advice will be given by NAHAT to help health authorities appropriately monitor the work of their registration officers.

Police Checks

31.   Circular HC(91)16 (LAC(91)4) set out the general scheme for disclosure of criminal background. Authorities are reminded that as a general rule, checks with the police on whether applicants for registration have criminal records should not normally be made in the case of directors and senior staff or organisations providing care who will not be closely involved in the day to day running of the home. Checks on such persons may however be made in certain circumstances including where there are grounds for concern about a named individual. Schedule 2 of the Nursing Homes and Mental Nursing Homes Regulations 1984 as amended by Regulation 5 of the Nursing Homes and Mental Nursing Homes (Amendment) Regulations 1991 (SI 1991 No. 2532) gives health authorities powers to inquire into criminal records only where the applicant is an individual.

Emphasis of Inspections

32.   Authorities should bear in mind that the purpose of inspection is to ensure that homes and hospitals reach the standards required by regulations to obtain and keep registration. It follows therefore that in carrying out inspections and making their subsequent recommendations inspectors should take an overall view of the standard of services, facilities and care provided. They should pursue individual matters only if health, safety or welfare are likely to be placed at risk or they are part of a pattern of inadequate standards overall.

33.   Registration officers should not attempt to raise standards by imposing unnecessary requirements on owners or managers. Inspection reports should quite clearly distinguish between requirements which must be accepted by owners and managers as a requirement of registration, or of continued registration, and recommendations which need not. It is the responsibility of health authorities to ensure that their registration officers do not impose requirements beyond their statutory responsibilities.

Monitoring Contracts for Services Provided by Nursing Homes and Private Hospitals

34.   Health authorities are reminded that contracting and inspection are two separate processes. Inspectors should not normally be involved in contract monitoring in ways which may compromise their regulatory functions. The aim of the Registered Homes Act 1984 is to ensure that adequate standards are provided and maintained. The Nursing Homes and Mental Nursing Homes Regulations 1984 define 'adequate' as meaning sufficient and suitable. Registration and inspection officers should not seek to impose standards in excess of those required for registration purposes.

35.   Purchasers of services may sometimes seek higher contract standards than those required for registration. Registration officers must avoid giving the impression that failure to reach such standards will affect registration.

Mother and Baby Homes

36. Regulations will be revised to exclude from the need to register as nursing homes those 'mother and baby' homes which do not provide nursing care and whose primary purpose is to provide social care in family centres. This change will reflect the view held by many health authorities that a group whose need is for social care and training in parenthood does not require the protection offered by the Registered Homes Act 1984.

Notifying Deaths in Hospices

37. The requirement in paragraph 8(1) of SI 1984 No. 1578 that deaths should be notified within twenty four hours is unduly prescriptive in the case of recognised hospices. Regulations will therefore be relaxed to allow recognised hospices to agree with their registering authorities longer times for notification.

Control Of Hot Water Temperatures

38. The Health and Safety Executive is reviewing this matter and may issue further guidance.

Enquiries

39. Any enquiries about this circular should be made to:

Judy Bennett
Social Care Group 2A
217 Wellington House
133-155 Waterloo Road
London   SE1 8UG

Tel: 0171 972 4033 (direct line)

40. Further copies of this circular may be obtained from:

Health Publications Unit
DSS Distribution Unit
Heywood Stores
Manchester Road
Heywood, Lancs OL10 2PZ

Please quote the serial number appearing at the top of this guidance. Telephone enquiries will not be accepted.

Summary of SI 1996 No. 706

NATIONAL HEALTH SERVICE (FUND-HOLDING PRACTICES) REGULATIONS 1996 SI NO. 706

These Regulations consolidate and amend previous SIs regulating fund-holding. A fund-holding practice means a practice of one or more medical practitioners who are providing general medical services in accordance with arrangements under section 29 of the NHS Act 1977 and which has been recognised as a fund-holding practice in accordance with section 14 of the NHS and Community Care Act 1990. A fund-holding practice is entitled to be paid an allotted sum in accordance with section 15(1) if the 1990 Act and may use that sum for purposes specified in these Regulations.

These Regulations cover:

- interpretation of the Regulations and their application to Wales (Part I);
- recognition as a fund-holding practice (Part II);
- renunciation and removal of recognition (Parts III and IV);
- determination of the allotted sum (Part V);
- the purposes for which the allotted sums may be applied (Part VI).

The Regulations also take account of the statutory changes brought about by the Health Authorities Act 1995 and the fact that Health Authorities since 1 April 1996 are responsible for services which came under the former Family Health Services Authorities and that fund-holders which previously reported to the Regional Health Authorities now report directly to the Secretary of State or (in Wales) to Health Authorities. The 'Arrangement of Regulations' is set out below.

PART I – *General*
1. Citation, commencement and interpretation
2. Application of Regulations in Wales

PART II – *Recognition*
3. Application for recognition as a fund-holding practice
4. Time of application
5. Grant of recognition as a fund-holding practice
6. Determination of application
7. Continuing recognition
8. Additions to existing fund-holding practices
9. Withdrawal or death of a member of a fund-holding practice
10. Application for change in status of a recognised fund-holding practice

PART III – *Renunciation of Recognition*
11. Renunciation of recognition
12. Consequences of renunciation of recognition

PART IV – *Removal of Recognition*
13. Grounds for removal of recognition
14. Procedure for removal of recognition
15. Removal of recognition with immediate effect
16. Procedure for removal of recognition with immediate effect
17. Consequences of removal of recognition

PART V – *Allotted Sum—Determination*
18. Determination of allotted sum

PART VI – *Allotted Sum—Authorised Purposes*
19. Payment for drugs, medicines and listed appliances
20. Payment for goods and services
21. Limit on provision of goods and services
22. Payments to staff
23. Payment for management expenses
24. Payments to a member of a fund-holding practice
25. Savings from the allotted sum

PART VII – *Miscellaneous*
26. Recovery of misapplied amounts
27. Transfer of functions
28. Revocations

SCHEDULES
1. Conditions for obtaining recognition as a fund-holding practice
2. Conditions for continuing recognition as a fund-holding practice

APPENDIX 7

Useful addresses

Action for Sick Children
Argyle House
29–31 Euston Road
London NW1 2SD

Tel 0171 833 2041
Fax 0171 837 2110

Action for the Victims of Medical Accidents
Bank Chambers
1 London Road
Forest Hill
London SE23 3TP

Tel 0181 291 2793

Age Concern
1268 London Road
London SW16 4ER

Tel 0181 679 8000

Alzheimer's Disease Society
Gordon House
10 Greencoat Place
London SW1P 1PH

Tel 0171 306 0606
Fax 0171 306 0808

Association for Public Health
Hamilton House
Mabledon Place
London WC1H 9TX

Tel. 0171 413 1896

Association for Quality in Healthcare
47 Southgate Street
Winchester
Hants SO23 9EH

Tel 01962 877700
Fax 01962 877701

Association for Residential Care
ARC House
Marsden Street
Chesterfield
Derbyshire S40 1JY

Tel 01246 555043
Fax 01246 555045

Association of Community Health Councils
30 Drayton Park
London N5 1PB

Tel 0171 609 8405

Association of Directors of Social Services
Devon County Council
County Hall
Topsham Road
Exeter
Devon EX2 4QR

Tel 01392 384947
Fax 01392 384984

Association of Medical Secretaries, Practice Administrators and Receptionists Ltd
Tavistock House North
Tavistock Square
London WC1H 9LN

Tel 0171 387 6005
Fax 0171 388 2648

Ataxia
The Stable Copse Edge
Wiggins Yard Thursley Road
Bridge Street Elstead
Godalming
Surrey GU7 1HW

Tel 01483 417111
Fax 01483 424006

Barnado's
Tanners Lane
Barkingside
Ilford
Essex IG6 1QC

Tel 0181 550 8822

Bridges
Greytree Lodge
Second Avenue
Greytree
Ross-on-Wye
Herefordshire HR9 7HT

Tel 01594 834120

British Association for Service to the Elderly
119 Hassell Street,
Newcastle under Lyme
Staffs ST5 1AX

Tel 01782 661033
Fax 01483 450667

British Association of Day Surgery
35–43 Lincoln's Inn Fields
London
WC 2A 3PN

British Association of Social Workers
16 Kent Street
Birmingham B5 6RD

Tel 0121 622 3911
Fax 0121 622 4860

British Colostomy Association
15 Station Road
Reading RG1 1LG

Tel 01734 391537
Fax 01734 569095

British Diabetic Association
10 Queen Anne Street
London W1M 0BD

Tel 0171 323 1531

British Epilepsy Association
Anstey House 40 Hanover Square
Leeds LS3 1BE

Tel 0113 2439393
Fax 0113 2428804

British Federation of Care Homes
840 Melton Road
Thurmaston
Leicester LE4 8BN

Tel 0116 2640095
Fax 0116 2640141

British Heart Foundation
14 Fitzhardinge Street
London W1H 4DE

Tel 0171 935 0185
Fax 0171 486 5820

British Homoeopathic Association
27a Devonshire Street
London W1N 1RJ

Tel 0171 935 2163

British Institute of Learning Disabilities (BILD)
Wolverhampton Road
Kidderminister
Worcs DY10 3PP

Tel 01562 850251
Fax 01562 851970

British Migraine Association
178a High Road
West Byfleet
Surrey KT14 7ED

Tel 01932 352468
Fax 01932 351257

British Red Cross
9 Grosvenor Crescent
London SW1X 7EJ

Tel 0171 201 5043

Cancer Relief Macmillan Fund
15–19 Britten Street
London SW3 3TZ

Tel 0171 351 7811

Carers National Association
20–25 Glasshouse Yard
London EC1A 4JS

Tel 0171 490 8818
Fax 0171 490 5824
Carers line: 0171 490 8898

Centre for Policy on Ageing
25–31 Ironmonger Row
London EC1V 3QP

Tel 0171 253 1787
Fax 0171 490 4206

Child Accident Prevention Trust
4th Floor Clerk's Court
18–20 Farringdon Lane
London EC1R 3AU

Tel 0171 608 3828
Fax 0171 608 3674

Child Growth Foundation
2 Mayfield Avenue
Chiswick
London W4 1PW

Tel 0181 995 0257/0181 994 7625
Fax 0181 995 9075

College of Occupational Therapists
6–8 Marshalsea Road
Southwark
London SE1 1HL

Tel 0171 357 6480
Fax 0171 378 1353

**College of Speech and Language
Therapists**
7 Bath Place
Rivington Street
London EC2A 3DR

Tel 0171 613 3855
Fax 0171 613 3854

**Community and District Nursing
Association UK**
Thames Valley University
8 University House
Ealing Green
London W5 SED

Tel 0181 231 2771
Fax 0181 231 278

Counsel and Care for the Elderly
Twyman House
16 Bonny Street
London NW1 9PG

Tel 0171 485 1550

Crossroads Caring for Carers
10 Regent Place
Rugby CV21 2PN

Tel 01788 573653
Fax 01788 565498

**Department of Health
(Address for information on the
Registered Homes Tribunal)**
Area 217 Wellington House
133–55 Waterloo Road
London SE1 8UG

Tel 0171 972 4035 or 4034

Diabetes Foundation
177a Tennison Road
London SE25 5NF

Tel 0181 656 5467

Disabled Living Foundation
380–384 Harrow Road
London W9 2HU

Tel 0171 289 6111

Elderly Accommodation Council
46A Chiswick High Road
London W4 1SZ

Tel 0181 995 8320 and
0181 742 1182

English National Board
Victory House,
170 Tottenham Court Road
London W1P 0HA

Tel 0171 388 3131
Fax 0171 383 4031

ENB Resource and Careers Department
as above

Equal Opportunities Commission
Overseas House
Quay Street
Manchester M3 3HN

Tel 0161 833 9244
Fax 0161 835 1657

Family Planning Association
27–35 Mortimer Street
London W1N 7RJ

Tel 0171 636 7866
Fax 0171 436 5723

Family Welfare Association
501–505 Kingsland Road
Dalston
London E8 4AU

Tel 0171 254 6251

Family Welfare Association of Manchester (FWA Ltd)
Gaddum House
6 Great Jackson Street
Manchester M15 4AX

Tel 0161 834 6069
Fax 0161 839 8573

Good Practice in Mental Health
380–384 Harrow Road
London W9 2HU

Tel 0171 289 2034/3060

Headway (National Head Injuries Association)
7 King Edward Court
King Edward Street
Nottingham NG1 1EW

Tel 0115 9240800
Fax 01159 240432

Help the Aged
16 St James Walk
Clerkenwell Green
London EC1R 0BE

Tel 0171 253 0253

Help the Hospices
34–44 Britannia Street
London WC1X 9JG

Tel 0171 278 5668

Ileostomy Association of Great Britain and Ireland
Ambelhurst House
PO Box 23 Mansfield
Notts NG18 4TT

Tel 01623 28099
Fax 01623 28099

Independent Healthcare Association
22 Little Russell Street
London WC1A 2HT

Tel 0171 430 0537
Fax 0171 242 2681

Independent Living (1993) and Independent Living (Extension) Fund
Government Building
Chalfont Drive
Nottingham NG8 3RB

Tel 0115 9428191
Fax 0115 9293156

Infection Control Nurses' Association of the British Isles
Clatterbridge Hospital
Bebington
Wirral
Merseyside L63 4JY

Tel 0151 334 4000

Institute of Child Health
30 Guilford Street
London WC1N 1EH

Tel 0171 242 9789
Fax 0171 831 0488

Joseph Rowntree Foundation
The Homestead
40 Water End
York YO3 6LP

Tel 01904 629241

Leonard Cheshire Foundation
26–29 Maunsel Street
London SW1P 2QN

Tel 0171 828 1822
Fax 0171 976 5704

Limbless Association
31 The Mall
Ealing
London W5 2PX

Tel 0181 579 1758

**Marie Curie Memorial Foundation
(Marie Curie Cancer Care)**
28 Belgrave Square
London SW1X 8QC

Tel 0171 235 3325
Fax 0171 823 2380

MENCAP
see Royal Society of Mentally
Handicapped Children and Adults

Mental After Care Association
25 Bedford Square
London WC1B 3HW

Tel 0171 436 6194

Mental Health Foundation
37 Mortimer Street
London W1N 8JU

Tel 0171 580 0145
Fax 0171 631 3868

Migraine Trust
45 Great Ormond Street
London WC1N 3HZ

Tel 0171 278 2676

**MIND (National Association for
Mental Health)**
Granta House 15–19 Broadway
Stratford London E15 4BQ

Tel 0181 519 2122

**Multiple Sclerosis Society of Great
Britain and Northern Ireland**
25 Effie Road
London SW6 1EE

Tel 0171 610 7171
Fax 0171 736 9861

**Muscular Dystrophy Group of
Great Britain and Northern Ireland**
7–11 Prescott Place
London SW4 6BS

Tel 0171 720 8055
Fax 0171 498 0670

**National Association for Voluntary
Hostels**
Fulham Palace
Bishops Avenue
London SW6 6EA

Tel 0171 731 4205

National Autistic Society
276 Willesden Lane
London NW2 5RB

Tel 0181 451 1114

**National Council for Hospice and
Specialist Palliative Care Services**
59 Bryanston Street
London W1A 2AZ

Tel 0171 611 1153
Fax 0171 724 4341

**National Council for Voluntary
Organisations**
Regent's Wharf
8 All Saint's Street
London N1 9RL

Tel 0171 713 6161

**National League of the Blind and
Disabled**
2 Tenterden Road
Tottenham
London N17 8BE

Tel 0181 808 6030

National Schizophrenia Fellowship
28 Castle Street
Kingston-upon-Thames
Surrey KT1 1SS

Tel 0181 547 3937
Fax 0181 574 3862

Occupational Therapists in Private Practice
c/o College of Occupational Therapists
6 Marshalsea Road
London SE1 1HL

Tel 0171 378 8094

Parkinsons Disease Society
22 Upper Woburn Place
London WC1H 0RA

Tel 0171 383 3513
Fax 0171 383 5754

Public Trust Office, Protection Division
Stewart House
24 Kingsway
London WC2B 6JX

Tel 0171 269 7000

Queen's Nursing Institute
3 Albemarle Way
Clerkenwell
London EC1V 4JB

Tel 0171 490 4227

Rainbow Trust
Surrey House
31 Church Street
Leatherhead
Surrey KT22 8EF

Tel 01372 363438

Richmond Fellowship for Community Mental Health
8 Addison Road
London W14 8DL

Tel 0171 603 6373
Fax 0171 602 8652

Registered Nursing Homes Association
Calthorpe House
Hagley Road Edgbaston
Birmingham B16 8QY

Tel 0121 454 2511
Fax 0121 454 0932

The Relatives Association
c/o Counsel and Care (see above)

RADAR Royal Association for Disability and Rehabilitation
12 City Forum
250 City Road
London
EC1V 8AF

Tel 0171 250 3222

Royal College of Nursing
20 Cavendish Square
London W1M 9AE

Tel 0171 409 3333

Royal Society for Mentally Handicapped Children and Adults (MENCAP)
MENCAP National Centre
123 Golden Lane
London EC1Y 0RT

Tel 0171 454 0454
Fax 0171 608 3254

Samaritans
10 The Grove
Slough SL1 1QP

Tel 01753 532713

Shaftesbury Society
16 Kingston Road
London SW19 1JZ

Tel 0181 542 5550
Fax 0181 239 5580

Stroke Association
CHSA House
Whitecross Street
London EC1Y 8JJ

Tel 0171 490 7999
Fax 0171 490 2686

Terrence Higgins Trust
52–54 Grays Inn Road
London WC1X 8JU

Tel 0171 242 1010 (helpline)
Tel 0171 831 0330 (administration)
Tel 0171 405 2381 (legal line, Weds 7–10 pm)

United Kingdom Central Council
for Nursing Midwifery and Health
Visiting
23 Portland Place
London W1A 1BA

Tel 0171 637 7181
Fax 0171 436 2924

**Welsh National Board for Nursing
Midwifery and Health Visiting**
Floor 13
Pearl Assurance House

Greyfriars Road
Cardiff CF1 3AG

Tel 01222 395535
Fax 01222 229366

**Women's Nationwide Cancer
Control Campaign**
Suna House
128/130 Curtain Road
London EC2A 3AR

Tel 0171 729 4688
Fax 0171 613 0771

Glossary

actionable *per se* a court action where the plaintiff does not have to show loss, damage or harm to obtain compensation, eg an action for trespass to the person

advocate a person who pleads for another – they could be paid and professional, such as a barrister or solicitor, or it could involve a lay advocate either paid or unpaid

arrestable offence an offence defined in section 24 of the Police and Criminal Evidence Act 1984 which gives to the citizen the power of arrest in certain circumstances without a warrant

arrested or incomplete development of mind a definition in the mental health act of a specific form of mental disorder (see below)

Bolam test the test laid down by Mr Justice McNair in the case of *Bolam* v. *Friern HMC* on the standard of care expected of a professional in cases of alleged negligence, ie that of an ordinary skilled professional (see page 115)

certiorari an action taken to challenge an administrative or judicial decision (literally: to make more certain)

charge a legal burden which can be placed upon property or land, often to ensure repayment of money, eg mortgage

conditional fee system a system whereby client and lawyer can agree that payment of fees is dependent upon the outcome of the court action

constructive knowledge knowledge which can be obtained from the circumstances and which the person is presumed to have

continuous service requirement the length of service which an employee must have served in order to be entitled to receive certain statutory or contractual rights which differs for the various rights concerned

contract an agreement enforceable in law

contract for services an agreement, enforceable in law whereby one party provides services, not being employment, in return for payment or other consideration from the other

contract of service a contract for employment

declaration a ruling by the court, setting out the legal situation

dispensing doctor a doctor who is able to dispense medication when pharmaceutical premises are more than a mile from the surgery, or in an emergency

dissenting judgment a judge who disagrees with the decision of the majority of judges in courts where three of five judges hear the case

distinguished (of cases) the rules of precedent (see **hierarchy**) require judges to follow decisions of judges in previous cases, where these are binding upon them but in some circumstances it is possible to come to a different

624

decision because the facts of the earlier case are not directly comparable to the case now being heard, and therefore the earlier decision can be 'distinguished'

ex gratia as a matter of favour, eg without admission of liability, of payment offered to a claimant

extended role a term used to describe a registered nurse practitioner carrying out work usually undertaken by another professional (usually a doctor) – see also *Scope of Professional Practice*

FP10 prescription the form on which the doctor writes a prescription

frustration (of contracts) the ending of a contract by operation of law, because of the existence of an event not contemplated by the parties when they made the contract, eg imprisonment, death, blindness

Re F ruling where a professional acting in the best interests of an incompetent person incapable of giving consent does not act unlawfully if he follows the accepted standard of care according to the Bolam test (see p. 50)

guardian *ad litem* a person with a social work and child care background who is appointed to ensure that the court is fully informed of the relevant facts which relate to a child and that the wishes and feelings of the child are clearly established – the appointment is made from a panel set up by the local authority

hierarchy the recognised status of courts which results in lower courts following the decisions of higher courts as a binding precedent – thus decisions of the House of Lords must be followed by all lower courts, unless they can be distinguished (see above)

in loco parentis in the place of parents, a doctrine which permits persons who are temporarily caring for children to have parental powers now to a certain extent formalised in section 3(5) of the Children Act 1989

interest in land a right to live in or title to, or estate in, any land

invitation to treat the early stages in negotiating a contract, eg an advertisement, or letter expressing interest – it will often precede an offer that when accepted leads to the formation of an agreement which, if there is consideration and an intention to create legal relations, will be binding

learning disabilities the term referring to those formerly known as mentally handicapped or mentally impaired

mandamus an order of the court, directing a person or body corporate to do some particular thing

Master an official of the High Court who does not hear cases but arbitrates on procedural disputes between the parties to an action

mental disorder defined in section 1(1) Mental Health Act 1983 as 'mental illness, arrested or incomplete development of mind, psychopathic disorder and any other disorder or disability of mind'

mental illness not defined in Mental Health Act 1983 but together with three other specified forms constitutes mental disorder (see above)

parens patriae literally, parent of the country, applied to the Queen, to indicate overall custodian

personal representative specifically an executor, if appointed in the will, or administrator, appointed in the absence of a will, whose duty it is to settle the affairs and dispose of the property of a deceased person

pleading in the alternative when a claim is brought or defended alternative arguments can be put which may be mutually incompatible and if one fails the other may still be successful

precedent see **hierarchy**

prima facie at first sight, or sufficient evidence brought by one party to require the other party to provide a defence

professional misconduct conduct unworthy of a nurse, midwife or health visitor

prohibition an order of the court requiring a person or corporate body or court not to undertake an activity

psychopathic disorder 'a persistent disorder or disability of mind (whether or not including significant impairment of intelligence) which results in abnormally aggressive or seriously irresponsible conduct on the part of the person concerned.' section 1(2) Mental Health Act 1983

quantum the amount of compensation, or the monetary value of a claim

rescission where a contract is ended by the order of a court, or by the cancellation of the contract by one party entitled in law to do so

restraint of trade a term in a contract that one party will not compete against the other following the ending of the contract – if framed too widely, it may be considered by the courts to be invalid

subpoena an order of the court requiring a person to appear as a witness (*subpoena ad testificandum*) or to bring records/documents (*subpoena duces tecum*)

tort a civil wrong excluding breach of contract – it includes: negligence, trespass (to the person, goods or land), nuisance, breach of statutory duty and defamation

ultra vires outside the powers given by law (eg of a statutory body or company)

user literal legal meaning is 'the enjoyment of property'

virement the ability to switch expenditure from the location allocated to it in a budget

ward of court a child under 18 placed under the protection of the High Court, which assumes responsibility for him or her – all decisions relating to his or her care must be made in accordance with the directions of the court

warrant a writ conferring some right or authority, eg search warrant

warranties terms of a contract which are considered to be less important than the terms described as conditions: breach of a condition entitles the innocent party to see the contract as ended, ie repudiated by the other party; breach of warranty only entitles the innocent party to claim damages

Wednesbury principle the court will intervene to prevent or remedy abuses of power by public authorities if there is evidence of unreasonableness or perversity – principle laid down by the Court of Appeal in the case of *Associated Provincial Picture House Ltd* v. *Wednesbury Corporation* [1948] 1 KB 233

without prejudice without detracting from or without disadvantage to – in the first sense very specific provisions in an Act can be stated not to limit or render invalid a wider, vaguer statement of the law, usually earlier in the Act, and in the second sense the use of the phrase prevents the other party using the information to the prejudice of the one providing it

Bibliography

Beddard R. *Human Rights and Europe* 3rd edition, Grotius Publications Ltd, 1992

Brazier Margaret *Medicine Patients and the Law*, Penguin, 1992

Clarkson C.M.V. and Keating H.M. *Criminal Law Text and Materials* 2nd edition, Sweet & Maxwell, 1990

Dale and Appelbe's *Pharmacy law and ethics* 5th edition, Pharmaceutical Press, 1993

Dimond B.C. *Legal Aspects of Nursing* 2nd edition, Prentice Hall, 1995

Dimond B.D. *Patients' Rights, Responsibilities and the Nurse*, Central Health Studies, Quay Publishing, 1993

Dimond B.C. *Legal Aspects of Midwifery*, Books for Midwives Press, 1994

Ellis Norman *Employing Staff* 5th edition, British Medical Journal, 1994

Gann Robert *The NHS A to Z* 2nd edition, The Help for Health Trust, 1993

Griffiths Gerwyn *Modern Law Review* 1990 vol. 53 page 255

Ham Chris *The New National Health Service*, NAHAT, 1991

Hoggett Brenda *Mental Health Law*, Sweet & Maxwell 1992

Hunt Geoffrey and Wainwright Paul, editors *Expanding the Role of the Nurse*, Blackwell Scientific Publications, 1994

Ingman Terence *English Legal Process*, Blackstone Press (for examples of the cases and uses of the prerogative powers)

James *Introduction to English Law*, 12th edition Butterworths, 1989

Jones Richard *Mental Health Act Manual* 4th edition, Sweet & Maxwell, 1994

Kidner Richard *Blackstone's Statutes on employment law* 3rd edition, Blackstone, 1993

Kloss Diana *Occupational Health Law* 2nd edition, Blackwell Scientific Publications 1994

Knight Bernard *Legal Aspects of Medical Practice* 5th edition, Churchill Livingstone, 1992

Mason David and Edwards Peter *Litigation: A risk management guide for midwives* Royal College of Midwives, 1993

Miers David and Page Alan *Legislation* 2nd edition, Sweet & Maxwell, 1990

Morgan Derek and Lee Robert G. *Human Fertilisation and Embryology Act 1990*, Blackstone Press Limited, 1991

Nurse's Handbook of Law and Ethics, Springhouse Corporation, 1992

Pyne R.H. *Professional Discipline in Nursing, Midwifery and Health Visiting* 2nd edition, Blackwell Scientific Publications, 1991

Rowson Richard *An Introduction to Ethics for nurses*, Scutari Press, 1990

Rumbold Graham *Ethics in Nursing Practice* 2nd edition, Baillière Tindall, 1993

Selwyn's *Law of Employment* 8th edition, Butterworths, 1993

Smith and Keegan *English Law* 10th edition, Pitman, 1992

Speller's Law Relating to Hospitals (edited by John Finch) 7th edition, Chapman Hall Medical, 1994

Steiner Josephine *Textbook on EC law*, 3rd edition, Blackstone Press Limited, 1992

Street on Torts (edited by Margaret Brazier) 8th edition, Butterworths, 1988

Thompson Robin and Thompson Brian
    Dismissal: A basic introduction to your legal rights
    Equal Pay
    Health and Safety at Work
    Injuries at Work and work related illnesses
    Women at work

All Published by Robin Thompson and Partners and Brian Thompson and Partners London 1993.

Tschudin Verena and Marks Maran Diane *Ethics a Primer for Nurses*, Baillère Tindall, 1993

Young Ann P. *Legal Problems in Nursing Practice*, Harper and Rowe, 1989

Young Ann P. *Law and Professional Conduct in Nursing* 2nd edition, Scutari Press, 1994

White Richard, Carr Paul and Lowe Nigel *A Guide to the Children Act 1989*, Butterworths, 1991

Table of Cases

Table of Legislation

Note: page references in bold italics denote where the section is quoted directly

STATUTES

REGULATIONS, ORDERS

Index

643